EDUCATION 92/93

Nineteenth Edition

Editor

Fred Schultz
The University of Akron

Fred Schultz, professor of education at the University of Akron, attended Indiana University to earn a B.S. in social science education in 1962, an M.S. in the history and philosophy of education in 1966, and a Ph.D. in the history and philosophy of education and American studies in 1969. His B.A. in Spanish was conferred from the University of Akron in May 1985. He is actively involved in researching the development and history of American education with a primary focus on the history of ideas and social philosophy of education. He also likes to study languages.

Annual Editions
A Library of Information from the Public Press

SCHOOL OF EDUCATION
CURRICULUM LABORATORY
UM-DEARBORN

Cover illustration by Mike Eagle

The Dushkin Publishing Group, Inc.
Sluice Dock, Guilford, Connecticut 06437

The Annual Editions Series

Annual Editions is a series of over 55 volumes designed to provide the reader with convenient, low-cost access to a wide range of current, carefully selected articles from some of the most important magazines, newspapers, and journals published today. Annual Editions are updated on an annual basis through a continuous monitoring of over 300 periodical sources. All Annual Editions have a number of features designed to make them particularly useful, including topic guides, annotated tables of contents, unit overviews, and indexes. For the teacher using Annual Editions in the classroom, an Instructor's Resource Guide with test questions is available for each volume.

VOLUMES AVAILABLE

Africa
Aging
American Government
American History, Pre-Civil War
American History, Post-Civil War
Anthropology
Biology
Business and Management
Business Ethics
Canadian Politics
China
Comparative Politics
Computers in Education
Computers in Business
Computers in Society
Criminal Justice
Drugs, Society, and Behavior
Early Childhood Education
Economics
Educating Exceptional Children
Education
Educational Psychology
Environment
Geography
Global Issues
Health
Human Development
Human Resources
Human Sexuality
International Business
Japan
Latin America

Life Management
Macroeconomics
Management
Marketing
Marriage and Family
Microeconomics
Middle East and the Islamic World
Money and Banking
Nutrition
Personal Growth and Behavior
Physical Anthropology
Psychology
Public Administration
Race and Ethnic Relations
Social Problems
Sociology
Soviet Union (Commonwealth of Independent States and Central Europe)
State and Local Government
Third World
Urban Society
Violence and Terrorism
Western Civilization, Pre-Reformation
Western Civilization, Post-Reformation
Western Europe
World History, Pre-Modern
World History, Modern
World Politics

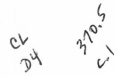

Library of Congress Cataloging in Publication Data
Main entry under title: Annual editions: Education. 1992/93.
1. Education—Periodicals. I. Schultz, Fred, *comp.* II. Title: Education.
370'.5   73-78580   ISBN: 1-56134-086-3
LB41.A673

Nineteenth Edition

Manufactured by The Banta Company, Harrisonburg, Virginia 22801

Editors/ Advisory Board

EDITOR

Fred Schultz
University of Akron

ADVISORY BOARD

Members of the Advisory Board are instrumental in the final selection of articles for each edition of Annual Editions. Their review of articles for content, level, currentness, and appropriateness provides critical direction to the editor and staff. We think you'll find their careful consideration well reflected in this volume.

STAFF

To the Reader

In publishing ANNUAL EDITIONS we recognize the enormous role played by the magazines, newspapers, and journals of the *public press* in providing current, first-rate educational information in a broad spectrum of interest areas. Within the articles, the best scientists, practitioners, researchers, and commentators draw issues into new perspective as accepted theories and viewpoints are called into account by new events, recent discoveries change old facts, and fresh debate breaks out over important controversies.

Many of the articles resulting from this enormous editorial effort are appropriate for students, researchers, and professionals seeking accurate, current material to help bridge the gap between principles and theories and the real world. These articles, however, become more useful for study when those of lasting value are carefully *collected, organized, indexed,* and *reproduced* in a *low-cost format,* which provides easy and permanent access when the material is needed. That is the role played by *Annual Editions.* Under the direction of each volume's *Editor,* who is an expert in the subject area, and with the guidance of an *Advisory Board,* we seek each year to provide in each *ANNUAL EDITION* a current, well-balanced, carefully selected collection of the best of the public press for your study and enjoyment. We think you'll find this volume useful, and we hope you'll take a moment to let us know what you think.

The quality of the debate over the state of education in North America continues to become more interesting. The winds of change are upon us. The early 1990s brought another deluge of creative new terms about education and its development on this continent. Terms like "deconstruction," "reconceptualization," and "postmodern" are being used to describe new visions in the enterprise of teaching and learning. There is little doubt that some major reinterpretation of our educational experience is in the process of development.

Possible choices open to us range from cultural literacy, to present-day child-centered and existentialist approaches to schooling as a therapeutic and empowering endeavor, all the way to vigorous debate over "deconstructing" and "reconceptualizing" how people are to be educated. Amidst this vigorous debate on the means and ends of education is the continuation and expansion of "knowledge-based" inquiry on the conduct of instruction and the organization of curriculum. Undergraduate curricula in teaching education programs continue to change as the recently developed revisions in teacher licensure and certification standards fall in place. The competition for the minds and hearts of those who teach in and those who govern educational systems is as intense as ever. This is a healthy situation, and it is adding significantly to the quality as well as the variety of research in the field.

Dialogue and compromise continue to be the order of the day. The various interest groups within the educational field reflect a broad spectrum of perspectives from various behaviorist and cognitive development perspectives to various humanistic ones. Practice-based approaches to field inquiry on teaching and learning in classrooms continue to produce fascinating alternatives to discovering the "knowledge base of teaching." Case study approaches to teaching teachers are opening up new directions for teacher education programs. The interests of students, parents, state or provincial governments, and the corporate world continue to challenge traditional views on how people should learn.

Although the Gulf War is behind us, military, economic, and diplomatic issues compete for the attention of government leaders along with educational issues. Yet several new major educational initiatives have been presented to North American legislative bodies in the past year. President Bush has sent to Congress a major legislative package to help the public school systems in the United States, but as always, there is continuing debate as to whether it is adequate. Improving the funding of national educational needs still requires much more attention.

In assembling this volume, we make every effort to stay in touch with movements in educational studies and with the social forces at work in the schools. Members of the advisory board contribute valuable insights, and the production and editorial staff at The Dushkin Publishing Group coordinates our efforts. Through this process we collect a wide range of articles on a variety of topics relevant to education in the United States and Canada.

The following readings explore the social and academic goals of education, the current condition of North American educational systems, the teaching profession, and the future of American education. In addition, these selections address the issues of change, the moral and ethical foundations of schooling, and the many varieties of educational experiences available to people in North America.

As always, we would like you to help us improve this volume. Please rate the material in this edition on the form at the back of the book and send it to us. We care about what you think. Give us the public feedback we need.

Fred Schultz

Fred Schultz
Editor

Contents

Unit 1

Perceptions of Education in North America

Four articles examine the present state of education in America. Topics include school reform, school quality, the future of teaching, and current public opinion on public schools.

Unit 2

The Reconceptualization of the Educative Effort

Four selections discuss the effects of equal opportunity, the reorganization of school programs, and the challenges facing education today.

The concepts in bold italics are developed in the article. For further expansion please refer to the Topic Guide and the Index.

Unit 3

Striving for Excellence: The Drive for Quality

Four articles discuss the current aims for excellence in American education. Topics include teacher quality and curriculum development.

The concepts in bold italics are developed in the article. For further expansion please refer to the Topic Guide and the Index.

Unit 4

Morality and Values in Education

Four articles examine the role of American schools in teaching morality and social values.

Unit 5

Managing Life in Classrooms

Three articles consider the necessity of judicious and effective discipline in the American classroom today.

The concepts in bold italics are developed in the article. For further expansion please refer to the Topic Guide and the Index.

Unit 6

Equal Opportunity and American Education

Seven articles discuss the current state of equality and opportunity in the American educational system. Racism, welfare reform, and the future of school desegregation are some of the topics considered.

The concepts in bold italics are developed in the article. For further expansion please refer to the Topic Guide and the Index.

Unit 7

Serving Special Needs and Humanizing Instruction

Seven selections examine some of the important aspects of special educational needs—mainstreaming, teen pregnancy, and education at home.

The concepts in bold italics are developed in the article. For further expansion please refer to the Topic Guide and the Index.

Unit 8

The Profession of Teaching Today

Five articles assess the current state of teaching in American schools. Topics include teacher accountability, teacher education, and the need for effective teaching.

Unit 9

A Look to the Future

Three articles look at the future of education in American schools. Curricula for the future, demographic changes, and educational reform are considered.

The concepts in bold italics are developed in the article. For further expansion please refer to the Topic Guide and the Index.

Topic Guide

This topic guide suggests how the selections in this book relate to topics of traditional concern to students and professional educators involved with the study of education. It is useful for locating articles that relate to each other for reading and research. The guide is arranged alphabetically according to topic. Articles may, of course, treat topics that do not appear in the topic guide. In turn, entries in the topic guide do not necessarily constitute a comprehensive listing of all the contents of each selection.

TOPIC AREA	TREATED IN:	TOPIC AREA	TREATED IN:
Abused Children	29. Children of Divorce	Diversity in Learners (cont'd)	22. Schools That Work 23. Chapter 1: A Vision for the Next Quarter Century 24. Search for Equity in School Funding 25. Losing Battle: Schools Fail Hispanics 26. *Perestroika* in Chicago's Schools 27. ABC's of Caring
Accountability	34. Accountability for Professional Practice		
Beginning Teachers	36. Schools and the Beginning Teacher		
Caring Kids and Teachers	14. Caring Kids: Role of the Schools 27. ABC's of Caring	Divorce and Children	29. Children of Divorce
Choice and Schooling	6. America's Public Schools: Choice *Is* a Panacea	Educational Leadership	2. Emerging Leadership Needs in Education 3. Education: Path to Urban Greatness 39. Improving Education for the Twenty-First Century
Classroom Design	17. Design a Classroom That Works		
Classroom Environment	7. Inside the Classroom: Social Vision and Critical Pedagogy 17. Design a Classroom That Works	Ethics and Teaching	13. Ethical Education in Our Public Schools: Crisis and Opportunity 14. Caring Kids: Role of the Schools 15. The Good, the Bad, and the Difference 16. Moral Education: An Idea Whose Time Has Gone
Classroom Management	17. Design a Classroom That Works 18. Quality School 19. Charm School for Bullies		
Communities and Schools	4. 23rd Annual Gallup Poll of Public Attitudes Toward the Public Schools 26. *Perestroika* in Chicago's Schools	Equity and Schooling	1. Suffer the Little Children 2. Emerging Leadership Needs in Education 3. Education: Path to Urban Greatness 23. Chapter 1: A Vision for the Next Quarter Century 24. Search for Equity in School Funding 25. Losing Battle: Schools Fail Hispanics 26. *Perestroika* in Chicago's Schools
Cooperative Learning	7. Inside the Classroom: Social Vision and Critical Pedagogy 9. What Really Counts in Schools 35. What, Why, and How of Cooperative Learning		
Creativity and Schools	31. World Finals of Creativity	Excellence and Schooling	7. What Really Counts in Schools 10. On Standardized Testing 11. Case for More School Days 12. Standards Debate Across the Atlantic
Critical Pedagogy	5. Down Side of Restructuring 7. Inside the Classroom: Social Vision and Critical Pedagogy 16. Moral Education: An Idea Whose Time Has Gone 38. "Our Children Are Dying in Our Schools"	Exceptional Children	27. ABC's of Caring
		Future of Education	23. Chapter 1: A Vision for the Next Quarter Century 39. Improving Education for the Twenty-First Century 40. Beyond the Melting Pot 41. Educational Renaissance: 43 Trends for U.S. Schools
Demographic Change	1. Suffer the Little Children 20. American the Multicultural 21. Multicultural Literacy and Curriculum Reform 25. Losing Battle: Schools Fail Hispanics 40. Beyond the Melting Pot		
		Gallup Poll of Public Attitudes	4. 23rd Annual Gallup Poll of Public Attitudes Toward the Public Schools
Discipline	17. Design a Classroom That Works 18. Quality School 19. Charm School for Bullies	Hidden Curriculum	7. Inside the Classroom: Social Vision and Critical Pedagogy 9. What Really Counts in Schools
Diversity in Learners	1. Suffer the Little Children 20. America the Multicultural 21. Multicultural Literacy and Curriculum Reform	Hispanics and Schools	25. Losing Battle: Schools Fail Hispanics

TOPIC AREA	TREATED IN:	TOPIC AREA	TREATED IN:
History of Education	8. "Restructuring" in Historical Perspective: Tinkering Toward Utopia	**"Reform" and Education**	6. America's Public Schools: Choice *Is* a Panacea 7. Inside the Classroom: Social Vision and Critical Pedagogy 8. "Restructuring" in Historical Perspective: Tinkering Toward Utopia 9. What Really Counts in Schools 10. On Standardized Testing 11. Case for More School Days 12. Standards Debate Across the Atlantic
Incentives for Change	6. America's Public Schools: Choice *Is* a Panacea		
Independent Schools	32. Different Drummers: The Role of Nonpublic Schools in America 33. What Is an Independent School?		
Longer School Year	11. Case for More School Days	**Restructuring Schools**	6. America's Public Schools: Choice *Is* a Panacea 7. Inside the Classroom: Social Vision and Critical Pedagogy 8. "Restructuring" in Historical Perspective: Tinkering Toward Utopia
Moral Education	13. Ethical Education in Our Public Schools: Crisis and Opportunity 14. Caring Kids: Role of the Schools 15. The Good, the Bad, and the Difference 16. Moral Education: An Idea Whose Time Has Gone		
		Standardized Testing	10. On Standardized Testing
Multicultural Education	20. America the Multicultural 21. Multicultural Literacy and Curriculum Reform 23. Chapter 1: A Vision for the Next Quarter Century 25. Losing Battle: Schools Fail Hispanics	**Standards and Schooling**	9. What Really Counts in Schools 10. On Standardized Testing 11. Case for More School Days 12. Standards Debate Across the Atlantic
Private Schools	32. Different Drummers: Role of Nonpublic Schools in America 33. What Is an Independent School?	**Teenage Pregnancy**	30. Teen-Age Pregnancy: Case for National Action
Profession of Teaching	34. Accountability for Professional Practice 35. The What, Why, and How of Cooperative Learning 36. Schools and the Beginning Teacher 37. Put to the Test: The Effects of External Testing on Teachers 38. "Our Children Are Dying in Our Schools"	**Testing and Teachers**	37. Put to the Test: Effects of External Testing on Teachers
		Urban Education	1. Suffer the Little Children 2. Emerging Leadership Needs in Education 3. Education: The Path to Urban Greatness 26. *Perestroika* in Chicago's Schools 40. Beyond the Melting Pot
Public Perceptions of Schools	1. Suffer the Little Children 2. Emerging Leadership Needs in Education 3. Education: Path to Urban Greatness 4. 23rd Annual Gallup Poll of Public Attitudes Toward the Public Schools	**Values and Teaching**	13. Ethical Education in Our Public Schools: Crisis and Opportunity 14. Caring Kids: Role of the Schools 15. The Good, the Bad, and the Difference 16. Moral Education: An Idea Whose Time Has Gone
Reconceptualizing Schooling	5. Down Side of Restructuring 6. America's Public Schools: Choice *Is* a Panacea 7. Inside the Classroom: Social Vision and Critical Pedagogy 8. "Restructuring" in Historical Perspective: Tinkering Toward Utopia		

Perceptions of Education in North America

There continues to be intense controversy among citizens as to the quality and adequacy of North American schools. Meanwhile the plight of many of this continent's children is getting worse, not better. Some have estimated that a child is molested or neglected in the United States once every 47 seconds; a student drops out of school once every 8 seconds. More than a third of the children in the United States have no health insurance coverage. The litany of tragedy for the continent's children and teenagers could be extended; however, I believe we all get the message. There is grave, serious business yet to be attended to by the social service and educational agencies that try to serve North American youth. After a decade of reform rhetoric in the 1980s, people are impatient to see some fundamental efforts to meet the basic needs of young people in the 1990s. The problems are the greatest in major cities and in more isolated rural areas. Public perceptions of the schools are affected by high levels of deprivation among large minority sectors of the population and the economic pressures that our interdependent world of today naturally produces as a result of international competition for the world's markets.

Studies conducted in the past few years, particularly the Carnegie Corporation's study of adolescence in America, document the plight of millions of young persons in North America. Some authors point out that although there was much talk about educational change in the 1980s, those changes were marginal and cosmetic at best. States responded by demanding more course work and tougher exist standards from school. However, the underlying courses of poor academic achievement received insufficient attention. With still more than 25% of school children in the United States living at or below the poverty level and almost a third of them in more economically and socially vulnerable nontraditional family setting, the overall social situation for young persons in North America continues to be difficult. The public wants more effective governmental responses to public needs.

The North American public has found certain proposed educational policy reforms of the 1980s very attractive. Various proposed approaches to greater parental choice in where their children attend school have gained in popularity. In the cities, magnet schools have achieved popularity for they also provide a wider range of school attendance choices for parents and students. There has been much written in the public trade press regarding proposals to encourage the competition between public and private schools. Alternative approaches to attracting new and talented teachers have received sympathetic support among many sectors of the general public, but these alternative teacher certification approaches have met with stiff opposition from large segments of the incumbents of North American education systems. Many states are exploring and experimenting with such programs at the urging of government and business leaders. Yet many of these alternative programs are too superficial and fail to teach the candidates in these programs the new knowledge base on teaching and learning that have been developed in recent years.

So, in the face of major demographic shifts and the persistence of many long-term social problems, the public watches closely how schools respond to new as well as old challenges. In recent years, these challenges have tended to aggravate rather than to allay the public's concerns about the efficacy of public schooling as it is conducted in most places. Alternative educational agendas continue to be articulated by various political, cultural, corporate, and philanthropic interests. At the same time, the "incumbents" of the educational system respond with their own educational agendas reflecting their views of the system from the inside. The well-being and academic progress of students is the motivating force behind the recommendations of all well-meaning interest groups in this dialogue. New national strategic goals for future educational development may come from this dialogue. The American public is more sensitive to the relevance of educational policy at the local, state, and national levels.

The public is concerned that several severe educational problems need to be addressed. They perceive the importance of teaching young children learning-readiness skills, and there is widespread concern to eliminate the severe drug usage problems among children and adolescents. The problem of illiteracy is important as a significant minority percentage of the American population are unable to read or write effectively. They are concerned about the increasing school dropout rate (around 24%) nationally—particularly in the large cities and rural poverty areas. Issues as to parent choice plans, extending the school day or year, and proposals for year-round school in areas experiencing rapid population growth are now being given serious public discussion. Recent declines in nationally standardized school achievement test scores have also created citizen concern for the quality of the teaching-learning process in American schools. Whether these public concerns for improvement in the conditions and outcomes of learning can be successfully resolved with effective new curricula (some of which involve the restoration of older, traditional educational ideals) remains to be seen. The decade is running pace, as all the others have, and "we have miles to go before we sleep" with any concrete assurance that these great educational issues can be resolved in the short-term future.

There have been massive shifts in American public opinion regarding the quality of the nation's schools throughout the history of the United States. Never have North American schools confronted a more pluralistic world-wide ideological and economic environment than the one they face today. The history of school reform efforts in nineteenth- and twentieth-century Canadian and American education reflects a continuing public concern for the quality of teachers and the quality of learning. Improving the qualitative outcomes of schooling has never been easy; today the American public sees the connections between effective schooling and national development in the light of dramatically changing national demographic and economic circumstances. (These circumstances are discussed further in the essays in unit 6.) If there is any optimism in public perceptions of the "state" of schooling in North America, it is a guarded optimism.

North Americans sense the present intense competition for world markets and the demands for a more literate, learning-oriented work force. There are public calls for curricular changes in schools that will better prepare American youth for the complex demands of becoming more literate and more able to work and to learn independently. The public seems to believe that American education problems are not additive or quantitative, but qualitative.

Fewer American young adults entering college or university studies today wish to consider seriously the possibility of becoming teachers. Teacher education enrollments are up significantly in some universities, but still not enough to meet anticipated national demands for teachers projected for the early and mid 1990s.

The public's perception of the costs and effectiveness of new school programs is vague at best, because we are uncertain as to the long-term success of certain models for innovation that are being placed in schools. For instance, some state departments of education are imposing 9th and 12th grade exit standards that are academically demanding, as well as "tiered diplomas" (qualitatively different exit credentials) for high school graduates. We are not sure what the overall public reactions to such innovations will be even though the competency testing has been going on in some states and provinces for some time.

There is public uncertainty, as well, as to whether state and provincial legislators will accept a greater state government role in funding needed changes in the schools. People are generally convinced that it is unreasonable to expect local communities to finance local educational systems to a much greater extent than they are at present. There is some public perception that the challenges confronting North American educational systems in the 1990s are different from those that were confronted in the 1960s and earlier.

Looking Ahead: Challenge Questions

What educational issues are of greatest concern to citizens today?

What ought to be the policy directions of national and state governments regarding educational reform?

What are the most important problems blocking efforts to improve educational standards?

What technological changes in the world economy influence the directions of educational change?

What economic factors affect educational development?

How can we best build a national public consensus regarding the structure and purposes of schooling?

What social factors encourage at-risk students to leave school early?

What are the differences between the myth and the reality of North American schooling? Have the schools done anything right?

What are the best ways to accurately assess public perceptions of the educational system?

What is the functional effect of public opinion on national public policy regarding educational development?

What generalizations can one draw concerning public schools in the United States from the Gallup poll data?

How can existing public concerns regarding schooling be addressed more effectively by state or provincial legislatures?

Suffer the Little Children

The world's leaders gather for an extraordinary summit and listen at last to a crying need.

Just how much is a child worth? To a father in northern Thailand, 10-year-old Poo was worth $400 when he sold her to a middleman to work in Madame Suzy's Bangkok brothel. To Madame Suzy, Poo is worth $40 a night while she's still young and fresh. But her price will soon come down.

To a quarry owner outside New Delhi, 12-year-old Ballu is worth 85¢ a day, the amount the child earns breaking rocks in an 11-hour shift. "I wanted to become an engineer," says Ballu. He glances sadly at his callused hands. "But now I have crossed the age for studies and will be a stonecutter all my life."

To local bosses in Mexico City, children are worth about $2.80 a day for scavenging food, glass, cloth and bones from three vast municipal dumps. The walls around the dumps enclose homes, families, even a church and a store. Many of the 5,000 children living there attend school in the dumps; they are not tolerated on the outside because of their smell.

Just how much is the very life of a child worth? A 10¢ packet of salt, sugar and potassium can prevent a child from dying of diarrhea. Yet every day in the developing world more than 40,000 children under the age of five die of diarrhea, measles, malnutrition and other preventable causes. An extra $2.5 billion a year could save the lives of 50 million children over the next decade. That is roughly equal, children's advocates note, to the amount that the world's military establishments, taken together, shell out every day.

Last weekend George Bush joined 34 other Presidents, 27 Prime Ministers, a King, a Grand Duke and a Cardinal, among others, at the United Nations for a meeting unlike any in history: the World Summit for Children. The leaders came to discuss the plight of 150 million children under the age of five suffering from malnutrition, 30 million living in the streets, 7 million driven from their homes by war and famine.

Shamed into action, the leaders endorsed a bold 10-year plan to reduce mortality rates and poverty among children and to improve access to immunizations and education. For once, this was more than a political lullaby of soothing promises; the very existence of the extraordinary summit held out hope to those who have fought to make children's voices heard. To lend support, more than a million people held 2,600 candlelight vigils earlier in the week—in South Korea's Buddhist monasteries, in London's St. Paul's Cathedral, in Ethiopia's refugee camps, around Paris' Eiffel Tower, in 700 villages in Bangladesh.

As the whole word directs its attention, however briefly, to those to whom the earth will soon belong, what kind of leadership can the United States offer? Americans cherish the notion that they cherish their children, but there's woeful evidence to the contrary. Each year thousands of American babies are born premature and underweight, in a country torn by neither war nor famine. The U.S. is one of only four countries—with Iran, Iraq and Bangladesh—that still execute juvenile offenders. And nearly 1 in 4 American children under age six lives in poverty. Congressmen wrestling with budget cuts, policymakers musing about peace dividends, voters weighing their options—all would do well to wonder what sort of legacy they will be leaving to a generation of children whose needs have been so widely ignored. And those needs go far beyond vigils and poignant speeches.

Shameful Bequests to The Next Generation

America's legacy to its young people includes bad schools, poor health care, deadly addictions, crushing debts—and utter indifference

NANCY GIBBS

 George Bush knows how to talk about children. With a sure sense of childhood's mythology, of skinned knees and candy apples and first bicycles, he campaigned for office in a swarm of jolly grandchildren and promised justice for all. In this year's State of the Union address, he mentioned families and "kids" more than 30 times—the electronic equivalent of kissing babies on the village green. "To the children out there tonight," he declared as he built to his finale, "with you rests our hope, all that America will mean in the years ahead. Fix your vision on a new century—your century, on dreams you cannot see, on the destiny that is yours and yours alone."

Forget the next century. Just consider for a moment a single day's worth of destiny for American children. Every eight seconds of the school day, a child drops out. Every 26 seconds, a child runs away from home. Every 47 seconds, a child is abused or neglected. Every 67 seconds, a teenager has a baby. Every seven minutes, a child is arrested for a drug offense. Every 36 minutes, a child is killed or injured by a gun. Every day 135,000 children bring their guns to school.

Even children from the most comfortable surroundings are at risk. A nation filled with loving parents has somehow come to tolerate crumbling schools and a health-care system that caters to the rich and the elderly rather than to the young. A growing number of parents with preschool children are in the workplace, but there is still no adequate system of child care, and parental leaves are hard to come by. Mothers and fathers worry about the toxic residue left from too much television, too many ghastly movies, too many violent video games, too little discipline. They wonder how to raise children who are strong and imaginative and loving. They worry about the possibility that their children will grow wild and distant and angry. Perhaps they fear most that they will get the children they deserve. "Children who go unheeded," warns Harvard psychiatrist Robert Coles, giving voice to a parent's guilty nightmare, "are children who are going to turn on the world that neglected them."

And that anger will come when today's children are old enough to realize how relentlessly their needs were ignored. They will see that their parents and grandparents have left them enormous debts and a fouled environment. They will recognize that their exceptionally prosperous, peaceful, lucky predecessors, living out the end of the millennium, were not willing to make the investments necessary to ensure that the generation to follow could enjoy the same blessings.

The natural case for taking better care of children would be made on moral grounds alone. A society cannot sacrifice its most vulnerable citizens without eroding its sense of community and making a lie of its principles. But having been left behind by a decade of political shortcuts, child advocates have adopted a more practical strategy. "If compassion were not enough to encourage our attention to the plight of our children," declares New York Governor Mario Cuomo, "self-interest should be." Marian Wright Edelman, the crusading founder of the Children's Defense Fund, goes further. "The inattention to children by our society," she warns, "poses a greater threat to our safety, harmony and productivity than any external enemy."

Spending on children, any economist can prove, is a bargain. A nation can spend money either for better schools or for larger jails. It can feed babies or pay forever for the consequences of starving a child's brain when it is trying to grow. One dollar spent on prenatal care for pregnant women can save more than $3 on medical care during an infant's first year, and $10 down the line. A year of preschool costs an average $3,000 per child; a year in prison amounts to $16,500.

But somehow, neither wisdom nor decency, nor even economics, has prevailed

with those who make policy in the state houses, the Congress or the White House. "We are hypocrites," charges Senator John D. ("Jay") Rockefeller IV, who is chairman of the National Commission on Children. "We say we love our children, yet they have become the poorest group in America." Nearly a quarter of all children under six live in households that are struggling below the official poverty line—$12,675 a year for a family of four.

In some cases the abandonment of children begins before they are even born. America's infant mortality rate has leveled off at 9.7 deaths per 1,000 births, worse

Between 1978 and 1987, spending on programs for the elderly rose 52%; spending on children dropped 4%

than 17 other developed countries. In the District of Columbia, the rate tops 23 per 1,000, worse than Jamaica or Costa Rica. Fully 250,000 babies are born seriously underweight each year. To keep these infants in intensive care costs about $3,000 a day, and they are two to three times more likely to be blind, deaf or mentally retarded. On the other hand, regular checkups and monitoring of a pregnant woman can cost as little as $500 and greatly increase the chances that she will give birth to a healthy baby.

Every bit as important as prenatal care is nutrition for the child, both before and after birth. "Of all the dumb ways of saving money, not feeding pregnant women and kids is the dumbest," says Dr. Jean Mayer, one of the world's leading experts on nutrition and president of Tufts University. During the first year of life, a child's brain grows to two-thirds its final size. If a baby is denied good, healthy food during this critical period, he will need intensive nutritional and developmental therapies to repair the damage. "Kids' brains can't wait for Dad to get a new job," says Dr. Deborah Frank, director of growth and development at Boston City Hospital, "or for Congress to come back from recess."

Congress understood the obvious benefits of promoting infant nutrition in the 1970s, when it launched the Special Supplemental Food Program for Women, In-

fants and Children. WIC provides women with vouchers to buy infant formula, cheese, fruit juice, cereals, milk and other wholesome foods, besides offering nutrition classes and medical care. It costs about $30 a month to supply a mother with vouchers—yet government funds are so tight that only 59% of women and infants who qualify for WIC receive the benefits. "A power breakfast for two businessmen is one woman's WIC package for a month," says Dr. Frank. "Why can't public-policy makers see the connection between bad infant nutrition, which is cheap and easy to fix, and developmental problems, which are expensive and often difficult to fix?"

The theme of prevention applies just as forcefully to medicine. This year the U.S. will spend about $660 billion, or 12% of its GNP, on medical services, but only a tiny fraction of that will go toward prevention. For children the most basic requirement is inoculation, the surest way to spare a child—and the health-care system—the ravages of tuberculosis, polio, measles and whooping cough. During the first 20 years after the discovery of the measles vaccine, public-health experts estimate, more than $5 billion was saved in medical costs, not to mention countless lives. And yet these days in California, the nation's richest state, only half of California's two-year-olds are fully immunized. Dallas reported more than 2,400 measles cases from last December through July, eight of them fatal, including one child who lived within six blocks of an immunization clinic.

Even parents who recognize the importance of preventive care are having a harder time affording it for their children. Most Americans over age 65 are covered by Medicare, the federal health-insurance plan under which the elderly—rich or poor—are eligible for benefits. Children's health programs, in contrast, are subject to annual congressional whims and budget cutting. Fewer and fewer employers, even of well-paid professionals, provide health benefits that cover children for routine medical needs. This means that health costs are the responsibility of individual parents, who make do as best they can, often at considerable sacrifice.

Some states and community groups are trying to help. Two years ago, Minnesota pioneered the Children's Health Plan to provide primary preventive care for children. The plan costs the state about $180 per child, but parents pay only $25: in the end everyone saves. Schools in Independence, Mo., established a health-care package to provide drug and alcohol treatment and counseling services for every child in the district. Cost to parents: $10 per child. In Pittsburgh 12,000 children have received free health care through a program crafted by churches, civic groups, Blue Cross and Blue Shield.

But too many kids are denied such care, and that starts a chain reaction. "You can't educate a child unless all systems are go, i.e., brain cells, eyes, ears, etc." says Rae Grad, executive director of the National Commission to Prevent Infant Mortality. A national survey in 1988 found that two-thirds of teachers reported "poor health" among children to be a learning problem. This is why Head Start, the model federal program providing quality preschool for poor children, also includes annual medical and dental screenings. But once again the money is not there: only about 20% of eligible children are fully served by the program.

Head Start and similar preschool strategies improve academic performance in the early grades and pay vast dividends over time. President Bush has promised enough funding to put every needy child in Head Start, which Congress says will require a fivefold increase by 1994 from the present $1.55 billion a year. Both the House and the Senate have approved higher funding levels, and lawmakers will soon meet to reconcile differences between the two bills. But as the deficit mounts, the peace dividend sinks into the Persian Gulf and the savings and loan crisis chews into basic budget items, politicians may have a hard time approving funding increases for a constituency that does not vote. Senator Orrin Hatch of Utah, a proponent of costly child-care legislation, says the outcome of the budget negotiations is "going to be terrible for kids."

Likewise, American society has, in the past generation, abandoned its commitment to providing a world-class system of secondary education. Education Secretary Lauro Cavazos himself calls student performance "dreadfully inadequate." From both the inner cities and the affluent suburbs comes a drumbeat of stories about tin-pot principals who cannot be fired, beleaguered teachers with unmanageable workloads and illiterate graduates with abysmal test scores. If they can possibly afford to, parents choose private or parochial schools, leaving the desperate or destitute in the worst public schools. Teachers, meanwhile, are aware that they are often the most powerful influences in a child's life—and that their job pays less in a year than a linebacker or rock star can earn in a week.

Across the board, people who deal with children are more ill-paid, unregulated and less respected than other professionals. Among physicians, pediatricians' income ranks near the bottom. In Michigan preschool teachers with five years' experience earn $12,000, and prison guards with the same amount of seniority earn almost $30,000. U.S. airline pilots are vigilantly trained, screened and monitored; school-bus drivers are not. "My hairdresser needs 1,500 hours of schooling, takes a written and practical test and is relicensed every year," says Flora Patterson, a foster parent in San Gabriel, Calif. "For foster parents in Los Angeles County there is no mandated training, yet we are dealing with life and death." The typical foster parent there earns about 80¢ an hour.

In France, Belgium, Italy and Denmark, at least 75% of children ages 3 to 5 are in some form of state-funded preschool program

Worst of all is the status of America's surrogate parents: the babysitters and day-care workers who have become essential to the functioning of the modern family. In the absence of anything like a national child-care policy, parents are left to improvise. The rich search for trained, qualified care givers and pay them whatever it takes to keep them. But for the vast majority, child care is a game of Russian roulette: rotating nannies, unlicensed home care, unregulated nurseries that leave parents wondering constantly: Is my child really safe? "Finding child care is such a gigantic crapshoot," says Edward Zigler, director of Yale's Bush Center in Child Development and Social Policy. "If you are lucky, you are home free. But if you are unlucky, well, there are some real horror stories out there of kids being tied into cribs."

The U.S. economy has long been geared to two-income families; many families could not afford a middle-class lifestyle without both parents working. The real median income of parents under age 30 fell more than 24% from 1973 to 1987, according to a study by the Children's Defense Fund and Northeastern University. But social programs rarely reflect those economic realities. Growing financial pressure all too often translates into fewer doctors' visits, more stress and less time spent together as a family. Between 1950 and 1989, the divorce rate doubled: 1.16 million couples split up each year. That makes the need for reliable support services for children all the greater.

In place of responses came rhetoric: a 1986 Administration report on the family titled "Preserving America's Future" called for a return to "traditional values," parental support of children and "lovingly packed lunch boxes." Time and again, Washington has failed to address the needs of working parents—most recently in June, when President Bush vetoed the family-leave bill on the ground that it was too burdensome for business. The bill would have allowed a worker to take up to 12 weeks a year of unpaid leave to care for a newborn, an adopted child or a sick family member.

That is abysmal compared with what other industrialized nations allow. Salaried women in France can take up to 28 weeks of unpaid maternity leave or up to 20 weeks of adoption leave, though they are less likely to need it since day care, health care and early education are widely available in that country. In France, as well as in Belgium, Italy and Denmark, at least 75% of children ages 3 to 5 are in some form of state-funded preschool programs. In Japan both the government and most companies offer monthly subsidies to parents with children. In Germany parents may deduct the cost of child care from their taxes. "Under our tax laws," observes Congresswoman Pat Schroeder of Colorado, "a businesswoman can deduct a new Persian rug for her office but can't deduct most of her costs for child care. The deduction for a Thoroughbred horse is greater than that for children."

If the troubles children face were all born of economic pressure on the family, then wealthy children should emerge unscathed. Yet the problems confronting affluent children are also profound and insidious. Parents who do not spend time with their children often spend money instead. "We supply kids with things in the absence of family," says Barbara Mac-Phee, a school administrator in New Orleans. "We used to build dreams for them, but now we buy them Nintendo toys and Reebok sneakers." In the absence of parental guidance and affirmation, children are left to soak in whatever example their environment sets. A childhood spent in a shopping mall raises consumerism to a varsity sport; time spent in front of a television requires no more imagination than it takes to change channels.

At Winchester High School in a cozy Boston suburb, clinical social worker Michele Diamond hears it all: the drug use, the alcohol, the eating disorders, the suicide attempts by children who are viewed as privileged. "Kids are left alone a lot to cope," she says, "and they sense less support from their families." Pressured to succeed, to "fit in," to be accepted by top colleges, the students handle their stress however they can. Some just dissolve their problems in a glass. In nearby Belmont, a juvenile officer finds that parents shrug off the danger. When their kids are caught drinking, he notes, "they say, 'Thank God it isn't cocaine. It's alcohol. We can handle that.' "

All too often it *is* cocaine, the poisonous solace common to the golf club and the ghetto. It is not only the violence of the drug culture that threatens children; it is also the lure of the easy money that turns 11-year-olds into drug runners. "Alienated is too weak a word to describe these kids," says Edward Loughran, a 10-year veteran of the juvenile-justice system in Massachusetts. "They don't value their lives or anyone else's life. Their values system says, 'I am here alone. I don't care what society says.' A lot of these kids are dying young deaths and don't care because they don't feel there is any reason to aspire to anything else."

Violence in the neighborhood is bad enough. Violence in the home is devastating. Reports of child abuse have soared from 600,000 in 1979 to 2.4 million in 1989, a searing testimony to the enduring role of children as the easiest victims. In New York City, half of all abuse reports are repeat cases of children who have had to be rescued before, only to be returned to an abusive home.

When two-year-old "Rebecca" accidentally soiled her underwear, her mother and the mother's boyfriend were not pleased. So they heated up some cooking oil, held Rebecca down and poured it over her. Then they waited a week or so before Rebecca's mother, unable to stand the stench of the child's legs, which were rotting from gangrene, took her to the hospital. After a month's stay that saved her legs, Rebecca was able to move to a foster home. From there she went to live with her paternal grandmother, who had plenty of room: all four of her sons were in state prison.

Around the country there are hundreds of thousands of other children who scream for help from overburdened teachers, understaffed social service agencies, crowded courts and a gridlocked foster-care system. To dismiss child abuse as a personal, private tragedy misses the larger point entirely. If children are not protected from their abusers, then the public will one day have to be protected from the children. To walk through death row in any prison is to learn what child abuse can lead to when it ripens. According to attorneys who have represented them, roughly 4 out of 5 death row inmates were abused as children.

A reordering of priorities toward protecting children would include far higher funding and staffing of Child Protective Services, the organization that investigates charges of abuse and can move to rescue children before the damage is irreparable. But even that would do little good if there is no place to put them. No solution will be possible without an overhaul of the foster-care system, which in many cities is on the verge of collapse. All too often, children are separated from siblings and shuttled from group homes to relatives to foster families, with no sense of the safety, security or stability they need to succeed in school and elsewhere. "If we don't have money for adequate care," says Ruth Massinga, a member of the National Commission on Children, "removing children from their homes is just another devastation."

Failure to make treatment available to drug addicts who seek it will ensure yet another generation of addicted babies and battered kids. In Los Angeles the number of drug-exposed babies entering the foster-care system rose 453% between 1984 and 1987. A survey of states found that drugs are involved in more than 2 out of 3 child abuse and neglect cases. Children born into a family of addicts are left with impossible choices: a life with the abusers they know, or a life at the mercy of a system filled with strangers—lawyers, judges, social workers, foster parents.

It is a common mistake to assume that all abuse is physical. The scars of other forms of abuse—like unrelenting verbal cruelty—can be just as apparent when children grow older, unloved and self-hating. "You can tell kids you love 'em, says April, a runaway in Hollywood. "But that's not the same as showing them. Broken promises is really what tears your heart apart." For April there is not much difference between insult and injury. "Beating kids will hurt kids. Sexual abuse will hurt a kid. But verbal abuse is the worst. I've had all three. If you're not strong enough as a person, and they've been telling you this all your life, that you can never amount to anything, you are going to believe it."

There have always been children who are survivors, who overcome the odds and find some adult—a teacher, a grandparent, a priest—who can provide the anchors the family could not. Touré Diggs, 18, grew up in a rough neighborhood of New Haven, Conn., and is now enrolled at Fairleigh Dickinson University. Since his parents separated three years ago, Touré has tried to help raise his brother Landis, who is 7. In the end Touré knows he is competing with the lure of the street for Landis' soul. "You got to start so young," Touré says. "It's like a game. Whoever gets to the kids first, that's how they are going to turn out."

Schools in particular have come to take that role very seriously, which accounts for the debate over how to teach values and self-discipline to a generation whose boundaries have been loosely drawn. But other institutions are slowly waking up to the implications of writing off an entire generation. The business community, in particular, wonders where it will find a trained, literate, motivated work force in the 21st century. The Business Roundtable, with representatives from the largest 200 companies, has made support for education its highest priority in the '90s. In Dallas, Texas Instruments helps fund the local Head Start program. Eventually, more and more companies may make parental leave a standard benefit, regardless of the messages coming from Washington.

In Des Moines business leaders are sponsoring a program called Smoother Sailing, which sends counselors like "Sunburst Lady" Toni Johansen into the city's elementary schools. National studies have shown that such support helps improve confidence, discipline and attitudes about school. With the extra funding, the city has been able to provide one guidance counselor for every 250 students, in contrast to a national average of one for 850.

But there will be no real progress, no genuine hope for America's children until the sense of urgency forces a reconsideration of values in every home, up to and including the White House. Polls suggest the will is there: 60% of Americans believe the situation for children has worsened over the past five years; 67% say they would be more likely to vote for a candidate who supported increased spending for children's programs even if it meant a tax increase.

When adults lament the absence of "values," it is worth recalling that children are an honest conscience, the perfect mirror of a society's priorities and principles. A society whose values are entirely material is not likely to breed a generation of poets; anti-intellectualism and indifference to education do not inspire rocket scientists. With each passing day these arguments become more apparent, the needs more pressing. Where is the leader who will seize the opportunity to do what is both smart and worthy, and begin retuning policy to focus on children and intercept trouble before it breeds?

—Reported by Julie Johnson/Des Moines, Melissa Ludtke/Boston and Michael Riley/Washington

(Article continues)

Struggling for Sanity

Mental and emotional distress are taking an alarming toll of the young

ANASTASIA TOUFEXIS

 The dozen telephone lines at the cramped office of Talkline/Kids Line in Elk Grove Village, Ill., ring softly every few minutes. Some of the youthful callers seem at first to be vulgar pranksters, out to make mischief with inane jokes and naughty language. But soon the voices on the line—by turns wistful, angry, sad, desperate—start to spill a stream of distress. Some divulge their struggles with alcohol or crack and their worries about school and sex. Others tell of their feelings of boredom and loneliness. Some talk of suicide. What connects them all, says Nancy Helmick, director of the two hot lines, is a sense of "disconnectedness."

Such calls attest to the intense psychological and emotional turmoil many American children are experiencing. It is a problem that was not even recognized until just a decade ago. Says Dr. Lewis Judd, director of the National Institute of Mental Health: "There had been a myth that childhood is a happy time and kids are happy go lucky, but no age range is immune from experiencing mental disorders." A report prepared last year by the Institute of Medicine estimates that as many as 7.5 million children—12% of those below the age of 18—suffer from some form of psychological illness. A federal survey shows that after remaining constant for 10 years, hospitalizations of youngsters with psychiatric disorders jumped from 81,500 to about 112,000 between 1980 and 1986. Suicides among those ages 15 to 19 have almost tripled since 1960, to 1,901 deaths in 1987. Moreover, the age at which children are exhibiting mental problems is dropping: studies suggest that as many as 30% of infants 18 months old and younger are having difficulties ranging from emotional withdrawal to anxiety attacks.

What is causing so much mental anguish? The sad truth is that a growing number of American youngsters have home lives that are hostile to healthy emotional growth. Psyches are extremely fragile and must be nourished from birth. Everyone starts out life with a basic anxiety about survival. An attentive parent contains that stress by making the youngster feel secure and loved.

Neglect and indifference at such a crucial stage can have devastating consequences. Consider the case of Sid. (Names of the children in this story have been changed). When he was three months old, his parents left him with the maid while they took a five-week trip. Upon their return, his mother noticed that Sid was withdrawn, but she did not do anything about it. When Sid was nine months old, his mother left him again for four weeks while she visited a weight-loss clinic. By age three, Sid had still not started talking. He was wrongly labeled feebleminded and borderline autistic before he received appropriate treatment.

As children mature within the shelter of the family, they develop what psychologists call a sense of self. They acquire sensitivities and skills that lead them to believe they can cope independently. "People develop through a chain," observes Dr. Carol West, a child psychotherapist in Beverly Hills. "There has to be stability, a consistent idea of who you are."

The instability that is becoming the hallmark of today's families breeds in children insecurity rather than pride, doubts instead of confidence. Many

As many as 7.5 million children—12% of those below the age of 18—suffer from some form of psychological illness

youngsters feel guilty about broken marriages, torn between parents and households, and worried about family finances. Remarriage can intensify the strains. Children may feel abandoned and excluded as they plunge into rivalries with stepparents and stepsiblings or are forced to adjust to new homes and new schools. Children from troubled homes used to be able to find a psychological anchor in societal institutions. But no longer. The churches, schools and neighborhoods that provided emotional stability by transmitting shared traditions and values have collapsed along with the family.

Such disarray hurts children from all classes; wealth may in fact make it harder for some children to cope. Says Hal Klor, a guidance counselor at Chicago's Lincoln Park High School: "The kids born into a project, they handle it. But the middle-class kids. All of a sudden—a divorce, loss of job, status. Boom. Depression."

Jennifer shuttled by car service across New York City's Central Park between her divorced parents' apartments and traveled by chartered bus to a prep school where kids rated one another according to their family cars. "In the eighth grade I had panic attacks," says Jennifer, now 18. "That's when your stomach goes up and you can't leave the bathroom and you get sweaty and you get headaches and the world closes in on you." Her world eventually narrowed so far that for several weeks she could not set foot outside her home.

The children who suffer the severest problems are those who are physically or sexually abused. Many lose all self-esteem and trust. Michele, 15, who is a manic-depressive and an alcoholic, is the child of an alcoholic father who left when she was two and a mother who took out her rage by beating Michele's younger sister. When Michele was 12, her mother remarried. Michele's new stepbrother promptly began molesting her. "So I molested my younger brother," confesses Michele. "I also hit him a lot. He was four. I was lost; I didn't know how to deal with things."

At the same time, family and society are expecting more from kids than ever before. Parental pressure to make good grades, get into college and qualify for the team can be daunting. Moreover, kids are increasingly functioning as junior adults in many homes, taking on the responsibility of caring for younger siblings or ailing grandparents. And youngsters' own desires—to be accepted and popular with their peers, especially—only add to the strain.

Children express the panic and anxiety they feel in myriad ways: in massive weight gains or losses, in nightmares and disturbed sleep, in fatigue or listlessness, in poor grades or truancy, in continual arguing or fighting, in drinking or drug abuse, in reckless driving or sexual promiscuity, in stealing and mugging. A fairly typical history among disturbed kids, says Dr. L. David Zinn, co-director of Northwestern Memorial Hospital's Adolescent Program, includes difficulty in school at age eight or nine, withdrawal from friends and family and persistent misbehavior at 10 or 11 and skipping school by 15. But the most serious indication of despair—and the most devastating—is suicide attempts. According to a report issued in June by a commission formed by the American Medical Association and the National Association of State Boards of Education, about 10% of teenage boys and 18% of girls try to kill themselves at least once.

Despite the urgency of the problems, only 1 in 5 children who need therapy receives it; poor and minority youngsters get the least care. Treatment is expensive, and even those with money and insurance find it hard to afford. But another reason is that too often the signals of distress are missed or put down to normal mischief.

Treatment relies on therapeutic drugs, reward and punishment, and especially counseling—not just of the youngster but of the entire family. The goal is to instill in the children a feeling of self-worth and to teach them discipline and responsibility. Parents, meanwhile, are taught how to provide emotional support, assert authority and set limits.

One of the most ambitious efforts to reconstruct family life is at Logos School, a private academy outside St. Louis that was founded two decades ago for troubled teens. Strict rules governing both school and extracurricular life are laid out for parents in a 158-page manual. Families are required to have dinner together every night, and parents are expected to keep their children out of establishments or events, say local hangouts or rock concerts, where drugs are known to be sold.

Parents must also impose punishments when curfews and other rules are broken. Says Lynn, whose daughter Sara enrolled at Logos: "My first reaction when I read the parents' manual was that there wasn't a thing there that I didn't firmly believe in, but I'd been too afraid to do it on my own. It sounds like such a cop-out, but we wanted Sara to be happy."

As necessary and beneficial as treatment may be, it makes better sense to prevent emotional turmoil among youngsters by improving the environment they live in. Most important, parents must spend more time with sons and daughters and give them the attention and love they need. To do less will guarantee that ever more children will be struggling for sanity. —*Reported by Kathleen Brady/New York, Elizabeth Taylor/Chicago and James Willwerth/Los Angeles*

Emerging Leadership Needs in Education

School systems across the country are crying out for leadership. Meanwhile, low-quality education and an increasing number of "at-risk" children demand a new response to educating our youth.

Michael Usdan

Michael Usdan is president of the Institute for Educational Leadership. This article is adapted from his presentation to the 96th National Conference on Governance, November 17, 1990, Baltimore, Md.

We need to reassess the traditional separation of schools and general-purpose government predicated on a demography that would compel such a reassessment in terms of the problems of children and family. This focus is justified by a broadening of the base of participation in education, extending to the business and political communities. This paper deals with the demographic changes in our communities, the continued active involvement of the business community, and the increased involvement of the political leadership, in terms of the saliency of educational issues, symbolically represented in the Charlottesville Education Summit, where for the third time in American history the governors and the president assembled to discuss education and the development of national educational goals.

The evolving demographics of our nation, particularly with respect to young children, will continue to compel linkages between schools and units of general-purpose government. George Bernard Shaw is alleged to have said that the mark of a truly well-educated man is the capacity to be moved by statistics. Last May, Columbia University's National Center for Children and Poverty completed a statistical profile of America's poorest young citizens, distilling data available on children aged six years and younger. The profile pulls together in frighteningly compelling ways the demographic realities that confront this society in terms of our "seed corn"—our children—and our future. The Columbia University study suggests that while those of us eligible for charter membership in AARP may be in a position to fade away gracefully (and comfortably), the prospects for our children and grandchildren are not so bright, and that we face the possibility of our country's becoming a banana republic within 15 to 20 years unless we address the conditions facing youth.

The percentage of children under the age of six living in poverty is greater than for any other age group in our nation. In fact, of the six national education goals identified by the Charlottesville summit, the learning readiness goal, without any question, is the most significant. If we do nothing else but focus on readiness we will make great progress. We have five million young children living in families below the poverty line; the nation's poorest citizens are its youngest. Twenty-three percent of children under six years of age surveyed by the Columbia study were living in poverty—abject poverty, according to the Census Bureau definition of 12,600 dollars a year for a family of four. In our largest and densest urban areas, where the cost of living is generally higher but incomes may modestly exceed the Census Bureau poverty cut-offs, enough children under six are growing up in abject poverty—or in such economically marginal circumstances to be close to the poverty line—to support the assertion that some 40 percent of young children are economically deprived.

Fifty percent of black children and 40 percent of Hispanic children under age six live in the abject poverty category with its attendant social problems and prospects, such as low achievement in school, repetition of grades, dropping out, delinquent and criminal behavior, unmarried teen parenting, welfare dependency, low earning prospects if employed, etc. Significantly, most of the children surveyed in the Columbia study had at least one working parent (i.e., only 25 percent of the families in the study were completely welfare dependent). Of great relevance to the political coalitions that will have to be forged to address these issues is the fact that more than half of the poor children in the United States live in suburbs and rural areas. One of the problems we face in framing the problem of poverty is the media's focus on major urban centers. If our knowledge of poverty were formed through newspaper and broadcast reporting alone, we would be inclined to think that poverty were a problem among inner cities exclusively. Poverty is pervasive, and there are constituencies to approach in rural and suburban settings, as well as cities. The coalition politics needed to address the problem comprehensively, however, is not being practiced very creatively.

Of the five million poor children identified by the 1987 data, 2.1 million were Caucasian (40 percent), 1.6 million were black, one million were Hispanic and 300,000 were other minorities. These critical and frightening demographic trends must trigger a whole new set of responses on the part of schools and other social service agencies. The schools have to be involved; located in every community in the United States, at the grass roots, no other institution has the social penetration of the schools.

The result of our century-long effort to keep the abuses of patronage politics out of schools has been to recreate them as public entities totally separated from general-purpose government, social service and health agencies, and the juvenile justice system. Moreover, school board elections are separated from general elections, with an amplification of the apathy expressed by low voter participation in political institutions. The separation is now dysfunctional. If 40 percent of children under six are growing up in poverty and need a set of comprehensive and integrated services, the disjointed and fragmented services now being offered them—without coordinated and systemic case management—must be re-evaluated. General government, including mayors and city councils, must become as aggressive in educational issues as the governors during the past five to eight years. The issues, of course, extend beyond education to include poverty. The earlier we intervene in the poverty and school-preparedness lifecycle—pre-natal would be ideal—the better off we will be as a society, and the greater return we will derive from our "investment," to couch the issue in crass economic terms, rather than terms of morality, equity and equalization.

The seminal reports that have been released by the Committee for Economic Development, "To Invest in Our Children" (1985) and "Children in Need" (1987), are wonderfully persuasive, offering a practical program for corporate investment in pre-school, early childhood intervention, and pre-natal health services. The Business Roundtable (BRT) initiative is a terribly important movement *politically*. If one looks at the demographic realities and the political equation, the number of adults with children in the public schools in the United States is now around 23 percent. Moreover, the constituency for public education is increasingly minority, economically disadvantaged, and politically disenfranchised.

The reality is that public education will have to build much broader political coalitions with other groups. Schools must break out of their provincialism and parochialism and recognize the political reality of these new constituencies and work with them. The Business Roundtable, the Committee for Economic Development, and the U.S. Chamber of Commerce's Education Center are increasingly involved. The BRT initiative, through which major corporations will be involved in the education reform movement nationwide, is terribly important. The dollars for this effort will have to come from the public sector and, pragmatically, the political support for this movement will be essential. In the future, one of the great ironies of American educational policy making will be that the American business community—of all groups—will be pushing national officials and others toward national standards and national expectations for schools. As this group proceeds to address the complex morass that is the governance of American public education (50 state systems, no constitutional procedure for education, 15,000 school systems of various kinds) it will discover the difficulty of changing the system. The business and political communities will be stressing accountability and national standards. The business community will stay involved because of issues such as work force and competitiveness. It will be these business leaders who will be pushing the national administration toward national standards and national expectations. Ideally, we will develop more eclectic and responsive measures of student productivity and achievement, instead of depending on more traditional means such as the multiple-choice tests. The College Board of the Educational Testing Service is already moving in this direction. Had educators suggested five or seven years ago that we needed national standards and accountability, these same organizations would have rejected the idea out-of-hand as a result of the deeply-rooted theology of localism in American education. While many people view these local school boards as a part of the problem rather than the solution, they cannot be ignored. Political and business leaders will continue to work through established local organizations as they seek change.

Conclusion

Collaboration in improving education is a central concept that is coming into vogue. Some view the current levels of collaboration among education, social services, welfare, and health services as somewhat hopeless—with few established incentives for further cooperation (indeed, there are disincentives in the public sector for education providers to cross governmental boundaries). Some cynically view collaboration as an "unnatural act." While collaboration will not be easy, it will be absolutely essential if we are serious about meeting the needs of children.

EDUCATION: THE PATH TO URBAN GREATNESS

The success of urban centers is linked to effective public education systems incorporating innovative approaches to school structure, learning and community involvement.

Kurt L. Schmoke

Kurt L. Schmoke is mayor of Baltimore, Md. This article is adapted from his remarks to the 96th National Conference on Governance, November 16, 1991, Baltimore, Md.

Baltimore is embarking on a brain-power revolution, a revolution in which the intellect of our citizens will propel us along the path to urban greatness. This path is education, and it is marked by new approaches to schools, learning, and community involvement. The role of education in achieving this future is well understood. When three hundred of the city's emerging leaders met this past spring to envision Baltimore in the year 2020, they divided into ten groups with each group discussing a particular issue such as public safety, economic development, housing and community development, race relations, and regionalism. Virtually every group linked a successful vision of their topic to education. Their consensus echoed our resolve to make Baltimore "The City That Reads."

From a political point of view, there are problems with making education the top priority of a mayoral administration. You can't see education; there are no ribbon-cuttings, it doesn't change the skyline, and improvements are slow and arduous in coming. But better schools and sharper minds are what Baltimore and other cities need most in the 1990s. Education is our future, and Baltimore has now fully embraced this vision.

How is education the path to urban greatness? Strong public school systems and highly-regarded universities will attract more families to central cities. A technologically-advanced work force will attract and support business. Ingenuity makes for productivity and—in the case of Baltimore—will ensure prominence in the international marketplace. Through education we can prevent social problems that drain our human and financial resources. Through education we can show people other options to early parenthood, substance abuse and crime. Through education we can

Strong public school systems and highly-regarded universities will attract more families to central cities.

dispel the ignorance that fuels prejudice. Education is both a moral imperative and an economic necessity.

The brain-power revolution in Baltimore is born of necessity and forethought. Already there is an increasing disparity between the knowledge-based jobs and the number of people in the work force with adequate skills and training. This trend must be reversed. In Baltimore—with Westinghouse Electric and Johns Hopkins University the largest area employers—we have taken steps to reduce the number of young people abandoning their public education careers at an early age.

To ensure Baltimore's high-tech future, we have launched projects such as The Christopher Columbus Center for Marine Research and Exploration. We intend for the city of Baltimore to become in the area of marine biotechnology what Cape Canaveral is to the space program. Maryland's recent sponsorship of a "High-Tech Week" also underscored the tremendous strides that area businesses and universities have made as leaders of the biotechnology boom. We have recognized that our economy now and in the future will rely heavily on the industries of the mind.

We also know that our education system is not now achieving all that it must. As a report from the National Endowment of the Humanities has confirmed, many of our public schools—the foundation of our education system—have serious problems. Why? We frequently try to answer this question by parcelling-out blame. We blame the parents, we blame increased societal demands, teachers, administrators, television, Nintendo, heavy metal and rap music, and of course, finally, we blame the children. Obviously we are right in looking for causes, but assessing blame does not move the problems closer to a solution.

First, despite severe financial problems in public education, there are islands of excellence. Our schools can work. There are countless examples in Baltimore of schools that succeed, and we know that teachers still can perform miracles in the classroom and that our children can excel. A local teacher, in fact, recently received the Presidential Award for Excellence in Science and Mathematics Teaching. In addition, a student graduated last year from one of our high schools while earning college credits and performing community service. These are just two examples of the educational system really working well.

How can we ensure that these examples of excellence are the rule and not the exception? How can we be sure that the system will always work? Often we begin problem-solving in the manner of fairy tales—"Once upon a time . . ."—but a fairy tale doesn't always come true. We need to free ourselves of old images of what education systems should be, and instead create a system that works for today. As they say in the health profession, we need to start with people "where they are."

Three Principles

We have looked at these islands of excellence. In looking at what works for our constituency we have developed three basic principles about the educational process. First and foremost is that an education process needs to support and encourage that primary relationship between teacher and student. The second

is that schools need to be fully integrated with the community. The third is that children, like adults, need to be motivated; they need to see education in the broader context of their lives.

With respect to the first principle of teachers and students, we are enhancing that teacher-student relationship in a number of ways. First, by increasing teachers' salaries and including them in the decision-making process. We have also reduced class sizes in the early elementary grades so that teachers can give more individual attention to their students. We have a number of programs to combat teenage pregnancy. Our pregnancy prevention programs help us make certain that adolescents are in school and not at home raising babies. We have located one such program in a large urban shopping mall so it is accessible to young people. To minimize distractions to learning, we have instituted a strict city-wide dress code and encouraged the adoption of uniforms. To illustrate the context, Baltimore has a population of roughly 750,000, with 105,000 students in our school system of 186 schools. The uniform dress code—a completely voluntary program which the parents and the PTA vote upon—in three years has expanded from six schools to approximately 70 schools. All of these projects are designed to help teachers concentrate on what they do best, which is encouraging young people to think, study, analyze and create.

Also central to supporting the educational process in the classroom is ensuring that our children arrive at school ready and able to learn. About 60 percent of our children are eligible for Chapter 1 funding of one sort

Through education we can show people other options to early parenthood, substance abuse and crime.

or another, meaning that they come from homes that are economically or socially disadvantaged. In Baltimore the efforts that address pressing social issues include an innovative outreach program to increase prenatal care, transitional housing, strong Head Start centers, and secure the establishment of 23 pre-school programs inside a public school building.

The final step to improving the classroom learning environment has been outside help, from parents and the private sector. We have learned that we cannot presume that all parents are literate or that they all believe in education. In Baltimore we are working diligently to increase our own adult literacy programs and make the schools more user-friendly for parents. Several private and nonprofit partners are supporting this effort. A group called the Citizens Planning and Housing Association produces individualized school report cards to give parents the information they need about their schools. Instead of the kids, the school gets a report card from CPHA which analyzes elements like drop-out rates, budget factors, equipment, tenure, etc. In this way parents learn more about the schools.

Baltimore schools are using more technology to support parents with information. Some schools have computerized systems for calling parents if their children are absent. Some schools have a homework hotline which parents can call to learn what has been assigned by each teacher. In Baltimore we have noted that cases of child abuse increase on "report card day." In response, report cards are distributed with an insert for parents (which they see before they get to the grades) that supplies information about encouraging the child instead of abusing the child.

We ask parents to do a lot, but sometimes parents either are not around or need help, so we try to give children additional outside partners. We have recently begun providing special help at library-based neighborhood homework centers—we converted a library into a homework center and provided mentors. Our mentorship programs have been very successful. One of these is called RAISE—Raising Ambition and Instilling Self-Esteem—whereby volunteers assist our young people and follow them through their school careers.

In Baltimore we believe firmly that schools need to be integrated with the community. Thanks to the changes in our lifestyles, schools now are perhaps the only community institutions that touch virtually every household, and while we often blame societal changes for placing additional burdens on the schools, these changes also provide us with the unique opportunity to use the schools as a focal point of the neighborhood. A school that is fully integrated with the community is a school that prepares children for future opportunities and challenges. To fill this role, schools must be flexible enough to adapt to change and receive adequate support. This means breaking down the walls between the communities and the schools. For too long parents

We need to free ourselves of old images of what education systems should be, and instead create a system that works for today.

have viewed schools as the outpost of some huge, monolithic, impenetrable system. School headquarters always seem mysterious and guarded.

The Berlin Wall is not the only wall that has fallen recently. In Baltimore we have spent the last two years first empowering the public to become involved in the schools and then developing systems to facilitate that involvement. The latest of these projects will begin in September, 1991 when a model school restructuring program will start in 20 schools. Each of those participating schools will have an advisory council: a governing council made up of parents, school officials and community representatives. The councils will assume responsibility and authority for governing the schools. The schools, in turn, will be much more accountable to their students, and we are going to increase the allocations to each of the schools that participates. We are engaged in restructuring for a positive impact on student performance, and eventually this reform program will be implemented in all of our public schools.

We have also invited community groups to participate in other ways. We have efforts such as business partnerships, and adopt-a-school programs; Chase Manhattan, for example, now sends employees to read to kindergarten and first grade students in one of our local elementary schools. They then give each of the first graders, after they finish reading, a copy of that book, so that the children are building up their own personal library. It has worked remarkably well.

Thanks to the changes in our lifestyles, schools now are perhaps the only community institutions that touch virtually every household.

Our school system now is 85 percent black. We are trying to revise the curriculum to include more of the contributions of African-Americans. A female 1990 MacArthur Fellowship winner is working with us on the effort to infuse more of the African-American experience into our curriculum to give our kids a real sense of history, culture, and self worth.

Baltimore's Commonwealth program has served as an outlet for church-based groups and community organizations interested in promoting the cause of public education. The program offers students with 95 percent attendance and passing grades a range of opportunities: employment, college assistance, and partnerships with businesses. Through the program, a number of our students have begun to change their attitudes and their outlooks as they see that with these guarantees education is going to work for anybody willing to work for an education.

Partnerships Do Not Replace Funding

One of the keys to improved education is ensuring equity in school finance, as many other states are now striving to do. Baltimore has a number of programs that demonstrate money *does* work. In one of our high schools we focused on a certain class; we gave them increased resources, we told them we would guarantee scholarships if they delivered a certain level of effort over the academic year, and we provided for one-on-one mentoring throughout the year. The result: In that class, 80 percent of the students graduated versus 45 percent in the class before them. Moreover, 80 percent of this class was accepted into college versus 9 percent in the previous class. Money can work if money is targeted in the right ways.

Through democracy and empowerment we can encourage the federal government to get involved once again in targeted ways with communities. We believe that there is an appropriate role for the federal government in education. Some argue that a quality education should be a federal guarantee to all at-risk children. If there is one area of education where the federal government should put its money, it is in early childhood education, to guarantee that every child who is eligible will in fact become a participant in the Head Start program. The United Negro College Fund slogan says it all: A Mind is a Terrible Thing to Waste. In this era of conservation we have at our disposal a major energy source, brainpower—a power source that is renewable, clean, efficient, and money-making. Baltimore is determined to run on this power along its path to urban greatness.

The 23rd Annual
GALLUP POLL
Of the Public's Attitudes
Toward the Public
Schools

Stanley M. Elam, Lowell C. Rose, and Alec M. Gallup

STANLEY M. ELAM (Indiana University Chapter) is contributing editor of the Phi Delta Kappan. *He was* Kappan *editor from 1956 through 1980 and has been coordinating Phi Delta Kappa's polling program since his retirement. LOWELL C. ROSE (Indiana University Chapter) is executive director of Phi Delta Kappa. ALEC M. GALLUP is co-chairman, with George Gallup, Jr., of the Gallup Organization, Princeton, N.J.*

THE STRATEGY announced by the Bush Administration last spring for achieving six national goals for education by the year 2000 receives strong public support in the 23rd annual Gallup/Phi Delta Kappa Poll of the Public's Attitudes Toward the Public Schools — even stronger than the goals themselves received in last year's poll. Americans remain highly doubtful, however, that the six goals, first announced in February 1990, can be attained by the target date. In addition, most of the specific measures for public school improvement endorsed by the Bush Administration receive strong support from the U.S. public.

There are at least 10 elements in the strategy for school improvement outlined by Bush and his new education secretary, Lamar Alexander. The first is parental choice of the school a child will attend, a proposal intended primarily to introduce more accountability and competition into what is considered a stultified and complacent monopoly. Accountability would also be promoted by a "voluntary" national system of achievement testing and by a national report card to provide clear and comparable information to the public on how schools, school districts, states, and the nation are progressing. To promote more effective teaching, teachers would receive extra pay for proven merit, for teaching "core" subjects (English, math, science, history, and geography), for teaching in dangerous or challenging settings, and for serving as mentors for new teachers. The school day and year would be extended, with attendance optional and parents paying the extra cost. Greater flexibility for schools would be en-

couraged; this means, presumably, that various forms of restructuring and shifting of responsibility would be rewarded. Other features of the strategy: the creation of 535 "New American Schools," one in each congressional district and two additional ones per state, each with as few restrictions as possible; the establishment of "America 2000 Communities," not yet defined; the setting of job-related skill standards; and the founding of "skill centers" in communities and workplaces.

Here is how the public views some of these reform ideas:

• People favor (by 62% to 33%) allowing students and parents to choose which public schools in their community the students attend, regardless of where they live. But few people with children in the public schools say that their children would change schools if given such a choice.

• People favor paying extra for particularly effective teaching (69% in favor, 24% opposed), for teaching in hazardous or challenging situations (63% in favor, 29% opposed), and for serving as mentors to new teachers (49% in favor, 39% opposed). But they oppose extra pay for teaching "core" subjects (39% in favor, 53% opposed).

• People overwhelmingly favor requiring the public schools in their communities to conform to national achievement standards and goals (81% in favor, 12% opposed). They also approve of requiring public schools in their communities to use a standardized national curriculum (68% in favor, 24% opposed). And they approve of requiring public schools in their communities to use standardized national tests to measure academic achievement (77% in favor, 17% opposed). More specifically, people approve of tests in English, math, science, history, and geography (88% in favor, 8% opposed); in problem-solving skills (84% in favor, 10% opposed); and in writing a clear composition or paper on some topic (85% in favor, 10% opposed).

• On the question of extending the school day and year, there is less agreement. However, for the first time since the

Reprinted by permission from *Phi Delta Kappan*, September 1991, pp. 41-56.

question was initially asked in 1982, a majority of respondents (51%) favor extending the school year, while 42% oppose the idea. Only 46% would lengthen the school day by an hour, while 48% oppose the idea. A sizable majority oppose the idea of making the longer school day or year optional, with parents who choose the option paying the extra cost; the vote was 36% in favor, 56% opposed.

• The first of the six national goals for education announced in February 1990 by President Bush and the nation's governors was that, by the year 2000, all American children will start school ready to learn. Not only did poll respondents give this goal a high priority, but they also endorsed preschool programs at public expense for parents who want them. Fifty-five percent favor such programs; 40% oppose them.

I N THE PAGES that follow, the findings on other questions related to the Administration's education agenda are presented, along with more details concerning the findings above and responses to questions on a number of other topics. The 1991 poll is the most comprehensive survey of American attitudes on education to be conducted in the series, which began in 1969. Gallup field interviewers asked a scientifically selected sample of 1,500 U.S. adults a total of 80 questions, twice the usual number.

America's Future Strength

The first question asked this year dealt with three sources of America's strength: education, industry, and the military. Only weeks after a military victory in the Persian Gulf, less than half (41%) of poll respondents considered "building the strongest military force in the world" to be very important. By contrast, 89% regarded "developing the best education system in the world" as very important. A smaller majority (59%) regarded "developing the most efficient industrial production system in the world" as very important. In short, Americans recognize that a strong education system is fundamental to national well-being; nothing will work without a well-educated citizenry.*

The question:

In determining America's strength in the future, say 25 years from now, how important do you feel each of the following factors will be — very important, fairly important, not too important, or not at all important?

	Very Important %	Fairly Important %	Not Too Important %	Not at All Important %	Don't Know %
Developing the best education system in the world	89	9	1	*	1
Developing the most efficient industrial production system in the world	59	32	5	*	4
Building the strongest military force in the world	41	39	15	3	2

*Less than one-half of 1%.

*A Yankelovich Clancy Shulman poll taken in early June for *Time/*CNN found that, if America decided to devote resources equal to those of the Persian Gulf War to domestic purposes, 73% of respondents wanted to spend them on providing American children with the best education of any nation in the world. Health care was second, with 64%; economic competitiveness was third, with 54%.

The same question was asked in three previous polls, with these results:

| | Very Important | | |
	1988 %	1984 %	1982 %
Developing the best education system in the world	88	82	84
Developing the most efficient industrial production system in the world	65	70	66
Building the strongest military force in the world	47	45	47

National Goals for Education

Shortly after the President and the nation's governors announced their six national goals for education in February 1990, interviewers for the 22nd Gallup/Phi Delta Kappa poll asked Americans three questions about the goals: What priority would you assign to each goal? How likely is it that each goal will be reached by the year 2000? Would you tend to vote for political candidates who support the goals? The public strongly supported each goal but expressed profound skepticism about attaining them. There was at least modest support for the idea of voting for political candidates who favor the goals.

The first two of these questions were asked again in 1991. The public gave even higher priorities to each goal, but public skepticism about reaching them was as high as last year. Once again, the highest priority was assigned to the sixth goal: making sure that, by the year 2000, every school is free of drugs and violence and offers a disciplined environment conducive to learning.

Support for the national education goals is consistent across every segment of the population: men and women; whites, nonwhites, Hispanics, and blacks; all age groups; Republicans, Democrats, and independents; all levels of education, from grade school dropouts through college graduates; people in all regions of the U.S. and in communities of various sizes; people in all major occupation groups; people at all income levels; and people with or without children in either public or private schools. Pessimism about the chances of reaching the goals was also consistent among the various demographic groups.

The first question:

This card describes several national education goals that have been recommended for attainment by the year 2000. First, would you read over the descriptions of the different goals on the card. Now, as I read off each goal by letter, would you tell me how high a priority you feel that goal should be given during the coming decade — very high, high, low, or very low?
A. By the year 2000, all children in America will start school ready to learn [i.e., in good health, having been read to and otherwise prepared by parents, etc.].
B. By the year 2000, the high school graduation rate will increase to at least 90% [from the current rate of 74%].

C. By the year 2000, American students will leave grades 4, 8, and 12 having demonstrated competency in challenging subject matter, including English, mathematics, science, history, and geography. In addition, every school in America will insure that all students learn to use their minds, in order to prepare them for responsible citizenship, further learning, and productive employment in a modern economy.

D. By the year 2000, American students will be first in the world in mathematics and science achievement.

E. By the year 2000, every adult American will be literate and will possess the skills necessary to compete in a global economy and to exercise the rights and responsibilities of citizenship.

F. By the year 2000, every school in America will be free of drugs and violence and will offer a disciplined environment conducive to learning.

Priority Assigned Each Goal

Goal	Very High % 1991	1990	High % 1991	1990	Low % 1991	1990	Very Low % 1991	1990	Don't Know % 1991	1990
A	52	44	38	44	6	6	1	2	3	4
B	54	45	37	42	5	8	1	1	3	4
C	55	46	35	42	6	7	1	2	3	3
D	43	34	41	42	11	16	2	3	3	5
E	50	45	36	37	9	11	2	3	3	4
F	63	55	23	26	6	9	5	6	3	4

The second question:

As I read off each goal by letter again, would you tell me whether you think reaching that goal by the year 2000 is very likely, likely, unlikely, or very unlikely?

Likelihood of Goal Attainment

Goal	Very Likely % 1991	1990	Likely % 1991	1990	Unlikely % 1991	1990	Very Unlikely % 1991	1990	Don't Know % 1991	1990
A	10	12	37	38	33	33	14	12	6	5
B	6	10	36	35	39	37	14	12	5	6
C	6	9	36	38	36	36	15	12	7	5
D	4	6	22	23	45	41	23	24	6	6
E	6	7	25	25	41	42	23	21	5	5
F	4	5	14	14	38	40	39	36	5	5

A National Report Card

Americans want to know what progress is being made toward attaining the national goals for education. By a margin of better than 3-1, they favor preparation and publication of "public school report cards" for individual schools, for each school district, for each state, and for the nation. Again, every category of respondent supports the idea of report cards on the schools, but parents of public school children are particularly enthusiastic.

The question:

It has been proposed that public school report cards be prepared and made public to show what progress is being made toward achievement of the national education goals. Would you favor or oppose such report cards?

	For Local Schools %	For Local District %	For the State %	For the Nation %
Favor	73	76	75	75
Oppose	22	19	19	19
Don't know	5	5	6	6

Accountability Measures

People appear to have more faith in the motivational force of the carrot than the stick. Generally, Americans believe that schools showing progress toward attainment of the national goals for education within a reasonable time should be financially rewarded, but they oppose withholding funds from less successful schools. Instead, they would fire the principals and teachers!

The questions:

If a public school in this community does not show progress toward the national goals within a reasonable time, would you favor or oppose withholding state or federal education funds from that school?

If a public school in this community does show progress toward the national goals within a reasonable time, would you favor or oppose awarding more state and federal education funds to that school?

If a public school in this community does not show progress toward the national goals within a reasonable time, would you favor or oppose not renewing the contracts of the principal and the teachers in that school?

	General Public Favor %	Oppose %	Don't Know %	Public School Parents Favor %	Oppose %	Don't Know %
If unsuccessful, withhold state and federal funds	33	57	10	29	61	10
If successful, award more state and federal funds	64	26	10	64	27	9
If unsuccessful, do not renew principal/teacher contracts	57	32	11	55	34	11

Longer School Day and Year

U.S. public school students spend considerably less time in school than do students in several other developed countries. In Japan, for example, most students attend school 240 days a year, which is about 60 more days or 33% longer, on average, than is the case in the U.S. But Americans have opposed lengthening the school day and year in previous Gallup/Phi Delta Kappa polls

In the 1982 poll, people were first asked these questions: "In some nations, students attend school as many as 240 days a year as compared to about 180 in the U.S. How do you feel about extending the public school year in this community by 30 days, making the school year about 210 days or 10 months long? How do you feel about extending the school day in the public schools in this community by one hour?" Respondents opposed both ideas by sizable margins — 53% opposed to, 37% in favor of lengthening the school year; 58% opposed to, 37% in favor of a longer day. Opposition was somewhat less strong when the question was asked again in 1983 and in 1984.

This year we found that, for the first time, a majority of Americans (51%) favor a school year of 210 days or 10 months. Opposition to a longer school day declined marginally: 48% oppose the longer day, while 46% favor it.

The longer school year is particularly favored by college graduates (62% in favor, 33% opposed), by professionals and businesspeople (60% in favor, 37% opposed), and by people in the western region of the U.S. (59% in favor, 36% opposed).

The questions:

In some nations, students attend school as many as 240 days a year as compared to about 180 days in the U.S. How do you feel about extending the public school year in this community by 30 days, making the school year about 210 days or 10 months long? Do you favor or oppose this idea?

How do you feel about extending the school *day* in the public schools of this community by one hour? Do you favor or oppose this idea?

	Extend School Year 30 Days				Extend School Day One Hour			
	1991 %	1984 %	1983 %	1982 %	1991 %	1984 %	1983 %	1982 %
Favor	51	44	40	37	46	42	41	37
Oppose	42	50	49	53	48	52	48	53
Don't know	7	6	11	10	6	6	11	10

In view of the recommendations in America 2000, a question was added this year to sample public opinion on the idea of making a longer school day or year optional, with parents who choose the option paying tuition to cover the extra cost. This idea was unpopular among virtually all population groups.

The question:

It has been suggested that public schools make it optional for students to attend a longer school day or longer school year. Parents of students who choose this option would pay tuition to cover the extra cost. Are you in favor of or opposed to this suggestion?

	National Totals		
	Favor %	Oppose %	Don't Know %
Longer school day or year optional, with parents who choose it paying extra cost	36	56	8

Publicly Supported Preschools

The first of the national goals announced by President Bush and the nation's governors calls for all children to start school ready to learn. Most educators believe that tax-supported preschool programs for 3- and 4-year-olds would advance this goal significantly. A question in the current poll shows that

the public tends to agree, although not all groups embrace the idea. Some 55% favor tax-supported preschool for children whose parents want it, while 40% oppose the idea.

Congress passed a law in 1971 (vetoed by President Nixon) that would have provided day care for millions of young children. A Gallup/Phi Delta Kappa poll in 1976 showed that public support for a measure that would provide child-care centers as part of the public school system was by no means universal in that era. Although nonwhites favored it (76% to 15%) and persons between the ages of 18 and 29 approved it (64% to 32%), overall support was only 46%, while opposition came from 49%. Five years later, the poll asked if parents of 3- to 5-year-olds participating in preschool programs operated by the public schools should pay for them. An overwhelming 83% said yes, and only 10% said no.

While *preschool programs* and *day care* are not necessarily synonymous, the findings reported above suggest that there has been a considerable change in public opinion on this issue since 1976. Majorities in all but a few major demographic groups now favor tax-supported preschools. Support is particularly strong among young adults, nonwhites, and persons with children in school. People over age 50 and people who are not in the labor force are less favorably disposed toward tax-supported preschool programs.

The question:

It has been proposed that the public schools make preschool programs available to 3- and 4-year-olds whose parents wish such programs. These programs would be supported by taxes. Would you favor or oppose such programs?

	Favor %	Oppose %	Don't Know %
NATIONAL TOTALS	55	40	5
Selected Demographic Groups*			
Race			
White	53	42	5
Nonwhite	70	26	4
Hispanic**	62	32	6
Black	72	26	2
Age			
18 - 29 years	70	27	3
30 - 49 years	56	40	4
50 and over	45	48	7
50 - 64 years	50	44	6
65 and over	39	53	8
Politics			
Republican	49	45	6
Democrat	59	37	4
Independent	56	38	6
Occupation			
Professional and business	60	38	2
Clerical/sales	58	40	2
Manual labor	58	37	5
Nonlabor force	47	45	8
Religion			
Protestant	52	44	4
Catholic	56	38	6
Parents of children under 18			
One child	65	32	3
Two children	60	36	4
Three or more children	65	32	3

*The full Gallup Organization report of this poll provides breakdowns of responses from 13 major demographic categories and 59 subgroups. Major categories not included in this table are education level, occupation of chief wage earner, sex, region of the country, income, community size, and children in school (none in school, public school parents, and nonpublic school parents).

**"Hispanic" includes all races with Hispanic connections.

National Curriculum, Standards, and Tests

If the public will governs, the following developments are inevitable in America: a national curriculum, national standards of achievement in five subjects and in thinking and writing skills; national tests to determine whether the national standards are being met; report cards for individual schools, school districts, states, and the nation; and an accountability strategy that includes firing teachers and administrators in failing school systems.

Public opinion on local, state, and national report cards and on accountability strategies was presented earlier. Findings on seven questions related to a national curriculum with its accompanying standards and tests are reported below. The first three of these questions have been asked in earlier polls. The last four were asked for the first time this year.

The first question:

Would you favor or oppose requiring the public schools in this community to use a standardized national curriculum?

Favor %		Oppose %		Don't Know %	
1991	1989	1991	1989	1991	1989
68	69	24	21	8	10

The second question:

Would you favor or oppose requiring the public schools in this community to conform to national achievement standards and goals?

Favor %		Oppose %		Don't Know %	
1991	1989	1991	1989	1991	1989
81	70	12	19	7	11

The third question:

Would you favor or oppose requiring the public schools in this community to use standardized national tests to measure the academic achievement of students?

Favor %		Oppose %		Don't Know %	
1991	1989	1991	1989	1991	1989
77	77	17	14	6	9

Respondents who answered "oppose" or "don't know" to the preceding question this year were also asked:

What if these standardized national tests were made optional for all public schools, so that the policy-making authorities in each district could decide whether or not to give the tests? Would you favor or oppose making these tests optional?

Favor %	Oppose %	Don't Know %
57	20	23

The fourth question:

Would you favor or oppose requiring the public schools in this community to use standardized testing programs to measure students' achievement in the following areas:
A. knowledge in five core subjects: English, math, science, history, and geography?
B. problem-solving skills?
C. ability to write a clear composition or paper on some topic?

Area	Favor %	Oppose %	Don't Know %
Core subjects	88	8	4
Problem-solving skills	84	10	6
Ability to write	85	10	5

The fifth question:

If standardized national tests were given to students in this community, how do you think they would score on these tests — above average, below average, or about average?

Above Average %	Below Average %	About Average %	Don't Know %
17	25	51	7

The sixth question:

Now, let's assume that national achievement standards and goals for a student's advancement to the next grade are adopted by the public schools of this community. Which one of these approaches do you think would be better for a student who fails to meet the standards: require the student to repeat the grade with remedial help, or promote the student to the next grade with remedial help?

Repeat Grade %	Promote %	Don't Know %
58	32	10

The seventh question:

When do you think remedial help should be provided — during the regular school day or outside the school day, such as after school, on Saturdays, and during summer breaks?

During School Day %	Outside School Day %	Both (Volunteered) %	Don't Know %
52	41	2	5

Opinion on these seven questions was fairly uniform among all demographic groups, but some differences are worth pondering:

• Sixty-one percent of parents who reported that their oldest child was above average academically favored a national curriculum. Even more parents (77%) who reported that their oldest child was average or below average favored it.

- Blacks were less enthusiastic about standardized national tests to measure academic achievement than the population as a whole (69% versus 77%).
- People in the East were more favorable toward national tests than those in other sections of the country (East, 84%; Midwest, 73%; South, 75%; West, 74%).

Vouchers, Choice, and The Public/Private School Issue

Several states are already experimenting with parental choice of the schools children attend, but the choice is generally limited to public schools. President Bush has said that he would like parental choice programs to include all schools that serve the public and are accountable to public authority, regardless of who runs them. Several questions in this year's poll were framed to see how this somewhat ambiguous position fares in the arena of public opinion.

As poll findings over the years show, school vouchers have never been particularly popular in this country. This year, however, support rose by six percentage points over 1987, when the question was last asked. Today, 50% of the public say they approve of vouchers, while 39% oppose them. These percentages are virtually the same as those reported for the year 1983, when the question was asked shortly after publication of *A Nation at Risk*, the government report that aroused widespread concern about the quality of the public schools.

The question:

In some nations, the government allots a certain amount of money for each child's education. The parents can then send the child to any public, parochial, or private school they choose. This is called the "voucher system." Would you like to see such an idea adopted in this country?

National Totals

	1991 %	1987 %	1986 %	1985 %	1983 %	1981 %	1971 %	1970 %
Favor	50	44	46	45	51	43	38	43
Oppose	39	41	41	40	38	41	44	46
Don't know	11	15	13	15	11	16	18	11

The voucher plan finds its strongest support among nonwhites and blacks (57% in both groups), inner-city dwellers (57%), people with children under 18 (58%), and nonpublic school parents (66%).

Opinion on parental choice has been explored in Gallup/Phi Delta Kappa polls since 1985. In 1989, when President Bush and the Department of Education backed experimentation with parental choice plans, respondents were asked whether they favored or opposed allowing students and their parents to choose the public schools the students attend, regardless of where they live. The same question has been asked each year since then, with results that are remarkably uniform. In 1991, support for school choice approaches a 2-1 majority in virtually every major population segment, including parents of public school children.

The question:

Do you favor or oppose allowing students and their parents to choose which public schools in this community the students attend, regardless of where they live?

	Favor		Oppose		Don't Know	
	1991 %	1990 %	1991 %	1990 %	1991 %	1990 %
NATIONAL TOTALS	62	62	33	31	5	7
Sex						
Men	61	61	35	34	4	5
Women	62	63	32	29	6	8
Race						
White	60	60	35	34	5	6
Nonwhite	69	72	25	18	6	10
Age						
18 - 29 years	71	72	26	23	3	5
30 - 49 years	66	63	30	31	4	6
50 and over	50	54	42	38	8	8
Community Size						
1 million and over	62	64	32	27	6	9
500,000 - 999,999	60	61	37	36	3	3
50,000 - 499,999	68	60	27	33	5	7
2,500 - 49,999	62	61	34	36	4	3
Under 2,500	57	60	38	33	5	7
Education						
College	61	62	35	33	4	5
Graduate	60	62	36	30	4	8
Incomplete	61	63	35	34	4	3
High school	64	65	31	28	5	7
Graduate	63	66	32	28	5	6
Incomplete	65	62	31	29	4	9
Income						
$40,000 and over	60	59	37	37	3	4
$30,000 - $39,999	64	62	32	32	4	6
$20,000 - $29,999	61	67	35	27	4	6
$10,000 - $19,999	63	60	30	30	7	10
Under $10,000	59	60	33	31	8	9
Region						
East	61	62	32	27	7	11
Midwest	58	57	39	38	3	5
South	63	66	32	28	5	6
West	62	62	30	34	8	4

This year President Bush has edged toward endorsement of some form of voucher system. He believes that choice programs should include "all schools that serve the public and are accountable to public authority, regardless of who runs them." This implies that so-called private schools — and perhaps parochial schools — should be an option for all parents, presumably at taxpayer expense. Therefore, a new question put the issue directly: "Do you favor or oppose allowing students and parents to choose a private school to attend at public expense?" Public opposition was overwhelming. More than two-thirds of the respondents to this question (68%) opposed the idea, and only 26% favored it, with 6% expressing no opinion.

Gallup interviewers then asked the 26% who favored the idea this follow-up question: "Do you think private schools that accept government tuition payments for these students should be accountable to public school authorities or not?" The tally was 63% in favor of public accountability for private schools that accept government tuition payments, 27% opposed, and 10% expressing no opinion. Thus even people who would tolerate government tuition payments to "private" schools believe that those schools should — in some manner as yet undefined — be held accountable to public school authorities for the use of the money.

If parental choice ever becomes a reality in more than a few experimental situations in America, parents will face new problems. What qualities and characteristics should they look for in their child's school? Do they have enough information to make wise choices? If not, will they find it difficult to get that information? The results of several questions bearing on these problems follow.

1. PERCEPTIONS OF EDUCATION IN NORTH AMERICA

The first question:

This card lists different factors that might be considered in choosing a public school for a child, assuming free choice of public schools were allowed in this community. As I read off each of these factors, would you tell me whether you consider it very important, fairly important, not too important, or not at all important in choosing a local school?

National Totals

	Very Important %	Fairly Important %	Not Too Important %	Not at All Important %	Don't Know %
Quality of the teaching staff	85	11	2	*	2
Maintenance of student discipline	76	20	2	*	2
Curriculum (i.e., the courses offered)	74	21	3	*	2
Size of classes	57	31	9	1	2
Grades or test scores of the student body	46	42	7	1	4
Track record of graduates in high school, in college, or on the job	45	39	12	1	3
Size of the school (number of students)	36	36	22	4	2
Proximity to home	29	45	20	3	3
Extracurricular activities, such as band/orchestra, theater, clubs	19	49	24	5	3
Social and economic background of the student body	22	32	35	8	3
Athletic program	16	37	34	11	2
Racial or ethnic composition of the student body	14	18	46	19	3

*Less than one-half of 1%.

In choosing a school, people say they would look first at the quality of the teaching staff, at the maintenance of discipline, at the curriculum offered, at the size of classes, at test scores, and at the track record of graduates. Interestingly, athletic programs and other extracurricular activities are not particularly important considerations.

Although "racial or ethnic composition of the student body" is at the bottom of the above list, nearly one-third of the public (32%) regards this as a very or fairly important consideration. In 1990 about half of poll respondents (48%) stated that racial and ethnic considerations were very important or fairly important in selecting a school.

When this question was asked in 1990, some students of the poll wondered what respondents had in mind when they said that racial and ethnic composition would be an important factor in their choice of schools. To find out, this year several follow-up questions were asked of those who felt that the issue was important. One asked about the ideal percentage of whites to have in a school, one was an open-ended question about *why* racial and ethnic composition is important, one asked whether it is very important or fairly important that there not be too many members of racial and ethnic minorities in a school, and one asked whether it is very important or fairly important that there not be too few members of these groups.

The findings are revealing. Only 3% of whites, for example, say that the schools should ideally be 100% white, and an identical percentage of nonwhites say that schools should enroll no whites at all. However, in reply to the open-ended "why" question, the most common response (made by about one-third of respondents) was "it is important to have a balanced racial mix." Only a few respondents gave answers that revealed racial prejudice.

On a final question, only 9% of whites say there are too many minority students in the schools, and 13% say there are too few. Blacks, on the other hand, are somewhat less satisfied with the status quo. Thirty percent of blacks say there are too few minority students in the schools, 15% say too many, and 29% say about the right number.

To find out how many parents would choose a school for their children different from the one they now attend, parents with children in the public schools were asked directly whether or not they would choose to change their children's schools.

The question:

If you could choose your children's schools among many of the public schools in this community, would you choose the ones they now attend or different ones?

	National Totals %
Would choose same as now	68
Different ones	23
Don't know	9

To determine whether parents would be well enough informed to make wise decisions in choosing a school, parents with children in school were asked how much they knew about the advantages and disadvantages of the schools in their community, whether they felt they had enough information to make a wise choice for their children, and, if *not*, how difficult they felt it would be to obtain this information.

Almost a third (31%) said that they knew little or nothing at all about the schools, and 38% claimed that they did not have enough information to make a wise choice. Of the latter group, almost half thought this kind of information would be "very difficult" or "fairly difficult" to obtain.

The first question:

How much would you say you know about the advantages and disadvantages of the different public schools in this community — a great deal, a fair amount, very little, or nothing at all?

	National Totals %
A great deal	19
A fair amount	43
Very little	29
Nothing at all	4
No response	5

The second question:

Suppose you could choose any school in this school district. Do you feel you have enough information about the different public schools in this community to make the best choice for a child, or not?

	National Totals %
Yes, know enough	51
No, don't know enough	39
Don't know	10

The third question (asked of those who felt they did not have enough information to make the best choice):

How difficult do you think it would be to obtain this kind of information — very difficult, fairly difficult, not too difficult, or not difficult at all?

	National Totals %
Very difficult	8
Fairly difficult	36
Not too difficult	42
Not difficult at all	7
Don't know	7

The above responses of parents hint at some of the problems that might arise if parents were allowed to choose the schools their children attend. For example, it is clear that many people are not sure they have — or even could easily get — the kind of information about schools that would make good choices possible.

Driver's Licenses and Dropping Out

The second national goal for the year 2000 embraced by the Bush Administration and the nation's governors calls for a dramatic reduction in school dropout rates, so that by the end of the century 90% of all young Americans will be graduating from high school. This goal was considered "very important" by 54% of respondents to this year's poll, although few mentioned dropouts as a major problem in their local public schools.

As every educator knows, there is no single answer to the dropout problem, just as students have no single reason for dropping out. A good strategy will employ many different tactics. One tactic that has caught the attention of legislators in several states is to deny driver's licenses to high school dropouts. As of February 1990, nine states had some form of license suspension for this purpose, including Arkansas, Florida, Indiana, Louisiana, Maine, Texas, Virginia, West Virginia, and Wisconsin. Twenty-five more states were considering legislation for the same purpose. Florida even suspends the licenses of students who have failing grades, and Florida's Dade County had suspended 10,000 licenses only six months into the program.

The general public favors driver's license suspension for dropouts by about a 2-1 margin: 62% in favor, 32% opposed. Support is fairly consistent across population groups; however, three groups that tend to overlap registered milder enthusiasm: blacks, adults who did not complete high school, and persons with incomes under $10,000.

The question:

As a way of keeping students in high school, one state has passed a law that takes away driver's licenses from school dropouts under age 18. Would you favor or oppose such a law in this state?

	National Totals %
Favor	62
Oppose	32
Already have such a law (volunteered)	1
Don't know	5

Children of low-income or ethnic minority parents are more likely than others to drop out of school. Asked to rate eight measures often suggested to help prevent such children from dropping out, poll respondents endorsed all of them, but they particularly favored firmer discipline, remedial classes and services, and preschool programs.

The question:

This card lists some suggestions that have been made for helping low-income and racial or ethnic minority students in school. As I read off each suggestion, one at a time, would you tell me whether you consider it an excellent, good, only fair, or poor way to help low-income and minority students?

Suggestions	Excellent %	Good %	Only Fair %	Poor %	Don't Know %
Firmer discipline	58	27	8	4	3
Special remedial classes and services	52	35	7	2	4
Preschool programs	49	35	8	4	4
Classwork of greater interest and relevance	44	37	10	4	5
Increased school funding	40	31	15	10	4
The chance to choose from a variety of educational programs at their school	36	44	11	5	4
Decisions on school policy made by parents, pupils, and teachers rather than by school district administrators and the school board	32	35	16	11	6
The chance to choose, with their parents, the local schools they attend	25	38	20	13	4

Teacher Pay, Preparation, and Quality

Because differential pay for teachers is being encouraged by the Bush Administration, current poll respondents were asked to judge four bases for differential pay favored by the Administration. They approved two, gave qualified approval to a third, and turned thumbs down on the fourth.

By an overwhelming margin (69% in favor, 24% opposed) people like the idea of extra pay for teaching "particularly effectively." This is no surprise to anyone who has followed these polls. As early as 1970, respondents to the second Gallup education poll were asked whether each teacher should be paid on the basis of the "quality of work" or on a "standard scale." Fifty-eight percent of the respondents chose "quality of work," only 36% chose "standard scale," and 6% were undecided. When the same question was asked in 1983, a slightly larger percentage (61%) chose "quality of work." In that same year, people were also asked whether, because of a shortage of teachers in science, math, and technical/vocational subjects, teachers in those areas should be paid extra. Fifty percent said yes, 35% no. In 1984, 65% of poll respondents favored and 22% opposed the idea of merit pay for teachers. In 1988, 84% of poll respondents favored

1. PERCEPTIONS OF EDUCATION IN NORTH AMERICA

"an increased pay scale for those teachers who have proved themselves particularly capable." Only 11% opposed it.

In the current poll, 63% of the respondents also approve of extra pay for teaching in "dangerous school environments," the equivalent of battle pay in the military. About half (49%) approve of extra pay for teachers serving as mentors for new teachers, but 39% oppose the idea, and a large 12% didn't respond, perhaps because the concept of mentors is not widely understood.

The Administration-backed policy of providing extra pay for teachers of the "core" subjects — English, math, science, history, and geography — proved unpopular: 53% opposed the idea; 39% favored it.

The question:

Do you favor or oppose extra pay for teaching particularly effectively; for teaching the basic "core" subjects — English, math, science, history, and geography; for teaching in dangerous school environments; and for serving as mentors for new teachers?

	Favor %	Oppose %	Don't Know %
For teaching particularly effectively	69	24	7
For teaching in dangerous environments	63	29	8
For serving as mentors for new teachers	49	39	12
For teaching the core subjects	39	53	8

A 1984 Gallup/Phi Delta Kappa poll showed that the general public rates the value of teachers' services to society just below those of the clergy and medical doctors and ahead of school principals, judges, lawyers, business executives, and bankers. The belief that teachers are underpaid is probably tied to this judgment. In six of these polls people have been asked if they think teacher salaries in their communities are too high, too low, or just about right. In every case, those who said too low outnumbered those who said too high by a wide margin. The widest divergence occurred in 1990, when 5% said that teacher pay was too high, 50% said that it was too low, and 31% said that it was about right.

This year the salary question was put in a new form, but the results are similar.

The question:

Would you favor or oppose raising teacher salaries in the public schools of this community at this time?

	National Totals %	No Children In School %	Public School Parents %	Nonpublic School Parents %
Favor raising salaries now	54	51	59	56
Oppose raising salaries now	32	33	30	34
Don't know or no opinion	14	16	11	10

This year several new questions related to teaching ability were asked. The findings show that the public tends to believe that teaching talent is "inborn" rather than the result of "training" but that education courses are very useful (53%) or fairly useful (35%). At the same time, a minority of people would be willing to hire as teachers (particularly for high schools) talented college graduates who are subject-matter specialists, even if they have had no courses in how to teach.

But they would prefer that these specialists demonstrate teaching talent.

The first question:

In your opinion, is the ability to teach or instruct students more the result of natural talent or more the result of college training about how to teach?

	National Totals %
Natural talent	40
College training	25
Both (volunteered)	32
Don't know	3

The second question:

In your opinion, how useful are education courses in training people how to teach or instruct students — very useful, fairly useful, not too useful, or not at all useful?

	Very Useful %	Fairly Useful %	Not Too Useful %	Not at All Useful %	Don't Know %
Education courses	53	35	6	1	5

The third question:

Assume that the people on this list have a college degree, received good grades in college, and wish to teach but have taken no courses in how to teach. Which of these people, if any, would you hire to teach in elementary school? Which would you hire to teach in high school?

	Elementary School %	High School %
People with a high degree of expertise or knowledge in a particular academic subject	26	36
"Experts" in certain nonacademic areas, such as business, industry, or technology	16	37
Persons with a high degree of expertise in a particular academic subject who also demonstrate a talent for teaching or instruction	77	68
Don't know	11	9

(Figures add to more than 100% because of multiple answers.)

Control of Schools

Many leaders of school reform are convinced that constructive change in the system will come only when local teachers and principals — and sometimes parents as well — have the freedom to make and implement policy decisions heretofore reserved for school boards and top administrators. Site-based management has become one of the foundation stones of the so-called restructuring movement.

The general public seems to share this view. In the current poll, 76% of the respondents favor giving principals and teachers more say in how their local schools are run; 14% oppose the idea. Moreover, the public favors giving policy-making power to councils composed of local principals and teachers, as has been done in Chicago, rather than leaving it with boards and top administrators. On this question the vote is even more lopsided: 79% in favor to 11% opposed.

This distrust of boards and central offices showed up in last year's poll. The public believes that parents should have more say in several policy areas, including the allocation of school funds, the curriculum, selection and hiring of administrators and teachers, teacher and administrator salaries, and selection of textbooks, instructional materials, and books placed in school libraries.

The first question:

In most school districts the school superintendent and school board have more to say about how the local public schools are run than the principals and teachers. Would you favor or oppose giving the principals and teachers more say about how the public schools in this community are run?

	National Totals %
Favor more say for principals and teachers	76
Oppose more say for principals and teachers	14
No opinion	10

The second question:

In most school districts, policy decisions and changes are made by the school board and its administrative staff. In a few districts, however, some of these decisions are made by councils composed of local public school teachers, principals, and parents. Which way would you prefer to have policy decisions made in the schools in this community — by the school board and its administrative staff or by a council of teachers, principals, and parents?

	National Totals %
Decisions by council of teachers, etc.	79
Decisions by school board, etc.	11
No opinion	10

School Finance

There are now 10 states in which the state's highest court has found the school finance system unconstitutional because of great disparities among school districts in per-pupil expenditures for education. (Most state constitutions "guarantee" equal educational opportunity for children.) The 10 offending states are, in chronological order of rulings, California (1971), New Jersey (1973 and 1991), Connecticut (1977), Washington (1978), Wyoming (1980), West Virginia (1982), Arkansas (1983), Kentucky (1989), Montana (1989), and Texas (1989). In another 14 states (including four — Idaho, Michigan, Oklahoma, and Oregon — in which challenged systems have been upheld in prior years), the school finance system is currently under court challenge. The other 10 states facing such challenges are Alabama, Illinois, Indiana, Kansas, Massachusetts, Minnesota, Missouri, North Dakota, Rhode Island, and Tennessee.*

As long ago as 1974 the Education Commission of the States (ECS) proposed an equal opportunity amendment to the U.S. Constitution, to do for the nation what the celebrated *Serrano* decision was expected to do for California, i.e., equalize per-pupil expenditures among school districts. In that same year the Gallup education poll found that the public favored such an amendment to the U.S. Constitution by a 3-1 margin. Nothing came of the ECS proposal.

The current poll reveals continued strong public support for more equality in per-pupil expenditures for education and for more court action to equalize expenditures.

The first question:

Do you think that the amount of money allocated to public education in this state from all sources should or should not be the same for all students, regardless of whether they live in wealthy or poor school districts?

	National Totals %	No Children In School %	Public School Parents %	Nonpublic School Parents %
Should be the same	80	78	84	75
Should not be the same	13	14	12	14
Don't know	7	8	4	11

The second question:

Suppose it were determined that certain districts in this state were spending a smaller amount of money per student than other districts. Would you favor or oppose court action to equalize expenditures per student?

	National Totals %	No Children In School %	Public School Parents %	Nonpublic School Parents %
Favor	62	61	62	59
Oppose	24	24	26	29
Don't know	14	15	12	12

The support for equal funding expressed in responses to both of these questions came in equal proportions from all demographic groups and all regions of the country.

Consistent with their approval of shifting decision-making authority to the people closest to the children being educated, poll respondents believe that local authorities — not federal agencies — should determine how federal education funds are spent.

The question:

When federal agencies appropriate money, they usually require the schools that receive this money to spend it as these agencies direct. Should, or should not, this be changed to give local authorities more say in how the money is to be spent?

	National Totals %	No Children In School %	Public School Parents %	Nonpublic School Parents %
Should	72	71	74	65
Should not	16	16	17	28
Don't know	12	13	9	7

---

*Finance systems have been upheld in Arizona, Colorado, Connecticut, Georgia, Maryland, New York, Ohio, and Wisconsin, in addition to Idaho, Michigan, Oklahoma, and Oregon. Source: "Education Finance in the 1990s," Education Commission of the States, November 1990.

Again, there were no significant differences among demographic groups on this question of local control. For example, 71% of Republicans support it, as do 74% of Democrats.

Tight Budgets, Tough Choices

Nearly every state in the union faced recession-related budgetary problems this year, and teachers were furloughed by the thousands in those states where the pinch was the greatest. People appear to have very definite opinions about strategies for dealing with budget deficits. Their responses to questions offering possibilities both for saving money and for raising money are remarkably discriminating.

Educators should be reassured by the strong opposition (78%) to reductions in teaching staff. Administrators should ponder the strong support (73%) for reductions of administrative staff.*

Surprisingly, in view of America's well-known resistance to new taxes, the public as a whole favors (55% to 40%) a 1% state sales tax dedicated specifically to financing schools. By a smaller margin (50% to 44%), the public also approves of a state income tax of one-half of 1%, earmarked for the same purpose. Public school parents in particular favor these measures, but support is fairly consistent across population groups.

The first question:

As you are probably aware, many states are having severe budgetary problems. If it becomes necessary to reduce spending for education in this state, would you favor or oppose the following measures in the public schools of this community?

	Favor %	Oppose %	Don't Know %
Elimination of all extracurricular activities	32	62	6
A freeze on all salaries	47	46	7
Reduction in the number of teachers	15	78	7
Reduction in the number of administrators	73	19	8

	Favor %	Oppose %	Don't Know %
Reduction in the number of support staff members (e.g., janitors, secretaries, nurses, and counselors)	47	45	8
Increases in class size	21	72	7
Elimination of certain courses	54	34	12

The second question:

Now, to raise money for education in this state, would you favor or oppose the following measures in the public schools of this community?

	Favor %	Oppose %	Don't Know %
Charging user fees for all extracurricular activities (e.g., sports, music groups, drama, special interest clubs)	49	44	7
A 1% state sales tax dedicated specifically to the public schools	55	40	5
A one-half of 1% state income tax dedicated to the public schools	50	44	6
Establishment of local education foundations to attract financial support from private companies and individuals	74	17	9

Knowledge of, Interest in, and Connections with the Schools

The final series of questions in the survey pertained to the American public's knowledge of, interest in, and connections with the local schools. The 1991 findings show some increase in levels of knowledge, interest, and participation since previous surveys. More significant for educators, however, is the fact that the more people know about their schools, the more likely they are to support and defend them. Correspondingly, the more interest people have in the schools and the more they participate in school-related activities, the more likely they are to support and defend the schools.

The first question:

How much do you know about the local public schools — quite a lot, some, or very little?

	National Totals		
	1991 %	1983 %	1969 %
Quite a lot	22	22	18
Some	47	42	40
Very little	30	29	42
Don't know	1	7	*

*Less than one-half of 1%.

The second question:

How much interest do you have in what is going on in the local public schools — quite a lot, some, very little, or none at all?

	National Totals %	No Children In School %	Public School Parents %	Nonpublic School Parents %
Quite a lot	38	27	63	51
Some	38	40	33	31
Very little	17	23	3	14
None at all	7	9	1	4
Don't know	*	1	*	*

*Less than one half of 1%.

The third question:

Since September, which of the following, if any, have you yourself done?

*In "Editor's Notes" for May 1991, Henry Muller, managing editor of *Time* magazine, quoted former Labor Secretary William Brock as saying, "There are more school administrators in New York State alone than in all 12 countries of the European Community. And the E.C. has a population of 320 million, vs. 18 million in the Empire State." Muller added that "only 38-41 cents out of every dollar actually gets to the classroom. The rest is eaten up along the way." Muller did not give a source for these obviously suspect figures or explain them further.

	National Totals	
	1991 %	1983 %
Attended a local public school athletic event	30	25
Attended a school play or concert in any local public school	30	24
Met with any teachers or administrators in the local public schools about your own child	27	21
Attended any meeting dealing with the local public schools	16	10
Attended a PTA meeting	14	14
Attended a school board meeting	7	8
Written a letter to the school board, newspaper, or any organization about the local public schools	6	4
None of the above	49	43
Don't know	2	4

(Figures add to more than 100% because of multiple answers.)

Grading the Public Schools

This year poll respondents were asked to assign seven sets of grades, which are summarized in the tables below. The first question:

Students are often given the grades A, B, C, D, and FAIL to denote the quality of their work. Suppose the *public* schools themselves, in this community, were graded in the same way. What grade would you give the public schools here — A, B, C, D, or FAIL?

Ratings Given the Local Public Schools

	1991 %	1990 %	1989 %	1988 %	1987 %	1986 %	1985 %	1984 %	1983 %	1982 %	1981 %
A & B	42	41	43	40	43	41	43	42	31	37	36
A	10	8	8	9	12	11	9	10	6	8	9
B	32	33	35	31	31	30	34	32	25	29	27
C	33	34	33	34	30	28	30	35	32	33	34
D	10	12	11	10	9	11	10	11	13	14	13
FAIL	5	5	4	4	4	5	4	4	7	5	7
Don't know	10	8	9	12	14	15	13	8	17	11	10

The preceding table shows that the public's ratings of its local public schools have remained basically stable since 1984. This followed a low point in 1983, when the poll was conducted shortly after the appearance of *A Nation at Risk*.

Other grades assigned by poll respondents this year are summarized in the table below.

Grades Assigned

	A&B %	A %	B %	C %	D %	F %	Don't Know %
By National Sample							
Public schools nationally	21	2	19	47	13	5	14
Public schools in this community	42	10	32	33	10	5	10
Public school teachers in this community	53	16	37	27	6	3	11
Public school principals and other administrators in this community	43	13	30	28	11	5	13
Public *elementary* school teachers in this community	57	19	38	22	5	2	14
Public elementary school principals and other administrators in this community	47	15	32	25	8	3	17
Public *high school* teachers in this community	40	10	30	28	9	4	19
High school principals and other administrators in this community	37	10	27	26	11	5	21
The school board in this community	30	8	22	30	12	8	20
Parents of students in the local schools for bringing up their children	30	5	25	37	16	7	10
By Public School Parents Only							
The school your oldest child attends	73	29	44	21	2	4	*
Teachers in the school your oldest child attends	72	31	41	21	4	2	1
Principals/administrators in the school your oldest child attends	61	29	32	24	6	4	5

*Less than one-half of 1%.

The most striking aspects of the tables above are: 1) the disparity between the grades people give their local schools (42% A or B) and the grades they give the nation's schools (21% A or B) and 2) the enormous confidence expressed by parents in the schools their oldest children attend (73% A or B) and in the teachers in those schools (72% A or B). The most plausible explanation for these disparities is that the more *firsthand knowledge* one has about the public schools, the more favorable one's perception of them. In short, familiarity with the public schools breeds respect.

Biggest Problems Facing Local Public Schools in 1991

For the first time, drug use, lack of discipline, and lack of school funding are virtually tied as the most frequently mentioned problem with which the local public schools must deal. This reflects a combination of a precipitous drop in the percentage mentioning drug use (from a high point of 38% in 1990 to 22% this year) and an increase in the percentage mentioning lack of proper financial support. The latter response rose from 13% in 1990 to 19% in 1991.

Percent Mentioning the Problem

	1991	1990	1989	1988	1987	1986	1985	1984	1983	1982
Use of drugs	22	38	34	32	30	28	18	18	18	20*
Lack of proper discipline	20	19	19	19	22	24	25	27	25	27

*Ranked third, below lack of proper financial support (22%).

The drug problem was mentioned most often by nonwhites (29%). People with no children in school, who make up two-thirds of the survey sample, mentioned drugs as a public school problem more frequently (24%) than did public school parents (17%).

It seems significant that in the following population groups lack of financial support was number one among all the concerns mentioned: persons who have attended college; professionals and businesspeople; and public school parents, particularly those with a college education and those with children who receive above-average grades in school.

The question:

What do you think are the biggest problems with which the public schools in this community must deal?

1. PERCEPTIONS OF EDUCATION IN NORTH AMERICA

	National Totals %	No Children In School %	Public School Parents %	Nonpublic School Parents %
Use of drugs	22	24	17	13
Lack of discipline	20	20	18	31
Lack of proper financial support	18	15	26	11
Difficulty in getting good teachers	11	11	11	6
Poor curriculum/poor standards	10	11	8	15
Large schools/ overcrowding	9	8	11	7
Parents' lack of interest	7	7	8	10
Pupils' lack of interest/ truancy	5	6	5	*
Integration/busing	5	4	5	10
Low teacher pay	4	5	3	*
Fighting/violence/gangs	3	4	4	1
Lack of family structure	3	3	4	8
Lack of needed teachers	3	3	4	3
Moral standards	3	3	1	5
Lack of dedicated teachers	3	3	2	4
Drinking/alcoholism	2	2	3	*
Dropouts	2	2	3	1
Lack of attention to/under- standing of students	2	2	2	3
Teachers' lack of interest	2	2	2	*
Crime/vandalism	2	2	2	2
School not interesting for students	2	1	3	*
Lack of respect for teachers/other students	2	1	3	4
There are no problems	1	1	2	1
Miscellaneous	21	21	27	32
Don't know	8	10	5	10

*Less than one-half of 1%.

Views on Discipline

The public is thoroughly consistent in its perceptions that 1) students in the public schools of the U.S. lack discipline and 2) improved discipline is the answer to many of the schools' problems.

In the 1991 poll the general public ranked discipline second among the biggest problems with which public schools in their communities must deal, gave a disciplined environment (free of drugs and violence) the number-one ranking among the six national goals, ranked maintenance of student discipline second among factors important to parents in choosing a public school for their child, and rated firmer discipline first among suggestions for helping low-income and racial or ethnic minority students succeed in school.

These perceptions clash with the opinions of teachers, who usually perceive discipline problems to be much less serious than parents' lack of interest and support, lack of proper financial support, and pupils' lack of interest and truancy as major problems.* Either the public has been misled, or the teachers are mistaken. Wherever the truth lies, this discrepancy in perceptions is a cause for serious concern.

*See Stanley Elam, *The Second Gallup/Phi Delta Kappa Survey of Public School Teacher Opinion: Portrait of a Beleaguered Profession* (Bloomington, Ind.: Phi Delta Kappa, 1989), p. 13.

Dissatisfied Groups

At least two population groups in America are highly critical of the public schools and favor radical changes in them. This finding derives from an analysis of the responses of the 59 subgroups for which the Gallup Organization provided data this year.

The two most disaffected groups are blacks and inner-city dwellers. Obviously, these groups overlap considerably; even so, they make up a sizable fraction of the total poll sample. A third group, persons between the ages of 18 and 29, also differs from the national sample on several crucial questions.

The table below shows how the responses of these groups differ from the national average on 10 questions that provide a measure of disaffection and desire for change.

	National Sample (N = 1,500) %	Blacks (N = 171) %	Inner-City Dwellers (N = 462) %	18- to 29-Year-Olds (N = 289) %
Give high grades (A or B) to local public schools	42	28	27	37
Give A or B grade to local public school teachers	53	40	39	50
Give A or B grade to local school board	30	21	17	28
Believe standard- ized national tests would show local stu- dents below average	25	39	40	28
Favor preschool programs at public expense	55	72	61	70
Favor a voucher system	50	57	57	60
Favor parental choice of any public school	62	70	70	71
Favor choice of private school at public expense	26	41	33	28

Research Procedure

The Sample. The sample used in this survey embraced a total of 1,500 adults (18 years of age and older). It is described as a modified probability sample of the nation. Personal, in-home interviewing was conducted in all areas of the nation and in all types of communities.

Time of Interviewing. The fieldwork for this study was carried out during the period of 3-17 May 1991.

The Report. In the tables used in this report, "Nonpublic School Parents" includes parents of students who attend parochial schools and parents of students who attend private or independent schools.

Due allowance must be made for statistical variation, especially in the case of findings for groups consisting of relatively few respondents, e.g., nonpublic school parents.

The findings of this report apply only to the U.S. as a whole and not to individual communities. Local surveys, using the same questions, can be conducted to determine how local areas compare with the national norm.

Composition of the Sample

Adults	%
No children in school	68
Public school parents	29*
Nonpublic school parents	5*

*Total exceeds 32% because some parents have children attending more than one kind of school.

Sex	%
Men	48
Women	52
Race	**%**
White	86
Nonwhite	14
Age	**%**
18-29 years	24
30-49 years	39
50 and over	37
Occupation	**%**
(Chief Wage Earner)	
Business and professional	30
Clerical and sales	6
Manual labor	39
Nonlabor force	17

Occupation	%
(Chief Wage Earner)	
Farm	2
Undesignated	6
Income	**%**
$40,000 and over	30
$30,000-$39,999	16
$20,000-$29,999	16
$10,000-$19,999	21
Under $10,000	11
Undesignated	6
Region	**%**
East	25
Midwest	24
South	31
West	20
Community Size	**%**
1 million and over	37
500,000-999,999	11
50,000-499,999	15
2,500-49,999	10
Under 2,500	27
Education	**%**
College	46
High school	48
Grade school	6

Acknowledgments

A panel of 15 distinguished educators and others interested in education helped frame the questions used in the 1991 Gallup/Phi Delta Kappa education poll. We wish to acknowledge their generous help.

Panelists were Harmon A. Baldwin, superintendent (retired), Monroe County (Ind.) Community School Corporation and member, MCCSC Board of Education; Robert W. Cole, Vice President, Center for Leadership in School Reform, and former editor of the *Phi Delta Kappan*; Larry Cuban, professor and associate dean, School of Education, Stanford University; H. Dean Evans, superintendent of public instruction, State of Indiana; Mary H. Futrell, past president, National Education Association, and senior fellow and associate director, George Washington University Center for the Study of Education and National Development; Bill Honig, superintendent of public instruction, State of California; Chris Pipho, director, Information Clearinghouse, Education Commission of the States; Carol O'Connell, education consultant and president, Phi Delta Kappa; Mary Anne Raywid, professor of education, Hofstra University; Joseph J. Scherer, executive director, National School Public Relations Association; Jo Seker, director, Concerned Educators Against Forced Unionism; Kenneth A. Sirotnik, professor and chair, Policy, Governance, and Administration, College of Education, University of Washington; Benjamin D. Stickney, director of program development, Board of Cooperative Educational Services, Colorado Springs; Donald R. Stoll, executive director, Educational Press Association of America; and Perry A. Zirkel, University Professor of Education and Law, Lehigh University. — SME

How to Order the Poll

The minimum order for reprints of the published version of the Gallup/Phi Delta Kappa education poll is 25 copies for $10. Additional copies are 25 cents each. This price includes postage for parcel post delivery. Where possible, enclose a check or money order. (If faster delivery is desired, do not include a remittance with your order. You will be billed at the above rates plus any additional cost involved in the method of delivery.) Send orders to Gallup Poll, Phi Delta Kappa, P.O. Box 789, Bloomington, IN 47402-0789. Ph. 812/339-1156.

Persons who wish to order the 649-page document that is the basis for this report should write to Sarah Van Allen at the Gallup Organization, 47 Hulfish St., Suite 200, Princeton, NJ 08542 or phone 609/924-9600. The price is $95 per copy, postage included. Besides complete demographic breakdowns of responses to all questions asked this year, that document contains answers to several questions bearing on race and ethnicity.

The Reconceptualization of the Educative Effort

There are attempts at reconceptualizing schooling underway. We have been hearing a lot about "restructuring" schooling and about how best to redefine the goals and processes of education in general. As education historian David Tyack noted in 1990, much of the talk about restructuring is a continuation of the rhetoric regarding the reform of education. There have been several reform efforts to reconceive how school services are delivered to people since the mid-nineteenth century. The conceptual tension between centralization vs. decentralization of educational institutions has been a source of debate throughout the twentieth century. There are several currently contending (and frequently conceptually conflicting) strategies for restructuring life in schools as well as the options open to parents in choosing the schools their children may attend. Tyack addresses this problem adroitly in the essay that anchors this unit. On the one hand, we have to find ways to empower students and teachers to improve the quality of academic life in classrooms. On the other hand, there appear to be powerful forces contending over whether control over educational services should be even more centralized or decentralized (site-based) and with control of personal and resources residing with parents and teachers at the school level. Those who favor greater parental and teacher control of schools support greater decentralized site management and community control conceptions of school governance. Yet the ratio of teachers to nonteaching personnel (administrators, counselors, school psychologists, and others) continues to decline as public school system bureaucracies get more and more "top heavy."

President Bush and the governors of the states have talked about redefining the way schools are conceived and run. Within the North American intellectual community, the literature on critical pedagogical reinterpretation of what schools are and how they affect the lives of children and youth has led to dialogue on how better to empower students to discover and develop their talents as persons.

In this unit, the efforts to reconceive, redefine, and deconstruct existing patterns of curriculum and instruction at the elementary and secondary levels of schooling are considered and related to the efforts to reconceive existing conflicting patterns of teacher education. There is a broad spectrum of dialogue developing in North America, the British Commonwealth, the Soviet Union, and other areas of the world regarding the redirecting of the learning opportunities of citizens.

Prospective teachers are encouraged to question their own educational experiences as a part of the process of becoming more reflective professional persons. Cultural institutions and values affect our ideas about curriculum content and the purpose of educating others. This is perceived as vitally important in the developing dialogue over liberating students' capacities to function as independent inquirers. The dramatic economic and demographic changes in North American society necessitate fundamental reconceptualization of how schools ought to respond to the social contexts in which they are located.

Fundamental rethinking is underway regarding the process of curriculum development in elementary and secondary schools and in teacher education. This has developed as an intellectual movement with participants in the dialogue coming from the entire range of ideological, political, and cultural perspectives reflected in public debate regarding the social purposes of educational systems and the quality of teaching and learning. The current efforts to restructure and to redefine professional purposes are closely related to the efforts to achieve meaningful qualitative improvement in what and how students learn in schools. The varied and pluralistic perspectives that shape the lives of students in their formal educational experiences in schools has been under critical review. This process is leading to fascinating reconception of what is possible in our efforts to educate others.

This movement in our thought about education is reflected in the views of school board members, school administrators, teachers, and students, as well as the views of scholars in teacher education and the arts and sciences. The effort to reassess and reconceive the education of others is a part of broader reform efforts in society, as well as a dynamic dialectic in its own right. How can schools, for instance, better reflect the varied communities of interest that they serve? How can they be better perceived as more just, fairer places in which young people seek to achieve learning and self-fulfillment?

This is not the first period in which North Americans have searched their minds and souls to redirect, construct, and, if necessary, deconstruct their understandings regarding formal educational systems. The debate over what ought to be the conceptual and structural underpinnings of national educational opportunity structures has continued since the first mass educational system was formed in the nineteenth century. The vital work in the development of critical perspectives of learning that has developed in the past thirty years is represented in the language of empowerment and personal liberation that helps students think critically and commandingly about self and others.

Alternative approaches to improving the quality of educational experiences for young people develop in most decades. In any given year, many interesting, innovative programs are initiated in some schools to facilitate and enrich student learning. When we think of continuity and change, we think of the conceptual balance between cherished traditions, and innovations that may facilitate learning without compromising cherished core values or standards. On the other hand, some innovations do challenge traditional ideas. This is a sensitive balance. When one thinks of change in education, one can be reminded of such great educational experiments of earlier times as (1) John Dewey's Laboratory School at the University of Chicago, (2) Maria Montessori's Casi di Bambini (children's houses), and (3) A. S. Neil's controversial Summerhill School in England, as well as many other earlier and later innovative experiments in learning theories. Our own time has seen similarly dramatic experimentation.

What constitutes desirable change is directly related to one's own core values regarding the purposes and content of educational experiences. When considering a proposed change in an educational system or a particular classroom, some questions to ask include: What is the purpose of the proposed change? What are the human and social benefits and costs of the proposed change (in teachers' work, in students' learning tasks, etc.)? What defensible alternatives are possible? What are our best ideas? How does the proposed change affect traditional practice? The past thirty or more years of research on teaching and learning have led us to be more concerned over the need to improve the quality of learning while also broadening educational opportunity structures for young people. Broadening opportunities structures provides a high degree of equity in access to educational services, as well as developing alternative educational experiences. We must strive to be fair with our colleagues and our students in the spirited debates now going on regarding changes needed to make school systems and teachers more effective.

It is still of some value to remind ourselves of that ideal expressed so well by Matthew Arnold in the late nineteenth century that education ought to be "the best that has been thought and said." It is necessary to confront the issue regarding what subjects should be retained in school curricula, as well as what new bodies of knowledge ought to be added. Part of this task involves consideration as to how knowledge from related areas can be developed in interdisciplinary curricular efforts. We must prepare young persons to be humane, caring individuals, and this needs to be done while also teaching them the technical skills that they need to persevere and to succeed in a highly competitive "high-tech" international marketplace. This dispute over the content of school and university curricula, as a part of the debate regarding general studies for all students, has been going on ever since Thomas Huxley and Matthew Arnold debated, in the late nineteenth century, the places of the sciences and the humanities in school curricula.

Each of the essays in this unit relates directly, in some relevant way, to the conceptual tension involved in reconceiving how educational development should proceed.

Looking Ahead: Challenge Questions

What are the most important problems to be considered when we talk about restructuring schools?

What concepts in our thoughts about education need reconceptualization?

What are the social forces that affect human responses to change?

What can teachers do to improve critical reasoning skills in themselves and their students?

To what extent can schooling be reconstructed to most effectively emphasize academic achievement as well as intangible but important factors such as character or initiative or freedom of thought?

Are there more political and economic pressures on educators than they can reasonably be expected to manage? Is this sort of pressure avoidable? Why or why not?

What knowledge bases (disciplines or interdisciplines) ought senior high school students study?

If it is true that there should be a common curriculum at the primary and middle grade levels, should there also be a common curriculum at the secondary level?

What values ought to be at the basis of any effort to reconceptualize the social purposes of schools?

Lack of Time Is the Problem

The D Side
O
W of Restructuring
N

Martin Carnoy

Martin Carnoy is Professor of Education, Stanford University, California.

THE latest round of educational reform, called restructuring, puts America's teachers center stage in educational change. Because committed teachers are the bottom line of improved education, this makes good sense, but it may also spell trouble for the reform, especially when the other constraints our schools and teachers face come into play.

Once past the media hype, governors' conferences, and presidential declarations, school restructuring really boils down to getting teachers and pupils more motivated about doing well in school. Taking a leaf out of recent business management techniques, a handful of school district leaders have turned over much responsibility for what goes on in their schools to teachers. Working with principals who, in one teacher's words, "know how to lead by allowing others to lead," activist teachers in these districts are developing new practices and new curriculum that work for their students.

There are many reasons why reform that brings responsibility for educational improvement down to the

> **The time and energy of teachers is what drives reform; it will not work unless they think it makes sense.**

school level should work. For one, no matter where the curriculum and evaluation criteria are produced, what happens to children educationally seems to be greatly influenced by school environment. How teachers and children feel about each other and how well they define their goals affect *what* they produce and the *effort* they expend in reaching such goals.

Schools are not like private companies, no matter how much the business community would like them to be. And it is not because private enterprises are efficient and public enterprises are bureaucratic and inefficient. A typical business—unlike a school—produces well-defined products for well-defined prices. Its bottom line is profit, which it can measure every quarter. And when chief executive officers make decisions for their businesses, they have every reason to believe the decisions will be carried out. Employees are usually closely supervised, and there are clear financial incentives to increase pro-

ductivity and clear sanctions against those who do not perform.

In education, products are fuzzier and prices even more vague. We would like to think that schools have an unequivocal mission to produce the most pupil achievement possible. But who defines "possible"? And are not schools also held accountable for developing good citizens and for protecting children from the worst excesses of life outside schools? Current restructuring reform argues that if each school has a say in defining what and how it produces, at least everyone will know what the product goal is and how they plan to reach it.

Neither are there direct command or incentive mechanisms in schools that translate educational decisions made at the state and district levels into classroom action. Teachers are not like most employees in private businesses. Getting more effort and more quality effort out of teachers is more complex. Teachers are independent professionals who—to a large extent—control what goes on in their production workspace and are fairly immune to direct orders from above.

Getting teachers to be more effective "producers" is complicated by another factor: Schools *share* responsibility for their product with parents and the community. This is like saying that the night shift at the auto plant is run by a different manage-

From *The Education Digest*, May 1991, pp. 3-6. Condensed from *Education Week*, 10 (November 7, 1990). Reprinted by permission.

ment and a different set of workers, and neither the day- nor night-shift team has much to say about how the other performs. If one team does its job exceedingly well, it does put pressure on the other to meet the standard. But if parents—who get the first crack at educating their children—are not very effective, teachers often feel that they can only do so much. In education, it is easy to point the finger at the other shift when "productivity" is low.

Enter restructuring. One key term is motivation—get the day shift motivated so that the standard goes up, effort in the classroom increases, and teachers turn on parents and the community. A motivated school can raise the quantity and quality of outside-school educational effort. The second key term is professionalization—give power to the teachers to organize curriculum, change practice, and initiate new programs. They are the only ones who can make the classroom an exciting place. The third key term is leadership—decentralize control so that innovative leaders can flourish at the school site and raise educational quality.

For a public demanding educational improvement, any reform that looks promising is immediately attractive. Restructuring provides another dimension—its broad political appeal. Conservatives like it because it smacks of entrepreneurial spirit and makes each "firm" a semi-independent operation. Progressives like it because it solves the labor problem (more effort) in a way that gives "workers" greater control of the workplace—schools become less hierarchical and more cooperative. In a nutshell, restructuring is highly consistent with American values of decentralization, individual initiative, and individual responsibility where "individual" in this case is the principal, the teacher, or the school team. It is a properly antibureaucratic idea that meets today's feelings about bigness and bureaucracy.

So, what's the problem? What could go wrong with a reform that is so consistent with both the institutional nature of schooling and our political culture? In a word, the problem is time. It is teachers' time and energy that drive the reform, and no matter how organizationally efficient or po-

> **Principals may resist restructuring to maintain control or avoid taking on more work.**

litically appealing, it won't work unless they think it makes sense.

The up side is that restructuring reprofessionalizes teachers, increasing their self-image and the psychic reward they derive from teaching. But it also places severe demands on an already precious resource—teacher time. Developing school goals and refining them as the school goes through changes requires lots of planning meetings. Getting parents involved also means meetings—many more than current parents' nights and school-site councils. In typical innovations, such as improving on the state-mandated curriculum, developing after-school programs for at-risk pupils, or providing increased contact between pupils, teachers, and counselors, active teachers (and the principal) have to put in a lot of extra time, including coming in on Saturdays.

The sense of teamwork is strong, making such commitments easier, but time away from families also often creates stress and other pressures. And since most teachers are women, already holding a second "job" at home, extra time is not always available. One teacher told me, "If you want to support this, we need to be provided with time in our regular workweek to implement these programs."

The added teacher time needed is greatest in those communities where the quality of parent input is the lowest. If educational outcomes are to improve for these at-risk pupils, either parents have to be brought into the process as active, better-informed participants, or the school has to substitute for lack of parent time and resources. In either case, teachers need to devote additional hours each day on top of an already relentless schedule.

It is not surprising that most teachers and principals are leery of the reform, and many of those who have bought in are verging on burnout. Surveys of restructuring around the

country show that the term has become a catch-all for any change in the way school districts organize education but is seldom the real thing. Even if teachers in a school want to initiate a full-fledged restructuring, principals often resist so that they do not lose control or have to take on more work.

The traditional answer to the time issue from teachers and their unions is higher salaries. Where teachers are grossly underpaid and nonunionized, higher pay would at least keep the best from moving away. Higher salaries nationwide might also create respect for teachers professionally (or greater resentment) and would certainly make teaching more attractive to the best and the brightest. But more income does not really solve the time problem.

Much of the solution lies in recognizing that restructuring requires a variety of supporting resources, both technical and financial. Often, where salaries are already attracting well-qualified teachers, more income is less the answer than resources strategically placed directly in the schools.

Resources of a more technical nature are also required. Teachers can set goals and have some know-how to achieve them effectively, but most are without the skills to convert well-thought-out aims into a clear-cut set of management decisions. Neither do most principals have the training to be managerial change agents. Along with the ideas of restructuring, someone has to provide new kinds of inservice assistance.

If we value good education and think that restructuring is the right idea at the right time, we should be ready to support committed, innovative schools with the kinds of strategic resources required to make the reform work. Young lawyers fresh out of Yale or Stanford might be willing to work 16 hours a day, seven days a week, for $85,000 a year, but they know that in 10 years, they will be earning three or four times that much and working at a quieter pace. Teachers are not in the same boat. For restructuring to succeed under today's fiscal constraints, they can look forward to 12-hour days, six days a week, for the rest of their professional lives. Most are not willing to sign on for that trip, and those who are will not last long without help.

America's Public Schools:

Choice *Is* a Panacea

John E. Chubb and Terry M. Moe

John E. Chubb, a senior fellow in the Brookings Governmental Studies program, and Terry M. Moe, professor of political science at Stanford University and a former Brookings senior fellow, are the authors of Politics, Markets, and America's Schools, *an analysis of 500 public and private high schools based on information gathered from more than 20,000 students, teachers, and principals, the most comprehensive data set on high schools ever assembled. This article is excerpted from the conclusion to that book.*

For America's public schools, the last decade has been the worst of times and the best of times. Never before have the public schools been subjected to such savage criticism for failing to meet the nation's educational needs—yet never before have governments been so aggressively dedicated to studying the schools' problems and finding the resources for solving them.

The signs of poor performance were there for all to see during the 1970s. Test scores headed downward year after year. Large numbers of teenagers continued to drop out of school. Drugs and violence poisoned the learning environment. In math and science, two areas crucial to the nation's success in the world economy, American students fell far behind their counterparts in virtually every other industrialized country. Something was clearly wrong.

During the 1980s a growing sense of crisis fueled a powerful movement for educational change, and the nation's political institutions responded with aggressive reforms. State after state increased spending on schools, imposed tougher requirements, introduced more rigorous testing, and strengthened teacher certification and training. And, as the decade came to an end, creative experiments of various forms—from school-based management to magnet schools—were being launched around the nation.

We think these reforms are destined to fail. They simply do not get to the root of the problem. The fundamental causes of poor academic performance are not to be found in the schools, but rather in the institutions by which the schools have traditionally been governed. Reformers fail by automatically relying on these institutions to solve the problem — when the institutions are the problem.

The key to better schools, therefore, is institutional reform. What we propose is a new system of public education that eliminates most political and bureaucratic control over the schools and relies instead on indirect control through markets and parental choice. These new institutions naturally function to promote and nurture the kinds of effective schools that reformers have wanted all along.

Schools and Institutions

Three basic questions lie at the heart of our analysis. What is the relationship between school organization and student achievement? What are the conditions that promote or inhibit desirable forms of organization? And how are these conditions affected by their institutional settings?

Our perspective on school organization and student achievement is in agreement with the most basic claims and findings of the "effective schools" literature, which served as the analytical base of the education reform movement throughout the 1980s. We believe, as most others do, that how much students learn is not determined simply by their aptitude or family background— although, as we show, these are certainly influential— but also by how effectively schools are organized. By our estimates, the typical high school student tends to

From *The Brookings Review*, Summer 1990, pp. 4-12. Copyright © 1990 by The Brookings Institute, Washington, DC.

learn considerably more, comparable to at least an extra year's worth of study, when he or she attends a high school that is effectively organized rather than one that is not.

Generally speaking, effective schools — be they public or private — have the kinds of organizational characteristics that the mainstream literature would lead one to expect: strong leadership, clear and ambitious goals, strong academic programs, teacher professionalism, shared influence, and staff harmony, among other things. These are best understood as integral parts of a coherent syndrome of organization. When this syndrome is viewed as a functioning whole, moreover, it seems to capture the essential features of what people normally mean by a team — principals and teachers working together, cooperatively and informally, in pursuit of a common mission.

How do these kinds of schools develop and take root? Here again, our own perspective dovetails with a central theme of educational analysis and criticism: the dysfunctions of bureaucracy, the value of autonomy, and the inherent tension between the two in American public education. Bureaucracy vitiates the most basic requirements of effective organization. It imposes goals, structures, and requirements that tell principals and teachers what to do and how to do it — denying them not only the discretion they need to exercise their expertise and professional judgment but also the flexibility they need to develop and operate as teams. The key to effective education rests with unleashing the productive potential already present in the schools and their personnel. It rests with granting them the autonomy to do what they do best. As our study of American high schools documents, the freer schools are from external control the more likely they are to have effective organizations.

Only at this late stage of the game do we begin to part company with the mainstream. While most observers can agree that the public schools have become too bureaucratic and would benefit from substantial grants of autonomy, it is also the standard view that this transformation can be achieved within the prevailing framework of democratic control. The implicit assumption is that, although political institutions have acted in the past to bureaucratize, they can now be counted upon to reverse course, grant the schools autonomy, and support and nurture this new population of autonomous schools. Such an assumption, however, is not based on a systematic understanding of how these institutions operate and what their consequences are for schools.

Political Institutions

Democratic governance of the schools is built around the imposition of higher-order values through public authority. As long as that authority exists and is avail-

The key to better schools, therefore, is institutional reform.

able for use, public officials will come under intense pressure from social groups of all political stripes to use it. And when they do use it, they cannot blithely assume that their favored policies will be faithfully implemented by the heterogeneous population of principals and teachers below — whose own values and professional views may be quite different from those being imposed. Public officials have little choice but to rely on formal rules and regulations that tell these people what to do and hold them accountable for doing it.

These pressures for bureaucracy are so substantial in themselves that real school autonomy has little chance to take root throughout the system. But they are not the only pressures for bureaucracy. They are compounded by the political uncertainty inherent in all democratic politics: those who exercise public authority know that other actors with different interests may gain authority in the future and subvert the policies they worked so hard to put in place. This knowledge gives them additional incentive to embed their policies in protective bureaucratic arrangements — arrangements that reduce the discretion of schools and formally insulate them from the dangers of politics.

These pressures, arising from the basic properties of democratic control, are compounded yet again by another special feature of the public sector. Its institutions provide a regulated, politically sensitive setting conducive to the power of the unions, and unions protect the interests of their members through formal constraints on the governance and operation of schools—constraints that strike directly at the schools' capacity to build well-functioning teams based on informal cooperation.

2. RECONCEPTUALIZATION OF THE EDUCATIVE EFFORT

The major participants in democratic governance— including the unions—complain that the schools are too bureaucratic. And they mean what they say. But they are the ones who bureaucratized the schools in the past, and they will continued to do so, even as they tout the great advantages of autonomy and professionalism. The incentives to bureaucratize the schools are built into the system.

Market Institutions

This kind of behavior is not something that Americans simply have to accept, like death and taxes. People who make decisions about education would behave differently if their institutions were different. The most relevant and telling comparison is to markets, since it is through democratic control and markets that American society makes most of its choices on matters of public importance, including education. Public schools are subject to direct control through politics. But not all schools are controlled in this way. Private schools — representing about a fourth of all schools — are subject to indirect control through markets.

What difference does it make? Our analysis suggests that the difference is considerable and that it arises from the most fundamental properties that distinguish the two systems. A market system is not built to enable the imposition of higher-order values on the schools, nor is it driven by a democratic struggle to exercise public authority. Instead, the authority to make educational choices is radically decentralized to those most immediately involved. Schools compete for the support of parents and students, and parents and students are free to choose among schools. The system is built on decentralization, competition, and choice.

Although schools operating under a market system are free to organize any way they want, bureaucratization tends to be an unattractive way to go. Part of the reason is that virtually everything about good education — from the knowledge and talents necessary to produce it, to what it looks like when it is produced— defies formal measurement through the standardized categories of bureaucracy.

The more basic point, however, is that bureaucratic control and its clumsy efforts to measure the unmeasurable are simply *unnecessary* for schools whose primary concern is to please their clients. To do this, they need to perform as effectively as possible, which leads them, given the bottom-heavy technology of education, to favor decentralized forms of organization that take full advantage of strong leadership, teacher professionalism, discretionary judgment, informal cooperation, and teams. They also need to ensure that they provide the kinds of services parents and students want and that they have the capacity to cater and adjust to their clients' specialized needs and interests, which this

> *What we propose is a new system of public education that relies on indirect control of the schools through markets and parental choice.*

same syndrome of effective organization allows them to do exceedingly well.

Schools that operate in an environment of competition and choice thus have strong incentives to move toward the kinds of "effective-school" organizations that academics and reformers would like to impose on the public schools. Of course, not all schools in the market will respond equally well to these incentives. But those that falter will find it more difficult to attract support, and they will tend to be weeded out in favor of schools that are better organized. This process of natural selection complements the incentives of the marketplace in propelling and supporting a population of autonomous, effectively organized schools.

Institutional Consequences

No institutional system can be expected to work perfectly under real-world conditions. Just as democratic institutions cannot offer perfect representation or perfect implementation of public policy, so markets cannot offer perfect competition or perfect choice. But these imperfections, which are invariably the favorite targets of each system's critics, tend to divert attention from what is most crucial to an understanding of schools: as institutional systems, democratic control and market control are strikingly different in their fundamental properties. As a result, each system structures individual and social choices about education very differently, and each has very different consequences for the organization and performance of schools. Each system puts its own indelible stamp on the schools that emerge and operate within it.

What the analysis in our book suggests, in the most practical terms, is that American society offers two basic paths to the emergence of effective schools. The first is through markets, which scarcely operate in the public sector, but which act on private schools to discourage bureaucracy and promote desirable forms of organization through the natural dynamics of competition and choice.

The second path is through "special circumstances,"—homogeneous environments free of problems—which, in minimizing the three types of political pressures just discussed, prompt democratic governing institutions to impose less bureaucracy than they otherwise would. Private schools therefore tend to be effectively organized because of the way their system naturally works. When public schools happen to be effectively organized, it is in spite of their system—they are the lucky ones with peculiarly nice environments.

As we show in our book, the power of these institutional forces is graphically reflected in our sample of American high schools. Having cast our net widely to allow for a full range of noninstitutional factors that might reasonably be suspected of influencing school autonomy, we found that virtually all of them fall by the wayside. The extent to which a school is granted the autonomy it needs to develop a more effective organization is overwhelmingly determined by its sectoral location and the niceness of its institutional environment.

Viewed as a whole, then, our effort to take institutions into account builds systematically on mainstream ideas and findings but, in the end, puts a very different slant on things. We agree that effective organization is a major determinant of student achievement. We also agree that schools perform better the more autonomous they are and the less encumbered they are by bureaucracy. But we do not agree that this knowledge about the proximate causes of effective performance can be used to engineer better schools through democratic control. Reformers are right about where they want to go, but their institutions cannot get them there.

The way to get schools with effective organizations is not to insist that democratic institutions should do what they are incapable of doing. Nor is it to assume that the better public schools, the lucky ones with nice environments, can serve as organizational models for the rest. Their luck is not transferable. The way to get effective schools is to recognize that the problem of ineffective performance is really a deep-seated institutional problem that arises from the most fundamental properties of democratic control.

The most sensible approach to genuine education reform is therefore to move toward a true institutional solution—a different set of institutional arrangements that actively promotes and nurtures the kinds of schools people want. The market alternative then be-

> *Of all the reforms that attract attention, only choice can address the basic institutional problem plaguing America's schools.*

comes particularly attractive, for it provides a setting in which these organizations take root and flourish. That is where "choice" comes in.

Educational Choice

It is fashionable these days to say that choice is "not a panacea." Taken literally, that is obviously true. There are no panaceas in social policy. But the message this aphorism really means to get across is that choice is just one of many reforms with something to contribute. School-based management is another. So are teacher empowerment and professionalism, better training programs, stricter accountability, and bigger budgets. These and other types of reforms all bolster school effectiveness in their own distinctive ways—so the reasoning goes—and the best, most aggressive, most comprehensive approach to transforming the public school system is therefore one that wisely combines them into a multifaceted reformist package.

Without being too literal about it, we think reformers would do well to entertain the notion that choice *is* a panacea. Of all the sundry education reforms that attract attention, only choice has the capacity to address the basic institutional problem plaguing America's schools. The other reforms are all system-preserving. The schools remain subordinates in the structure of public authority — and they remain bureaucratic.

In principle, choice offers a clear, sharp break from the institutional past. In practice, however, it has been forced into the same mold with all the other reforms. It has been embraced half-heartedly and in bits and pieces — for example, through magnet schools and limited open enrollment plans. It has served as a means of granting parents and students a few additional options or of giving schools modest incentives to compete. These are popular moves that can be accomplished without changing the existing system in any fundamental way. But by treating choice like other system-preserving reforms that presumably make democratic control work better, reformers completely miss what choice is all about.

Choice is not like the other reforms and should not be combined with them. Choice is a self-contained reform with its own rationale and justification. It has the capacity *all by itself* to bring about the kind of transformation that reformers have been seeking to engineer for years in myriad other ways. Indeed, if choice is to work to greatest advantage, it must be adopted *without* these other reforms, since they are predicated on democratic control and are implemented by bureaucratic means. The whole point of a thoroughgoing system of choice is to free the schools from these disabling constraints by sweeping away the old institutions and replacing them with new ones. Taken seriously, choice is not a system-preserving reform. It is a revolutionary reform that introduces a new system of public education.

A Proposal for Real Reform

The following outline describes a choice system that we think is equipped to do the job. Offering our own proposal allows us to illustrate in some detail what a full-blown choice system might look like, as well as to note some of the policy decisions that must be made in building one. More important, it allows us to suggest what our institutional theory of schools actually entails for educational reform.

Our guiding principle in the design of a choice system is this: public authority must be put to use in creating a system that is almost entirely beyond the reach of public authority. Because states have primary responsibility for American public education, we think the best way to achieve significant, enduring reform is for states to take the initiative in withdrawing authority from existing institutions and vesting it directly in the schools, parents, and students. This restructuring cannot be construed as an exercise in delegation. As long as authority remains "available" at higher levels within state government, it will eventually be used to control the schools. As far as possible, all higher-level authority must be eliminated.

What we propose, more specifically, is that state leaders create a new system of public education with the following properties.

The Supply of Schools

The state will be responsible for setting criteria that define what constitutes a "public school" under the

> *Choice, unlike the other education reforms, is self-contained, with its own rationale and justification.*

new system. These criteria should be minimal, roughly corresponding to the criteria many states now use in accrediting private schools — graduation requirements, health and safety requirements, and teacher certification requirements. Any educational group or organization that applies to the state and meets these minimal criteria must then be chartered as a public school and granted the right to accept students and receive public money.

Existing private schools will be among those eligible to participate. Their participation should be encouraged, because they constitute a supply of already effective schools. Our own preference would be to include religious schools too, as long as their sectarian functions can be kept clearly separate from their educational functions. Private schools that do participate will thereby become public schools, as such schools are defined under the new choice system.

School districts can continue running their present schools, assuming those schools meet state criteria. But districts will have authority over only their own schools and not over any of the others that may be chartered by the state.

Funding

The state will set up a Choice Office in each district, which, among other things, will maintain a record of all school-age children and the level of funding — the "scholarship" amounts — associated with each child. This office will directly compensate schools based on the specific children they enroll. Public money will flow from funding sources (federal, state, and district governments) to the Choice Office and then to schools. At no point will it go to parents or students.

The state must pay to support its own Choice Office in each district. Districts may retain as much of their current governing apparatus as they wish — superintendents, school boards, central offices, and all their staff. But they have to pay for them entirely out of the revenue they derive from the scholarships of those children who voluntarily choose to attend district-run schools. Aside from the governance of these schools, which no one need attend, districts will be little more than taxing jurisdictions that allow citizens to make a collective determination about how large their children's scholarships will be.

As it does now, the state will have the right to specify how much, or by what formula, each district must contribute for each child. Our preference is for an equalization approach that requires wealthier districts to contribute more per child than poor districts do and that guarantees an adequate financial foundation to students in all districts. The state's contribution can then be calibrated to bring total spending per child up to whatever dollar amount seems desirable; under an equalization scheme, that would mean a larger state contribution in poor districts than in wealthy ones.

While parents and students should be given as much flexibility as possible, we think it is unwise to allow them to supplement their scholarship amounts with personal funds. Such "add-ons" threaten to produce too many disparities and inequalities within the public system, and many citizens would regard them as unfair and burdensome.

Complete equalization, on the other hand, strikes us as too stifling and restrictive. A reasonable trade-off is to allow collective add-ons, much as the current system does. The citizens of each district can be given the freedom to decide whether they want to spend more per child than the state requires them to spend. They can then determine how important education is to them and how much they are willing to tax themselves for it. As a result, children from different districts may have different-sized scholarships.

Scholarships may also vary within any given district, and we strongly think that they should. Some students have very special educational needs — arising from economic deprivation, physical handicaps, language difficulties, emotional problems, and other disadvantages — that can be met effectively only through costly specialized programs. State and federal programs already appropriate public money to address these problems. Our suggestion is that these funds should take the form of add-ons to student scholarships. At-risk students would then be empowered with bigger scholarships than the others, making

> *Each student must be guaranteed a school, as well as a fair shot at getting into the school he or she most wants.*

them attractive clients to all schools — and stimulating the emergence of new specialty schools.

Choice Among Schools

Each student will be free to attend any public school in the state, regardless of district, with the student's scholarship — consisting of federal, state, and local contributions — flowing to the school of choice. In practice most students will probably choose schools in reasonable proximity to their homes. But districts will have no claim on their own residents.

To the extent that tax revenues allow, every effort will be made to provide transportation for students who need it. This provision is important to help open up as many alternatives as possible to all students, especially the poor and those in rural areas.

To assist parents and students in choosing among schools, the state will provide a Parent Information Center within its local Choice Office. This center will collect comprehensive information on each school in the district, and its parent liaisons will meet personally with parents in helping them judge which schools best meet their children's needs. The emphasis here will be on personal contact and involvement. Parents will be required to visit the center at least once, and encouraged to do so often. Meetings will be arranged at all schools so that parents can see firsthand what their choices are.

The Parent Information Center will handle the applications process in a simple fashion. Once parents and students decide which schools they prefer, they will fill out applications to each, with parent liaisons available to give advice and assistance and to fill out the applications themselves (if necessary). All applications will be submitted to the Center, which in turn will send them out to the schools.

Schools will make their own admissions decisions, subject only to nondiscrimination requirements. This step is absolutely crucial. Schools must be able to define their own missions and build their own programs in their own ways, and they cannot do that if their student population is thrust on them by outsiders.

Schools must be free to admit as many or as few students as they want, based on whatever criteria they think relevant — intelligence, interest, motivation, special needs — and they must be free to exercise their own, informal judgments about individual applicants.

Schools will set their own "tuitions." They may choose to do so explicitly, say, by publicly announcing the minimum scholarship they are willing to accept. They may also do it implicitly by allowing anyone to apply for admission and simply making selections, knowing in advance what each applicant's scholarship amount is. In either case, schools are free to admit students with different-sized scholarships, and they are free to keep the entire scholarship that accompanies each student they have admitted. That gives all schools incentives to attract students with special needs, since these children will have the largest scholarships. It also gives schools incentives to attract students from districts with high base-level scholarships. But no school need restrict itself to students with special needs, nor to students from a single district.

The application process must take place within a framework that guarantees each student a school, as well as a fair shot at getting into the school he or she most wants. That framework, however, should impose only the most minimal restrictions on the schools.

We suggest something like the following. The Parent Information Center will be responsible for seeing that parents and students are informed, that they have visited the schools that interest them, and that all applications are submitted by a given date. Schools will then be required to make their admissions decisions within a set time, and students who are accepted into more than one school will be required to select one as their final choice. Students who are not accepted anywhere, as well as schools that have yet to attract as many students as they want, will participate in a second round of applications, which will work the same way.

After this second round, some students may remain without schools. At this point, parent liaisons will take informal action to try to match up these students with appropriate schools. If any students still remain unassigned, a special safety-net procedure — a lottery, for example — will be invoked to ensure that each is assigned to a specific school.

As long as they are not "arbitrary and capricious,"

> *The state must refrain from imposing any structures or rules that specify how authority is to be exercised within individual schools.*

schools must also be free to expel students or deny them readmission when, based on their own experience and standards, they believe the situation warrants it. This authority is essential if schools are to define and control their own organizations, and it gives students a strong incentive to live up to their side of the educational "contract."

Governance and Organization

Each school must be granted sole authority to determine its own governing structure. A school may be run entirely by teachers or even a union. It may vest all power in a principal. It may be built around committees that guarantee representation to the principal, teachers, parents, students, and members of the community. Or it may do something completely different.

The state must refrain from imposing *any* structures or requirements that specify how authority is to be exercised within individual schools. This includes the district-run schools: the state must not impose any governing apparatus on them either. These schools, however, are subordinate units within district government—they are already embedded in a larger organization—and it is the district authorities, not the schools, that have the legal right to determine how they will be governed.

More generally, the state will do nothing to tell the schools how they must be internally organized to do their work. The state will not set requirements for career ladders, advisory committees, textbook selection, in-service training, preparation time, homework, or anything else. Each school will be organized and operated as it sees fit.

Statewide tenure laws will be eliminated, allowing each school to decide for itself whether or not to adopt a tenure policy and what the specifics of that policy will be. This change is essential if schools are to have the flexibility they need to build well-functioning teams. Some schools may not offer tenure at all, relying on pay and working conditions to attract the kinds of teachers they want, while others may offer tenure as a supplementary means of compensating and retaining their best teachers.

Teachers, meantime, may demand tenure in their negotiations (individual or collective) with schools. And, as in private colleges and universities, the best teachers are well positioned to get it, since their services will be valued by any number of other schools. School districts may continue to offer districtwide tenure, along with transfer rights, seniority preference, and whatever other personnel policies they have offered in the past. But these policies apply only to district-run schools and the teachers who work in them.

Teachers will continue to have a right to join unions and engage in collective bargaining, but the legally prescribed bargaining unit will be the individual school or, as in the case of the district government, the larger organization that runs the school. If teachers in a given school want to join a union or, having done so, want to exact financial or structural concessions, that is up to them. But they cannot commit teachers in other schools, unless they are in other district-run schools, to the same things, and they must suffer the consequences if their victories put them at a competitive disadvantage in supplying quality education.

The state will continue to certify teachers, but requirements will be minimal, corresponding to those that many states have historically applied to private schools. In our view, individuals should be certified to teach if they have a bachelor's degree and if their personal history reveals no obvious problems. Whether they are truly good teachers will be determined in practice, as schools decide whom to hire, observe their own teachers in action over an extended period of time, and make decisions regarding merit, promotion, and dismissal.

The schools may, as a matter of strategy, choose to pay attention to certain formal indicators of past or future performance, among them: a master's degree, completion of a voluntary teacher certification program at an education school, or voluntary certification by a national board. Some schools may choose to require one or more of these, or perhaps to reward them in various ways. But that is up to the schools, which will be able to look anywhere for good teachers in a now much larger and more dynamic market.

> *When it comes to performance, schools will be held accountable from below, by parents and students who are free to choose.*

The state will hold the schools accountable for meeting certain procedural requirements. It will ensure that schools continue to meet the criteria set out in their charters, that they adhere to nondiscrimination laws in admissions and other matters, and that they collect and make available to the public, through the Parent Information Center, information on their mission, their staff and course offerings, standardized test scores (which we would make optional), parent and student satisfaction, staff opinions, and anything else that would promote informed choice among parents and students.

The state will not hold the schools accountable for student achievement or other dimensions that call for assessments of the quality of school performance. When it comes to performance, schools will be held accountable from below, by parents and students who directly experience their services and are free to choose. The state will play a crucial supporting role here in monitoring the full and honest disclosure of information by the schools — but it will be only a supporting role.

Choice as a Public System

This proposal calls for fundamental changes in the structure of American public education. Stereotypes aside, however, these changes have nothing to do with "privatizing" the nation's schools. The choice system we outline would be a truly public system — and a democratic one.

We are proposing that the state put its democratic authority to use in creating a new institutional framework. The design and legitimation of this framework would be a democratic act of the most basic sort. It would be a social decision, made through the usual processes of democratic governance, by which the people and their representatives specify the structure of a new system of public education.

This framework, as we set it out, is quite flexible and admits of substantial variation on important issues, all of them matters of public policy to be decided by representative government. Public officials and their constituents would be free to take their own approaches to taxation, equalization, treatment of religious schools, additional funding for disadvantaged students, parent add-ons, and other controversial issues of public concern, thus designing choice systems to reflect the unique conditions, preferences, and political forces of their own states.

Once this structural framework is democratically determined, moreover, governments would continue to play important roles within it. State officials and agencies would remain pivotal to the success of public education and to its ongoing operation. They would provide funding, approve applications for new schools, orchestrate and oversee the choice process, elicit full information about schools, provide transportation to students, monitor schools for adherence to the law, and (if they want) design and administer tests of student performance. School districts, meantime, would continue as local taxing jurisdictions, and they would have the option of continuing to operate their own system of schools.

The crucial difference is that direct democratic control of the schools — the very *capacity* for control, not simply its exercise — would essentially be eliminated. Most of those who previously held authority over the schools would have their authority permanently withdrawn, and that authority would be vested in schools, parents, and students. Schools would be legally autonomous: free to govern themselves as they want, specify their own goals and programs and methods, design their own organizations, select their own student bodies, and make their own personnel decisions. Parents and students would be legally empow-

ered to choose among alternative schools, aided by institutions designed to promote active involvement, well-informed decisions, and fair treatment.

Democracy and Educational Progress

We do not expect everyone to accept the argument we have made here. In fact, we expect most of those who speak with authority on educational matters, leaders and academics within the educational community, to reject it. But we will regard our effort as a success if it directs attention to America's institutions of democratic control and provokes serious debate about their consequences for the nation's public schools. Whether or not our own conclusions are right, the fact is that these issues are truly basic to an understanding of schools, and they have so far played no part in the national debate. If educational reform is to have any chance at all of succeeding, that has to change.

In the meantime, we can only believe that the current "revolution" in public education will prove a disappointment. It might have succeeded had it actually been a revolution, but it was not and was never intended to be, despite the lofty rhetoric. Revolutions replace old institutions with new ones. The 1980s reform movement never seriously thought about the old institutions and certainly never considered them part of the problem. They were, as they had always been, part of the solution—and, for that matter, part of the definition of what democracy and public education are all about.

This identification has never been valid. Nothing in the concept of democracy requires that schools be subject to direct control by school boards, superintendents, central offices, departments of education, and other arms of government. Nor does anything in the concept of public education require that schools be governed in this way. There are many paths to democracy and public education. The path America has been trodding for the past half-century is exacting a heavy price — one the nation and its children can ill afford to bear, and need not. It is time, we think, to get to the root of the problem.

Inside the Classroom: Social Vision and Critical Pedagogy

William Bigelow

Jefferson High School, Portland, Oregon

Bigelow, a secondary school teacher in Portland, Oregon, believes that public schooling in the United States serves social and economic class interests very unequally, and that one justifiable response for the educator is to help equip students to understand and critique the society in which they live. This article portrays students and teachers engaging in the kind of structured dialogue that Bigelow says is essential to the critical pedagogy he employs.

There is a quotation from Paulo Freire that I like: he writes that teachers should attempt to "live part of their dreams within their educational space."[1] The implication is that teaching should be partisan. I agree. As a teacher I want to be an agent of transformation, with my classroom as a center of equality and democracy—an ongoing, if small, critique of the repressive social relations of the larger society. That does not mean holding a plebiscite on every homework assignment, or pretending I do not have any expertise, but I hope my classroom can become part of a protracted argument for the viability of a critical and participatory democracy.

I think this vision of teaching flies in the face of what has been and continues to be the primary function of public schooling in the United States: to reproduce a class society, where the benefits and sufferings are shared incredibly unequally. As much as possible I refuse to play my part in that process. This is easier said than done. How *can* classroom teachers move decisively away from a model of teaching that merely reproduces and legitimates inequality? I think Freire is on the right track when he calls for a "dialogical education."[2] To me, this is not just a plea for more classroom conversation. In my construction, a dialogical classroom means inviting students to critique the larger society through sharing their lives. As a teacher I help students locate their experiences socially; I involve students in probing the social factors that make and limit who they are and I try to help them reflect on who they *could* be.

STUDENTS' LIVES AS CLASSROOM TEXT

In my Literature in U.S. History course, which I co-teach in Portland, Oregon, with Linda Christensen, we use historical concepts as points of departure to explore themes in students' lives and then, in turn, use students' lives to explore history and our society today. Earlier this year, for instance, we studied the Cherokee Indian Removal through role play. Students portrayed the Indians, plantation owners, bankers, and the Andrew Jackson administration and saw the forces that combined to push the Cherokees west of the Mississippi against their will. Following a discussion of how and why this happened, Linda and I asked students to write about a time when they had their rights violated. We asked students to write from inside these experiences and to recapture how they felt and what, if anything, they did about the injustice.

Seated in a circle, students shared their stories with one another in a "read-around" format. (To fracture the student/teacher dichotomy a bit, Linda and I also complete each assignment and take our turns reading.) Before we began, we suggested they listen for what we call the "collective text"—the group portrait that emerges from the read-around.[3] Specifically, we asked them to take notes on the kinds of rights people felt they possessed; what action they took after having their rights violated; and whatever other generalizations they could draw from the collective text. Here are a few examples: Rachel wrote on wetting her pants because a teacher would not let her go to the bathroom; Christie, on a lecherous teacher at a middle school; Rebecca, on a teacher who enclosed her in a solitary confinement cell; Gina, who is black, on a theater worker not believing that her mother, who is white, actually was her mother; Maryanne, on being sexually harassed while walking to school and her subsequent mistreatment by the school administration when she reported the incident; Clayton, on the dean's treatment when Clayton wore an anarchy symbol on

From *Teachers College Record*, Vol. 91, No. 3, Spring 1990, pp. 437-448. Reprinted by permission of the publisher from William Bigelow, "Inside the Classroom: Social Visions & Critical Pedagogy" in Tozer, Steven, Anderson, Thomas H. and Armbruster, Bonnie B., eds. FOUNDATIONAL STUDIES IN TEACHER EDUCATION: A RE-EXAMINATION, pp. 139-150.
(New York: Teachers College Press, © 1990 by Teachers College, Columbia University. All rights reserved.)

his jacket; Bobby, on convenience store clerks who watched him more closely because he is black. Those are fewer than a quarter of the stories we heard.

To help students study this social text more carefully, we asked them to review their notes from the read-around and write about their discoveries. We then spent a class period interpreting our experiences. Almost half the instances of rights violations took place in school. Christie said, "I thought about the school thing. The real point [of school] is to learn one concept: to be trained and obedient. That's what high school is. A diploma says this person came every day, sat in their seat. It's like going to dog school." A number of people, myself included, expressed surprise that so many of the stories involved sexual harassment. To most of the students with experiences of harassment, it had always seemed a very private oppression, but hearing how common this kind of abuse is allowed the young women to feel a new connection among themselves—and they said so. A number of white students were surprised at the varieties of subtle racism black students experienced.

We talked about the character of students' resistance to rights violations. From the collective text we saw that most people did not resist at all. What little resistance occurred was individual; there was not a single instance of collective resistance. Christie complained to a counselor, Rebecca told her mother, many complained to friends. This provoked a discussion about what in their lives and, in particular, in the school system encouraged looking for individual solutions to problems that are shared collectively. They identified competition for grades and for positions in sought-after classes as factors. They also criticized the fake democracy of student government for discouraging activism. No one shared a single experience of schools' encouraging groups of students to confront injustice. Moreover, students also listed ways—from advertising messages to television sitcoms—through which people are conditioned by the larger society to think in terms of individual problems requiring individual solutions.

The stories students wrote were moving, sometimes poetic, and later opportunities to rewrite allowed us to help sharpen their writing skills, but we wanted to do more than just encourage students to stage a literary show-and-tell. Our larger objective was to find social meaning in individual experience—to push students to use their stories as windows not only on their lives, but on society.

There were other objectives. We hoped that through building a collective text, our students—particularly working-class and minority students—would discover that their lives are important sources of learning, no less important than the lives of the generals and presidents, the Rockefellers and Carnegies, who inhabit their textbooks. One function of the school curriculum is to celebrate the culture of the dominant and to ignore or scorn the culture of subordinate groups. The personal writing, collective texts, and discussion circles in Linda's and my classes are an attempt to challenge students not to accept these judgments. We wanted students to grasp that they can *create* knowledge, not simply absorb it from higher authorities.[4]

All of this sounds a little neater than what actually occurs in a classroom. Some students rebel at taking their own lives seriously. A student in one of my classes said to me recently, "Why do we have to do all this personal stuff? Can't you just give us a book or a worksheet and leave us alone?" Another student says regularly, "This isn't an English class, ya know." Part of this resistance may come from not wanting to resurface or expose painful experiences; part may come from not feeling capable as writers; but I think the biggest factor is that they simply do not feel that their lives have anything *important* to teach them. Their lives are just their lives. Abraham Lincoln and Hitler are important. Students have internalized self-contempt from years of official neglect and denigration of their culture. When for example, African-American or working-class history *is* taught it is generally as hero worship: extolling the accomplishments of a Martin Luther King, Jr., or a John L. Lewis, while ignoring the social movements that made their work possible. The message given is that great people make change, individual high school students do not. So it is not surprising that some students wonder what in the world they have to learn from each other's stories.

Apart from drawing on students' own lives as sources of knowledge and insight, an alternative curriculum also needs to focus on the struggle of oppressed groups for social justice. In my history classes, for example, we study Shays's Rebellion, the abolition movement, and alliances between blacks and poor whites during Reconstruction. In one lesson, students role-play Industrial Workers of the World organizers in the 1912 Lawrence, Massachusetts, textile strike as they try to overcome divisions between men and women and between workers speaking over a dozen different languages.

STUDYING THE HIDDEN CURRICULUM

In my experience as a teacher, whether students write about inequality, resistance, or collective work, school is *the* most prominent setting. Therefore, in our effort to have the curriculum respond to students' real concerns, we enlist them as social researchers, investigating their own school lives. My co-teacher and I began one unit by reading an excerpt from the novel *Radcliffe*, by David Storey.[5] In the selection, a young boy, Leonard Radcliffe, arrives at a predominately working-class British school. The teacher prods Leonard, who is from an aristocratic background, to become her reluctant know-it-all—the better to reveal to others their own ignorance. The explicit curriculum appears to concern urban geography: "Why are roofs pointed and not flat like in the Bible?" the teacher asks. She humiliates a working-class youth, Victor, by demanding that he stand and listen to her harangue: "Well, come on then, Victor. Let us all hear." As he stands mute and helpless, she chides: "Perhaps there's no reason for Victor to think at all. We already know where he's going to end up, don't we?" She points to the factory chimneys outside. "There are places waiting for him out there already." No one says a word. She finally calls on little Leonard to give the correct answer, which he does.

Students in our class readily see that these British schoolchildren are learning much more than why roofs are pointed. They are being drilled to accept their lot at the bottom of a hierarchy with a boss on top. The teacher's successful effort to humiliate Victor, while the others sit watching, undercuts any sense the students might have of their power to act in solidarity with one another. A peer is left hanging in the wind and they do nothing about it. The teacher's tacit alliance with Leonard and her abuse of Victor legitimate class inequalities outside the classroom.[6]

We use this excerpt and the follow-up discussion as a preparatory exercise for students to research the curriculum—both explicit and "hidden"[7]—at their own school (Jefferson High School). The student body is mostly African-American and predominately working class. Linda and I assign students to observe their classes as if they were attending for the first time. We ask them to notice the design of the classroom, the teaching methodology, the class content, and the grading procedures. In their logs, we ask them to reflect on the character of thinking demanded and the classroom relationships: Does the teacher promote questioning and critique or obedience and conformity? What kind of knowledge and understandings are valued in the class? What relationships between students are encouraged?

In her log, Elan focused on sexism in the hidden curriculum:

> In both biology and government, I noticed that not only do boys get more complete explanations to questions, they get asked more questions by the teacher than girls do. In government, even though our teacher is a feminist, boys are asked to define a word or to list the different parts of the legislative branch more often than the girls are. . . . I sat in on an advanced sophomore English class that was doing research in the library. The teacher, a male, was teaching the boys how to find research on their topic, while he was finding the research himself for the girls. Now, I know chivalry isn't dead, but we are competent of finding a book.

Linda and I were pleased as we watched students begin to gain a critical distance from their own schooling experiences. Unfortunately, Elan did not speculate much on the social outcomes of the unequal treatment she encountered, or on what it is in society that produces this kind of teaching. She did offer the observation that "boys are given much more freedom in the classroom than girls, and therefore the boys are used to getting power before the girls."

Here is an excerpt from Connie's log:

> It always amazed me how teachers automatically assume that where you sit will determine your grade. It's funny how you can get an A in a class you don't even understand. As long as you follow the rules and play the game, you seem to get by. . . . On this particular day we happen to be taking a test on chapters 16 and 17. I've always liked classes such as algebra that you didn't have to think. You're given the facts, shown how to do it, and you do it. No questions, no theories, it's the solid, correct way to do it.

We asked students to reflect on who in our society they thought benefited from the methods of education to which they were subjected. Connie wrote:

> I think that not only is it the teacher, but more importantly, it's the system. They purposely teach you using the "boring method." Just accept what they tell you, learn it and go on, no questions asked. It seems to me that the rich, powerful people benefit from it, because we don't want to think, we're kept ignorant, keeping them rich.

Connie's hunch that her classes benefit the rich and powerful is obviously incomplete, but it does put her on the road to understanding that the degrading character of her education is not simply accidental. She is positioned to explore the myriad ways schooling is shaped by the imperatives of a capitalist economy. Instead of being just more of the "boring method," as Connie puts it, this social and historical study would be a personal search for her, rooted in her desire to understand the nature of her *own* experience.

In class, students struggled through a several-page excerpt from *Schooling in Capitalist America* by Samuel Bowles and Herbert Gintis. They read the Bowles and Gintis assertion that

> major aspects of educational organization replicate the relationships of dominance and subordinancy in the economic sphere. The correspondence between the social relation of schooling and work accounts for the ability of the educational system to produce an amenable and fragmented labor force. The experience of schooling, and not merely the content of formal learning, is central to this process.[8]

If they are right, we should expect to find different hidden curricula at schools enrolling students of different social classes. We wanted our students to test this notion for themselves.[9] A friend who teaches at a suburban high school south of Portland, serving a relatively wealthy community, enlisted volunteers in her classes to host our students for a day. My students logged comparisons of Jefferson and the elite school, which I will call Ridgewood. Trisa wrote:

Now, we're both supposed to be publicly funded, equally funded, but not so. At Jefferson, the average class size is 20–25 students, at Ridgewood—15. Jefferson's cafeteria food is half-cooked, stale and processed. Ridgewood—fresh food, wide variety, and no mile-long lines to wait in. Students are allowed to eat anywhere in the building as well as outside, and wear hats and listen to walkmen [both rule violations at Jefferson].

About teachers' attitudes at Ridgewood, Trisa noted: "Someone said, 'We don't ask if you're going to college, but what college are you going to.' "

In general, I was disappointed that students' observations tended to be more on atmosphere than on classroom dynamics. Still, what they noticed seemed to confirm the fact that their own school, serving a black and working-class community, was a much more rule-governed, closely supervised environment. The experience added evidence to the Bowles and Gintis contention that my students were being trained to occupy lower positions in an occupational hierarchy.

Students were excited by this sociological detective work, but intuitively they were uneasy with the determinism of Bowles and Gintis's correspondence theory. It was not enough to discover that the relations of schooling mirrored the relations of work. They demanded to know exactly who designed a curriculum that taught them subservience. Was there a committee somewhere, sitting around plotting to keep them poor and passive? "We're always saying 'they' want us to do this, and 'they' want us to do that," one student said angrily. "Who is this 'they'?" Students wanted villains with faces and we were urging that they find systemic explanations.

Omar's anger exploded after one discussion. He picked up his desk and threw it against the wall, yelling: "How much more of this shit do I have to put up with?" "This shit" was his entire educational experience, and while the outburst was not directed at our class in particular—thank heavens—we understood our culpability in his frustration.

We had made two important and related errors in our teaching. Implicitly, our search had encouraged students to see themselves as victims—powerless little cogs in a machine daily reproducing the inequities of the larger society. Though the correspondence theory was an analytical framework with a greater power to interpret their school lives than any other they had encountered, ultimately it was a model suggesting endless oppression and hopelessness. If schooling is always responsive to the needs of capitalism, then what point did our search have? Our observations seemed merely to underscore students' powerlessness.

I think the major problem was that although our class did discuss resistance by students, it was anecdotal and unsystematic, thereby depriving students of the opportunity to question their own roles in maintaining the status quo. The effect of this omission, entirely unintentional on our part, was to deny students the chance to see schools as sites of struggle and social change—places where they could have a role in determining the character of their own education. Unwittingly, the realizations students were drawing from our study of schools fueled a world view rooted in cynicism; they might learn about the nature and causes for their subordination, but they could have no role in resisting it.

THE "ORGANIC GOODIE SIMULATION"

Still stinging from my own pedagogical carelessness, I have made efforts this year to draw students into a dialogue about the dynamics of power and resistance. One of the most effective means to carry on this dialogue is metaphorically, through role play and simulation.[10]

In one exercise, called the "Organic Goodie Simulation," I create a three-tiered society. Half the students are workers, half are unemployed,[11] and I am the third tier—the owner of a machine that produces organic goodies. I tell students that we will be in this classroom for the rest of our lives and that the machine produces the only sustenance. Workers can buy adequate goodies with their wages, but the unemployed will slowly starve to death on their meager dole of welfare-goodies. Everything proceeds smoothly until I begin to drive wages down by offering jobs to the unemployed at slightly less than what the workers earn. It is an auction, with jobs going to the lowest bidder. Eventually, all classes organize some kind of opposition, and usually try to take away my machine. One year, a group of students arrested me, took me to a jail in the corner of the room, put a squirt gun to my head, and threatened to "kill" me if I said another word. This year, before students took over the machine, I backed off, called a meeting to which only my workers were invited, raised their wages, and stressed to them how important it was that we stick together to resist the jealous unemployed people who wanted to drag all of us into the welfare hole they are in. Some workers defected to the unemployed, some vigorously defended my right to manage the machine, but most bought my plea that we had to talk it all out and reach unanimous agreement before any changes could be made. For an hour and a half they argued among themselves, egged on by me, without taking any effective action.

The simulation provided a common metaphor from which students could examine firsthand what we had not adequately addressed the previous year: To what extent are we complicit in our own oppression? Before we began our follow-up discussion, I asked students to write on who or what was to blame for the conflict and disruption of the previous day. In the discussion some students singled me out as the culprit. Stefani said, "I thought Bill was evil. I didn't know what he wanted." Rebecca concurred: "I don't agree with people who say Bill was not the root of the problem. Bill was management, and he made workers feel insecure that the unemployed were trying to take their jobs." Others agreed with Rebecca that it was a divisive structure that had been created, but saw how their own responses to that structure perpetuated the divisions and poverty. Christie said: "We were so divided that nothing got decided. It kept going back and forth. Our discouragement was the root of the problem." A number of people saw how their own attitudes kept them from acting decisively. Mira said: "I think that there was this large fear: We have to follow the law. And Sonia kept saying we weren't supposed to take over the machine. But if the law and property hurt people why should we go along with it?" Gina said: "I think Bill looked like the problem, but underneath it all was us. Look at when Bill hired unemployed and fired some workers. I was doin' it too. We can say it's a role play, but you have to look at how everything ended up feeling and learn something about ourselves, about how we handled it."

From our discussion students could see that their make-believe misery was indeed caused by the structure of the society: The number of jobs was held at an artificially low level, and workers and unemployed were pitted against each other for scarce goodies. As the owner I tried every trick I knew to drive wedges between workers and the unemployed, to encourage loyalty in my workers, and to promote uncertainty and bickering among the unemployed. However, by analyzing the experience, students could see that the system worked only because they let it work—they were much more than victims of my greed; they were my accomplices.

I should hasten to add—and emphasize—that it is not inherently empowering to understand one's own complicity in oppression. I think it is a start, because this understanding suggests that we can do something about it. A critical pedagogy, however, needs to do much more: It should highlight times, past and present, when people built alliances to challenge injustice. Students also need to encounter individuals and organizations active in working for a more egalitarian society, and students need to be encouraged to see themselves as capable of joining together with others, in and out of school, to make needed changes. I think that all of these are mandatory components of the curriculum. The danger of students' becoming terribly cynical as they come to understand the enormity of injustice in this society and in the world is just too great. They have to know that it is possible—even joyous, if I dare say so—to work toward a more humane society.

TEACHERS AND TEACHER EDUCATORS AS POLITICAL AGENTS

At the outset I said that all teaching should be partisan. In fact, I think that all teaching *is* partisan. Whether or not we want to be, all teachers are political agents because we help shape students' understandings of the larger society. That is why it is so important for teachers to be clear about our social visions. Toward what kind of society are we aiming? Unless teachers answer this question with clarity we are reduced to performing as technicians, unwittingly participating in a political project but with no comprehension of its objectives or consequences. Hence teachers who claim "no politics" are inherently authoritarian because their pedagogical choices act on students, but students are denied a structured opportunity to critique or act on their teachers' choices. Nor are students equipped to reflect on the effectiveness of whatever resistance they may put up.

For a number of reasons, I do not think that our classrooms can ever be exact models of the kind of participatory democracy we would like to have characterize the larger society. If teachers' only power were to grade students, that would be sufficient to sabotage classroom democracy. However, as I have suggested, classrooms can offer students experiences and understandings that counter, and critique, the lack of democracy in the rest of their lives. In the character of student interactions the classroom can offer a glimpse of certain features of an egalitarian society. We can begin to encourage students to learn the analytic and strategic skills to help bring this new society into existence. As I indicated, by creating a collective text of student experience we can offer students practice in understanding personal problems in their social contexts. Instead of resorting to consumption, despair, or other forms of self-abuse, they can ask why these circumstances exist and what can they do about it. In this limited arena, students can begin to become the subjects of their lives.

When Steve Tozer of the University of Illinois asked me to prepare this article, he said I should discuss the implications of my classroom practice for people in social foundations of education programs. First, I would urge you who are teacher educators to model the participatory and exploratory pedagogy that you hope your students will employ as classroom teachers. Teachers-to-be should interrogate their own educational experiences as a basis for understanding the relationship between school and society. They need to be members of a dialogical community in which they can experience themselves as subjects and can learn the validity of critical pedagogy by doing it. If the primary aim of social foundations of education coursework is to equip teachers-to-be to understand and critically evaluate the origins of school content and processes in social context, then the foundations classroom should be a place for students to discuss how their own experiences as students are grounded in the larger society, with its assumptions, its inequities, its limits and possibilities.

As you know, a teacher's first job in a public school can be frightening. That fear mixed with the conservative pressures of the institution can overwhelm the liberatory inclinations of a new teacher. Having *experienced,* and not merely having read about, an alternative pedagogy can help new teachers preserve their democratic ideals. Part of this, I think, means inviting your students to join you in critiquing *your* pedagogy. You need to be a model of rigorous self-evaluation.

The kind of teaching I have been describing is demanding. The beginning teacher may be tempted to respond, "Sure, sure, I'll try all that when I've been in the classroom five or six years and when I've got a file cabinet full of lessons." I think you should encourage new teachers to overcome their isolation by linking up with colleagues to reflect on teaching problems and to share pedagogical aims and successes. I participated in a support group like this my first year as a teacher and our meetings helped maintain my courage and morale. After a long hiatus, two years ago I joined another group that meets bi-weekly to talk about everything from educational theory to confrontations with administrators to union organizing.[12] In groups such as this your students can come to see themselves as creators and evaluators of curriculum and not simply as executors of corporate- or administrative-packaged lesson plans.

It is also in groups like this that teachers can come to see themselves as activists in a broader struggle for social justice. The fact is that education will not be *the* engine of social change. No matter how successful we are as critical teachers in the classroom, our students' ability to use and extend the analytic skills they have acquired depends on the character of the society that confronts them. Until the economic system requires workers who are critical, cooperative, and deeply democratic, teachers' classroom efforts amount to a kind of low-intensity pedagogical war. Unfortunately, it is easy to cut ourselves off from outside movements for social change—and this is especially true for new teachers. As critical teachers, however, we depend on these movements to provide our students with living proof that fundamental change is both possible and desirable. It seems to me you cannot emphasize too strongly how teachers' attempts to teach humane and democratic values in the classroom should not be

isolated from the social context in which schooling occurs.

In closing, let me return to Freire's encouragement that we live part of our dreams within our educational space. Teachers-to-be should not be ashamed or frightened of taking sides in favor of democracy and social justice. I hope *your* students learn to speak to *their* students in the language of possibility and hope and not of conformity and "realism." In sum, your students ought to learn that teaching is, in the best sense of the term, a subversive activity—and to be proud of it.

NOTES

1. Paulo Freire and Donaldo Macedo, *Literacy: Reading the Word and the World* (South Hadley, Mass.: Bergin and Garvey, 1987), p. 127.

2. See especially Ira Shor and Paulo Freire, *A Pedagogy for Liberation* (South Hadley, Mass.: Bergin and Garvey, 1983.)

3. See Linda Christensen, "Writing the Word and the World," *English Journal* 78, no. 2 (February 1989): 14–18.

4. See William Bigelow and Norman Diamond, *The Power in Our Hands: A Curriculum on the History of Work and Workers in the United States* (New York: Monthly Review Press, 1988), pp. 15–23.

5. David Storey, *Radcliffe* (New York: Avon, 1963), pp. 9–12. I am grateful to Doug Sherman for alerting me to this excerpt.

6. While most students are critical of the teacher, they should always be allowed an independent judgment. Recently, a boy in one of my classes who is severely hard of hearing defended the teacher's actions. He argued that because the students laughed at Leonard when he first entered the class they deserved whatever humiliation the teacher could dish out. He said the offending students ought to be taught not to make fun of people who are different.

7. See Henry Giroux, *Theory and Resistance in Education: A Pedagogy for the Opposition* (South Hadley, Mass.: Bergin and Garvey, 1983). See especially Chapter 2, "Schooling and the Politics of the Hidden Curriculum," pp. 42–71. Giroux defines the hidden curriculum as "those unstated norms, values, and beliefs embedded in and transmitted to students through the underlying rules that structure the routines and social relationships and classroom life" and points out that the objective of critical theory is not merely to describe aspects of the hidden curriculum, but to analyze how it "functions to provide differential forms of schooling to different classes of students" (p. 47).

8. Samuel Bowles and Herbert Gintis, *Schooling in Capitalist America* (New York: Basic Books, 1976), p. 125.

9. See Jean Anyon, "Social Class and the Hidden Curriculum of Work," *Journal of Education* 162 (Winter 1980): 67–92, for a more systematic comparison of hidden curricula in schools serving students of different social classes.

10. There is an implication in many of the theoretical discussions defining critical pedagogy that the proper role of the teacher is to initiate group reflection on students' outside-of-class experiences. Critics consistently neglect to suggest that the teacher can also be an initiator of powerful in-class experiences, which can then serve as objects of student analysis.

11. Bigelow and Diamond, *The Power in Our Hands*, pp. 27–30 and pp. 92–94. See also Mike Messner, "Bubblegum and Surplus Value," *The Insurgent Sociologist* 6, no. 4 (Summer 1976): 51–56.

12. My study group gave valuable feedback on this article. Thanks to Linda Christensen, Jeff Edmundson, Tom McKenna, Karen Miller, Michele Miller, Doug Sherman, and Kent Spring.

"Restructuring" in Historical Perspective: Tinkering toward Utopia

David Tyack

Stanford University

As U.S. education enters the 1990s, *restructuring* has become a magic incantation. A colleague who discusses education reform with businessmen says that when she describes the everyday realities of life in classrooms, their eyes glaze over, but when she mentions restructuring, their eyes pop open. The term is now gaining the popularity of *excellence* in the early 1980s or *equality* in the 1960s. Veteran reformer John Goodlad thinks that "we are rapidly moving toward the use of the word 'restructuring' whenever we talk about school reform at all. And if we have enough conferences on it, we'll assume that the schools have been restructured." But what does it signify?[1]

The present is an intense and often contradictory phase in a long history of Americans tinkering toward utopia through reforming the schools. It is no accident that a *vague* word like restructuring has also become a *vogue* word. "School restructuring has many of the characteristics of what political and organizational theorists call a 'garbage can,' " writes Richard F. Elmore, adding that "the theme of restructuring schools can accommodate a variety of conceptions about what is problematical about American education, as well as a variety of solutions."[2] Restructuring has become a general

For critical comments on an earlier draft my thanks go to Larry Cuban, Elisabeth Hansot, Michael Kirst, John Meyer, Daniel Perlstein, Dorothy Shipps, and Marshall Smith (who have sense enough not to be contaminated by my errors). Also my gratitude for the support of the Spencer Foundation and the Stanford Center for the Study of Families, Children, and Youth.

label for new strategies of school reform that respond to disillusionment with the results of state legislation of the middle 1980s that sought to mandate stiffer standards for students and teachers. The wall charts comparing the performance of states with each other and the United States with other nations seemed to show that top-down reform was not producing the dramatic changes reformers sought.

People regard restructuring as a synonym for the market mechanism of choice, or teacher professionalization and empowerment, or decentralization and school site management, or involving parents more in their children's education, or national standards in curriculum with tests to match, or deregulation, or new forms of accountability, or basic changes in curriculum and instruction, or some or all of these in combination. Slogans suitable for bumper stickers proclaim the new dogmas: Choice is the answer; small is beautiful; blame the bureaucrats.

Proposals for restructuring in school governance go every which way, with people urging the troops to march in different directions. Consider these as examples:

President Bush and the Governors have recently called for "clear, national performance goals" and "detailed strategies" for reaching those targets. This moves toward something that would recently have been anathema—a national curriculum (it was not so long ago that over a hundred members of Congress voted to call the U.S. Commissioner of Education the Commissar of Education). One wonders how that ardent states rights advocate, Thomas Jefferson, might have reacted when they called their statement "A Jeffersonian Compact." With President Bush declaring that "the American people are ready for *radical* reforms," the Charlottesville fifty-one also called for "decentralization of authority and decision-making responsibility to the school site, so that educators are empowered to determine the means for accomplishing the goals and to be held accountable for accomplishing them."[3]

From *Teachers College Record*, Vol. 92, No. 2, Winter 1990, pp. 171-191. Copyright © 1990 by Teachers College, Columbia University. Reprinted by permission.

2. RECONCEPTUALIZATION OF THE EDUCATIVE EFFORT

In 1986 the National Governors Association urged states to take over and run districts that failed to educate children, reflecting widespread distrust of a traditional bastion of local control, elected school boards. One state (New Jersey) has officially taken over all direction of a school district (Jersey City).[4]

Chicago, by contrast, bids fair to take us back to the kind of extreme decentralization in city school governance that was anathema to the professional elites of an earlier era. In 1904 in Philadelphia there were 545 members on the ward and central school boards—537 more than were needed to run an efficient system, thought the reformers of that time. Chicago today would make that system seem elitist, not populist; under the new reform law it has over 6,500 school board members and a complex network of central, middling, and ancillary authorities.[5]

Under the banner of choice, a number of reformers like William Bennett want to give parents and students a chance to choose their school at the same time that they want to curb if not eliminate choice of elective subjects to study. Such reforms could produce a national template for curriculum and a free market in schooling.[6]

RESTRUCTURING THE BIG APPLE

As usual, New York City provides an interesting window on school reform. The new chancellor, Joseph A. Fernandez, arrived fresh from an exemplary attempt to restructure the Miami public schools, in part by negotiating school site management with the teachers' union. In New York, he found that neither centralization nor decentralization was working according to plan; it was not clear who had been in charge, if anyone. His office windows were dirty, so he called an engineer to clean them. Sorry, he learned, by contract the engineers cleaned windows only once a year. Asking his secretary to order highlighting pens, he was informed that delivery would take four weeks. Some of the thirty-two decentralized school boards were under investigation for corruption and incompetence, and Fernandez challenged their ability to appoint superintendents without his approval. He declared that he would take over schools that did not meet acceptable academic standards, and he negotiated a pact with the principals' union that enabled him to move ineffective principals, changing the policy that gave them a tenured fiefdom in a particular building.[7]

Far from being either an efficiently centralized system or a fully decentralized one, New York illustrates the baronies and "fragmented centralization" found in much educational governance today. The present system is a product of a history that shows in microcosm many of the issues I will examine in this article. In successive waves of attempted change in governance over the last century, New York reformers have sought to find the one best system for running their schools—to restructure them, in current lingo.

In 1893, Joseph M. Rice declared the city too large to be one district. He believed it should be divided into twenty separate ones. Elite reformers at the turn of the century disagreed: New York needed to abolish its ward boards, to centralize control in a small board, and delegate decision making to an expert superintendent and specialists in the central office. In the 1930s some far-sighted educators like Leonard Covello tried to build community-based schools within the massive bureaucracy that was the New York system. In the 1960s, angered by the glacial pace of racial integration achieved by the central board of education, black activists called for community control of schools. They got not what they really wanted but the thirty-two "decentralized" districts that Fernandez now copes with. In the last thirty years, the federal and New York state legislatures enacted dozens of categorical programs and new mandates. These produced mid-level administrators at 110 Livingston Street to supervise, coordinate, or obscure the inconsistencies in these categorical programs; accounting to state and federal officials became a bureaucratic art form.[8]

This involuted history of attempted restructurings in New York City produced a complexity in decision making that only a Rube Goldberg could understand, much less appreciate. Tired of the turmoil, a skeptical New York teacher had this to say about yet another restructuring: "School Reform Again? (Sigh)."[9]

The New York system is, of course, a special case. In the 1960s the city had more educational administrators than all of France. But writ large in this biggest of U.S. cities is a set of historical changes that are worth exploring in more detail in a national context. This broader history suggests both the difficulty of fundamental change today, given the institutional legacy and vested interests created by earlier attempts to reorganize American public schools, and the importance of being clear about educational purposes. Many long-term historical trends in American public education have gone directly counter to reforms urged today.[10]

There are so many diagnoses and solutions and such varied actors who press for restructuring today, as Elmore says, that it is unlikely that schools will be full transformed from standardized and externally regulated bureaucracies into a new model based on "school inquiry and problem solving, school autonomy, professional norms, and client choice." He points out that the political interests involved "cut across almost every major institutional, jurisdictional, and professional boundaries [sic] in education." Further, he detects inconsistency in the notion that

> systemwide change will occur by lodging greater responsibility with people who work in schools. If this is really the central insight of school restructuring, then it seems contradictory to argue that all schools will or should change in the same way as a result of school restructuring, since to do so, schools would all have to arrive spontaneously at more or less the same solutions to highly complex problems of content, pedagogy, technology, organization, and governance. Lodging a high degree of discretion with schools is, in other words, inconsistent with broad uniform effects.[11]

It is still possible, as Elmore argues, that an "adaptive realignment" may occur as leaders in states and school districts respond to critical social, economic, and educational problems.[12] The pressures are surely there: concerns about economic competitiveness, the failure to educate the children of the poor effectively, and worry about attracting and retaining good teachers. Although there is much hype in talk about restructuring schools, there is also hope if aims become more realistic and if different groups can work toward that common agenda. At the end of this article I will return to the present moment in education reform and comment on two current strategies: decentralizing authority and seeking to make the classroom a more lively and challenging workplace for teachers and students.

POLICY TALK AND TRENDS IN PRACTICE

To understand the history of education reform in the United States, waves of trendy talk need to be distinguished from long-term trends in institutional development. Policy discourse may produce little change in the schools. On the other hand, trends in practice may go counter to popular rhetoric. Some reformers ride trends, others buck them.

Statistical trends—some of which I will present later— demonstrate that American public education has changed dramatically over the last century, although it is a common lament of reformers that little ever changes. The achievements of one generation of reformers have often become the targets of reformers in the next era of change. Such is the case today.

Reform periods in education are typically times when concerns about the state of the society or economy spill over into demands that the schools set things straight. The discovery of some problem—America losing in economic competition, the threat of Russian science, poverty, racial injustice, unassimilated immigrants—triggers such policy talk. Policymakers translate these anxieties and hopes into proposals for educational reform. These solutions are often very modest in scope compared with the crises they are expected to solve; home economics, for example, was supposed to halt the rising divorce rate and supposedly excessive ambitions of "the new woman" early in the twentieth century. Some reforms become enacted or adopted, and a few of them are even implemented. Often reforms pushed by outsiders—lay activists—have a short half-life in the schools, however, and concerns and policies tend to recycle in waves.[13]

Another kind of reform typically has had a more lasting impact on the schools: changes proposed by key decision makers within education. Such reforms in the past century have largely been justified on grounds of professionalism (for example, certification of teachers), science (IQ testing and tracking), and specialization of function leading to efficiency (the creation of new structures like the junior high school or new categories of employees).[14]

The history of education reform is a complex tale of open and covert politics, contending ideologies, tugs-of-war between decentralization and centralization, and tensions between teaching the "basics" and expanding the curriculum. Out of that past I select a few turning points to analyze what seem to me to be major reorganizations of schooling—times when reformers sought to restructure education, though they did not use that term and construed reorganization in differ-

ent ways. In looking at these reforms I concentrate on governance, school organization, and instruction, for these are key issues in what is today called restructuring. I also examine what the reformers meant by what today is called "accountability."

As a starting point I begin with the late nineteenth century, a time when highly decentralized rural schools coexisted with what was perhaps the most centralized systems of instruction that have existed in the United States, the uniform urban school bureaucracies of that period.

In the years from about 1900 to 1950 a cohesive group of professional educators sought to "take the schools out of politics" and to reorganize them from the top down to the bottom. They worked to consolidate school districts, to increase the size of schools, to diversify the curriculum, and to centralize control according to "scientific" expertise and new hierarchical patterns of authority.

In the late 1950s and 1960s new actors entered school politics to challenge this "closed system" of policymaking in education. Protest groups consisting of people who had lacked influence over education policy sought to make schools more responsive to social differences and social justice. In some communities activists demanded community control or new ethnically based programs such as bilingual education. Protest groups turned to allies in federal and state legislatures and to the courts to secure their rights or to create new categorical programs. As a result of the new politics of education, new entitlements and programs, regulations, and litigation, the older centralization of power in hierarchical local districts became fragmented.

The 1980s saw a swing in school reform to uniform state mandates. The conventional wisdom of that period was that the previous generation of school reform had resulted in educational mayhem, and this in turn had resulted in educational mediocrity. Back to basics, to required courses, to testing and upgrading of standards—these were the hallmarks of this attempt to reform schooling. These reforms immediately preceded the current interest in restructuring.[15]

If one looks only at policy talk, each wave of reform appears to wash over the schools only to be succeeded by another, often contradictory, set of policies. In fact, however, there were institutional trends that persisted through decades, congruent with some kinds of reform and contradictory to others. Since these trends have inexorably shaped the context for current attempts to restructure the schools, I examine these basic institutional trends before returning to the present moment in education reform.

THE LATE NINETEENTH CENTURY: PATTERNS OF DIVERSITY

Throughout most of the nineteenth century, American public education was highly decentralized, far more so than schools in any other nation. One reason was the dispersal of the population, which was mostly rural and educated in one-room schools. Another reason was a deep-rooted American distrust of centralized government, a fear that led citizens to write state constitutions that hobbled the powers of state governments. When states did try to control districts, citizens resisted state encroachment on local prerogatives. Control and funding of schools, with few exceptions, lay in the hands of local school trustees, who formed by far the largest group of elected officials in the United States, probably in the world. In 1890, state departments of education had an average of two employees, but close to a half-million local school trustees ran schools in their communities.[16]

Thus there was "school-based management" and community control to a degree unimaginable in today's schools. Local trustees and parents selected the teachers, supervised their work, and sometimes boarded them in their homes. The teacher's performance as reflected in the students' learning was visible to anyone who wanted to come to the frequent "exhibitions" (or public events, often held on Fridays, in which locals gathered to hear the children recite poems or compositions, give "declamations" on political or moral themes, and conduct spelling bees). Here accountability meant doing what the local community wanted. "Look with suspicion upon the teacher who tells you how he bosses the school board," observed a teacher in Kansas. "He is either a liar or a one-termer, and the probabilities are that he is both."[17]

Today the one-room rural school may seem a model of community-based education, but in the nineteenth century many career teachers regarded the rural school as a pedagogical slum, the urban system as a mecca. Rural schools paid meager salaries; teachers were typically young and paid youths' wages. Teachers' private lives as well as public performance were there for all to monitor. The demands of teaching all subjects to children of different ages strained even the most ingenious instructors. They had to improvise learning from whatever textbooks were available, to find ways to satisfy the conflicting tastes of their patrons (as the local citizens were called), and to devise their own systems of discipline and teaching. In the nineteenth century, educational leaders often wanted to consolidate one-room district schools and to turn them into graded schools on the urban model, but they did not succeed in large-scale consolidation of schools until well into the twentieth century.[18]

Urban schools of the latter half of the nineteenth century contrasted sharply with the decentralized rural schools. Cities paid teachers much more than did the rural communities, retained them much longer, and buffered them from community demands. Although the early city schools were rather haphazard in control and curriculum, leading urban superintendents managed to reorganize them into uniform, hierarchical systems. They prescribed the textbooks. They devised achievement tests covering the content of this curriculum. These tests determined promotion of pupils from grade to grade and supposedly calibrated the competence of teachers. Principals inspected teachers to make sure that they were toeing the line, like the pupils, and following the curriculum guide. Many cities had special normal (or teacher-training) divisions in their high schools to prepare young women to teach the city's course of study (including practice, in Washington, D.C., in prescribed exercises in "Yawning and Stretching" as a mid-morning ritual).[19]

This urban regime offered tightly controlled, orderly, standardized, direct instruction. Its institutional regime resembles the exam-driven, centralized curriculum and instruction characteristic of many nations today. Many educators at the turn of the twentieth century, however, thought this form of schooling a pedagogical disaster. They pointed out that in some cities half the children were lumped in the first two grades: enormous numbers were "retarded" (held back in grade), and dropped out at the earliest opportunity—often in the fourth or fifth grade. This one-size-fits-all, rigid education, they believed, needed to be reorganized and differentiated.[20]

"REORGANIZATION": TEMPLATE FOR REFORM, 1900–1950

The reformers of the period from 1900 to 1950 whom I call the "administrative progressives" were a group unified by similar training, interests, and values. They were the first generation of professional leaders educated in the new schools of education, men (there were few women in the group) who carved out lifelong careers in education as city superintendents, education professors, state officers, or foundation officials. They shared a common faith in "educational science" and in lifting education "above politics" so that experts could make the crucial decisions.[21]

The administrative progressives advocated innovations that would produce efficiency, equity (in their own definition), accountability, and expertise. They called their program of reform "reorganization," and during the years from 1900 to 1950 they were remarkably successful. Basically they did most of what they planned to do. Indeed, the momentum of many of their reforms continued during the thirty years after 1950, at a time when the older leadership of the administrative progressives was challenged by new actors in school politics.

By reorganization these leaders meant the opposite of what many people today mean by restructuring. They wanted to centralize control of urban schools in small, elite boards and to delegate decision making to experts; they thought that the old decentralized ward system of running schools was atavistic and corrupt. They worked successfully to consolidate small rural districts and to abolish one-room schools; they celebrated largeness, not smallness. They wanted to differentiate the curriculum to match the supposed differences of ability and economic destiny of students, not to give all students a solid grounding in academic subjects. They sought to create hierarchies of curriculum experts and supervisors to tell teachers what and how to teach, not to give them greater autonomy in the classroom, and they tried to replace the vagaries of local lay politics with the authority of educational science.[22]

Although educational leaders talked about "taking the schools out of politics"—in itself a smart political strategy—they knew that they needed allies. In the early twentieth century, business and professional elites dominated school boards and took an active interest in reorganization. One of the reasons the administrative progressives were so effective was that their aims aligned with those of the power holders of the time. Then as now, businessmen were worried about international economic competition and wanted efficient schools to help Americans meet the challenge of a new industrial and commercial giant, Germany.[23]

Supremely confident, the administrative progressives proclaimed that their reforms were in the national interest and in the interest of the schoolchildren. They tended to dismiss their opponents as ignorant or self-interested. They denounced decentralized urban ward boards of education as corrupt and meddling in professional matters. They regarded the rural foes of school consolidation as backward yokels who did not know what was good for their children. The big school was better because it permitted more differentiation of curriculum, and school boards and parents who did not recognize this were behind the times. Teachers who opposed guidance by expert administrators were unprofessional troublemakers.[24]

Influential educators used their professional organizations to pressure state legislatures to consolidate and standardize schools and to impose new certification requirements for education professionals. One reason for their success was that educators seemed to speak with one voice about what reforms were needed—or at least there was substantial consensus among the administrators, who dominated the National Education Association (NEA).

A symbiosis developed between university education schools and administrators, the new mandarins of education. New specialties generated new training programs; Teachers College, Columbia University, for example, prepared graduates for fifty-four different educational positions. Education barons placed their students in key superintendencies and then were invited to survey city school systems to measure how well they matched the new template of reorganization.[25]

The new educational ideology of science and efficient management gave the appearance of turning educational policy into a process of rational planning. The administrative progressives believed that children had different abilities and destinies in life and that hence schools should be differentiated. They devised IQ tests to sort pupils and standardized achievement tests to measure what they learned. They gave different labels to students who did not fit their definition of "normal," and they created tracks and niches for them. Reorganization to these experts meant a place for every child and every child in his or her place.[26]

The administrative progressives promised public *accountability* for their leadership, but it signified something quite different from its current meaning in the literature of restructuring. They mostly focused on structure and process, not results in academic learning, when they talked about accountability. They used many kinds of tests for internal management of students but they normally did not release test results to the public (that did not become common practice until the last generation).

By contrast, today many people say that in the restructured school teachers should be held responsible—that is, accountable—for *what* students learn but should have autonomy to decide *how* to accomplish that result. In this version, the process of learning is deregulated, the product specified and monitored, usually by tests whose results become public.

If being accountable means never needing to say you are sorry, the administrative progressives demonstrated their virtue and forestalled criticism by collecting enormous amounts of data to illustrate responsible modern management. They promised fiscal accountability and calculated to the last penny the cost of a lesson in Latin or welding. They claimed to use the latest technologies of instruction. They documented enrollments and the adoption of new programs. The accountability of the educational system came not from assessing the results of instruction but from demonstrating conformity of the structure and processes of schooling with what the public was taught to think was standard and up-to-date, the correct institutional grammar of the modern school.[27]

All in all, the restructuring of public schools that went by the name of "reorganization" produced clear institutional changes. Enrollments ballooned, schools grew larger and curricula more complex, the ranks of specialists swelled, numbers of districts sharply declined, and per-pupil funding rose steadily. The administrative progressives managed to persuade the public, by and large, to accept their notion of what was normal and desirable in education. The years from 1900 to 1950 have sometimes been labeled the golden age of the school superintendent, corroborated by political scientists of the 1950s who called local school districts "closed systems."

CHALLENGE IN THE 1960s: NEW ACTORS, PROGRAMS, PURPOSES

Beginning in the middle 1950s and growing in intensity and diversity in the 1960s, critics began to challenge some of the basic assumptions and achievements of the reorganization of schools during the previous half-century. Groups that had little voice in the old system demanded a role in decision making. The new politics of education undermined the status quo and modified old structures of power and school programs. As educators incorporated these changes into the existing system, however, no coherent new model of governance emerged. Indeed, the organizational responses to the new activists produced larger and more complex and fragmented bureaucracies.[28]

The *Brown* desegregation decision and the civil rights movement were major catalysts of change. Militant blacks demonstrated that people who had been segregated and largely excluded from the old politics of education could influence a system that had relegated them to powerlessness. This message was not lost on groups like Hispanics, feminists, or parents of handicapped children.[29]

Finding local systems of schools resistant to their demands, outsiders turned to higher levels of government—to state and federal legislatures and courts—for redress. One result was increased impact of federal and state governments on a system in which decision making had remained largely a local prerogative well into the 1950s. Legislatures and courts provided legal leverage for a variety of reforms: racial desegregation, the attack on institutional sexism, new bilingual programs, the introduction of ethnic curricula, new attention to the needs of the handicapped, and the equalization of school finance.

Reformers in the 1960s demanded dispersion and decentralization of educational decision making as well as an increased role for federal and state governments. Indeed, state and federal legislation itself sometimes mandated greater parental involvement through school-community councils in educational programs financed by these levels of government. Militant blacks called for community control of schools in the vast urban ghettoes. Largely as a result of pressures from disaffected students, school districts greatly expanded the number of electives and created alternative schools, storefront academies, schools within schools, and schools without walls. Such reforms gave greater choice to the students themselves. Activists attacked IQ testing and tracking, those familiar tools of the administrative progressives. Teachers demanded greater power over their work lives, achieved by unionization and by innovations such as teacher centers. Organizations like the NEA that once had joined administrators and teachers in one large if not always happy family split apart, the better to pursue their separate interests.[30]

The result of the new politics of education in the 1960s was neither the decentralization characteristic of nineteenth-century schools nor the modest centralization at the state and district levels achieved by the administrative progressives. Instead, governance resembled what John Meyer calls "fragmented centralization." Put another way, everybody and nobody was in charge of public schooling in that tumultuous decade. The insiders—the educational leaders—lost their sense of control over schooling.[31]

Federal and state laws created dozens of new categorical programs such as Title (later Chapter) I, which sought to funnel resources to needy students, or Public Law 94-142, which prescribed ways to educate handicapped children. As in the case of vocational education—which since 1918 had developed its own bureaucratic apparatus at federal, state, and local levels—many of the new programs produced new specialists at each level charged with seeking and disbursing funds and overseeing the new programs. Often these new categorical programs were uncoordinated, and sometimes they conflicted with one another.

One result of such fragmented centralization was that accountability often became accounting, and school bureaucracies grew at a rate never before equaled. New midmanagers became accountants for new categorical programs, compartmentalized domains that linked local bureaucrats more to state and federal officials than to the local district. John Meyer suggests that in the face of possibly contradic-

tory mandates and requirements, a sensible strategy for school superintendents was calculated ignorance or incompetence rather than the masterful planning that was the aim of their predecessors.[32]

The older faith in a science of education and universal solutions to educational problems did not disappear in the 1960s, however. Indeed, educational research was a growth industry in that decade. In particular, the number of evaluators expanded rapidly as government agencies demanded that someone assess the success of reforms. As a new version of accountability, much early evaluation was based on a rational model of planning and implementation—calibrating how well practice matched design. Sophisticated scholars soon concluded, however, that evaluation, like education itself, is a complex social and political process fraught with assumptions and interests ignored by the rational model.[33]

Indeed, as definitions of equity and efficiency changed, accountability became a cloak of many colors. One concept of accountability was responsiveness to the many protest groups that demanded attention to their agendas. This might take the form of introducing black history, for example, or appointing a Title IX coordinator to correct gender injustices. Accountability also became compliance with legal mandates resulting from the expansion of litigation in education, for districts had to respond to court-ordered desegregation, protection of procedural rights for students and teachers, and abandonment of prayers and Bible reading. Still another kind of accountability consisted of offering students more choices, as in electives or alternative schools, though this was considered by many people an abdication of educational responsibility.

THE 1980s: BACK TO BASICS, REFORM FROM THE TOP DOWN

By the 1980s a popular diagnosis of crisis in education was that educational ferment in the previous generation had disrupted learning. The decline in educational achievement, in turn, had endangered the nation's competitiveness in a tough world. Test scores, both across the years in the United States and in international comparisons, constituted the chief evidence for decay in schooling. The key reform report of the 1980s—*A Nation at Risk* (1983)—proclaimed rigor as the remedy—or, as a state legislator put it, "we need to make the little buggers [students] work harder."[34]

If anyone wanted proof that evaluation had broader social and political causes and consequences, the use of test scores in this period gave dramatic evidence. Made public, such standardized tests purported to measure what American students were learning. Policymakers came to regard tests as the chief measure of accountability. The message they gave was not reassuring: In absolute terms, students did not know as much as people thought they should, as students did in many other nations, or as they imagined American youth did in the golden age of the past; in relative terms, the situation seemed to be getting worse.[35]

This time the initiative in reform did not come from

protest groups or academics or educators or foundations, the people who had pressed the innovations of the 1960s. Rather, the new activists were people who had often been on the sidelines during that period: state governors and legislators and business organizations. During the late 1970s and early 1980s, when retrenchment had been the order of the day, state politicians took little interest in the schools (who wanted to be associated with decline?). The rhetoric of crisis in *A Nation at Risk,* amplified by the media and federal spokespeople, linked prosperity to learning—albeit in somewhat questionable ways—and made education once again a public priority. The Reagan administration did not want to spend more federal money on schools. Instead, William Bennett used his bully pulpit as secretary of education to chastise and cheer.[36]

The legislative action was in the states. Following the lead of *A Nation at Risk,* and sometimes anticipating it, almost all the states increased graduation requirements by specifying more academic courses in fields like English, mathematics, science, and social studies. Concurrently, states often raised requirements for admission to state colleges and universities. Many introduced or intensified standardized testing programs, sometimes specifying that they should be used to determine promotion or graduation. Twenty-seven legislatures set a minimum grade-point average for beginning teachers; forty-six required some kind of test for certification; many developed requirements for evaluating teachers; and some passed merit pay, career ladder, or mentor teacher programs—all designed to reward outstanding teachers.[37]

California illustrates how one state sought to increase academic rigor. In 1968 there were only three course requirements for graduation: American history, American government, and physical education. Essentially districts had a free hand in curriculum and instruction. In 1983 the legislature passed a law requiring students to take thirteen courses. The state department of education developed a more detailed and prescriptive course of study, pressured textbook publishers to intensify academic content and to stress "higher-order thinking," sought to align instruction with the new state framework, and developed statewide tests geared to the new curriculum.[38]

State reformers wanted to undo the curricular laissez-faire of the 1960s—the expansion of elective courses, for example—and to impose new requirements from the top down on teachers and students. Reformers insisted that their goal was to intensify—restore?—the traditional academic side of learning, but the means they chose—state mandates—did tilt governance strongly toward centralization. By the mid-1980s there was a new consensus on what accountability meant: results in learning, largely measured by test scores. This shift in the meaning of accountability was a fundamental, not an incremental, change in educational policy and practice that together with centralized state mandates and a growing interest in federal standards for learning might be considered a basic shift in educational policy. Implicit in all this was a transfer of power to a set of experts located in private organizations—the testers—who, like textbook corporations,

were not directly accountable to democratic decision making.[39]

It is still much too early to judge the impact of the state-imposed reforms of the mid-1980s, but by the end of the decade policymakers were already pointing anxiously at the numbers on wall charts of statistics of achievement that compared the states with one another and the United States with other nations. As leaders examined these Dow-Jones indices of scholastic achievement, some of them began to wonder if top-down state reforms were really producing the results they expected.[40]

Today many people believe that effective reform must restructure education, not simply issue new orders from the top in the dream of restoring some imagined era of academic virtue. As I have mentioned, advocates of restructuring often call for greater decentralization in governance, more autonomy for teachers and collegial decision making, more attention to the difficult tasks of getting students to think and demonstrate their competence, more parental involvement, smaller schools, and much more. Periodically in the last century reformers have advanced quite similar proposals. In assessing the chances of success and the wisdom of such reforms today, however, it is helpful first to look at persistent institutional trends in public schools over many decades.

LONG-TERM STRUCTURAL TRENDS IN PUBLIC SCHOOLS

For over a century, Americans have used statistics to demonstrate social crises and to justify educational remedies. Reformers have publicized crime rates, the influx of immigrants, numbers of child laborers, health problems, drug consumption, and declining test scores in order to advance their particular agendas. Much less often has policy talk about reform been compared with secular trends in schooling that may reveal what has happened over the long term, the institutional context within which proposals must be implemented.

If one looks at such long-term trends rather than at waves of policy talk (usually called periods of reform), the development of American schools looks much more linear and consistent than changes in rhetoric might suggest—and the direction of these statistics goes counter to major tenets of restructuring today.

Consider first the notion that the control of schools should be decentralized and lay people should be involved more. The major historical trends have moved in the opposite direction. By eliminating small school districts and their local trustees—reducing the number of districts from nearly 130,000 in 1931 to fewer than 16,000 in 1987—reformers of the past decimated the number of school trustees, thereby erasing in those communities the major form of lay input in educational decision making. In addition, early in the twentieth century the administrative progressives succeeded in nearly eliminating ward-based school boards in cities and reduced the average size of central boards from 21 to 7.[41]

2. RECONCEPTUALIZATION OF THE EDUCATIVE EFFORT

There has been much more talk about decentralization of urban schools in the last three decades than real changes in practice. In 1980 Allan C. Ornstein found that over half of the largest cities *claimed* that they had decentralized their schools, but when he checked again in 1988 only one-quarter said that they were decentralized. On closer inspection, even these cities looked dubious. When Ornstein compared the numbers of administrators in the central office with those in outlying offices, only two of these supposedly decentralized cities (New York and St. Louis) had more administrators outside than inside the central office. Some had ten to twenty times more administrators in the central office. Decentralization often turns out to be little more than another layer of bureaucracy, with little of the public involvement that is commonly attributed to decentralized governance.[42]

Second, today reformers want to create schools on a smaller, more intimate scale, but the number of students per school has jumped more than six-fold in the last half-century. The one-room school has become a vanishing breed, dropping from over 150,000 in 1930 to fewer than 1,000 today. Early in the twentieth century the model high school had perhaps 100 students, but by 1986 over half enrolled more than 1,000 students. The total number of high schools remained fairly constant—at about 24,000—between 1930 and 1980 while the number of high school graduates jumped in those years from 592,000 to 2,748,000. Until recently, most educators agreed that larger high schools were superior to small. Reformers today who want smaller, more personal environments must create them in much bigger buildings—hardly impossible, but not easy either.[43]

Third, some reformers today want to restructure curriculum and instruction so that students will focus on fewer subjects and treat them in greater depth. This goes against the grain of almost a century of differentiation of curriculum to fit the supposed abilities and later destinies of students, especially at the secondary level. The number of subjects and tracks vastly multiplied between 1900 and 1950. During the late 1960s demands for electives and alternative forms of schooling (including ethnic curricula) further expanded the course of study. Since the state reforms of the 1980s there has been some drop in enrollments in fields like vocational education and the arts, but the curriculum is still highly diverse, and tracking—obvious or covert—is still very common.[44]

Fourth, reformers now want to pare down middle management, regulation, and paperwork, but these have been growth industries. Getting rid of administrators has proved to be easier to propose than to accomplish; even during the time of retrenchment in the late 1970s, far more teachers were dropped, proportionately, than administrators. Accurate numbers on middle management are notoriously hard to find, but it appears that the number of middle managers in school districts more than doubled in the last forty years, much of it a result of fragmented centralization. There was one central office administrator for 746 pupils in 1950 and one for 520 in 1980. Handling the new paperwork empires were secretaries and clerical workers, who increased from 31,824 in 1950 to 223,647 in 1980. In 1890 there was, on average, one staff member in state departments of education for every 100,000 pupils, in 1974 one for about every 2,000. Regulations have ballooned: In California the state education code took about 200 pages in 1900, in 1985 more than 2,600.[45]

Fifth, reformers now argue that teachers are the heart of the education enterprise. They should have autonomy to make decisions. Funding should focus on their work. In recent decades, however, the growth of principals and non-teaching staff has far outpaced the relative growth of teachers. The word *principal* used to mean "principal teacher," and in the early decades of the twentieth century the principal was also a teacher in most schools, except in the larger cities. By the middle of the twentieth century, however, as schools grew larger, the job typically became a full-time administrative position. In 1946 fewer than one-quarter of schools had a principal; by 1980 there was more than one principal in all schools. In 1950 teachers constituted 70 percent of all staff employed per school, but in 1986 they were only 53 percent of the total, for other instructional and support staff increased markedly. There was one adult school employee for every 19 students in 1950, one for 9 in 1986; during this period the pupil-teacher ratio dropped much less (though still substantially, from 27 to 18).[46]

One way of interpreting the disparity among these five sets of long-term trends and some of the current proposals for restructuring is to regard the trends as evidence of the need for radical change, to say that the direction education has taken is fundamentally wrong, as shown by the present presumably critical failings of public schooling. Hence restructuring is mandatory. A counter argument would cast doubt on the possibility of basic change, given the way trends have persisted despite many vigorous attempts to alter the fundamental character of schooling in the past.

EDUCATION REFORM TODAY

I suggest that neither stance—the cheerleader for change or the wet-blanket approach—really captures the most appropriate uses of history in policy analysis. History is better suited to posing issues for decision makers to consider than providing set answers. Restructuring means so many things I cannot comment on all its ramifications. Let me focus on two facets of the movement, one structural and the other pedagogical: decentralization of authority and making the classroom a lively and challenging workplace for teachers and students.

First, then, let us consider the issue of centralization versus decentralization in education decision making. Perhaps the key question for reformers is to decide what decisions can best be made through relatively centralized or relatively decentralized decision-making structures. It is apparent that there is no easy way to characterize the governance of U.S. schools as either centralized or decentralized—the web of interactive relationships is far too complex for that. It is easy to bash bureaucrats, but in experiments in restructuring school districts superintendents and principals have proven to be key leaders.[47]

There has been much ebb and flow in talk about centralization/decentralization. In practice, however, history reveals a steady growth in state and then federal regulation, the size of districts, and the number of administrative staff. The administrative progressives set the ball of centralization rolling in the early twentieth century; the trend accelerated partly because it matched what was happening in other social, economic, and political institutions. In the 1960s federal and state categorical programs and litigation produced fragmentation in governance that greatly expanded administration and regulation. New state mandates of the 1980s centralized control of schools at the state level.

Decentralization and deregulation, by contrast, are remedies that appeal now to reformers across the political spectrum. Some of this discourse is populist or corporate rhetoric, some of it carefully reasoned strategies for change. With ritualistic regularity Americans have created and then bemoaned bureaucracies. A common pattern in the 1960s, for example, was to identify some problem and then designate an administrator to take care of it. Americans have also been ambivalent about regulations, often deciding that "there ought to be a law," then grousing about red tape.

Bureaucracies and regulations are not simply perverse and malign growths. In their origins they usually seemed reasonable responses to perceived problems. Much of the growth in nonteaching staff, for example, resulted from a conscientious desire to provide children with services—nutrition, day care, transportation, libraries, and counseling—that otherwise would have been absent. Today, indeed, some reformers talk about locating more, not fewer, social services in the schools, which would mean adding more nonteaching staff.

Regulation in American education has often aimed at correcting serious inequities such as segregation of blacks or neglect of disabled or immigrant children. Wholesale deregulation has the potential of reintroducing social injustices. As Americans have learned painfully in the savings and loan fiasco of the Reagan years, deregulation can have its not-so-hidden costs.

School governance will continue to be an uneasy and shifting balance between centralized and decentralized control, but the two modes of decision making are not equally appropriate for all tasks. Equalizing school funding or securing civil rights, for example, has demanded considerable centralization. To the degree that school governance is now characterized by fragmented centralization, we may have the worst of both worlds: many accountants to higher state and federal authorities but few people really accountable to students or parents. Eliminating overlapping jurisdictions and unnecessary paperwork may require both more centralization and more decentralization, depending on the particular function.

If one looks at the second issue I raised—reforms designed to make the classroom a livelier and more challenging workplace for teachers and students—I think it is fair to say that pushing changes in pedagogy from above has a spotty

and largely disappointing history. The most clear-cut example was the autocratic regime of nineteenth-century urban schools described above; teachers were simply told what to do and policed to see that they did it. Improving classroom instruction—the most important kind of reform, especially in poor and minority communities—has typically succeeded best when teachers were active partners in the process, and this is the key, I believe, to decentralized strategies of change.

Some of the most articulate advocates of restructuring call now for professionalizing teaching and decentralizing instructional decision making in individual schools. They seek to attract capable teachers, give them more autonomy and more chance to experiment along with colleagues, and enable them to respond effectively to their students. It is important not to start with an a priori notion of what professionalism is or to assume that teachers are hankering to run everything in schools. As Susan Moore Johnson has shown, teachers have typically rejected schemes like merit pay or career ladders because they fostered competition among teachers. Many have also objected to forms of school governance that placed an organizational overload on them. The goal of delegating decision making about classroom instruction to teachers does, however, hold the promise of matching school reforms to the aspirations and needs of teachers and their students. There are hopeful models of such change evident today, as in the Central Park East Schools of New York City.[48]

Enabling teachers to do their job better by giving them the autonomy and resources to create lively learning is quite different from traditional reform patterns of adding a new program to an existing structure. It is fundamentally an idea that needs to be developed by those who carry it out. Such reforms have historically been the most difficult to bring about. There is far more talk about restructuring teaching than action to bring it about. One point seems clear: The notion that reforms in instruction should be or can be permanent ignores historical experience and violates the principle that teachers should have the autonomy to adapt ways of learning to their students. And if teachers are really to be free to experiment, they may also fail, as do doctors or politicians.

Progress in improving classroom instruction will come slowly and in small and perhaps temporary increments, I suspect, not in millennial bursts. Larry Cuban's historical study *How Teachers Taught* should make us wary of expecting rapid or permanent changes. As he says, various winds of reform have ruffled the surface of the educational sea, but a fathom deep, in the classroom practices remained remarkably consistent over time. Teachers have become experts in accommodating to, deflecting, or sabotaging changes they do not desire.[49]

When teachers do buy into reforms, however, when they make them their own, the experience can energize them and their students. This kind of change is hard to set in concrete; some reforms in classroom learning have had a short, happy life. An example is the Eight-Year study of the 1930s. In that experiment, teachers in thirty secondary schools reorganized curriculum and instruction along progressive lines, free of college entrance requirements. By most accounts, students found learning an exciting experience in high school and also performed better in higher education than a comparison group educated in more traditional ways. A decade or so after the reforms were evaluated, however, a researcher found that "little remained of the experimental programs."[50]

No magic wand of restructuring can set things permanently straight. We will always have waves of education reform that seek to alter the substantial structures we have built, for values differ, interests conflict, generational perspectives change. For the last century Americans have been constantly tinkering toward utopia in school reform. It has been our way of creating the future that we want.

NOTES

1. John I. Goodlad quoted in Lynn Olson, "The 'Restructuring' Puzzle: Ideas for Revamping 'Egg-Crate' Schools Abound, but to What Ends?" *Education Week*, November 2, 1988, p. 7.

2. Richard F. Elmore and Associates, *Restructuring Schools: The Next Generation of Educational Reform* (San Francisco: Jossey-Bass, 1990), p. 4; and William A. Firestone, Susan H. Fuhrman, and Michael W. Kirst, *The Progress of Reform: An Appraisal of State Education Initiatives* (New Brunswick, N.J.: Center for Policy Research in Education, 1989), pp. 10, 13. Michael Kirst observes that restructuring is "almost a Rorschach test. It's all in the eye of the beholder" (quoted in Olson, "Restructuring Puzzle," p. 7); see also "Cavazos Issues 'Terrible' Report on U.S. Schools," *Los Angeles Times,* May 3, 1990, p. A3.

3. *New York Times*, October 1, 1989, Section 4, pp. 1, 22 (emphasis added to *radical*).

4. Michael W. Kirst, "Who Should Control Our Schools: Reassessing Current Policies," Center for Educational Research at Stanford, School of Education, Stanford University, 1988; reported in *New York Times,* March 23, 1990, p. A-9.

5. Chester E. Finn, Jr., and Stephen K. Clements, "Reconnoitering Chicago's Reform Efforts: Some Early Impressions," Occasional Paper, Joyce Foundation, July 1988; and Herbert J. Walberg et al., "Reconstructing the Nation's Worst Schools," *Phi Delta Kappan* 70 (June 1989): 802–05.

6. William Bennett, *American Education: Making It Work* (Washington, D.C.: GPO, 1988).

7. On Miami's experiment, see Jane L. David, "Restructuring in Progress: Lessons from Pioneering Districts," in Elmore, *Restructuring,* pp. 212–15; *New York Times*, January 6, 1990, pp. A-1, 16; January 19, 1990, A-16; March 9, 1990, A-1, 16.

8. Joseph M. Rice, *The Public School System of the United States* (New York: Century, 1893); Diane Ravitch, *The Great School Wars* (New York: Basic Books, 1974); Leonard Covello, *The Heart Is the Teacher* (New York: McGraw-Hill, 1958); and David Rogers, *110 Livingston Street* (New York: Random House, 1968).

9. Julius Gordon, "School Reform Again? (Sigh)," *New York Times,* January 29, 1990, p. A-19.

10. In thinking about these issues I am indebted to a penetrating essay by David K. Cohen, "Governance and Instruction: The Promise of Decentralization and Choice" (essay for May 1989 conference sponsored by the LaFollette Institute of Public Policy at the University of Wisconsin, Madison).

11. Elmore, *Restructuring,* pp. 290–92.

12. Ibid., pp. 2–3, 293. Jane L. David writes that "the goals of restructuring are to decentralize authority, create more professional workplaces, and focus resources on teaching and learning" ("Restructuring in Progress," p. 211).

13. Larry Cuban, "Reforming Again, Again, Again, and Again," *Educational Researcher* 19 (1990): 3–13; Thomas James and David Tyack, "Learning from Past Efforts to Reform the High School," *Phi Delta Kappan* 64 (1983): 400–06; Thomas S. Popkewitz, "Educational Reform: Rhetoric, Ritual, and Social Interest," *Educational Theory* 38 (1988): 77–93; and Michael W. Kirst and Gail Meister, "Turbulence in

14. David Tyack and Elisabeth Hansot, *Managers of Virtue: Public School Leadership in America* (New York: Basic Books, 1982), Part II.

15. Michael W. Kirst, "Recent State Education Reform in the United States: Looking Backward and Forward," *Educational Administration Quarterly* 24 (1988): 319–28.

16. David Tyack, Thomas James, and Aaron Benavot, *Law and the Shaping of Public Education, 1785-1954* (Madison: University of Wisconsin Press, 1987), chs. 2–3.

17. Marion G. Kirkpatrick, *The Rural School from Within* (Philadelphia: Lippincott, 1917), pp. 39–40; and Wayne E. Fuller, *The Old Country School: The Story of Rural Education in the Middle West* (Chicago: University of Chicago Press, 1982).

18. David B. Tyack, *The One Best System: A History of American Urban Education* (Cambridge: Harvard University Press, 1974), Part 1.

19. John D. Philbrick, *School Systems in the United States* (Washington, D.C.: GPO, 1885); pictures of "yawning and stretching" in Frances Benjamin Johnston photograph collection in the Library of Congress.

20. Leonard P. Ayres, *Laggards in Our Schools: A Study of Retardation and Elimination in City School Systems* (New York: Charities Publication Committee, 1909).

21. Tyack and Hansot, *Managers of Virtue*, Part 2.

22. George D. Strayer, "Progress in City School Administration during the Past Twenty-five Years," *School and Society* 32 (1930): 325–45.

23. Tyack, *One Best System*, Part 4.

24. For the views of one fascinating "troublemaker," see Margaret Haley, "Why Teachers Should Organize," in National Education Association, *Addresses and Proceedings, 1904*, pp. 145–52.

25. Tyack and Hansot, *Managers of Virtue*, Part 2.

26. Larry Cuban and David Tyack, "Match and Mismatch—Schools and Children Who Don't Fit Them," in *Accelerated Schools*, ed. Henry Levin (Falmer Press, forthcoming).

27. Raymond E. Callahan, *Education and the Cult of Efficiency* (Chicago: University of Chicago Press, 1962); and John W. Meyer and Brian Rowan, "Institutionalized Organizations: Formal Structure as Myth and Ceremony," *American Journal of Sociology* 83 (1977): 340–63.

28. Edith Mosher, Anne H. Hastings, and Jennings Wagoner, Jr., *Pursuing Equal Educational Opportunity: The New Activists* (New York: ERIC Clearing House on Urban Education, 1979).

29. Richard Kluger, *Simple Justice: The History of Brown v. Board of Education and Black America's Struggle for Equality* (New York: Vintage Books, 1977); and David Tyack and Elisabeth Hansot, *Learning Together: A History of Coeducation in American Public Schools* (New Haven: Yale University Press and Russell Sage Foundation, 1990), ch. 9.

30. Henry Levin, ed., *Community Control of Schools* (Washington, D.C.: Brookings, 1970).

31. John W. Meyer, "The Impact of the Centralization of Educational Funding and Control of State and Local Educational Governance" (Stanford: Institute for Research on Educational Finance and Governance, Stanford University, 1980); and idem, W. Richard Scott, and David Strang, "Centralization, Fragmentation, District Complexity," *Administrative Science Quarterly* 32 (1987): 186–201.

32. Meyer, "Centralization," pp. 6, 17.

33. Milbrey Wallin McLaughlin, "Learning from Experience: Lessons from Policy Implementation," *Educational Evaluation and Policy Analysis* 9 (1987): 171–78.

34. Kirst, "Recent State Education Reform," p. 320.

35. Myths abounded about how much students had learned in the golden age of the past, but it is exceedingly difficult to compare past and present achievement. Despite the widespread use of standardized achievement tests in schools since the early 1920s, the results were generally not made public but instead were kept within the bureaucracy for internal decision making.

36. For the political agenda and media blitz behind *A Nation at Risk*, see Peter S. Hlebowitsh, "Playing Power Politics: How *A Nation at Risk* Achieved Its National Stature," *Journal of Research and Development in Education* 23 (1990): 82–88; and Lorraine M. McDonald and Milbrey W. McLaughlin, *Education Policy and the Role of the States* (Santa Monica, Calif.: Rand Corporation, 1982).

37. Firestone, Fuhrman, and Kirst, *Progress of Reform*.

38. Ibid., ch. 2.

39. Cohen, "Governance and Instruction"; *New York Times,* March 21, 1990, p. B7.

40. "Cavazos Issues 'Terrible' Report on U.S. Schools," p. A3.

41. National Center for Education Statistics, *Digest of Education Statistics, 1988* (Washington, D.C.: NCES, 1988), Table 67; and Tyack, *One Best System,* Part 4.

42. Allan C. Ornstein, "Centralization and Decentralization of Large Public School Districts," *Urban Education* 24 (1989): 233–35; in New York, the voter turnout in elections for district school boards is typically minuscule.

43. NCES, *Digest, 1988,* Table 67.

44. John Francis Latimer, *What's Happened to Our High Schools?* (Washington, D.C.: Public Affairs Press, 1958); and Firestone, Furhman, and Kirst, *Progress of Reform,* pp. 23–26.

45. NCES, *Digest, 1988,* Table 61; and John W. Meyer et al., *Bureaucratization without Centralization: Changes in the Organizational System of American Public Education, 1940–1980,* Project Report No. 85-A11 (Stanford: Institute for Finance and Governance, Stanford University, 1985), Table 1. I am indebted to Jane Hannaway for the information on the California Code.

46. NCES, *Digest, 1988,* Table 61; and Meyer et al., *Bureaucratization,* Table 1.

47. David, "Restructuring in Progress."

48. Theodore Sizer, *Horace's Compromise: The Dilemma of the American High School* (Boston: Houghton Mifflin, 1984) and Carnegie Forum on Education and the Economy, *A Nation Prepared* (New York: Carnegie Foundation, 1986); David Bensman, *Quality Education in the Inner City: The Story of the Central Park East Schools* (New York: Community School Board, District 4, 1987); Susan Moore Johnson, "Schoolwork and Its Reform," in *The Politics of Reforming School Administration,* ed. Jane Hannaway and Robert Crowson (New York: Falmer Press, 1989), pp. 95–112; and idem, "Redesigning Teachers' Work," in Elmore, *Restructuring,* ch. 5. Thomas Timar points out that state mandates and regulations often stymie local efforts at restructuring—see "The Politics of School Restructuring," *Phi Delta Kappan,* December 1989, pp. 265–75.

49. Larry Cuban, *How Teachers Taught: Constancy and Change in American Classrooms, 1890–1980* (New York: Longman, 1984).

50. Wilford M. Aiken, *The Story of the Eight-Year Study* (New York: McGraw-Hill, 1942); and Lawrence A. Cremin, *The Transformation of the School: Progressivism in American Education, 1876–1957* (New York: Vintage, 1964), p. 256, n. 6.

Striving for Excellence: The Drive for Quality

For several years now, there have been frequent, and sometimes conflicting, visions of what constitute excellent outcomes of schooling. Life in schools has been examined from several pedagogical, social, economic, and ideological perspectives. We see some fascinating alternatives that could be opened to us if we have the will to make them happen. In the decade of the 1980s, those reforms which were to lead us to a higher level of qualitative growth in the conduct of schooling tended to be what education historian David Tyack referred to in *The One Best System* (Harvard University Press, 1974) as "structural" reforms: demands for standardized testing of students and teaching, reorganization of teacher education programs, legislative actions to provide alternative routes into the teaching profession, efforts to recruit more talented people into teaching, and laws to enable greater parental choice as to where their children may attend school. Some of these issues were explored in unit 2 on the reconceptualization of our educational efforts. But these structural reforms cannot, as Tyack noted as early as 1974, in and of themselves, produce higher levels of student achievement. We need to explore a broad range of possible and deeply important aims of schooling requiring a broadly conceived conception of what it means to be a literate person. Also, we need to reconsider what is implied in speaking of the "quality" of the effects of our children having been schooled.

Children and adolescents need the opportunity to discover, create, and master inquiry skills that will enable them to cope effectively with the dramatic changes occurring in an ever more interdependent world. Yes, they must be literate in the narrow sense of that term. They must learn to read, write, and compute at levels appropriate to the technologically advanced world they will encounter in their early adulthoods. The cognitive goals of schooling cannot be de-emphasized, but we cannot "deskill" (Apple, *Education and Power*, 1982) students by denying them the opportunity to learn how to be skilled inquirers, persons able to reason well on their own.

In brief, when we speak of quality and excellence as aims of education, we must remember that these terms encompass *aesthetic* as well as cognitive processes. Young people cannot achieve that full range of intellectual capacity to solve problems on their own simply by being obedient and memorizing factual data. How students encounter their teachers in classrooms and how teachers interact with their students are concerns that encompass aesthetic as well as cognitive dimensions. We see re-flected in the current literature on this topic critical reactions to standardized testing as well as vigorous defenses of it. Perhaps, and this is probably the case, there is a need to enforce intellectual (cognitive) standards and to make schools creative places in which to learn where students learn to explore and to imagine and to hope.

Perhaps standardized testing is not the answer. European nations give more qualitative forms of examinations in the sciences and mathematics and written essay examinations in the humanities and social sciences, as well as oral exit examinations from secondary school by committees of teachers. Perhaps we really do have to rethink how we strive for excellence in education. There has always been tension between quality and equality of opportunity in the educational policy debate. "Top down" solutions have been traditional to educational problems in the United States, Canada, and the rest of the world. Perhaps this is not avoidable due to the logical necessity of governmental financing of public, tax-supported school systems. However, the top-down pattern of national-state (provincial) policy development for schooling needs to be tempered by even more "bottom-up," grass-roots efforts at improving the quality of schools such as is now underway in many school systems across the North American continent. Imaginative inquiry and assessment strategies need to be developed by teachers working in their classrooms with the support of professional colleagues and parents.

Excellence is the goal: the means to achieve it is what is in dispute. There is a new dimension to the debate over the assessment of the academic achievement of elementary and secondary school students. In addition, there is a continuing struggle of conflicting academic (as well as political) interests over improving the quality of preparation of future teachers.

Few conscientious educators would oppose the idea of excellence in education; as with motherhood and one's nation, some things are held in deep and generalized reverence. The problem in gaining consensus over excellence in education is that excellence is always defined against some standard. Since there are fundamentally opposing standards for determining what constitutes excellent student and teacher performances, it is sometimes debatable which standards of assessment should prevail. The current debate over excellence in teacher education in the United States clearly demonstrates how conflicting academic values can clash and lead to conflicting programmatic recommendations for educational reform.

The 1980s brought North American educators many important individual and commission reports on bringing qualitative improvement to the educational system at all levels. Some of the reports addressed higher education concerns (particularly relating to general studies requirements and teacher education), but most of them focused on the academic performance problems of elementary and secondary school students. There were literally dozens of such reports. In this area, the activities of the Bush administration and the National Governors' Conference in the United States may foster additional items for the educational reform agenda. There have been some common themes in those reports on school reform sponsored by government, philanthropic, and corporate bodies. There has been some thematic commonality in those reports issued to date by affected groups of educators. However, there are professional teaching organizations that take exception to what they believe to be too heavily laden hidden business and political agendas underlying some of the public rhetoric on school reform. Educators in teacher education are not in agreement either.

As the United States and Canada debate the educational tradeoffs involved in alternative strategies for school reform, they can learn which educational attitudes, values, and performance outcomes must prevail. These spirited, generalized public debates over educational policies and programs should produce great learning societies.

The following are types of questions that can be considered when developing policy alternatives for improvement of student achievement. Should schools with different missions be established at the secondary level as they are in some parts of Europe? If specialization is considered desirable or necessary at the second level, what specific types of specialized secondary schools should be established? Or should there be a common secondary school curriculum for all secondary school students? If existing American and Canadian elementary and secondary schools are not producing desired levels of academic competency, what specific course changes in school curricula are required? What forms of teacher education and in-service reeducation of teachers are needed? Who pays for any of these programmatic options? Where and how are funds raised or redirected from other budgetary priorities to do these things? Will Americans ever adopt the "streaming" and "tracking" models of secondary school student placement that exists in Europe? How can we best assess (evaluate) academic performance? Will North

Americans accept structural realignments in the educational system? How will handicapped learners be scheduled in schools? Is there a national commitment to heterogeneous grouping of students, and to mainstreaming handicapped students in the United States? Many individual, private, and governmental reforms efforts have failed to address and resolve the reform agenda issues these questions raise.

Other industrialized nations have championed the need for alternative secondary schools to prepare young people for varied life goals and civic missions. The American dream of the common school translated into a comprehensive high school in the twentieth century. It was to be a high school for all the people with alternative diploma options and its students "tracked" into different programs. What is the next step? What is to be done? To succeed in improving the quality of student achievement, concepts related to our educational goals must be clarified, and political motivation must be separated from the demonstrable realities of student performance. We must clarify our goals. When we do this we come down to getting clearer on "what knowledge is of most worth?" Which educational values and priorities are to prevail?

Looking Ahead: Challenge Questions

Try to identify some of the different points of view on achieving excellence in education. What value conflicts can be defined?

Do teachers see educational reform in the same light as governmental, philanthropic, or corporate-based school reform groups? On what matters would they agree? On what matters might they disagree?

What can be learned from recent reports on the state of American education? What are your views of the recommendations being offered to improve the quality of schooling?

How could school curricula and instructional practices be modified to encourage excellence in teaching and learning?

What are the minimum academic standards that all high school graduates should meet?

What are the most significant issues to be addressed in the development and use of minimum competency testing?

Is there anything new in the struggle for excellence? What can be learned from the history of efforts to reform education?

What Really Counts in Schools

Our understanding of the mission of schooling
must go beyond the merely measurable to a
consideration of more profound purposes.

ELLIOT W. EISNER

Elliot W. Eisner is Professor of Education
and Art, Stanford University, School of
Education, Stanford, CA 94305.

Deciding what really counts in
our schools is the first order of
our educational mission. The
second is to create the conditions that
are consistent with that mission. There
is no shortage of opinion about our
mission. We hear from the highest
offices in our land that American
schools are in a dismal state. We hear
from others that they are in a state of
crisis. We read in the mass media
about our lowly position, not in the
arms race, but in the "education race."
Education has become the front line in
our quest for international supremacy.
For many, there is no mistaking it:
Education is not only a business, it is a
competitive race.

We are told that we must get our
house in order, in order to continue to
reside in our house—others are waiting in the wings. The mark of our
success will be our position among
other nations on tests that purportedly
measure what counts.

I have more than severe reservations about such prescriptions for educational supremacy. Neither supremacy nor the metaphor of the race are, I
believe, appropriate for thinking
about the kinds of lives we would like
our children to lead. A president who,
when campaigning for office, spoke of
the need for "a kinder and gentler
America" cannot logically view our
nation's schools as instruments for
beating others. There is in such obser-

vations, at the very least, a tinge of
inconsistency.

It is time to think about what really
counts in schools. I think that our
analysis ought to penetrate the simplistic, the merely measurable, and the
superficial. This article is my effort to
make that penetration.

A Starting Point
I start with certain premises about
human nature and the mission of education. I start with the premise that
when children come into the world,
they do not possess minds. People
acquire minds during the course of
their lifetimes; the task is not completed when students finish the 12th
grade. Children *do* come into the
world with brains; brains are biological. Minds are cultural. Minds are
forms of cultural achievement, and the
kinds of minds that children come to
own depend, in large measure, on the
kinds of experiences they are afforded
during the course of their lifetimes.

We all know what a *culture* is. In the
biological sense, a culture is a place
for growing things. Schools are cultures for growing minds. The major
instruments that we use to create
minds are the kinds of programs we
offer and the quality of teaching we
provide. Like the systole and diastole
of the beating heart, curriculum and
teaching are the most fundamental aspects of our schools. Decisions that we
make about what to include and what
to exclude from the programs we offer are of the foremost importance.
But programs, no matter how well-

conceived, must always be mediated if
they are to influence the lives of those
with whom we work. This process of
mediation, at its best, is an artistic
activity. We call it *teaching*. When
teachers transform the inevitably limited and schematic conceptions of
school programs into the kinds of
activities that genuinely engage students, when they create the environments that open up new vistas and
provide for deep satisfactions, they
make a difference in the lives that
children lead. No curriculum teaches
itself, it always must be mediated, and
teaching is the fundamental mediator.

Teaching, however, as a form of
human mediation, is not the only important influence on children. How
we organize the "envelope" within
which teaching and curriculum activities occur also matters. That is, how
schools are structured, the kind of
values that pervade them, the ways in
which roles are defined and assessments made are a part of the living
context in which both teachers and
students must function. Make no mistake about it, these pervasive organizational features define the kind of
place that schools are; they also teach.
Dreeben (1968) refers to these features as the non-pedagogical aspects
of instruction.

**Six Aims That Count in
Schools**
What really counts in school, from my
perspective, may not appear on anyone's list of national educational im-

By Elliot W. Eisner, "What Really Counts in School," *Educational Leadership*, Vol. 48, No. 5, February 1991, pp. 10-11, 14-17.
Reprinted with permission of the Association for Supervision and Curriculum Development. Copyright © 1991 by ASCD. All
rights reserved.

peratives. Yet, I believe they are imperative. Let me share them with you.

The Journey Is the Reward

First, what really counts in schools is teaching children that the exploration of ideas is sometimes difficult, often exciting, and occasionally fun.

I know that such a prosaic aspiration for educational practice as a fundamental aim of education must seem simple. In one sense, it *is* simple. It is certainly an aim that is simple to articulate. It is not so simple to achieve. But it is of the utmost importance educationally.

We sometimes seem to believe that the importance of what we do in school is determined by how well children do on tasks they will encounter later in schools or in colleges or universities. I take issue with such a conception. The major goals of schooling are not realized by performances on tasks defined in classrooms or within schools. The important effects of schools are located in the kinds of lives that children lead outside school and the kinds of satisfactions they pursue there. In research terms, the major dependent variables of schooling are not scores on standardized achievement tests, whether norm- or criterion-referenced: they are the kinds of ideas children are willing to explore on their own, the kinds of critical skills they are able to employ on tasks outside classrooms, and the strength of their curiosity in pursuing the issues they will inevitably encounter in the course of their lives. Indeed, a much better index for school achievement than standardized achievement test scores is the level and quality of the conversations children engage in away from their classrooms.

The reason it is so important for youngsters to enjoy what they study in school is because without such satisfactions, the likelihood that they will pursue their studies outside our institutions is small.

There are, it is said, three reasons that motivate people to do things. The first of these is to secure satisfactions that are intrinsic to the activity itself. Both sex and play are paradigm cases of such satisfactions. In both, activities are pursued for the intrinsic satisfactions that they yield. That is why, I think, intellectual activity at its highest level is often associated with play.

When children enjoy playing with ideas and dealing with problems in a playful way, when they secure the kinds of satisfactions that they get from activities that they choose, they are engaged in the kind of activity I am talking about.

A second reason for doing something is not because the activity itself is pleasurable, but because the results are. Most people like to have a clean kitchen, but I suspect few of us enjoy kitchen-cleaning chores. Many people work at jobs whose processes they don't enjoy, but they do take pride and satisfaction in the work once done.

A third reason for doing something is not because the process is satisfying, nor because the results are, but because one likes the payoff in the form of a paycheck. Too many people, lamented Hannah Arendt (1958), are engaged in this kind of activity as a way of securing a livelihood. For Arendt, such activity constitutes labor. Work, by contrast, is related to the first and second forms of motivation.

I happen to think that in our schools many children are inadvertently motivated by extrinsic reward systems that teach them that the important reason for engaging in an activity is to secure a reward that typically has little or nothing to do with the activity itself. We call such motivators "stars," "brownie points," "grades," and "honor classes." What will happen to those students when those motivators are no longer available? Will they take the journey? They will, if in the context of schools and classrooms they discover that the journey is the reward.

Formulating Questions, Seeking Answers

A second aim that really counts in schools is helping youngsters learn how to formulate their own problems and how to design the tactics and strategies to solve them. We often talk in education about the importance of problem-solving skills, and clearly the ability to solve problems is important. But the most difficult of intellectual tasks is not primarily in solving problems but in formulating the questions that give rise to them. We place great emphasis in our schools on setting tasks for students and expecting them to pursue them. We call these tasks "assignments." They emanate from teachers and are directed to students.

The child's job is not to question why, but, as they say, to do or die.

Some writers (Apple 1982) have referred to this process as a process of *deskilling*. What is deskilled when such a process dominates classrooms and schools is the child's ability to assume responsibility for the aims as well as the means he or she might employ in dealing with them. Since in the course of life the ability to conceptualize what is problematic and to formulate interesting questions is fundamental in maintaining one's intellectual autonomy, it does not seem unreasonable that schools should be places in which students could practice such skills. This would require giving children an opportunity to formulate their own aims, to conceptualize their own problems, and to design the ways in which such problems might be addressed. It means that finding out what students want to know about *after teaching* is as important as determining whether they possess the answers we hoped they would. The kinds of questions students can formulate is as important an educational outcome—perhaps even more so—as how well they can converge upon the correct answers that populate our textbooks.

Providing school programs that make it possible for students to formulate their own problems increasingly as they get older and to work on tasks related to them would, undoubtedly, lead to increased heterogeneity in the classroom. I am fully aware that it is neither feasible nor desirable for such activities to be all that is provided in our curriculums. There does need to be some common fare and some effort at cooperative group activity. Every child going off on his or her own track in an utterly independent way is not what I have in mind. But what I do envision is providing children with opportunities to learn how to formulate their own goals, questions, and problems. Providing such opportunities will, of course, make the process of evaluation more complicated and difficult. However, our educational aspirations should not be defined by the current limits of our testing technology. We need to reach for more.

Multiple Forms of Literacy

A third aim that counts in schools is the development in the young of multiple forms of literacy. Literacy is typically thought of as the ability to read and write. Literacy surely includes such skills, but I conceptualize it in broader ways (Eisner 1985). Literacy is, broadly speaking, the ability to encode or decode meaning in any of the forms used in the culture to represent meaning. Aristotle observed long ago that "man by nature seeks to know." The *knowing* that Aristotle talked about is embedded in human experience, and human experience, in turn, is influenced by the forms of representation that we can meaningfully employ. School programs ought to develop literacy, that is, the ability to secure meaning, from the wide range of forms that are used in culture to express meaning. This surely includes far more than the literal use of language or the ability to write precise "standard" English. Language itself takes many forms. There is the literal use of language, the literary use, the figurative, the poetic, and the vernacular use of language. Language is diverse: the kinds of meaning that can be represented and secured in poetry, for example, are simply unavailable to those limited to prose.

Similarly, the meanings that are engendered through choreography, through music, and through the visual arts are unique or special to their forms. There are some meanings that can be grasped through visual form that cannot be described in language or in quantitative form. Toshiba, IBM, Apple, and other computer companies have long recognized that spreadsheets, pie charts, scattergrams, and visuals in living color increase the meaningfulness of some kinds of information; they know that the way in which we construct meaning depends upon the way in which forms of representation are configured. Not everything that we want to say can be said in language. Not everything that we want to convey can be reported in number. The moral here for school programs is clear: those that neglect or marginalize the fine arts, for example, embrace an educational policy guaranteed to graduate students who are semi-literate. The great ceramic figures of the Zapotec, the bronze vessels of the Han Dynasty, the egg tempera madonnas of 14th century Italy, the Abstract Expressionism of the 1950s will be for our students other people's pleasures if

The imagination is, fundamentally, an important dimension of human consciousness and, at bottom, the engine of cultural and social progress.

they are denied the opportunity to learn how to see and understand what these works make possible.

At present, American schools are embarked on a set of educational priorities that are both narrow and shortsighted. We think about literacy in the tightest, most constipated of terms. We need a more generous conception of what it means to know and a wider conception of the sources of human understanding. The poet, the painter, the composer, the playwright, as well as the physicist, the chemist, the botanist, the astronomer have something to teach us. Paying adequate attention to such forms of understanding in schools is the best way to make them a meaningful part of our students' intellectual lives.

In Praise of Wonder, Imagination

A fourth aim that really counts in schools is teaching the young the importance of wonder. So much of what we teach in schools seems to undermine the importance of wonder. Indeed, wondering, even daydreaming has been regarded as an "off-task" activity. The tacit image of pedagogical virtue conveyed by so much of our educational literature is an image of youngsters with their heads buried in workbooks who never come up for air. Academic engaged time, by itself, is no virtue. Whether being academically engaged is or is not a virtue depends, at minimum, on the nature of the task in which one is engaged. Often times daydreaming and wonderment are forms of respite from activities that children find meaningless and distasteful. They are means children

use to maintain their psychological equilibrium.

But more than the satisfactions afforded by escape from meaninglessness are the potential worlds that wonder makes possible. The imagination is, fundamentally, an important dimension of human consciousness and, at bottom, the engine of cultural and social progress. It is a resource distinctive to our species. Some people have argued that bees are great architects and proceed to support their case by pointing out that bees use a material that is soft and malleable to build not only beautiful architectural structures of great proportion and precision, but structures of great strength as well.

The fact of the matter is, however, that bees are not great architects. Bees create honeycombs because they can do nothing else. They have been creating these same honeycombs for years now, and I suspect that they will continue to do so in the future. What architects require, and what humans possess, is imagination. Humans create buildings that take the forms they do by virtue of wonderment and by the strength of imagination. When bees are able to create Baroque beehives I might change my mind, but until then I am unwilling to regard bees as creative architects.

Wonder and imagination are fundamental not only in architecture, but also in science and in all creative aspects of human affairs. I believe our schools should create the kind of environment and provide the kind of tasks that elicit and develop respect for wonder and stimulate the imagination. One of the features of schooling that dampens the inclination toward wonder and that limits the imagination are the kinds of assessment practices we typically employ. If there's any single lesson that multiple-choice tests teach, it is that for every question there is a single correct answer and for every problem a single correct solution. The correct solution is known by the testmaker or the teacher, and the student soon learns that his or her task is to converge upon the correct one. The tacit message is a message of convergence, of singularity, of homogeneity.

If we created teaching practices that put a premium on the imaginative aspects of learning, if we encouraged children to maintain that wonderful fantasy and speculative ability they possessed when they started school, we would be better able to create a culture that was much more receptive to the possibilities of human experience and much more educationally productive.

In speaking of the development of the imagination and the enhancement of wonder, I risk the possibility of seeming to talk about aims that are "pie in the sky." I do not believe such aims are "pie in the sky." I believe they can be attained. Their attainment will require a shift in what we consider really important in school. Equally as important, we will need to invent curriculum activities that afford youngsters opportunities to use their imagination and to engage in wonder. I have no doubt whatsoever that such activities can be designed, even in subjects that appear to be literal and highly rule-governed.

The School as Community
A fifth aim of fundamental importance in schools is helping children realize that they are part of a caring community. Such a realization will not occur unless the school itself becomes a community. Many schools lack a sense of community; and many students, particularly during the time they are most vulnerable, their adolescence, are in institutions in which sustained and intimate contact with a caring adult is limited. Departmentalized school structures, which are the norm at the middle and senior high school levels, often provide adolescents with no adults in a counseling capacity nor any who are responsible for their pastoral care. Typically, a student will have five to seven teachers, will often see these teachers each day for 45 to 50 minutes, and in some schools will have access to a school counselor, but more often than not when such contact occurs, it is for purposes of vocational or academic counseling or for discipline. In few schools is there someone in touch with the emotional and social aspects of the students' lives. Whether we're students or teachers, all of us inevitably bring our personal lives into our classrooms.

The absence of pastoral care for students might not be so significant if the communities in which they lived were characterized by strong nuclear families and strong social bonds. The fact of the matter is that 25 percent of

My hope is that educators will be moved to begin the kind of dialogue that leads to genuine reform in education, a reform that pays attention to what really counts.

school-aged children are raised in single-parent homes; 52 percent of minority school children are raised in single-parent homes. Very often these children come home to a home with no one at home. We call them latchkey children. The seven to eight million latchkey children in America are twice as likely to use drugs as those who have a parent working at home. Since we have approximately 46 million students in public schools, seven to eight million latchkey children represents approximately 20 percent of our school population. In short, the school has always had a caring role to play, but this role is considerably more critical today. Developing an ethic of caring and creating a community that cares is, as far as I know, on no one's list of educational priorities—but it ought to be.

Each Student's Personal Signature
A sixth aim I believe to be of fundamental importance in schools is teaching children that they have a unique and important personal signature. Much that we teach by virtue of the curriculum content we emphasize and how we choose to evaluate what students have learned diminishes their sense of personal signature. The tasks we use to teach beginning arithmetic, spelling, punctuation, writing, and even reading emphasize the acquisition of social conventions. It is, of course, appropriate for schools to assign great importance to enabling the young to learn those social conventions we call the three R's. One of the features of these social conventions is

that the child's task is to take conventions from the outside and, so to speak, to internalize them. These tasks can be regarded as requiring the skills of *impression*: they are intended to impress the child. And indeed they must. There are no teachers I know who seek from their students ingenuity in spelling. We want students to be able to communicate, to possess a shared set of conventions, and knowing which letters are to appear in what words in what order is a part of that aspiration. And it should be.

The problem is that such tasks dominate school programs. Children need opportunities not only to acquire the skills of impression, but also the skills of *expression*. In expressive activities the source of content is not located primarily outside the child. It is not simply a matter of acquiring those skills that demonstrate that social conventions have been learned but, rather, helping students reach down into their unique beings in order to find content that can be made visible in the public world. Again, the fine arts, including creative writing, are fields in which personal signature is particularly important. When a teacher gives a class of students the same words to spell, the pedagogical end-in-view is uniformity of outcome. The teacher wants all of the students to spell all of the words correctly, and that means the same way.

When that same teacher asks children to write a creative story, or paint a landscape, or choreograph a dance, or compose a piece of music, the last thing the teacher wants is uniformity of outcome. What the teacher seeks is heterogeneity, diversity, idiosyncracy, works that attest to the distinctive ways in which individual children see, feel, and imagine.

I am not arguing that such tasks should monopolize our programs, but we should at least have some semblance of balance. The provision of such opportunities and the inclusion of the fine arts and related subjects make it possible for children not only to realize, some for the first time, their own positive uniqueness, but also to find a place in our educational sun. Equity is achieved in education not only by giving students an opportunity to come to school, it is also influenced by what they find when they arrive. School programs that create a very narrow eye of a needle through which all children must pass diminish educational equity. Thus, the social—and indeed the moral conditions—that ought to prevail in our schools are those that broaden the eye of the needle and make it possible for all children to discover their aptitudes. Such programs would expand considerably our conception of giftedness. Indeed, if we provided opportunities in school for them to display their interests and talents, we would find that virtually all children were gifted in some way. At present, the game is far too narrow.

Related to this outcome is another, and that is the view that the genuinely good school does not diminish individual differences, it expands them. Virtue in the context of education is not achieved by bringing all children to the same destination; it is achieved by helping them learn how to become who they are. Variance, not homogeneity, is what counts in schooling, and we ought to design the environments and invent the activities that will make that variance possible.

Our Legacy to Students

The aims that I have identified concerning what really counts in schools are not those inscribed in *A Nation at Risk* (NCEE 1983), they are not on the list generated by President Bush during his September 1989 education summit, and, as far as I know, they are not on any state department of education's educational priorities. Yet, for me, they are central to any adequate conception of education. The realization of such aims will require more than the appearance of articles in *Educational Leadership* or speeches at ASCD's Annual Conference. The centerpiece of change is the teacher and the central location, the classroom and the school.

I have no doubt that the creation of the conditions instrumental to the achievement of these values is possible. I also have no doubt that their realization will require the active engagement of teachers and the serious support of school administrators. It will, most certainly, also require the support of communities, who often need to understand better than they do at present what education is about and what really counts in schools, not only in the short term, but in the long run.

My hope is that educators will be moved to begin the kind of dialogue that leads to genuine reform in education, a reform that pays attention to what really counts. Genuine reform will require attention not only to the mission of our schools, but to their educational ecology. It will require attention not only to our intentions, but to the ways in which we organize our workplaces, to the scope of the programs that we provide, to the quality of our teaching, and to the means through which we assess what really matters. The agenda is large, formidable, and important. But the creation of that agenda and its realization are the legacy that we have the privilege to leave to our students. What other legacy could be more important?

References

Apple, M. (1982). *Education and Power* Boston: Routledge and Kegan Paul.
Arendt, H. (1958). *The Human Condition*. New York: Doubleday.
Dreeben, R. (1968). *On What Is Learned in School*. New York: Addison-Wesley.
Eisner, E. (1985). *The Educational Imagination*. 2nd ed. New York: Macmillan.
National Commission on Excellence in Education. (1983). *A Nation at Risk*. Washington, D.C.: U.S. Government Printing Office.

On Standardized Testing

A Position Paper of the Association for Childhood
Education International by Vito Perrone

Vito Perrone is a faculty member of the Harvard Graduate School of Education, where he is also Director of Programs in Teacher Education and Chair of the Teaching, Curriculum and Learning Environments Program. In addition, he is a senior fellow at the Carnegie Foundation for the Advancement of Teaching.

In 1976—the middle of a decade when standardized testing of young children was approaching unprecedented levels and test results were being used for decisions about kindergarten entry, promotion and retention, and placement in curricular programs— ACEI issued a position paper calling for a moratorium on standardized testing in the early years of schooling (ACEI/AESP/Perrone, 1976). Recognizing that it was making primarily a moral statement, ACEI hoped that its action might encourage serious discussion about the effects of testing and the active pursuit of assessment directions that honored developmental traditions and were educationally sounder than standardized tests.

Pressures to test children continued in the latter years of the 1970s, but there was also vigorous debate about the negative effects of testing. And support for more authentic forms of assessment, rooted in close observation and systematic documentation of children's learning, became more common. After publication of A Nation at Risk (National Commission on Excellence in Education, 1983), however, the climate changed dramatically. Testing programs expanded greatly, especially in kindergarten and the primary grades. The results have been deleterious, particularly for poor and minority children.

A moratorium is more necessary now than in 1976. It is time for teachers, school administrators and parents to say more forcefully than ever that testing and its uses in the primary years must be brought to an end and reduced in frequency thereafter. This 1991 ACEI position paper is dedicated to that end.

3. STRIVING FOR EXCELLENCE

Given the power of standardized testing in society, it comes as a surprise to many that the history of this form of testing is so short. Produced in 1909, the *Thorndike Handwriting Scale* was, for example, the first popular standardized achievement test used in the public schools.[1] A wide variety of achievement and aptitude tests quickly followed.

By the 1930s, a majority of schools in the United States and Canada engaged in some form of standardized testing, but the scope was exceedingly small by today's standards. Few people who completed high school before 1950, for example, took more than three standardized tests in their *entire* school careers.[2] The results were hardly ever discussed, parents didn't receive the scores and school-wide results were not grist for local newspapers. By contrast to this earlier period, those who complete high school in 1991 will have taken, on average, from 18 to 21 standardized tests; many will have taken more, the majority of them in the K-5 years.[3] And test scores will not only fill newspapers, but also become part of the sales-pitch of real estate brokers, especially if test scores are high in a particular district. To understand the overall magnitude of the shift, it should be noted that since 1950 the volume of testing has grown at the annual rate of 10-20 percent (Haney & Madaus, 1989).

While the tests are problematic at all ages and levels of schooling, they are particularly questionable for children in the primary grades. These are years when children's growth is most uneven, in large measure idiosyncratic; the skills needed for success in school are in their most fluid acquisitional stages. Implications of failure in these years can be especially devastating.

SOME HARD QUESTIONS ABOUT STANDARDIZED TESTING

Acknowledging that standardized tests overwhelm much of classroom practice, Harvard psychologist Sheldon White suggests that we are contending with "an affair in which magic, science, and myth are intermixed" (1975). He is offering, of course, an understatement! How many of us actually believe that an individual's intelligence, achievement and competence can be represented adequately by any of the standardized tests that fill our schools? Or that *one* distribution curve—whatever the metric—is capable of classifying all children? Or that a particular score on a test can provide a genuinely defensible demarcation between those who should be promoted to the next grade level and those who should be retained? Between those who should be provided enrichment and those needing remediation? Such assumptions defy almost everything we have come to understand about children's growth, as well as their responses to particular educational encounters. Teachers and parents know this. When they have a chance to step back and reflect on their children, few will accept that any test score can define any child.

Even if one fails to take note of the implicit assumptions of the tests—essentially that children's knowledge and competence *can be measured* by the number of correct answers they supply—an examination of the test items and the composition of the tests (something those in schools need to do more often) ought to cause some measure of pause, if not enormous concern.[4] Are the questions clear? Do they address the particular educational concerns of teachers of young children or of parents? Do the tests as a whole provide useful information about individual children? About a class? Do they help children in their learning? Do they support children's intentions as learners? Do they provide *essential* information to children's parents? In our experience with teachers and parents, we have encountered few who can provide an affirmative response to *any* of these questions. That teachers and parents can offer so little positive response surely suggests problems with the tests and the emphasis given to them.

In contrast, however, almost all teachers respond affirmatively to the following questions: Do you feel any pressure to teach to the tests? If the tests were not given or used for the evaluation of individual children, teachers and schools, would you use fewer skill sheets, workbooks and other simple-response pedagogical materials? Would you use a broader range of instructional materials, giving more attention to integrated learning? Would expectations for *all* children enlarge? Would you devote more attention to active, inquiry-oriented programs in mathematics and science? Would you give more time to the arts? Would the curriculum be more powerful, more generative? Do you feel that you can assess children's learning in more appropriate ways than the use of standardized achievement tests?

Used for major educational decisions, as they are in many settings, the various tests clearly limit educational possibilities for children. We need to understand this well, for the pressure to use more tests for more purposes continues to mount.

CHILDREN AND TESTS

More on the History of Testing

As noted, testing programs began a substantial upward spiral after 1950; more often than ever before, they became the basis for selection and retention in numerous educational programs and grade levels. *But prior to 1965, the tests were not used often in the early grades.* This is important to understand. A consensus associated with the traditions of kindergarten, as well as a developmental perspective, guided the primary grades as a whole: the early years were "special," a time for natural growth and development. Where serious testing programs existed, they generally began in grade 3 or 4.

Testing exploded in the period after 1965, however, especially with regard to its uses. As evaluation demands grew with the influx of new federal and state resources for schools, the tests were quickly seen as inexpensive and easy-to-use measures for meeting the requirements. And with the accountability movement of the 1970s, the tests became the definers of standards in almost all curricular areas.

Yearly testing, beginning in grade 3, became more the norm, although in many school districts accountability demands contributed to the use of annual fall and spring testing as a means of determining "gains" in achievement. By the late 1970s, testing started to invade the primary grades. Developmental understandings began to erode as early years' testing became the big growth area. By the end of the 1980s, testing of young children had become commonplace. Sixteen states in the U.S. and districts in 21 other states now require children to take a standardized test before entering kindergarten; districts in at least 42 states require students to pass a standardized test before "graduating" from kindergarten. It is now the exceptional school district that *doesn't* test K-2 children (National Commission on Testing and Public Policy, 1990).

The Tests and Their Uses

While many of the *prekindergarten* tests are of the paper-pencil variety, most have a more individual, performance-oriented quality. For measuring physical development, children are asked to skip or stand on one foot for 20 seconds; on the cognitive level, they are asked, for example, to retell a story in its proper sequence. With regard to social and environmental experience, they are asked to count to 10, recognize colors and shapes, manipulate a crayon or pencil, and follow directions. The results of these "screening" activities are often the basis for cautioning parents to "wait another year before starting your child in kindergarten." They are also used as a means of "early identification" of individuals who, as the preschool screeners say, might be expected to have difficulty in school and might need special assistance (essentially an early process of labeling). Although scant evidence exists that such early screening is beneficial for either children or schools, it has, nonetheless, become almost universal.

In kindergarten, children typically receive their first paper-pencil test, which ostensibly gauges "reading readiness." Those who score in the bottom quartile are encouraged, in some settings required, to spend another year in kindergarten; or they are placed in a K-1 transitional setting that often leads to later retention. The underlying rationale is that children benefit from the knowledge teachers gain from this kind of testing. Yet, teachers gain little if any important knowledge from such tests. With so little evidence that reading readiness scores correlate with reading success, their use is unwarranted. It is a scandal to retain children on the basis of such tests (Shepard, 1987).

Beginning in grade 1 and continuing through the elementary grades, children in most schools complete at a minimum (and many children take even more) an annual achievement test battery such as the Metropolitan Reading Test, Metropolitan Achievement Test, California Test of Basic Skills, Stanford Achievement Test or Iowa Test of Basic Skills. In a small minority of districts (particularly those serving middle class, mostly white populations), the tests are rather benign. They are, as the administrators say, the sources for "staying in-touch with overall achievement levels." If scores go down significantly, that fact would likely prompt discussion in these districts, but changes in scores tend not to be dramatic enough to raise too much concern.

Given the pressures of the past two decades, however, the tests in the majority of school districts have expanded in their purposes. For example, how well individual children score determines whether they will be placed in a gifted and talented program or become eligible for special tutoring. The results of annual achievement testing also determine eligibility for a variety of enrichment programs, special classes, foreign language instruction, and the like. The tests also determine a student's academic level. They become the basis for early tracking and then ongoing tracking, reflecting the belief that homogeneous achievement groups facilitate more efficient and effective teaching and learning. That such grouping on the basis of a test leads mostly to inequity has not been sufficiently considered. And in recent years, test results have been used increasingly to determine whether a child should advance from one grade to another. This represents a new dimension (Meisels, 1989; National Association for the Education of Young Children, 1988).

What Testing Means for Children and Teachers

All in all, increased testing results in increased pressure on teachers and children. In a school guided by developmental concerns, teachers place much less emphasis on the tests. If, however, tests play a significant role in grade advancement, or the tests are the primary basis for the school's so-called accountability, teachers feel compelled to spend considerable time preparing children to take the tests. In such settings, the tests become the school curriculum.

Preparation usually begins many weeks before the actual testing. During this period, two to three hours a day are often devoted to practice tests and related exercises, all alien to the ongoing instruction and the usual student response patterns. The teachers readily acknowledge that the questions comprising the practice exercises, similar to those on the real test, are "trivial and unimportant." Moreover, the possible responses contain words that children likely have never seen and certainly don't use. The practice time is wasted time, yet some teachers believe it is important to waste the time: *they are preparing students for the test.*

By the time the three days of real testing is completed—after children have been admonished to "get a lot of sleep," "remember that this test is very important," "take all your books off your desks," "leave your calculators at home," "keep your eyes down on your own papers" and "ask no one for help"—weeks, sometimes months, will have passed. Time for real books will have been sacrificed for time spent reading isolated paragraphs and then answering several multiple-choice questions. Rather than posing problems for which math might be used, in the process coming to a natural and deeper understanding of math concepts, time will have been spent on reviewing skills such as addition, subtraction, multiplication, fractions, division—all in isolation. Little time will have been given to science and social studies, other than the concentration on factual information that isn't particularly useful or generative of ongoing interest. Time is a valuable commodity; it should not be wasted in this manner.

When it's over, the frustration of teachers in these schools will be high. They will feel that their own intentions have been undermined. They will not have had an opportunity to look carefully at the tests—to see what individual children did with various questions, to inquire why children selected particular responses as a way of getting closer to their logic, to get some sense of patterns in various sections of the test, or to determine how closely *any* of the questions got to their purposes. In the world of standardized testing, such issues are not viewed as particularly important. And the scores, when they come back several months later, will be of little use. Yet, because of their seeming authenticity, the scores will stand for how well each class and the school as a whole performed for the year. The scores may also affect the opportunities afforded individual students. This is all travesty! The substance and integrity of education are missing.

An educator's principal purpose is to enhance the growth of *every* child. When children are labeled "unready" or "slow learners" because of standardized test results, their educational opportunities generally become narrow, uninteresting and unchallenging. One-dimensional tasks such as those found in skill sheets, workbooks and drills figure prominently in their education. Who are the ones who tend most often to be labeled? A high proportion of children from lower socioeconomic populations, including large numbers of minorities, are represented in special education and lower-level tracks.[5] This ought to give us serious pause! Our commitment to democratic practice and equality of educational opportunity forces us to speak out strongly against any process that consistently produces such results.

Reasons for caution in the use of tests include the possible loss of children's self-esteem, the distortion of curriculum, teaching and learning, and the lowering of expectations. Other concerns relate to the tests themselves. For example, tests used in grades 1 and 2 are different from those used in grades 3-6. The early tests are picture and vocabulary dependent, while the later ones place greater stress on content. Consequently, high scores in early testing may not carry over to later testing. Because tests include diverse subject areas, they may or may not relate directly to what children have been taught or evoke from particular children any intrinsic interest. In addition, the multiple-choice format of standardized tests confuses many children who are not accustomed to sharing their understandings in that manner. Moreover, for a host of reasons having little to do with their reading ability, children who read very well may select "wrong" answers from among the limited choices available.

Peculiarities of testing abound. Children who have been routinely encouraged to be cooperative learners are forbidden to talk while testing. Children who have been taught to work problems out slowly are told speed is essential. Children who have come to understand that *they* must construct answers to problems, that many answers are possible, are confronted with someone else's answers and told that only one answer is possible. The message is clear: "Don't take your time—guess if necessary and forget what you have been learning day in and day out." Such conditions cause many children undue anxiety, even if the ultimate consequences of test-taking are not devastating. And we have only touched the surface.

The Value of Responsive Educational Environments

Educators of young children have long believed that children learn in many different ways, demonstrating in the process that they have multiple patterns of growth and achievement. This belief has given direction to programs with diversified aims and goals. In these programs, children are respected, regardless of racial background or socioeconomic class. Their interests become basic

starting points for learning. Such developmental programs tend to support more formal instruction in reading, for example, only when children are ready and not simply because they are 6 years of age.

Because teachers in such settings commit themselves to increasing successful learning experiences and improving children's self-esteem, many learning options are made available. The clock then tends not to determine to such a large degree when children begin and end learning activities. Peer interaction and communication are encouraged. Creative and expressive forms of communication that develop feeling—the most personal of human possessions—become integral, rather than peripheral, to a child's life in these classrooms. (Too often a teacher does little with the creative and expressive arts because they don't relate particularly well to the normative testing programs. They are not basic enough!)

Static expectations for children, rooted in an array of basal materials and common curricula, do not reflect the diversity that actually exists in primary schools. Yet, standardized tests are rooted in standard curricular materials (basal textbooks, syllabuses, state or provincial guidelines) that have predetermined expectations all children must meet. To actually develop a responsive, developmental classroom environment is to risk lower scores on standardized tests. Teachers and children do not need this kind of external pressure.

Evaluation Consonant with Purpose

The need is to engage in assessment that is not only related to the best practice, but also rooted directly in the instructional process itself. While many possible entry points to such assessment exist, we share first the way a group of elementary teachers in New York City responded to a new city-wide science test for use in grades 3 and 5. We believe the example is instructive for other assessment areas, as well as other grade levels.

This group of teachers argued that *the* test (not science assessment itself) was inappropriate for use in their classrooms. It 1) covered too much ground too superficially and didn't get close enough to what children actually knew and understood; 2) didn't honor their slower, more intense, meaning-making, hands-on, observational and experience-oriented approaches to science; and 3) was a distraction at a time when serious

WHERE DOES ACEI STAND?

In 1976, ACEI called for a moratorium on all standardized testing in the early years of schooling. The Association also affirmed the *importance* of evaluation in classrooms and schools, acknowledging that careful evaluation was the key "to the qualitative improvement of educational practice and the learning of children." ACEI's position remains similar now with one exception. We now believe firmly that *no standardized testing should occur in the preschool and K-2 years*. Further, we question seriously the need for testing every child in the remainder of the elementary years.

ACEI is not alone in such a position. The National Commission on Testing and Public Policy recently reached that conclusion after five years of studying standardized testing intensively. The National Association for the Education of Young Children, in one of its policy imperatives of 1988, called for an end to K-2 testing. In its new primary program released in 1990, the Province of British Columbia outlined steps intended to eliminate all deficit-based assessment and evaluation in the early grades. And the state of North Carolina, after a decade of heavy high-stakes testing of K-2 children, ended all such testing in 1988. What we are seeing is a growing understanding that teaching to tests increasingly has become the curriculum in many schools, especially in the early years when test scores are most affected by such a direction.

The fact that test scores are increasing is no longer causing much celebration. We have mounting evidence that the curriculum is becoming a matter of worksheets, workbooks and simple skills; higher order thinking skills and deeper levels of understanding are being sacrificed; reading for meaning is being set aside; the arts are becoming nonexistent; exploration of real materials, the science and mathematics of the world, isn't being "risked"; and time for play, what most teachers and parents understand to be the work of children, is being seen as a frill.

Such understandings have brought a growing realization that the curriculum in many schools is not powerful enough, that it doesn't lead to large understandings or commitments to extended learning. And increasingly, teachers are becoming more vocal about wanting opportunities to create a more thoughtful and expansive curriculum. In the process, they are making clear that they know how to address accountability issues through good documentation of children's actual work rooted in a solid and generative curriculum. This bodes well for change.

---

science inquiry was becoming well-established. Working with a research psychologist at the Educational Testing Service, the teachers developed a science assessment that used the district's objectives and the questions asked on the city-wide test, but made the basic questions open-ended. They wanted to demonstrate the larger possibilities in an open-ended, less restricted assessment format.

In the document they prepared as part of their oppositional process, the teachers wrote that:

. . . the multiple-choice format. . . allows no room for pupils to construct or generate answers based upon their knowledge and thought. . . . Further, tests which consist solely of questions for which there is only one correct response constitute an inappropriate assessment or model for science education. We are concerned that testing in this form will undercut science as a process, the investigative, experimental components of our science program which entail observation, experiment, and field work. (Chittenden, 1986)

Their critique is worthy of more attention.

The city-wide test asked, "Which of the following trees can be found growing along the streets of our city? a) Redwood, b) Palm, c) Rubber, d) Maple." While not suggesting that the question was important, the teachers asked in their alternative test, "Name some trees that grow along the streets of New York." The 30 3rd-grade children who took the alternative test named 73 different species of trees (including the "Central Park tree"). For instructional purposes, teachers gained entry points they hadn't thought about.

Rather than ask, as the city-wide test did, "Which of the following planets is the largest? a) Venus, b) Mars, c) Pluto, d) Jupiter," the test prepared by the teachers asked students to draw a picture of the solar system. The drawings were enormously revealing. The teachers and the ETS researcher didn't argue that the questions they asked were wonderful, fully generative, connected to many of the issues they believed were critical. They did conclude, however, that their open-ended process provided information more useful to their ongoing instruction and got closer to children's understandings than the multiple-choice, city-wide test.

Assessment for purposes that go beyond the school—and that is what most current accountability efforts are about—need not, of course, have an *individual*, every-student basis. More open-ended, performance-oriented processes that typically take more time and demand more materials, for example, would likely be seen as more feasible if sampling were to be used. Sampling could also involve teachers in schools much more directly, making assessment more than a process "owned and operated" by some distant bureaucracy.

Centrality of the Teacher in Classroom-Based Assessment

Work in the area of writing represents the most serious break yet in the power of standardized testing. Those concerned about writing in the schools argue convincingly that writing cannot be assessed validly outside the instructional process itself and that writing to a real audience is central. Further, they assert that writing at its best is *situated*—in this sense, not easily standardized in current psychometric or technological terms.

Understanding children's writing cannot begin with one task, a single piece of work, or with writing that has not been completed within the norms of powerful classroom practice. Such writing isn't likely to bring forth students' best and most committed efforts. That understanding alone has changed the assessment landscape enormously. Teachers who encourage active writing programs make clear that serious writing takes thought and time, is close to personal experience or interest and connects to an individual's way of interpreting the world. Children write what they *know* and *feel* about their world—understandings that extend to all curricular areas, including social studies, science, math and the arts.

Teachers recognize that children have *much more* to talk and write about in settings where the ongoing school experience of the students is rich: teachers read a great deal to children, giving emphasis to authorship and personal style; books are plentiful; active learning is promoted; the world is permitted to intrude, to blow through the classroom. In this sense, writing is not something apart; rather, it has a context and that context is important to understanding the writing. Most writing assessment efforts that have existed, including those of NAEP (National Assessment of Educational Progress), provide little knowledge of contextual issues.

Experience has also shown that the best person to judge students' writing, who can monitor their progress as writers, is the teacher closest to them. That shouldn't surprise anyone. The classroom teacher knows, for example, the questions a particular child has been raising about various aspects of classroom learning. When reading a piece of writing, the teacher can refer to previous writing efforts, a book the child is currently reading, genres of authors the child is most inclined toward at the moment, a painting just completed, a trip recently taken, the new baby sister, the spring flooding across the community's many glacial lakebeds, the special meadow colors, the classroom's human mosaic. Thoughtfully responding to the surrounding context, which is never really separate from the text, the teacher can better interpret the writing.

It is that teacher, deeply involved with the child as writer, who knows the next question to raise, when to push and when not to, who can judge the meaning and quality of a piece of that child's writing. This outlook governs our perspective about evaluation issues as a whole.

The foregoing becomes clear when reading children's work in the various publications of the Teachers and Writers Collaborative (see Landrum, 1971; Murphy, 1974) or the accounts prepared by Don Graves and Lucy Calkins. And we have seen similar creative and energetic writing in large numbers of elementary schools where active writing programs have been established.

As we read the wonderful writing, knowing that each of the pieces was completed over time—not at one sitting, not without conversation, not without several tries, not without some peer response and early teacher response—we wonder what would have been produced had these writers been forced to write on April 1 at 10:00 a.m., knowing they had 30 minutes and the readers would be persons far away. Actually, we don't wonder too much. We have seen the writing and it isn't the same. And we talk with enough teachers to know that they don't believe what students produce on those days represents anything approximating their best work. Many of the students, often the most skilled writers, leave much of the writing assessment page blank.

Teachers who honor children's work as the genuine product of thought, capable of evoking thought, can certainly describe their students' writing. They are authentic readers. And they have been convincing in their view that any talk of assessment is doomed intellectually if it doesn't acknowledge the importance of being close to the student writer and the surrounding context.

So where does this lead us regarding an assessment program? Having acknowledged the centrality of the classroom setting, the classroom teacher and work over time, we are convinced the principal direction is rooted in carefully organized and considered classroom documentation. Classroom teachers can, for example, systematically preserve copies of drafts of students' writings as well as finished pieces. Two to three pieces a month would provide a reasonable collection. Reviewing them periodically can inform a teacher's ongoing efforts to assist particular students, an important purpose of documentation. At year's end, the accumulation—organized chronologically—can be subjected to a careful review, with some of the following questions serving as a framework: Over time what are the salient features, dominant motifs? How much invention? What about complexity? Choice of topics? Discourse frameworks? Connections to ongoing academic and social strengths? Diversity of word use? Voice? Use of conventions?

This review often provides a perspective missed in the course of addressing work that stands alone. Such a portfolio is almost always enormously revealing to parents, bringing the kind of overview, or large picture, that parents often miss as they interact with their children about the school experience.

Classroom-based review addresses concerns about the ongoing support of individual students and informs further instructional practice. It also serves as a way for a teacher to describe children's growth as writers over the course of a year, as well as inform their subsequent teacher more fully. In addition, students learn to bring careful self-examination and more solid interpretation to their own efforts as writers. Such an opportunity should not be missed.

For purposes of a larger school-wide review, randomly selected students from each classroom in a school might be asked to choose five or six pieces of their writing to be read by groups of teachers in the school as a whole—providing the readers with a context of the individual works. At the level of the school, using such samples as a base—knowing that they were written within the instructional program itself and not apart from it in a forced, unsituated exercise—provides readers with more confidence about describing, for example, the writing of 4th-graders in a particular school. And they should be able to do it with good authority.

Further, as "a community of readers of writing," the teachers involved in this school-wide review can actually enlarge *their* understandings of writing, in the process becoming better teachers and facilitators of writing. If the evaluation effort doesn't produce these kinds of results, it is quite clearly a failed and faulty exercise.

A School District's Assessment Effort

Having argued that the best evaluation is classroom and school-based, it is still possible to extend the logic of making use of multiple samples, embedded in best practice, to a school system where a community of readers linked to shared beliefs can be formed. With each step from the classroom, however, confidence levels must, of necessity, begin to decline.

With that, we want to share an assessment effort conducted by a school district that is moving in a more positive direction. The example comes from Grand Forks, North Dakota, where the Superintendent of Schools agreed to experiment with a classroom-based, instructionally oriented writing assessment planned by teachers. Grade 6 was selected as a focus. The Grand Forks teachers began by examining as a group samples of children's writing. Further, they read collectively some of the writings of Don Graves, Lucy Calkins and Jerome Harste, among others. They learned about the diverse ways 6th-grade teachers throughout the system worked with writing, and they also became deeply involved in a writing-workshop approach to the teaching of writing.

Documenting their own practices, reflecting together on their experiences, and reading work produced by their children in the workshop setting, the teachers acquired a healthy outlook on the district-wide mandate for assessment that would get them close to children's writing and inform their ongoing practice.

For the assessment studies, they decided to ask students to complete a personal narrative of their own choosing, within the framework of the ongoing instruction. In some classrooms, a process approach provided the structure; in other settings, different processes prevailed. Six hundred fifty narratives were produced. A holistic process, using as criteria clear message, logical sequence, voice and mechanics, enabled the teachers to respond descriptively and quantitatively to the question of "How well do 6th-graders in the Grand Forks public schools write?"

While not perfect, the process was embedded within classroom practice. Further, it enlarged school system-wide discussion about writing and writing process, provided teachers with more experience as readers of written discourse and broadened insights into the teaching of writing.

A community of writing teachers, persons able to link the teaching of writing to the classroom context as well as understand ways to make connections between writing and evaluation, is being formed. This is empowerment of a high order. In addition, because of the way the evaluation process was organized, large numbers of students have learned to evaluate their own writing. This contributes more to improving writing in the schools than any process that stands apart from teachers and their ongoing instructional efforts. Although the focus has been on writing, the connections to other subject fields should be clear.

The foregoing hardly covers all the possibilities in what is increasingly being defined as "authentic assessment" or "performance-based assessment." Basic to such efforts is the close tie of assessment to the instructional process itself. The interest is not in what students can give back in terms of information but what they can do, the relationships they are able to make, the understandings they are able to develop and extend to other learnings.

In addition to the benefits discussed and implied from systematic record-keeping, our experience reveals that teachers who document children's learning through carefully organized records tend also to be more knowledgeable about children and learning. They become the "students of teaching" that schools need and parents desire. Teachers able to describe children's learning in great detail are teachers who are trusted and capable of helping reestablish parental confidence in schools.

CONCLUSION

This Association for Childhood Education International position paper decries the continuing potency of standardized testing in primary school programs. Stressing the inappropriateness of standardized testing, it argues that teachers and parents should oppose using test results to make *any* important judgment about a child. And it sets forth unequivocally the belief that *all* testing of young children in preschool and grades K-2 and the practice of testing every child in the later elementary years should cease. To continue such testing in the face of so much evidence of its deleterious effects, its opposition to most of what we know about the developmental needs of young children, is the height of irresponsibility. We know, for example, that testing:

■ Results in increased pressure on children, setting too many of them up for devastating failure and, consequently, lowered self-esteem.

■ Does not provide useful information about individual children, yet often becomes the basis for decisions about children's entry into kindergarten, promotion and retention in the grades, and placement in special classes.

■ Leads to harmful tracking and labeling of children.

■ Compels teachers to spend precious time preparing children to take the tests, undermining their efforts to provide a developmentally sound program responsive to children's interests and needs.

■ Limits educational possibilities for children, resulting in distortion of curriculum, teaching and learning, as well as lowered expectations.

■ Fails to set the conditions for cooperative learning and problem-solving.

In emphasizing the critical need to seek more constructive directions for staying close to children's growth, this position paper also presents teachers and schools with a means of entering the assessment arena systematically and beneficially. The classroom setting and the teacher are acknowledged as central to an assessment program that, over time, is rooted in carefully organized and considered documentation. This kind of systematic, classroom-based review can inform not only a teacher's efforts to help individual children, but also ongoing instructional practice. Additionally, children learn to subject their work to careful self-examination and interpretation. Most important, authentic, performance-based assessment guarantees a greater understanding of the growth of individual children, which should reduce the need for any of the testing programs that currently exist.

References

Association for Childhood Education International/National Association of Elementary School Principals. Perrone, V. (1976). Position paper. On standardized testing and evaluation. *Childhood Education, 53*, 9-16.

Chittenden, E. (1986). *Alternatives to the New York City science test* (p. 4). Princeton, NJ: Educational Testing Service.

Haney, W., & Madaus, G. (1989). Searching for alternatives to standardized tests: Whys, whats, and whithers. *Phi Delta Kappan, 70*, 383-387.

Landrum, R. (Ed.). (1971). *A day dream I had last night.* New York: Teachers & Writers Collaborative.

Meisels, S. J. (1989). High-stakes testing in kindergarten. *Educational Leadership, 46*(7), 16-22.

Murphy, L. (Ed.). (1974). *Imaginary worlds: Notes for a new curriculum.* New York: Teachers & Writers Collaborative.

National Association for the Education of Young Children. (1988) *Testing of young children: Concerns and cautions.* Washington, DC: Author.

National Commission on Excellence in Education. (1983). *A nation at risk: The imperative for educational reform.* Washington, DC: Government Printing Office.

National Commission on Testing and Public Policy. (1990). *From gatekeepers to gateway: Transforming testing in America.* Chestnut Hill, MA: Boston College.

Shepard, L. (1987, January). *The assessment of readiness for school: Psychometric and other considerations.* Presentation at the National Center for Educational Statistics, Washington, DC.

White, S. (1975). Social implications of IQ. *National Elementary Principal, 54*(4), 10.

Footnotes

[1] Alfred Binet began his work on "mental ability" tests in 1904. This work, which contributed to the development of achievement tests, resulted in the Stanford-Binet test (and the "IQ score") in 1916. While IQ testing became popular in many schools, particularly as a means of separating children for various special education programs, it has been reduced substantially in the past two decades because of court-imposed limitations. We begin this position paper with the premise that all IQ testing should end. Such testing serves *no* educational purpose. When we speak here of standardized testing, we are referring to the array of readiness and achievement tests that continue to be so dominating in the schools.

[2] Students in New York state, who pursued regents' diplomas, were among those who would have taken more. There were also some school districts—generally in urban communities—that made more frequent use of tests for purposes of promotion and graduation. These were, however, exceptions.

[3] The difference in numbers is matched by the magnitude of their meaning. The tests were used for many more purposes. They determined a good deal about the educational experiences made available to children and whether they would be promoted or retained; they also became a basis for evaluating classrooms, schools and teachers.

[4] A large number of publications have provided thoughtful critiques of sample test items from a variety of popularly used standardized tests. See, among others: D. Meier, *Reading Failure and the Tests* (New York: Workshop Center for Open Education, 1973); D. Meier, H. Mack & A. Cook, *Reading Tests: Do They Hurt Your Child?* (New York: Community Resources Institute, 1973); B. Hoffman, *The Tyranny of Testing* (New York: Collier Books, 1964); *National Elementary Principal* (Mar./Apr. 1975 and Aug. 1975); *Standardized Tests and Our Children* (Cambridge: FairTest, 1990).

[5] J. Mercer, *Labelling the Mentally Retarded* (Berkeley: University of California Press, 1972). See also P. Olson, "Power and the National Assessment of Education Progress," *National Elementary Principal* (July/Aug. 1975) for some of the cultural problems with tests as well as a review of some of the important related court cases. M.E. Leary, "Children Who Are Tested in an Alien Language: Mentally Retarded?" *New Republic* (May 23, 1970), pp. 17-19, discusses the *Diana et al. vs California State Board of Education* case regarding the placement of Mexican-American and Black children in special education classes on the basis of test scores. *Hobson vs Hanson*, Civil Action No. 82-66, U.S. District Court for Washington, DC, 1968, provides an excellent review of standardized tests and teaching. For readers interested in an excellent review of the serious problems of standardized testing and minorities, see R. Williams, Chairperson, "Position Paper of the American Personnel and Guidance Association Committee on Standardized Testing and Evaluation of Potential Among Minority Group Members," 1975; N. Medina & M. Neill, *Fallout from the Testing Explosion: How 100 Million Standardized Exams Undermine Equity and Excellence in America's Public Schools* (Cambridge: FairTest, 1988); and A. Hilliard, "Testing African-American Students," *Negro Educational Review*, 1987.

*Call it Huck Finn's law:
The authentic American flourishes in
spite of schooling, not because of it. As applied,
this has meant that American kids
have one of the shortest school years in the Western
world. It shows. Today what Huck Finn
didn't know would hurt him*

THE CASE FOR MORE
SCHOOL
DAYS

MICHAEL J. BARRETT

Michael J. Barrett represents Cambridge, Belmont, Water-town, and the Allston-Brighton neighborhood of Boston in the Massachusetts State Senate. He is a Harvard graduate and holds a law degree from the Northeastern University School of Law. Barrett writes often on public-policy issues. He is the author of legislation that would extend the school year in Massachusetts to roughly 220 days.

Off and on for the surprising stretch of forty years, beginning in 1949, the Gallup organization has polled the American public on the delicate subject of whether to lengthen the school year. For many years, though the wording of the question changed, the results held steady: by substantial margins people indicated that they did not like the idea. Even in 1959, during the era of *Sputnik* and intensified concern over what young Americans were learning, 67 percent of those polled were opposed to "increasing the number of days per year spent in school" for high school students, while a mere 26 percent were in favor.

In the 1980s something different began to happen. In line with the growing concern about economic competitiveness, Gallup retooled the question to make explicit comparisons with other countries. Interviewees were told that students in some nations attend school for as many as 240 days a year, compared with 180 in the United States. In light of this, Gallup asked, how do you feel about extending the school year by thirty days, to a total of 210? In 1984, fifty percent were against, 44 percent approved—a finding that, however consistent with past opposition, showed a distinct narrowing of the gap. In 1989 came the breakthrough. A new question maintained the comparative focus: "In some nations students spend about 25% more time in school than do students in the U.S. Would you favor or oppose increasing the amount of time that students in this community spend in school?" Forty-eight percent said they were in favor, 44 percent said they were opposed, and eight percent were undecided.

Read together, these figures record a sea change in public feeling, but the dike has not exactly burst; state legislatures and local school committees have not rushed to do anything dramatic. I can offer a personal perspective on the reasons why. As a Massachusetts state legisla-

tor, I discuss education with parents, children, and teachers, and as someone who believes in the need for a dramatic extension of the school year, I hold up the unpopular end of many conversations. Education involves matters intimately familiar to people—their kids, the rhythms of family life, their own memories of school—and everybody has an opinion.

Asked how she and her neighbors would feel about lengthening the school year, a constituent of mine, a parent of three school-aged daughters, stiffens and says, "People don't want their options taken away from them. They want freedom of choice in these things." A student just out of high school, told about the long school year in Japan, says, "I don't want to be Japanese. I like my summers. I work hard enough as it is."

If these soundings and others like them are any guide, America's attachment to the 180-day school year is still strong. In a world already reeling from future shock, the notion of extending the year seems punitive, an assault on the idea of summer itself. It raises the specter of joyless cramming. It implies that American parents have somehow failed their children.

Still, with people worried about the direction of the country, the strength of the economy, and the emerging competition from our friends in Europe and Asia, it is time to give the matter another look. It is time, too, to examine the peculiarly American roots of the dug-in resistance to change, and to consider how, in an era of short money and diminished confidence in government, the switch to a longer school year might be achieved.

The accumulating data on comparative education, itself a relatively new preoccupation of policy specialists, point up two trends. First, compared with their peers in

Asian and European countries, American students stand out for how little they work. Second, compared with Asians and Europeans, American students stand out for how poorly they do.

Bottom Dogs

A S TO THE FIRST: CONSIDER A LIST, GARNERED from a variety of sources, of the varying number of days in a standard school year. This list was hard to put together—which tells us something about the neglect of this subject in U.S. educational circles.

Japan	243	New Zealand	190
West Germany	226–240	Nigeria	190
South Korea	220	British Columbia	185
Israel	216	France	185
Luxembourg	216	Ontario	185
Soviet Union	211	Ireland	184
Netherlands	200	New Brunswick	182
Scotland	200	Quebec	180
Thailand	200	Spain	180
Hong Kong	195	Sweden	180
England/Wales	192	**United States**	**180**
Hungary	192	French Belgium	175
Swaziland	191	Flemish Belgium	160
Finland	190		

Of course, bare counts of school days do not tell us everything we might like to know about academic calendars. Japan's Ministry of Education, Science and Culture prescribes a minimum of 210 calendar days of classroom instruction, including half-days on Saturdays. Local school boards have the option of adding more time, and typically call for a total of about 240 days, often using the bulk of the additional days for field trips, sports activities, student festivals, and graduation ceremonies. In the United States the 180-day school year must accommodate field trips, school-wide assemblies, in-service training for teachers, and anything else that needs doing, reducing the real number of days of classroom instruction to something considerably less than 180.

The gap in classroom time between Japan and the United States widens when student attendance at *juku* is taken into account. *Juku* are the private, profit-making tutorial services that have become ubiquitous in Japan since the 1970s. Operating after school and on weekends —but in such a way as to parallel the regular education system—they provide enrichment, preparatory, remedial, and cram courses to an education-hungry young population. By ninth grade more than 47 percent of Japanese students attend *juku*, averaging five hours a week in addition to regular school time.

Presumably, multinational counts of days of instruction will be refined, in time, to provide more detail. In the meantime, an observer might note several things about the list presented above. Highly ranked are Japan, West Germany, South Korea, and Israel, four nations noted for their discipline and drive. Hungary, an Eastern-bloc country whose quality of education has not received much attention in the West, also asks for a good deal of time from its students. Swaziland and Nigeria, members of the Third World, are reasonably demanding. And the United States, which has been known to celebrate its own capacity for discipline and drive, comes in near the bottom. Conceivably such an order of finish supports the cherished American idea that the Japanese have a deviant propensity to work harder than almost anyone else. In any event, it certainly supports the idea that Americans have a deviant propensity to work less than almost anyone else.

That there should be an identifiable American school year at all is remarkable in itself. The federal system in the United States is supposed to encourage variety, in line with the famous dictum by U.S. Supreme Court Justice Louis Brandeis: "There must be power in the States and the Nation to remould, through experimentation, our economic practices and institutions to meet changing social and economic needs. . . . It is one of the happy incidents of the federal system that a single courageous State may, if its citizens choose, serve as a laboratory; and try novel social and economic experiments without risk to the rest of the country."

THE ACCUMULATING DATA ON COMPARATIVE EDUCATION POINT UP TWO TRENDS. FIRST, COMPARED WITH THEIR PEERS IN ASIAN AND EUROPEAN COUNTRIES, AMERICAN STUDENTS STAND OUT FOR HOW LITTLE THEY WORK. SECOND, COMPARED WITH ASIANS AND EUROPEANS, AMERICAN STUDENTS STAND OUT FOR HOW POORLY THEY DO.

State law, rather than any act of Congress, governs the number of days that a given school system is open. Brandeis would approve, we may assume. But no single courageous state with a choosy citizenry has undertaken to remold its schools to meet changing social and economic needs. Instead, conformity rules with an iron hand. According to the Education Commission of the States, fully forty-six of the fifty states mandate school years of 175 to 180 days or the equivalent number of hours. One state requires just over 180; three require under 175.

The lack of variety is all the more extraordinary given that state law typically prescribes the number of school days as a minimum. This means that thousands of towns, cities, counties, and independent school districts in the United States are legally free, sometimes subject to state review, to extend the school year—to, say, somewhere within the West German range of 226 to 240 days. Yet to judge from the available literature, across the entire range of American education, embracing the fifty states

and the thousands of subdivisions within those states, nary a public school system has broken the mold in a lasting way. Occasional reports, scattered sightings, are made of useful but tentative experiments. Beginning with the 1988–1989 academic year two inner-city elementary schools in New Orleans have operated on a 220-day calendar, and this past spring the Stanley elementary school in Kansas City, Kansas, won an RJR Nabisco Foundation grant to add forty-six days to its school year. Presumably these are approximations of the European and Asian models, involving more classroom instruction for everybody. They are also precarious, with no permanent basis in law, no institutionalized existence in the local community, and no long-term funding mechanisms.

Elsewhere we find programs built on the traditional notion of summer school, either for remedial purposes or for enrichment, with participation voluntary except for students who fail courses. These represent valuable extensions of educational time, but when attendance is significantly less than 100 percent of the class, the regular curriculum cannot be lengthened and enriched without throwing the next fall's semester into chaos.

Some will maintain that uniformity is a boon to the mobile American family, as it moves from community to community and state to state. But a uniform school year does not provide a uniform education, or anything like it, because the curriculum varies from place to place. The mobile American family is guaranteed a generous, mobile summer vacation, but that is it.

Quantity Into Quality

I N THE 1960S THE INTERNATIONAL ASSOCIation for the Evaluation of Educational Achievement (IEA) began to tackle the thorny problem of assessing educational quality across the gulfs of nationality, language, and culture. The undertaking, enormous in its complexity, produced the first installments of a multinational data base on how the world's children are doing in mastering the common languages of the emerging world economy: mathematics and the sciences.

When the IEA conducted its most recent mathematics assessment, in 1981–1982, the results were disheartening for Americans. In an eighth-grade match-up, among twenty school systems surveyed, the American students ranked tenth in arithmetic, twelfth in algebra, and sixteenth in geometry. Japan, our principal economic competitor, finished first in all three of these categories. In an intimation of the economic times that might lie ahead, Hungarian students finished ahead of Americans in all three categories. Even Thailand, until recently considered a Third World country rather than a member of the thriving Pacific rim, saw its students finish ahead of the Americans in geometry.

3. STRIVING FOR EXCELLENCE

These international comparisons have attracted their share of critics. For example, one point commonly made is that secondary education in the United States is universal—that the system is open to all children, with 1988 figures showing that 71 percent of those who begin high school go on to graduate—while systems elsewhere are closed or elite, with a consequent creaming effect that inflates test scores.

The universality of American education is, in fact, a great potential strength. Self-congratulation is not in order, however. Other nations, including Japan, currently set the pace for universality. According to 1984 figures from the U.S. Department of Education, 88 percent of Japanese students who began high school went on to graduate. Moreover, in part because of a tendency to "track" students into either academic or vocational channels, and in part because of the unevenness of the curriculum in our peculiarly decentralized educational network, the U.S. system winds up being inclusive without necessarily being either egalitarian or first-rate. As one aspect of its 1981–1982 study, the IEA identified twelfth-grade students from various countries who were engaged in the serious study of mathematics, defined for the United States as those in classes requiring as prerequisites at least two years of algebra and one year of geometry. By such a definition a strikingly small proportion of the American student body qualified for this part of the study. According to the IEA, a serious mathematics education was provided to 50 percent of Hungarian students,

THE UNITED STATES FACES A TIME-IN-SCHOOL DEFICIT EVERY BIT AS SERIOUS AS THE TRADE DEFICIT AND THE BALANCE-OF-PAYMENTS PROBLEM: EACH YEAR, AMERICAN CHILDREN RECEIVE HUNDREDS OF HOURS LESS SCHOOLING THAN MANY OF THEIR EUROPEAN OR ASIAN MATES, AND THE RESULTING HARM PROMISES TO BE CUMULATIVE AND LASTING.

30 percent of students in British Columbia, 15 percent of Finnish students—but only 13 percent of students in the United States.

Defenders of the status quo also argue a contrary point: not that the United States does well by its great mass of students but that our best students achieve as much as any in the world. Quite apart from the irony of a 200-year-old democracy's arguing in terms of the performance of its elites, the data give defenders shaky grounds for hope. Keeping in mind that the American contingent in the IEA's comparison of serious twelfth-grade math stu-

dents is only 13 percent of the relevant U.S. age group, consider a representative portion of the results for three subjects:

Student Achievement by Subject Area
(U.S. 12th-Grade Equivalent)

Advanced Algebra	Functions/Calculus	Geometry
1. Hong Kong	1. Hong Kong	1. Hong Kong
2. Japan	2. Japan	2. Japan
3. Finland	3. England/Wales	3. England/Wales
4. England/Wales	4. Finland	4. Sweden
5. Flemish Belgium	5. Sweden	5. Finland
6. Israel	6. New Zealand	6. New Zealand
7. Sweden	7. Flemish Belgium	7. Flemish Belgium
8. Ontario	8. Ontario	8. Scotland
9. New Zealand	9. Israel	9. Ontario
10. French Belgium	10. French Belgium	10. French Belgium
11. Scotland	11. Scotland	11. Israel
12. British Columbia	12. **United States**	12. **United States**
13. Hungary	13. Thailand	13. Hungary
14. **United States**	14. Hungary	14. British Columbia
15. Thailand	15. British Columbia	15. Thailand

The students were tested in three other areas of mathematics as well. The results were similar to those above, with the United States finishing below the average across the board.

In an alternative effort to measure the performance of elites, the IEA calculated the average achievement score of the top one percent of the twelfth-graders in each country. The United States came out as the lowest of any country for which data were available. In other words, our most able students scored lower in algebra than their top-notch peers in any other country. The findings were little better in calculus, for which the same analysis was conducted.

The IEA did a science assessment in 1983–1986. Among ten-year-olds in fifteen countries where tests were conducted, the Americans ranked eighth. Confirming indications in other studies that American students fall further behind with every passing year in school, our fourteen-year-olds were in a three-way tie, with students from Singapore and Thailand, for fourteenth place among students from seventeen countries. In yet another attempt to evaluate our elites, the IEA surveyed the scores of a special group of secondary school pupils who could be considered advanced science students: seniors pursuing a second year of study within a particular discipline. In rankings with similar students from twelve other nations, the Americans placed eleventh in chemistry, ninth in physics, and last in biology.

The association between American effort and American results is illuminated by "Opportunity to Learn" studies, which seek to identify the material that has actually been taught to various groups of students and the proportion of the intended curriculum that the teacher has managed to cover. OTL researchers focus on a practical question that puzzles parents and students all over America: Why is it that no class ever seems capable of actually getting through its textbook, or even coming close? Why is so much material covered in a rush, in the closing weeks of the year? Granted, books are big in order to give teachers a choice of lessons, but the sheer volume of material left uncovered is disquieting. Accompanied by Chris Berner, a member of my staff, I was recently "teacher for a day" in a seventh-grade class in Cambridge, Massachusetts. It was the end of the school year. Students reported that they had reached page 126 of a 400-page math text. They were halfway through the social-studies book.

The IEA's data on international math achievement become a little less perplexing when analyzed in accord with OTL principles. OTL researchers asked the students from each country who took part in the exercise, Had the mathematics required to answer each question on the international exam been taught to them at any time in class? The findings were fascinating. The typical Japanese twelfth-grade student had been taught how to solve 92 percent of the problems on the tests for algebra, geometry, and calculus. In England and Wales the comparable figure was 85 percent, in Hungary 67 percent, in Thailand 63 percent—and in the United States only 54 percent.

It seems, then, that students in other countries master more material largely because they get further along in their courses. OTL analysis lends authority to a conclusion that the lay person might reach as a matter of common sense: imperfect as American education might be, forty or so more days of it a year would mean more material covered and more material learned. The United States faces a time-in-school deficit every bit as serious as the trade deficit and the balance-of-payments problem: each year, American children receive hundreds of hours less schooling than many of their European or Asian mates, and the resulting harm promises to be cumulative and lasting.

Huck Finn's Law

IF THE INTERNATIONAL DATA LOOK BLEAK AND OTL analysis points to a lack of learning time as crucial, the question must be asked, Why, when our students do so badly, do we continue to ask them to do so little?

In 1988, looking back at the five years that had passed since the report *A Nation At Risk* was issued, William Bennett remarked on the lack of progress:

A Nation At Risk also noted that it is not unusual for high school students in other industrialized countries to spend eight hours a day at school, 220 days each year. In the United States, by contrast, a typical school day lasts six hours, and the school year runs 175 to 180 days. *A*

Nation At Risk recommended that school districts and state legislatures consider increasing instructional time by implementing a seven-hour school day and a 200- to 220-day school year, a recommendation that has been largely ignored.

American teachers prefer their current nine- or ten-month contracts, and their union leaders have opposed most legislative efforts to lengthen the school day or year. Since 1983, such proposals have been considered in 37 states. But a longer school year has been adopted in only nine of them—and all of those states merely extended their unusually short calendars to the more common 180-day standard. Only five states have lengthened the school day—none to more than six-and-a-half hours.

Bennett's finger-pointing should extend to the average citizen. As the Gallup numbers show, for years there has been weak public demand for more education, "more" meaning greater amounts of time spent in the schools helping children to learn. Once the public realizes the need for change and momentum builds, the school year and the school day will be lengthened, regardless of which other interests are opposed.

The 1989 Gallup poll hints at the beginning of a turn-around in public opinion—but only the beginning. Many parents would insist that their reservations are immediate and practical. They see summer as special, as a time for young people to be with their families, to do something that helps them grow—even if it is only attending summer camp—or to earn some money. Push these parents a little, and the objections become more emotional: kids need a chance to play, darn it, and they're under a lot of pressure as it is. What happened to the idyllic side of childhood? Is life to be all work? When will there be time for young people to explore the quirky and personal magic of their own creativity?

These questions are hard, and those of us who believe in the necessity of more schooling must not answer them glibly. But these questions are also rhetorical, and loaded. They rely for their effect on an idealized image of childhood which does not correspond to the down-to-earth, day-to-day summer experience of even middle-class kids. A school environment can be humane and true to the curiosity of children, and learning to read and write and compute and analyze is the key to unlocking the creative urge, not squelching it. For that matter, extended schooling can allow time not only for more instruction but also for more play. And surely summer is special for many families. But a school year that stretched into the last week of July would still leave more than a month for a family vacation, a stint at camp, or both. If Americans could tolerate going to school Saturday mornings, the break could start earlier.

As it is, American kids have one of the longest summer vacations in the Western world. Like everything in life, this comes at a cost. For years educators have devoted considerable effort to documenting a phenomenon that many parents know from practical observation: the tendency of kids to forget during the summer what they learned in the spring. In 1978 a study of retention conducted for the New York Board of Regents reported, "Numerous research studies indicate that long extended summer vacations result in forgetting much that was learned during the regular school year. . . . In order to start a new year effectively, teachers in most elementary schools tend to devote four or more weeks [to] review and reteaching activities."

As for earning money, some students hold jobs because of genuine financial need, and others because their parents believe that doing so builds character. But many students work to maintain a level of conspicuous consumption that they and their families would do well to avoid. In any event, given the evolving world economy and the changing nature of employment, the financial stakes for all these students figure to be the same: to be strapped for today or to be strapped for life. Personal income correlates with education and one's position in what is fast becoming a global economy; we must expect the time to come when young people in Germany, Hungary, Japan, South Korea, and the United States will compete more or less directly to do the same work, with the jobs going to those who are best prepared to hold them. A nation intent on having its men and women able to afford a decent standard of living will insist that adolescent earnings be forgone today so that adult earnings are not lost tomorrow. The stakes are very high. The urgent priority of young Americans today is to learn.

Public resistance to more education rides on a surface of practical objection but draws its power from deeper sources: American mythology, defined as the country's collection of ideas about itself; American complacency; and, of late, American defensiveness. A subsidiary issue is the resistance of the American educational establishment, both the theorists at the university level and the ranks of unionized teachers at the elementary and secondary levels. Then comes the question of money: how to finance a change that must bring with it more pay for teachers, curriculum redesign, and capital improvements like air-conditioning.

A bit of educational history is in order. In many states school attendance was not mandatory for much, if not most, of the nineteenth century. Many schools operated almost in the fashion of public libraries: that is to say, they were open for a great deal of the year but did not require local youths to be on the premises. Children would drop in and out as family responsibilities and personal inclinations dictated.

In 1847 Horace Mann, an educational reformer serving the state of Massachusetts as secretary of the Board of Education, in his annual report called for a mandatory minimum period of school attendance by students. Five years later the Massachusetts legislature enacted the nation's first compulsory-attendance law, requiring parents to send their children to school for at least twelve weeks.

Similar mandates were established throughout the country, but they could still be outdone by truancy; the United States was one place where submission to the regimentation of formal schooling was regarded with great ambivalence. Spending time in a classroom was not easy to reconcile with an affection for personal freedom and wide-open spaces,

especially when the work involved abstruse subjects like math and grammar. Huckleberry Finn said it pretty well:

> Well, three or four months run along, and it was well into the winter, now. I had been to school most all the time, and could spell, and read, and write just a little, and could say the multiplication table up to six times seven is thirty-five, and I don't reckon I could ever get any further than that if I was to live forever. I don't take no stock in mathematics, anyway.
>
> At first I hated the school, but by and by I got so I could stand it. Whenever I got uncommon tired I played hookey, and the hiding I got next day done me good and cheered me up.

Call it Huck Finn's law: the authentic American flourishes in spite of schooling, not because of it. Of course, the demands of modern industrial life made inroads nevertheless. From 1890 to 1974 school enrollment among American fourteen- to seventeen-year-olds—the children around Huck Finn's age—grew from seven percent to 92 percent. In the same period the average length of the school year in the United States increased from 135 days to 179, and the average number of days of real attendance increased from 81 to 160.

The short and thoroughly modern life of the 180-day school year undercuts the theory that it survives from a time when the academic calendar followed the agricultural cycle. Not even this degree of intention can be discerned. Instead, the historical record gives evidence that the period of mandatory school attendance increased steadily over time as it was shaped by two broad influences: on the one hand, the always growing demand for an educated work force, and on the other, the instinct to spare children from formal schooling during the hottest months of the year, regardless of whether they had any role to play in farming. Even if the agricultural theory fit the facts, it would not explain very much. Other countries have agricultural pasts too, but this has not stunted the growth of their educational calendars.

A NEW YORK BOARD OF REGENTS STUDY REPORTED, "NUMEROUS RESEARCH STUDIES INDICATE THAT LONG EXTENDED SUMMER VACATIONS RESULT IN FORGETTING MUCH THAT WAS LEARNED DURING THE REGULAR SCHOOL YEAR. . . . IN ORDER TO START A NEW YEAR EFFECTIVELY, TEACHERS IN MOST ELEMENTARY SCHOOLS TEND TO DEVOTE FOUR OR MORE WEEKS [TO] REVIEW AND RETEACHING ACTIVITIES."

It is true that the common public school spread rapidly in nineteenth-century America. The ideal product, however, was not the academic high achiever but the yeoman-citizen able to read and write well enough to be self-sufficient and to express his own opinion. Learning in and of itself was not thought to be the key to success; native ingenuity and self-directed hard work were. Richard Hofstadter, in his *Anti-intellectualism in American Life*, outlined "the ideal assumptions" of the case against getting a lot of education.

Intellectuals, it may be held, are pretentious, conceited, effeminate, and snobbish; and very likely immoral, dangerous, and subversive. The plain sense of the common man, especially if tested by success in some demanding line of practical work, is an altogether adequate substitute for, if not actually much superior to, formal knowledge and expertise acquired in the schools.

Huck Finn's special dislike for mathematics is an American refrain picked up more recently by social-science research. Harold Stevenson, of the University of Michigan, has done pathbreaking work in comparing Japanese, Taiwanese, and American attitudes toward learning and education. In 1987 he observed,

Americans generally do not consider mathematics as important as reading in elementary school. According to our classroom observations, American teachers spend more class time on reading (language arts) than on math-

ematics at both first and fifth grades. Chinese and Japanese teachers, however, divide their time more evenly between these two subjects. . . . Despite the greater amount of time devoted to language arts in the U.S. as compared to the Asian countries, American mothers most frequently said that reading should be given more emphasis in elementary school. Japanese mothers were nearly three times as likely as American mothers to mention a need for greater emphasis on mathematics.

Even in the era of high tech, American mythology has adapted cleverly rather than given way. According to Hofstadter, the American scientist singled out for respect is the practical person who moves quickly to translate exotic research into something commercially marketable. Thomas Edison and the electric light, the Wright brothers and the airplane, Steven Jobs and the user-friendly computer—it is the figure of the American inventor-entrepreneur, not the American scientist-thinker, who nicely reconciles, in a technological age, our drive for achievement with our mistrust of the bookworm and the nerd.

The country's lukewarm feelings about academic high achievers, Hofstadter argued, arose out of our democratic and egalitarian traditions. As the nineteenth century drew to a close, this instinct to downplay intellectual effort had to confront two powerful new forces, the theories of Darwin and of Freud. Both lent authority to the idea that native predispositions, aptitudes, and innate traits—including intellect—were critically important. In truth, these theories seemed to say, people really are quite different from one another. Divisive as the message might have been, Americans found a way to reconcile it with egalitarianism. A belief in innate traits and personal aptitudes could be said, after all, merely to mimic the individualistic strain in American culture. People might be different, and some might be stronger intellectually than others, but who cared in a country where success could come through grit and hard work?

Effort Versus Aptitude

A LINE OF REASONING THAT SOUGHT TO MINImize the importance of intellect while accepting high-powered theories of intellectual differences was bound to break down as education and academic achievement came to mean more and more in the economy. In present-day American culture observers like Harold Stevenson and Merry White, a professor of sociology at Boston University, see a terrible inversion at work. Embracing the credo that every child is different, we make early efforts to pinpoint differences in ability and interests. Then we channel children into tracks according to what we think we have found. Thus a practice rooted in the American celebration of the individual operates to subvert the real-life chances of many American students.

3. STRIVING FOR EXCELLENCE

Stevenson, detecting an infatuation with ability grouping in his interviews with parents and students, wrote,

> Compared to the Asians we interviewed, Americans placed more emphasis on differences in innate ability as the basis for variations in achievement. American children, for example, were much more likely than Chinese or Japanese children to agree with the statement, "The tests you take can show how much or how little natural ability you have." Conversely, American children were least likely to agree that "everybody in your class has the same amount of ability in math."
>
> These beliefs are in line with those of their mothers. American mothers did not agree that people have the same amount of ability in mathematics. When asked about the role of effort, Chinese and Japanese mothers were more likely than American mothers to believe that any student can be good at mathematics if he or she works hard enough. American mothers also expressed stronger beliefs than Chinese and Japanese mothers that their children were born with their math abilities.

If aptitude rather than effort is seen as the key to achievement, the result will be to undermine the work ethic, at least as it applies to education. Time spent in a classroom will not seem very important.

As Stevenson indicates, among those who disagree with Americans on the relative importance of effort are none other than the Japanese. Their culture puts little stock in the notion of traits and aptitudes, placing paramount emphasis instead on what White calls "the path of pure endeavor." Here is a Japanese challenge more profound than economic competition. Granted, the Japanese have the advantage of a homogeneous population, but they still deserve credit for using the work ethic as a way around the politics of class. In stressing equal opportunity based on effort—and, for that matter, in being unapologetic boosters for effort itself—the Japanese threaten to embarrass us, by taking aspects of the American creed and applying them with more conviction than we do.

Today in American culture hard work is good if it is done for oneself or one's family, whether to meet one's own standards or to better oneself economically. We put great stock in individual striving and individual freedom. But hard work is not so good when it is done at the behest of others (except possibly in wartime). No one gets easy points in this country for toeing the line, taking orders, or going along with authority.

It follows that there is a deeply ambivalent reaction—part of human nature but exaggerated in the American character—to being told by elites to "work harder." The situation is exacerbated because so many of today's parents grew up in the 1960s, when anti-establishment values were at their zenith. Before the 1960s came the Eisenhower era, condemned for excessive conformity, for the oppressive sameness documented in William Whyte's *The Organization Man* and David Riesman's *The Lonely Crowd*. In the Baby Boom generation's put-down of present-day Japanese values there is an echo of the same generation's put-down of the American 1950s.

Failing Students, Contented Parents

AMERICAN MYTHOLOGY MAKES COMMON CAUSE with another formidable force: American complacency. Harold Stevenson's work in 1979–1980 with children, mothers, and teachers from three countries suggests the problem, by contrasting performance and attitudes. In one statistical exercise he rated the mathematics achievement of equal numbers of students from Japan, Taiwan, and the United States. Among the top 100 first-graders there were only fifteen American children. Almost unbelievably, among the top 100 fifth-graders there was only one American child. In contrast, among the bottom 100 first-graders fifty-eight were American, and among the bottom 100 fifth-graders sixty-seven were American.

There was more. The shocker came in the attitude surveys. More than 40 percent of the American mothers were "very satisfied" with how their children were doing in school, whereas less than five percent of the Japanese and Chinese mothers were "very satisfied." Nearly a third of the Chinese and Japanese mothers said they were "not satisfied" with their children's performance, but only 10 percent of the American mothers expressed dissatisfaction.

The jarring enthusiasm of the Americans persisted when it came to attitudes toward the quality of the schools themselves. Ninety-one percent judged that the school was doing an "excellent" or a "good" job. Only 42 percent of the Chinese mothers and 39 percent of the Japanese mothers were this positive.

Stevenson's paradox—low measures of student performance and high measures of parental satisfaction—prompted him to utter a despairing thought:

> Given these findings, one wonders how practical it is to push now for educational reform in the United States. Schools can only respond to the needs expressed by the parents and citizens who provide their financial support. There is little indication in these data that large numbers of American parents find sufficient basis for dissatisfaction to alter their attitudes toward American education.

Happy in Their Work

THE GOOD NEWS IN 1990 IS THAT AMERICAN complacency is giving way; these days everybody talks about the hardworking Asians and the buoyant Europeans. The bad news is that the newest emotions are American discouragement, defensiveness, and paranoia. Polling in 1989 showed nearly half the public in this country subscribing to the notion that the United States is in "decline." But that doesn't mean we admire the competition. Rather than acknowledging that Americans put out less effort than do students in a multitude of other countries, we define the issue narrowly, as a choice between our values and those of our strongest competitor, Japan. Having set up the straw man, we then bridle at the thought of "becoming Japanese," shorthand for our fear of being dragooned into conformity and workaholism, all in the name of meeting stiff economic competition.

Instead of examining Japanese culture, rejecting many of its features but accepting others in order to improve our own, we Americans focus on claims that the Japanese are imitators, not creators; that they pirate our technology; and that they cheat to gain advantage in international trade. These impressions are used time and time again to disparage proposals to extend the school year. All you

RATHER THAN ACKNOWLEDGING THAT AMERICANS PUT OUT LESS EFFORT THAN DO STUDENTS IN A MULTITUDE OF OTHER COUNTRIES, WE DEFINE THE ISSUE NARROWLY, AS A CHOICE BETWEEN OUR VALUES AND THOSE OF OUR STRONGEST COMPETITOR. HAVING SET UP THE STRAW MAN, WE BRIDLE AT THE THOUGHT OF "BECOMING JAPANESE."

ever get by doing that, people argue, is a pocketful of misery, in terms of uncreative children and diminishing interest in classwork.

Such defensiveness misses the mark, and should be forsworn so that we might indulge instead an American habit. After all, we are energetic imitators of the good ideas of others, born appropriators of bits and pieces of Old World practice, great borrowers from the different cultures that have shaped our immigrants. In 1810–1812 did not Francis Cabot Lowell, of Massachusetts, give himself a grand tour of textile plants in the British Isles, memorize the design of the great power looms in order to outwit English laws against technology transfer, and return home to establish the first modern factory in America? Robert Dalzell, Jr., a historian at Williams College, writes that Lowell's feat is viewed as a "stunning act of industrial piracy." We Americans take pride in our pragmatism, our flexibility; no fixed principle is more important to us than the principle that nothing is fixed. If there are things dogged and determined in Japanese attitudes that we admire, if there are features of their educational system that seem to work—even if there are few points to be gleaned about equal opportunity—we should be shamelessly American and adapt them for ourselves.

In any event, dwelling on the negative cannot carry us very far. Our understanding of the way the Japanese live is growing more sophisticated all the time, and some of the self-serving truisms of today are not likely to hold up very well. One staple of conversation among American parents is the supposed association between the rigors of Japanese education and suicide among Japanese youths. The figures were once more troubling than they are today. According to a report by the U.S. Department of Education, in 1975 the suicide rates in Japan for the age groups ten to fourteen, fifteen to nineteen, and twenty to twenty-four were all higher than the U.S. rates. But by 1984 the Japanese numbers for the three age groups had gone down and the American numbers had more or less held steady, with the result that the American suicide rates were higher for all three age groups.

Japanese students do seem to be under considerable pressure to excel, but they do not seem especially unhappy, at least in the early elementary grades. Merry White, in her short and useful book *The Japanese Educational Challenge: A Commitment to Children,* wrote,

Because of our preconceptions of Japanese schooling, a walk into a typical fifth grade classroom in Japan may shock us. We might easily expect an environment suffused with rote learning and memorization, a structured and disciplined setting with an authoritarian teacher in control. This is far from the reality of most classrooms. Walking into a fifth grade math classroom, I was at first surprised: the mood was distinctly chaotic, with children calling out, moving spontaneously from their desks to huddled groups chatting and gesticulating. An American teacher would wonder "Who's in charge here?" and would be surprised to see the teacher at the side of the room, calmly checking papers or talking with some students. When I came to understand what all this meant, I realized that the noise and seeming chaos was in fact devoted to the work of the class; children were shouting out ideas for possible answers, suggesting methods, exclaiming excitedly over a solution, and *not,* as we might suppose, gossiping, teasing each other, or planning something for recess or after school. The teacher was not at all upset as long as total engagement in the appointed set of tasks persisted; she actually felt that the noise level was a measure of her success in inspiring the children to focus and work.

At its national convention last July the American Federation of Teachers criticized "treadmill schedules" that set out to cover the curriculum at all costs and do not provide teachers or students with adequate time for such things as reflection and planning. The proposed solution implied a reduction in teaching time. A far better one is suggested by the work of James Stigler and Ruth Baranes, observers of Japanese, Taiwanese, and American classrooms. Their research points to one of the contributions to quality made possible by a quantitative improvement in the school year: the pace at any given moment can allow for leisurely teaching and leisurely learning. Only teachers in Japan, they reported, were ever observed spending an entire forty-minute math lesson on one or two problems. In fact, their analysis revealed that the typical Japanese math lesson was less hectic than the American. "Japanese teachers," they wrote, "seem not to rush through material, but rather are constantly pausing to discuss and explain."

This is not to say that at the high school level the pace is relaxed. While the payoff for hard work is great in terms of student achievement, the side effects generate controversy and soul-searching among the Japanese public. Recently a fifteen-year-old girl died when she rushed to get into school just at starting time and a teacher, intent on locking out late students, slammed a heavy metal school gate on her head. The resulting uproar, which focused on the enforcement of rigid rules and discipline, suggests two general truths about education in present-day Japan: first, things are very far from perfect, and second, the system is not unyielding but subject to pressure and criticism—and presumably improvement as well.

American efforts to debunk the achievement orientation of the Japanese always seem to overreach. After all, Americans have taken considerable satisfaction in their own culture's work ethic. Any present-day rationalizations that, in effect, concede the willingness of the Japanese to outwork Americans probably concede more than this society can afford. The current stage of anxious anticipation is still an early one. In not so many more years, if things do not change, the evidence of Asian and possibly European superiority, first in economic productivity and then in standard of living, will be overwhelming. The creed of American exceptionalism is powerful and volatile; it is an open question whether this society can exist successfully with the conviction that it is second-rate. If the price of avoiding psychological dislocation later is to adjust the culture now in order to make more room for academic achievement, the price would seem to be well worth paying.

James Fallows, the Washington editor of *The Atlantic*, argues that American defensiveness is wasted motion. Fallows contends that the world can become multi-polar, and can have many thriving economies. The United States need not be unilaterally dominant in order for American culture to work. Neither must we be slavish in our imitation of the Japanese. Presumably Americans will perform best in an environment that stresses openness and freedom, as opposed to the conformity bred by the Japanese system. In other words, we can, to echo the title of Fallows's recent book, succeed by becoming "more like us." But we do have to succeed. The bottom line for learning and working had better be the same: more or less equivalent effort leading to more or less equivalent results.

Quality Versus Quantity

GET PAST THE QUICKSAND OF AMERICAN MYTHology, American complacency, and American defensiveness, and the argument for extending the school year comes up against the educational establishment. One group of professionals has created a large and complicated body of literature, riven with statistical analysis, on the question of "time and learning." Two of the premises are unassailable. First, additional time by itself does not guarantee successful learning. More is not necessarily better, because other factors come into play, ranging from the quality of the teacher to the quality of the textbooks to the health of the student. Second, time is a commodity that comes in different sizes. The length of the school year, the length of the school week, the length of the school day, the number of minutes diverted to "classroom management" and lost to instruction, the number of minutes allocated to a particular subject, the amount of homework, the rate of pupil attendance and absenteeism—these blocks of time interrelate, and the importance of any one of them cannot be analyzed without considering its impact on the others.

Generally speaking, these theorists are not interested in the larger, garden-variety units of time such as the school year, the school week, or the school day. They prefer to deal with the smaller units, rearranged according to concepts of their own devising: "time on task," "engaged time," and "academic learning time." Nancy Karweit, of the Johns Hopkins University, does work that is representative of the group. In one article she presented a graph, based on her observation of twelve classrooms, to contrast what she termed "scheduled time," "instructional time," and "engaged time" in math class. Scheduled time was the number of minutes in a week that a teacher allotted for math instruction. Instructional time was the time left in scheduled time after classroom-management time and interruptions were deducted. Engaged time was the time left in instructional time after student inattention was deducted.

Karweit's aim was to take the official class period of forty-five or so minutes and, after close observation and careful counting, lop off all the minutes that were not used well. Her eye is on the micro-management of the educational experience. The focus is on using scheduled class time more effectively, shortening the transitions between tasks, minimizing distractions to learning, increasing the proportion of the class period in which the teacher is actively engaged with students, and increasing the quality and appropriateness of instruction. The length of the school year, in contrast, is what she calls a "global time measure." Whether to increase it is a question that might interest the generalist, but for her it is simply too big a clump of time to matter; too many other factors intervene to affect learning.

Time-and-learning theory finds a statistical relationship between the amount learned, as measured by achievement-test scores, and the time spent learning, but it is not a strong one. The reason is that so much else affects the student. Herbert Walberg, of the University of Illinois, has surveyed the literature to identify, in all, nine "educational productivity factors." Three have to do with personal characteristics: ability, chronological development, and motivation. Four have to do with psychological environments: home life, the classroom social group, the general peer culture, and television viewing. Only two have to do explicitly with instruction: the quality of teaching, ranging from the curriculum to the individual teacher's method, and, finally, the amount of time students are engaged in learning.

The Walberg list suggests that those who oppose a longer school year because they favor "quality" over "quantity" draw a misplaced contrast. Seven of Walberg's nine factors involve neither the quality nor the quantity of education but other considerations altogether. What is significant is that with the exception of lengthening the school year or school day, both of which can be done for thousands of students at a time, these productivity factors defy easy improvement by interested human beings. For masses of people across the entire society, personal qualities, psychological environments, and the quality of teaching will be slow to change.

The educational theorists concede as much; the prevailing mood in their ranks is either outright pessimism or a cautious allowance that things might improve at the margins. While they are quick to criticize proposals for change, they hesitate to put forward concrete alternatives of their own. For all the seeming precision gained by measuring learning in relation to engaged time rather than the raw number of days in the school year, these researchers are quite vague about how much to increase engaged time per day or per week. "How long can teachers be expected to productively interact with their stu-

UNDOUBTEDLY A HOST OF INFLUENCES, SOME OF THEM SUBTLE MATTERS OF CULTURE, ARE AT WORK WHEN AMERICAN KIDS DO POORLY AND OTHERS DO WELL. BUT WE ARE NOT LIKELY SOON TO BANISH THE PROBLEMS THAT ARE TOO NUMEROUS, NOR ARE WE LIKELY TO BANISH THOSE THAT ARE TOO SUBTLE. EQUALIZING THE

dents?" Karweit wonders. "How long can students be expected to be on-task?" Summarizing the current state of the literature for the Consortium on Educational Policy Studies at Indiana University, three researchers wrote, "Increased instructional time does have modest effects on student achievement; unfortunately, research is inconclusive on the most effective and practical ways to increase time."

There is a hidden irony, in any event, in the efforts of Karweit and others to boost "quality time" in the classroom. At first, those who speak of quality rather than quantity will always claim the higher moral ground. But the casual observer of American education comes away with the impression that past a certain point, gains in learning per hour will always be elusive—slipping and sliding in every school system with changes in teachers, administrators, teaching techniques, theories of learning,

curriculum additions, and who knows what else. By its very nature, teaching is an extraordinarily decentralized human activity dependent on the personality of the teacher, the personalities of the students, and the chemistry among them. Trying to get the teacher and the students to bridge the gap between Japan and the United States by stepping up learning per hour—as the time-and-learning theorists do—is a great deal more daunting than creating a longer school year in which to cover more of the curriculum. Images come to mind of forced feeding and assembly-line speed-ups.

Unfortunately, these same theorists go out of their way to criticize proposals to extend the school year. Their major insight, as noted, is that playing with big variables like the school year won't help much if little things go wrong. For example, increasing the school year will do no good if all the additional time is lost to absenteeism. Points like these seem so self-evident as not to merit much repeating, but in the professional literature they appear all the time, slightly dressed up in academic verbiage.

In their current roles time-and-learning theorists are not much help; they stifle the political debate over education in this country. Every unit of learning time that they regard as important just happens to be a micro-measure too esoteric for convenient public discussion. Conversely, every unit of time that the public can talk about, think about, or do anything about is disparaged as a source of false hope. This is anti-democratic and elitist, and eventually self-defeating even for the social scientists. Educational improvements in a democracy need a mobilized constituency. Parents will not march to the town hall under the banner of increasing engaged time. They will not yet march under the banner of increasing the school year, either. But at least they can understand the idea without a course in statistics, and can take part in the debate—elementary, perhaps, but the first step toward change.

Nonetheless, the micro-theorists have something to contribute to the debate about how to improve education. Engaged time is a useful idea; nobody can argue with teacher-training efforts that focus on productivity within the classroom and the reduction of distractions and interruptions. For that matter, big and important debates about American education can continue within the context of a longer school year as well. Questions about curriculum, class size, teacher autonomy, school-based management, competency testing, dropout prevention, minority isolation, student services and counseling—there is much to preoccupy us. A longer school year, while hardly sufficient in itself to reclaim quality in American education, is a superstructure under which other changes can be made. A school year of, say, 220 days will serve as a big tent. A number of things may go into the tent to make it a better place; to accommodate them all and to arrange them in proper order requires the space the tent provides.

3. STRIVING FOR EXCELLENCE

The micro-theorists mount a highly technical assault on the longer school year. Many others within the educational establishment attack on grounds broader and more general, although not so closely reasoned. The arguments of these writers and thinkers vary but in the end boil down to the familiar preference for quality rather than quantity. In fact their stock in trade is not quality but complexity; they view the problem of American education as so knotty, with contributing factors so numerous and solutions so uncertain, that it can never be solved, only written about. These professionals seem incapable of coming up with a short list of concrete priorities for reform, let alone of describing how to get from the present to the future along the highly political road that reform must travel. Undoubtedly a host of influences, some of them subtle matters of culture, are at work when American kids do poorly and other kids do well. But we are not likely soon to banish the problems that are too numerous, and neither are we likely to banish those that are too subtle. Equalizing the time we commit to learning is the way that we will begin to come back. In lamenting that it is all very complicated, the professionals do nothing to advance the argument for dramatic change; in practical, political terms, they advance the argument for little change, or no change at all.

Lester Thurow, of the Massachusetts Institute of Technology, has lost patience with all the foot-dragging. In 1985 he wrote,

> The standard American response to proposals for a longer school year is to argue that Americans should learn to more efficiently use the current 180 days before they worry about adding more days. Such a response is to get the whole problem backwards. Instead of starting with what is easy to do—work longer and harder—Americans start with what is very difficult to do—work smarter. The argument is also a form of implicit American arrogance. Americans think that they can learn in 180 days what the rest of the world takes 220 to 240 days to learn. It also forgets that the rest of the world is trying to use its 220 or 240 days more efficiently.

The Matter of Leadership

WHAT, THEN, IS TO BE DONE? AS THE DEBATE over lengthening the school year is joined, how is public apprehension to be overcome, a public consensus to be formed?

First, there is the matter of leadership. Recall that in the late 1950s, after *Sputnik*, Americans did not balk at being challenged to run a race with the Soviets for world scientific supremacy. In fact, this nation has always reacted well to competitions summed up in muscular imagery by our leaders: Americans run races, go for the gold, vie for championships, all with admirable zest.

But these days the message of civic, political, and intellectual leaders is different. The tone is unrelentingly dour. Americans are not dared to run a race; they are told that the race has already been run, the United States has lost, and they are to blame—because they did not "work harder." Both the political right and the political left have generated cottage industries centered on the person of the scold, the critic, the moralist. These entrepreneurs of gloom engender a very mixed reaction, because people are ambivalent about being lectured to. When Roger Porter, a presidential aide for economic and domestic policy, labels American education "depressing and uninspiring," dismay at our prospects dampens our appetite for meeting the challenge. The end-of-the-American-century, fall-of-a-great-power talk has gone too far.

Where education is concerned, the Gallup polls tell us that people are now open to a message of change. Complacency is no longer holding us back. But the tone of the message must be optimistic, and resonant with the American themes that lend themselves to the task of mobilizing for change—specifically, the notions that we have always risen to the challenge of competition, felt free to adapt the good ideas of others, worked like demons when the prize was self-improvement, and had a special knack for exploiting the practical fruits of learning.

Americans are up to the game of international educational competition, but we need to know what the rules are. When the rest of the world plays a twenty-minute period, American students cannot be expected to rack up as many points in fifteen. Our toughest competitors are, in fact, playing a school year of 220 days or so, with results that bode poorly for America's future. It is up to this country's leaders to get the word out, in a way that inspires rather than dispirits their audiences.

Once these leaders make the effort, they will find that many people are way ahead of them, and not only because of concern about international competition. An entirely different dynamic is also at work, one that promises to tip popular opinion further in favor of more schooling. Aspects of it were detected by the 1988 Gallup poll on education, in response to the question "Would you favor or oppose the local public schools' offering before-school and after-school programs where needed for so-called latch-key children, that is, those whose parents do not return home until late in the day?"

To those familiar with public resistance to extending the school year and school day, the response was stunning. Seventy percent of the sample were in favor, 23 percent opposed—a spread repeated when Gallup asked the question, in slightly different form, last year.

The forces at work here are formidable. More than 25 million women in the United States have children under the age of thirteen, and most of those women work at least part-time. Latchkey children, who spend some part of the working day at home without adult supervision, arouse particular concern. A 1987 Harris survey indicates that 12 percent of elementary, 30 percent of middle school, and 38 percent of high school students are left to care for themselves after school "almost every day."

In the seventh-grade class I taught for a day, the majority of the students lived in housing projects. They were not averse to the idea of a longer school year. Instead, they volunteered that kids would be kept off the streets, that now they were "spoiled" by too much TV and too much Nintendo, and that there was nothing to do over the long summer vacation. The students also had suggestions about what a longer school year might include: more sports, more time to study, and more opportunity to take courses in subjects that interested them.

The issue here extends beyond latchkey children to touch all manner of middle-class, working-class, and poor families. Many parents who cover all the bases for their children are doing so just barely, and at a cost in terms of missed wages that they cannot sustain forever. All told, an enormous potential constituency exists for a longer school day, folded into a longer school year.

The Vision of Justice Brandeis

T HE COMPLAINT WILL BE HEARD THAT A SCHOOL cannot be all things to all people—cannot be place of education, health-care clinic, settlement house, and neighborhood recreation center rolled into one. The pragmatic response is that a school must in fact be all these things.

In most communities the best facility for accommodating large numbers of children is the school building. The best adults to be with these children are teachers, and the best way to structure the hours involved is through a curriculum that permits ample time for physical exercise, creative activity, and play, as well as learning. Almost nothing else—neither healthy civic institutions nor trained personnel—is available to the children, either at the end of the abbreviated school day or at the end of the abbreviated school year.

Despite the size of the potential popular constituency, a big problem remains. Teachers tend to be opposed to an extension of the school day and school year. Most prefer their summer vacations. But significant increases in pay are also very important to this financially pressed group. Teachers must recognize that the school-year and school-day issues are the levers they have been looking for; better pay and big extensions of school time go hand in hand.

Which leads to the subject of how, in this complicated country, the transition to a world-class school year can be made, and how members of the public, many of them not parents, can be induced to pay the costs.

Matters already discussed are crucial. Leaders must emerge among parents, educators, civic activists, and politicians. The issue must be thrust into the public domain, the international data disseminated, the economic stakes made clear. Bills must be introduced at the state level (I am sponsoring one in Massachusetts) to increase the minimum length of the school year. As obvious as this step is, it raises a question of fairness that dogs reform in the American system.

In the 1830s and 1840s Horace Mann struggled to rescue the floundering American school system and per-

suade a divided public of the need to educate children more thoroughly. As secretary of the Massachusetts Board of Education, Mann firmly staked out a position against maximum local control of the schools—an undertaking as controversial then as it is now. He undercut hiring prerogatives by proposing statewide standards for teachers, and infringed on curriculum-setting power by pushing for uniformity in textbooks. His influence soon extended across the country. Various state legislatures stepped up the pace of educational reform, passing laws whose effects were to increase drastically the number of children in school, the length of time they spent there, and the cost and quality of the instruction they received.

Here came a dose of messy politics: These same legis-

FOR YEARS THERE HAS BEEN WEAK PUBLIC DEMAND FOR MORE EDUCATION, "MORE" MEANING GREATER AMOUNTS OF TIME SPENT IN THE SCHOOLS HELPING CHILDREN TO LEARN. ONCE THE PUBLIC REALIZES THE NEED FOR CHANGE AND MOMENTUM BUILDS, THE SCHOOL YEAR WILL BE LENGTHENED, REGARDLESS OF WHICH OTHER INTERESTS ARE OPPOSED.

latures declined to assume the cost of funding these good acts. Instead, the new laws took the form of state-imposed mandates on municipalities, to be paid for out of property taxes. Legislatures had the right to do this because then, as now, state constitutions placed local communities under the power of state governments.

Mandates made people upset. One hundred and fifty years later they still do. When the state dictates to the city and town, critics object either that the content of the mandate is bad or that the content is fine but the dictator should foot the bill. The mandating power, these critics say, makes accountability impossible, places a financial burden on the lower governments, and offends the unwritten but powerful tradition of home rule.

True enough, but mandates have an overriding virtue: awkward in principle, they work in practice. Systems of government must somehow sort out responsibilities. In the American system the sorting out gets done by the U.S. Constitution and the constitutions of the various states, as interpreted by the courts, and by the U.S. Congress and the state legislatures. From the start, the public schools have been left to local communities to run—but the ground rules have been written elsewhere, and they have changed as the country and world have changed.

Those who insist that states fully fund their education mandates would lead us into the political bog, and soon be stuck themselves. Legislatures and Congress might respond by declining to set higher standards, which would be disastrous. More likely, these bodies would set the standards, assume the costs—and then extend their influence even further, into day-to-day policy-making, which should be left to local people. Full funding would have the effect, ironic for the locals who demanded it, of leading inexorably to more state encroachment and oversight. It is an axiom of political finance, and probably of human nature: If you pay for it, you will want to run it. It follows that if a healthy measure of control over schools is to remain at home, local officials must live with mandates, and without insisting on full funding.

One is able, then, to lay one's hands on a blunt but historically effective tool of change: the mandate. One can envision the pattern of change, true to federalism and the maxim of Louis Brandeis: a leapfrog trail from one state to the next, as each works out the problems of persuasion, politics, and finance. One can describe several elements of change. A longer school year should be phased in over some period, because time will be needed to plan, and because local governments cannot tax their citizens into penury, even when mandated to do so. Stepped-up revenue-sharing should come from state legislatures, because while full funding of the mandate is neither possible nor desirable, a generous partnership is.

And one must insist upon some help from the federal government. The Chief Executive of the United States must be asked to be the education President he says he wants to be, and to sponsor and sign into law a program of federal aid to school districts as they switch to a longer year. The federal government's tax base is broad enough to help finance the expansion of the school year. Nothing is more critical to national security in the post–Cold War era than schooling our children, yet education's share of the federal budget in fiscal year 1990 was an abysmal 1.9 percent. The issue here is priorities, not capabilities. The question, as the old saw goes, is not whether we can afford to do it but whether we can afford not to.

While a broad-based movement builds, more immedi-ate levers of change present themselves. If civic or political leaders are determined to see a 220-day school year in their state by the year 2000, they might begin by raising private-sector and public-sector matching funds to extend the year for ten or so medium-sized districts, spread among the poor, the middle-class, and the well-to-do. And if this arrangement does not work, a handful of affluent districts can take the plunge on their own, using their taxing power and their long-standing prerogative to go beyond state minimums in setting the local school year. This would be financially feasible in the short term and politically formidable in the long term. In my own state of Massachusetts, what Lexington does today, Concord will feel impelled to do in relatively short order.

Some will hesitate, in the well-intentioned belief that the school year should not change for any district until it changes for all. But, as a matter of tactics, this is not shrewd. The issue is not whether all schools change to 220 days; the issue is whether no schools whatsoever change, depriving us of the chance to get the process started. Once the trend begins in earnest, the courts or the legislatures will come under mounting pressure to do the right thing by poorer communities. In the past two years the supreme courts of New Jersey, Kentucky, Texas, and Montana have handed down landmark decisions on inequities in the financing of rich and poor school districts. If the aim is social justice, it becomes important to set a longer school year as the standard of record, even for a handful of wealthier districts, so that poorer districts can then be brought up to par.

Find a way to begin the process, and watch it build on itself. Who will abide having his children receive forty fewer days of education every year than the kids in the next town over? For that matter, who will abide, for much longer, having her children receive less education than the kids in the country the next continent over? The world is shrinking. Change is inevitable. It is only a matter of time.

The Standards Debate Across the Atlantic

As European countries become integrated into the European Community, they are examining each other's standards and the standards of the U.S. and Japan.

MICHAEL G. BRUCE

Michael G. Bruce was an educational consultant, associated with Webster University's London campus. He had taught widely in the United States and had extensive contacts with the field of international education throughout Europe. His last major piece of work was for the European Commission, on the position of teacher education in Europe. Michael G. Bruce died in 1991 at age 54.

Standards in education are by no means a unique concern of the U.S. They also concern the "other United States," the European Community (EC) of 320 million citizens balancing the U.S. on the other side of the Atlantic.

In recognition of European integration and in anticipation of 1992, the deadline for the next major step toward this end, Europeans are looking to their own educational standards. Sometimes each nation looks internally, at its own standards—British, French, Dutch, German, Spanish, or Italian. But European countries are also looking with ever-increasing interest at each other's standards, and Europe as a whole is measuring its own performance against that of the U.S. and Japan.

A recent survey of education in the European Community, *70 Millions d'Eleves, l'Europe de l'Education* (*Seventy Million Students, Educational Europe*) refers to the "Etats-Unis d'Europe" (United States of Europe),

and the author asserts that American work on school effectiveness is "valid for Europe."[1]

The British and the French

Yet there are considerable differences between Europe and the U.S., and one of the most profound is the process used to determine high school graduation. The French baccalaureate and the British General Certificate of Education, Advanced Level, are typical examples of the European system.

Despite differences between British and French practices of high school graduation assessment, their similarities are most striking when both are

Immigrants are enriching the European language pool, and their presence reinforces the European awareness that bilingualism is a normal, widespread human skill.

compared with American procedures. Both British and French procedures are based on terminal assessment, with little or no weighting for grades accumulated in previous years of study. Both place heavy reliance on formal written answers to question papers that are classified and unseen by either the candidates or their teachers until the examination. Both use open-ended questions and attach considerable importance to the students' ability to develop their arguments in extended prose. Candidates' answers are dispatched to national agencies, where they are graded.

As Grant Wiggins (see Educational Leadership, February 1991, p. 18) mentions, the British use elaborate moderating procedures to ensure comparability of standards among individual exam graders, who grade hundreds of thousands of exams; and the French have similar mechanisms to ensure objectivity. naturally, considerable public interest is attached to what is the culmination of 13 years of schooling. In Britain, the local papers commonly comment on the performance of the most successful students—and on their schools. In France, the best exam answers are published in the national press.

Since European universities are selective in different ways from their American counterparts, this achievement is important for the individual student. Success on these formal school examinations is the normal qualification for entry to the university; and, in much of Europe, universities are obliged to accept all successful candidates. Students therefore attach great importance to their performance. Indeed, in France, successful students do not "pass," they are "recus" (received), with all the word implies about being admitted to a special body, the university.

All European universities charge home students merely nominal fees or offer universal fee remission; and all countries have elaborate systems of student finance designed to ensure that monetary problems should never be a barrier to university study. But the tough academic hurdle represented by the French baccalaureate, the British "Advanced Levels," the German *Abitur*, and by similar formal national standards in other countries limits university entrance. The intention is to make standards criterion-referenced, although the public is sometimes suspicious that politicians may "adjust" pass levels in order to fine-tune the university population.

British and French schools have eliminated the pressure that students or parents might exert on their teachers to inflate their grades by having papers graded by anonymous graders who are usually far away from the schools. As a high school teacher in the 1960s, I was able to say to my students, "Together, we will get good grades—and I can help you." Since grades were not my gift to bestow, students saw me as an ally, while someone else was the judge.

Common Concerns
Despite these differences from the U.S., there are still similar concerns about standards, often expressed by employers and frequently discussed by the press. Such concerns commonly relate to basic skills or to the work ethic of students.

Anxiety over literacy rates runs high. A British report early this year, alleging falling standards in the primary schools, was recently echoed in France. The educational establishment has accused both the British and the French reports of scaremongering, but both have found support in the press and with the business community. Allegations and counterallegations, research evidence and conflicting re-

search evidence—this scenario will seem familiar to anyone who follows educational debate in the States.

One major social change may be reflected in falling language skills standards. In the past three decades, massive immigration to meet the growing manpower needs of the more prosperous countries of Northern Europe has produced a rapid increase in the number of students whose mother tongue is not a European language. In Britain, France, and the Netherlands most immigrants come from former colonies; in Germany, most come from southern European or near-European countries, such as Yugoslavia, Greece, and Turkey. In all countries, most immigrants have arrived with non-European languages as their mother tongues. And, unlike the sizable population of Hispanic immigrants in the U.S., their languages (Arabic, Turkish, Rudu, or Gujerati, for example) are outside the European family of languages; often they employ a different alphabet.

Such immigrants are enriching the European language pool, and their presence reinforces the European awareness that bilingualism is a normal, widespread human skill. But they have also introduced into Europe a variety of foreign accents and non-standard forms of European speech and writing. So far as I know, none of the research purporting to detect a decline in literacy has attempted to disaggregate performances of native Euro-Caucasian students from that of first- or second-generation immigrant students. Indeed, any attempt to do so would be politically inept and dangerously divisive. But in the absence of such evidence, it is at least feasible that literacy rates are falling in the schools with large immigrant student populations who have unique language needs of their own.

"Added Value"—Real or Insignificant?
Discussion of good, effective schools took a major new turn in the 1980s with the publication of two major studies, *Fifteen Thousand Hours* by Michael Rutter and associates and *School Matters* by Peter Mortimer and associates.[2] Rutter and Mortimer noted a striking paradox: on the one hand, there is research, much of it American, alleging that the impact of schooling on stu-

dents' life chances is minimal; on the other hand, British parents go to considerable lengths to choose (within the publicly funded state system) the schools where they want their children to study. Are the parents' instincts wrong? Or are there real differences in outcome between schools, which research has not detected?

Using sensitive measures of behavior and academic performance, Rutter and Mortimer uncovered significant differences in "added value" between schools. Differences in outcome, including retention and dropout rates, percentage of students who go on to higher education, and employment success, reflected *actual* differences in schools, even when full allowances had been made for the social, attitudinal, and educational differences of students on entry. As Rutter and Mortimer put it in their now famous phrase, "Schools make a difference." But differences between schools are particularly conspicuous when we recognize that the term *standards* denotes more fields of behavior than intellectual performance alone.

The work of Rutter and Mortimer presupposes that parents can select the schools to which they will entrust their children. Indeed, pressure on educational systems to raise standards (however measured) can be most effective when schools realize that they need to win, and then to retain, the confidence of the parents in their community in order to remain in business. This is the free-market view, and, paradoxically, where public schools are concerned, it is more in evidence in Europe than in the States.

Europe Has More Choice
No EC country has the principle of secularity, as embodied in the Constitution of the U.S. On the contrary, European governments have historically had close association with the churches; and much public education in Europe was once provided by the churches. Today, throughout all EC countries, national networks of church schools coexist with schools funded directly by the state. But, in contrast to the U.S., church schools are funded by the government and offer free, or nearly free, education. At the very least, therefore, European parents have a choice between a state (usually secular) school and a church school

(which usually offers the same curriculum but within a Christian framework and is financed from state funds). The two systems are often competitive, and in a largely secular age parents are as likely to choose the school in whose teaching they have the most confidence as the school that corresponds to their religious faith. Indeed, there is growing evidence that parents choose church schools because they believe they offer firmer discipline, a more structured ethos, and more traditional teaching—"standards," at least in one sense of the word. Parental choice within the free, publicly funded state system is carried still further in Britain, Denmark, and the Netherlands. The Dutch, for historic reasons, have no less than four competing school systems, reflecting past religious divisions. They offer parents a wider range of choice than most other European countries. In Denmark, the government permits individuals or groups to set up their own private schools and apply for state funding.

Recent changes have been most marked in the United Kingdom; yet, despite the controversy surrounding moves under the Thatcher administration to reinforce parental choice, the practice of choice is nothing new. Schools have always been conceived of as communities, with something of the characteristics of a family (teachers are officially *in loco parentis*), and it is considered right that different schools, even when in the same neighborhood and under the same "Office," will have distinct communal personalities and ethos distinctively their own. Given that each school has its own team of teachers and develops its own priorities, it follows that it is right for parents to choose the type of school they consider appropriate for their sons and daughters.

The Standards Debate Here and There

One of the many fascinating differences between Europe and the U.S. lies in the vocabulary of the standards debate. As an outside observer of American educational debate, I detect that in America accusations of falling standards are commonly directed at *systems*—state governments, school boards, curricular practices, educational innovations, patterns of teacher education. On a different level, the finger may be pointed at individual teachers, with reference to personal accountability for student performance or to competency testing.

On my side of the Atlantic, the pressure for standards seems to be directed at *institutions*—especially the individual school. Parents do not as a rule choose individual teachers, nor do they really exercise an educational choice when they move into a particular community and accept the educational system that goes with it. But they do exercise considerable choice in selecting the schools to which they will entrust their offspring. We are undergoing a consumer revolution; and where schools are concerned, parents as clients are becoming more discriminating and more exigent.

As the two economic giants of the industrial world, the U.S. and the EC have come to the realization that their long-term futures depend on their human resources. The schools will ensure our future—or will imperil it. In the current debate, we have much in common, as we defend similar democratic, pluralistic values and work to further the well-being of our citizens; and we draw upon complementary traditions. For each of us, there is a rich treasury of educational experiences on the other side of the Atlantic. We shall be foolish indeed if we do not draw on it.

[1]F. Vaniscotte, (1989), *70 Millions d'Eleves, l'Europe de l'Education*, (Paris: Hatier).

[2]M. Rutter et al., (1979), *Fifteen Thousand Hours*, (London: Open Books); and P. Mortimer et al., (1988), *School Matters*, (Wells: Open Books).

Morality and Values in Education

What part ought the schooling experience play in the formation of such things as character, informed compassion, conscience, honor, and respect for self and others? From Socrates forward (and before him) we have wrestled with these concerns. We address these things here as educators in every human generation have had to address them. Aristotle noted in his *Politics* that there was no consensus as to what the purposes of education should be in Athens, that people disputed what Athenian youth ought to be taught by their teachers, and that youth did not always address their elders with respect. Apparently we do not have a new problem on our hands here. It is one, however, of great importance that every generation of citizens in every nation addresses in one manner or another. Certainly the issue of public morality and the question as to how best to educate for individually and collectively responsible social behavior is a matter of great significance in North America today.

Some teachers have developed very meaningful ways to help their students learn to make decisions about the well-being and best interests of themselves and others. There are certain classroom environments where children and adolescents are not given the opportunity to engage in evaluative lines of discussion as to what constitutes, or would have constituted, more responsible lines of action among persons involved in literary, historical, or current issues. We know that children benefit from practice in decision-making of all kinds, including moral decision-making. Developing a sense of moral consciousness and confidence in one's capacity to make reasoned moral judgments is, or it should be, a very important part of each student's encounter with life in school.

Some authors, such as David Purpel, have reminded us that some of the past efforts by educators to promote programs of moral education in the schools have had great shortcomings or have been actually counterproductive. He and others have argued that teachers need to help students develop within themselves a sense of critical social consciousness and a genuine concern for social justice. The debate on this issue continues in professional literature. Insight into the nature of use of moral decision-making should be taught in the context of real current and past social problems and lead students to develop their own skills in social analysis relating to the ethical dilemmas of human beings.

There is a need for teachers to develop principles of professional practice that will enable them to respond reasonably to the many ethical dilemmas they face. The knowledge base on how teachers derive their knowledge of professional ethics is developing. The study of how teachers come to be aware of their basic values and of how these values shape their professional practice is very important. Educational systems at all levels are based on the desirability to teach certain fundamental beliefs and the disciplines of knowledge (however they may be organized in different cultures). School curricula are based on certain moral assumptions (secular or religious) as to the worth of knowledge, and the belief that some forms of knowledge are more worthy than others. Schooling is not only to transmit national and cultural heritage, including the intellectual heritage, of a people; it is also a fundamentally moral enterprise. "Moral bases of education" is the evaluation of choices and the making of decisions on the knowledge and academic skills that ought to be taught. How persons answer the questions implied by the above remarks reflects their own ideological biases.

We see, therefore, that when we speak of morality and education there are process issues as to the most basic knowledge-seeking, epistemological foundations of learning. Hence, the controversy over morality in education deals with more than just the tensions between secular and religious interests in society, although to know about such tensions is a valuable, important matter. Moral education is also more than a debate over the merits of methods used to teach students to make morally sound, ethical choices in their lives—although this also is critically important and ought to be done. Thus, we argue that the construction of educational processes and the decisions as to the substantive content of school curricula are also moral issues, as well as epistemological ones having to do with how we discover, verify, and transmit truth.

One of the most compelling responsibilities of Canadian and American schools is the responsibility of preparing young persons for their moral duties as free citizens of free nations. The Canadian and American governments have always wanted the schools to teach the principles of civic morality based on their respective constitutional traditions. Indeed, when the public school movement began in the United States in the 1830s and 1840s, the concept of universal public schooling as a mechanism for instilling a sense of national identity and civic morality was supported. In every nation, school curricula have certain value preferences imbedded in them.

Significant constitutional issues are at stake in the forms and directions moral education should take in the schools. Both theistic and nontheistic conceptions of what constitutes moral behavior compete for the loyalties of teachers and students. Extremist forces representing the ideological left and right, both religious and secular, wish to see their moral agendas incorporated into school curricula. The pressures from these groups can be extreme.

The cherished civil freedoms of all young people must be protected. These freedoms include the freedom to believe or not to believe matters of doctrine unrelated to the shared civic values that form the basis for our free, democratic social order. These doctrinal matters, including such fiercely controverted social issues as abortion and sexual morality, raise a number of questions. Do teachers have a responsibility to respond to student requests for information on sexuality, sexual morality, communicable diseases, etc.? Or should they deny these requests? For whom do the schools exist? Is a teacher's primary responsibility to his or her client, the student, or to the student's parents? Do secondary school students have the right to study and to inquire into subjects not in officially-sanctioned curricula? What are the moral issues surrounding censorship of student reading material? What ethical questions are raised by arbitrarily withholding information regarding alternative viewpoints on controversial topics?

Schools cannot avoid reflecting some values because, as noted previously, the values underlying the content of any curriculum are easily identified by most students from the middle grades upward. Likewise, teachers cannot hide all of their moral preferences. However, they can learn to conduct just, open discussions of moral topics without succumbing to the temptation to deliberately indoctrinate students with their own views.

Teaching students to respect all people, to revere the sanctity of life, to uphold the right to dissent on the part of any citizen, to believe in the equality of all people before the law, to cherish the freedom to learn, and to respect the right of all people to their own convictions—these are principles of democracy and ideals worthy of being cherished. An understanding of the process of ethical decision-making is needed by the citizens of any free nation; thus, this process should be taught in a free nation's schools.

The essays in this unit constitute a comprehensive overview of moral education with considerable historical and textual interpretation. Topics covered include public pressures on schools and the social responsibilities of schools. The unit can be used in courses dealing with the historical or philosophical foundations of education.

Looking Ahead: Challenge Questions

What is moral education? Why do so many people wish to see a form of moral education in schools?

What are the differences in moral education issues in public and private schools?

Are there certain values about which most North Americans can agree? Should they be taught in schools?

Should local communities have total control of the content of moral instruction in local schools, as they did in the nineteenth century? Why or why not?

What are some of the problems with the manner in which ethics and ethical decision-making skills have been taught in schools?

What is civic education? How do states encourage civic education in the schools?

Should schools be involved in teaching people to reason about moral questions? Why or why not? If not, who should do it? Why?

What is the difference between indoctrination and instruction?

Is there a national consensus concerning the form that moral education should take in schools? Is such a consensus likely if it does not now exist?

What attitudes and skills are most important to a responsible approach to moral decision-making?

How can we learn about how teachers' values affect their professional relationships with students?

Ethical Education in Our Public Schools: Crisis and Opportunity

WALDO BEACH

Waldo Beach is professor emeritus, Duke University Divinity School, Durham, North Carolina.

In recent years, the news media has focused on the decline in the quality of public education, especially at the secondary school level. This decline is measured quantitatively, by graphs showing the downturn in national SAT scores, the rising dropout rate of students, the burn-out rate of teachers, and the low literacy scores, not only in English but in math and science. The depressing conclusion drawn from the data is that our public education system is failing to equip our citizenry to cope with the demands of a technological culture. The hidden assumption in all of this data is that the central purpose of education is technical. Unless we can teach our young people how to run our machines, we will continue to lose our markets to the Japanese and slide down the economic slope into a depression.

But there is another dimension of the educational process, both public and private, which is impossible to graph exactly but which is certainly just as crucial: the nurture of conscience and character. Education in moral responsibility, in behavior that sustains a civil society, is as imperative as training in science and math.

The American public has been alerted to the urgency of our situation by news accounts of the gross moral misbehavior on the part of many of our teenage youths. A recent article in the *New Yorker* (Finnegan 1990) describes vividly the life-style and practices of teenagers in the depressed inner-city neighborhoods of New Haven, Connecticut. Gangs of boys, engaged in drug trafficking on street corners, are involved in violence, shootings, and the destruction of property. The number of babies born to unwed teenagers is on the rise. This situation is particularly shocking to me, as I was reared in New Haven. I had my schooling at Hillhouse High School under the benign shadow of Yale University, an atmosphere where the ethics of responsible civility, of respect for persons and property, were generally observed. Currently, most of the stu-dents at Hillhouse High School are poor and often from broken homes. Academic achievement is low, the dropout rate scandalously high, and stealing and looting, even drug trafficking on school grounds, are common practice. This same pattern is duplicated in many inner-city areas, from South Boston to Los Angeles.

A recent report by the Carnegie Council on Adolescent Development (1989) analyzes the cultural factors that have brought us to this sorry state. They emanate not so much from within the schools as from the larger socioeconomic cultural forces at work in the lives of all American adolescents. The enormous impact of commercial TV is certainly one. High school students as well as younger children are nurtured daily in the values celebrated by commercial TV, much more than by their formal schooling: values of speed, power, violence, comfort, convenience, glamor, and sensual enjoyment. As the aforementioned *New Yorker* article mentions, in describing a drug trafficker named Terry, "A vast part of what Terry knows and believes about the world he learned from television, and on critical topics such as violence and drugs his electronic education has been a toxic soup of mixed moral messages. . . . His own religion, his ideology—consumer individualism—imbibed since childhood from commercial television, is itself profoundly rooted" (17 September 1990, 74).

A second factor that influences the lives of adolescents is the growing gap between the haves and the have-nots, between the wealthy and the poor. This gap makes a mockery of the TV image of the good life of comfort and high consumerism that teenagers watch while living in shacks. Little wonder that gangs of high school students become drug peddlers on the street corner in order to make easy money, to live high. Little wonder that stealing and violence are on the increase or that prostitution among teenage girls is on the rise, for these are ready ways to get money for drugs.

Another cultural impact on the moral attitudes and behavior of adolescents is in the area of sex. The mass media celebrates daily the ritual devotions of sexual activity. It should come as no surprise to learn from the recently published report by the Carnegie Council on

From *The Clearing House*, Vol. 64, No. 5, May/June 1991, pp. 313-315. Reprinted with permission of the Helen Dwight Reid Educational Foundation. Published by Heldref Publications, 1319 Eighteenth St., N.W., Washington, DC 20036-1802. Copyright © 1991.

Adolescent Development, *At the Threshold* (1990), that "since the late 1960s, adolescents have been sexually active in greater numbers and at younger ages than ever before. . . . [A]t age eighteen 67 percent of boys and 44 percent of girls are sexually experienced. By their 20th year, the figures have gone up to 80 percent for males and 70 percent for females" (25). Sex education in schools seems to have little influence on these figures. Although sexual activity has decreased slightly because of the fear of AIDS, the pregnancy rate among teenage girls remains high. The sorry consequence of this, of course, is that girls with babies must drop out of school and shift for themselves. And with the disintegration of the supportive and close family unit, especially among poor, inner-city minorities, the problems posed for framers of education and public policy are horrendous.

Many more problems might be cited as the demons that invade our schools, such as looting, deceit in academic performance, and endemic racial and religious prejudices that set one group of students against another and often erupt into gang violence. Yet our task in this symposium is not to catalog our woes, but to seek to find positive strategies to counteract these negative forces and devise realistic programs of moral education in secondary public schools.

The two most widely known and practiced programs of moral education today are the values clarification method (VC) and Lawrence Kohlberg's cognitive-development theory. Readers of *The Clearing House* are surely familiar with the main motifs of these programs, and they need not be reviewed here in any detail. VC attempts to have students sort out the values at stake in their actions, both in and out of school, to decide which are desirable and which are not, and to act upon the values they esteem. This can be done through formal instruction, but preferably by a guidance and counseling program. The chief article of faith in the VC *credo* is neutrality; because of the religious and ethnic pluralism of the public school, no teacher should "indoctrinate" the many pupils in a class with one "official" moral axiom. This approach holds that each student should decide the norms of right and wrong for him- or herself. Here is where the chief fault of VC becomes evident. A complete ethical neutrality on the part of teachers, parents, administrators, and counselors is impossible and irresponsible. In effect, it says to students, "Go ahead —do what you want. If you prefer getting a high grade by stealing that assigned paper from someone else rather than writing it yourself—that's your business." It is this moral anomie or normlessness that has lately turned school administrators and teachers from VC.

A program of ethical education more substantial and widely used is Kohlberg's cognitive-development theory, with its six stages of moral development. A child moves from stage one, where the good versus bad option is determined by the reward versus punishment con-

sequence, to stage six of moral maturity where, as Kohlberg puts it, "Right is defined by the decision of conscience in accord with self-chosen ethical principles appealing to logical consistency, universality, and consistency" (Purpel and Ryan 1976, 215). This sounds very much like Kant's Categorical Imperative. The principles of justice, equality of rights, and respect for the worth of persons set moral education on much more solid ground than the shifting sands of VC's anomie.

Where the cognitive-development theory of moral education falls short, in my opinion, is that it lays so much stress on the *cognitive* aspect of learning and not enough on the *affective* or volitional; it emphasizes the mind rather than the heart. Presumably, according to Kohlberg, the pupil would do as he or she knows, at whatever stage he or she may be. A corrective to Kohlberg's theory can be found in the Judeo-Christian religion, where morality is more a matter of the loves of the heart than the insights of the mind. It is the *affective* more than the *cognitive* aspect of growth that is crucial in the education of conscience into responsible behavior.

What are some positive moral education strategies that might overcome the shortcomings of the VC and the cognitive-development theories in public schools? To answer first the basic premise question, Should schools engage in moral education, the answer is an unequivocal yes.

This can and should be done through the visible curriculum. In social studies, health sciences, history, political science, economics, and literature, responsible instruction deals with the hard facts, yes, but also with the value-dimensions and quandaries that permeate all of this data. How could one possibly teach American history and avoid the issues of the moral basis of the Bill of Rights and its ethical limits, or Negro slavery, or American foreign policy? Teaching literary classics, such as *Hamlet, Moby Dick,* and *The Diary of Ann Frank,* should point students to the moral dilemmas in these pieces of literature but also sensitize them to the moral norms of integrity and responsibility. A sex education class in health sciences should move beyond the facts about sexual relations and the statistical data about AIDS to deal with moral responsibilities, the relation of sex to love, and the cultivation of "habits of the heart" in dating relationships that are not exploitive, that do not "use" the other person for self-gratification.

The most effective and significant part of moral education—in all public schools but secondary schools in particular—is carried on not so much in the visible curriculum as in the "hidden" curriculum—that is, in the structures and style of interpersonal relationships of the teachers, administrators, guidance counselors, and coaches with students. Also of great importance for morality is the relationship of the teachers and parents. A sensitive teacher, alert to the particular domestic circumstance of the troubled boy in her eleventh-grade English class, can help him by friendly encouragement to develop a more positive attitude toward his schoolwork. Or where there is a strong PTA, even in a depressed inner-city area, guidance counselors and other staff members can help improve academic performance, as well as moral behavior, by offering parents techniques for monitoring TV-watching and helping with homework. To be sure, in many schools this remedy of individualized concern is thwarted by the current student/teacher ratio—itself the consequence of budgetary squeeze. But the normative answer is clear: smaller size classes, more guidance counselors, and closer PTA ties.

Another positive strategy in the "hidden curriculum" is to create a greater sense of moral responsibility on the part of students in all the activities that foster a sense of community responsibility within the school. Such activities include an honor code, whereby students are held responsible for their integrity in academic performance; a peer-counseling tutorial program, in which talented older students can tutor younger students, and a local chapter of SADD (Students Against Drunk Driving). Programs such as these have been shown to change moral attitudes and behavior for the better.

Other programs of community service, such as those proposed by the Educators for Social Responsibility or the Josephson Institute for the Advancement of Ethics,[1] involve students in civic activities that serve the needs of the poor nearby or far away or help to clean up the natural environment. Such involvement may turn the stu-

dents' internal moral heart-set from "me-itis" to a sense of social responsibility. Walk in the annual CROP (Christian Rural Overseas Program) Walk for World Hunger. Give blood to the Red Cross. Work in the local Habitat for Humanity program. The problem here, of course, is that high school students, especially those of limited income, often must carry part-time jobs outside of school hours to help make ends meet. This strategy is more realistic for students of more means who also need to be cured of "me-itis." Yet even for students in an inner-city school, programs of community service can cultivate a social conscience and a sense of obligation to serve neighbors across town and on the other side of the globe.

NOTE

1. Readers who want to inquire further about such programs may contact these organizations as follows: Educators for Social Responsibility, 23 Garden Street, Cambridge, Massachusetts 02138, and Josephson Institute for the Advancement of Ethics, 213 Washington Street, Suite 104, Marina Del Ray, California 90292.

BIBLIOGRAPHY

Carnegie Council on Adolescent Development. 1989. *Turning points: Preparing American youth for the twentieth century.* New York: Carnegie Corporation of New York.
———. 1990. *At the threshold.* New York: Carnegie Corporation of New York.
Finnegan, W. 1990. A street kid in the drug trade. 2 parts. *New Yorker* (10 September): 51–86 and (17 September): 60–90.
Purpel, D., and K. Ryan, eds. 1976. *Moral education . . . It comes with the territory.* Berkeley, Calif.: McCutchan.

Caring Kids

The Role of the Schools

Psychological research, common sense, and the experience of an important pilot project in California offer specific guidance for helping children to grow into caring adults. Mr. Kohn provides the details.

Alfie Kohn

Alfie Kohn is an independent scholar living in Cambridge, Mass., who writes and lectures widely on human behavior and education. His books include The Brighter Side of Human Nature: Altruism and Empathy in Everyday Life *(Basic Books, 1990) and* No Contest: The Case Against Competition *(Houghton Mifflin, 1986). © 1991, Alfie Kohn.*

"Education worthy of the name is essentially education of character," the philosopher Martin Buber told a gathering of teachers in 1939.[1] In saying this, he presented a challenge more radical and unsettling than his audience may have realized. He did not mean that schools should develop a unit on values or moral reasoning and glue it onto the existing curriculum. He did not mean that problem children should be taught how to behave. He meant that the very profession of teaching calls on us to try to produce not merely good learners but good people.

Given that even the more modest task of producing good learners seems impossibly ambitious—perhaps because of a misplaced emphasis on producing good test-takers—the prospect of taking Buber seriously may seem positively utopian. But in the half-century since his speech, the need for schools to play an active role in shaping character has only grown more pressing. That need is reflected not only in the much-cited prevalence of teenage pregnancy and drug use but also in the evidence of rampant selfishness and competitiveness among young peo-

ple.* At a tender age, children learn not to be tender. A dozen years of schooling often do nothing to promote generosity or a commitment to the welfare of others. To the contrary, students are graduated who think that being smart means looking out for number one.

I want to argue, first, that something *can* be done to rectify this situation because nothing about "human nature" makes selfishness inevitable; second, that educators in particular *should* do something about the problem; and third, that psychological research, common sense, and the experience of an important pilot project in California offer specific guidance for helping children to grow into caring adults.

MUCH OF what takes place in a classroom, including that which we have come to take for granted, emerges from a set of assumptions about the nature of human nature. Not only how children are disciplined, but the very fact that influencing their actions is viewed as "discipline" in the first place; not merely how we grade students, but the fact that we grade them at all; not simply how teachers and students interact, but the fact that

---

*Our society's current infatuation with the word *competitiveness*, which has leached into discussions about education, only exacerbates the problem by encouraging a confusion between two very different ideas: excellence and the desperate quest to triumph over other people.

interaction *between students* is rarely seen as integral to the process of learning — all of these facts ultimately rest on an implicit theory of what human beings are like.

Consider the fact that most conversations about changing the way children act in a classroom tend to focus on curbing negative behaviors rather than on promoting positive ones. In part, this emphasis simply reflects the urgency of preventing troublesome or even violent conduct. But this way of framing the issue may also tell us something about our view of what comes naturally to children, what they are capable of, and, by extension, what lies at the core of our species. Likewise, it is no coincidence, I think, that the phrase "it's just human nature to be . . ." is invariably followed by such adjectives as selfish, competitive, lazy, aggressive, and so on. Very rarely do we hear someone protest, "Well, of course he was helpful. After all, it's just human nature to be generous."

The belief persists in this culture that our darker side is more pervasive, more persistent, and somehow more real than our capacity for what psychologists call "prosocial behavior." We seem to assume that people are naturally and primarily selfish and will act otherwise only if they are coerced into doing so and carefully monitored. The logical conclusion of this world view is the assumption that generous and responsible behavior must be forced down the throats of children who would otherwise be inclined to care only about themselves.

The belief persists in this culture that our darker side is more pervasive . . .

A review of several hundred studies has convinced me that this cynicism is not realism. Human beings are not only selfish and self-centered, but also decent, able to feel — and prepared to try to relieve — the pain of others. I believe that it is as "natural" to help as it is to hurt, that concern for the well-being of others often cannot be reduced to self-interest, that social structures predicated on human selfishness have no claim to inevitability — or even prudence. This is not the place for rehearsing the arguments and data that support these conclusions — in part because I have recently done so at book length.[2] But I would like to mention a few recent findings from developmental psychology that speak to the question of whether educators can aim higher than producing a quiet classroom or a nondisruptive child.

To start at the beginning, newborns are more likely to cry — and to cry longer — when they are exposed to the sound of another infant's crying than when they hear other noises that are equally loud and sudden. In three sets of studies with infants ranging in age from 18 to 72 hours, such crying seemed to be a spontaneous reaction rather than a mere vocal imitation.[3] In the view of Abraham Sagi and Martin Hoffman, who conducted one of the studies, this finding suggests the existence of "a rudimentary empathic distress reaction at birth."[4] Our species may be primed, in other words, to be discomfited by someone else's discomfort.

As an infant grows, this discomfort continues and takes more sophisticated forms. Marian Radke-Yarrow, Carolyn Zahn-Waxler, and their associates at the National Institute of Mental Health have been studying toddlers for nearly 20 years, having in effect deputized mothers as research assistants to collect data in the home instead of relying on brief (and possibly unrepresentative) observations in the laboratory. A 10- to 14-month-old child, they have found, can be expected to show signs of agitation and unhappiness in the presence of another person's distress, perhaps by crying or burying her

head in her mother's lap. As a child develops the capacity to undertake more deliberate behavior, in the period between 18 and 24 months, his response to distress will become more active: patting the head, fetching a toy, offering verbal expressions of sympathy, finding an adult to help, and so forth.[5]

I should add that, like all parents, researchers have also observed hostile and selfish actions on the part of children. To say that sympathy or helping behavior is pervasive and precocious is not to claim that every child is an angel or to deny that toddlers — particularly in a society preoccupied with possessiveness — will sometimes snatch back a toy ("Mine!") or throw it across the room. But it is to argue that the *antisocial* is no more basic or natural than the *prosocial*.

By the time children are of preschool age, comforting, sharing, and helping are regular occurrences. One study of preschoolers during free play discovered that 67 of the 77 children shared with, helped, or comforted another child at least once during only 40 minutes of observation.[6] After counting such behaviors in similar experiments of her own, Arizona State University psychologist Nancy Eisenberg became curious about why children were acting this way. To find out, she came up with a technique that few research psychologists had thought to use: she *asked* the children.

Eisenberg and a colleague simply followed 4- and 5-year-olds around a preschool and watched for unprompted prosocial behavior. Each time such an act was observed, the child was asked why he or she did it. ("How come you gave that to John?") None of the children intended to conform to adult expectations or expressed any fear of punishment. Very few said that they expected to benefit in some way by helping—such as by impressing their peers. Among the most frequent explanations heard was the simple observation that the other child had needed help.[7] This, when you come right down to it, is the heart of altruism.[8] And it is enough to suggest that parents and educators hoping to raise a child who

is responsive to the needs of others already have "an ally within the child," in Martin Hoffman's lovely phrase.

IF WE HAD to pick a logical setting in which to guide children toward caring about, empathizing with, and helping other people, it would be a place where they would regularly come into contact with their peers and where some sort of learning is already taking place. The school is such an obvious choice that one wonders how it could be that the active encouragement of prosocial values and behavior — apart from occasional exhortations to be polite — plays no part in the vast majority of American classrooms. This would seem to stem either from a lack of interest in the idea or from some objection to using the schools in particular for this purpose. Both factors probably play a role, but I will concentrate here on the latter and consider three specific reservations that parents, teachers, policy makers, and others may have — or at least may hear and thus need to answer — about classroom-based programs to help children develop a prosocial orientation.

The first objection is that an agenda concerned with social and moral issues amounts to teaching values — a dangerous business for a public institution. In response, we must concede that a prosocial agenda is indeed value-laden, but we should immediately add that the very same is true of the status quo. The teacher's presence and behavior, her choice of text, the order in which she presents ideas, and her tone of voice are as much part of the lesson as the curriculum itself. So, too, is a teacher's method of discipline or classroom management saturated in values, regardless of whether those values are transparent to the teacher. In short, to arrange our schools so that caring, sharing, helping, and empathizing are actively encouraged is not to introduce values into a neutral environment; it is to examine the values already in place and to consider trading them in for a new set.

It is sometimes said that moral conformance. The development of prosocial values is realized as an unintended bonus.

EDUCATION of character in Buber's sense asks of teachers something more than the mere elimination of behavior problems in the classroom. The absence of such problems is often seen as an invitation to move past behavioral and social issues and get on with the business at hand, which is academic learning. I am arguing, by contrast, that behavioral and social issues, values and character, are very much part of the business at hand. But whether we are talking about addressing misconduct or about taking the initiative to help students become more responsive to one another, a teacher can take any of several basic orientations. Here are four approaches to changing behaviors and attitudes, presented in ascending order of desirability.

1. Punishing. A reliance on the threat of punishment is a reasonably good indication that something is wrong in a classroom, since children have to be bullied into acting the way the teacher demands. Apart from the disagreeable nature of this style of interaction — which cannot be disguised, incidentally, by referring to punishment as "consequences" — it is an approach distinguished mostly by its ineffectiveness. Decades of research have established that children subjected to punitive discipline at home are *more* likely than their peers to break rules when they are away from home.

Isolating a child from his peers, humiliating her, giving him an F, loading her with extra homework, or even threatening to do any of these things can produce compliance in the short run. Over the long haul, however, this strategy is unproductive.

Why? First, at best, punishment teaches nothing about what one is supposed to do — only about what one is not supposed to do. There is an enormous difference between not beating up one's peers, on the one hand, and being helpful, on the other.

Second, the child's attention is not really focused on the intended lesson at all ("pushing people is bad"), much less on the rationale for this principle, but primarily on the punishment itself. Figuring out how to get away with the misbehavior, how to avoid detection by an authority, is a perfectly logical response. (Notice that the one who punishes be-

---

cerns and social skills ought to be taught at home. I know of no one in the field of education or child development who disagrees. The problem is that such instruction — along with nurturance and warmth, someone to model altruism, opportunities to practice caring for others, and so forth — is not to be found in all homes. The school may need to provide what some children will not otherwise get. In any case, there is no conceivable danger in providing these values in both environments. Encouragement from more than one source to develop empathic relationships is a highly desirable form of redundancy.

The second concern one hears — and this one dovetails with the broader absence of interest in the prosocial realm — is the fear that children taught to care about others will be unable to look out for themselves when they are released into a heartless society. The idea that someone exposed to such a program will grow up gullible and spineless, destined to be victimized by mean-spirited individuals, can be traced back to the prejudice that selfishness and competitiveness are efficacious social strategies — a sterling example of what sociologist C. Wright Mills used to call "crackpot realism." In fact, those whose mantra is "look out for number one" are actually at a greater disadvantage in any sort of society than those who are skilled at working with others and inclined to do so. Competition and the single-minded pursuit of narrowly conceived self-interest typically turn out to be counterproductive.

By contrast, a well-designed program of prosocial instruction will include training in cooperative conflict resolution and in methods of achieving one's goals that do not require the use of force or manipulation. But even without such a component, there is nothing about caring for others that implies not caring for or looking after oneself. A raft of research has established that assertiveness, healthy self-esteem, and popularity are all com-

patible with — and often even correlates of — a prosocial orientation.[9]

The final objection to teaching children to be caring individuals is that the time required to do so comes at the expense of attention to academics — a shift in priorities apt to be particularly unpopular at a time when we entertain ourselves by describing how much students don't know. In fact, though, there is absolutely no evidence to suggest that prosocial children — or the sort of learning experiences that help to create them — are mutually exclusive with academic achievement. To the contrary, the development of perspective-taking — the capacity to imagine how someone else thinks, feels, or sees the world — tends to promote cognitive problem solving generally. In one study, the extent to which girls had these skills at age 8 or 9 was a powerful predictor of performance on reading and spelling tests taken two years later — an even better predictor, in fact, than their original test scores.[10]

Not only are the ingredients of a prosocial orientation conducive to academic excellence, but the educational process itself does not require us to choose between teaching children to think and teaching them to care. It is possible to integrate prosocial lessons into the regular curriculum; as long as children are learning to read and spell and think critically, they may as well learn with texts that encourage perspective-taking. Indeed, to study literature or history by grappling with social and moral dilemmas is to invite a deeper engagement with those subjects. Meanwhile, literally hundreds of studies have shown that cooperative learning, which has an important place in a prosocial classroom, enhances achievement regardless of subject matter or age level.[11] So consistent and remarkable have these results been that schools and individual teachers often adopt models of cooperative learning primarily to strengthen academic per-

---

> **There is nothing about caring for others that implies not caring for oneself.**

> # Like sticks, carrots are artificial attempts to manipulate behavior.

comes transformed in the child's eye into a rule-enforcer who is best avoided.) Social learning theory tells us that this attention to the punishment is also likely to *teach* the child to be punitive and thus exacerbate the behavior problems; a teacher's actions do indeed speak louder than words.

Finally, punishment breeds resistance and resentment. "The more you use power to try to control people, the less real influence you'll have on their lives," Thomas Gordon has written.[12] Since such influence is associated with helping children to develop good values, the use of power would seem ill-advised.

2. Bribing. There is no question that rewards are better than punishment. On the other hand, what these two methods share is probably more important than the respects in which they differ, and herein lies a tale that will be highly disconcerting to educators enamored of positive reinforcement. Psychological—and particularly developmental—theory and research have come a long way since the simplistic behaviorism of the last generation, but many well-meaning teachers continue to assume that what works for training the family pet must be appropriate for shaping children's actions and values as well.

Gold stars, smiley faces, trophies, certificates, high grades, extra recess time, candy, money, and even praise all share the feature of being "extrinsic" to whatever behavior is being rewarded. Like sticks, carrots are artificial attempts to manipulate behavior that offer children *no reason to continue acting in the desired way when there is no longer any goody to be gained.* Do rewards motivate students? Absolutely. They motivate students to get rewarded. What they fail to do is help children develop a commitment to being generous or respectful.

In fact, the news is even worse than this. Not only is bribing someone to act in a particular way ultimately ineffective, but, like the use of threats, it can actually make things worse. Consider the effects of rewards on achievement. Yale psychologist Robert Sternberg recently summed up what a growing number of motivation researchers now concede: "Nothing tends to undermine creativity quite like extrinsic motivators do. They also undermine intrinsic motivation: when you give extrinsic rewards for certain kinds of behavior, you tend to reduce children's interest in performing those behaviors for their own sake."[13] Once we see ourselves as doing something in order to get a reward, we are less likely to want to continue doing it in the absence of a reward — even if we used to find it enjoyable.

Readers of the *Kappan* were first exposed to research demonstrating this phenomenon more than 15 years ago,[14] and the data have continued to accumulate since then, with some studies concentrating on how extrinsic motivators reduce intrinsic interest and others showing how they undermine performance, particularly on creative tasks.[15] A number of explanations have been proposed to account for these remarkably consistent findings. First, people who think of themselves as working for a reward feel controlled, and this lack of self-determination interferes with creativity. Second, rewards encourage "ego involvement" to the exclusion of "task involvement," and the latter is more predictive of achievement. Third, the promise of a reward is "tantamount to declaring that the activity is not worth doing for its own sake," as A. S. Neill put it;[16] indeed, anything construed as a prerequisite to some other goal will probably be devalued as a result.

What is true for academic learning also applies to behavior. A little-known series of studies has pointed up the folly of trying to encourage prosocial behavior through the use of extrinsic incentives. Children who received rewards for donating to another child—and, in another experiment, adults who were paid for helping a researcher—turned out to be less likely to describe themselves in words suggesting intrinsic motivation to help than were people who received nothing in return.[17] In another study, women offered money for answering a questionnaire were less likely to agree to a similar request two or three days later, when no money was involved, than were women who had not been paid for helping with the first survey.[18]

The implication is that, when someone is rewarded for prosocial behavior, that person will tend to assume that the reward accounts for his or her actions and thus will be less likely to help once no one is around to hand out privileges or praise. Indeed, elementary school students whose mothers believed in using rewards to motivate them were less cooperative and generous than other children in a recent study.[19] Such findings are of more than theoretical interest given the popularity of Skinnerian techniques for promoting generosity in schools. A recent *New York Times* article described elementary schools where helpful children have their pictures posted in hallways, get to eat at a special table in the cafeteria, or even receive money.[20] Such contrivances may actually have the effect of undermining the very prosocial orientation that their designers hope to promote.

3. Encouraging commitment to values. To describe the limitations of the use of punishments and rewards is already to suggest a better way: the teacher's goal should not be simply to produce a given behavior — for example, to get a child to share a cookie or stop yelling — but to help that child see himself or herself as the kind of person who is responsible and caring. From this shift in self-concept will come lasting behaviors and values that are not contingent on the presence of someone to dispense threats or bribes. The child has made these behaviors and values his or her own.

A student manipulated by currently fashionable behavioral techniques, however, is unlikely to internalize the values underlying the desired behaviors. At the heart of "assertive discipline," for example, is control: "I want teachers to learn that they have to take charge," Lee Canter explained recently.[21] I don't. I want *children* to become responsible for what they do and for what kind of people they are. The teacher has a critical role to play in making sure that this happens; in criticizing manipulative approaches I am not suggesting that children be left alone

From preschool to high school, children should learn why helping others is good.

to teach themselves responsibility. But the teacher ought to be guided less by the need to maintain control over the classroom than by the long-term objective of helping students to act responsibly because they understand that it is right to do so.

I will have more to say below about strategies for facilitating this internalization, but first I want to mention a version of this process that I believe is even more desirable — the ideal approach to helping children become good people.

4. Encouraging the group's commitment to values. What the first two approaches have in common is that they provide nothing more than extrinsic motivation. What the first two share with the third is that they address only the individual child. I propose that helpfulness and responsibility ought not to be taught in a vacuum but in the context of a community of people who learn and play and make decisions together. More precisely, the idea is not just to internalize good values *in* a community but to internalize, among other things, the value *of* community.

Perhaps the best way to crystallize what distinguishes each of these four approaches is to imagine the question that a child is encouraged to ask by each. An education based on punishment prompts the query, "What am I supposed to do, and what will happen to me if I don't do it?" An education based on rewards leads the child to ask, "What am I supposed to do, and what will I get for doing it?" When values have been internalized by the child, the question becomes "What kind of person do I want to be?" And, in the last instance, the child wonders: "How do we want our classroom (or school) to be?"

EDUCATORS eager to have children think about how they want their classrooms to be — which is to say, educators who do not feel threatened at the prospect of inviting children to share some of the responsibility for creating norms and determining goals — need to think in terms of five broad categories: what they believe, what they say, what they do, how they relate to students, and how they encourage students to relate to one another. Let us consider each in turn.

What educators believe. The famous Pygmalion effect refers to the fact that a teacher's assumptions about a child's intellectual potential can affect that child's performance. Such self-fulfilling prophecies, however, are by no means limited to academics; they also operate powerfully on a child's actions and values. Write off a student as destructive or disruptive, and he or she is likely to "live down to" these expectations. Conversely — and here is the decisive point for anyone concerned with promoting generosity — attributing to a child the best possible motive that is consistent with the facts may set in motion an "auspicious" (rather than a vicious) circle. We help students develop good values by assuming whenever possible that they are already motivated by these values — rather than by explaining an ambiguous action in terms of a sinister desire to make trouble.

However, what we assume about a given student is also colored by our assumptions regarding human nature itself. While I am not aware of any research on this question, it seems reasonable to suppose that an educator who thinks that self-interest motivates everything we do will be suspicious of individual instances of generosity. Someone who takes for granted that a Hobbesian state of nature would exist in a classroom in the absence of a controlling adult to keep children in line, who believes that children need to be leaned on or "taught a lesson" or bribed to act responsibly, is likely to transfer these expectations to the individual child and to produce an environment that fulfills them. The belief that children are actually quite anxious to please adults, that they may simply lack the skills to get what they need, that they will generally respond to a caring environment can create a very different reality. What you believe matters.

What educators say. An immense body of research has shown that children are more likely to follow a rule if its rationale has been explained to them and that, in general, discipline based on reason is more effective than the totalitarian approach captured by the T-shirt slogan "Because I'm the mommy, that's why." This finding applies not only to discouraging aggression but to promoting altruism. From preschool to high school, children should learn why — not merely be told that — helping others is good. Pointing out how their actions affect others sensitizes students to the needs and feelings of others and tacitly communicates a message of trust and responsibility. It implies that, once children understand how their behavior makes other people feel, they can and will choose to do something about it.

How such explanations are framed also counts. First, the level of the discourse should be fitted to the child's ability to understand. Second, the concept of using reason does not preclude passion. A prohibition on hurting people, for example, should not be offered dispassionately but with an emotional charge to show that it matters. Third, prosocial activity should not be promoted on the basis of self-interest. "Zachary, if you don't share your dump truck with Linda, she won't let you play with her dinosaur" has an undeniable appeal for a parent, but it is a strategy more likely to inculcate self-regarding shrewdness than genuine concern for others. The same goes for classroom exhortations and instruction.

A series of studies by Joan Grusec of the University of Toronto and her colleagues is also relevant. Her research provides a concrete alternative to the use of rewards or praise to elicit generosity. "Children who view their prosocial conduct as compliance with external authority will act prosocially only when they believe external pressures are present," she has written. Far preferable is for children to "come to believe that their prosocial behavior reflects values or dispositions in themselves."[22]

This result is best achieved by verbally attributing such values or dispositions to the child. In one experiment, in which children gave away some of their game winnings after watching a model do so, those who were told that they had made the donation "because you're the kind of person who likes to help other people" were subsequently more generous than those who were told that they had donated because they were expected to do so.[23] In another study, the likelihood of children's donating increased both when they were praised and when they were led to think of themselves as helpful people. But in a follow-up experiment, it was the latter group who turned out to be more generous than those who had received verbal reinforcement. In other words, praise increased generosity in a given setting but ceased to be effective outside of that setting, whereas children with an intrinsic impulse to be generous continued to act on that motivation in other circumstances.[24]

A study of adults drives home the point. Subjects who were told that a personality test showed that they were kind and thoughtful people were more likely to help a confederate who "accidentally" dropped a pile of cards than were those who were told that they were unusually intelligent or those given no feedback at all. This finding is important because it implies that being led to think of oneself as generous does not affect behavior merely because it is a kind of reinforcement or a mood-enhancer; this label apparently encourages prosocial action because it helps to build a view of the self as altruistic.[25]

This is not to suggest that a teacher's every utterance must be — or can be — geared toward internalization. Simply making sure that a classroom is a safe environment conducive to learning can require the sort of behavioral interventions on a day-to-day basis that don't do much to strengthen a child's prosocial self-concept. But the more teachers attend to the latter, the fewer problems they are likely to have over the long run.

What educators do. Children of all ages, from before the time they can read until after the time they start seeking distance from adults, learn from what they see. Studies show that children who watched, even briefly, as someone donated to charity were themselves likely to donate more than other children — even if months had elapsed since the exposure to the model.[26] The extent to which a teacher expresses concern about people in distress and takes the initiative to help

— which applies both to how the teacher treats the students themselves and how he or she refers to people outside the classroom — can set a powerful example and be even more effective than didactic instruction in promoting a sense of caring in students.

There is no shortage of suggestions about how to devise lessons that address social and ethical issues, ranging from explicit training in perspective-taking or moral reasoning to discussions about values that can, in turn, include either "clarification" of the beliefs that students already hold or old-fashioned lectures on character or morality. Most of the debate on the subject occurs between proponents of just such programs, each accusing the other of being relativistic or of seeking to indoctrinate. Far less consideration is given to the possibility of integrating such issues into the regular curriculum.

A distinction, though not a sharp one, can be made between teaching morality (or about morality) as such and helping children to be positively connected to others. The latter is my focus here, and some writers have argued that, particularly for younger children, it ought to be the primary focus in the schools, too. "Unless the young child has acquired a positive propensity towards other persons," says one educator, "subsequent moral education will become virtually impotent."[27]

As an alternative to special units devoted to one of these approaches, children can use texts in conventional subject areas that encourage perspective-taking. This option should allay the concern that moral instruction will distract us from academics.

How educators relate to students. Preceding and underlying specific techniques for encouraging particular behaviors is the practice of nesting all kinds of discipline and instruction in the context of a warm, nurturant, and empathic relationship with students. Children whose parents are interested in and supportive of them usually distinguish themselves as socially competent and psychologically healthy on a range of measures, and there is no reason to think that the teacher/student relationship is any different.

Warm, caring, empathic adults do several things at once. They provide the child with a benevolent, safe place in which to act. (If a child's experience with others leaves him or her feeling threatened rather than safe, this is likely to fos-

ter psychological damage control at the expense of any inclination to help others.) I hope that few educators take seriously the absurd dictum that teachers should display no warmth until well into the school year — after firm control of the classroom has been won. Instead, teachers should establish themselves from the beginning as the students' allies, adults with whom they can work to solve the problems that emerge during the normal course of development. In meeting a child's emotional needs we give him or her the emotional freedom to meet the needs of others.

How educators encourage students to relate to one another. Anyone interested in children as social beings must recognize the need to attend to the interactions among them in the classroom. In most American schools, children are forced to work either against one another (by competing) or apart from one another (by learning individually). The chance to work *with* one another, to learn social skills and caring, is left to happen by itself during recess, at lunch, or after school. This single fact goes a long way toward explaining why people in our society tend to regard others as potential obstacles to their own success. David Johnson and Roger Johnson of the University of Minnesota have emphasized that the relationship between student and student is at least as important as that between student and teacher or between student and curriculum. Their reference to student/student relationships is offered in the context of creating good learners, and it is all the more true in terms of creating good human beings.

How, specifically, should teachers encourage student interaction? First, students can be put in pairs or small groups so as to help one another learn. This concept, known as cooperative learning, embraces many disparate models for implementation: some depend on grades and other extrinsic incentives to insure that students work together, some involve cooperation among as well as within groups, some provide for a strict division of labor in completing assignments. A substantial number of studies have found that cooperative learning of various types has the potential to help students feel good about themselves, feel good about each other, feel good about what they are learning, and learn more effectively.

Cooperation, by virtue of being an interaction in which two or more people

Do quiet children learn more effectively or merely make fewer demands on teachers?

work together for mutual benefit, is not itself an example of prosocial behavior as the term is usually used. Neither does its successful use presuppose the existence of prosocial motives in all children. Rather, by creating interdependence and a built-in incentive to help, cooperative learning *promotes* prosocial behavior. Having children learn from one another creates powerful bonds between them and sends a message very different from that sent by a classroom in which each child is on his or her own — or, worse still, one in which the success of each is inversely related to the success of the others.[28]

In one study, fifth-graders who studied grammar in cooperative learning groups were more likely to give away prize tokens to a stranger than were those who studied on their own; in another, kindergartners who participated in cooperative activities acted more prosocially than their peers in a traditional classroom.[29] But the consequences are not limited to generosity per se. Carefully structured cooperative learning also promotes a subjective sense of group identity, a greater acceptance of people who are different from oneself (in terms of ethnicity or ability level), and a more sophisticated ability to imagine other people's points of view.[30] Cooperation is an essentially humanizing experience that predisposes participants to take a benevolent view of others. It allows them to transcend egocentric and objectifying postures and encourages trust, sensitivity, open communication, and prosocial activity.

Second, teachers can move the idea of discipline not only away from punishments and rewards but also away from the premise of these strategies — namely, that teachers should simply be figuring out by themselves how to elicit compliance with a set of rules or goals that they alone devise. The realistic alternative is not for the teacher to abdicate responsibility for what happens in the classroom but rather to bring in (and guide) children so that they can play a role in making decisions about how their

classroom is to be run and why. (Must hands always be raised or only during certain kinds of discussions? What is the best way for the class as a community to balance principles of fairness and the spontaneity that encourages participation?)

Discipline would thus be reconfigured as collaborative planning and mutual problem solving. Such an approach will be preferred by anyone who favors the idea of autonomy and democratic decision making — but it can also be argued that purely practical considerations recommend it, since children are more likely to follow rules that they have helped to create than rules dictated to them. This, of course, assumes that following rules is in itself a desirable goal. More broadly, educators need to ask themselves and each other about the ultimate objective of discipline. Even if one of the conventional programs of behavior control succeeded in keeping children quiet, do quiet children learn more effectively or merely make fewer demands on the teacher? (The Johnsons like to say that a principal walking through the school corridors should be concerned if he or she hears no sound coming from a classroom; this means that real learning probably is not taking place.) And which approach is most likely to help children come to care about one another?

To invite children to participate in making decisions not only about classroom procedures but also about pedagogical matters (what is to be learned, how, and why) and housekeeping matters (how to celebrate birthdays or decorate the walls) is to bring them into a process of discussion, an opportunity to cooperate and build consensus. To this extent, it is a chance for them to practice perspective-taking skills, to share and listen and help. In short, involving children in planning and decision making is a way of providing a framework for prosocial interactions that supports other such opportunities; it turns a routine issue into another chance to learn about and practice caring—and, not so incidentally, thinking as well.[31]

Finally, educators can provide students with opportunities to be responsible for one another so that they will learn (prosocial values and skills) by doing. Ideally, this can include interaction with those of different ages. For an older child to guide someone younger is to experience firsthand what it is to be a helper and to be responsible for someone who is dependent on him or her. For the younger child, this cross-age interaction presents an opportunity to see a prosocial model who is not an adult.

ONE OF THE most exciting and innovative educational programs now in operation, the Child Development Project (CDP), is devoted specifically to helping children become more caring and responsible.[32] The experience of the CDP offers lessons in the systematic application of many of the ideas discussed here; indeed, I owe my formulation of some of these ideas to the work done by Eric Schaps, Marilyn Watson, and others involved with the project.

The CDP is the first long-term, comprehensive, school-based project in prosocial education. After being invited a decade ago to work in the San Ramon Valley (California) Unified School District, about 30 miles east of San Francisco, the staff carefully matched two sets of three elementary schools in the district for size and socioeconomic status. A coin flip then determined which of these sets would receive the program and which would serve as the comparison group. The first teachers were trained before the start of the 1982–83 school year. Staff researchers focused on a group of children in the experimental schools (then in kindergarten and now in junior high school) to assess whether their attitudes, behavior, and achievement differed significantly from those of their counterparts in the comparison schools. In the fall of 1988, the program was introduced into two elementary schools in nearby Hayward, a district more ethnically diverse than the white, affluent suburbs in San Ramon Valley,

Prosocial values come from a synthesis of adult inculcation and peer interaction.

and Schaps is now seeking funding to take the program to eight more sites around the country.

"How do we want our classroom to be?" is exactly the question that the CDP would have children ask. Rejecting punishment and rewards in favor of strategies geared toward internalization of prosocial norms and values, the CDP invites teachers and students to work together to turn their classrooms into caring communities. The primary components of the program intended to bring this about are these:

• a version of cooperative learning that does not rely on grades or other extrinsic motivators;

• the use of a literature-based reading program that stimulates discussion about values and offers examples of empathy and caring even as it develops verbal skills;

• an approach to classroom management in which the emphasis is on developing intrinsic motives to participate productively and prosocially, in which teachers are encouraged to develop warm relationships with the children, and in which periodic class meetings are held so that children can play an active role in planning, assessing progress, and solving problems; and

• a variety of other features, including pairing children of different ages to work together, setting up community service projects to develop responsibility, giving periodic homework assignments specifically designed to be done (and to foster communication) with parents, and holding schoolwide activities that may involve whole families.

In their writings, members of the CDP staff have distinguished their way of teaching values from the approaches of better-known models. Unlike certain kinds of character education, the CDP approach emphasizes helping students understand the reason for a given value rather than simply insisting that they ac-

cept it or behave in a certain way because they have been told to do so. Unlike purely child-centered approaches, however, the CDP is committed to the importance of adult socialization: the teacher's job is to teach, to guide, to enforce, to facilitate cooperation, to model behaviors — in short, to be much more than a passive bystander. Prosocial values come from a synthesis of adult inculcation and peer interaction, and these values — in contrast to the programs developed by some theorists in the area of moral reasoning — emphasize caring for others as well as applying principles of fairness.

Prior to the implementation of the CDP, students randomly selected from the three experimental and the three comparison schools proved to be similar not only demographically but also on a range of social attitudes, values, and skills. Once the program was implemented, however, structured interviews and observations turned up significant differences between students participating in the program and those in the comparison schools on some, though not all, measures.

Children taking part in the CDP engaged in a greater number of spontaneous prosocial behaviors in class, seemed better able to understand hypothetical conflict situations, and were more likely to take everyone's needs into account in dealing with such situations. They were more likely to believe that one has an obligation to speak up in a discussion even if one's position seems unlikely to prevail (which should answer those concerned about the assertiveness of caring children). While the CDP's emphasis has not required any sacrifice of conventional achievement (as measured by standardized test scores), neither has it given participants a consistent academic advantage over students in comparison schools. (In part, this finding may be due to a ceiling effect: students in the district already score in the top 10% of California school-

children, so there is not much room for improvement.) By the time the CDP group reached sixth grade, though, they were outscoring their counterparts in the comparison schools on a measure of higher-order reading comprehension (essays written about stories and poems).

It remains to be seen whether and in what ways the values and behaviors of children from schools using the CDP will continue to distinguish them from those who attended comparison schools now that they are all in junior high school. But this pilot project provides real evidence for the larger point I am making here: it is both realistic and valuable to attend to what students learn in the classroom about getting along with their peers. Children can indeed be raised to work with, care for, and help one another. And schools must begin to play an integral role in that process.

1. Martin Buber, *Between Man and Man*, trans. Ronald Gregor Smith (New York: Macmillan, 1965), p. 104.

2. Alfie Kohn, *The Brighter Side of Human Nature: Altruism and Empathy in Everyday Life* (New York: Basic Books, 1990).

3. Marvin L. Simner, "Newborn's Response to the Cry of Another Infant," *Developmental Psychology*, vol. 5, 1971, pp. 136-50; Abraham Sagi and Martin L. Hoffman, "Empathic Distress in the Newborn," *Developmental Psychology*, vol. 12, 1976, pp. 175-76; and Grace B. Martin and Russell D. Clark III, "Distress Crying in Neonates: Species and Peer Specificity," *Developmental Psychology*, vol. 18, 1982, pp. 3-9.

4. Sagi and Hoffman, p. 176.

5. See, for example, Carolyn Zahn-Waxler and Marian Radke-Yarrow, "The Development of Altruism: Alternative Research Strategies," in Nancy Eisenberg-Berg, ed., *The Development of Prosocial Behavior* (New York: Academic Press, 1982).

6. Marian Radke-Yarrow and Carolyn Zahn-Waxler, "Dimensions and Correlates of Prosocial Behavior in Young Children," *Child Development*, vol. 47, 1976, pp. 118-25.

7. Nancy Eisenberg-Berg and Cynthia Neal, "Children's Moral Reasoning About Their Own Spontaneous Prosocial Behavior," *Developmental Psychology*, vol. 15, 1979, pp. 228-29. Eisenberg and another colleague have observed that appeals to authority or punishment (which were completely absent here) are what one would expect if the chil-

dren were at Lawrence Kohlberg's first stage of moral reasoning and that the apparently altruistic needs-oriented explanations have often — and presumably unfairly — been coded as stage 2, that is, as an immature, "preconventional" way of thinking about moral problems (see Nancy Eisenberg-Berg and Michael Hand, "The Relationship of Preschoolers' Reasoning About Prosocial Moral Conflicts to Prosocial Behavior," *Child Development*, vol. 50, 1979, pp. 356-63).

8. The tendency to define *altruism* so narrowly that only Mother Teresa would qualify for the label both reflects and perpetuates a cynical view of human nature. It would never occur to us to define *aggression* so as to exclude everything short of mass murder.

9. Kohn, Ch. 3.

10. Norma Deitch Feshbach and Seymour Feshbach, "Affective Processes and Academic Achievement," *Child Development*, vol. 58, 1987, pp. 1335-47. For more research on cognitive skills and perspective-taking, see David W. Johnson and Frank P. Johnson, *Joining Together: Group Theory and Group Skills*, 3rd ed. (Englewood Cliffs, N.J.: Prentice-Hall, 1987), p. 244.

11. For example, see David Johnson et al., "Effects of Cooperative, Competitive, and Individualistic Goal Structures on Achievement: A Meta-Analysis," *Psychological Bulletin*, vol. 89, 1981, pp. 47-62; David W. Johnson and Roger T. Johnson, *Cooperation and Competition* (Edina, Minn.: Interaction Book Co., 1989), especially Ch. 3; and Robert E. Slavin, *Cooperative Learning: Theory, Research, and Practice* (Englewood Cliffs, N.J.: Prentice-Hall, 1990), especially Ch. 2.

12. Thomas Gordon, *Teaching Children Self-Discipline* (New York: Times Books, 1989), p. 7.

13. Robert J. Sternberg, "Prototypes of Competence and Incompetence," in Robert J. Sternberg and John Kolligian, Jr., eds., *Competence Considered* (New Haven: Yale University Press, 1990), p. 144.

14. Mark R. Lepper and David Greene, "When Two Rewards Are Worse Than One: Effects of Extrinsic Rewards on Intrinsic Motivation," *Phi Delta Kappan*, April 1975, pp. 565-66.

15. See, for example, Edward Deci and Richard Ryan, *Intrinsic Motivation and Self-Determination in Human Behavior* (New York: Plenum Press, 1985); Mark R. Lepper and David Greene, eds., *The Hidden Costs of Reward* (Hillsdale, N.J.: Erlbaum, 1978); and the work of John Nicholls, Teresa Amabile, Judith M. Harackiewicz, Mark Morgan, and Ruth Butler. I have reviewed some of this re-

search in "Group Grade Grubbing Versus Cooperative *Learning*," *Educational Leadership*, February 1991, pp. 83-87.

16. Quoted in Mark Morgan, "Reward-Induced Decrements and Increments in Intrinsic Motivation," *Review of Educational Research*, vol. 54, 1984, p. 5.

17. Cathleen L. Smith et al., "Children's Causal Attributions Regarding Help Giving," *Child Development*, vol. 50, 1979, pp. 203-10; and C. Daniel Batson et al., "Buying Kindness: Effect of an Extrinsic Incentive for Helping on Perceived Altruism," *Personality and Social Psychology Bulletin*, vol. 4, 1978, pp. 86-91.

18. Miron Zuckerman, Michelle M. Lazzaro, and Diane Waldgeir, "Undermining Effects of the Foot-in-the-Door Technique with Extrinsic Rewards," *Journal of Applied Social Psychology*, vol. 9, 1979, pp. 292-96.

19. Richard A. Fabes et al., "Effects of Rewards on Children's Prosocial Motivation," *Developmental Psychology*, vol. 25, 1989, pp. 509-15.

20. Suzanne Daley, "Pendulum Is Swinging Back to the Teaching of Values in U.S. Schools," *New York Times*, 12 December 1990, p. B-14.

21. Quoted in David Hill, "Order in the Classroom," *Teacher Magazine*, April 1990, p. 77.

22. Joan E. Grusec and Theodore Dix, "The Socialization of Prosocial Behavior: Theory and Reality," in Carolyn Zahn-Waxler, E. Mark Cummings, and Ronald Iannotti, eds., *Altruism and Aggression: Biological and Social Origins* (Cambridge: Cambridge University Press, 1986), p. 220.

23. Joan E. Grusec et al., "Modeling, Direct Instruction, and Attributions: Effects on Altruism," *Developmental Psychology*, vol. 14, 1978, pp. 51-57.

24. Joan E. Grusec and Erica Redler, "Attribution, Reinforcement, and Altruism: A Developmental Analysis," *Developmental Psychology*, vol. 16, 1980, pp. 525-34.

25. Angelo Strenta and William DeJong, "The Effect of a Prosocial Label on Helping Behavior," *Social Psychology Quarterly*, vol. 44, 1981, pp. 142-47.

26. See James H. Bryan and Nancy H. Walbek, "Preaching and Practicing Generosity," *Child Development*, vol. 41, 1970, pp. 329-53; James H. Bryan and Perry London, "Altruistic Behavior by Children," *Psychological Bulletin*, vol. 72, 1970, pp. 200-211; Martin L. Hoffman, "Altruistic Behavior and the Parent-Child Relationship," *Journal of Personality and Social Psychology*, vol. 31, 1975, pp. 937-43; and Marian Radke-Yarrow, Phyllis M.

Scott, and Carolyn Zahn-Waxler, "Learning Concern for Others," *Developmental Psychology*, vol. 8, 1973, pp. 240-60.

27. Ben Spiecker, "Psychopathy: The Incapacity to Have Moral Emotions," *Journal of Moral Education*, vol. 17, 1988, p. 103.

28. For an analysis of the harms of competition in the classroom and elsewhere, see Alfie Kohn, *No Contest: The Case Against Competition* (Boston: Houghton Mifflin, 1986).

29. David W. Johnson et al., "Effects of Cooperative Versus Individualized Instruction on Student Prosocial Behavior, Attitudes Toward Learning, and Achievement," *Journal of Educational Psychology*, vol. 68, 1976, pp. 446-52; and Bette Chambers, "Cooperative Learning in Kindergarten: Can It Enhance Students' Perspective-Taking Ability and Prosocial Behaviour?," unpublished manuscript, Concordia University, Montreal, 1990.

30. See, for example, the research cited in David W. Johnson and Roger T. Johnson, "The Socialization and Achievement Crisis: Are Cooperative Learning Experiences the Solution?," in Leonard Bickman, ed., *Applied Social Psychology Annual 4* (Beverly Hills, Calif.: Sage, 1983), p. 137; and Elliot Aronson and Diane Bridgeman, "Jigsaw Groups and the Desegregated Classroom: In Pursuit of Common Goals," *Personality and Social Psychology Bulletin*, vol. 5, 1979, p. 443.

31. Another classroom management issue is raised by Carolyn Zahn-Waxler. She warns that a teacher who routinely and efficiently takes care of a child in distress in order to preserve order in the classroom may unwittingly be teaching two lessons: 1) that "people do not react emotionally to upset in others" and 2) that, "if someone is hurt, someone else who is in charge will handle it" ("Conclusions: Lessons from the Past and a Look to the Future," in Zahn-Waxler, Cummings, and Iannotti, p. 310).

32. For more about the Child Development Project, see Alfie Kohn, "The ABC's of Caring," *Teacher Magazine*, January 1990, pp. 52-58; and idem, *The Brighter Side of Human Nature*, Ch. 6. For accounts written by members of the staff, see Victor Battistich et al., "The Child Development Project: A Comprehensive Program for the Development of Prosocial Character," in William M. Kurtines and Jacob L. Gewirtz, eds., *Moral Behavior and Development: Advances in Theory, Research, and Applications* (Hillsdale, N.J.: Erlbaum, 1989); and Daniel Solomon et al., "Cooperative Learning as Part of a Comprehensive Classroom Program Designed to Promote Prosocial Development," in Shlomo Sharan, ed., *Cooperative Learning: Theory and Research* (New York: Praeger, 1990).

The Good, The Bad And The DIFFERENCE

BARBARA KANTROWITZ

Like many children, Sara Newland loves animals. But unlike most youngsters, she has turned that love into activism. Five years ago, during a trip to the zoo, the New York City girl learned about the plight of endangered species, and decided to help. With the aid of her mother, Sara— then about 4 years old—baked cakes and cookies and sold them on the sidewalk near her apartment building. She felt triumphant when she raised $35, which she promptly sent in to the World Wildlife Fund.

A few weeks later, triumph turned into tears when the fund wrote Sara asking for more money. "She was devastated because she thought she had taken care of that problem," says Polly Newland, who then patiently told her daughter that there are lots of big problems that require continual help from lots of people. That explanation worked. Sara, now 9, has expanded her causes. Through her school, she helps out at an inner-city child-care center; she also regularly brings meals to homeless people in her neighborhood.

A sensitive parent can make all the difference in encouraging—or discouraging—a child's developing sense of morality and values. Psychologists say that not only are parents important as role models, they also have to be aware of a child's perception of the world at different ages and respond appropriately to children's concerns. "I think the capacity for goodness is there from the start," says Thomas Lickona, a professor of education at the State University of New York at Cortland and author of "Raising Good Children." But, he says, parents must nurture those instincts just as they help their children become good readers or athletes or musicians.

That's not an easy task these days. In the past, schools and churches played a key role in fostering moral development. Now, with religious influence in decline and schools wavering over

> **A sensitive parent is crucial in encouraging a child's sense of morality and values**
> —

the way to teach values, parents are pretty much on their own. Other recent social trends have complicated the transmission of values. "We're raising a generation that is still groping for a good future direction," says psychologist William Damon, head of Brown University's education department. Many of today's parents were raised in the '60s, the age of permissiveness. Their children were born in the age of affluence, the '80s, when materialism was rampant. "It's an unholy combination," says Damon.

These problems may make parents feel they have no effect on how their children turn out. But many studies show that parents are still the single most important influence on their children. Lickona says that the adolescents most likely to follow their consciences rather than give in to peer pressure are those who grew up in "authoritative" homes, where rules are firm but clearly explained and justified—as opposed to "authoritarian" homes (where rules are laid down without explanation) or "permissive" homes.

The way a parent explains rules depends, of course, on the age of the child. Many adults assume that kids see right and wrong in grown-up terms. But what may be seen as "bad" behavior by an adult may not be bad in the child's eyes. For example, a young child may not know the difference between a fanciful tale and a lie, while older kids—past the age of 5—do know.

Many psychologists think that in children, the seeds of moral values are emotional, not intellectual. Such traits as empathy and guilt— observable in the very young—represent the beginning of what will later be a conscience. Even newborns respond to signs of distress in others. In a hospital nursery, for example, a bout of crying by one infant will trigger wailing all around. Research on children's attachment to their mothers shows that babies who are most secure (and those whose mothers are most responsive to their needs) later turn out to be leaders in school: self-directed and eager to learn. They are also most likely to absorb parental values.

The first modern researcher to describe the stages of a child's moral development was Swiss psychologist Jean Piaget. In his groundbreaking 1932 book, "The Moral Judgment of the Child," he described three overlapping phases of childhood, from 5 to 12. The first is the "morality of constraint" stage: children accept adult rules as absolutes. Then comes the "morality of cooperation," in which youngsters think of morality as equal treatment. Parents of siblings will recognize this as the "If he got a new Ninja Turtle, I want one, too," stage. In the third, kids can see complexity in moral situations. They can understand extenuating circumstances in which strict equality might not necessarily mean fairness ("He got a new Ninja Turtle, but I got to go to the ball game, so it's OK.")

Although Piaget's conclusions have been expanded by subsequent researchers, his work forms the basis for most current theories of moral development. In a study begun in the 1950s, Lawrence Kohlberg, a Harvard professor, used "moral dilemmas" to define six phases. He began with 50 boys who were 10, 13 and 16. Over the next 20 years, he asked them their reactions to carefully constructed dilemmas. The most famous concerns a man named Heinz, whose wife was dying of cancer. The boys were told, in part, that a drug that might save her was a form of radium discovered by the town pharmacist. But the pharmacist was charging 10 times the cost of manufacture for the drug and Heinz could not afford it—although he tried to borrow money from everyone he knew. Heinz begged the pharmacist to sell it more cheaply, but he refused. So Heinz, in desperation, broke into the store and stole the drug. Kohlberg asked his subjects: Did Heinz do the right thing? Why?

Kohlberg and others found that at the first stage, children base their answers simply on the likelihood of getting caught. As they get older, their reasons for doing the right thing become more complex. For example, Lickona says typical 5-year-olds want to stay out of trouble. Kids from 6 to 9 characteristically act out of self-interest; most 10- to 13-year-olds crave social approval. Many 15- to 19-year-olds have moved on to thinking about maintaining the social system and being responsible.

Over the years, educators have used these theories to establish new curricula at schools around the country that emphasize moral development. The Lab School, a private preschool in Houston, was designed by Rheta DeVries, a student of Kohlberg's. The teacher is a "companion/guide," not an absolute authority figure. The object of the curriculum is to get kids to think about why they take certain actions and to think about consequences. For example, if two children are playing a game and one wants to change the rules, the teacher would ask the other child if that was all right. "Moral development occurs best when children live in an environment where fairness and justice is a way of life," says DeVries.

Not everyone agrees with the concept of moral development as a series of definable stages. Other researchers say that the stage theories downplay the role of emotion, empathy and faith. In "The Moral Life of Children," Harvard child psychiatrist Robert Coles tells the story of a 6-year-old black girl named Ruby, who braved vicious racist crowds to integrate her New Orleans school—and then prayed for her tormentors each night before she went to bed. Clearly, Coles says, she did not easily fall into any of Kohlberg's or Piaget's stages. Another criticism of stage theorists comes from feminist psychologists, including Carol Gilligan, author of "In a Different Voice." Gilligan says that the stages represent only *male* development with the emphasis on the concepts of justice and rights, not female development, which, she says, is more concerned with responsibility and caring.

But many psychologists say parents can use the stage theories to gain insight into their children's development. At each phase, parents should help their children make the right decisions about their behavior. In his book, Lickona describes a typical situation involving a 5-year-old who has hit a friend over the head with a toy while playing at the friend's house. Lickona suggests that the parents, instead of simply punishing their son, talk to him about why he hit his friend (the boy played with a toy instead of with him) and about what he could do next time instead of hitting. The parents, Lickona says, should also discuss how the friend might have felt about being hit. By the end of the discussion, the child should realize that there are consequences to his behavior. In Lickona's example, the child decides to call his friend and apologize—a positive ending.

For older children, Lickona suggests family "fairness meetings" to alleviate tension. If, for example, a brother and sister are constantly fighting, the parents could talk to both of them about what seem to be persistent sources of irritation. Then, youngsters can think of ways to bring about a truce—or at least a cease-fire. Children who learn these lessons can become role models for other youngsters—and for adults as well. Sara Newland tells her friends not to be scared of homeless people (most of them rush by without even a quick glance, she says). "Some people think, 'Why should I give to them?'" she says. "But I feel that you should give. If everyone gave food, they would all have decent meals." One recent evening, she and her mother fixed up three plates of beef stew to give out. They handed the first to the homeless man who's always on their corner. Then, Sara says, they noticed two "rough-looking guys" down the block. Sara's mother, a little scared, walked quickly past them. Then, she changed her mind and asked them if they'd like some dinner. "They said, 'Yes, God bless you'," Sara recalls. "At that moment, they weren't the same people who were looking through a garbage can for beer bottles a little while before. It brought out a part of them that they didn't know they had."

With Tessa Namuth *in New York and* Karen Springen *in Chicago*

111

Moral Education: An Idea Whose Time Has Gone

DAVID E. PURPEL

David E. Purpel is a professor at the School of Education, University of North Carolina at Greensboro.

Simply put, the most important and troubling of all human tasks (and hence a challenge for educators) is to be able to know what it means to live the virtuous life. No challenge is more central, more complex, or more conflictual; for, as history so cruelly shows us, differences in moral orientations have led to deep personal pain and enormous social tragedy. Such issues are inherently of incredible complexity, and they are made even more problematic by our particular historical and cultural traditions. Our democratic roots, our pluralistic society, and our memories of political and ideological authoritarianism make us extremely wary of any particular or singular moral code or creed. These traditions leave us in a state of continuous skepticism, if not distrust, ever on guard lest we fall under the domination of any moralistic hegemony.

Our reluctance as a culture to accept any moral vision save the broadest and most general is reinforced by our devotion to Enlightenment traditions of science, rationality, and humanism. Scholarship and research continue to erode what were once considered to be universal truths, everlasting values, and permanent visions. Knowledge and virtue have been relativized, contextualized, deconstructed, and demystified, if not devalued and discounted. Ironically and tragically, the brilliance and force of this scholarship has made the once bedrock assumption of education—namely, that "the truth shall make you free"—seem quaint if not hollow. Indeed, the once-liberating solutions to cultural arbitrariness, political autocracy, and intellectual rigidity that marked the Enlightenment have created anguishing problems of their own.

Our skepticism, our individuality, and our criticalness have left us alone, fragmented, and lost. In an era when we yearn to believe, our intellect cautions; in a time when we ache for community, our impulse for autonomy intervenes; and in an era when we desperately seek meaning, our rationality scorns. Our tragedy is that this predicament not only produces personal existential anguish but takes on the proportion of catastrophe in the face of our current massive social and cultural crises.

Our liberal traditions have led us to respond to social problems pragmatically, rationally, and sensibly, with the assumption that careful planning and technical knowledge can significantly ameliorate if not solve any problem. Auschwitz, Hiroshima, Cambodia, and the Gulag, as metaphors of this orientation gone mad, not only have shocked and horrified us but have also seriously aggravated our despair and paralysis. Indeed, we have come to understand that the destructive forces in our world are as powerful as ever, and today we find our entire planet and civilization to be at risk. Solutions to crises of this magnitude involve much more than good ideas and effective programs. What is required is a transformation in consciousness from our present one of competition, mastery, personalism, and success to one of cooperation, justice, community, and harmony.

This to me constitutes the fundamental challenge for education and more particularly for our profession, and yet the most painful characteristic of current educational professional efforts is the puniness of its response to our current social and cultural crises. The culture cries out for the imagination and courage to avoid the horrors of war, pollution, starvation, and disease, and the profession responds with initiatives such as career ladders, assertive discipline, and effective teaching. Alas, this timidity and blandness even extends to those more daring educators who have ventured into that troublesome area called moral education. It is always important to reiterate that education has perforce at least implicit moral dimensions, and, in that sense, there has always been and always will be "moral education." Moreover, we have had a history of more explicit efforts at providing direct moral education. The focus of this article is on the most recent efforts to conceptualize programs for moral education. As much as I admire the courage, imagination, and seriousness of these efforts, their success and shortcomings tell us much of the weaknesses of the profes-

From *The Clearing House*, Vol. 64, No. 5, May/June 1991, pp. 309-312. Reprinted with permission of the Helen Dwight Reid Educational Foundation. Published by Heldref Publications, 1319 Eighteenth St., N.W., Washington, DC 20036-1802.

sion's better efforts. My critique focuses not only on those hardy authors of moral education theories but also on their critics and those professionals who choose not to involve themselves at all with the issues of what constitutes a morally valid education. What we are left with after all the efforts, criticisms, and nonefforts in this recent moral education movement is a situation in which the profession is without an energizing moral discourse that responds to our critical social crises. Instead, we have the scattered remnants of a movement that, ironically, contributed to our moral paralysis, either through misguided efforts to be neutral or ill-guided efforts to preserve conventional morality or both.

To demonstrate my point, I focus (briefly) on the three most prominent recent approaches—the Simon and Raths values clarification approach; Kohlberg's cognitive-developmental theory; and the pro-social movement, perhaps best represented by the writings of Kevin Ryan.

The values clarification program involves an ingenious and deceptively simple pedagogy designed to encourage students to reflect on their personal feelings and "values" and to come to choose and affirm them. There is no particular effort to distinguish among categories of values, but the intent seems to be mainly one of encouraging and supporting individuals to be in close touch with their feelings and attitudes, to confront the responsibility of freely choosing, and thereby to achieve a sense of personal confidence and well-being. There is an attempt to avoid predetermined standards, to encourage open discussion and inner-reflection, but without reference to any particular intellectual or moral paradigm.

The so-called Kohlberg approach is, on the other hand, grounded in psychological and philosophical theories, particularly developmental psychology and naturalist philosophy. Although Kohlberg maintained a sense of hierarchy, it is a hierarchy he claimed to be rooted in nature. Thus he was able to present his scheme as descriptive and scientific. In contrast, values clarification eschews any judgmental orientation and posits itself as a neutral pedagogy; with its reliance on intense subjectivity, values clarification reveals an orientation toward the individual as the key decision-making unit. However, there is a similarity between the approaches. Although Kohlberg once boasted of the objectivity of his approach and the values clarification people of the subjectivity of theirs, both focus on the individual and both present their programs as "unbiased," intent only on facilitating natural processes that have been unnecessarily blocked.

In addition, both share a deficiency, namely, the failure to provide for any serious contemporary political, contextual, historical, or social analysis. It is as if there were no larger present and compelling context than hypothetical cases—as if the issues could be discussed without regard to particular social/political circumstances. (It should be pointed out that some of the Kohlberg-related research does commit itself generally to promoting democracy, but the fact remains that the focus on these

moral education programs is heavily psychological, with an emphasis on personal, cognitive, and emotional processes and without critical reference to political and social contingencies.) The emphasis then is on dealing with moral issues in a political vacuum, which, of course, is impossible if not disingenuous given what we now know about the hidden curriculum.

It seems that there are substantial elements of the public and the profession who are very wary about dealing explicitly and directly with values. Raising moral questions is, to some, troubling, disquieting, and threatening, and, to others, moral analysis is not scientific or objective enough to constitute valid research. Still others fear any effort that seriously questions the status quo. This attachment of scientism, with its aversion to anything not measurable, to the consolidation of the power of the dominant culture has led to the naive notion that education needed to be objective and free from ideology.

The recent research into the hidden curriculum, however, has revealed that the agenda of the schools is larger than the explicit list of courses, syllabi, and programs. Schools also are themselves influenced by particular social and cultural orientations, values, and beliefs. We have come to see in recent research how the schools are not and cannot be neutral, that they are active participants in cultural politics. Schools inevitably make morally important decisions in such areas as grading, tracking, curriculum, and what constitutes appropriate teacher and student behavior. Indeed, it was Ronald Reagan who repeatedly told the American public that education cannot be value neutral, a position long held by radical critics. Ironically, the moral thrust of both the Kohlberg and values clarification programs was quite modest and well within existing cultural boundaries. Kohlberg's ideas lay grounded in a commitment to justice and democracy but only in broad and familiar terms, and there was surely no attempt to promote a political agenda or a social movement. The values clarification approach does not even affirm these broad social values, opting instead for a concern for psychological well-being. However, what these mild-mannered programs did accomplish was to disturb the superficial tranquility of an imposed and distorted moral consensus. Perhaps more significant and revealing than these programs in their own terms was the nature of the criticisms they suffered.

These movements were criticized on scholarly grounds (faulty theory, questionable methodology, and spongy findings) as well as on ideological grounds. In the case of values clarification, there was the criticism that there were no criteria for moral validity, while Kohlberg was criticized for the opposite reason. These movements were attacked from academia at the same time that they came under fire from various public groups. For the most part, the academic discourse has been weighty, measured, sophisticated, apt, cool, and dispassionate, whereas the public attacks have often been emotional, if not hysterical, misinformed, and fearful. Basically, these movements were quashed by the combined weight of professional smugness and public passion.

The successful efforts to at least marginalize the Kohlberg and values clarification programs can be seen as part of the larger backlash of the educational reform movements of the 1960s and 1970s. This vacuum has, of course, been filled with a new reform movement that emphasizes skills mastery, basic education, academic achievement, and competence-based education. Ironically, although the moral dimensions of these new movements are very clear if not explicit, the concept of moral education itself is hardly a driving force in current educational practice. In other words, the decline of the moral education movement carries with it a decline in explicit moral analysis of education. The brief and unhappy life of moral education at least provided an opportunity for an important debate, a debate that was silenced by public fear and professional blindness. Are we then left with a situation in which we have twin roads to moral paralysis —one marked by critical, dispassionate, noncommittal discourse and the other by passionate and intolerant commitment? Can we not be critical of the efforts to add a moral discourse to education while compassionately supporting and collaborating in the struggle to ground education in a moral vision?

Both conservatives and radicals seem to be increasingly reticent to integrate political, moral, and educational analysis. Radicals have boldly and forcefully developed a powerfully illuminating discourse on political and economic domination, social oppression, and intellectual hegemony, courageously challenging the major sacred cows of liberal capitalism. However, they seem shy and hesitant in the face of their responsibility to be other than negative, suspicious, and damning. This problem of shyness is not shared by neoconservatives, who have filled part of the vacuum left by the weakening of the values clarification and Kohlberg movements with the so-called pro-social moral education approach. This approach is a throwback to the old character education approach, one that focuses on socializing and acculturating students to conventional norms of "good" behavior.

The orientation of this movement resonates with neoconservative concerns for social stability, the preservation of conventional canons of schooling, and the restoration of the primacy of the old-fashioned bag of virtues—hard work, perseverance, respect for authority, delay of gratification, obedience, endurance, and courage. This is surely a moral orientation, but it is one that is rooted in denial, complacency, and sentimentality. It is also a moral consciousness that has contributed to our present predicament in that it blindly refuses to go beyond superficial pieties to an examination of the underlying values of hierarchy, privilege, competition, and success that characterize our culture and schools. Its refusal to provide a critical examination of our social, historical, political, and cultural context mark it as less moral than moralistic and less intellectual than didactic.

Perhaps it is time to put an end to efforts at explicit moral education programs. They have not only failed in their own goal of being integrated into the schools; they have also had the deleterious effect of reification and reductionism. Moral educators have managed to compartmentalize a basic, perhaps the most basic, dimension of education by engaging in a discourse of programs, courses, and techniques. In so doing, they have echoed the dualistic notion that there are two kinds of education, one of which is moral and the other where "moral" is irrelevant. Indeed, the most truly moral analysis of education has come not from the moral educators but from people who have instead developed sensitive and penetrating moral critiques of the school/society/cultural matrix. Critics and scholars such as Maxine Green, Paulo Freire, Henry Giroux, Michael Apple, and William Pinar are the true moral educators in that they demand that the public and the profession confront our primary moral issues, those emerging from barriers to a life of justice, meaning, community, love, and joy.

What we need instead of moral education is much more moral discourse and analyses, but not just on the specific ethical implications of living in schools—as in what happens when students cheat or steal. We also need to ground our educational policies and practices in a larger moral analysis of our culture and society. We need to confront the intersection of moral beliefs and educational policies and practices in such questions as the balance between individual autonomy and social responsibility, between the values of competition and cooperation; we need to confront the moral problematics of excellence, testing, grading, and hierarchy; and we need to respond as educators to these issues. By this, I mean that we accept both the necessity and complexity of such a task, or, as Sharon Welch (1985) has put it, "to have absolute commitment and infinite suspicion." We *don't* need more moral education programs; we *do* need a moral mode of analysis for education, one that helps us to understand our moral needs and aids us in responding as educators to them. Yet, this is still not enough.

We also need to ground that language in a moral vision, a far more demanding, more problematic, and more vital requirement than analysis. Moral education without affirmation and commitment is a contradiction in terms, an evasion, and an act of irresponsibility. However, not any affirmation will do; it is simply not enough, given the very harsh realities of our time, to affirm empty pieties and self-serving nostrums—for example, rationalizing self-indulgence as the preservation of civilization. Nor is it enough in these extraordinary times to try to pump up those sagging, tired values of liberal capitalism—reliance on good will, patience, forbearance, and the preservation of the status quo. What we must do is to accept the reality that the "long run" is here, that is, that there is sufficient reason to believe that we are very close to having used up the beneficial energies of existing conceptions of liberalism and enlightenment. It is a new era with both heightened dangers and exhilarating possibilities and a time for deepening our moral imagination, not our moralist fears. It is a time to reaffirm our historical commitments, not to restore nostalgic fantasies, and a time for courage and hope, not defensiveness and despair.

It is time for our culture in general and our profession in particular to confront both the difficulties and possibilities for such an endeavor, given the diversity, pluralism, and divisions in our society. I believe with many others of different times and places that there is very real evidence of a human impulse that is capable not only of greed and aggression but also of caring and compassion. Our myths, narratives, and traditions are surely full of such hopes, aspirations, and commitments, and educators are as much in touch with these impulses as any other professional group. Indeed, educators have a marvelous opportunity to participate in this most important cultural project of our time—the creation of a renewed common vision. Elements of this vision are available from our traditions of fundamental commitments to love, human dignity, and social justice grounded in a quest for a life of meaning. An education that is fully dedicated to this quest is what will make it moral. Nothing else will do.

REFERENCES

Giroux, H., and D. Purpel. 1983. *Moral education and the hidden curriculum: Deception or discovery*. Berkeley: McCutchan.

Kohlberg, L. 1984. *The psychology of human moral development: Essays in moral development*. San Francisco: Harper and Row.

Raths, L., H. Merrill, and S. Simon. 1978. *Values and teaching: Working with values in the classroom*. Columbus: Charles Merrill.

Welch, S. 1985. *Communities of resistance and solidarity: A feminist theology of liberation*. Maryknoll, N.Y.: Orbis.

Managing Life in Classrooms

We have witnessed in recent years the massive development of a knowledge base on life in the classroom, on teacher-student interaction in the teaching-learning process. Much of this knowledge has come from field-based research by teachers, psychologists, anthropologists, and others who have sought to explore "life" in classroom settings. We speak of managing life in classrooms because we now know that there are many factors that go into building effective teacher-student and student-student relationships. The traditional term discipline is too narrow and tends to refer only to teacher reactions to undesired student behavior. We better understand methods of managing student behavior when we look at the *totality* of what goes on in classrooms with teacher responses to student behavior as a part of that totality. Teachers have tremendous responsibility for the emotional climate that is set in a classroom. Whether students feel secure and safe and whether they want to learn depends to an enormous extent on the psychological frame of mind of the teacher. Teachers must be able to manage their own selves in order to be able to manage effectively the development of a humane and caring classroom environment.

Teachers bear moral and ethical responsibilities for being witnesses to and examples of responsible social behavior in the classroom. There are many models of observing life in classrooms. When one speaks of life in classrooms, arranging the total physical environment of the room is a very important part of the teacher's planning for learning activities. Teachers need to expect the best work and behavior from students that they are capable of achieving. Respect and caring are attitudes a teacher must communicate to receive them in return. Reasonable expectations, emphasis on doing the best work one can, and communicating faith in the capacity of one's students to do *their* best work do wonders in developing positive classroom morale. Open lines of communication between teacher and students create the possibility for congenial, fair, dialogical resolution of problems as they occur.

Developing a high level of task orientation among students and encouraging cooperative learning and shared task achievement will foster camaraderie and self-confidence among students. Shared decision-making will build an *esprit de corps*, a sense of pride and confidence, which will feed on itself and blossom into high-quality performance. Good class morale, well managed, never hurts academic achievement. The importance of emphasizing quality, helping students to achieve levels of performance they can feel proud of having attained and encouraging positive dialogue among them leads them to take ownership in the educative effort. When that happens, they literally empower themselves to do their best.

When talking with teachers and prospective teachers regarding what concerns them about their roles (or prospective roles) in the classroom, it is usual that "discipline," the management of student behavior, will rank near or at the top of their list. A teacher needs a clear understanding of what kind of learning environment is most appropriate for the subject matter and age of the students. Any person who wants to teach must also want his or her students to learn well and in a manner that helps them to learn basic values of respect for others and how to become more effective citizens. Humane and caring ways to do this are most valuable and effective.

There is considerable debate among educators regarding certain approaches used in schools to achieve a form of order in classrooms that also develops respect for self and others. The dialogue about this point is spirited and informative. The bottom line for any effective and humane approach to discipline in the classroom and the necessary starting point is the teacher's emotional balance and capacity for self-control. This precondition creates a further one—that the teacher wants to be in the classroom with his or her students. Unmotivated teachers have great difficulty motivating students.

Helping young people learn the skills of self-control and self-motivation to become productive, contributing, and knowledgeable adult participants in society is one of the most important tasks that good teachers undertake. These are teachable and learnable skills; they do not relate to heredity or social condition. They can be learned by any human being who wants to learn them and who is cognitively (intellectually) able to learn them. We further know that these skills are learnable by virtually all but the most severely cognitively disabled persons. There is a large knowledge base on how teachers can help students to learn self-control. All that is required is the willingness of teachers to learn these skills themselves and teach them to their students. Some might say that this is a task for specialists in methods of teaching and educational psychology. I profoundly disagree with those who would make such an exclusionary academic claim. No topic is more fundamentally related to any thorough examination of the social and cultural foundations of education.

There are many sound techniques that new teachers can use to achieve success in managing students' classroom behavior. They should not be afraid to ask colleagues questions and to develop peer support groups. These peer support groups should be composed of those colleagues with whom they work with confidence and trust. Educators at all levels encounter some behavioral problems with some students. Even educators of adults sometimes have behavioral management problems in training activities or educational programs. Young teachers starting out in the elementary and secondary schools are always concerned about how they will manage disruptive, disorderly, or disobedient students.

Teachers' core ethical principles come into play when deciding what constitutes defensible and desirable standards of student conduct. As in medicine, realistic preventive techniques combined with humane but clear principles of procedure seem to be effective. Teachers need to realize that, before they can control behavior, they must identify what student behaviors are desired in their classrooms. They need to reflect, as well, on the emotional tone and ethical principles implied by their own behaviors. To optimize their chances of achieving the classroom atmosphere they wish, teachers must strive for emotional balance within themselves; they must learn to be accurate observers; and they must develop just, fair strategies of intervention to aid students in learning self-control and good behavior. A good teacher is a good model of courtesy, respect, tact, and discretion. Children learn by observing how other persons behave as well as by being told how they are to behave.

Confidence in one's own innate worth and in one's ability to teach effectively goes a long way toward reducing or eliminating discipline problems in educational settings. Teachers often function as role models for their students without even being aware of it. Later in life, they might be told by former students what an impact they had; these revelations are precious to them. From the first day of the first year of teaching, good teachers maintain firm but caring control over their classes by means of continuing observation of and reflection on classroom activities. There is no substitute for positive, assertive teacher interaction with students in class.

This unit addresses many of the topics covered in basic foundations courses. The selections shed light on classroom management issues, teacher leadership skills, the legal foundations of education, and the rights and responsibilities of teachers and students. In addition, the articles can be discussed in foundations courses involving curriculum and instruction or individualized approaches to

testing. This unit falls between the units on moral education and equal opportunity because it can be directly related to either or both of them.

Looking Ahead: Challenge Questions

What are good general rules, subject to amendment, which can guide a first-year teacher's initial efforts to manage student behavior?

What are some of the best techniques for helping someone to learn self-control?

What ethical issues may be raised in the management of student behavior in school settings?

What reliable information is available on the extent and severity of school discipline problems in North America? What sources contain such information?

What are some of the best techniques for helping someone to learn self-control?

What civil rights do students have? Do public schools have fewer rights than private schools in controlling student behavior problems? Why or why not? What are the rights of a teacher in managing student behavior?

Do any coercive approaches to behavioral management in schools work better than noncoercive ones?

Why is teacher self-control a major factor in just and effective classroom management strategies?

What are the moral responsibilities of teachers in managing student behavior?

What are some ways a teacher can help students take pride in their own work and in that of their classmates?

Take the Lead!

Design a Classroom That Works

Teacher Frank Garcia knows that the best classroom environments don't just happen; they're carefully designed. Here, he shares his do's and don'ts for designing the right kind of learning environment.

JOAN NOVELLI

JOAN NOVELLI *is an associate editor at* INSTRUCTOR.

Quick! Draw a picture of your classroom last year. Are the desks in clusters, rows, facing each other, or maybe shaped like a horseshoe? How far is the furthest child from the blackboard? Where is your desk? How is the rest of the floor space utilized? What about wall space? How is your room like the one next door? What makes it different?

Next think about your teaching style. Do you do a lot of whole-class teaching? Is peer tutoring part of your program? What is the level of student interaction during the course of a day? Is cooperative learning at work in your classroom?

Now look at your drawing again. Does the room's organization reflect your teaching style? If your students frequently participate in small-group activities, will the desk arrangement accommodate those meetings with ease? When it's time for whole class instruction, will there be an easy transition? If direct instruction is your primary teaching method, will some students miss out by being on the outer edge of the seating arrangement?

Finally, consider what you know about the way kids learn and how you will incorporate that knowledge into your classroom. The choices you make in designing this year's classroom can help you put your instructional goals into action. So turn your paper over and plan an environment that will incorporate the floors, walls, and furniture of your classroom into your teaching style.

A TEACHER TELLS YOU HOW

Frank Garcia, a sixth-grade teacher at Dove Hill School in San Jose, California, knows that creating great classrooms takes careful thought. As the Evergreen School District's mentor teacher for classroom environment, Garcia has given workshops and seminars on classroom design and is called on throughout the year to assist teachers in his school and district in setting up

classrooms that help make learning happen.

While teachers often experiment with variations in classroom configuration, Garcia points out that universities generally don't prepare teachers to deal with the physical space of a classroom. Garcia believes that with careful planning, reflection on personal teaching style, awareness of curriculum needs, and knowledge of the way children learn, teachers can create classroom environments that are conducive to learning.

One of Garcia's objectives is to make the learning environment an exciting place and, he says, organization and structure are part of this excitement. Garcia recommends beginning with a floor plan locating chalkboards, electrical outlets, sinks, and storage areas. These areas, which are generally stationary, help determine where desks, audiovisual equipment, art materials, and other classroom resources should go.

For example, whether instruction is based on cooperative learning, direct instruction, or a combination of the two, most teachers need to direct everyone's attention to the board at some point during the day. When deciding on a seating plan, Garcia recommends that you think about arranging desks so that as many students as possible have easy access to the board. To encourage self-directed learning in your classroom, use lower storage shelves for materials that students can help themselves to—manipulatives, books, ongoing projects, unfinished assignments, or free-time work. The space around these bookshelves or cabinets makes a versatile, small-group meeting space, with a variety of materials close at hand. What does all of this add up to? Less time getting situated for learning and more time doing it!

WHAT ABOUT WALLS?

Garcia says that walls are the most neglected space in classrooms. "My pet peeve," he says, "is drab classrooms with a few posters tacked up and that's it. Walls have to live!" Some would argue that wall materials are potentially distracting. But knowing that kids are going to look at their surroundings, Garcia believes in creating walls that are sources of enjoyment, inspiration, and learning.

Paula Maciel, a third-grade teacher at Dove Hill School with 21 years of teaching experience, agrees. She always felt something was missing from her classroom and called on Garcia for some advice. Together they looked at parts of Garcia's room that Maciel wanted to implement in her own room. Then they went to work on Maciel's room.

The main problem, Garcia found, was the wall space. He points out that if you want kids to notice materials on walls, the displays have to stand out. In Maciel's room, this meant redoing bulletin boards and creating frames or backgrounds for displayed materials. Step one was creating new bulletin-board borders to replace the standard, prefabricated two-inch corrugated paper strips. Maciel followed Garcia's advice, using some black in every bor-

der, accentuating the contrast between the border and the background to bring out what she wanted kids to see. Continuing with this strategy, Maciel framed other wall displays, including prints, posters, and student work, with black paper.

Garcia, who has been known to change a wall display three or four times before being satisfied, advises stepping back from the area to get the full view. He recalls being taught that certain colors don't mix, but his philosophy is: If it looks good, mix it!

Maciel checked for variety in angle and positioning of materials as well as an overall visually exciting look. The result of this careful attention is a classroom that comes alive. And that's a classroom, Maciel found, where kids are drawn to learn.

Ready to get to work on your classroom? Read the details below and find out how.

The Details...

Smart Seats

Because Frank Garcia's teaching style is a mix of both cooperative learning and direct instruction, he finds clusters of three an optimum desk setup. Clusters of four worked well for group activities but left too many kids with their backs to the board. Whatever the configuration of desks and chairs, Garcia says one thing is certain: You need easy access to every student. That means leaving space around rows or clusters so you can move through the seating area comfortably.

Kids need to be able to move around them comfortably, too. Garcia suggests considering the size of the students when planning seating arrangements. Sixth-grade kids will most likely need more space between rows or clusters than first graders.

Deck the Walls

Other colors just don't bring out material on walls like black, says Garcia. He uses black construction paper to frame everything. This may seem overpowering, but, as Garcia points out, there's very little black in most of what goes on walls.

Interactive and decorative bulletin boards are an important part of Garcia's wall planning, and borders get just as much attention as the displays themselves. He finds that kids don't pay much attention to preformed borders, so he designs his own with

paper patterns, colors, and geometric shapes. Garcia's not afraid to go a little wild here: He's used three-dimensional shapes, reflective tape, even tiny tree lights to create effective bulletin-board borders.

Changing Places

After seating 31 students, Garcia still has room for two small tables. He uses them to give small groups of kids close-up attention and to review lessons with students as needed. Kids use the area to work on projects or just to get a change of scenery.

Nearby shelves hold portable learning centers that children can bring back to the table or back to their desks. Garcia emphasizes that because most teachers don't have the space to use a different part of the room for every activity, versatility is what makes an area like this work.

Test Drive

Is this room ready for action? Garcia recommends a trial run before students arrive for their first day.

Sit in the kids' seats. Is the board visible? Are any seats going to be particularly prone to distractions? For example, is one too close to the door, the sink, or the "in" box? Walk through the aisles. Is there a comfortable amount of space?

Help yourself to materials you'll

encourage kids to get and return on their own. Are they easy to find, reach, and put away?

Look around. Do the walls feel friendly? Are interactive bulletin boards accessible from a child's point of view? If something is meant to be read, is it at a child's eye level?

Now step outside the room. Walk back in, as though it's the first day of school. Is this an exciting place to be?

Software Staples

This software storage strategy doubles as a self-directed learning motivator. Stapling sleeves to the wall keeps titles in full view, making the software easy to select and put away. And unlike a traditional filing system, Garcia says this display reminds students of the variety of software available for their use, encouraging them to try something different.

Personal Touch

In this corner, stuffed animals, plants, and knickknacks invite kids to shelves stocked with books, puzzles, map activities, and more. These decorative additions do more than just keep shelves from becoming overcrowded and inaccessible. They also create a warm, welcoming feeling. And "anytime you're in an environment where you feel good," says Garcia, "good things are going to happen."

The Quality School

The accepted attitude for at least half of the students in our boss-managed, adversarial schools is to be anti-education, according to Dr. Glasser. He suggests that we try to overcome this problem through a new method of managing schools that focuses on quality.

WILLIAM GLASSER

William Glasser, M.D., is a board-certified psychiatrist and founder and president of the Institute for Reality Therapy, Canoga Park, Calif.

There is no shortage of good ideas about ways to solve the problems of our schools, any more than there is a shortage of good teachers or capable students. To the contrary, the *Kappan* alone has published article after article explaining such outstanding educational practices as outcome-based education and cooperative learning. Many teachers have been able to use these ideas successfully with students who had previously shown little motivation to learn.

Good as they are, however, ideas such as these have not taken hold and will not take hold, because of the way almost all our schools are managed. Nearly all superintendents, principals, and teachers use a method of management that not only prevents new ideas from being introduced into the system but is also the cause of many of the problems we have been trying to solve. Before anything else will work, we need to replace the way we manage now with a new method of management that focuses on quality.

THE ONLY ANSWER TO OUR SCHOOL PROBLEMS

Try to picture students in a required academic class at a typical secondary school as a gang of street-repair workers. If they were working as hard as they do in class, half or more would be leaning on their shovels, smoking and socializing, perfectly content to let the others do the work. Of those who were working, few would be working hard, and it is likely that none would be doing high-quality work.

It is apparent, however, that students have a good idea of what parts of their schooling are of high quality. I have talked at length to groups of high school students about this subject. Most of them see quality in athletics, music, and drama, and a few find quality in advanced placement courses or in shop classes. Almost none find anything of high quality in regular classes. All except a very few admit that, while they believe that they are capable of doing high-quality work in class, they have never actually done any and have no plans to do any in the future. My aim here is to explain how to manage students so that a substantial majority actually *do* high-quality schoolwork. Nothing less will solve the problems of our schools.

Does it make that much difference whether a student stays in school and "leans on a shovel" or drops out?

If we accept the idea that the purpose of any organization, public or private, is to build a high-quality product or perform a high-quality service, then we must also accept the idea that the workers in that organization must do high-quality work and that the job of the manager is to see that this occurs. In our schools, the students are the workers, and today almost none are doing high-quality work in their regular academic classes. Those who manage in the schools — teachers who manage students directly and administrators who manage both teachers and students — are in most cases highly dedicated, humane people who have tried very hard but have yet to figure out how to manage so that students do significant amounts of high-quality work.

Is this problem unsolvable? Should we do as we now seem to be doing: give up on the idea of many students doing high-quality work and make more of an effort to increase the amount of low-quality work? When we settle for such measures as trying to reduce the number of dropouts, isn't that exactly what we are doing? If high-quality education is what we need, does it make that much difference whether a student stays in school and "leans on a shovel" or drops out and "leans on a shovel"?

*T*oday almost none of our students are doing high-quality work in their regular academic classes.

Or should we look for organizations in which almost all the workers are working hard and doing a high-quality job and try to apply to the schools the techniques that managers use in these places? Though they may not be widely known or applied in this country, far better management practices exist than most school managers use. What is significant about these more effective practices is that they are specifically aimed at persuading the workers to do high-quality work. In today's world, only organizations whose products and services are of high quality will thrive—and our schools are far from thriving.

When we look into who has taught managers to manage so that almost all workers do high-quality work, one name stands out. "The man who taught the Japanese to achieve high quality at low cost (after World War II) is an American, Dr. W.

Edwards Deming," according to Myron Tribus, one of Deming's disciples. "The Japanese faced an 'export or die' situation. They had a reputation for shoddy products. . . . With the aid of the MacArthur government, they located Dr. Deming, and he proceeded to teach them the methods rejected by our managers. The rest is history."[1]

And what this history tells us is that, led by managers trained by Deming, the Japanese workers produced very high-quality products (especially automobiles and electronics) and made them available at prices the average person could afford. Given an opportunity to get high quality for the same price as low quality, consumers have been stampeding to "made in Japan," and the result has been a tidal wave of money cascading toward the Japanese.

I will explain below how Deming's ideas can be brought undistorted into our schools so that, instead of the elitist system we now have, in which just a few students are producing high-quality work, almost all students will have this experience. Once they have this experience, which for almost all students is a totally new one, they will find it highly satisfying. They will no more turn down the chance to continue doing this kind of work than does the well-managed factory worker.

But further, as I will soon explain, students are not simply the workers in the school; they are also the products. Once they see that they, themselves, are gaining in quality, they will work to continue the process, just as we continue to buy the high-quality products of Japan.

What I propose to do that will help administrators and teachers to accept these new management ideas is to continue to explain *control theory*, with which I have been identified for the past decade. Control theory explains far better than any other existing theory both why and how we behave. Control theory explains both why Deming's ideas — when they are used correctly — work so well and how these ideas can be brought into schools. Moreover, I believe that teachers and administrators need to understand control theory. I do not believe that those who manage students will change what they do significantly if they do not clearly understand the reasons for changing.

There are remarkable parallels between the American manufacturers who ignored Deming when he suggested that they make quality their number-one priority after World War II and the school managers who seem unconcerned that only a few students in any secondary school do what we — or even they — would call high-quality work. Like the automakers in the Seventies, who concentrated on building a lot of low-quality, high-profit cars and who might have gone bankrupt if competition had been unrestricted, our schools have been primarily concerned with trying to get more students to do enough work to reach the low standard of quality required for high school graduation. Yet, as long as "getting more of them to do enough to get through" is our goal, not only will we not reach it but we will fall even further behind.

As difficult as this assertion is for most teachers to believe, I contend that the continuing drop in student performance is caused by the fact that our traditional system of managing students sends the clear message that low-quality work is acceptable. Probably less than 15% of our students do high-quality academic work in school, and even many of that group do far less than they are capable of doing. We fail to recognize that the way we manage schools ignores the fact that very few people will expend the effort needed to do high-quality work unless they believe that there is *quality* in what they are asked to do. While a manager cannot make workers do high-quality work — control theory contends that no one can make anyone do anything — it is the job of the manager to manage so that it is easy for workers (or students) to see a strong connection between what they are asked to do and what they believe to be worth doing.

While an exact definition of *quality education* that would apply to all situations is extremely elusive, we are generally capable of recognizing quality when we see it. Ask any school administrator to take you through his or her school and show you some high-quality work in any subject area, and I am certain that you will agree that what you are shown is of high quality. What is similar about all the work you would be shown is that none of it could be graded or evaluated by machine. True quality never can be. Furthermore, it is almost impossible for us to do or see anything without making a fairly accurate appraisal of the quality of what we see or do.

I continue to rely on the industrial analogy that compares workers and managers to students and teachers because I think it is both accurate and appropriate. The students are the workers of the school. And, like workers in most service industries, the difference between the success and failure of the organization depends on the quality of their work, be it waiting on tables or learning academic subjects. The teachers are the first-level managers, and the administrators are the middle- and upper-level managers. And the productivity of any school depends mostly on the skill of those who directly manage the workers—that is, the teachers. According to Deming, their success in turn depends almost completely on how well they are managed by the administrators above them.

The major complaint we all had as students was not that the work was too hard but that it was boring. This complaint was — and still is — valid. By *boring* we usually meant that we could not connect what we were asked to do with its usefulness in our lives. For example, it is deadly boring to work hard memorizing facts that neither we nor anyone we know will ever use except for a test in school. The distinguishing characteristic of the effective teachers we remember is that they were *not* boring; somehow or other what they asked us to do was satisfying to us. Here, perhaps, is a major difference between a teacher who understands the role of manager and one who does not. The manager is willing to expend effort to assign work that is not boring because he or she knows that it is almost impossible for bored workers to do high-quality work.

Effective teachers manage students without coercion. Yet, if increasing the number of teachers who manage students without coercion is the only solution to the pressing problem of getting students to do high-quality work, no one in power seems to want to address the issue. For example, none of the recommendations in *A Nation at Risk* focused on how teachers manage students. That report claimed that we needed a longer school day and year, stiffer graduation requirements, and more homework — all coercive practices. But longer hours and harder courses with the same teachers for whom students were not doing high-quality work would change nothing, and it is hardly surprising that this report led to no significant improvements in the schools.

However, as the work of Linda McNeil of Rice University has shown, magnet schools and other structurally innovative schools can also fail if traditional coercive management prevails.[2] Thus many such schools are now doing much less than they could. Their shortcomings do not stem from a faulty structure but from the fact that many teachers who have made an effort to improve the way they manage students are being hampered by administrators who tell them that the high-quality work both they and their students are doing is not acceptable.

According to McNeil's research, it is not acceptable because it does not include enough of the low-quality schoolwork that standardized, state-mandated achievement tests measure. Nothing of high quality, including schoolwork, can be measured by standardized, machine-scored tests. If we are truly interested in measuring what successful teachers in magnet schools are doing, we will need to conduct thorough interviews with them, collect observations of a statistically significant sample of them, and carry out follow-up studies to see if the future academic performance of their students is enhanced. It is a symptom of the illness that afflicts our self-destructive system that students are made aware in a wide variety of coercive ways that the low-quality work that is measured by machines is the top administrative priority in almost all school systems.

This fact is beautifully illustrated by the academic equivalent of the Boston Tea Party, reported in the 27 April 1989 *Los Angeles Times*:

> A group of seniors at Torrance's academically rigorous West High School intentionally flunked the latest California Assessment Program test in an attempt to send a message to administrators whom they believe place too much emphasis on the exam. . . . At the school Wednesday, student body President Kelle Price, who said that she did not intentionally fail the test, said some seniors became disgruntled when some teachers interrupted classes to prepare them for the . . . [state] tests. She said students also believed that administrators — who visited classes to stress the importance of doing well — were too concerned with maintaining the school's image. . . . At West High, there was much debate Wednesday about who — if anyone — places too much emphasis on the tests. Bawden [the principal] blamed the state Department of Education and the press which does not publish other indicators of school performance. . . . Bill Franchini, who heads the Torrance Teachers Assn. . . . blamed it on a trickle-down effect, saying the pressure starts with the state Dept. . . . and works its way down through the local school districts, principals, teachers and eventually students. "I think [students] are feeling like pawns in a game that is much bigger than they are," he said.

Everyone is correct. It is the push from the top to do well on low-quality tests that the intelligent students who want high-quality education are rebelling against. Coercion begets coercion; anyone who knows history knows this is true.

This article is about managing schools for quality and, in doing so, changing any school from what it is into what I call a *quality school*. I will focus on how teachers can manage students more effectively and on how administrators can use the same strategies to manage teachers. The management method that I will offer is very different from the school management that is now in place in most schools. As I have already hinted, it is based on control theory and uses the proven methods of W. Edwards Deming. It is almost unused in schools, though it is being used with great success in a few corporations, such as the Ford Motor Company.

As good as Deming's ideas are, I believe that it is unlikely that they will spread as widely as they should — or even continue to be used as much as they now are — unless many more managers realize that these ideas are based on an understandable and usable theory. Although there may be the beginnings of a management revolution in a few major industries, the changes are far from widespread, and almost none of them have reached the schools. Teachers and students are being managed today in the same way they have always been managed. It is the same way that people have been managed for centuries — by a method based on the ancient, commonsensical theory of how we function that is best known as stimulus/response theory.

But stimulus/response theory is mistaken. When it is used to manage people, it leads to a traditional management method that from now on I will call *boss-management*. Boss-management is ineffective because it relies on coercion and always turns workers and managers into adversaries. Bossing rarely leads to consistent hard work — and almost never to high-quality work. Nowhere is this fact more obvious than in the schools. Managing for quality demands a new noncoercive method of management that I call *lead-management*, which I will explain in detail below.

As many of you know, this is not the first time that I have written about the use of control theory in the schools. My 1986 book, *Control Theory in the Classroom*, focused on how knowledge of this new theory can persuade teachers to use cooperative learning to replace lecturing and individual seatwork.[3] While the feedback from the schools that have implemented this important change has been very positive, progress has been slow. And it is now apparent to me that progress will continue to be slow until we are able to change from boss-management to lead-management.

Cooperative learning works well because it gives students power. Lead-managers support this approach because they have discovered that the more they are able to empower workers, the harder workers will work. By contrast, bosses want to be in charge. They are not comfortable with giving as much power to the workers as is required by cooperative learning.

Moving from boss-management to lead-management means breaking with tradition, and this is always very hard to do. In the schools it will be especially hard, even harder than in industry, because at least one major obstacle that is not found in other workplaces is intrinsic to education: effective teaching may be the hardest job there is.

THE HARDEST JOB

It is unlikely that we will ever move from boss-management to lead-management unless we recognize explicitly how difficult it is to teach effectively. Our failure to do so allows us to continue to think that, if only we buckled down and really tried, we could easily boss our teachers into doing better. Nothing could be further from the truth. What makes this obstacle so difficult to overcome is that most people, educators included, do not see it as an obstacle.

Almost everyone in our society shares a huge misconception about teaching. By *everyone* I mean not only the general public but also nearly all teachers, parents, administrators, school board members, politicians, education reporters, and teacher educators. What almost all these people misunderstand is that being an effective teacher may be the most difficult of all the common jobs in our society.

Before I explain why this is so, let me define what I mean by *effective teaching*. An effective teacher is one who is able to convince not one-half or three-quarters, but essentially *all* of his or her students to do high-quality work in school. This means to work up to their capacity so that there is no need to divide students into tracks and reserve a large number of spaces in a low track for those who "lean on their shovels." All the measures of school failure that are widely reported—

such as dropout rates, low test scores, and students' unwillingness to take "hard subjects" (e.g., math and science)—are the result of students' failing to expend the effort to do high-quality work. The few teachers who can consistently persuade almost all the students they teach to do high-quality work are, without doubt, succeeding at the hardest job there is.

In order to explain why effective teaching is such a hard job, I must first briefly discuss work in general. I think it is safe to say that all work falls into one of two major categories: managing things or managing people. When we manage things, the essence of the job is performing an operation on a thing or even on a person (who is acting as passively as a thing) that improves the value of that thing or person. What is characteristic of a thing or of a person behaving as a thing is that, hard as the operation we perform may be, the person managing the operation is never actively resisted.

*T*he more the work that students are asked to do satisfies their needs, the harder they will work.

When we manage things, which have no personal agendas, we are much more in control of what we do than we are when we manage people. This control makes managing things, no matter how much skill or creativity is required, much easier than managing people. Regardless of the skill and creativity of the manager, managing people depends for its ultimate success on the cooperation of the people being managed. The less the people being managed are willing to do as the manager says, the harder the job of managing them becomes. All teachers are people managers, and nearly everyone acknowledges that students seem to be among the most resistant of all workers. When teachers are blamed for failing to do what many of them believe is nearly impossible — for example, teaching academically unmotivated students — they perceive this blame as unfair, and this makes their job harder still.

Another factor that makes effective teaching in the U.S. much harder than it is in other countries is that we do not have the strong cultural support of education that is taken for granted in such countries as Korea, Japan, France, and Germany. What we have is a wide variety of subcultures, many of which do not value the education offered in most of our schools. Or, if they do value it, they do not value the way it is offered. While it may be overstating the case to say that some of our subcultures are anti-intellectual, there are certainly a great many families in which what is commonly referred to as book learning is not highly prized.

Many teachers are accepting the expedient view that students should be stuffed with low-quality fragments.

Even most of our colleges receive far more publicity for athletics than for academics. We take pride in the fact that someone who did not do well in school or who had little formal schooling — the so-called self-made man or woman — can go far in our society. A person with a doctorate who wishes to run for high office might find the degree to be as great a handicap as a moral indiscretion. This ethos may be more democratic and less elitist than that of foreign cultures, but it does not help our teachers. This means that our teachers have a much harder job than those who teach in some foreign countries, because foreign students are much more likely to be persuaded by their families and by the society at large to work hard in school and to do as the teacher says.

As student "achievement" becomes more and more a political issue, state after state has begun to "measure" achievement by "objective" tests. And the scores have been deemed too low. Most state departments of education, driven by the fear that they will be blamed for these low scores, are making desperate efforts to "reform" teaching in ways that are directly (and, I believe, blindly) aimed at raising test scores.

As McNeil's research clearly shows, teachers are increasingly being asked to objectify and standardize their teaching. As they do so, education is being fragmented and mystified, and content areas that might be controversial (and interesting), such as the Vietnam War, are being omitted from the curriculum. As this happens, teachers are being treated more and more as nonintellectual "things" and less and less as capable professionals. McNeil writes:

> Such reforms render teaching and the curriculum inauthentic. If we are to engage students in learning, we must reverse this process. When school knowledge is not credible to students, they opt out and decide to wait until "later" to learn "what you really need to know." Mechanical teaching processes knowledge in a way that guarantees it will be something other than credible. Centralized curriculum, centralized tests of outcomes, and standardized teacher behaviors can only frustrate those teachers whose passion for teaching has shown students (and the rest of us) what education should be about.[4]

In order to conform to this new and widespread concern that all that is taught be measured, teachers are required to turn their backs on a basic axiom of control theory: for workers, including students, to do high-quality work, they must be managed in a way that convinces them that the work they are asked to do satisfies their needs. The more it does, the harder they will work.

Instead, teachers are being required to try to stuff students with fragments of measurable knowledge as if the students had no needs of their own — almost as if they were things. Education is defined in terms of how many fragments of information these student/things can retain long enough to be measured on standardized achievement tests. Most competent teachers recognize, however, that the effort to stuff students with measurable fragments of knowledge has little or nothing to do with high-quality education. Yet their input has been either ignored or depreciated by the politically motivated standardizers and fragment measurers who are now in charge.

Because this low-quality, standardized, fragmented approach is so unsatisfying to students (and to teachers), more and more students are actively resisting. Their resistance is seen as a discipline problem, and school administrators fall into the trap of thinking that discipline problems—not unsatisfying educational experiences—are the cause of low levels of achievement. This explains the increased emphasis on strict rules of deportment (more coercion) that further define good students as passive things rather than as involved, questioning, at times dissenting, active learners.

This failure to take into account the needs of students or teachers has made what is already the hardest job nearly impossible. Any method of teaching that ignores the needs of teachers or students is bound to fail, and we are now paying the price for that failure in the coin of increased use of drugs and high rates of delinquency and teen pregnancy.

The use of boss-management produces most of the discipline problems that we try to prevent.

Therefore, teachers, who must manage better than all other managers if they are to succeed at all, are being asked to accept working conditions that practically insure that they will fail to persuade a great many of their students to do even low-quality work. For competent teachers, it has become a miserable Catch-22. If they teach conceptually and challenge students to think and defend their ideas, the students will have a chance to learn something worthwhile. But, since the students may not do well on the tests that measure fragments, such teachers will be labeled as troublemakers and failures. On the other hand, if they teach the way they are told to teach, the students will fail to learn anything that the students believe is worthwhile. But their teachers will be praised as successful team players, and the students will be blamed as incompetent.

Caught in this trap, many teachers are giving up on what they believe and accepting the politically expedient view that students should be treated as things and stuffed with fragments of low quality. So they emphasize facts and right answers, avoid controversy and discussion, give a lot of homework, test frequently, and tailor what they teach to state testing programs. In doing so, they become much more impersonal than they would like, and they teach less of what they want to teach and of what their students want to learn. Nothing makes a job harder than having to give up on what you believe.

There are probably other obstacles to overcome if we are to make the switch from boss-managing to lead-managing. But if we can overcome this one, we have a good chance of overcoming the others. If we continue to take lightly the skill and art of teaching, to think that almost anyone can do it, and to stop most formal training when teachers start to teach, we will not make any progress. Teaching is a very hard job that needs to be well-compensated and that requires considerable on-the-job training throughout a teacher's career. Less than this will not suffice.

NONCOERCIVE MANAGEMENT

Having established that teaching is perhaps the most difficult of all management jobs, I can now begin to take a detailed look at how to replace boss-management with lead-management so that we can begin the move toward quality. Boss-management is wrong because it limits both the quality of the work and the productivity of the worker. Furthermore, as I will explain shortly, its use actually produces most of the discipline problems that we try to prevent.

In education the prevalence of boss-management has effectively limited the number of students who will do *any* significant work to about 50% in the best neighborhoods and down to 10% in areas where there is little support for learning in students' homes. Therefore, given the hardest of management jobs, teachers (and administrators) are burdened with a method of management that limits their ability to succeed no matter how competent they are in other respects.

The most obvious reason for the overwhelming preponderance of boss-managers is tradition. It is "natural" for the strong to try to dominate the weak, and students are always younger, less knowledgeable, and thus weaker than teachers. Moreover, administrators tend to see students as subordinates, a situation tailor-made for boss-management. And since schools have always been boss-managed, most teachers and administrators do not spend much time questioning what they do. Indeed, many are not even aware that a better, noncoercive method of management exists.

There is always the fear in education, especially among the measurers and fragmenters, that too great a concern with quality means that students inevitably cover less ground; that is, as quality increases, productivity declines. Deming has shown that the opposite occurs: quality always leads to increased productivity. Many people do not believe this, because it seems so contrary to their "common sense."

Boss-management is also difficult to challenge, because in most schools enough students are willing to work so that any teacher can point to them and say, "Look at all the students who are doing well because they are doing what they are told." But their success is not a result of the way they are managed; it is a result of the homes they come from. These students succeed *despite* the way they are managed. If boss-management were truly effective, many more students would succeed.

But as much as boss-management promises control, it totally fails to deliver on this promise. In most schools there are plenty of students who neither work nor follow rules. Teachers who get severely frustrated by these resistant students tend to request such sanctions as detention, suspension, and corporal punishment. As they use these sanctions, they become more bosslike and so less effective.

They fail to see that these very sanctions stand in the way of achieving the quality that is essential if the school workplace is to become highly productive. The reason is that, as soon as a boss uses coercion, especially punishment, the worker becomes an adversary. There is no way around it. And while people will work for an adversary (huge numbers do, and some even work hard), they do so because of their own needs. The boss is ignored, avoided, disliked, or ridiculed. The boss is seen either as unnecessary or as an obstacle to completing the job.

The adversarial relationship between teachers and students that is so detrimental to the quality of learning begins early. As early as first grade, any child who does not do as the teacher says is apt to be boss-managed, and the coercion starts. It does not make much difference whether the coercion is subtle or overt: a child knows when he or she is being coerced. As soon as this occurs, a child's main agenda becomes resistance, the personal power struggle between teacher and pupil starts, and education is forgotten. It becomes a vicious cycle: the child learns less and resists more; the teacher coerces more and teaches less. For many children, this adversarial relationship is in place by early elementary school, and their formal education becomes secondary to a never-ending power struggle in which all involved are losers.

While boss-management is ineffective at all levels, the higher the level at which it is employed, the more damage it does to the quality of the work and to the productivity of the worker. Teachers who use boss-management exclusively will limit the learning in their classes. A principal who is a dedicated boss-manager will make it so hard for his teachers to use lead-management that the whole school will be negatively affected. A superintendent following this philosophy will cast a pall over a whole district. And when this is the management philosophy in the state office, as it is today in the many states that demand that learning be fragmented and standardized so that the standard fragments can be measured, the whole state will suffer.

In contrast to the coercive core of boss-management, persuasion and problem solving are central to the philosophy of lead-managment. The lead-manager spends all of his or her time and energy figuring out how to run the system so that the workers will see that it is to their benefit to produce high-quality work. Keeping these points in mind, I offer the following four essential elements of lead-management.

• The leader engages the workers in a discussion of the quality of the work to be done and the time needed to do it so that the workers' input can be considered. The manager makes a continual effort to fit the job to the skills and the needs of the workers.

• The leader (or a worker designated by the leader) models the job so that the workers who are to perform the job can see exactly what the manager thinks is the best way to work. At the same time, the workers are continually asked for their input regarding better ways to do the job.

• The leader asks the workers to inspect or evaluate their own work for quality, with the understanding that the manager will listen to what they say because they know a great deal about how to produce high-quality work.

• The leader is a facilitator in that he or she tries to show the workers that everything feasible has been done to provide them with the best possible tools and workplace, as well as a noncoercive and cooperative atmosphere in which to do the job.

To see how these elements would work in the classroom, all students, both as individuals and as a group, could be asked to evaluate their classwork, homework, and tests and to put their evaluation of the quality of their work on everything they do. Just how they would do this would be discussed and agreed on as part of the continual give-and-take in a lead-managed class. Following Deming, the constant aim would be to get the students involved in evaluating the quality of their own work. Students would be encouraged to keep their own records of the quality of what they do so that they always know exactly how far they have come.

> *Because coercion is never an option, the lead-manager and the workers cannot become adversaries.*

Once the students discover that they are being taught in a way that allows them to see that they are actually doing high-quality work, they will experience a satisfaction that almost no students now get in their boss-managed classes. Only the discovery that they can do quality work can lead to motivation, a subject I will discuss in more detail in my explanation of control theory below. There would never be any coercion, and it is unlikely that there would be any discipline problems in such a noncoercive atmosphere.

A lead-manager emphasizes that problems are never solved by coercion; they are solved by having all parties to the problem figure out a better way that is acceptable to all. If the first solution doesn't work, the problem is addressed again. Because coercion is never an option, the lead-manager and the workers cannot become adversaries.

This means that lead-management and the concepts of quality will not flourish in our classrooms unless they are implemented at the building level. The principal is the crucial element in education reform. The principal who wants to be a successful lead-manager must learn the social and administrative skills needed to be a buffer between the bosses above and the teachers he or she lead-manages.

It would be good if these ideas were accepted by administrators higher than the building principal, and I am sure that, at times, this will be the case. But the political power struggles in the central office will almost always intrude. Bossing and kowtowing are so deeply ingrained at the higher levels of the education system that my hopes for reform are pinned on finding enough principals who are willing to give up bossing and start leading.

CONTROL THEORY AND MOTIVATION

In the schools, boss-management is a major reason that so few students are involved in high-quality honors courses. What makes this situation even worse is that, as long as the boss-managers prevail, there is little chance that we will ever be able to increase this small number, because boss-managers totally misunderstand what has become one of the most common buzz words in management: *motivation*. Boss-managers firmly believe that people can be motivated from the outside; they fail to understand that all of our motivation comes from within ourselves.

When it comes to understanding motivation, boss-managers are looking for something that does not exist. Yet they keep looking because, like almost everyone, they believe in stimulus/response theory, the ancient commonsense theory that explains that our behavior is almost always motivated by a stimulus that exists outside of ourselves.

I do not mean to suggest that what happens outside of ourselves means nothing. Far from it. What happens outside of ourselves has a lot to do with what we choose to do, but the outside event does not *cause* our behavior. What we get—and all we ever get—from the outside is information. How we choose to act on this information is up to us. Therefore, the information that the students get from the teacher, which includes the way this information is given to them, is very important. But the students are the ones who make the final judgment about how important it is to them. The more important they think the information is, the more they will do what they are asked, and the better they will do it.

If I point a gun at you and ask for your wallet, the entire sequence of events is information for you. You will do what you think is best. Most of you will give up your wallets because you decide that your lives are more important than your wallets. But some of you might not do so. The difference between a lead-manager and a boss-manager lies in the information each gives to the workers or students — and this is a vast difference. In practice, it is the main difference between students who work and students who "lean on their shovels."

A boss-manager always responds to the quality of a worker's work with a coercive message — be it reward or punishment — because bosses think that this is the best way to "motivate" workers. Bosses like to point guns more than they like to raise salaries, and they are always looking for bigger guns. Effective lead-managers *never* use coercive messages. Instead, a lead-manager will try to give workers the kind of information that will persuade them to do as directed because it is as much to the workers' benefit as it is to the manager's.

If they know control theory, lead-managers also know what things we, as humans, are always looking for. Using this knowledge, an effective lead-manager always makes an effort to combine what all workers are looking for (actually what all humans are looking for) with what he or she is asking them to do. Moreover, students are not exceptions to the axiom of control theory that states that all living creatures are always motivated by the basic needs of their species.

Therefore, to begin to understand what motivation actually is, we must start with the contention of control theory that all human beings are born with five basic needs: survival, love, power, fun, and freedom. Throughout our lives we must attempt to live in a way that best satisfies these needs. *Control theory* is a descriptive term because all of our lives we try to control our own behavior so that what we choose to do is the most need-satisfying thing we can do at the time.

But when we find ourselves managing people, knowledge of these needs is more than helpful; it is essential. For example, when I present my ideas to teachers and administrators, I usually interview six junior or senior high school students in front of a large audience. Because for young people the need for power is very difficult to satisfy, I ask, "Where in school do you feel important?" To the students, this question always seems to come from outer space; they look at me as if I had asked them something ridiculous. For almost all students— even for the very good ones, who are usually selected as the group for me to interview—feeling important (powerful) in school is an alien experience.

However, when I persist, what most of them tell me is that they feel important in their extracurricular activities. Sports, music, and drama are most frequently mentioned. What are almost never mentioned are academic classes. When I ask why this is so, they say that, in the extracurricular situations, where they almost always work together as a group or on a team, they work harder and accomplish more because they help one another and because it's more fun. They emphasize that they are more comfortable and less bored because it is accepted that they socialize while they work in these situations, a practice that is not acceptable in their regular classes. From the standpoint of control theory, what these students are saying is that it is very hard for them to satisfy their needs in academic classes, because most work is done alone and, in most classes, there is little or no class discussion.

---

*T*hroughout our lives we must attempt to live in a way that best satisfies our basic human needs.

To remedy this, I strongly suggested in my 1986 book, *Control Theory in the Classroom*, that we teach students in cooperative groups in their academic classes. Learning together as a member of a team satisfies the needs for power and for belonging much better than does learning alone. Good lead-managers recognize that, when they can promote and support cooperation among workers, they have laid the foundation for high-quality work. Had I not written that book, I would have to argue extensively for this approach here. But I need not repeat those arguments.

By late middle school or early high school there is a state of almost total antagonism between the teachers and the "non-working" students, whose numbers reach as high as 90% in some schools in economically deprived neighborhoods. When a great many students and teachers are involved, this angry atmosphere saps energy from both groups. They tend to slip into a kind of sullen, apathetic truce: "I won't bother you if you don't bother me." But this truce is fragile. When it is broken, which happens frequently when teachers or students get excessively frustrated, the anger can be explosive.

But this sad state of affairs also prevails for as many as 50% of the students in even our best public secondary schools. The atmosphere may be less explosive, but the sullen antagonism is just as high. And no matter what we try to do to improve the situation, unless we eliminate the boss-management that does not address itself to the needs of students, we will stay right where we are — or perhaps lose even more ground. We need to accept the fact that the majority of boss-managed students see little chance of satisfying their needs by working hard in school, and we cannot boss them into doing more.

Assuming that administrators manage teachers in the same way that I suggest teachers manage students, what I have proposed here may sound marvelous to teachers who have read this far. However, I can also hear them saying that I have described a pipe dream: "No one would let me teach this way or treat me like this." What they are saying is that lead-teaching and lead-managing go against the central premise of the traditional boss-management that dominates almost all education: neither students nor teachers can be trusted to do what is best for themselves. They must be told what to do and coerced into doing it. Therefore, even when lead-teachers get results (as they consistently will), what they do to get these results might be seen as a threat both to those who boss them and to many of the boss-teachers who teach alongside them.

Even if their students are working, lead-teachers may be told that their discipline is lax because there is laughter in their classrooms. If they are creative, as they necessarily need to be to teach in a need-satisfying way, they might be told that they are deviating from the time-tested (and deadly dull) way of planning lessons: lecture and hand out a lot of dittoed worksheets for students to do by themselves at their desks. One group of high-performing students told me they were being "dittoed to death" in their high school.

Successful lead-teachers will also be criticized for caring too much and told that too much personal involvement is unprofessional. They will be admonished to keep the state assessment tests in mind and to fragment the subject matter so that students will do better on these tests, even though this traditional boss-management practice fails to capture the attention of more than half of the students. Lead-teachers will quickly learn that, in schools dominated by boss-managers, they will be unpopular for what they believe and especially for what they do. They will see many boss-teachers failing miserably. Yet most of those who run the "system" will continue to support what the boss-teachers do as right and to criticize the actions of the lead-teachers as wrong.

It is this kind of boss-thinking that leads to the totally destructive stimulus/response premise that school must be a struggle between two ancient and traditional adversaries: the teachers (bosses) and the students (workers). In this view, if the bosses relax even for a moment, the students will destroy the school. However, the sad truth is that many of our schools are already very close to being destroyed. Some schools in our central cities are no longer even semblances of places of learning, and the more we depend on boss-managers to solve the problem, the more we will lose of the little we have left.

What is high quality at McDonald's is more obvious to students than what is high quality in English or math class.

I contend that teachers and administrators who are successful use control theory, whether they are aware of it or not. Yet the majority of teachers will not make the effort to learn this theory unless they are firmly and warmly supported in this major learning process by administrators who are also conversant with control theory. If what teachers do as they attempt to become lead-managers is merely tolerated, boss-management will prevail. Teachers need to be led, which means encouraged and praised by administrators who go into their classrooms and compliment them and their students on any high-quality work they do. Lead-managers must actively promote the satisfaction of needs at all levels of the system. Doing any less will not work.

HIGH-QUALITY SCHOOLWORK

Anyone who understands control theory would predict what Deming found to be true: workers will not work hard unless they believe that there is quality in what they are asked to do. Working hard will not satisfy our need for power when we are engaged in what we believe to be a low-quality task. For example, busywork is the epitome of low-quality school work. Although quality is a hard concept to define, it is still something that most of us can recognize, and most students do not see quality in the work they are asked to do in their academic classes.

For example, look into a typical required academic class, such as 10th-grade English. On most days fewer than 10 students will be working hard; the rest do little more than sit there. If you ask the idle students why they are not working, they will tell you that the work is boring, that they don't need it, and that no one cares what they think. While the work may have value to the teacher, the *students* do not see much value in what they are being asked to do.

If you ask the slackers why the few students who are working bother to make the effort, they'll make a few disparaging remarks about the type of students who work (*nerds* is the current word). But it will become apparent to you that they really don't know the answer to your question. If you then ask those who are working why they bother, they will usually say that they need a good grade or that they don't want to disappoint their parents—rather than that the work has value or quality. More than almost any other place where work is done, school (with its many compulsory academic subjects) suffers from the inability to attach the image of quality to the work that workers are asked to do.

When students say that they "hate school," one of the things they are saying is that they hate being asked to work hard at something that does not fulfill their needs. Many of these same students will say that they want only to get out of school and go to work. A variety of unskilled and semiskilled part-time jobs are available to young people today, and many of them are working much harder at after-school jobs than in school. One reason is that most of them see what they are asked to do at work, menial as it is, as more satisfying than schoolwork.

Although the money students earn at these jobs is satisfying, there is another, more subtle factor operating. For most students, it is easier to see the quality in what they are asked to do at work—e.g., be clean, courteous, and quick— than to see the quality in the reading and calculating that they do at school. I don't believe this situation would continue if most of these students felt that they had to spend the rest of their lives working in a fast-food restaurant. In the short run, however, what is high quality at McDonald's is more obvious to them than what is high quality in English or math class.

On the other hand (and this may seem contradictory), if you ask some students working at McDonald's whether they want a good education, their answer is always yes. They all have some sort of vague picture of what constitutes a good education, though few of them really understand the concept. It is a lot easier for them to see quality on the job than at school. To find out why this is so requires asking a few more questions.

For example, if you ask whether it takes hard work to get a good education, most young people will say that it does. They are not clear about what a good education is, but they believe that it takes hard work to get it. Furthermore, if you ask them whether they are smart enough to get a good education, almost all will say that they are — even if they don't know exactly what it is that they have to be smart enough to do.

But if you then ask them whether they're working hard in school, most will say no. As much as they want that vague something that to them is a good education, which they know takes hard work, they do not have any clear idea of how schoolwork as they know it relates to what they want. Until they have a much clearer idea about what a quality education is and about how it relates to what they are asked to do in school, they will not work hard in school.

The public schools in Johnson City, New York, where Albert Mamary is superintendent, are probably the best model in the U.S. of what could be called quality schools. But we need more than a few models like Johnson City. After all, there were always a few quality foreign cars around, but no one paid attention until they arrived in quantity. Even the schools that border on Johnson City have paid little attention to the good work going on there.

As Linda McNeil has pointed out, we are making the serious mistake of assuming that a high-quality school is one in which everyone is well-behaved and getting low-quality "passing" scores on nonquality achievement tests. Led (actually *mis*led) by state departments of education, we are striving to do in our schools what nearly destroyed the auto industry. A lot of ill-designed and poorly built cars were able to pass minimal inspection standards, and, not knowing better or having no better ones available, people bought them. People still support our public schools, but discontent is rife. If there were more and better-publicized models of a better way of doing things, people would demand the same quality from their school systems.

What the U.S. auto industry failed to recognize until foreign imports started to penetrate the market was that the domestic cars were low in quality. In the same way, our boss-dominated education establishment fails to recognize that quiet, conforming students who pass achievement tests that measure only minimal knowledge and low-quality skills are not doing high-quality schoolwork.

Nevertheless, I think it is also safe to say that most of those who manage our schools do not manage for quality and that most teachers do not even think of quality when they face students. The goals on their minds are those of the top-level management: raise the test scores a little, get more students through, and keep discipline problems low. There is no way that anyone will ever confuse these minimal goals with quality, and the result is that less than 15% of all students do quality work of any kind. When a lot of quality suddenly appears in classes where it had never been seen before, as was documented in the movie *Stand and Deliver*, it is so unusual that it borders on the unbelievable and becomes the stuff of real-life drama.

What all of us — workers and students alike — do when we do high-quality work is to evaluate carefully what we are doing and come to the conclusion that it is worth working hard because it feels good. What few managers realize is that coercion prevents this necessary self-evaluation, because the workers and students spend most of their time and effort evaluating the boss instead of evaluating their own work.

For instance, consider again the example of the good students at West High School in Torrance, California, who purposely failed the state-mandated tests because they resented the amount of time that preparation for these low-quality tests took from the high-quality work that they felt they should be doing. These students focused their resentment on the boss-administrators who pushed this meaningless assessment program. The students then did what we all tend to do when we are being coerced: they wasted time and effort evaluating the coercers and trying to outwit them. If they had not been coerced, these good students would have ignored the tests and spent their time and effort furthering their education by evaluating their own work and raising its quality. They would still have done reasonably well on the tests that they made so much effort to mess up. When effort is diverted from the task at hand, as happens in every coercive situation, quality suffers.

Think of the times in your life when you did high-quality work. Didn't you do it because you were supported and encouraged enough so that you were willing to evaluate what you were doing and work to make it better and better? As you improved, didn't the work itself become more and more important to you? Or did you do it because you were badgered and wanted to get rid of the pressure from the manager or teacher?

In education more than in industry, when we try to make the move to quality, it is the rare student who can recognize quality when he or she starts a new subject. For example, in *Stand and Deliver*, the true story of a group of Hispanic high school students who successfully learned calculus, it is clear that the students had no idea that there was quality to calculus when they started. What they recognized quickly, however, was that their teacher, Jamie Escalante, was a high-

quality teacher. They began to accept the fact that, if he taught calculus, it too must have quality.

But quality goes beyong doing well on tests and assignments, and in a sense it goes beyond mastery learning. In our quest for quality, what we need to strive for is students' setting their own standards for quality, not just doing well on tasks the teacher assigns. Deming points out that, given the encouragement and the tools, workers will build better products than boss-managers ever dreamed possible.

When we see the record-breaking performances of athletes in the Olympic games, the importance of self-motivation is obvious. In many cases, athletes perform far beyond the expectations of even their coaches. For example, when you listen to the gymnasts after their performances (even if they didn't win), what they are most proud of is that, good as they are, they have improved. The concept of quality has taken hold inside them. This is what we need to try to do with our students: start early, and talk to them about quality. Give them tools and lots of encouragement. Then stand back and see where they go once the idea of quality education gets inside their heads.

While there is much to be worked out as these ideas are put into practice, Deming has shown that "working it out" is the easy part. The hard part is deciding to make the change and getting rid of the adversarial boss-managed atmosphere. I can offer no guarantee that we will be able to achieve quality by doing what I have suggested here, but there is good evidence that, if we don't do something like this, we will never achieve quality. The good news is that quality is contagious, and we see this contagion in extracurricular activities. You don't have to coerce a student into putting effort into playing basketball, singing in the chorus, or acting in the school play.

If we can achieve quality in our classrooms, as I believe we can, then academic quality will become contagious as well. Many students who work hard now are treated as pariahs by the other students because the accepted attitude for at least half of the students in our boss-managed, adversarial schools is to be anti-education. The only way to defeat this destructive attitude is to make quality as much a part of academics as it is now part of athletics. Once quality becomes central to our coursework, students will be proud of what they do, and this pride will become as contagious as pride anywhere else. It is only too obvious that few students or teachers are proud of what is going on now in too many of our classrooms.

1. Myron Tribus, *Selected Papers on Quality and Productivity Improvement* (Washington, D.C.: National Society of Professional Engineers, 1988), p. 5. Copies of this book are available for $15 from NSPE, P.O. Box 96163, Washington, DC 20090-6163.

2. Linda M. McNeil, *Contradictions of Control: School Structure and School Knowledge* (New York: Methuen/Routledge & Kegan Paul, 1986).

3. William Glasser, *Control Theory in the Classroom* (New York: Harper & Row, 1986).

4. Linda M. McNeil, "Contradictions of Control, Part 3: Contradictions of Reform" *Phi Delta Kappan,* March 1988, p. 485.

CHARM SCHOOL FOR Bullies

**Aggressive kids
are learning to
negotiate instead
of throwing tantrums
and punches.**

Deborah Franklin is a staff writer.

NATHAN'S A SLAMMER. He'll stomp out of class when somebody crosses him, banging the door behind him. Though bright, the burly fifth-grader taunts and teases to get what he wants. He hates his classmates and they hate him.

Unlike Nathan, who seeks a spotlight, Joe keeps mostly to himself. But when he feels he's been pushed too far—which happens several times a day—he comes back swinging. It's usually the nose of a smaller, weaker kid that gets in the way.

While Nathan and Joe are equally agile in terrorizing their classmates, they don't ordinarily collaborate. But once every week during a recent quarter, Harvard University psychologist Robert Selman brought the two bullies together for a little experiment. Under his tutelage in a counseling office at their Cambridge, Massachusetts, elementary school, the boys learned and practiced socially acceptable methods of manipulating each other.

In each session, Selman would hand Nathan and Joe a construction set, and tell them to play *together*. If they shared the blocks, they could build a space station or castle, complete with turrets and a working drawbridge. Working alone, they would have only enough time and resources to build irregular piles of interlocked plastic.

In their first encounter, the boys ignored each other; Nathan tipped his chair back at one end of the table giving loud Bronx cheers, while Joe, his jacket zipped to his chin, a wedge of rusty hair hiding his eyes, worked silently at the other end. But by the third session, Joe began to perk up. He put a few pieces together and zoomed them around like a jet, loudly bombing invisible enemies. "Do you like my aircraft, Nathan?" he asked, still not looking at the other boy. No response. Nathan was working on his own project, and was missing a piece. He eyed the tail of Joe's jet.

"If I had a piece like you have," Nathan said, "I could sure use it." No response. Nathan began fishing around in a box of 80 or 90 loose pieces. "Help me find one of those things, Joe," he said without looking at him. "I could use it." Joe continued to fly his jet in sweeping arcs, and the bombing grew more intense. Nathan scowled. "If you asked *me* for help, Joe, I'd give it to *you*," he said. A loud buzzer signaled the end of the play period.

Selman, who had silently watched the interaction from a few feet away, wasted no time getting to the point. "So, you guys did a good job of playing today, but it seemed as though you had a problem." He walked through the conflict, getting Nathan to explain what he'd wanted. "You know," Selman said, "I bet that if you guys worked together on a project you could make something really cool."

Nathan nodded his head, and seemed interested. Joe tucked his chin and stared at the floor. "I'd rather each build our own stuff," he said quietly. "When we work together, we get into fights."

Selman nodded. "Yeah, I know that happens sometimes," he said. "But maybe it's worth *trying* to work together, so that you could make the spaceship."

Such odd little scenes of confrontation and mediation are unfolding at a handful of "charm schools" for bullies around the country. The underlying theory of these experimental programs, based on the research of developmental psychologists in the last decade, is that most bullies are made, not born. Search the past of a teenage extortionist, and you're likely to find a fourth-grader who never learned to negotiate. Help the troubled fourth-grader brush up on his social skills, and you may nudge him away from the joys of intimidation—and maybe even toward an appreciation of the other guy's perspective. But in order to learn these skills, all children—especially bullies—need a safe place for lots of practice.

"We would never expect a kid to learn to read or write just from hearing a lecture," says Steven Brion-Meisels, a Cambridge educator who has adapted some of Selman's techniques for use by teachers in the classroom. "And we shouldn't expect them to learn social skills that way either."

If all this sounds like the finely spun theory of naive academics, consider one view from the trenches. Stella Sadofsky has been a social worker in New Jersey schools for 22 years, and knows an educational fad when she sees it. This time she thinks the academics are on to something.

"Teachers are already spending inordinate and increasing amounts of time dealing with kids' social problems," Sadofsky says. "Separating kids and breaking up fights takes time, too. Instead, in the same amount of time, we can teach children to solve their own problems. They start to see that there are many solutions that don't involve slugging it out."

Children don't outgrow aggression. Of 11,000 junior high and high school students surveyed nationally in 1987, almost half the boys, and more than one-fourth of the girls, reported having taken part in at least one fight during the previous year that involved fists or weapons. More than a third had been physically threatened, 14 percent had been robbed, and 13 percent had been attacked while at school or on a school bus. Even students who haven't been beaten up are scared: One-fourth of the students in a similar survey said that the possibility of being bullied is one of their biggest fears.

In the long run, bullying may hurt the aggressor even more than the victim. One study that followed nearly 600 children from age eight to 30 showed that those who bullied in elementary school—acted rudely to the teacher and other children, started fights over nothing, took classmates' toys without asking—were five times more likely than their less belligerent classmates to have been convicted of crimes by age 30. They were also much more likely to have low-paying jobs, to be abusing their spouses, and to be raising contentious children of their own.

"It's unquestionably in the best interests of these kids and society to intervene early," says Selman. He and others who run similar programs focus on children who are not hardened criminals, but who simply spend most of their school hours on the edge of aggression.

Some teachers and parents might question the value of teaching these children Machiavellian reasoning—telling Nathan and Joe, for instance, that sharing is good because it helps *you* get what *you* want. But Selman defends his tactics. "If you try more sophisticated reasoning on kids before they're ready, they'll flat out ignore you," he says. "Recognizing that the other guy has rights independent of your own is a concept that many teenagers and even adults have trouble with." For most bullies, there are only two ways to resolve conflicts: fighting or running.

That's not surprising if you look at the first place children learn about conflict, the family. Leonard Eron, a psychologist at the University of Illinois in Chicago, found that the parents of aggressive children he studied tended to punish their offspring both harshly and capriciously, alternately blowing up at them for minor infractions and ignoring them for long stretches of time. Other researchers say that such parents punish more according to their own moods than in response to the child's behavior.

After these early lessons in erratic parental attacks, some children naturally become wary and misinterpret the actions and intentions of others. Vanderbilt University psychologist Kenneth Dodge says about half the aggressive boys he studies see slights or hostilities where none are meant—even in videotaped scenes of conflict involving other children. "This is the kid who gets angry easily, has temper tantrums, and might get into a lot of fights, but doesn't necessarily start them," says Dodge. "Somebody calls him a name or jostles him in the hallway and instead of tossing it off with a joke as other children do, he overreacts."

To help fifth- and sixth-grade boys who fit that description, psychologist John Lochman of Duke University holds weekly sessions in the Durham, North Carolina, public schools. In role-playing sessions, one kid becomes the bully, another the victim; just before the conflict's climax, the boys freeze, and one group member interviews each actor about when he first noticed a problem, what he was thinking and feeling as the conflict escalated, and what he was likely to do next. Afterwards the group discusses alternate solutions that might have helped both boys get what they wanted without violence. Other exercises are spiced-up versions of counting to ten before blowing your stack: One child holding a puppet concentrates on reciting the alphabet, while five other children taunt the puppet.

Initially, instead of trying to change a bully's desire to dominate, Lochman builds on it. "We'll tell a child, 'Look—if you let those guys get to you, *they're* controlling *you*. They like it when you act out and get in trouble.'" Only later, after the child has mastered staying cool under fire, will Lochman suggest that there might be rewarding alternatives to intimidation.

Of course, not all school districts can afford to pull aggressive children out of class once a week for an hour of intensive training in negotiation. But proponents of these charm schools suggest that teachers can provide some of the same kinds of practice during class meetings held once or twice a week. There, for 30 minutes or an hour, children can have a chance to air complaints and to see that others often have a different viewpoint. Gradually they'll learn that they can take and give criticism without bringing the world down around their ears. Brion-Meisels recalls one such meeting of sixth-graders in Boston: "Rules come up a lot in these meetings, and this particular day, the kids wanted to discuss the rules we should have about swearing." In the midst of the discussion, Eddie, the class bully, said he thought he alone should be allowed to swear, and anyone else who did should be kicked out of class.

"Most of the other kids groaned and called him a jerk," Brion-Meisels says. "But Donald, a kid he sort of admired, spoke up and said, 'Wait a minute, man. You mean that if I swore you'd think I should be kicked out?' Eddie thought about it and said, 'No, I don't know as you'd have to leave. You and I could swear, and that'd be okay.'

"That's a beginning," says Brion-Meisels, "just a tiny chink in the armor on which you can build." The following week in reading group, Eddie's teacher coaxed him to note the perspectives of different children in the story, and paired Eddie and Donald together to work on an art project—small steps in learning to collaborate. "I could have lectured Eddie for a week about the importance of thinking about the other guy, and he wouldn't have gotten it," says Brion-Meisels. "He didn't get it until he started practicing."

Eight weeks into their sessions in Cambridge, Joe and Nathan quietly reached their own milestone. Bored with the simple toys they'd managed to construct individually, the boys decided for the first time to pull together and attempt the space station. As Nathan perspired over the instruction sheet, he crowded Joe, reaching across him for a particular piece. This time, Joe didn't withdraw or as he had in one previous session, strike back. Instead, he tried to negotiate.

"We don't *need* that part for the next step, Nathan," he said. "This time let *me* put it together."

Nathan backed off, a little surprised, a little relieved. "Okay, we'll take turns, and the next time I'll do it," he said, handing over the half-built toy.

Selman was jubilant. "We had them talking," he says. "That's a big deal for these kids.

"We're not saying that ten weeks like this can turn these kids completely around," Selman adds, "or that it's enough for every child. Some kids have serious emotional problems, and need in-depth counseling." It's also too soon to tell whether the lessons Nathan and Joe have learned will stick. But a study that Lochman has just finished on his aggressive kids in North Carolina is encouraging: Several years after their negotiation sessions ended, the children had more self-esteem, better problem-solving skills, and lower rates of drug and alcohol abuse than similar children who hadn't been in the program.

By the end of the term, Nathan still took the noisy lead in any decision, while Joe's first impulse was to sulk. But gradually, they got better at dreaming up solutions to problems. During the last session, the boys finally built the space station, and both wanted to take it home. Instead, they agreed to keep snapshots of the project. The two class bullies stepped close together behind the structure, swung their arms around each other, and hammed for the camera.

Equal Opportunity and American Education

North America is as multicultural a region of the world as exists anywhere on earth. Our enormous cultural diversity encompasses populations from many indigenous "First Americans" as well as peoples from every European culture, plus many peoples of Asian, African, and Latin American nations and the Central and South Pacific Island groups. There is spirited controversy among Americans as to how best to help all Americans to better understand the multicultural heritage of America. There are spirited defenders and opponents to the traditional eurocentric heritage of the established North American knowledge base. We must deal with this controversy as well as with many others having to do with issues regarding what constitutes equality of opportunity from different perspectives.

The problems of inequality of educational opportunity are still of great concern to American educators. One in four American children do not have all of their basic needs met and live under poverty conditions. Almost one in three live in single-parent homes, not that this is necessarily a disadvantage, but under conditions of poverty it often is. More and more concern is expressed over how to help children of poverty. The equity agenda of our time has to do with many issues related to gender, race, and ethnicity. All forms of social deprivation or discrimination are aggravated by great disparities in family income and accumulated wealth. How can children and adolescents be helped to have an equal opportunity to succeed in school? We have wrestled with this great practical and moral dilemma in educational policy development for decades. How can we advance the just cause of the educational interests of our children and adolescents more effectively?

We are several decades into one of the greatest human rights movements in human history, and the international situation has led to the apparent end of the cold war with the Soviet Union. However, other grave and pressing economic and military challenges still divert previous economic resources from the need to create more effective opportunity structures for the young. Can you imagine a more worthwhile use of precious national resources than for the health, education, and safety of our children and young adults? Discrimination on the basis of sex and race is still a great challenge to North American societies in spite of the great progress we have made. We must resolve never to stop the just and right struggle to secure equal rights for all our youth.

Some of us are still proud to say we are a nation of immigrants. There are powerful demographic and economic forces impacting on the makeup of the populations of Canada and the United States. In addition to the traditional minority-majority group relationships in the United States, new waves of immigrants are making concerns for achieving equality of opportunity in education as important as ever. The new immigrations from Asia and Latin America reemphasize the already preexistent reality that we are a nation forged from many cultures. Both Canada and the United States are deeply committed to improving intercultural relations in education and the society at large. The sociological and demographic changes in North American population development are very significant, and they represent trends that assure that we will remain multicultural democracies.

The social psychology of prejudice is something North American psychiatrists, social psychologists, anthropologists, and sociologists have studied in great depth since the 1930s. Tolerance, acceptance, and a commitment to the unique worth of every person are teachable and learnable attitudes. The dream of the founders and of the martyrs for human rights lives. It will never die.

The struggle for equality of opportunity is an endless challenge; poverty reduces windows of opportunity for those affected by it. A just society is constantly challenged to find meaningful ways to raise human aspirations, to heal human hurt, and to help in the task of optimizing every citizen's potential. Education is a vital component of all efforts to alleviate, or even eradicate, the causes of poverty. Yet poverty is not the only obstacle to equality of opportunity. Any form of discrimination against persons because of their identity or socioeconomic status is an impediment to democratic social aspirations. Educational systems and the teachers who labor within them can be a bulwark and a source of hope for those who struggle to overcome these impediments and fulfill the full promise of their humanity.

The fulfillment of the full promise of humanity is what democracy is all about. The freedom to teach, the freedom to learn, the freedom to become the best we can be—that is what the schools of free peoples provide. Teachers have enormous opportunities to reach out to their students as examples of justice and fairness in their day-to-day instructional activities. They can incorporate into their lessons an emphasis on acceptance of difference, toleration of and respect for the beliefs of others, and the skills of reasoned debate and dialogue.

The civil rights of students and teachers in schools is a question that is often raised before state and federal courts. The equal treatment of students under national constitutional guidelines is of great importance. Many decisions made by the courts concern issues that affect students and teachers, including the study of religion in schools, prayer and scripture reading in schools, racial desegregation, bilingual education, and academic freedom. The federal judiciary in the United States has established important precedents in all of the above areas. In both Canada and the United States, great importance is attached to the development of workable opportunity structures in national educational systems. The interpretation of these opportunity structures has evolved over many years, as reflected in the evolution of lines of argument in the courts on these matters.

Equality of the interests of citizens of democratic societies is based on the belief that, in any free society, a plurality of interests must be protected. In addition, the dignity and opportunity of each individual citizen must be protected. The unjust limitation of freedom of expression or the limitation of the opportunity to become adequately educated are intolerable in a democratic state.

Americans have witnessed one of the greatest struggles for equality before the law in all of human history. That struggle is especially well known to educators. More than 30 years ago, the Supreme Court of the United States arrived at the first in what was to be a long chain of decisions affecting majority-minority relations in American schools. The famous 1954 decision of the United States Supreme Court in *Brown v. Board of Education of Topeka* and other decisions expanded equality of educational opportunity to include women, linguistic minorities, cultural minorities, the aged, and the defenseless. These decisions constitute a triumphant testimony to the possibility of social justice under the law. Future generations of Americans and other free peoples will forever look with awe at the struggle for civil rights in American schools from 1954 to the closing years of the present century. Rarely have free people asserted their rights under the law as forcefully and effectively as the American people

have on the question of equality of educational opportunity.

The closing years of this century can be approached with renewed hope and confidence in regard to the issue of educational opportunity. A vast body of research on this issue has evolved from the many federal court decisions since 1954. Problems of inequity in the schools have been well documented, and the nation is developing increased sophistication and effectiveness in finding solutions to these problems. The desegregation of American schools has been forcefully initiated throughout the nation, and progress is continuing in majority-minority relations in the schools. It is not only cultural minorities who have benefited from the federal school desegregation cases, however. Affirmative action in employment and admission to professional schools, the students' rights issue, and the rights of women and the aged have been based on the same constitutional arguments and precedents established in the major school desegregation cases and the Civil Rights Act of 1964. The right of linguistic minorities to learn the English language in public schools has been based on these same constitutional principles. Every American has benefited, either directly or indirectly, from this triumph of constitutional law over racist tradition.

Looking Ahead: Challenge Questions

What do you know about how it feels to be poor? How do you think it would feel in school? How would you respond?

If you are a female, have you ever felt that you were discriminated against, or at least ignored?

If you are a male, have you ever felt that you were being favored?

How can schools address more effectively the issue of gender bias?

How do children learn to be prejudiced? How can they learn tolerance?

What were the constitutional precedents for the school desegregation cases?

What academic freedoms should every teacher and student have?

What do you understand to be the interrelationship between the effects of poverty and racial or sexual discrimination?

How can a classroom teacher help his or her students adopt tolerant multicultural perspectives?

AMERICA THE MULTICULTURAL

ROBERT J. COTTROL

Robert J. Cottrol is a specialist in American legal history and an associate professor of law at Rutgers School of Law in Camden, New Jersey. He is the author of The Afro-Yankees: Providence's Black Community in the Antebellum Era *and many articles about race and law in the United States. This article is drawn from a speech he delivered at the AFT conference, "Building Alliances for Youth at Risk."*

I GREW UP in the fifties, in an era when public schools, with few exceptions, presented a picture of the world that was relentlessly monocultural and, I might add, monochromatic. World history classes presented us with an impressive array of European heroes and villains, King John I (who I confess made a greater impression on me as the villain of numerous Robin Hood movies than as the grantor of the Magna Carta), Charlemagne, Columbus, Louis XIV, Napoleon, Kaiser Wilhelm, Adolf Hitler, Winston Churchill, and the list goes on. Rarely did the standard world history class examine the lives of the great figures from Africa, Asia, Latin America, or the indigenous populations of the Americas. Likewise, in American history class it was possible to go through the school year learning about Washington, Jefferson, Adams, Lincoln, Roosevelt, Wilson and other great men of U.S. history, with only a pause, in February, during what was then called "Negro History Week," to spend a brief moment on George Washington Carver and his experiments on the peanut.

So my views on multicultural education are informed, in part, by childhood memories. But my views also have been informed by my adult experiences. I have spent my adult life studying the role of race in American legal and social history. This study has left me with an appreciation for the diversity of American culture and for America's opportunity to contribute further to global civilization.

LET ME first say what multicultural education is not, or at least should not attempt to be. It should not simply be a program designed for minority students. There is a temptation to believe that multicultural education can somehow provide a quick fix for the ills that plague inner-city education. If only we teach inner-city students about the African Kingdom of Mali in the Middle Ages instead of dwelling on Medieval England, if we present less Abraham Lincoln and more Frederick Douglass, if we offer more of the writings of Malcolm X and less discussion of the Eisenhower administration, then students who previously had been turned off by school will suddenly become scholars, enthusiastic and interested in their school work. Would that this were so! We then could easily switch to a more Afro-centric or Hispano-centric or Asia-centric curriculum, confident that a change in subject matter would produce diligent, enthusiastic students. The increase in language and analytical skills alone that would result from their new studiousness would more than justify any subject matter deficiencies such a curriculum might produce. These could be corrected later.

Unhappily, multicultural education has only a marginal ability to bring about such a transformation. The students most at risk—those from decaying inner city neighborhoods, those from broken families, those who join gangs in fear of their lives, those who are the heirs of a culture of despair that has developed in all too many of our ghettoes in the last generation—will not be inspired nor have their lives radically changed by the addition of a multicultural dimension to their educations, however much we might hope so. The addition of black, or Hispanic, or Asian, or Indian heroes and role models might inspire a few such students, but multicultural education cannot be seen as a remedy for society's neglect of its cities, the poor people that dwell in them, and the urban schools that will shape the next generation of Americans.

Nor should multicultural education be the occasion for building up false ethnic pride or for substituting myths about people of African, Asian, or Latin American descent for myths concerning people of European descent. Multicultural education should not be an excuse for replacing the myth of "America the Perfect" with "America the Reprobate." In an honest, serious multicultural education, one in which students encounter the rich diversity of the American heritage, our students should learn about the greatness of Thomas Jefferson's ideas *and* that, as a slaveholder, he betrayed America's ideals. Our students should learn about the great achievement that was the opening of the American West *and* about the tremendous price America's indigenous populations paid in the process.

The fact is that American history—like any history—offers no simple, pure truths. Our history is neither great nor terrible, but a complicated mix of both, with good growing from evil, and evil growing from good. It is this complexity that makes history interesting and challenging. We shouldn't deny students of any color the richness of this American dilemma.

THE TEACHING of history is probably the most important part of multicultural education because it is the major means by which the culture, values, and legacy of our civilization are passed from one generation to the next. American history, like history generally, tells us the ways in which our civilization is unique, and yet, properly taught, it reminds us of our kinship with others who share the human experience.

Every student who passes through our school system needs to be made aware that the cultures of peoples from every corner of the earth have made significant contributions to the American experience. This means teachers must bring some of the newer historical scholarship into the classroom. At one time those who wrote about and taught history believed their mission was to relate the stories of the great men and public events of each age and to ignore the day-to-day lives of ordinary people. We would learn about George Washington but little about the lives and motivations of the farmers, shopkeepers, and artisans who served with him in the Continental Army. Or we would learn about the Lincoln-Douglas debates but little about the agonies of the slaves who were at the heart of those debates. We learned about the building of the transcontinental railroad but nothing about the day-to-day living conditions of Irish and Chinese laborers who carved that railroad out of the American wilderness.

> *At every point in our nation's history, American culture has been transformed, and our democratic ideals tested and strengthened, by America's black, brown, red, and yellow citizens.*

Much recent scholarship—by focusing more on the lives and contributions of minorities; on the political and social lives of ordinary Americans; and by exploiting such historical sources as census data, court records, and voting statistics—has given us a more complete picture of the American past. It is important that this new, more historically accurate picture be painted for our students as early in their education as possible. The incorporation of that scholarship will tell us and our students much concerning the civilization that we Americans of all colors have built on the North American continent.

Our civilization began with an English base. We need not deny nor underplay this fact even when we are teaching children of African, Latin American, Asian, American Indian, and I might add, Eastern and Southern European descent. Our notions of law and politics, of constitutionalism in the broadest sense of that term, are English in origin. It was in England that modern concepts of limited, representative government, due process in criminal trials, the rights to organize politically and challenge the government through orderly political processes took their modern form. These ideas have captured the imagination of the world; they have been adopted as ideals and, increasingly, as practices by people of every race. The great Latin American liberator Simon Bolivar took American ideas of constitutionalism and incorporated them into the fundamental charters of a number of South American countries. He went the American Constitution one step better by, in many cases, abolishing slavery immediately upon attainment of independence. And these constitutional ideals have been spread by Americans of every race. Japanese-Americans helped draft Japan's postwar democratic constitution. The great African-American lawyer and jurist Justice Thurgood Marshall helped draft Kenya's first constitution as an independent nation.

The spread of Anglo-American constitutionalism has been a multiracial enterprise as was the creation of English as a universal language. The English language was spread by British colonial administrators and by Americans of every description, by Jewish-American tourists, by Polish-American students studying in foreign universities, by Hispanic Peace Corps volunteers, by the Negro and Nisei GIs who played a large part in liberating Italy and France during World War II.

BUT THE story of America is not just about how Anglo-American ideas were spread by a multicultural citizenry. At every point in our nation's history, American culture has been transformed, and our democratic ideals tested and strengthened, by America's black, brown, red, and yellow citizens. This is a story all students need to know. We should tell students about anthropological historian Peter Wood, whose work on eighteenth-century South Carolina, "*Black Majority*," shows us that much of the American cowboy culture had West African origins. Our students should know that at the time of the Constitution's formation that the issues of slavery and black citizenship were hotly debated, and they should know that black people were not passive bystanders in that debate. The odyssey of early American freedom is not complete unless students learn of Paul Cuffee's successful struggle to attain black suffrage in eighteenth-century Massachusetts or that Richard Allen established an independent black church in eighteenth-century Philadelphia because he and his congregation refused to participate in a segregated church. A student who walks away from an American history class unaware that the nineteenth-century war between the United States and the Seminole nation of Florida occurred because Seminole chief Osceola regarded the fugitive slaves who lived among the Seminole as an integral part of the Seminole nation and refused to return them to their former masters has missed an important chapter in the history of the struggle for freedom in this country. Nor should we neglect to tell our students that the Texas War for Independence (the war in which the battle of the Alamo was fought) occurred, in part, because Mexico had abolished slavery and refused to allow American settlers in Texas to maintain slaves.

The struggles to end segregation and slavery and to build a more just society in their aftermath, provide the most vivid examples of how a multicultural population changed this country and helped enlarge the definition of freedom here, and indeed around the world. An Afro-American culture was formed in slavery, a culture different from the West African culture from which its people were descended—a fact we should never lose sight of, for if we do, we run the risk of asking black students to substitute an ersatz African culture for the rich African-American culture that is theirs. The Afro-American culture formed in slavery was an American culture and one that influenced not only black Americans but white ones as well. Who can look at American music, storytelling, and cooking without seeing this Afro-American culture? Who can look at southern white Protestantism and its fervent religiosity and deny the Afro-American influence?

But the impact of black people on the story of American freedom is broader and deeper than these examples. No student should leave our schools without having encountered the life of Frederick Douglass, preferably in one of his magnificent autobiographies. Douglass, one of nineteenth-century America's great statesmen and men of letters overcame handicaps even greater than those of his legendary friend Abraham Lincoln. Born a slave, he had a bootlegged education as a child, clandestinely taught to read and write by his master's wife. He escaped and had an incredible career as an abolitionist, journalist, and statesman. His concern for human freedom extended far beyond the precincts of slavery and race. He was an early advocate of women's suffrage and the betterment of working class whites. While still a fugitive, he stayed in England for a time. Notwithstanding his gratitude to his English hosts and his appreciation for their support of the American abolitionist cause, he did not hesitate to criticize England's treatment of Ireland and to befriend the Irish statesman Daniel O'Connell. During the Civil War, Douglass played a courageous role in persuading Lincoln to move beyond simple unionism to embrace the antislavery cause. No American student can truly be said to have

had a complete education without studying the life of this remarkable man.

But there are others who must be studied. The slaves and free black men who rallied to the American cause and served with the Union forces during the Civil War helped write a new chapter in American constitutionalism. Students should become familiar with these lives, and I would heartily recommend the movie *Glory* as one way to discover that chapter in American history. We need to teach our students about former slaves who in the aftermath of Appomattox worked to unite and rebuild the many families that had been separated during slavery. We must tell our students about how much freed men valued education. Whole families would till the soil for twelve or fourteen hours a day and then go to school because they believed that education would bring about a better life for their children. We also need to tell our students that the dashing of those hopes led to the frustration that is at the root of many of today's urban problems. Our students also need to be taught that one of the most important cases establishing the principle of equal treatment under law came when a Chinese immigrant named Yick Wo insisted on an equal right to run his small business—a laundry.

Students studying twentieth-century America need to learn of A. Philip Randolph's struggle to bring dignity and economic justice to black workers. We must tell them about Walter White's attempts to stop lynchings, of Judge William Hastie's efforts to bring a measure of justice to the Jim Crow army of World War II, and of the incredible heroism of the Japanese-Americans of the 442nd regiment in that war and how they and black troops, two groups singled out for second-class military and civilian citizenship, helped to liberate Dachau. Students' knowledge of America will be enriched immeasurably by studying the lives of Americans of all races who were active in the civil rights movement. Children cannot appreciate the richness and poverty of the twentieth-century American experience without examining the world through the eyes of labor leader Cesar Chavez, or walking down the mean streets of East Harlem with Piri Thomas.

These too are part of the American story. They are the legacy of all Americans as much as are our more familiar memories of Washington and Lincoln. These stories should not be put to one side, reserved for students of some races but not others or marginalized as sidebars to American history. This *is* American history.

WE ARE coming to the end of a remarkable, and in many ways terrible, century. In this period, we have seen extraordinary technological progress, moving testimony to the human capacity for the acquisition and application of knowledge. But we have also seen another, darker side of human character. We have seen the rise of totalitarian forces made more potent and more terrible by that same technological progress. I do not know how the history of the world in the twentieth-century will be written in the future. I suspect that future historians will note that the United States played an admirable, indeed leading, role in vanquishing those totalitarian forces—Imperial Germany in the first World

War, Nazism, Fascism, and Japanese militarism in the Second, and more recently Communism, in what was once termed by John Kennedy the long twilight struggle of the Cold War. Our record in this regard has by no means been perfect. There were compromises between our ideals and our policies. We have, for example, been slow to anger over the tyrannies that rule in China, and South Africa, in Uganda and Iraq. But still the American people—through great expenditure of resources, including our most valuable resource, the lives of the nation's sons and daughters—have not only done much to vanquish tyranny but much to advance the cause of freedom as well. Ours is a remarkable record for a nation that was not counted among the great powers at the beginning of this century.

But there is another great contribution we can make to the world. At the beginning of this century, W. E. B. Du Bois said that the problem of the twentieth-century would be the color line. How prophetic he was. With slight modification, we can see that the problem for the next century remains the same. The problems of ethnic strife and multiculturalism plague nations around the globe. We need not look beyond our northern neighbor, Canada, to see language and ethnicity dividing a peaceful and prosperous country. Our former adversary, the Soviet Union, now faces ethnic conflict that may engulf the country in a civil war that could threaten the entire world. Eastern Europe's difficult road to democracy is made more so by the release of long pent-up ethnic hatreds. Western Europeans who once looked with amazement and scorn at American racial problems have suddenly become very quiet on the subject in the face of large-scale immigration from Asia and Africa. The nations of Africa are divided by tribalism. The problem of South African racism and tribalism still mocks universally held values. Japan has scarcely begun to address the question of justice for Koreans and other ethnic minorities. Irish Protestants and Catholics still quarrel over issues that had their origins during the reigns of Tudor and Stuart monarchs.

For all its faults and for all the faults that a multicultural education will uncover and report, the United States remains the most successful multi-ethnic and multiracial society of our time, perhaps of all time. This too is the American story. And so we return to the real teaching challenge: telling the very complicated story of American history to students—complicated because it includes so much that is terrible and so much that is remarkable. It is a history of contradiction and dilemmas. Ultimately, we should judge the quality and success of our multicultural education programs not strictly according to how many individuals of color are noted—such an approach could easily lead just to more sidebars, which is not the point. In judging a particular multicultural education effort, we should ask whether it tells the story of how American culture was shaped and transformed by a multicultural population. And we should ask whether it helps our students come to grips with the contradictions at the core of our history.

Moreover, multicultural education should include, as part of its fundamental *corpus*, the teaching of the democratic ideas—tolerance, justice, rule by law, individual rights, majority rule, and more—that have made possible our incredibly diverse, prosperous and—relatively speaking—amicable society.

Perhaps our most important contribution to the twenty-first century will be to demonstrate that people from different races, cultures, and ethnic backgrounds can live side by side; retain their uniqueness; and, yet, over time form a new common culture. That has been the American story. It is a history that has much to tell the world. It must be told by American educators.

Multicultural Literacy and Curriculum Reform

Changes in our demographic make-up and in the nature of the work force are among several factors contributing to a growing recognition of the need for curriculum reform. James Banks suggests a curriculum designed to foster multicultural literacy—one that helps students and teachers to know, to care, and to act in ways that develop and cultivate a just society.

James A. Banks

JAMES A. BANKS is professor of education at the University of Washington, Seattle.

MOST reports urging educational reform in the 1980s paid scant attention to helping citizens develop the knowledge, attitudes, and skills necessary to function effectively in a nation and world increasingly diverse ethnically, racially, and culturally.[1] Two of the most influential works published late in the decade not only failed to describe the need for multicultural literacy and understanding, but also ran counter to the U.S. multicultural movement.[2]

E. D. Hirsch's and Allan Bloom's widely reviewed and discussed books, both published in 1987, were regarded by many as having cogently made the case for emphasizing the traditional western-centric canon dominating school and university curricula, a canon threatened, according to Bloom and other western traditionalists, by movements to incorporate more ethnic and women's content into curric-

ula.[3] Hirsch's works appear more sympathetic to ethnic and women's concerns than Bloom's. However, Hirsch's formulation of a list of memorizable facts is inconsistent with multicultural teaching, since it ignores the notion of knowledge as a social construction with normative and political assumptions.[4] Regarding knowledge as a social construction and viewing it from diverse cultural perspectives are key components of multicultural literacy.

There is growing recognition among educators and the general public that tomorrow's citizens should acquire the knowledge, skills, and attitudes critical to functioning in a diverse, complex world. Several factors contribute to this growing recognition, including the *demographic imperative,*[5] significant population growth among people of color, and increasing enrollments of students of color in the na-

Reprinted with permission from *Educational Horizons*, Vol. 69, No. 3, Spring 1991, pp. 135-140. *Educational Horizons*, quarterly journal of Phi Lambda Theta, National Honor and Professional Association in Education, Bloomington, IN 47407-6626.

tion's schools. Because of higher birth-rates among people of color compared to whites and the large influx each year of immigrants from Asia and Latin America, one in three Americans is forecast to be a person of color by the turn of the century.[6] Between 1981 and 1986, about 89 percent of legal immigrants to the United States came from non-European nations. Most came from Asia (47 percent) and Latin America (38 percent).[7] This significant population growth will have tremendous impact on the nation's social institutions, including the work force, the courts, the economic system, and the schools. The ethnic texture of the nation's schools will become increasingly diverse as well as low income as we enter the twenty-first century. About 46 percent of school-age youths will be of color by the year 2000.[8] This will contrast sharply with the ethnic and racial makeup of teacher populations; teachers of color are expected to decline from about 12.5 percent of the nation's teaching force in 1980 to about 5 percent by the year 2000.[9]

Growing recognition of the changing nature of the nation's work force and the predicted gap between needs and skills are other factors motivating educators and the general public to focus on multicultural concerns. When the twenty-first century arrives, there will be a large number of retirees and too few new workers. People of color will constitute a disproportionate share of the work force in the next century. Between 1980 and 2000, about 83 percent of new entrants to the labor force will be women, people of color, or immigrants; native white males will make up only 15 percent.[10] However, if the current educational levels of students of color are not increased significantly, most students will not have the knowledge and skills to meet the requirements of a global, primarily service-oriented job market. Consequently, corporations will export work to foreign nations that have more skilled workers—a trend that already has begun. While work opportunities are exported, low-income inner-city residents become increasingly disempowered in the process.

THE RASH of recent racial incidents on the nation's campuses is yet another factor stimulating discussion and concrete action regarding multicultural education and curriculum reform. More than two hundred such incidents were reported in the press between 1986 and 1988[11]; an unknown number has not been publicized. Racial incidents have occurred on all types of campuses, including liberal ones like the University of California, Berkeley; Stanford University; and the University of Wisconsin, Madison. African Americans and Jews have been frequent victims in such incidents, which have stunned and perplexed administrators and motivated many students of color and their white allies to demand ethnic studies requirements and reform of required general studies courses to include ethnic content.

Despite rough beginnings and a tenuous status, ethnic studies courses are becoming institutionalized at most major universities, including Berkeley, the University of Minnesota, and Bowling Green State University. The ethnic studies program at Berkeley, for example, grants a doctoral degree; the University of Washington has established an interdisciplinary Department of American Ethnic Studies. Amid a bitter campus controversy and national debate, Stanford replaced a required freshman western culture course with one called "Culture, Ideas, and Values," which includes the study of at least one non-western culture and works by women, minorities, and people of color.

Ethnic studies courses in high schools have not fared as well as those at universities. Most school districts have tried to incorporate such content into the existing curriculum rather than establishing separate courses. The rationale for this approach is intellectually defensible and laudable, but the approach has had mixed results. In most schools, the *textbook* is the curriculum. In the early 1970s, when the civil rights movement was at its apex and publishers were being pressured to integrate textbooks, large bits and pieces of ethnic content were introduced.

But when the civil rights movement lost much of its momentum and influence during the Reagan years, the impetus for textbook publishers to include this content waned, and publishers consequently slowed their pace. However, the momentum has now resumed as a result of changing demographics and pressure exerted by people of color, especially those in large urban school districts and in populous states with state textbook adoption policies, such as California and Texas.

The Curriculum Canon Battle

Parents and students of color are now pushing for reforms that go beyond separate ethnic studies courses and programs. They are urging public school educators and university faculties to integrate ethnic content into mainstream curricula and to transform the canons and paradigms on which school and university curricula are based. Acrid and divisive controversies have arisen on several campuses over attempts to incorporate ethnic content into the mainstream curriculum or to require all students to take ethnic studies courses. A heated and bitter debate also has arisen over attempts to incorporate ethnic content into public school curricula.[12] Much of this controversy focuses on attempts to infuse curricula with content about African Americans and African contributions to western civilization—efforts often called *Afrocentric*.[13] Today's curriculum controversies are in some ways more wrenching than those of the 1960s and 1970s, when attempts were made to establish separate ethnic studies courses and programs.

At universities throughout the United States, a vigorous debate is raging between those who defend the established Eurocentric, male-dominated curriculum and those who argue that the curriculum and its canon must be transformed to more accurately reflect race, ethnic, and cultural diversity.

A canon is a "norm, criterion, model or standard used for evaluating or criticizing."[14] It is also "a basic general principle or rule commonly accepted as true, valid and fundamental."[15] A

*H*istory is replete with examples of dominant groups defining their own interests as being in the public interest.

specific and identifiable canon is used to define, select, and evaluate knowledge in school and university curricula in the United States and other western nations. Rarely is this canon explicitly defined or discussed, and it is often taken for granted, unquestioned, and internalized by writers, researchers, teachers, professors, and students. Consequently, it often marginalizes the experiences of people of color, Third World nations and cultures, and the perspectives and histories of women.

African-American scholars such as George Washington Williams, Carter G. Woodson, and W.E.B. DuBois challenged the established canon in social science and history in the nineteenth and twentieth centuries.[16] Their scholarship was influential in the African-American academic community but largely ignored by the white world. The ethnic studies movement, growing out of the civil rights movement of the 1960s and 1970s, seriously challenged the Eurocentric canon. Later, this canon also was challenged by the women's studies movement. These movements are forcing an examination of the canon used to select and judge knowledge imparted in school and university curricula.

Feeling that their voices often have been silenced and their experiences minimized, women and people of color are struggling to be recognized in the curriculum and to have their important historical and cultural works canonized. This struggle can best be understood as a battle over who will participate in or control the formulation of the canon or standard used to determine what constitutes a liberal education. The guardians and defenders of the traditional, established canon apparently believe it best serves their interests and, consequently, the interests of society and the nation.[17]

A struggle for voice has emerged because of a powerful resistance movement to multicultural studies. Two organizations were founded to resist multicultural curriculum reform: the Madison Center, organized by William Bennet when he was secretary of education, and the National Association of Scholars. Resistance

also has been articulated in a series of popular and education articles and editorials severely critical of the multicultural education movement.[18]

Special Interests and the Public Interest

Ethnic and women's studies often are called *special interests* by individuals and groups now determining and formulating curricula. *Special interest* is defined as a "person or group seeking to influence policy often narrowly defined."[19] The term implies an interest that is particularistic and inconsistent with the paramount goals and needs of the nation. To be in the public good, interests must extend beyond the needs of a unique or particular group.

An important question is, Who formulates the criteria for determining what is a *special interest*? Powerful, traditional groups already have shaped curricula, institutions, and structures in their image and interests. The dominant culture tends to view a special interest as any one that challenges its power, ideologies, and paradigms, particularly if interest groups demand that institutional canons, assumptions, and values be transformed. History is replete with examples of dominant groups defining their own interests as being in the public interest.

One way those in power marginalize and disempower those who are structurally excluded from the mainstream is by labeling such individuals' visions, histories, goals, and struggles as "special interests." This serves to deny excluded groups the legitimacy and validity of full participation in society and its institutions.

Only a curriculum that reflects the collective experiences and interests of a wide range of groups is truly in the national interest and consistent with the public good. Any other curriculum reflects only special interests and, thus, does not meet the needs of a nation that must survive in a pluralistic, highly interdependent global world. Special interest curricula, such as history and literature emphasizing the primacy of the West and the history of European-American males, are detrimental to the public good, since they do not help students acquire life skills and perspectives essential for surviving in the twenty-first century.

The ethnic and women's studies movements do not constitute efforts to promote special interests. Their major aims are to transform the curriculum so that it is more truthful and inclusive and reflects the histories and experiences of the diverse groups making up American society. Such movements serve to democratize school and university curricula, rather than strengthen special interests.

For a variety of complex reasons, including the need to enhance our nation's survival in a period of serious economic and social problems, it behooves educators to rethink such concepts as special interests, the national interest, and the public good. Groups using such terms should be identified, along with their purposes for using them, and the use of these terms in the context of a rapidly changing world should be evaluated.

Our concept of cultural literacy should be broader than Hirsch's, which is neutral and static. Knowledge is dynamic, changing, and constructed within a social context. Rather than transmitting knowledge in a largely uncritical way, as Hirsch suggests, educators should help students recognize that knowledge reflects the social context in which it is created and that it has normative and value assumptions.

A Multicultural Curriculum

It is imperative that curricula be transformed to help students view concepts, issues, and problems from diverse cultural perspectives. Merely inserting ethnic and gender content into existing curricular structures, paradigms, and assumptions is not enough. Totally transformed, multicultural curricula motivate students to view and interpret facts, events, concepts, and theories from varying perspectives.

Students and teachers also bring their own biases and points of view to the knowledge they encounter. What students learn reflects not only what they encounter in the curriculum, but also the perceptions of the medium (the teacher). The multicultural classroom is a place where multiple voices are both heard and legitimized, including the vanquished and victims, students and teachers, the textbook writer, and those whose culture is transmitted by oral traditions.

Hirsch's contention that all U.S. citizens should master a common core of knowledge is logical and defensible.[20] But who will participate in formulating this knowledge? And whose interests will it serve? There must be broad participation in identifying, constructing, and formulating the knowledge we expect all our citizens to master. Such knowledge should reflect cultural democracy and serve the needs of all citizens.

Knowledge that satisfies these criteria can best be described as multicultural, and when mastered by students, multicultural literacy is acquired. Multicultural literacy is far preferable to cultural literacy, which connotes knowledge and understanding selected, defined, and constructed by elite groups within society. Multicultural literacy, on the other hand, connotes knowledge and understanding that reflect the broad spectrum of interests, experiences, hopes, struggles, and voices of society.

Knowledge as Social Construction

The knowledge construction process is an important dimension of multicultural education.[21] It describes ways teachers help students understand, investigate, and determine how implicit cultural assumptions, frames of references, perspectives, and biases within a discipline influence how knowledge is created. This process teaches students that knowledge reflects the social, political, and economic context in which it is created. Knowledge created by elite and powerless groups within the same society also tends to differ in significant ways.[22]

Students can analyze the knowledge construction process in science, for example, by studying how racism has been perpetuated by genetic theories of intelligence, Darwinism, and eugenics. In his important book, *The Mismeasurement of Man*, Stephen Jay Gould describes how scientific racism developed and was influential in the

Multicultural literacy is far preferable to cultural literacy, which connotes knowledge and understanding selected, defined, and constructed by elite groups within society.

nineteenth and twentieth centuries.[23] Scientific racism also has influenced significantly the interpretations of mental ability tests in the United States.[24] When students are examining how science has supported racist practices and ideologies, they also should examine how science has contributed to human justice and equality. Biological theories about the traits and characteristics that human groups share, as well as anthropological theories that challenged racist beliefs during the post-World War II period, especially the writings of Franz Boas and Ruth Benedict, are good examples of how science and scientists have helped eradicate racist beliefs, ideologies, and practices.[25] Students should learn how science, like other disciplines, has been both a supporter and eradicator of racist beliefs and practices.

Students can examine the knowledge construction process in the social sciences and humanities when they study such units and topics as the European discovery of America and America's westward movement. Students can discuss the latent political messages contained in these concepts and how they are used to justify the domination and destruction of Native American cultures.

Students can be asked why the Americas are called the *New World* and why people from England are often called *settlers* and *pioneers* in textbooks, while people from other lands are usually called *immigrants*. Students can be asked to think of words that might have been used by the Lakota Sioux to describe the same people that a textbook might label *settlers* and *pioneers*. Such terms as *invaders, conquerors,* and *foreigners* may come to their minds. The goal of this exercise is not to teach students that Anglo immigrants who went West were invaders, but to help them view settlers from the perspectives of both Anglos and Lakota Sioux.

Other important goals are to help students develop empathy for both groups and to give voice to all the participants in U.S. history and culture. Students will gain a thorough understanding of the settlement of the West as well as other events only

when they are able to view these from diverse ethnic and cultural perspectives and construct their own versions of the past and present.

When studying the westward movement, a teacher might ask, Whose point of view does the westward movement reflect, European Americans' or the Lakota Sioux's? Who was moving West? How might a Lakota Sioux historian describe this period in U.S. history? What are other ways of thinking about and describing the westward movement?

The West, thus, was not the West for the Sioux; it was the center of the universe. For people living in Japan, it was the East. Teachers also can help students look at the westward movement from the viewpoint of those living in Mexico and Alaska: The West was the North for Mexicans and the South for Alaskans. By helping students view the westward movement from varying perspectives, teachers can help them understand why knowledge is a social construction that reflects people's cultural, economic, and power positions within a society.

Teaching Students to Know, to Care, and to Act

The major goals of a curriculum that fosters multicultural literacy should be to help students to know, to care, and to act in ways that will develop and foster a democratic and just society where all groups experience cultural democracy and empowerment. Knowledge is an essential part of multicultural literacy, but it is not the only component. Knowledge alone will not help students develop empathy, caring, and a commitment to humane and democratic change. To help our nation and world become more culturally democratic, students also must develop commitment to personal, social, and civic action as well as knowledge and skills to participate in effective civic action.

ALTHOUGH knowledge, caring, and action are conceptually distinct, in the classroom they are highly interrelated. In my multicultural classes for teacher education students, I use historical and sociological knowl-

Students should learn how science, like other disciplines, has been both a supporter and eradicator of racist beliefs and practices.

edge about the experiences of different ethnic and racial groups to inform as well as enable students to examine and clarify their personal attitudes about ethnic diversity. These knowledge experiences are also vehicles that enable students to think of actions they can take to actualize their feelings and moral commitments.

Knowledge experiences that I use to help students examine their value commitments and think of ways to act include reading *Balm in Gilead: Journey of a Healer*, Sara Lawrence Lightfoot's powerful biography of her mother, one of the nation's first African-American child psychiatrists; the historical overviews of various U.S. ethnic groups in my book, *Teaching Strategies for Ethnic Studies*; and several video and film presentations, including selections from "Eyes on the Prize II," the award-winning history of the civil rights movement produced by Henry Hampton.[26] To enable students to focus their values regarding these experiences, I ask them such questions as, How did the book or film make you feel? and Why do you think you feel that way? To enable them to think about ways to act on their feelings, I ask such questions as, How interracial are your own personal experiences? Would you like to live a more interracial life? What are some books you can read or popular films you can see that will enable you to act on your commitment to live a more racially and ethnically integrated life? The power of these kinds of experiences is often revealed in student papers, as illustrated by this excerpt from a paper by a student after he had viewed several segments of "Eyes on the Prize II":

I feel that my teaching will now necessarily be a little bit different forever simply because I myself have changed . . . I am no longer quite the same person I was before I viewed the presentations—my horizons are a little wider, perspectives a little broader, insights a little deeper. That is what I gained from "Eyes on the Prize II."[27]

The most meaningful and effective way to prepare teachers to involve students in multicultural experiences that will enable them to know, care, and participate in democratic action is to involve teachers themselves in multicultural experiences that focus on these goals. When teachers have gained knowledge about cultural and ethnic diversity, looked at that knowledge from different ethnic and cultural perspectives, and taken action to make their own lives and communities more culturally sensitive and diverse, they will have the knowledge and skills needed to help transform the curricular canon as well the hearts and minds of their students.[28] Only then will students in our schools and colleges be able to attain the knowledge, skills, and perspectives needed to participate effectively in next century's global society.

1. National Commission on Excellence in Education, *A Nation at Risk: The Imperative for Educational Reform* (Washington, DC: U.S. Department of Education, 1983); Task Force on Federal Elementary and Secondary Education Policy, *Making the Grade* (New York: Twentieth Century Fund, 1983).
2. Allan Bloom, *The Closing of the American Mind* (New York: Simon and Schuster, 1987); E.D. Hirsch, Jr., *Cultural Literacy: What Every American Needs to Know* (New York: Vintage Books, 1987).
3. Bloom, *The Closing of the American Mind*.
4. Peter L. Berger and Thomas Luckman, *The Social Construction of Reality: A Treatise in the Sociology of Knowledge* (New York: Doubleday, 1966).
5. James A. Banks, *Teaching Strategies for Ethnic Studies*, 5th ed. (Boston: Allyn and Bacon, 1991), 4-5.
6. American Council on Education and the Education Commission of the States, *One-Third of a Nation: A Report of the Commission on Minority Participation in Education and American Life* (Washington, DC: American Council on Education, 1988).
7. Bureau of the Census, *Statistical Abstract of the United States: 1989*, 109th ed. (Washington, DC: GPO, 1989).
8. Aaron M. Pallas, Gary Natriello, and Edward L. McDill, "The Changing Nature of the Disadvantaged Population: Current Dimensions and Future Trends," *Educational Researcher* 18 (June-July 1989): 16-22.
9. American Council on Education and the Education Commission of the States, *One-Third of a Nation*.
10. William B. Johnston and Arnold H. Packer, *Work force 2000: Work and Workers for the 21st Century* (Indianapolis: Hudson Institute, 1987).
11. Philip G. Altbach, "The Racial Dilemma in American Higher Education" in *The Racial Crisis in American Higher Education*, ed. Philip G. Altbach and Kofi Lomotey (Albany, NY: State University of New York Press, 1991), 8.
12. Arthur Schlesinger, Jr., "When Ethnic Studies Are Un-American," *Social Studies Review* 5 (Summer 1990): 11-13; Andrew Sullivan, "Racism 101," *The New Republic*, 28 November 1990, 18-21; "Common Culture and Multiculture," *Social Studies Review* 7 (Winter 1991): 1-10.
13. Molefi Kete Asante, *Afrocentricity* (Trenton, NJ: African World Press, Inc., 1988); Asa G. Hillard III, Lucretia Payton-Stewart, and Larry Obadele Williams, eds., *Infusion of African and African American Content in the School Curriculum* (Morristown, NJ: Aaron Press, 1990).
14. *Webster's New International Dictionary*, 3rd ed., s.v. "canon."
15. Ibid.
16. John Hope Franklin, *George Washington Williams: A Biography* (Chicago: University of Chicago Press, 1985); Carter G. Woodson, *The History of the Negro Church* (Washington, DC: Associated Publishers, 1921); W.E.B. DuBois, *Black Reconstruction in America 1860-1880* (New York: Harcourt, Brace; Russel & Russel; Philadelphia: A. Saifer, all 1935; Atheneum, 1962).
17. Irving Howe, "The Value of the Canon," *The New Republic*, 18 February 1991, 40-44.
18. John Leo, "Teaching History the Way it Happened," *U.S. News and World Report*, 27 November 1989, 73; Gerald Sirkin, "The Multiculturalists Strike Again," *Wall Street Journal*, 18 January 1990; Diane Ravitch, "Multiculturalism Yes, Particularism, No," *The Chronicle of Higher Education*, 24 October 1990, p. A44.
19. *Webster's Ninth Collegiate Dictionary*, s.v. "special interest."
20. Hirsch, *Cultural Literacy*.
21. James A. Banks, "The Dimensions of Multicultural Education," *Multicultural Leader*, in press.
22. Karl Mannheim, *Ideology and Utopia: An Introduction to the Sociology of Knowledge* (New York: Harcourt Brace, 1936).
23. Stephen Jay Gould, *The Mismeasurement of Man* (New York: W. W. Norton and Company, 1981).
24. Jane R. Mercer, "Alternative Paradigms for Assessment in a Pluralistic Society," in *Multicultural Education: Issues and Perspectives*, ed. James A. Banks and Cherry A. McGee Banks (Boston: Allyn and Bacon, 1989), 289-304.
25. See Franz Boas, *Race, Language and Culture* (New York: Macmillan, 1948) and Ruth Benedict, *Patterns of Culture* (Boston: Houghton Mifflin, 1934).
26. Sara Lawrence Lightfoot, *Balm in Gilead: Journey of a Healer* (Reading, MA: Addison-Wesley, 1988); Banks, *Teaching Strategies*; *Eyes on the Prize II*, a television series produced by Blackside, Inc. for public television station WGBH, Boston, 1990.
27. Kevin Muir, "Eyes on the Prize: A Review" (Paper submitted to James A. Banks as partial requirement for EDUC 423, "Educating Diverse Groups," University of Washington, Seattle, 1990).
28. James A. Banks and Cherry A. McGee Banks, eds., *Multicultural Education: Issues and Perspectives* (Boston: Allyn and Bacon, 1989).
EH

SCHOOLS THAT WORK

Magnet schools that limit admissions are a proven way to educational excellence, but they raise some difficult questions about equity

On the diffusion of education among the people rests the preservation and perpetuation of our free institutions.

The speaker was Daniel Webster in 1837, and the sentiment he expressed has been the philosophical bedrock of American education since the nation's birth. Now, however, a quiet revolution is underway that may fundamentally alter the educational compact espoused by the Founding Fathers. Amid intensifying economic competition abroad and deep dissatisfaction with academic achievement at home, public school systems across America have been breaking with their egalitarian roots and establishing a network of richly endowed "magnet" schools aimed primarily at nurturing the brightest and most motivated of the nation's students.

Building on the examples set by a few unusual public schools such as New York's Bronx High School of Science and Boston Latin, educators have at least quadrupled the number of magnet schools in the United States in the past decade. Although magnets come in many forms, they typically share several qualities: They are rigorously academic and teach a specialized curriculum in math and science, for instance, or foreign languages or the arts. Many use nontraditional teaching techniques, and they deliberately draw their students from beyond traditional neighborhood boundaries, often selecting them for their special talents. One quarter to one third of all magnet schools select students on the basis of grades and test scores; others enroll on a first-come, first-served basis or through lotteries. Even those that do not use academic admission standards to screen applicants have demanding programs that in effect exclude many students.

Just 20 years ago, the notion of "public prep schools" with highly selective admission policies would have been roundly attacked. And in fact the proliferation of magnet schools does raise some serious issues of equity: In particular, critics complain that magnets are too elitist, lavishing resources on the best and brightest while relegating a majority of students to the mediocrity of ordinary neighborhood schools.

But in many of the nation's major metropolitan school systems, the "magnetizing" of American education is already largely a *fait accompli*. There are perhaps as many as 5,000 magnet schools nationwide today; no fewer than 20 percent of high-school students in and around U.S. cities now attend such programs. In a few localities, such as Seattle and Birmingham, Ala., mag-

net attendance has reached 40 percent of total high-school enrollment. Since the onset of the public school reform movement in the early 1980s, North Carolina, Illinois and half a dozen other states have even established public boarding schools that recruit top students from the entire state. Officials in Alabama, Arizona and elsewhere are contemplating similar schools.

This rapid increase in magnets comes at a time when the Bush administration is urging that a wide range of schools— public, private, religious and even profit making—should receive public funding. Bush education chief Lamar Alexander argues that encouraging parental "choice" in the kinds of schools kids attend will spur innovation in American education. What is generally unappreciated, however, is the fact that the magnet schools already established provide an excellent test of whether the choice strategy works. In its call last month for the creation of 535 new schools that "break the mold" of traditional schooling and increase students' educational options, the Bush administration was merely signing on to a movement that is already well advanced.

So far the results have been impressive. Magnet students took five of the top 10 honors in this year's Westinghouse Science Talent Search competition—historically an excellent predictor of success in scientific fields. They made up as many as half of the 650 recipients of the rigorous International Baccalaureate diploma in 1990. And by all accounts magnet schools are graduating disproportionately high numbers of National Merit Scholarship winners (see accompanying stories).

Equally important, magnets are supplying a crucial model for improving the education of all students—not merely the academically elite. "Magnets can be the yeast that leavens the whole loaf," says Charles Glenn, a Massachusetts school official who has written widely on the subject. They demonstrate the value of giving students a say in where they go to school and what they study. And they show how learning improves when teachers are liberated from the bureaucratic entanglements and assembly-line atmosphere of many public schools.

Roots of change. It was not the pursuit of educational excellence that initially sparked the spread of magnets but the goal of school desegregation. As early as 1969, for instance, the Boston School Committee established a magnet program at Trotter Elementary School to attract white students into the predominantly black neighborhood of Roxbury. Quickly, magnets gained popularity as an alternative to mandatory busing, the hugely divisive school desegregation strategy that became widespread in the early 1970s. The federal government helped fuel the nascent magnet movement by establishing a funding program in 1976 for school systems using magnets to desegregate. Today that Department of Education program remains a major source of magnet funding, supplying $110 million every year to school systems from Boston to San Diego.

In many cities, magnets have been successful in improving the racial mix of schools. But increasingly, it is the nation's demands for educational excellence that have propelled the spread of the movement. In cities from Syracuse to Sacramento, where neighborhood schools clearly weren't working for either blacks or whites, school officials have embraced magnets as a means of providing top students with more advanced academic work. The result has been a rapidly expanding network with a wide array of schools. In Los Angeles today, 31,000 of the city's 625,000 students are attending 98 magnet programs. They range from the Sherman Oaks Center for Enriched Studies, an elementary program where the tradition of grouping students by age and grade has been abandoned, to the Animal and Biological Sciences Center, a science high school located next to the Los Angeles Zoo, where officials have opened their

VIRGINIA

Excellence out of plenty

The story of Thomas Jefferson High School for Science and Technology, a regional magnet in Fairfax County, Va., is not exactly one of triumph over adversity. The keys for success—money, brains and vision—were all there for the taking. High-tech giants of Northern Virginia, such as TRW and Honeywell, poured over $4 million into building 11 state-of-the-art laboratories in an old neighborhood school that had been declining in enrollment. Seven school districts choosing to send students to Jefferson agreed to spend as much as $3,500 more for each one. Students were recruited from the region's affluent, college-educated families. And the state threw its support behind Jefferson, naming it the governor's school; it now contributes up to 8 percent of the school's $11.5 million budget. "In my 23 years working in education, I never had more confidence in the potential of a project," says David Sawyer, the former assistant superintendent of Fairfax County schools who designed the school's plan.

Yet the success of Jefferson has surpassed even Sawyer's dreams. Nearly 2,000 students, all highly qualified, applied for the 400 spots in this year's freshman class. Selections are based primarily on how well a student scores on the special admissions test and prior grades. The course catalog reads like a major university's, with classes in subjects like elements of artificial intelligence and DNA biotechnology and interdisciplinary courses such as biology/English/engineering. Each student completes at least one year-long research project during senior year, with titles like "A Pacemaker Prototype" and "A Study in the Storage of Digitized Infrared Data Signals." Half of the required credits for graduation are in math and science.

Students don't just memorize facts and formulas. They learn to be analytical. "We want students to be the ones asking the questions and framing the problems, as well as answering them," says Principal Geoffrey Jones of the school's approach. "We want to teach students to be lifetime learners." Freshmen in the required "Principles of Engineering and Technology" course, for instance, work through eight sophisticated problems during the year in order to learn the basics of science and technology. They might build a vehicle powered by the energy stored in the spring of a mousetrap, or design rocket-boosted gliders. Students in the Life Science and Biotechnology lab don white lab coats and clone african violets, a painstaking procedure, and juniors in the Industrial Automation and Robotics laboratory build their own robotic arms.

The list of other achievements is equally laudable: A $1 million supercomputer sits proudly in the Computer Systems laboratory, the first-prize award of a national student competition in computer programming. In the prestigious Westinghouse Science Talent Search contest, 16 Jefferson students placed in the top 300, with three among the 40 finalists. Last year, students took over 1,200 Advanced Placement exams, with 92 percent scoring a 3 or higher, and 44 percent the highest score of 5. And their mean score in math for the Scholastic Aptitude Test was 695, compared with the national mean of 476.

Jefferson also tries to be a good neighbor, serving other schools in the region by providing teacher training seminars and summer programs for non-Jefferson students. But its main mission is to invest in a world-class education for some of the nation's best science students. There is no doubt it is succeeding.

NANCY LINNON

research facilities to the school's students. In Buffalo, 14,000 magnet students specialize in everything from the visual and performing arts to finance and computer science.

Reservoirs of ideas. Many of the magnets at the secondary level are cells within schools rather than independent institutions. Teachers often play a critical role in both designing and running these programs—a rarity in a field that has traditionally made sharp distinctions between labor and management.

Next fall, for instance, a new "aerospace magnet" will open as a 120-student school-within-a-school at Los Angeles's Westchester High School, located adjacent to the city's airport and near aerospace giants Hughes Aircraft and Northrop Corp. The five magnet teachers are working with local scientists and engineers on a new curriculum that will include such courses as space geography, robotics and meteorology. In Community School District 4 in New York City's East Harlem, where 20 school buildings house no fewer than 52 specialized programs, teachers can serve as magnet "directors," with the authority to set curricula and hire staff.

Granting teachers a greater say in the running of these schools is paying big dividends. Not only has it tapped a deep but rarely exploited reservoir of imaginative instructional ideas, but it has increased the teachers' stake in their school's success. In the words of Russell Link, a theater-arts teacher at the Buffalo Academy for Visual and Performing Arts: "If I fail, I'm responsible for what I've failed in; it's my own curriculum."

Indeed, magnet programs are offering teachers exactly the sorts of decision-making opportunities that school reformers insist are needed to attract talented candidates into teaching and keep them there. The distinctive curriculum and classroom strategies of magnets frequently require teachers to work closely together—making it difficult for unmotivated instructors to hide behind their classroom doors. To help ensure that magnet teachers all share in a program's educational philosophy, Los Angeles, Buffalo and a number of other cities have even abandoned the traditional, union-backed practice of assigning teachers strictly on the basis of seniority. Instead, they allow the teachers and principals in magnets to hire new staffers themselves. Not surprisingly, a number of studies indicate that teacher absenteeism and attrition rates are significantly lower in magnet schools.

When considering choice as a reform strategy, some educators have worried that students would not bother to explore and take advantage of their options. The magnet school experience shows clearly that they will. Los Angeles, for example, receives 32,000 applications for the 10,000 magnet seats it fills annually; Buffalo receives 8,900 applications for 2,300 spaces.

Educators suspect, in fact, that the very act of selecting a school contributes powerfully to a student's performance there. "The key is ownership," says Seymour Fliegel, an architect of New York City's School District 4 magnet system and now a fellow at the Manhattan Institute, "and ownership comes from choice." Magnet students frequently forge strong ties to the schools they attend because they have selected them. According to Richard Battaglia of the magnet school program in Los Angeles: "Kids in 'special' schools start to act 'special.'"

Intimacy's payoff. Classroom chemistry is a crucial if intangible ingredient in the success of magnets. With enroll-

CALIFORNIA

Creating a port in a storm

Back in the 1970s, school officials at Long Beach Polytechnic High School got tired of their school's reputation for racial turmoil and gang problems. They closed off the sprawling campus to outsiders, imposed strict discipline on the 3,500 students (no hats, no gang insignia, no smoking, no drugs) and began patrolling the halls and grounds with walkie-talkies.

They also reacted with imagination, introducing a magnet program called the Center for International Commerce, or CIC. In part because Long Beach is the West Coast's largest port, school officials decided to capitalize on the connection to Pacific Rim commerce, designing a curriculum to prepare Poly graduates for professional careers in international relations and global business.

High finance. There are no basket-weaving classes in CIC. Freshmen and sophomores must take eight courses, including either Japanese, Chinese or Russian, international marketing, accounting, computers, world history and English. Juniors and seniors continue their language training while branching out into physics and calculus, international relations and world literature. Electives include Asian studies, international and maritime law and international banking.

Greta McGree, the CIC director since its inception, recruits potential students from 15 Long Beach lower schools, selecting 160 each year from among some 300 applicants. She looks for students with good grades, conduct and attendance, but also attempts to include minority kids from dysfunctional families who are struggling. Many have gone from failure to the honor roll at CIC.

Does CIC training pay off? One graduate, Bill Cheney, thinks it already is yielding dividends even though he is still in college. A junior at the University of California at San Diego, he's spending a year in Tokyo at Sophia University and working part time at Nagainitto Co., a shipping company. He studied Japanese for four years at Poly and got a job through CIC with a U.S. shipper in Long Beach that has a joint venture with Nagainitto. After graduation, he wants to work in Japanese-American trade. "CIC taught me there's more to business than just America," he says. "It helped me get rid of my ethnocentrism."

MIKE THARP

ments typically ranging from 200 to 500 students and smaller student-teacher ratios, there's greater personal contact between the students and teachers than in traditional neighborhood schools. "It's like a family here, you don't get lost in the shuffle," says junior Susan Writer of Los Angeles's "Zoo" school. Studies bear Writer out, showing that alienation and apathy are generally much lower among magnet students. In New York, for example, truancy and dropout rates are markedly lower in magnets than in other schools. "Teachers can teach well only if they can get inside kids' heads," says Theodore Sizer, chairman of the Coalition of Essential Schools, a network of 98 reform-minded schools. "And when students are part of a 'community,' a 'village,' they feel loyalty."

Unfortunately, the price of "magnetizing" schools can be imposing. For instance, it will cost Los Angeles nearly $2 million to launch five new magnets next September. It's not just that start-up costs for planning and construction are high: Future operating budgets must be adjusted upward as well. Houston spends as much as $1,300 more per student at some of its 79 magnets than it does at neighborhood schools. At the North Carolina School of Science and Mathematics in Durham, a much touted public boarding school where 550 11th and 12th graders are given room and board, top teachers and the latest lab equipment, per-student spending is $12,000—three times the state average. Richmond, Calif., recently learned these fiscal facts the hard way. The 31,000-student school district landed in bankruptcy court and was nearly forced to close its doors this spring after running up a $60 million debt, caused partly by the expenses incurred in trying to start up 47 new magnet programs.

Costs and equity. Even where the money for magnets does exist, many oppose the schools on equity grounds. American public schools have no business giving some students what can amount to a lifetime advantage over others, they argue. A recent study of

No borders to learning

The International Baccalaureate program has been described as "a prep school education at the end of a yellow bus ride." And for Coral Gables Senior High student Jeff Gonzalez—born in Cuba, living in Miami's Little Havana and heading to MIT this fall on an 80 percent scholarship—nothing could be more true. "If I had stayed at my local high school, I would never even have tried to get into MIT," says Gonzalez. "The IB program has widened my horizons."

Gonzalez is one of 450 students at Coral Gables participating in the IB program, a rigorous, two-year liberal-arts program that emphasizes sciences, languages and arts and requires both fluency in a second language and a minimum of one afternoon a week of community service. It culminates with a 4,000-word essay and a daunting series of internationally accredited examinations accepted at both American and foreign universities. The exams—totaling approximately 23 hours—consist mostly of essay questions, plus some math and science and one hour of oral exams, a half-hour of which must be taken in a second language.

The IB exams put a premium on critical thinking. In order to prepare, students take classes like "The Theory of Knowledge," a two-year epistemology course equivalent to about 100 hours of classwork, which focuses on the nature of inquiry. It forces students to ask questions about the nature of learning: How do we acquire our sense of history? What is the best way to develop a scientific understanding of the world? "It teaches kids how to ask questions," says CG Principal Ralph Moore. "It makes the IB program a living organism rather than disassociated courses."

Started 25 years ago in private international schools as a way to establish secondary-education norms for extremely mobile students, the IB is offered at more than 400 secondary schools worldwide. In the United States, 135 high schools, 90 percent of them public, offer IB diplomas. For a large, urban school like Coral Gables, which has more than 2,500 students representing 56 nationalities, the IB magnet has been a way to meet the needs of many ethnic minorities. "IB gives youngsters a vision of something that might not have been," says Jenny Oren Krugman, the IB coordinator. "We can take youngsters from a disadvantaged educational background and give them time and space." This year, Coral Gables received 500 applications for 150 IB spaces and the kids were better qualified than ever before; selections are based on grades, test scores and academic potential.

Students who receive an IB diploma have a big advantage after graduation. American universities are increasingly interested in the IB program as a way of identifying highly qualified minority students, and the diploma allows graduates to skip up to one full year of college. Last year, Coral Gables students moved on to MIT, Harvard and Wellesley, among other fine schools, most on some kind of scholarship. Florida offers a $2,500 annual stipend to all students with IB diplomas who attend colleges and universities in the state

Both in the United States and abroad, many who test for the IB diploma do not receive it--testimony to its difficulty. The pressure on IB students is so intense that Coral Gables has created a special "teacher mentor" program to monitor and assist them. Of this year's 96 IB seniors at Coral Gables, about 15 are expected to graduate with full IB diplomas; the rest will receive IB certificates in individual subjects. But what's most important, says Krugman, is not whether students finish with a full diploma or certificates but that they experience the intellectual rigor of the program. "It prepares them," she says, "for the demands and diversity of university life." For the teachers in Coral Gables's IB program, the reward is in reaching and expanding the expectations of students as gifted as Jeff Gonzalez.

ANNE MONCREIFF ARRARTE

---

tion—the best and brightest get the best," says Suzanne Davenport, the study's principal investigator. Increasingly, she contends, parents must enroll their children in high-achieving magnet elementary schools to give them a chance to get into top magnet high schools.

Davenport's charges go to the heart of the equity issue, for there *are* inequities between magnets with selective admissions and other public schools. As she points out, magnets can be a double whammy for students who don't make the grade. Not only are these children often stuck in mediocre schools, but the best teachers in those schools can be lured away by magnets offering top-flight students, abundant resources and greater professional prestige. At top schools like Bronx Science or San Francisco's Lowell Alternative High School, for instance, teachers are as likely to have Ph.D.'s in their subject areas as they are to have education degrees, in no small part because these well-endowed schools often have the money to pay them salaries higher than those of the ordinary high-school teachers.

These inequities are often compounded by confusing or unfair admission policies that handicap poor students. In many school systems, Davenport and her colleagues argue, the magnet-admission process is "a maze of complex requirements that aren't generally publicized." Nor are test scores and other measures of magnet schools' performance readily available to parents. As a result, students don't always select magnets for the right reasons: One ninth grader from New York's District 4 reported that she selected the school system's Maritime Academy magnet because the school offered students an opportunity to swim three times a week. To avoid such misunderstandings, a number of Massachusetts school systems have recently established "parent information centers" in their communities to help families evaluate magnet options.

Politics and favoritism have also undermined the placement process at times. In Chicago, where there is a lottery system to allot places in the magnet schools, a 1988 *Chicago* magazine investigation found disproportionately large numbers of politicians' and celebrities' children enrolled in top-ranked magnets. Admission policies can be unfair even where they're not patently illegal. First-come, first-served magnet-admission policies, for example, can work to the disadvantage of low-income parents, who can't always afford the baby sitters or time off from work needed to wait in line to claim a coveted opening.

Fair play. While problems like these are real, proponents argue that they

---

magnet programs in New York, Boston, Philadelphia and Chicago concluded that magnets with academic admission requirements "operate as separate, virtually private, schools." These cities, the critics charged, are moving toward a two-tiered system of public education: Selective schools skim off top students and teachers and garner a disproportionate share of resources, leaving nonselective neighborhood schools to struggle with disproportionate numbers of tough-to-educate low-income students. "It's a Social Darwinist philosophy of educa-

MINNESOTA

Fostering academic rivalry

South High, once the most abysmal school in Minneapolis, is today among the best in the state, and the key to its success is tension. Its two magnet programs — one called simply the Magnet School and the other the Open School — foster friendly competition between two groups of students who appear to have little in common besides being among the smartest kids in the city.

South's Open School serves nearly 600 kids with an unstructured 1960s approach, which sends them into the city for independent projects and puts them in front of the class to teach their peers. The Open School approach is epitomized by an English class conducted at the Guthrie Theater, an acclaimed repertory theater, where 18 students put in two hours daily watching props being built, talking with dramatists, even studying box-office operations.

Young orators. The more traditional Magnet School pumps 500 liberal-arts students with a demanding course load of world literature, advanced placement history and foreign languages. The program has its own magic. At a recent orientation for incoming freshmen, magnet students dominated the stage with skillful,

learned oratory. First up was a confident young man delivering a comic monologue about going crazy; by the time Amy Alexander finished portraying a mother mourning her dead baby in Euripides's "The Trojan Women," members of the audience were discreetly dabbing their eyes.

Open and Magnet came to South in 1982, when the school board closed two foundering high schools and poured the cream of their faculty and students into the prisonlike building at South. By 1984, South was attracting the brightest students from schools citywide. Open students are selected on the basis of letters attesting to creativity, while Magnet students are chosen for their high grades; in student vernacular, the Open kids are creative flakes, the Magnet students "oh, so rigid." But whatever the dynamic at work, the mix has resulted in a creative synergy for Minneapolis's top students, and it yields results. South has the highest number of National Merit Scholars in the state each year, with Magnet and Open contributing about equally. And students from the contrasting programs often find themselves competing for slots at Yale, Princeton and other top schools.

PATRICK BARRY

magnet (box, preceding page) on total school achievement has been just "a step short of amazing," says principal Ralph Moore.

Defenders argue that magnets with tough admission standards are not elitist, simply meritocratic. They "reward top talent, pure and simple," says Braughn Taylor, a deputy director of the North Carolina math and science boarding school.

Such attitudes are rarely questioned in countries like Japan and Germany, which are the United States' toughest economic rivals today. There, rigorous standards are imposed through a national curriculum and a national examination system, with successful exam takers being sent on to the countries' very best institutions of higher learning. At each stage, schools receive government funding on an equal basis so that the playing field for advancement is level. Our overseas competitors "really can't grasp the tension we Americans see between excellence and equity," says Denis Doyle, an education expert at the Hudson Institute.

Not all magnets have been successful, to be sure. Drafting innovative curricula or revamping the way teachers teach is tough and time-consuming. In some cases, schools claiming to be magnets have merely changed their names, says Douglas Archbald, a University of Delaware education professor who has studied the movement. In other instances, magnets have been created mainly to silence nagging middle-class parents, and the lack of commitment has shown clearly in the uninspired results at those schools.

Public excellence. Still, the many strong qualities of magnets make them important models of educational achievement. They underscore the value of small, close-knit, specialized schools that have a clear mission shared by teachers, principals, parents and students alike. With excellence as their goal, magnets are providing a compelling alternative to the large comprehensive high schools that have been charged with meeting students' every conceivable need in this country for many years.

Above all else, the magnet school experience suggests that America's youth can still get a world-class education in the public schools. Without that assurance, Daniel Webster's prayer for "the preservation and perpetuation of our free institutions" through public education would stand little hope of being answered.

should not obscure the promise of magnets. What's so wrong with offering top students the opportunity to take full advantage of their academic abilities, asks David Sawyer, a former assistant superintendent of schools in Fairfax County, Va. Many school systems, for example, spend an average of two or three times more per capita on handicapped and other "special education" students. Similarly, school districts have paid for vocational education programs for years without being attacked for being inequitable. Selective magnets are "no different than any other special program designed to serve the needs of a select population," says Sawyer, adding that the return on the investment in highly motivated, high-achieving students "is bound to be substantial."

Supporters also stress that the student bodies of many of the nation's most selective magnets are no longer as racially skewed as they once were. At the Bronx High School of Science,

where for many years the student body was largely Jewish, enrollment today is 30 percent Asian, 15 percent black, 8 percent Hispanic and 47 percent white and "other." Fully a fourth of Bronx Science students qualify for federal aid to the poor. Many minority parents, in fact, defend elite public schools on the ground that they represent real avenues to success for minority students. When San Francisco proposed in the early 1970s that Lowell make admissions noncompetitive so that it could better serve residents of the neighborhood, the NAACP helped lead the opposition to the plan.

It is also true that when magnets are housed with other, more traditional programs, they can have a "halo effect." By setting high standards, they can spark a healthy schoolwide competition among students. At sprawling Coral Gables Senior High School in Miami, for example, the impact of a demanding International Baccalaureate

THOMAS TOCH WITH NANCY LINNON, AND
MATTHEW COOPER IN ATLANTA

Chapter 1: A Vision for the Next Quarter Century

Chapter 1 can be much more than it is today,
Mr. Slavin avers. It can be an engine of change in the
education of disadvantaged children.

ROBERT E. SLAVIN

ROBERT E. SLAVIN is co-director of the Early and Elementary Education Program at the Center for Research on Effective Schooling for Disadvantaged Students, Johns Hopkins University, Baltimore. This article was written under a grant from the Office of Educational Research and Improvement, U.S. Department of Education (No. OERI-R-117-R-90002). However, the opinions expressed are those of the author and do not necessarily represent OERI positions or policies.

ONCE UPON a time (or so the story goes), there was a train company experiencing a high rate of accidents. The company appointed a commission to look into the matter, and the commission issued a report noting its major finding: when accidents occurred, damage was primarily sustained to the last car in the train. As a result of this finding, the company established a policy requiring that, before each train left the station, the last car was to be uncoupled.

All too often in its nearly 26-year history, compensatory education has pursued a "last-car" strategy in providing for the needs of low-achieving students. The attention and resources of Chapter 1 and of its predecessor, Title 1, have gone primarily into identifying and remediating the damage sustained by individual children. Yet the fault lies not in the children but in the system that failed to prevent the damage in the first place, just as the damage to the last car was due to the train system and had nothing to do with the last car itself.

However, recent discussions of Chapter 1 have made it clear that change is in the air. The Hawkins-Stafford Amendments of 1988, which reauthorized Chapter 1, introduced new flexibility in the use

From *Phi Delta Kappan*, April 1991, pp. 586-592. Reprinted by permission of Robert E. Slavin and *Phi Delta Kappan*.

of Chapter 1 funds and shifted the focus of Chapter 1 monitoring toward *outcomes* for children. The legislation also made it easier for schools serving highly impoverished populations to use Chapter 1 funds for all children, not just for those identified as low achievers. Furthermore, significant increases in Chapter 1 funding will create new opportunities. The program's annual budget for 1991-92 of $6.2 billion represents an increase of $1.9 billion over the 1987-88 level. The popularity of Chapter 1 is at an all-time high; its 1988 reauthorization passed both houses of Congress nearly unanimously. However, all these changes create only the possibility of significant reform. They do not guarantee that reform will actually take place, much less that students will actually benefit.

In this article I will discuss what Chapter 1 has achieved thus far and propose a vision of what Chapter 1 could become in its second quarter century.

A VISION FOR THE FUTURE

In their first 25 years, Title I and Chapter 1 have made an important contribution to the education of low-achieving disadvantaged students. The Sustaining Effects Study of the 1970s found that Chapter 1 students learned more than other "needy" children but did not bridge the substantial gap that separated them from "non-needy" students.[1] Perhaps the best evidence of the contribution made by Title I/Chapter 1 is indirect: the slow but steady reduction in the achievement gap between African-American and Hispanic students and white students is often perceived as an effect of Title I/Chapter 1.[2] Yet it is always possible to make a good program better.

Chapter 1 can be much more than it is today. It can be an engine of change in the education of disadvantaged children. It can help our nation's schools put a floor under the achievement expectations for all children who are not mentally handicapped, so that every student will have the basic skills necessary to profit from regular classroom instruction. It can help schools move toward the teaching of a full and appropriate curriculum for all students — but particularly for those who, by virtue of being "at risk," too often receive a narrow curriculum that emphasizes isolated skills. It can make the education of disadvantaged and at-risk students a top priority for all schools.

For more than 25 years, Title I and

WE KNOW MORE TODAY ABOUT EFFECTIVE PROGRAMS FOR AT-RISK STUDENTS.

Chapter 1 have primarily provided remedial services to children who are falling behind in basic skills by removing them from their regular classes for separate instruction.[3] There is a trend toward alternatives to pullouts, such as in-class and after-school services, and schools serving large numbers of disadvantaged students are increasingly taking advantage of new opportunities to use their Chapter 1 dollars schoolwide.[4] Yet Chapter 1 is still primarily a remedial program serving individual children.

We know a great deal more today than we did 25 years ago about effective programs for at-risk students and about how to help teachers successfully implement these programs. If compensatory education were just beginning today, it would probably be structured quite differently from the way it has been. In this article I am proposing a research-based vision of what Chapter 1 could become.

PREVENTING EARLY READING FAILURE

Perhaps the most important objective of compensatory education should be to ensure that children are successful in reading the first time they are taught and never become remedial readers. The importance of reading success in the early grades is apparent to anyone who works with at-risk students. The consequences of failing to learn to read in the early grades are severe. Disadvantaged students who have failed a grade and are reading below grade level are extremely unlikely to graduate from high school.[5] Chapter 1 itself has few effects beyond the third grade.[6] Retentions and special education referrals are usually based on early reading deficits.

The level of reading performance of African-American and Hispanic students is improving, but it is still far too low.

On the 1988 National Assessment of Educational Progress, 62% of all 9-year-olds could read at what is called the "basic" level, but only 39% of African-American 9-year-olds could do so.[7] Moreover, the basic level is hardly stellar performance for any 9-year-old, as indicated by this sample item:

Read the story below so that you can answer a question about it without looking back at the story.

Timothy wasn't big enough to play ball. In the summer he sat on the steps of his brownstone building and watched things. People washing cars. Children playing games. Teenagers standing in circles talking about how hot it was. Workers tearing down the building across the street.

DO NOT LOOK BACK!

Without looking back at the story, answer the following question.

What were the teenagers talking about?

    A Timothy
    B Music
    C How hot it was
    D The people washing cars
    E The building across the street[8]

In schools serving large numbers of disadvantaged students, the situation with respect to reading achievement is, of course, much worse. In our own research on the Success for All program, we found that in inner-city Baltimore the lowest 25% of students *not* in our program could hardly read at all at the end of first grade. They averaged a grade-equivalent score of 1.2 on individually administered reading tests. This means, for example, that these students were unable to read and comprehend the following simple passage from the Durrell Silent Reading scale: "I have a little black dog. He has a pink nose. He has a little tail. He can jump and run."[9]

One outcome of widespread reading failure is a high rate of retentions in urban districts. In many districts 20% or more of first-grade students are retained, and more than half of all students have repeated at least one grade by the time they leave elementary school.[10] In the early grades, performing below grade-level expectations in reading is the primary reason for retention in grade.

Almost all children, regardless of social class or other factors, enter first grade full of enthusiasm, motivation, and self-confidence, fully expecting to succeed in school.[11] By the end of first grade, many of these students have al-

> By the end
> of first grade,
> many students
> have begun to
> see school as
> punishing and
> demeaning.

ready discovered that their initial high expectations were not justified, and they have begun to see school as punishing and demeaning. Trying to remediate reading failure later on is very difficult, because by then students who have failed are likely to be unmotivated, to have poor concepts of themselves as learners, to be anxious about reading, and to hate it. Reform is needed at all levels of education, but no goal of reform is as important as seeing that all children start off their school careers with success, confidence, and a firm foundation in reading. Success in the early grades does not guarantee success throughout the school years and beyond, but failure in the early grades does virtually guarantee failure in later schooling.

A growing body of evidence from several sources indicates that reading failure in the early grades is fundamentally preventable. For example, Reading Recovery, which provides at-risk first-graders with one-to-one tutoring from specially trained and certified teachers, has been found to increase these students' achievement substantially.[12] These improvements have been found to persist into the later elementary grades. Another program, Prevention of Learning Disabilities, provides tutoring to at-risk first- and second-graders, with a focus on perceptual skills that are often lacking in learning-disabled students. This program has also had markedly positive effects.[13]

Our Success for All program provides all students in highly disadvantaged schools with research-based preschool programs, kindergarten programs, and early reading programs; with family support services; and with one-to-one tutoring from certified teachers, beginning in

first grade, for students who are falling behind their classmates. After three years, not a single third-grader is two years behind in reading; 10% of matched control students are at least this far behind. Thus the evidence suggests that reading failure is preventable for nearly all children, even a substantial portion of those who are typically categorized as learning disabled.

If reading failure *can* be prevented, it *must* be prevented. Chapter 1 is the logical program to take the lead in giving schools serving disadvantaged students the resources and programs necessary to see that all children learn to read.

Preventing early reading failure is not only a matter of implementing first-grade tutoring programs. A commitment to success for all students from the beginning of their school careers also requires a focus on appropriate programs before first grade.[14] While there are questions about the long-term effects of preschool and extended-day kindergarten,[15] the short-term effects are clear. With appropriate interventions in first grade and beyond, the promise of early intervention can be fulfilled.

We have evidence in hand to indicate that literacy for all students is a practical goal. We do not have comparable evidence with respect to other skills, but it should certainly be feasible to aim for competence in those areas as well.

ENHANCING REGULAR CLASSROOM INSTRUCTION

One of the fundamental principles of Title I/Chapter 1 has been that compensatory funds must be focused on the lowest-achieving students in qualifying schools. In principle this makes sense, in that it avoids spreading Chapter 1 resources too thinly to do low achievers any good, but in practice this requirement has led to many problems, including a lack of coordination between regular and Chapter 1 instruction, disruption of children's regular classroom instruction, labeling of students who receive services, and unclear responsibility for children's progress.[16]

It is time to recognize that the best way to prevent students from falling behind is to provide them with top-quality instruction in their regular classrooms. I would propose that some substantial portion of Chapter 1 funds (say 25%) be set aside for staff development and the adoption of programs known to be effective.

For example, by hiring one less aide, schools could instead devote $20,000 per year to staff development, a huge investment in terms of what schools typically spend but a small one in terms of what Chapter 1 schools receive. No one could argue that the educational impact of one aide could approach that of a faithful and intelligent implementation of effective curricula and instructional practices in regular classrooms throughout the school. Indeed, research on the achievement effects of instructional aides finds that they make little or no measurable difference in achievement.[17]

In one school, $20,000 (about $1,000 per class in elementary schools) could pay not only for needed materials and supplies but also for extensive inservice training, in class follow-up by trained "circuit riders," and released time for teachers to observe one another's classes and to meet to compare notes. The achievement benefits of effective classroom instruction for the entire day would far outweigh the potential benefits of remedial service.

There are many examples of approaches that have been much more successful for low-achieving students than remedial services. In a review of the literature on effective programs for students at risk, we identified several such approaches, including cooperative learning, peer tutoring, and a variety of continuous-progress models.[18] Programs directed at improving classroom management skills often increase achievement as well. In addition, with the support of Chapter 1 funds, poor schools could adopt many of the exciting innovations in curriculum that are currently being discussed but that have thus far been beyond their reach.

Many programs for schoolwide change could also be supported by Chapter 1 staff development funds. One example is our Success for All program. Others include James Comer's model, Theodore Sizer's Re:Learning approach, and Henry Levin's Accelerated Schools model.[19]

To change the focus of Chapter 1 to staff development and program adoption, several steps would have to be taken at the federal level. First, the government would have to sponsor research and development to create and evaluate programs that would be likely to make a difference with students in general and with students eligible for Chapter 1 in particular.[20] It would be necessary to support both promising development projects and independent evaluations by researchers

Planned Evaluations of Chapter 1

BY VALENA PLISKO AND ELOIS SCOTT

THE IDEA of program evaluation does not usually generate much enthusiasm, but these are exciting and promising times for Chapter 1 evaluation. The U.S. Department of Education (ED) is planning and conducting numerous evaluations that will tell us not only how well Chapter 1 is working and for whom, but also which elements are working best and how they can be extended so that all low-achieving children can receive their benefits.

Several priorities guide our planning for the evaluation of elementary and secondary programs. First, the numerous mandated studies reflect congressional emphasis on assessing the delivery of services, the allocation of funds, and program outcomes in a number of key programs. The public's concerns about accountability, the quality of curriculum and instruction, and the identification of exemplary programs and practices also guide our plans. Evaluation of the federal effort in compensatory education takes on increased importance as we work on strategies to support the national education goals. These evaluation activities will provide Congress and ED with essential information on elementary/secondary programs as they consider how well Chapter 1 is working and new directions for the program for the reauthorization in 1993.

REAUTHORIZATION

Our evaluation plan is keyed to the Chapter 1 reauthorization cycle and, with it, to the need to assess the impact of new statutory provisions and to consider al-

VALENA PLISKO is director of the Elementary and Secondary Division of the Planning and Evaluation Service, Office of Planning, Budget and Evaluation, U.S. Department of Education, where ELOIS SCOTT is an education evaluation specialist and director of the Prospects Longitudinal Study.

THE ED EVALUATION PLAN IS KEYED TO THE CHAPTER 1 REAUTHORIZATION CYCLE.

ternative strategies to improve program effectiveness.

To evaluate the impact of the 1988 Hawkins-Stafford Amendments on Chapter 1, ED is conducting several analyses of the program's new accountability features and other new provisions. The Implementation Study of Chapter 1 that is examining the new Chapter 1 provisions in the context of the program's administration and operation will be expanded in the 1991 fiscal year to examine the impact of the Hawkins-Stafford Amendments at the school level. Plans for that fiscal year also include an in-depth examination of the process of program improvement in selected sites. These evaluations will suggest not only how extensive an impact the provisions for program improvement have had on Chapter 1 but also how such accountability provisions might be applied to other federal programs.

In addition to the evaluation of program operations in schools and classrooms, we are also planning a study of resource allocation at the district and school levels in order to replicate and expand on the 1986 assessment. We will synthesize the findings of these various studies, along with those of the preliminary mandated assessment of Chapter 1, prior to reauthorization.

OUTCOMES

Further guiding our evaluation plan is a focus on outcomes, which have not been examined for a decade and a half. Congress has mandated that ED examine the long-term outcomes associated with Chapter 1 participation. ED is interested in identifying promising practices in all program areas. In order to justify the expense of conducting large-scale studies, we must go beyond describing typical programs to examine in great detail those projects and strategies that hold the most promise of producing desirable results.

The mandated Longitudinal Study of Chapter 1 will provide the opportunity to pursue such an in-depth examination. Beginning early in fiscal year 1991, the study will track students through several years of participation in Chapter 1, in other supplemental programs, and in regular instruction. Studies of promising approaches in urban and suburban/rural sites, commissioned in fiscal year 1990, will parallel the national longitudinal study to yield a better understanding of effective Chapter 1 practices and to guide improvements in existing programs.

PROVIDING GUIDANCE

There are six Chapter 1 technical assistance centers and 10 rural technical assistance centers whose purpose is to help states and local districts evaluate and improve their programs. The centers will be conducting intensive technical assistance with selected urban and rural sites and implementing program improvements. We see this work as a formative evaluation, in that the centers will be offering extensive assistance in program improvement at the same time as we are examining the improvement process through independent evaluators.

DISSEMINATING WHAT WORKS

Underlying our evaluation effort is the notion that it is not enough simply to describe what is; rather, we need to guide programs and projects in what could be by highlighting effective strategies that can be adapted to local circumstances.

For example, we are identifying effective practices for at-risk students through an International Study of Children and Youth at Risk, which we are conducting jointly with the Organization for Economic Cooperation and Development. The objective of the study is to compare our nation's experience in compensatory education with that of other countries and to identify and highlight effective strategies for serving those young people in Chapter 1. Particular attention will be given to strategies that focus on providing integrated services and have a strong component of parent and community involvement.

CURRENT EVALUATIONS

Chapter 1 evaluations currently under contract include an observational study of early education programs, a study of the integration of education and human services for preschool and elementary children, a national evaluation of Even Start, and a study of family education and transition programs to help retain the benefits of preschool for disadvantaged children. A study of academic instruction for the disadvantaged, three studies of special strategies/best practices for educating disadvantaged children, and a study of the teaching of advanced skills to Chapter 1 students are currently under way. In addition, a national study of migrant education and one on Chapter 1 eligibility and services for students with limited proficiency in English are currently being conducted. ED has funded a survey of state Chapter 1 directors and plans a follow-up study of the implementation of the new Chapter 1 amendments. Finally, ED has contracted for the production of a design for the Chapter 1 Longitudinal Study and is currently examining proposals to conduct that congressionally mandated evaluation. **K**

other than the developers. Independent evaluations of programs already in existence would be an excellent place to begin. Research is also needed on methods for disseminating and replicating effective practices in Chapter 1 schools.

Second, the federal government should provide support for the dissemination of effective programs to Chapter 1 schools. One model for doing this is the National Diffusion Network, which funds developer/disseminators to set up dissemination programs and state facilitators to bring validated programs to the attention of schools in their states. In addition, funds might be provided to state facilitators and state departments of education

THE DEMAND FOR EFFECTIVE METHODS REIN- FORCES THE IMPORTANCE OF CONTINUED R & D.

to provide training services to schools to help them adopt effective instructional models. A key element of such a program would be to make certain that teachers and parents, as well as administrators, have a role in choosing the programs to implement in their schools.

For this approach to work, it is critical that schools have a wide choice of methods that are known to be effective for Chapter 1 children (and others), and this demand for effective methods reinforces the importance of continued research and development. At the district and school levels, program facilitators or circuit riders who are experts in given programs could be provided to help individual teachers and schools implement those programs.[21]

Chapter 1 should not be only a staff development program; there is still a need for services that target individual children (e.g., tutoring for first-graders having difficulty in reading). However, without a major investment in staff development,

Chapter 1 services will always be shoveling sand against the tide, trying to compensate for individual children's deficits while having no effect on the source of the problem — the quality of instruction in the regular classroom.

Under current regulations, schools can use a small proportion of their Chapter 1 dollars for staff development, but these funds are rarely applied to the kind of training, follow-up, and assessment needed for the effective implementation of validated programs. One-day workshops with no follow-up are far more typical. Sometimes additional inservice training is provided to schools that qualify for program improvement, but these offerings are usually quite limited. And giving inservice training only to schools that had low scores may not be well received. Staff development directed at the adoption of effective practices should be available to all Chapter 1 schools.

The obvious objection to devoting substantial resources to staff development is that students who are not eligible for Chapter 1 would benefit from Chapter 1 dollars at least as much as those who are eligible. This objection can be answered in three ways. First, accountability procedures for Chapter 1 programs should continue to focus entirely on the achievement of students who are eligible for Chapter 1, so that schools implementing programs for all students will have to make certain that they are making a difference with low achievers. Second, to withhold effective and cost-effective programs from eligible students because noneligible students might also benefit is perverse; it is like withholding funds intended for water treatment because not all children have typhoid. Third, research finds that, regardless of their own personal characteristics, poor students in schools with large numbers of poor children are lower achievers than equally poor students in less-disadvantaged schools.[22] There is a corresponding case to be made that students in schools serving disadvantaged children deserve assistance even if they are not low achievers themselves.

We should be particularly concerned about poor and minority students who may be doing well enough to avoid Chapter 1 identification but who are still not achieving up to their full potential. Such children do not need direct services, but there is certainly a strong rationale for using federal assistance to improve the quality of their regular classroom instruction.

IMPROVING ASSESSMENT AND ACCOUNTABILITY

Chapter 1 has increasingly become an accountability program as well as an instructional program. Chapter 1 students have long been assessed on norm-referenced tests, and the results of these assessments have been used to identify effective and ineffective Chapter 1 programs. In districts with high Chapter 1 participation, performance on assessments mandated by Chapter 1 is a major factor in evaluations of principals and teachers.

In the 1988 Hawkins-Stafford Amendments, new accountability provisions were introduced under the general heading of "program improvement." Schools are now evaluated principally on the basis of year-to-year gains in normal curve equivalents (NCEs). The idea is that students should gain in percentile rank from year to year, which is to say that they should improve relative to the test's norming population. For example, a student who scored at the 50th percentile in the third grade and again at the 50th percentile in the fourth grade would be said to have made "no gain," even though he or she has in fact gained one grade equivalent in one year. A student who scores at a lower percentile rank in fourth grade than in third is said to have made "negative gain."

Each state sets a criterion of what constitutes an adequate NCE gain. As of this writing, most states had set a standard of any gain more than zero, but under federal pressure these expectations are being increased in most states. Schools that do not attain the state's standard are identified for program improvement, which means that they must submit a plan to the state explaining changes they will make in order to meet the standard in the future. They may also receive staff development services. The program improvement procedures not only identify schools that fall short but are also intended to recognize and reward schools whose Chapter 1 students score well.

In theory, the program improvement guidelines represent a major step forward, in that they change the focus of state monitoring of Chapter 1 from compliance with regulations to the achievement of children. However, in practice, the standards have some serious flaws.[23] First, schools are rewarded for students' NCE gains *starting in the second grade*. This means that effective early interventions, such as preschool, extended-day kindergarten, or first-grade tutoring, do not contribute to success in NCE gains and, in fact, may make such gains more difficult to achieve by raising the end-of-first-grade scores that are usually used as a base line.

Second, using NCE gains as a standard rewards schools that have high retention rates in grades 2 and up. Students who are retained typically show gains of from 10 to 20 NCEs or more solely because they are a year older and take the same test.[24]

Third, any accountability system based on traditional group-administered, norm-referenced standardized tests can reward teaching to the narrow set of skills that appears on the test. As a result of accountability pressures since the late 1970s, many districts have closely aligned their curricula and instruction with the standardized tests and have consequently cut down instruction in such areas as social studies, science, and writing that do not appear on the standardized tests.[25]

For Chapter 1 accountability to result in solid improvements in student performance, several changes are needed. First, the assessments must be changed to measure the full set of skills and understandings that we want students to have, so that "teaching to the test" will produce exactly the breadth and appropriateness of instruction we desire for all children.[26]

Second, we need to include kindergartners and first-graders in the assessment scheme, so that investments in early intervention will contribute to a school's success in meeting accountability goals. Assessment of young children will require individually administered tests of language and reading rather than group-administered tests, but the expense of providing such tests can be justified in that they would focus the attention of Chapter 1 programs on early intervention.

Finally, scores used for Chapter 1 accountability purposes must be adjusted for retention. For example, if a test gives a 20-NCE "bonus" to retained children (as is now often the case), then 20 NCEs could be subtracted from the scores of retained students. This would correct the system that now inadvertently rewards schools for retaining large numbers of children.

TARGETING CHAPTER 1 RESOURCES

As the regulations now work, Chapter 1 resources are distributed to districts and schools according to the percentage of students in poverty and are then distributed within schools according to students' actual performance. However, the required percentage of students in poverty is very low; more than 90% of school districts receive Chapter 1 funds, and one in every nine students receives Chapter 1 services. This is why school districts serving middle-class communities often receive significant Chapter 1 resources — and why 58% of students who receive Chapter 1 services are not themselves from poor families.[27] These policies create a bizarre phenomenon. Most large districts concentrate their Chapter 1 funds in their poorest schools. This means that the "poorest" school in a wealthy district may receive significant Chapter 1 funds, while a far poorer school in a large urban district will not, because it is not as poor as others in its district.

The broad targeting of Chapter 1 helps maintain the political popularity of the program, but it is otherwise hard to justify. Congress has addressed this issue by setting aside funds for "concentration grants" to districts with large numbers of children in poverty, but there is still a need to target Chapter 1 funds far more on schools that serve students from poor communities.

THE CURRENT SYSTEM INADVERTENTLY REWARDS SCHOOLS FOR RETAINING LARGE NUMBERS OF CHILDREN.

Chapter 1 is extremely important to our most vulnerable children. For 25 years it has focused attention and resources on low-achieving students in disadvantaged schools. Yet Chapter 1 can be much more than it is today. It can prevent learning problems rather than merely react to them by remediating problems that are already serious. It can ensure literacy for every child, it can become a major force in bringing effective programs into schools serving disadvantaged students, and it can reward schools for doing a good job with at-risk students. Chapter 1 provides only 2.5% of all education funding, but, if properly directed, this 2.5% can leverage the other 97.5% to help see that students in all schools achieve at the level we now expect of our best schools.

1. Launor F. Carter, "The Sustaining Effects Study of Compensatory and Elementary Education," *Educational Researcher*, August/September 1984, pp. 4-13.

2. See, for example, John B. Carroll, "The National Assessments in Reading: Are We Misreading the Findings?," *Phi Delta Kappan*, February 1987, pp. 424-30.

3. Mary M. Kennedy et al., *The Effectiveness of Chapter 1 Services* (Washington, D.C.: Office of Educational Research and Improvement, U.S. Department of Education, 1986).

4. U.S. House of Representatives Committee on Education and Labor, *Chapter 1 Survey of the Hawkins-Stafford School Improvement Amendments*, 101st Cong., 2nd sess., 1990, H. Rept. 101-M.

5. Dee N. Lloyd, "Prediction of School Failure from Third-Grade Data," *Educational and Psychological Measurement*, vol. 38, 1978, pp. 1193-1200; and Francis J. Kelly, Donald J. Veldman, and Carson McGuire, "Multiple Discriminate Prediction of Delinquency and School Dropouts," *Educational and Psychological Measurement*, vol. 24, 1964, pp. 535-44.

6. Kennedy et al., op. cit.

7. Ina V. S. Mullis and Lynn B. Jenkins, *The Reading Report Card, 1971-88: Trends from the Nation's Report Card* (Princeton, N.J.: Educational Testing Service, 1990), p. 26.

8. Ibid., p. 27.

9. Donald D. Durrell and Jane H. Catterson, *Durrell Analysis of Reading Difficulty* (New York: The Psychological Corporation, 1980).

10. Gary D. Gottfredson, "You Get What You Measure, You Get What You Don't: Higher Standards, Higher Test Scores, More Retention in Grade," paper presented at the annual meeting of the American Educational Research Association, New Orleans, April 1988.

11. See, for example, Doris Entwisle and Leslie Hayduk, "Academic Expectations and the School Achievement of Young Children," *Sociology of Education*, vol. 54, 1981, pp. 34-50.

12. Gay Su Pinnell, "Reading Recovery: Helping At-Risk Children Learn to Read," *Elementary School Journal*, vol. 90, 1989, pp. 161-82.

13. Archie A. Silver and Rosa A. Hagen, *Disorders of Learning in Childhood* (New York: Wiley, 1990).

14. Nancy L. Karweit, "Effective Preschool Programs for Students at Risk," in Robert E. Slavin, Nancy L. Karweit, and Nancy A. Madden, eds., *Effective Programs for Students at Risk* (Boston: Allyn and Bacon, 1989), pp. 75-102; and idem, "Effective Kindergarten Programs and Practices for Students at Risk," in Slavin, Karweit, and Madden, pp. 103-42.

15. See, for example, Constance Holden, "Head Start Enters Adulthood," *Science*, vol. 247, 1990, pp. 1400-1402.

16. Mary Kay Stein, Gaea Leinhardt, and William Bickel, "Instructional Issues for Teaching Students at Risk," in Slavin, Karweit, and Madden, pp. 145-94.

17. Patricia Schuetz, *The Instructional Effectiveness of Classroom Aides* (Pittsburgh: Learning Research and Development Center, University of Pittsburgh, 1980); and Elizabeth Word et al., *Student/Teacher Achievement Ratio (STAR): Tennessee's K-3 Class Size Study* (Nashville: Tennessee State Department of Education, 1990).

18. Slavin, Karweit, and Madden, op. cit.

19. James P. Comer, "Educating Poor Minority Children," *Scientific American*, vol. 259, 1988, pp. 42-48; Theodore R. Sizer, *Horace's Compromise: The Dilemma of the American High School* (Boston: Houghton Mifflin, 1984); and Henry Levin, "Accelerated Schools for Disadvantaged Students," *Educational Leadership*, March 1987, pp. 19-21.

20. Robert E. Slavin, "Making Chapter 1 Make a Difference," *Phi Delta Kappan*, October 1987, pp. 110-19; and idem, "On Making a Difference," *Educational Researcher*, April 1990, pp. 30-34.

21. Slavin, "Making Chapter 1 . . . ," p. 115.

22. Mary M. Kennedy, Richard K. Jung, and Martin E. Orland, *Poverty, Achievement, and the Distribution of Compensatory Education Services* (Washington, D.C.: Office of Educational Research and Improvement, U.S. Department of Education, 1986).

23. Robert E. Slavin and Nancy A. Madden, *Chapter 1 Program Improvement Guidelines: Do They Reward Appropriate Practices?* (Baltimore: Center for Research on Effective Schooling for Disadvantaged Students, Johns Hopkins University, 1990).

24. Ibid.

25. Lorrie Shepard, *'Inflated Test Score Gains': Is It Old Norms or Teaching the Test?* (Los Angeles: Center for Research on Evaluation, Standards, and Student Testing, University of California at Los Angeles, 1990).

26. Grant Wiggins, "Teaching to the (Authentic) Test," *Educational Leadership*, April 1989, pp. 41-47.

27. Kennedy, Jung, and Orland, op. cit.

The Search for Equity In School Funding

Spending more in poor districts is one way to equality. But in many states, the solution is spending caps for wealthy districts.

Jeffrey L. Katz

Students, parents and administrators from poor school districts know how to strike fear in the hearts of legislators and state educators. All they need to say is, "See you in court."

That's not an idle threat. Four state Supreme Courts have ruled on the fairness of their state's school financing systems during the past two years. Each time, the disparities between rich and poor districts were considered so stark that the funding systems were struck down as unconstitutional. And there's more to come: Court cases challenging state school finance systems are pending in at least another 19 states.

Education experts are describing this wave of litigation over school funding as more revolutionary than the one that began two decades ago. In the cases considered so far, the courts have become less tolerant of inequities among school districts in educational opportunities as well as in spending. As a result, more state spending for poor school districts seems to be in order. But more money alone isn't likely to bridge the gap between rich and poor districts. Many states are finding the only way to get there is through spending caps imposed on wealthy districts, prompting a concern that equity will be achieved mainly by making the better schools worse.

It's enough to make the arcane, complicated world of school finance formulas absolutely gripping to people who don't normally understand them, many state legislators included.

Even when funding equity issues aren't on the agenda, lawmakers are afflicted with "printout-itis," says Mary Fulton, a policy associate at the Education Commission of the States, refer-ring to the tendency to pore over computer-generated analyses of funding formulas. "What they really want to know is how their district is going to fare." Now legislators are increasingly being forced to deal with broader implications of school funding issues.

Legislators are key participants in the process because the states solely determine what constitutes educational equity. Efforts to reach out for federal jurisdiction were blunted in 1973, when the U.S. Supreme Court refused to focus on issues of educational funding within a state.

Most state charters do provide for education as a fundamental right, so challenges to school financing equity have ended up in state courts. Plaintiffs had mixed results when challenging the constitutionality of school finance systems in more than half of the states between 1970 and 1983. Only seven state school finance systems were declared unconstitutional during that time. Some other states were spurred by litigation to restructure their funding, although few made radical changes.

The courts seemed more tolerant of financing disparities in the '70s and '80s than they do now. School funding systems passed constitutional muster even when some of the high courts agreed that property-poor districts were denying educational opportunities to children, as the courts did in Maryland and New York.

CONCERNS ABOUT EDUCATION FInance equity became secondary throughout much of the '80s to such topics as improving student performance and teacher competence. That changed abruptly in 1989, when state school financing systems were struck down in Montana, Texas and Kentucky, followed by a similar result last year in New Jersey and a raft of lawsuits in other states.

Disputes over school financing plans don't end with high court decisions, of course. Although the courts have been quite explicit in declaring what financing elements are unconstitutional, they are generally vague about the proper remedies. After Texas' school finance system was struck down, for example, the legislature's initial response was also ruled unconstitutional. The Texas Supreme Court rejected a financing system that the state had claimed would have enabled 95 percent of the students to receive substantially equal funding. This April, lawmakers approved yet another financing plan that, among other things, shifts about $400 million in property tax revenues from wealthy to poorer districts.

John Augenblick, a partner in a Denver-based education consulting firm, attributes the heightened activity nationally to several factors: New state funding that doesn't account for the fiscal capacity of districts, aging school finance systems that don't consider changes in the districts, and the early successes of litigation.

Each case has its own idiosyncrasies. Outcomes depend on what issues plaintiffs raise and what they can prove, the history and tradition of the state, the phrasing and interpretation of constitutional requirements, and demographics. So it is not surprising that

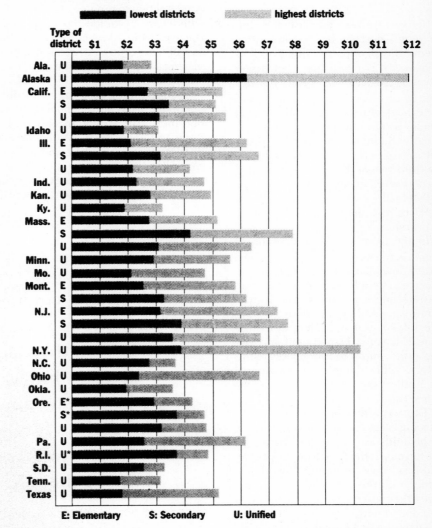

THE RANGE OF SCHOOL FUNDING

Average per-pupil expenditures, in thousands of dollars, for the 10 highest and 10 lowest school districts in states where court cases challenging school finance systems are pending or have been decided since 1989; figures are for the 1986–87 school year.

■ lowest districts   ▨ highest districts

E: Elementary   S: Secondary   U: Unified

*Because of the small number of districts meeting enrollment size criteria, only the lowest and highest five districts were considered.

Source: Congressional Research Service, based on data from U.S. Census Bureau

what constitutes equality in one state does not necessarily constitute equality in another.

One aspect most states share is a "foundation system" to distribute the bulk of their school funds. The state sets a base level of funding per pupil as well as a minimum tax level for districts. If a district sets its tax rates at this minimum level but falls short of the per-pupil funding rate, the state makes up the difference with what is

called a foundation grant. Problems occur when the state doesn't provide enough funding or sets the base funding level too low.

The courts are expecting states to give enough money to property-poor districts so that the same tax effort in every district will produce similar revenues. Some of the latest decisions have been based on comparisons of per-pupil expenditures regardless of local tax rates. And the courts have expanded their scope to include the overall education students receive. "How equal is equal is no longer a question of dollars," says Susan H. Fuhrman, co-director of the Center for Policy Research in Education. "It's a gauge of programs and what the dollars buy."

In New Jersey, for instance, the Supreme Court emphasized disparities in educational opportunities as well as in finances. It found that poor urban districts provided inadequate instruction in core curriculum subjects and were neglecting "special educational needs" by not offering such programs as early childhood education and dropout prevention. The court ruled that children in poor districts were entitled to per-pupil expenditures "substantially equal" to those in more affluent districts, regardless of property values or tax rates.

In the most sweeping decision of them all, the Kentucky Supreme Court struck down not only the state's school finance system but all of its education statutes and regulations. The legislature responded by revamping the entire school system, scaling down the state Education Department and giving more control to the schools themselves, while pumping an additional $1.3 billion into the system over two years.

The unpredictability of school financing cases can be just as unsettling to plaintiffs as it is to defendants. "If the formula is the devil to many people, and it is," says consultant Augenblick, "at least it's the devil you know. Many times the court turns out to be the devil you don't know," he adds, noting that the decision in Kentucky went far beyond what the plaintiffs sought.

WITH THE MOVEMENT TOward stiffer judicial standards on school funding equity still unfolding and each state's situation a little different, it is difficult to say how a state can best defend its existing financing plan.

Augenblick advises states to be able to rationalize their funding as much as possible in terms that do not relate to the wealth of a district. Rather, states that can attribute school spending to such elements as a district's size, enrollment, rate of growth, cost of living and teacher training and experience

will be most successful in court. It is easier to defend a system where the wealthiest districts are that way because they have higher tax rates than one where districts are wealthy on the basis of high property values alone.

States can preempt a court challenge or take action to prompt a lawsuit to be withdrawn. Colorado did so in 1988. But even Colorado achieved that at the cost of taking the controversial step of placing a cap on expenditures by local school districts.

Such spending caps can be terribly unpopular in wealthy school districts, but there are strong incentives for states to impose them. Without caps, districts that are willing and able to spend large amounts of money for education can obligate states to pour money into all of the other districts to

Spending caps are unpopular in wealthy districts, but there are strong incentives for states to impose them.

keep funding equitable. Few states can afford to do that. "It's very difficult to address the equity issue if you're going to do that only by bringing up those that are the low spending," says John Myers, education program director for the National Conference of State Legislatures. "That costs a lot of money." Spending caps also have the benefit of giving wealthy districts a vested interest in seeing state funding as a whole increase.

States have taken different tacks to limit local spending. Colorado divided its school districts into eight sub-

groups, based on needs and characteristics. The districts are assigned a local funding level and cannot exceed that amount by more than 7.5 percent. In Kentucky, by contrast, it is possible for a district to exceed the funding of other districts by nearly 50 percent. "That's an illustration of two states that have addressed the equity issue and come up with two very different results," says Augenblick, "and yet both states would tell you that they are achieving equity."

New Jersey originally sought to equalize spending by gradually shifting the cost of teacher pensions from the state to local districts. That was supposed to be a greater burden to wealthier districts that pay teachers more, but local opposition prompted the state to impose a two-year moratorium on the plan. New Jersey did establish overall caps on local district spending, however. A sliding scale was created that limited the wealthiest districts to a 7.5 percent increase in spending from the previous year. Some districts complained that the cap, combined with large increases in health insurance and other fixed costs, left them little choice but to cut educational programs.

That's the great fear about spending caps—that they will achieve equity primarily by making the better districts worse. "Leveling down," in other words, rather than "leveling up." This is particularly hard to swallow when even some of the best school districts don't necessarily measure up to the nation's educational ambitions. Some policy makers argue that there ought to be districts that can serve as models for others and that without them, well-to-do families will be more likely to leave the school system entirely and send their children to private schools.

There are also concerns about the vulnerability of depending too much on state funding in order to achieve equity, especially during a recession.

California illustrates the perils of emphasizing school financing equity while revenues are limited, says Allan Odden, co-director of the Center for Policy Research in Education. State funding accounts for a particularly high proportion of school aid in California, in part because of Proposition 13's limits on local property tax increases. The relatively low proportion of local spending also keeps discrepancies among districts low; 95 percent of the school districts are spending within $250 per pupil.

But depending on one branch of government for so much money has helped restrain overall school funding in California, despite the state's relatively high per capita income. California was tied for 30th among the states in overall expenditures per pupil in 1988-89; in 1977-78, it ranked 20th. Similarly, the state's abnormally high ratio of pupils per classroom teacher ranked it 49th in the fall of 1989, compared to its 34th ranking in 1978-79.

Odden thinks states ought to be able to balance the goals of education equity and excellence. He says it's no coincidence that while the Midwest and Northeast, which depend proportionally more on local revenues for school funding, have more disparities among school districts, they also have some of the nation's best schools.

"If you have equality of dollars, you end up with a mediocre system," Odden says. "The dilemma is whether you can have a world-class education system and equal spending across school districts."

If the courts continue the recent trends in school funding cases, we'll soon find out.

Losing Battle

Schools Fail Hispanics, Whose Dropout Rates Exceed Other Groups'

Cultural, Linguistic Barriers Stymie the Best Efforts Of Sunset High in Dallas

Rene Pena's Uphill Struggle

Alfredo Corchado

Special to The Wall Street Journal

DALLAS—The U.S. is losing its war to keep Hispanic kids in school.

About one third of Hispanic students drop out before completing high school, a rate higher than that of any other ethnic group and more than twice the national average for students generally.

Despite a publicized campaign by the departing Secretary of Education Lauro F. Cavazos to reverse the trend, Hispanic groups such as the National Council of La Raza, in Washington, predict the rate will exceed 50% by 1995.

The dropout crisis is made worse by poverty, by parents poorly educated themselves, and by difficulties students have with English and with Anglo culture. Its effect is to trap families in a cycle of failure and despair. Though the U.S. Latino population is approaching 25 million, the education shortfall could impede Hispanics' hopes for developing commensurate political power.

A month-long look at Dallas's Sunset High this year and last shows how hard it is to keep dreams alive. By rights, Sunset should be making great strides. The school has established an acclaimed anti-dropout program. Its for-

mer principal, Richard Marquez, is a Department of Education adviser. American business has taken a keen interest, too. Mobil Corp. gave Sunset High $68,000 to finance two years of dropout prevention efforts. Apple Computer Inc. donated a dozen personal computers. Others have given money to improve Sunset's library and to replace antiquated microscopes in the science lab. Donated pens, T-shirts and caps are given out as rewards for good attendance records. The YMCA runs a nearby day-care center for teen-age mothers so they can keep going to school.

Problems Persist

But notwithstanding the efforts, Sunset's dropout problems persist; indeed, they are particularly acute. About 50 of the 80 students in Mobil's anti-dropout program in September 1989 had dropped out by June.

"We're winning a few battles at Sunset," says Rene Pena, a guidance counselor. "But overall, we're still losing the war. This is more than just students at risk. It's families, communities, America's fabric."

Sunset High, built in 1925 to accommodate 1,100 students, once taught middle-class students with names like Kelly, Allen and Jones. They lived in a pleasant neighborhood of Dallas known as Oak Cliff. As times have changed, so have the demographics. Today, the neighborhood complains of crime. It now is primarily Mexican-American, and Sunset's 2,100 students, 82% of them Hispanic, strain facilities.

Despite the ethnic mix there are relatively few bilingual or Mexican-American teachers. Of 107 members of the faculty, just 12 are Hispanic.

And on any given morning, 300 students are AWOL. Those present squeeze through aging, poorly lighted hallways so narrow and crowded that tensions flare into scuffles. Teachers stand outside their rooms to sweep students from class to class.

"Move it!" screams Danny Sullivan, a 30-year-old assistant vice principal dressed in cowboy hat, boots and jeans. He isn't reluctant to use the foot-long paddle he keeps in his back pocket. He concedes that discipline would improve if only he could speak Spanish. "You have no control," he says. When he talks to parents, he often has to invite in their children as translators. He has begun to take Spanish lessons.

For Jose "Flaco" Rodriguez, a tall, wiry 18-year-old who roams the halls with a red bandanna tied around his forehead, language problems seem to have ruined his school career at the outset. At least that is his view of the matter. He cites an upsetting experience he had at the age of 10 that soured him on school. In broken English, the native of Piedras Negras, Mexico, explains that his attempt eight years ago to borrow a piece of paper and a pencil from a teacher created a misunderstanding that got him sent to the principal's office.

"The teacher was confused," Jose says. "The principal looked confused. I become shy. I no talk . . . no more."

By the end of school last June, young Mr. Rodriguez had been written off as incorrigible because, after three years in the ninth grade, he still hadn't been promoted. Now a dropout, he is holding down two jobs—as a landscaper and a fast-food cook. His objective is to raise $500 for his sister's wedding.

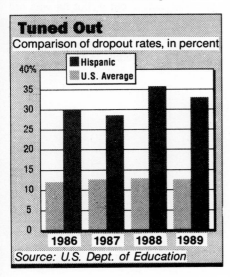

Tuned Out
Comparison of dropout rates, in percent

Source: U.S. Dept. of Education

It isn't that he detests school. Indeed, he is something of a truant-in-reverse. He continues to sneak back from time to time, lured by a history class taught by Abiel Garza, one of the few Hispanic teachers at Sunset.

A high-school dropout himself who went back to school—and ultimately graduated from college—Mr. Garza left Mexico as a child and grew up in public housing, poverty and a Spanish-speaking milieu in South Texas. "I see myself in those kids," he says. "I tell them, 'Don't make excuses for yourselves. We're from the same background. We share the same experiences. You, too, can succeed.' "

That message, at least in Mr. Garza's class, does filter down. Here, attendance and class participation are high. Students take notes and read newspapers and magazines to prepare for current-events questions. Spanish and English slang flies freely. *"Vamos a tirar chancle, profe!"* says a student when asked what he plans to do over the weekend. The literal translation: "We're going to throw shoes around." The meaning: "We're going dancing."

Mr. Garza takes pains to emphasize the Mexican elements of Texas history. A number of Hispanics were heroes of the Alamo, he tells his students, including a man named Juan Seguin, who later became mayor of San Antonio.

"I feel comfortable in his class," says Mr. Rodriguez. "He speaks like us—with a Mexican accent."

Recruitment Blues

School administrators would like to hire more teachers like Mr. Garza, but they are scarce. "Sometimes I feel like I'm at a dance and nobody wants to dance with me," complains Hector Flores, a minority recruiter for the Dallas Independent School District, who often returns empty-handed from hiring trips around the country.

It's a vicious circle: There aren't a lot of qualified Hispanic teachers because so few Hispanics make it to college—in part because Hispanic teachers are so scarce.

Competition for Hispanic teachers is intense among cities with large Latino populations. Los Angeles, Chicago, Miami and New York all are vying to hire. Los Angeles offers salaries as high as $33,000 for first-year Hispanic teachers. That is several thousand dollars more than Anglos who aren't bilingual get.

Dallas, the nation's eighth-largest school district, has less to offer inexperienced new teachers—just $21,000 a year.

More than 50 of Dallas's 181 public schools don't have a single Hispanic teacher. Although roughly a third of the district's estimated 44,000 students are Hispanic, only 9% of teachers are.

According to a popular stereotype, Hispanic families are close-knit and headed by hard-working parents devoted to their children. Why, then, don't the kids go to school?

For one thing, educators say, the stereotype doesn't hold true. About a third of Hispanic youths between the ages of 12 and 17 live in single-parent households, according to census figures. Some of these students themselves are heads of households. For them, earning a living comes before carrying books to class.

In Mr. Pena's cramped office one day, Sostenes Espino, a tall, muscular boy, nervously chips at a table with a paper clip. Above him on the wall is an American flag the counselor put up to make a point. It honors "Hispanic high-school dropouts who may go to war in the Middle East."

Responsibilities at Home

At the age of 15, Mr. Espino doesn't remember his father very well. When Sostenes is home, he and his mother argue about money, overdue electric bills and the rent payments. He currently lives with cousins, who recruited him for their street gang, called *Los Primos*. Several years back, his 16-year-old cousin took a bullet in the chest and died.

Mr. Espino works 14-hour days cleaning Dallas high-rises, and he turns over much of his pay to his mother. Every few months, he pops up at Sunset High. He doesn't earn credits toward a diploma because his attendance is so poor. He comes to relax.

"It was time for a vacation," he quips when Mr. Pena asks why he is back.

"Do you want to be a janitor for the rest of your life?" the counselor presses.

"I'm not a janitor," Mr. Espino responds. "I'm a maintenance worker."

Hispanic parents do buy into the truism that education is a way to escape poverty and despair. Yet, because of their own frequently limited experience with formal education, they often are intimidated by a system that seems alien to them.

And sometimes parents have muddled priorities. Esteban Tafoya, a 16-year-old freshman, enrolled in school three weeks late. The reason he gave was that his mother had insisted he attend his uncle's funeral in Laredo. And, after that, she wanted him to stick around a few extra days to participate in his cousin's *quincenera,* or 15th-birthday party. School officials, incredulous, checked out the boy's story and found it to be true.

Cultural Awareness

Although Sunset administrators try to acknowledge students' Hispanic heritage, their efforts sometimes are thwarted. One day last spring, students were bused to nearby Adamson High School, which also is predominantly Hispanic, for a cultural awareness seminar. What they got, instead, was an off-key rendition of "Blue Suede Shoes," which the guitarist said he had chosen because Elvis Presley was a high-school dropout.

Then, a rap musician performed a few numbers that seemed to have no relevance to Hispanic culture. Finally, a former gang member in T-shirt and blue jeans took the microphone to warn students against a life of crime: "Don't end up like me," he said.

But then he threw away his prepared text and plunged into an angry diatribe that seemed to undercut his message: "You come from a proud culture, a proud race, and you refuse to be treated without respect!"

Then Chaos

The speech brought about chaos. A member of the AV Boys ("AV" standing for Always Violent) from Sunset winked at the girlfriend of a member of Los United Homeboys. Fists flew, knives were drawn, and the remainder of the event was canceled.

"We tried," shrugs Mr. Pena.

Jesse Lopez, 17, who dropped out this fall, says he is a poor reader, a bad speller, and lousy at math. But he sailed through high school without flunking a grade, a feat even he finds bizarre. "I have no idea how I got this far," he says.

Teachers have been known to pass students from grade to grade just to get rid of them. An even more insidious practice leads to understating the number of dropouts in official statistics: A school will transfer unruly students to other schools, then make no effort to find out whether they ever arrived. "You want to get rid of a student?" says one counselor. "Transfer him."

Cele Rodriguez, Sunset's principal since March, concedes that some teachers "give up on my students. They lower their own expectations."

Making Allowances

In one class, physics teacher John Brening is discussing how pigeons find their way home at night. In his East Texas twang, Mr. Brening nonchalantly explains several theories but interrupts himself when he notices that most of the kids either are asleep, yawning or fidgeting in their chairs.

"How do I get your attention?" he asks, half-joking, throwing his hands in the air. "Do you want me to dance?"

"No," responds Bridget Contreras. "Change your accent."

Suddenly, Claudia Lozano, the school's dean of instruction, enters the classroom and wakes a student. She later meets with Mr. Brening and dresses him down for not "setting higher standards."

Mr. Brening admits he tolerates low performance levels from his students, because, in his opinion, they come to him with poor reading skills and short attention spans. "It gets to the point where you know what these Hispanic kids' limitations are."

Since September, Mr. Pena has been revising the anti-dropout program. He wants to bring in psychologists to counsel disturbed youngsters.

Last year 80 students were enrolled in the anti-dropout program; this year 350 kids are on Mr. Pena's list. The files that are sent along with the students include little profiles written by teachers and counselors describing problems and offering suggestions. Some sample comments:

• "Mike skips often. He does devious things (whistles in class, talks under his breath, leaves class even if I ask him to stay)." Suggestions: "I have not been able to reach his parents, but once. I've sent letters (they never return). I've kept him from leaving class, if he comes to class. Mike is a definite concern."

• "Ray has not been to class enough to evaluate him." Suggestions: "Ray did not see the importance of going to school. He wrote a paper once explaining why it was better if he sold dope. I spoke to him about it, but he was not convinced."

• "Pedro is very, very, immature." Suggestions: "Army boot camp. I'm open to suggestions. Help."

Perestroika in Chicago's Schools

By creating Local School Councils,
Chicago has introduced a vehicle for
fundamental reform of the public schools, but,
as in Eastern Europe, the real work lies ahead,
after the "walls" have come down.

WILLIAM AYERS

William Ayers is Assistant Professor, University of Illinois at Chicago, College of Education, Box 4348, Chicago, IL 60680. From September 1989 to June 1990, he served as an assistant to the deputy mayor for education in Chicago.

The most far-reaching restructuring of a big-city school system ever attempted got under way in October 1989, when more than 310,000 Chicagoans turned out to elect representatives to newly formed Local School Councils. The local councils are the centerpiece of reform legislation signed by Illinois Governor James Thompson in December 1988. The intent of the law is clear: power is to shift from a Byzantine central office to each local school site, and a command-style system is to be replaced by a democratic, radically decentralized one. The new model is to be a series of concentric circles with the school at the center, and circles of service, information, and resources available as needed. Under any circumstances, this kind of shift would be difficult and complex. In the Chicago context, the upheaval was sure to be dramatic and intense.

In a sense, school reform is Chicago's *perestroika*. As in Europe, an authoritarian, survivalist bureaucracy has collapsed, almost of its own weight; and a radical democracy is proposed as the solution to years of paralysis and backwardness. People who are ill-equipped—in temperament as well as experience—to run their own affairs are thus thrust into positions of authority. As an insulated central office loses its authority, there is a certain blood-letting, some bringing down to human size of those who had once been powerful; but it is tentative, almost token. The overall experience is characterized by intense hope and the glow of optimism. And as in Europe, the euphoria of bringing down walls guarantees nothing. What lies ahead is unclear; it depends on what people decide to do next.

School Crisis

Chicago's schools have been on the boundary of collapse for years. Indicators of that crisis abound:

● Nearly 50 percent of students who enter Chicago high schools drop out or fail to graduate with their classes. Of those who do graduate on time, only about one-third can read at grade level.

● Reading scores in almost half of Chicago's schools are in the lowest 1 percent of the nation.

● About 35,000 students (or 11 percent) are absent on any given day. Almost half of those absent students are considered chronically truant.

The list goes on. The causes of school crisis in Chicago are the same conditions found in most large urban districts. First is the inequitable distribution of educational resources. For example, more than half of the poorest children and 80 percent of the bilingual children in Illinois attend Chicago schools; and yet Chicago operates on substantially less money per child than surrounding districts. This is in part the result of a funding system based on property taxes. But Chicago is disadvantaged in relation to other resources as well. The city's students attend school in overcrowded and aging physical plants; they contend with an inadequate transportation system; they cannot enter school buildings after school hours; and they have more limited access to libraries, parks, and other public facilities than do students in neighboring districts. On every measure, Chicago children need more, and yet they have less.

A second cause of crisis is the stubborn will of a range of self-interested bureaucracies to work against any common purpose. For example, as in most big systems, Chicago schools require a firefighter in every building. There are five high-pressure boilers left in the entire system, and yet no school can be open without a firefighter on site. The expense of this kind of contractual agreement would be comic if it weren't tragic. Big school systems are less a single monolith than a collection of warring factions, with many programs entrenched as a result of court orders or federal and state laws. The central curriculum office, for example, contains 125 people. If only 1 administrative position were closed, the funds could double the supply budget at 12 schools or provide a 5-teacher team at 20 schools with 2 hours of planning every week for a year.

A third cause of failure is a rigid, unresponsive classroom culture. We have experienced enormous and fundamental changes in our society, but most schools today look exactly as schools looked 50 or 100 years ago. And in spite of all we now know about how people grow and learn, classrooms are still little lecture halls with teachers dispensing bits and pieces of wisdom called curriculum. Children learn best in an environment that nurtures and challenges a range of interests, where they are active in making choices, and where they are engaged in matters of real importance to them. Children learn when they are safe and respected. All the heavy machinery of schooling—the lockstep conformity and ironclad rules—run counter to the requirements of learning communities.

Finally, not only have the content and organization failed to evolve with a changing world, but knowledge of and respect for students have failed the test of reality as well. Schools, frankly, have not responded to the dazzling array of needs and potentials that youngsters bring to school today. Too many schools are organized with a mythical child in mind, someone like

Beaver from "Leave it to Beaver." When the children who arrive at the schoolhouse door don't look or act anything like Beaver, don't have his wry sense of humor or his experiences and skills, they are too often deemed unteachable by inflexible and narrow schools.

At the time, no one in Chicago denied the need for reform. The fact that the schools were in crisis was broadly experienced and widely understood. It was in this context of stagnation and unresponsiveness that the Chicago Teachers Union led a walkout in September 1987. It was the ninth teachers' strike in 18 years.

School Reform

Lasting a record 19 school days, the teachers' strike became the catalyst that forged a workable coalition of parents, community groups, and business leaders. The presence of this reform coalition soon guaranteed that, regardless of any agreement between the board and the union, there would be no return to business as usual. It became the vehicle for people to express their anger and frustration with the full range of school problems. Over the next several months, this coalition hammered out a reform package and a successful legislative strategy.

principal for its school and negotiates a four-year performance contract. This provision brings an end to principal tenure and a system of city exams that dramatically limited candidates for leadership positions. Second, councils draft school improvement plans consistent with federal and state regulation but free of city wide curriculum mandates. And finally, councils control school budgets and decide how to spend funds consistent with their visions of change.

The reform legislation is, of course, only a step toward real school improvement. Any law is imperfect, just as any court order is inadequate. The real work of school improvement is long-term and complex, and no single step can turn around years of failure. Still, today in Chicago there is hope, and a release of energies is powering the beginnings of change.

Next Steps

The initiative to restructure Chicago schools came from below; thus, the course of reform has a rough and improvisational look. And there are vast problems to encounter and overcome as reform moves into its second year.

To begin with, everyone in Chicago uses the language of reform, but there is still a long path to travel if power and resources are really to shift from

---

A Radical Experiment in School Reform

If you would like to follow Chicago's experiment in school reform, subscribe to *Catalyst: Voices of Chicago School Reform.* "Created to document, analyze, and support school improvement efforts in Chicago's public schools," *Catalyst* is published nine months of the year by the Community Renewal Society. The publication is free for Illinois residents, $10/year for non-Illinois residents. For more information, contact CRS, 332 S. Michigan Ave., Chicago, IL 60604–9863.

The Chicago School Reform Act created Local School Councils at 542 attendance centers. Each council consists of 6 parents, 2 teachers, 2 community representatives, and the principal. Members are elected by constituent groups: parents vote for parent representatives, teachers for teacher representatives, and so on. This method of representation was designed so that local schools can be run by local people, and as a safeguard against corruption or a takeover by self-interested groups.

Local School Councils have real power. First, each council hires the

the center to the base. Local initiatives are still routinely frustrated, and the central office still regularly issues commands. For example, last spring, after several councils had developed upgraded school security plans, using neighborhood resources and citizens, the central office announced a new security arrangement between the schools and the city police. The superintendent directed local schools to discontinue their programs and refused to allow funds to be used for them. Councils were enraged at another instance of business as usual.

Further, the people who have the power to propose and implement dramatic change will not necessarily do so. This is the *perestroika* problem: If one has lived in Rumania a long time, one is out of practice in exercising freedom. In Chicago, as Local School Councils draft improvement plans, they often fall back on the taken-for-granted and the commonplace; they propose things like higher test scores, less truancy, and so on. This lack of imagination, this paucity of visions, frustrates the council members' ability to propose something dramatically different. And yet, if they don't try something dramatically different, there is little chance they can create dramatically different schools. And if the schools do not break with their tradition of failure, then failure will remain their constant companion.

Finally, the most serious obstacle to reform is the failure of the reformers to capture the imaginations and en-

The fact that 6,000 citizens are convening regularly and focusing their energies on the schools is a positive thing.

ergies of teachers. Under reform, teachers have significantly expanded their power; yet the parent-led local councils suggest *parent control,* a term that has, to teachers' ears at least, a punitive ring to it. The failure to build an authentic partnership between parents and teachers could undo much of what has been positive to date.

As in Europe, the outcome of upheaval in Chicago is far from certain. The conditions for fundamental change exist. But whether or not positive change for children, families, and teachers is the result depends on decisions made and initiatives enacted. The fact that 6,000 citizens are convening regularly and focusing their energies on the schools is a positive thing. It is now necessary for that energy to bring about dramatic change in specific schools.

This unprecedented reform is based on a sense that the solution to the problems in a democracy is more democracy, that the people with the problems are also the people with the solutions, and that experience in changing things will bring wisdom to the next steps. Our options are open, lighthouses of hope and possibility are beginning to be put in place, long-term change can proceed from a base of support. Can we do it?

Serving Special Needs and Humanizing Instruction

A broad spectrum of special social problems continues to create exceptional needs for many North American students as they encounter life in school. The effects of factors such as divorce, domestic violence, abuse, and neglect take an awesome toll on children. Young people who experience the effects of major social upheavals and/or personal disabilities need special intervention strategies to assist them in school. In the face of the many special problems facing tax supported public schools, a significant minority of parents choose to send their children to independent school settings or even to school at home. This traditional means of opting out of the world of public schooling presents other sets of special problems for teachers, parents, and students. The choice to not use the public schools always reflects preferences and beliefs to those who make this decision.

Several specific issues have had a particularly severe impact on individual students' lives. Problems of addiction, teenage parenthood, social alienation, sexually transmitted diseases, insufficient employment opportunities for the poor and the working middle classes, and disaffection with the whole idea of going to school at all are some of the major problems that affect many youths of our time. Every school system is struggling to address these and similar issues. But there are specific curriculum and instruction issues in schools related to the fashion among some educators in recent years to use the old approach of grade retention to attempt remediation of students' school performance. These policies are now under critical scrutiny by some researchers and scholars. Anything students experience while they are in school can, and often does, have long-term emotional and intellectual consequences. Therefore, how we address the special needs of students is very important.

Some issues that confront teachers and their students are unique to the teacher-student relationship. Other issues that affect teachers in their work with students have their origin in the problems of society at large. These problems impact on teachers because students bring these social problems to school with them. Since first issued in 1973, this anthology has aimed to provide discussion of special social or curriculum issues affecting the teaching-learning conditions in schools. Fundamental forces at work in North American culture during the past several years have greatly affected millions of students. The social, cultural, and economic pressures on families have produced several special problems of great concern to teachers. There is demand for greater degrees of individualization of instruction and for greater development and maintenance of stronger self-concepts by students. The number of students who are either in single-parent situations or who have both parents working and maintaining careers has been growing. School systems and the teachers who work within them have been confronted with student populations that experience many problems that, traditionally at least, they were not expected to address. Teachers have an opportunity to shape the lives of young people by being good examples of stable personalities themselves, and through individualizing interactions with their students. All children and adolescents do not have the same opportunity to be exposed to untroubled and stable men and women.

A teacher needs to see the work of the school as integrated with the activities of the general society that created and sustains it. There is too much superficial conceptualizing of schooling as not related to, or somehow separated from, the rest of the world. Teachers need to be good observers of the learning styles of their students. They should be willing to modify instructional planning to provide learning experiences that are best for their students. It is a reality of the current social foundations of education that in the past 20 years (or more) special problems have emerged in the national culture that have affected teacher-student relations. These include development of mainstreaming, problems of drug abuse among youth, increase in the rate of teenage suicide, collapse of the traditional American family unit (except among the most conservative religious and social groups), the women's rights movement, and the evolution of nontraditional parenting patterns. To elucidate these problems is to gain a sense as to how teachers are facing the special instructional needs of students living in a time of economic and social upheaval without traditional family support systems.

Teachers should become aware of the extraordinary circumstances under which many children and young adults strive to become educated. Teachers are interested in studying their options to respond constructively to the special needs of their students. They want to know how they can help build self-confidence and self-esteem in their students, and how they can help them to want to learn in spite of all of the distracting forces in their lives.

There are even those who argue that all teachers can benefit from practicing certain parenting skills in their interactions with students. Development of constructive, positive student-teacher relationships to assist students in facing difficult life situations is a common theme in talk about curriculum and instruction.

We are all human beings sharing the same universe and the common heritage of our species; yet, marvelously, each of us is exceptional in some way. We all have special gifts and special limitations. The ancient Greeks believed every person could be educated to the optimum extent to perfect his or her excellent qualities. To a certain degree, we can also be educated to compensate for disabilities. Children are born into many special circumstances and different social atmospheres. Some must fight to survive and maintain their sense of dignity and self-worth. What constitutes the most appropriate learning atmosphere for each student has become a serious legal and moral question in recent years.

The special needs and abilities that people possess are often called exceptionalities. Exceptionalities of certain kinds, whether they be physical or cognitive (mental), sometimes require special intervention or treatment skills. How can education address the unique needs, interests, abilities, and exceptionalities of students? How can teachers best serve their students' needs for attention and intellectual stimulation, demonstrate concern for the students, and also meet regular instructional responsibilities? Many children are not aware of their special needs and academic and social capabilities. School systems must find ways to help students discover these needs and potentials, and they must create conditions for students to progress both academically and socially.

The Education of All Handicapped Children Act of 1975 (PL 94-142) was passed by Congress to address the special needs of handicapped learners by placing them in least restrictive learning environments. This law has increased sensitivity to the educational requirements of exceptional students. Gifted persons are exceptional, too, and their least restrictive learning environments can require special intervention strategies. Herein lies one of the dilemmas of special education: There are many special and exceptional students, and they all need carefully planned and individualized educational strategies. A liberating classroom climate for one student may be a stifling and boring climate for another. The nation's schools are called upon to address a range of special needs so vast that the schools are financially and professionally stressed to their limits.

Mainstreaming is an educational policy response to the 1975 federal legislation regarding the handicapped. There is a big gap between the hopes and expectations for mainstreaming and the realities of implementing it. The debates between proponents and opponents of mainstreaming as a required educational policy in the United States have grown more intense. Many teachers complain that the inadequate implementation of the policy in many school systems and the difficult teaching conditions created by the policy prevents quality teaching for all students from occurring.

The issues discussed in this unit are ones that critically impact the working conditions of teachers. These issues have been produced either by social forces outside of the schools, or by the thought of improving how we serve students' needs as a profession. They are relevant to the social foundations of education when the cultural foundations of learning are comprehensively conceived. These concerns are likewise relevant to the study of issues in curriculum and instruction and curriculum construction.

Looking Ahead: Challenge Questions

What would be a philosophical justification for improving self-esteem as a general claim of education?

What ought to constitute a teacher's attitude toward learning?

What is meant by least restrictive placement? What would be an example of such placement for a handicapped child? For a gifted child?

What is meant by individualization of instruction? How can it be accomplished? Do elementary and secondary teachers encounter different problems when it comes to individualizing instruction?

What is the present state of drug use or chemical dependency in the United States?

What are the best strategies for helping teenagers who become parents? Why do some people leave school altogether?

List a set of reasons as to why some parents teach their children at home. Why do you think they do it?

What would be the primary reason for choosing an independent school? What needs can an independent school meet that many public schools fail to meet?

The ABC's Of Caring

A California experiment replaces traditional classroom approaches with methods aimed at teaching children to be more cooperative and compassionate

Alfie Kohn

Alfie Kohn is the author of The Brighter Side of Human Nature: Altruism and Empathy in Everyday Life, *published by Basic Books, and* No Contest: The Case Against Competition, *published in paperback by Houghton Mifflin. He lives in Cambridge, Mass., and lectures widely on educational issues.*

RUBY TELLSWORTH STILL TALKS about the day she returned to her classroom after a break to find her 2nd graders sitting in a group, earnestly discussing something. When she asked what was going on, they told her a problem had come up during recess and they had convened a class meeting to work it out. They proceeded to resolve the problem on their own while she finished her coffee.

Tellsworth's students did not drop out of some teacher heaven. They had come to care about each other—and to take responsibility for what went on in their classroom—because of her patient efforts, day after day, to elicit just such attitudes. Those efforts result from her participation in a landmark study in social, moral, and academic education that has been under way in California's San Ramon Valley since the early 1980's. It is a study designed to discover whether schools can help children learn to look out for others instead of just for themselves.

For the last seven years, the educators and psychologists involved in this pioneering effort, known as the Child Development Project, have been training teachers, designing schoolwide activities, and reaching out to parents. Supported by a grant of roughly $1-million each year from the William and Flora Hewlett Foundation, CDP has suggested changes in what is taught, how it is taught, how classrooms operate, how discipline is conceived, and how teachers regard their task and relate to students and to each other. It is by far the most ambitious program of its kind ever attempted—and it seems to be working.

"I've watched a variety of character education fads sweep through the schools," says Bill Streshly, superintendent of San Ramon Valley Schools. "Most of them have been little add-on programs for whatever the social problem is: sex, drugs, patriotism, kindness to animals. They're not part of the basic mission of the schools, and they fade out. But CDP incorporates its ethical mission in every part of the school day."

In some schools where CDP is not in place, Streshly continues, an occasional class period is devoted to values education. "Then it's, 'take out your math books, do the problems, first one through gets an M & M,' " he says. "That is when the real values come out." Those values aren't always obvious, but they are potent nonetheless. Students are implicitly taught that other people are to be regarded as obstacles to their own success. They also get the message that their achievement, like their behavior, is a function of external rewards and punishments.

CDP, by contrast, is based on the idea that "we need to get them to internalize ethics," Streshly says. "There aren't enough M & M's to keep people on track, to manipulate behavior once they leave the high-surveillance school setting." Project teachers, he adds, "teach cooperation because cooperation is a part of citizenship that we want."

The actual program being implemented in the San Ramon schools has several distinct components. First, there is its approach to classroom management. In place of authoritarian, sit-down-and-shut-up discipline or gimmicks to reward obedience, CDP teaches teachers to work together with children to decide how the classroom should be organized and how behavior problems should be handled. Instead of wondering, "What rules am I supposed to follow?" a child is encouraged to ask, "What kind of classroom do we want to have?" Teachers also are urged to develop warm and respectful relationships with students—and to avoid attributing unnecessarily negative motives to their actions—so there will be fewer behavior problems that have to be solved.

That explains why, when some of Tellsworth's 2nd graders at Rancho Romero School were rude to her, she took them aside, reminded them that she had never treated them like that, and let them know how awful they had made her feel. (They have been more considerate ever since.) And when one of Mary Korzick's 1st grade students at the Walt Disney School threw a rock during recess, she solicited the class's opinion on whether a prohibition on rock throwing was a reasonable rule, and why. (They decided it did make sense.)

The second part of the program emphasizes cooperative learning: Children spend part of the day working on assignments with a partner or in larger groups. With respect to both achievement and social skills, CDP staff members believe that allowing children to jointly devise problem-solving strategies makes at least as much sense as either of the two dominant American classroom models—working against each other (competition) and working apart from each other (individualized learning). Hundreds of studies have shown that cooperative learning helps students feel more positive about themselves, each other, and the subject matter. It also has been found to boost academic achievement regardless of the child's ability level or age—perhaps because, in the words of 10-year-old Disney student Justin Wells, "It's like you have four brains."

Joel Thornley, superintendent of the neighboring Hayward school system, where CDP began the second phase of its program in 1988, overcame his doubts about cooperative learning only after watching it in practice. "Once we saw the kinds of responses they get in San Ramon, we had no reservations," he explains. "Cooperative learning works. If there's a single bet we've missed over the years, it's making kids sit quietly at their desks instead of letting them work with each other."

CDP's third component is a curriculum designed to display and reinforce what psychologists call "prosocial" values: caring, sharing, and helping. Students learn to read by being immersed in works of literature whose themes and characters get children to think about how other people feel and to respond empathetically.

Today, for example, Ann Cerri's 6th graders are discussing a story about a white boy who meets his first black—an entirely realistic premise in the predominantly white schools of San Ramon Valley. The story's narrator worries that his new acquaintance will be insulted if asked whether his forebears were slaves.

Cerri puts down the book and asks her students whether this is a reasonable concern. It depends on whether or not they actually were slaves, one girl suggests. It depends on how the question is asked, says a boy. It depends on the area of the country they're in, someone else offers. Soon the whole class is discussing the matter animatedly, imagining themselves in the position of the narrator and of the black man. One student recalls how he felt when people kept asking him about his grandfather's death.

Beyond the individual classroom, CDP has arranged for the schools to provide activities that give children practice at being helpful to, taking responsibility for, and learning about others. Each child is assigned a buddy in another class, for instance, so a 5th grader and a 2nd grader periodically have a chance to work together or socialize, and older children can set an example.

Eric Schaps, CDP's director, is especially proud of this part of the project. He shows a visitor a photograph of a bus full of children returning from a field trip. A 1st grader in the foreground has fallen asleep, his head resting on his 5th grade buddy's shoulder. "What 5th grade kid do you know who would do this?" he asks. American schools have "systematically deprived kids of this kind of cross-age interaction. It's the experience of caring about another person, not being responsible for cleaning the erasers, that makes one a kind, nurturing person," he says. And the younger child, Schaps adds, learns that he is cared for.

Schaps ticks off some of the other elements of the program. Older students can give up some free time to tutor younger children—and many do. Classes don't just collect toys for something called "charity": each adopts one needy family, whose names are withheld but whose circumstances are described to the children in detail. Students hear firsthand about the experiences of people who are handicapped or from different cultures.

Then there are the aspects of CDP that follow students home. Some homework, for example, is specifically designed to be done with parents. A 2nd grader may bring home a poem about a child who is teased by a sibling. Parents are invited to share their own childhood memories, to help their child compose a poem or story on the same subject.

By themselves, reflects 6th grade teacher Bob Brown, none of these components were "foreign or shocking or new." He notes, however, that CDP "brought several elements together" that added up to a significant change "in the way you look at kids and the way kids learn."

THE CHILD DEVELOPMENT PROJECT WAS born in the mind of Dyke Brown, now 74, who, three decades after helping to start the Ford Foundation, was troubled by what he calls the "increasing degree of self-preoccupation in our students." Drawing on solid research showing that cooperative learning promotes higher achievement than individualized or competitive approaches, that attention to social skills or moral values doesn't have to come at the expense of academics, and that children are more likely to follow rules when they know the reason for them or have had a hand in creating them, he developed the CDP concept. After securing a massive seven-year grant from the Hewlett Foundation in 1980, Brown found Schaps, a social psychologist who had enough experience working with educators to successfully run a program and who had the methodological expertise to evaluate whether it was doing any good.

Schaps hired a staff, designed a program and a research plan, and then began looking for some receptive schools in which to try them out. They eventually set up shop in San Ramon Valley, a cluster of suburban communities about an hour's drive east from San Francisco. There they chose six of the district's 13 elementary schools—two groups of three, carefully matched for size and socioeconomic status—that seemed especially eager to be part of the project. A coin was ceremoniously flipped to determine which three would be the program schools (Walt Disney, Rancho Romero, and Country Club) and which would be the comparison schools to serve as a control group.

They started training teachers in 1982. The training began—as it has each year since then—with a one-day introduction in May, followed by a full week in August, and then one day each month throughout the next school year. Teachers meet in groups of about 13 and get some hands-on practice working together. This serves the dual purpose of reducing their professional isolation and giving them a taste of the approach they will be using in their own classrooms. Someone from the CDP staff observes each teacher weekly and offers advice on how to handle a disruptive child, how to run a class meeting, how to structure cooperative learning, and how to make the best use of texts to promote prosocial values.

The staff now admits to having made mistakes in its early training procedures. CDP worked with kindergarten teachers the first year, 1st grade teachers the next year, and so on. But it took too long to involve the whole faculty that way. Moreover, teachers were expected to master the new concepts and skills almost immediately.

Since then, various aspects of the program have been changed, many based on suggestions from teachers. Some experienced teachers, in fact, have been hired to coach their colleagues and bring the program to other schools in the area. Says Schaps,

"Our hope is that the district eventually will spread this on its own, using these teachers to do it."

Indeed, most San Ramon teachers—even some of those who had misgivings in the beginning—have become believers. "I couldn't see it at first and I found it very difficult" to learn, says Phil Wallace, who traces his traditional approach to classroom discipline to his military background. But now, having just retired from teaching 4th grade, Wallace works part time as a substitute and sometimes runs across his former students.

"There's a tremendous difference" between those taught by CDP-trained teachers and the other children, he says. "It's a wonderful thing to see; these kids are helping each other, caring for each other. I said to myself, 'Holy Mackerel! Don't tell me this actually works!' "

Because the main group of children being tracked by CDP experimenters are now in junior high school, the research doesn't require that the original batch of teachers keep using the project's approach. Many, however, have no intention of going back to the way they used to do things.

"I'll be using this as long as I teach," says Tellsworth. "It's a way of life now. If I was put in a school where I had to use Assertive Discipline [a currently fashionable approach in which teachers use a system of rewards and penalties to enforce rules that they alone specify], I would leave."

THIS, OF COURSE, DOESN'T MEAN THAT THE CDP approach was easy for teachers to master. It requires them to abandon the idea that a "good" classroom is a quiet roomful of children who passively absorb information, obey someone else's rules, and keep their eyes on their own work. It means agreeing to question the assumption that bribes or threats—even if called by fancier names—will induce students to care about learning or about each other.

Janet Ellman, a 1st grade teacher at the Longwood School in Hayward, Calif., laughs as she recalls her occasional frustration when she first tried out CDP's suggestions for classroom management last year. "Sometimes they just wouldn't shut up. It was tempting to fall back on external kinds of reinforcement for quiet behavior. But this year, it has been much easier for me to get quiet from my children by bringing them into the process and showing them how it's difficult to learn sometimes when there's talking going on."

Not all teachers remain open to these unsettling proposals long enough to make them work. "Some people were very opposed to CDP because it was very frightening to them," says Sharon Kushner, a 3rd grade teacher at Disney. "After you teach for a number of years, you fall into a pattern and do things automatically. It doesn't get changed very easily."

That was the case for Ann Cerri at first. "A lot of us felt that the structure was being pulled out from under us" when traditional beliefs about discipline were challenged, she says. "I remember feeling a little overwhelmed. [The CDP approach] wasn't a formula that you tried out and everything was hunky-dory from then on. It was hard work. But in my gut I thought it was the right way to work with kids. I like the way the class feels now, the way the kids and I relate to each other."

Tellsworth tells a story that illustrates another side of the program. A mother was concerned that her daughter didn't stand up for herself with her peers. But midway through a school year, the mother overheard her talking on the phone with a bossy classmate and was amazed to find that her daughter was explaining why she didn't want to play with the other girl, enumerating the behaviors that bothered her, and making it clear that they would get together only if the girl controlled them.

Such tales don't surprise Schaps, the project's director. Getting kids to stand up for themselves is part of what the project is after, he points out. "We're looking for a healthy balance of concern for self and concern for others. We don't want to turn kids into doormats." In fact, results of CDP's tests show that children in the program schools are more likely to stand up for their own views than those in other area schools.

The project teaches children that "you shouldn't please your peers at the expense of your integrity and what you think is right," says Marilyn Watson, who is in charge of the teacher training component. Social problem-solving is encouraged, she explains, as is "articulating dissenting opinions"—and there is nothing about caring for others that conflicts with these goals.

Watson, who used to teach education at Mills College in Oakland, Calif., burns calories just having a conversation; her head, hands, and shoulders are always in motion. "We're not saying there's no self-interest," she emphasizes. "We're saying there's more to work with than just self-interest."

TODAY, WATSON IS SERVING AS AN INFOR-mal tour guide through one of San Ramon's non-program schools. It is typical of affluent, suburban elementary schools. In the back of a 1st grade classroom is a box of books, one of which, *Being Destructive*, is packed with "do nots" and "you shoulds." The book informs readers, "If you are destructive because you do not care, you may need to be punished."

In the front of the room, the teacher is speaking in a sharp voice and snapping her fingers. "Boys and girls, when I get to zero, you must be looking at me. Five . . . four . . ." She points ominously at "CLASS WARNING" written on the blackboard. "You must stay in your seats!" she insists. "If you raise your hand, I will come to you." She lines the children up so they can look at a map one at a time. She often refers to herself in the third person.

Watson later points out how this teacher, presum-ably well-meaning and well-trained, is making the children compete with each other rather than learning to work together, how she is encouraging them to depend on her rather than taking responsibility for their own learning and behavior, and how she keeps herself distant from them at the same time.

In a 5th grade room down the hall, only the A plus papers are tacked to the wall. The teacher's discipli-nary approach is traditional, yet the room is far more chaotic than CDP classrooms. "I'm waiting!" she yells to a group of oblivious 10-year-olds. "Anyone talking now will be sure their name won't get in the paper."

Next door, a teacher proudly shows off her "checking account" system of class control: A poster board lists how much a student "pays" for late work or a messy desk and how large a deposit he or she will get for an A on a test.

Afterward, Watson concedes that such a system may produce quiet classrooms and perhaps it might even result in higher test scores in the short run. "But you're aiming for the long run, for them to do it because they want to learn, not because they want money," she explains. "You can get the [desired] behavior this way. What you can't get is a commitment to the behavior, a sense that 'I'm in charge,' a sense of personal responsibility."

The shift in focus that Watson advocates is beginning to generate considerable excitement among educators. The Child Development Project has been honored by the American Association of School Administrators and the National Council for the Social Studies and has been certified by the U.S. Department of Education's Pro-gram Effectiveness Panel. Hundreds of requests for information about the project have been rolling in from schools and school districts, many of which are eager to begin adopting it.

Closer to home, a visitor has to look hard to find any critics of CDP in San Ramon Valley. Bob DuPont, part of a solid conservative majority on the local school board, says he knows of no opposition to the project. "We can—and have to—provide the basic values of positive citizenry in the schools," he says. "What's the alternative? If the schools don't do it, no one will."

Some parents were nervous when the idea was first presented to them. Fred Messreni, a 44-year-old corporate manager who is on the city council, remembers asking, "What is this program that's going to be experimenting with the behavior of my [daughter]?"

But, he says, "the concern rapidly evaporated and became excitement about the opportunity she was given. It's difficult to argue with constructive, positive influ-ences that bring results."

Another family, the Greningers, say they have mod-ified their approach to parenting after watching what the project has done for their three children at Disney. "We've incorporated it into our home," which means holding family meetings to resolve conflicts, says Barb Greninger. "Every time we've included [the children] in the decisionmaking process, it has worked out better."

"I swear," her husband, Dave, a Little League coach, chimes in. "The kids who are the troublemakers around here"—he waves at the neighborhood beyond his sliding glass doors—"don't go to Disney."

One teacher who does express reservations about CDP is Bill Randall, who recently completed a year of training for his 6th grade classroom. "It takes an undue amount of time," he says. "People in education are giving so much. You have to ask yourself, 'Why am I here? To teach study skills or to teach behavior skills?' But my main concern is, Does it last? Does it stick in the kids? Is there really a noticeable difference? The ideals sound fine, but what's the reality?"

The CDP researchers asked the same questions, unsatisfied with mere anecdotal accounts of success. Not all the tests administered to children—or the systematic monitoring of 67 classrooms each spring by observers who weren't told what the study was about—have shown consistent and statistically significant differences between the program schools and the comparison schools.

One possible explanation—which does not call into question the fundamental soundness of the CDP concept—is that some teachers were less effective at grasping and implementing the principles of the program. Another is that all of the comparison schools have independently become convinced of the value of cooperative learning and have begun encouraging their own teachers to use it—making a true test of CDP's comparative effectiveness difficult.

Nevertheless, some of the results are striking. Children in CDP classrooms are more likely to be spontaneously helpful and cooperative, better able to understand conflict situations, and more likely to take everyone's needs into account in resolving them than their counterparts in other schools. Newer research with a group of younger children in the project schools also shows some positive effects, which means that at least some of the teachers who were trained are continuing to use CDP techniques on their own.

These findings also have apparently impressed the Hewlett Foundation. "If the hypotheses hadn't been borne out, we'd be folded up by now," says Dyke Brown, the father of CDP. Instead, the grant was extended for an extra three years so that two critical questions can be answered: First, will the positive effects persist now that the students have moved on to junior high school and begun to mix with children who haven't been taught to care and cooperate? And, second, will such a program work in a less affluent, more ethnically heterogeneous school district—a district such as Hayward?

There are no data yet to answer the first question, and it's too soon to know for sure about Hayward. Initial signs regarding the latter are promising enough, however, that director Schaps wants to go even further. He will soon be seeking funding to take the program beyond California. If all goes well, 10 sites around the country will be chosen to receive CDP training over a period of four years. Ideally, teams of teachers and administrators in those districts will then be qualified to train still others.

Can teachers just adopt the program on their own? Some aspects—pairing buddies from different classes, for example—could be put into place tomorrow in any school. But other parts, such as the approach to discipline, are more difficult to implement than it might appear. Teachers need extended guidance and support, says Schaps, and they would have particular difficulty making major changes in classroom management without the backing of their colleagues and principal.

Project teachers tend to agree with this. At first, says Kushner, "the classroom was so noisy and I worried about what other people would think. I can't imagine trying to do this without other people in the school knowing that the kids aren't going to be sitting down in rows."

Implementing the program requires intensive teacher training, concedes Paul Mussen, a developmental psychologist who served on the CDP's advisory board. "It does present real practical problems," he says. "But the project proves that one can, with great effort, make great differences in how kids interact with each other. It shows that schools can have an effect."

Becoming the Child's Ally— Observations in a Classroom for Children Who Have Been Abused

Carol Caughey

Carol Caughey, M.A., provides individual and group treatment for troubled children and their parents in Federal Way, Washington. An experienced child caregiver as well as psychotherapist, she has worked in child abuse prevention programs that combine parenting classes with a free preschool.

The children formed a circle, and the student teacher gave them handled bells, instructing them to ring these "over your heads, by your shoulders, near your knees," in time to bouncy music. Three boys, Bernie, Tex, and Jeremy, had decided they didn't want to join us and were working quietly with Tinker Toys™ in a corner of the room. When they said they wouldn't take part in our circle, I hesitated to leave them alone. Two of these boys had been given to occasional bursts of flight around the room, during which they had knocked down everything in sight, and left chaos in their wake. Although recently their frenzied behavior seemed to have subsided, I still felt uneasy. Maybe a fight would break out. All of these boys were three-year-olds. At this age, children often begin to cooperate, but I had seen none of them play cooperatively before this morning.

Our circle continued its bell ringing. As our song came to an end, the three boys stood up. Jeremy was wearing a wooden crown and carried a scepter topped with a sun form, both made of Tinker Toys. Tex, standing behind him, also carried a scepter. This one, a round block stuck on a stick, was simpler than Jeremy's. Bernie followed. He was beating on the Tinker Toy container with a mallet that he had made. Jeremy began a chant and the others joined in. "Mungo. Mungo. Mungo." Bernie beat time. The others thrust their scepters to the rhythm he established. All chanted and began to march with solemnity.

They stepped high. Jeremy began to chuckle between the "mungos." Suddenly the intensity seemed to turn to great exuberance and delight. A spontaneous ritual had sprung up in our room, and our circle shut down. We all turned to watch, and then began to chant as we joined the line and followed the marching boys. "Mungo. Mungo."

Later I wondered at this ritual. It seemed like a celebration, as if these boys had reached a new stage in their growth and required a way to declare their accomplishments. I reviewed the ten weeks that we had been together, and saw that each boy had taken steps toward maturity. The cooperative act of inventing together was itself an impressive accomplishment. Jeremy, who was initially a willing victim, letting others grab things from him or hit him, had started to defend himself, to say "No." Tex had begun to engage in manipulating materials like clay and corn meal, tactile experiences which had not been available to him before. This process had extended his concentration to long, serene times when he was deeply involved in the activities so necessary to his early development. Bernie had recently surprised me. One morning I found that someone had discovered the triangle shapes

> **It seemed like a celebration, as if these boys had reached a new stage in their growth and required a way to declare their accomplishments.**

in our different sets of toys, had gathered them together and lined them up on one table. When I remarked at the surprise collection, Bernie admitted to it only by grinning. Several days later, I noticed him sneaking around and collecting to create a triangle surprise again. Together and quite accidentally, we had developed a triangle game, something with the same delightful stealth as the old fairy tale of the shoemaker and his nocturnal, secret helpers, the elves.

The "mungo ritual" might as well have been my own celebration. As a member of a team which had developed parenting classes for families at risk of child abuse and neglect, one of my responsibilities had been to set up a preschool for children whose parents were attending classes and would receive some instruction in the children's setting. This ritual occurred toward the end of our initial presentation of the course.

From *Young Children*, Vol. 46, No. 4, May 1991, pp. 22-28. Reprinted by permission of the publisher, the National Association for the Education of Young Children.

Teaching for self-realization

I had come to this task with the same assumptions about children's lives that had guided my previous teaching. These sprang from my resonance with Jung's concept of the inner self which guides one toward wholeness. Sullwold speaks of this concept in relationship to children as a pattern of being which is potentially defined, "much as the acorn 'contains' the oak or the caterpillar the butterfly" (p. 239). The urge of this pattern to take form is described by Axline as "a powerful force within each individual which strives continuously for complete self-realization" (p. 10).

In a classroom setting that provides a variety of materials and respects choice, children unfold through creative expression and through their own inclinations for interaction both with the environment and with others. In any setting, whether at-risk children are present or not, the first responsibility of a teacher is to provide an environment which is safe, both physically and psychologically, and rich with potential for exploration—one which offers new opportunities at the request or apparent requirement of the children. According to Featherstone's observations, "Giving children choices within a planned environment helps them develop initiative, competence, and an ability to think for themselves" (1973, p. 135). The teacher attempts to follow the children's lead, what Ashton-Warner calls, "the gracious movement from the inside out" (p. 95). And in developmentally appropriate programs, "adults provide opportunities for child-initiated, child-directed practice of skills as a self-chosen activity" (Bredekamp, p. 7).

According to this model, the teacher's second responsibility is to interact with children in a way which enhances their self-realization. To see and to communicate to the child that she is seen had been central to my experience of teaching. Within the interaction, the adult sees, learns, and

appreciates; the child acts, feels recognition, and internalizes appreciation for herself and her learning. The teacher witnesses and narrates the child's activities, expressions of feeling, or simply the child's presence. Seeing is the power that permits. The mystery of a child can't be interpreted. Yet, if we accept the child always as the revelation of her own mystery, we are open to her individuality, to what may be uniquely hers, or to what she may be ready to form that has not yet been seen or formulated into theory.

Our setting, which accommodated children from chaotic homes, was set up as an open environment which respected the children's own volition. Because these children had difficulty in ordering both their perceptions of the environment and their behavior within it, limits had to be stated frequently and precisely. For some, times of concentration were brief and infrequent. Nevertheless, I had seen children discover pride in their autonomy and take the steps that were celebrated in the mungo ritual.

The "world view" of an abused child

I also made discoveries in this setting. I recognized that the self emerges and strives to take form even through powerful inhibitions to its growth. I had come to a definition of the effects of abuse, which relates to the concept of the emerging self. That is, areas of the child's creative self have been cut off through the exploitive intervention of adult power. Recovery of the path to self-realization is achieved through the child's creative activities. As Ashton-Warner observed, "I see the mind of a five-year-old as a volcano with two vents, destructiveness and creativeness. And I see that to the extent that we widen the creative channel, we atrophy the destructive one" (p. 33).

Through normal developmental processes, children who have been abused evolve behaviors which limit

their growth. According to Piaget, the child's task, during the first five years, is to internalize a world plan through her interactions with the environment. He described two means by which this structure of knowledge is accomplished—assimilation and accommodation. Through assimilation, a child absorbs and records experience which is congruent with his existing structures, which fits with concepts that are in place. Accommodation occurs when the child meets and tries to incorporate experiences that don't fit. He is then required to change his structures so that they will be able to contain his new experience. Accommodation is accompanied by discomfort, an experience of disequilibrium. In the following observations of the children I met in our setting, I will refer to this model in interpreting their behavior and their learning.

Children whose parents are violent and unpredictable create a world view in which danger may erupt at any time. The children continually watch out for their survival. "Among the most poignant characteristics found by researchers is the abused child's hypervigilance, a tendency to be wary and watchful of the world—as if expecting the next unreasonable blow to fall at any moment" (Segal & Yahres, p. 181).

Chauncy, age 3, liked to play with cars and airplanes. He always situated himself near the door for this play. One morning, as I sat with him to talk about his stories of cars and planes, I noticed that, as he told the story of his play, he also developed a secondary monologue. "Someone walking. Closing the door. Opening a cabinet." When I listened carefully, I could hear what he was describing. He accurately noted every sound in the hall and office next door. I had not noticed until then that the movements beyond the door were audible. Once I did notice the sounds, I was not able to discriminate the meaning of each sound as precisely as he did. He had lived in a violent home, where drug use was frequent, and had incorporated a world view in which adults could suddenly transform and unexpected violence could threaten at any time. For reasons of survival he had become hypervigilant. It was automatic for him to check continually on what was going on in the unseen world next door and to describe it to himself. A certain portion of his intelligence was always invested in keeping himself safe, even while he was undertaking activities essential to his healthy development. His deepest sense of himself in the world was that he was always in danger.

The self as a "controller of abuse"

As well as maintaining a surveillance for expected violence, children who have been abused also attempt to control the expected abuse. If the child expects to be hit, she can maintain some sense of power over her world if she believes she can control the occasions when she is hit. She therefore seeks to maintain a view of herself as the cause of violent behavior in the adults around her. A child, then, may attempt to provoke abuse to avoid resigning herself to the feelings of helplessness, which would undermine initiative. Resignation would exclude the power of her own initiative from the child's world view, and she would establish what Krystal calls "the surrender pattern" (Krystal, 1988). Since initiative is required for the evolution of self, children may act in apparently destructive ways in order to maintain this sense of initiative. Of apparent maladaptive behaviors, Axline says, "It could be that it is the most effective way that he has discovered to control the situation and is therefore a satisfaction to him, because it is an expression of his power to direct and individualize himself" (p. 21).

During our early sessions, Tex was active and easily distracted. When he settled, it was often at the clay table where his initial haphazard engagement extended to exploration of texturing, cutting, and creating forms, particularly as a teacher observed

and narrated his activity. One morning I commented on his effort. "You've been working here a long time. It looks like you enjoy the clay." Immediately he threw one of the tools across the room, barely missing another child, ran from the table, and rushed to knock down a tower someone had been building. My comment seemed to startle him from his concentration and bring his activity up short. My expressed view of him as a boy who works and enjoys may have been inconsistent with his internalized self-view. In Piaget's terms, in order to receive this new knowledge, he was required to accommodate his self-concept to it. His destructive behavior might then have been an expression of the anxiety over this conflict, his disequilibrium. It might also

have been an attempt to maintain his view of himself as victim and to control the anticipated abuse. Most certainly, it was the appropriate behavior for this child in this moment.

I do not mean to infer that the process in a negative self-view is conscious. The power of the process is that behaviors which are consistent with it are incorporated into the muscles long before the responses become conscious. "The child's thought process is his physical actions" (Pearce, p. 111). The adult cannot help the child to change this pattern of response by reasoning, explaining, criticizing, or questioning. The new experience of a consistent environment will enable change. Tex's behavior was met with a two-minute time-out, enforced without judgment or any explanation except, "I don't want other people to knock

your things down. And I don't want you to knock theirs down."

During one session I set out corn meal on trays with materials for pouring, ladling, and measuring. As I worked, Tex watched in grave silence, but with building excitement. Could this be something he would be allowed to do? He asked simply by pointing to himself. I nodded. He seemed to fall in love with the corn meal play. As he worked, his posture opened and gained assurance. I sat with him and narrated. "You've almost filled that container. I wonder if you're going to fill it to the top." His response was to smile and fill it quickly, and then to carefully level it off. There was an air of reverence in the way he worked. He seemed to be saying, "This is what I

Children whose parents are violent and unpredictable create a world view in which danger may erupt at any time. The children continually watch out for their survival.

---

was designed to do and it's respected here." I suspect that, before he came to us, he had experienced only criticism and interruption when expressing his curiosity and need for tactile engagement and ordering of the world. He had developed the idea that what he most naturally wanted was wrong.

Changing the "world is dangerous" view

A child who has been abused has devised her world view through chaotic situations, independently, and often in profound loneliness. This view has been developed to cope with the world as she has experienced it. The child has a right to this view until, and unless, she discovers that she no longer needs it and can allow it to change. It will

The harsh brutality suggested by children's play, the specific images in their release of pent-up anger, often make us uncomfortable. But, because anger has an energy of its own, it will be expressed, one way or another. The alternatives to this kind of expressive play are hurting someone, something, or oneself.

change as she has new experiences that require her to evolve new structures and postures. These changes may occur in small increments since anxiety inhibits experience and intelligence. "Concern over survival, safety, or well-being immediately forces an evaluation of experience before that experience can take place" (Pearce, p. 11). If one is to respect the child, one must respect self-views that may seem negative to the caregiver. By respect I do not mean agree with, but rather recognize without judgment. While the caregiver communicates respect for the child's view, she can also offer her own view as a perspective for the child, perhaps offering a new experience. Two perspectives then are clarified by the caregiver—the child's and her own. She offers her own, not as a negation of the child's, but simply as a means of maintaining the truth between them. She does not deny the child's view, but does present a perception which could lead the child to amend that view.

David, age 5, rarely completed a task. Halfway through, he usually destroyed his work, saying, "This is ugly. I hate it. I can't do this." I narrated his perspective and my own. "You don't like your picture. It just doesn't seem the way you want it to be. I feel disappointed that you're ripping it up. I liked it and wanted to look at it some more." While respecting his right to make decisions about his work, I also expressed my own response to his work and his decision. After months of destroying his work, David did, in fact, begin to complete and hold onto it. Once he made a long and careful project in

clay which was fired for him to keep.

Carolyn, also 5, sought out small children and bit them, leaving an ugly mark and a lot of pain. She was determined to do this and would go willingly to the time-out chair after the deed was accomplished. When an adult was assigned to keep an eye on her, she twice managed to evade that adult just long enough to get in an aggressive bite. One morning I was cutting up potatoes for printing. She wanted a piece of potato. I gave her one and noticed her enjoyment of biting. The potato resisted just enough for a satisfying and angry bite, and she fully indulged her desire for that. I said, "It looks as if you really like to bite." She nodded wholeheartedly. "I want you to have a chance to bite," I told her, "and I want to help you to do that without hurting anyone." We made an agreement that I would give her a piece of raw potato whenever she wanted it and that she would bite it instead of people. In the following weeks, she did bite another child once, but there was considerably less biting than before our agreement. The potato agreement changed our relationship. She seemed to feel I was an ally, announced frequently that I was her friend, and, most wonderfully, began coming to me with affection, something she had avoided in our room.

The teacher as ally to the inner self

This method—setting out the adult perspective against the child's—is useful when a child expresses a de-

structive view of herself or the world. Besides that part of the ego that has built in a negative view, there is an inner child who knows her own innocence and seeks to grow and realize her urges, her visions, through her interactions with the world. This inner self needs an ally. To create an alliance I sit beside the child and describe what I see her doing or hear her saying. To narrate the child's activity helps her realize a positive experience of herself, one free of adult judgment. It shows her that the adult sees and appreciates her. It nourishes, not only the child's self-love, but the integration of that feeling into her verbal and nonverbal learning, her exploration. This narration also serves to lead the adult to a deeper awareness and appreciation of the child.

The opportunity for this alliance arises when the child is engaged, when her guard is down, when her curiosity and eagerness for creative expression are active. With some children such moments are brief. If the teacher joins the child, times of intense concentration will expand. Seeing is permitting. If adults have seen and described only destructive behavior, only destructive behavior has been permitted.

Sometimes silence is enough to maintain the flow of activity, but it must be a deeply interested silence, because it is the adult's quality of feeling and witnessing that nourishes the child most deeply. "To feel as well as hear what someone says requires whole attention" (Ashton-Warner, p. 2).

Children will frequently indicate what they want from a teacher, move to her lap for closeness, or shake their heads at some part of the teacher's narration to tell her that the activity has a meaning different from the one she is giving it. Some children will take over parts of the narration themselves, so that teacher and child tell the story mutually.

Narrating a new world view

Carrie, age 4, led a chaotic life. Her mother saw her only as a possible means to meet the demands of her own emotional deprivation. Her father was in prison. In our room, Carrie moved from one area to another, lethargic, neither reaching out to anyone, nor committing herself to any activity. My attempts to focus her attention by describing what she was doing, or more often, what she was watching seemed to go unnoticed. One morning, after many sessions of passivity, she found the blocks in a corner and, in solitude, began to build a structure. I went to sit with her. She worked silently building an enclosure. The walls were beautifully ordered, displaying patterns formed from colors and shapes. After I described to her what I was seeing, she began to talk about the enclosure. She described it as a private house for herself, and placed in it symbols for things she valued or longed to have. Her story of the private, varied, and carefully ordered life she could live there was elaborate. At the same time, her use of geometry and symmetry was subtle, accurate, and, I thought, beautiful. I witnessed this activity for more than 30 minutes and, when Carrie was finished, we both breathed deeply. The experience had been intense. It was one of those times when the intelligence, feelings, and symbolic knowledge of the child are brought to bear on a single activity, which seems to be a statement of a place of completion and harmony, a place to move forward from. I felt privileged to have been part of the activity and told her so. This marked a beginning for her. Now she came into our room with ideas of activities she wanted.

She began to pose in front of the mirror in dress-up clothes. She began to paint, with deep concentration, enormous, round, and friendly faces. She also frequently commanded my attention as if it were her due, which it certainly was.

Providing for anger to be safely expressed

Steve, age 5, was a loner. He played independently, avoided adults, and refused group activities.

his use of tools, particularly if they had any dangerous potential. After we discouraged that behavior, she attempted verbally to direct his every move. Now it was observation time, and Kenny's mother was sitting beside him.

Steve continued his angry drama with the clay. I narrated at first, but when Kenny joined in, I stopped, expecting that they might want to talk together. They took over the narration, while shyly engaging one another's interest with both noises

---

A child may attempt to provoke abuse to avoid resigning herself to the feelings of helplessness, which would undermine initiative.

One morning he was building with Lego™ blocks, and I went to his table. Because he'd shown a preference for solitude, I asked permission to join him and took his indifferent glance as acceptance. He had made two small towers and was butting them against one another. I said, "Those guys are bumping into one another." He shook his head and slammed the objects into one another with much more force. I amended by statement. "Oh, I was wrong. They are really hitting each other." He nodded and began a fight between the two, an equal fight in which no one seemed to be winning, but each jumped on, plowed into, and finally destroyed the other. As I narrated, "They really look mad. They seem to want to do each other in," the battle between the Lego people elevated in intensity. When both were destroyed, Steve got up and moved to the clay table. I followed.

He sat down across from Kenny, 5, another loner. Kenny was compliant, and took part in all of our activities with great seriousness. He displayed no enthusiasm and usually held his body in rigid control. When his mother visited our room for the first time, she held his hands to control

and sentences. "This guy's gonna smash him. Let's jump on this one. I'm really gonna stab him." I simply set limits that kept them safe—no tools lifted above shoulder level, stay in the chairs, etc. I also helped Kenny's mother to stay out of it. This was probably the expression of Kenny's anger that she had been trying to avoid. At the end of the session, the boys pulled easily out of the anger and smiled at one another. Kenny put his arm around Steve's shoulders. "I made a friend today," he said.

The harsh brutality suggested by children's play, the specific images in their release of pent-up anger, often make us uncomfortable. But, because anger has an energy of its own, it will be expressed, one way or another. The alternatives to this kind of expressive play are hurting someone, something, or oneself. Ashton-Warner says, "I have always been more afraid of the weapon unspoken than of the one [depicted] on the blackboard" (p. 94). Neither of these boys had ever shown a tendency to hurt anyone. I think their avoidance of others, even at the age when social play can be all-consuming and rich, may have been prompted in part by their own ethics, their reluctance to get too close for fear they might unleash their rage on someone else. This inhibition can itself be destructive, since it denies them a vital part of their growth.

Waiting for the inner self to emerge

These two incidents have about them a quality of completion. All three children took large steps in expressing some truth about their lives and in finding postures for moving forward. They had been in our room for about ten sessions, and I had sat by them frequently and talked to seemingly deaf ears. I had felt helpless to find ways to facilitate the children's desire to move forward. This process itself may have been a testing time, a time to check out the safety of our room and our trustworthiness before the children would reveal themselves. When I find no clear path to the inner child, I become impatient with the process, think I need to exert more active control. What I need, I expect, is to become more receptive to the child's inner and constructive self.

On the last day of our group meetings, Tex found a way to develop his inner self. We had, in our room, a tunnel, a cylindrical wire frame covered with blue vinyl. Children often used it for birthing stories. They especially liked to pretend they were birds, and liked to be touched through the vinyl and to hear stories about baby birds pecking their way out of eggs. The tunnel play was one of the ways children used to ask for physical affection. Three-year-old Tex had never done that. His name mirrored his apparent search for a strong, aggressive, masculine identity, one which didn't accommodate physical affection. This morning I was sitting at one end of the tunnel watching children crawl through. Tex started dashing around me. He poked me in the arm and tried to get me to chase him. Fearing that any unsolicited touch might increase his anxiety, I did not reach for him or hug him. Finally he wanted to crawl through the tunnel. He said that it was a bear's cave, then growled ferociously and showed his claws before he entered. A ferocious bear entered the tunnel, but before he came out, a change occurred. He told me, "I'm a baby bear and you're the mother." He emerged crawling with a small fierceness and tumbled into my lap.

For further reading

Curry, N. E., & Johnson, C. N. (1990). *Beyond self-esteem: Developing a genuine sense of human value.* Washington, DC: NAEYC.

McCracken, J. B. (Ed.). (1986). *Reducing stress in young children's lives.* Washington, DC: NAEYC.

Maier, H. (1978). *Three theories of child development.* New York: Harper.

Miller, A. (1983). *For your own good.* New York: Farrar, Strauss, & Giroux.

O'Gorman, N. (1978). *The children are dying.* New York: Signet.

Rogers, C. S., & Sawyers, J. K. (1988). *Play in the lives of children.* Washington, DC: NAEYC.

Warren, R. M. (1977). *Caring: Supporting children's growth.* Washington, DC: NAEYC.

Wickes, F. (1972). *The inner world of childhood.* New York: Appleton-Century.

References

Ashton-Warner, S. (1986). *Teacher.* New York: Simon and Schuster.

Axline, V. M. (1969). *Play therapy.* New York: Random House.

Bredekamp, S. (Ed.). (1987). *Developmentally appropriate practice in early childhood programs serving children from birth through age 8.* Washington, DC: NAEYC.

Featherstone, J. (1971). *Schools where children learn.* New York: Liveright.

Featherstone, J. (1973). A unified approach to learning. In C. Silberman (Ed.), *The open classroom reader* (pp. 134–138). New York: Random House.

Kalff, D. (1981). *Sandplay, a psychotherapeutic approach to the psyche.* Los Angeles: Sigo Press.

Krystal, H. (1988). *Integration and self-healing: Affect, trauma, alexithymia.* New York: Analytic Press.

Pearce, J. C. (1977). *Magical child.* New York: Dutton.

Segal, J., & Yahres, H. (1978) *A child's journey.* New York: McGraw-Hill.

Sullwold, E. (1984). Treatment of children in analytical psychology. In M. Stein (Ed.), *Jungian analysis* (pp. 235–255). Boulder, CO: Shambhala.

How Teachers Can Help Ease the Pain

Children of Divorce

Candy Carlile

Candy Carlile is Assistant Professor of Education, University of Mary Hardin-Baylor, Belton, Texas.

The structure of the American family is rapidly changing. In the 1960s 60 percent of American families could be described as traditional, with two parents, one at home, and two or three children. Only about 7 percent of U.S. families are now considered to be "traditional" (Elkind, 1986). Today we can expect 50 percent of all first marriages to end in divorce (Glick, 1984; Weitzman, 1985), with an even higher rate of divorce for remarriages (Berns, 1985). By the year 2000, it is expected that 60 percent of all U.S. children will spend some part of their lives in single-parent homes (Jellinek & Klavan, 1988).

Literally millions of children in classrooms across America are desperately trying to adjust to the personal tragedy of divorce. This process can be made easier for these children when sensitive, caring teachers work to create a safe, nurturing classroom environment that promotes the recovery and healing necessary for a child's well-being.

The Pain of Divorce
Even in the best of situations, divorce is a painful process for every-one. Although children of all ages are affected, perhaps the most vulnerable are those at the elementary school level. Ironically, when these children need parental love, assurance and support the most, their parents are least able emotionally to provide it. Unfortunately, the turmoil often does not stop after the divorce is final. Parental hostility and bitterness may escalate through the years and continue to cause needless pain and suffering that could result in psychological damage to the child.

A 10-year study of children of divorce conducted by Wallerstein and Kelly (1980) cited a number of symptoms that children in such cases might experience. Of these behaviors, the following might be observed in the elementary school classroom: anxiety, depression, regression, asthma, allergies, tantrums, daydreaming, overaggressive behavior, withdrawal from relationships, poor school performance, frequent crying or absence of emotion, and difficulty in communicating feelings. If any of these symptoms persist, professional counseling should be sought immediately for the child.

Children are remarkably resilient, however. Although they experience a great deal of pain and feelings of loss, most can and will recover from the trauma of divorce (Bienenfeld, 1987). With the help of an understanding teacher, the classroom can become the brightest spot in a child's life during this difficult time.

Things To Know About Divorce
Although children react differently to divorce depending upon age, maturity and individual situations, teachers need to be aware of some generalities to fully understand the plight of their students.

■ Children of divorce, as well as parents, go through a classic mourning process after divorce, much like after a death in the family. They experience disbelief, then anxiety, anger, sadness, depression and eventually, if given reassurance, acceptance of the divorce (Bienenfeld, 1987).

■ 80 to 90 percent of children recover from the initial shock of divorce in about a year (Jellinek & Klavan, 1988).

■ Boys react more intensely than girls to the loss of their fathers from the home. They are sometimes angry with their mothers for either causing the divorce or driving their fathers away (Dodson, 1987). From elementary school right through high school, boys from single-parent homes were more often classified as "low achievers" than children from intact families (NAESP & Charles F. Kettering Foundation, 1980).

From *Childhood Education*, Vol. 67, No. 4, Summer 1991, pp. 232-234. Reprinted by permission of Candy Carlile and the Association for Childhood Education International, 11141 Georgia Avenue, Suite 200, Wheaton, MD. Copyright © 1991 by the Association.

■ A common reaction of children of divorce who have been rushed into adult roles and responsibilities is to seek early escape from their childhoods. In such cases, these feelings can result in girls becoming sexually precocious and contemptuous of the parent who has been overdependent on them (Hetherington, 1981).

■ 95 percent of divorced parents with custody are mothers (Dodson, 1987). On an average, divorced women and their minor children experience a 73 percent decline in their standard of living in the first year after divorce (Weitzman, 1985). This may result in children having to move into less expensive dwellings and perhaps assume new or increased latchkey responsibilities as mothers struggle to make ends meet financially.

■ Children of divorce are more apt to be late to school or late more often and to miss school altogether. They are also more likely than their counterparts from intact families to spontaneously skip school (NAESP & Charles F. Kettering Foundation, 1980).

■ Teachers have discovered that Mondays and Fridays are especially difficult days for children of divorce (Francke, 1983). Leaving one parent at the end of the week and the other on Sunday can often be too much of an emotional overload for a young child. Anxiety, sadness and tears in the classroom on those days may be a result of the added stress.

A Place To Heal

If children are to recover from the trauma of divorce, they must have a buffer zone between them and parental conflict. Bienenfeld (1987) encourages parents to establish such a neutral zone by refraining from fighting and arguing when their children are present. Unfortunately, this doesn't always happen, and the classroom provides the only "conflict-free" haven for these children. With a little extra effort and planning, we can make our elementary school classrooms much more than simply havens. We can make them places where children can begin to heal and become whole again.

What Teachers Can Do To Help

■ *Know your children.* Children of divorce are usually not eager to talk about their family problems for fear of being perceived as different. It is a teacher's responsibility to identify children of divorce at the beginning of each school year, either through school records or information derived from other teachers. It's also helpful to know when the parents separated to determine approximately where the child is in terms of the healing process. Confer with parents of all students as often as possible to remain aware of other family crises that may occur during the school year.

■ *Talk about feelings.* In a survey of approximately 100 children of divorce, preschool through teen, two emotions were discovered to be predominant in interviews with the children: anger and sadness (Francke, 1983). Guilt, grief, loss, helplessness, loneliness, rejection and anxiety are also common emotions experienced by children before, during and after divorce. Children need to know that it's okay to have these feelings and that they are not alone. If they hesitate to verbalize their feelings, they should be given the opportunity to express themselves in other ways. The use of puppets and dolls (Francke, 1983), unstructured drawings (Bienenfeld, 1987), role-playing and creative writing are a few of the strategies found to be successful in the classroom.

■ *Bibliotherapy.* Using fictional books to help children through difficult times in their lives is certainly not a new strategy for elementary school teachers. Fortunately, a number of noteworthy juvenile books deal with the topic of divorce. Some are for independent reading by children, but I have found the most effective use of these books is to read them aloud to students and then discuss them together. This way the teacher is able to reach everyone—those who are dealing with divorce on a personal level and the other children who can always benefit from a lesson in understanding and kindness. (See Figure 1 for titles.)

■ *Make children aware they are not alone.* Through instructional activities, teach children about the many different types of family structures in today's society. Have children make individual booklets that tell about their families. Construct a class bulletin board using photos of family members. As a

---

Figure 1. Children's Books and Other Sources

Bienenfeld, F. (1980). *My mom and dad are getting a divorce.* St. Paul: EMC Corporation.

Blue, R. (1972). *A month of Sundays.* New York: Franklin Watts.

Brown, L. K., & Brown, M. (1986). *Dinosaur's divorce.* New York: Atlantic Monthly.

Cain, B., & Benedek, E. (1976). *What would you do? A child's book about divorce.* Indianapolis: The Saturday Evening Post Co.

Goff, B. (1969). *Where is daddy? The story of a divorce.* Boston: Beacon.

Kindred, W. (1973). *Lucky Wilma.* New York: Dial.

Lexau, J. (1971). *Me day.* New York: Dial.

Perry, P., & Lynch, M. (1978). *Mommy and daddy are divorced.* New York: Dial.

Pursell, M. S. (1977). *A look at divorce.* Minneapolis: Lerner.

Sitea, L. (1974). Zachary's divorce. In M. Thomas & C. Hart (Eds.), *Free To Be You and Me* (pp. 124-7). New York: McGraw-Hill.

Stanek, M. (1972). *I won't go without a father.* Chicago: Albert Whitman.

Zolotow, C. (1971). *A father like that.* New York: Harper & Row.

cooperative learning activity, have children cut pictures from magazines illustrating different types of family structures. These pictures can be placed in a classroom story-starter file or glued to a piece of posterboard to make a collage.

■ *Modify your language.* Be sure home correspondence, assignments, classroom assignments and school events allow for the variety of family structures represented within your classroom. A child may want to bring a grandparent to Open House or create a Mother's Day card for an aunt, a stepmother or the teacher down the hall. While divorce is no longer considered a social stigma, a child who attends Parents' Night with someone other than a parent can needlessly experience a great deal of personal embarrassment due to unthinking school personnel and children's insensitivity.

■ *Be tolerant of behavior changes.* The majority of children trying to cope with divorce experience a change in behavior. An increase in anxiety, restlessness, decreased concentration and daydreaming may be observed. The change may be immediate or gradual—with children responding to their own internal timetables (Wallerstein & Kelly, 1980). Lonely children may arrive at school early and stay late to receive as much time and attention from the teacher as possible (Francke, 1983).

Teachers must be patient with these children and deal with each case individually. When a child has had an especially bad day, extra time may need to be given for work that was not completed, or perhaps the child might be granted a "time out" from the classroom. Sometimes, a few classroom rules may need bending in order for children to regain some control of their emotions and their lives.

■ *Keep communication open with parents.* Divorce tends to complicate communication between teachers and parents. Simply scheduling parent-teacher conferences can become a major ordeal. Both parents may demand separate conferences, or neither parent may be able to come for the time you have scheduled. For the child's sake, it's important to make the extra effort necessary to keep parents informed of what's happening at school and to stay informed yourself. If necessary, make adjustments in conference times, or make evening telephone calls when parents are home from work.

Also keep in mind that the child may be having to adjust to two households now; books, homework assignments and notes about school progress or upcoming events may be left one place when they are needed at another. An additional matter to consider is that the child's transportation to and from school may also change with parental separation. With the increase in kidnappings by noncustodial parents, it is helpful for school personnel to be informed of which parent has been awarded legal custody of the child. Then, at least, it is possible for the custodial parent to be notified in case someone else arrives to pick the child up during school hours.

The Classroom and Beyond
The trend toward divorce in America is definitely not on the decline. Female-headed families are increasing 10 times as quickly as two-parent families. As a result, the number of emotionally troubled children in classrooms continues to grow with each new semester. In many cases, teachers are providing the only safety net for these children (Francke, 1983). Schools can no longer ignore the problem and must begin to support teachers by providing training that en-ables them to better understand and deal with children of divorce. In addition, budgets must be stretched to ensure that guidance counselors are in place at the elementary school level. Unless more progress is made toward reaching out to these children, some predict that as many as three out of four children of divorce will themselves get divorced. Can we afford having this prediction become a reality?

References
Berns, R. M. (1985). *Child, family, community.* New York: Holt, Rinehart & Winston.
Bienenfeld, F. (1987). *Helping your child succeed after divorce.* Claremont, CA: Hunter House.
Dodson, F. (1987). *How to single parent.* New York: Harper & Row.
Elkind, D. (1986). Helping parents make healthy educational choices for their children. *Educational Leadership, 44*(3), 36-38.
Francke, L. B. (1983). *Growing up divorced.* New York: Linden Press/Simon & Schuster.
Glick, P. C. (1984). Marriage, divorce and living arrangements: Prospective changes. *Journal of Family Issues, 5,* 7-26.
Hetherington, E. M. (1981). Children and divorce. In R. W. Henderson (Ed.), *Parent-child interaction: Theory, research and prospects* (p. 52). New York: Academic Press.
Jellinek, M., & Klavan, E. (1988, September). The single parent. *Good Housekeeping,* p. 126.
National Association of Elementary School Principals & Charles F. Kettering Foundation. (1980). One-parent families and their children: The schools' most significant minority. *Principal, 60,* 31-37.
Wallerstein, J. S., & Kelly, J. B. (1980). *Surviving the breakup.* New York: Basic Books.
Weitzman, L. J. (1985). *The divorce revolution.* New York: The Free Press.

■ TEEN-AGE PREGNANCY

The Case for National Action

FAYE WATTLETON

Faye Wattleton is president of Planned Parenthood Federation of America.

In 1983 a 25-year-old woman with a 9-year-old daughter gave the following testimony before Congress:

> In the tenth grade, my girlfriends and I were all sexually active, but none of us used birth control. I had hopes of a career and I wanted to go to college. One day my mother said, "Towanda, you're pregnant." I asked her how she knew. She said, "I can just tell."
> My mother wouldn't even consider abortion. I had nothing to say about a decision that would alter my entire life. A few weeks after the baby was born, my mother said, "You'll have to get a job." The only job I could get was in a bar.
> I spent two years dealing with the nightmare of welfare. Finally I went to the father of my child and asked him to take care of her while I went back to school. He agreed.
> I am now making some progress. I went to business school and I now have a job working in an office in Washington. But my life has been very difficult. . . . I had ambitions as a child, but my hopes and dreams were almost killed by the burden of trying to raise a child while I was still a child myself.

This young woman's story is relived around us every day. The United States has the dubious distinction of leading the industrialized world in its rates of teen-age pregnancy, teen-age childbirth and teen-age abortion. According to a study of thirty-seven developed nations published by the Alan Guttmacher Institute in 1985, the teen pregnancy rate in the United States is more than double the rate in England, nearly triple the rate in Sweden and seven times the rate in the Netherlands. Throughout the 1970s, this rate rose in the United States, while it declined in such places as England, Wales and Sweden. Each year, more than 1 million American teen-agers become pregnant; about half of these young women give birth.

Teen pregnancy is both cause and consequence of a host of social ills. The teen-agers likeliest to become pregnant are those who can least afford an unwanted child: those who are poor, those who live with one parent, those who have poor grades in school and those whose parents did not finish high school. As the National Research Council points out, teen mothers face "reduced employment opportunities, unstable marriages (if they occur at all), low incomes, and heightened health and developmental risks to the children. . . . Sustained poverty, frustration, and hopelessness are all too often the long-term outcomes." Compounding the tragedy is the fact that children of teen-age mothers are more likely to become teen parents themselves. The burden is felt by the entire society: The national costs of health and social service programs for families started by teen-agers amount to more than $19 billion a year.

Media accounts have tended to represent teen-age pregnancy as primarily a problem of the black community, and implicitly—or explicitly, as in the case of the 1986 CBS Special Report on the "vanishing" black family by Bill Moyers—they have attempted to blame the problem on the so-called degeneracy of the black family. Such distortions of fact are particularly dangerous because they coincide all too neatly with the insensitivity to blacks and the blame-the-victim ideology that the Reagan Administration so disastrously fostered.

High rates of teen pregnancy actually are as all-American as apple pie. Even when the figures for "nonwhite" teens were subtracted from the calculations, the rate of teen pregnancy in the United States in 1981 (83 per 1,000) far exceeded the teen pregnancy rates in all other major industrialized nations. In England and Wales, our closest competitors, the rate for teens of all races was just 45 per 1,000.

The fact of the matter is that teen-age pregnancy rates in the United States have a great deal more to do with class than they do with race. The majority of poor people in this country are white, and so are the majority of pregnant teen-agers. In a report published in 1986, the Guttmacher Institute examined interstate differences in teen pregnancy rates.

It found that the percentage of teens who are black is relatively unimportant as a determinant of overall state variations in teen-age reproduction. It is states with higher percentages of poor people and of people living in urban areas—whatever their race—that have significantly higher teen pregnancy and birth rates.

Teen pregnancy is as grave a problem within many black communities as are poverty and social alienation. One-third of all blacks, and one-half of all black children, live in poverty. And today the pregnancy rate among teens of color is double that of white teens. One of every four black children is born to a teen-age mother; 90 percent of these children are born to unwed mothers. Such patterns can only intensify the problems already facing the black community. Disproportionately poor, blacks are disproportionately affected by the social and economic consequences of teen-age pregnancy.

We need only look to other Western nations to recognize both the cause and the solutions to our teen pregnancy problem. American teens are no more sexually active than their counterparts in Europe; and teen-agers abroad resort to abortion far less often than do those in the United States. There is a major cause for our higher rates of teen pregnancy and childbirth: the fundamental discomfort of Americans with sexuality. Unlike other Western societies, we have not yet accepted human sexuality as a normal part of life. The result is that our children, and many adults as well, are confused, frightened and bombarded by conflicting sexual messages.

Most parents recognize their role as the first and most important sexuality educators their children will have, providing information and sharing family values from the time their children are born. Nevertheless, many parents are unable to talk with their children about such sensitive issues as sex and human relationships. Schools do not fill the gap. Only seventeen states and the District of Columbia mandate comprehensive sex education. As a result, many teen-agers are abysmally ignorant about their reproductive functions.

The mass media, particularly television, only exacerbate the problem. Many teen-agers spend more time in front of the television than they do in the classroom, and their sexual behavior in part reflects what they have learned from this thoroughly unreliable teacher. Nowhere is it more apparent than on television that America suffers from sexual schizophrenia: We exploit sex, and at the same time we try to repress it. Programs and advertisements bombard viewers with explicit sexual acts and innuendo. One study indicates that in a single year, television airs 20,000 sexual messages. Yet rarely is there any reference to contraception or to the consequences of sexual activity.

A substantial number of teens believe that what they see on television is a faithful representation of life. Many believe that television gives a realistic picture of pregnancy and the consequences of sex. And large numbers of teens say they do not use contraceptives because they are "swept away" by passion—surely a reflection of the romanticized view of sex that pervades the mass media.

Network executives, though they apparently have few qualms about exploiting the sexual sell twenty-four hours a day, have the hypocrisy to claim that good taste forbids them to carry ads for contraceptives. Some of the networks recently decided to accept condom ads, though not during prime time, and those ads promote condoms only as protection against AIDS, not against pregnancy. It should not surprise us, then, that America's youths are sexually illiterate, or that 67 percent of sexually active teens either never use contraceptives or use them only occasionally.

We have not failed to resolve this problem for lack of majority agreement on how to do it. A 1988 Harris public opinion survey done for Planned Parenthood found a strong consensus about both the severity of the teen pregnancy problem and about how to solve it:

§ Ninety-five percent of Americans think that teen-age pregnancy is a serious problem in this country, up 11 percent from 1985.
§ Seventy-eight percent of parents believe that relaxed discussions between parents and children about sex will reduce unintended teen-age pregnancy.
§ Eighty-nine percent endorse school sex education.
§ Eighty percent support school referrals of sexually active teens to outside family-planning clinics.
§ Seventy-three percent favor making contraceptives available in school clinics.

School-linked clinics that offer birth control as part of general health care are growing in number in many areas of the country. Community support and involvement are crucial to their development, to insure that the programs are consistent with community values and needs.

Clearly the vast majority of Americans, regardless of racial, religious or political differences, strongly supports the very measures that have proven so effective in reducing teen pregnancy rates in other Western nations. Unfortunately, an extremist minority in this country has an entirely different outlook on sexuality—a minority that has a level of influence out of all proportion to its size. Eager to cultivate the anti-family planning, antiabortion fringe, the Reagan-Bush Administration and its cohorts in Congress sought to whittle down Federal funds for domestic and international family planning, limit sex education in the schools, eliminate confidentiality for birth control and abortion services and block the development of school-linked clinics. These vocal opponents object to everything that has proven successful elsewhere in the industrialized world. Their one and only solution to the problem of teen-age pregnancy is, "Just say no!" But just saying no prevents teen-age pregnancy the way "Have a nice day" cures chronic depression.

There is nothing inherent in American life that condemns us permanently to having the highest teen pregnancy rate in the Western world—nothing that Sweden, England, France, the Netherlands and Canada have been able to do that we cannot.

Parents must talk with their children about all aspects of sexuality—openly, consistently and often—beginning in early childhood. Every school district in the country should provide comprehensive sex education, from kindergarten through twelfth grade. Community groups need to support the development of school-linked health clinics. The media must present realistic, balanced information about relationships and the consequences of sex. Television, in particular, must end the restrictions on contraceptives advertising. Government—at the local, state and Federal levels—must live up to its obligation to eliminate any financial barriers to family-planning education and services and to foster a community environment in which our children can flourish and aspire to a productive and fulfilling life.

But we must also recognize that the teen pregnancy problem cannot be solved through sexuality education and family-planning services alone. If our efforts are to succeed, society must provide all our young people with a decent general education, tangible job opportunities, successful role models and real hope for the future.

It is only by placing such a comprehensive national agenda at the top of the priority list that our society can protect the creative and productive potential of its youth.

THE WORLD FINALS OF CREATIVITY

Half a million young people vie to solve the tantalizing problems in the Odyssey of the Mind competition. Why did the China team's rubber-powered airplane fly 100 times as far as it was supposed to?

C. Samuel Micklus

C. Samuel Micklus, professor of technology at Glassboro State College in New Jersey, has written about industrial design and creative problem-solving in eight books and many articles and teachers' manuals. He founded Odyssey of the Mind in 1978 with his first problem: How do you lead a team member down a path with only nonverbal cues to guide him?

It was a cold, damp, overcast day in Budapest as we walked up and down its hilly streets. Finally we arrived at a building that may have been standing for well over a hundred years. Its ceramic tile floors were of beautiful Hungarian design. Down three flights of dimly lit stairs we came to a storage area. At one end was a door with a sign that read "Odyssey of the Mind"—the name of the international competition in creative problem-solving that has grown from its New Jersey beginnings to include more than half a million young people around the world.

The first Hungarian competitors, a team of seven teenage boys, had just painted the old concrete walls to improve their "space," said Eva Petho, one of the thousands of adults who give their time as Odyssey of the Mind (OM) coaches. We arrived as her team was working on several problems with every intention of competing in OM's 1991 World Finals, which [brought] 12,000 parents, teachers, friends, and members of 650 teams to the University of Tennessee in Knoxville on May 23-25.

I couldn't help remembering the first year a team from China reached the world finals. The problem was to design a series of model airplanes, one of which had to be propelled by a rubber band and fly at least 30 feet. An error was made in the Chinese translation. The Chinese were told the plane had to fly *300* feet, and when a team member launched their plane, it flew...and flew...and flew. I would conservatively say it flew more than 3,000 feet—going all the way to the top of the University of Maryland's Cole Field House, while the thousands of spectators cheered.

"I just sat there in awe," said Wayne Kehrlis, coach of a US team and a physical design engineer for IBM, OM's corporate sponsor. "I couldn't figure out their strategy. The tighter you twist a rubber band, the faster it spins. The kids had figured they needed to keep it up in the air a long time, so they created a friction device to slow it down. I sure learned something that day, as a coach as well as an engineer."

BALSA STRIPS HOLDING 978 POUNDS

During a dozen years of designing problems for these competitions, I have seen how children can outdo themselves when offered an interesting challenge and the adult encouragement to meet it—but not adult *help*, which OM coaches are forbidden to give.

"You kind of learn how to learn on your own," said a boy on the team from Urbandale High School in Iowa.

"Every time something messes up, someone has to fix it," said a high school girl from Greenville, Texas, explaining why she had to learn a lot about electronics.

I never know what will happen with the structure problem that is assigned each year. Teams start with 36-inch strips of one-eighth-inch square balsa wood, which they cut and glue to build a structure eight inches tall. The structure's assigned weight limit varies each year, usually from 10 to 18 grams, less than the weight of three letter-size envelopes. If a team uses roughly 10 strips of balsa wood, how much weight could these structures hold? Teams began making structures holding 500 pounds and more. It became difficult to get enough weights for some of our regional competitions.

In order to weaken the structures, I wrote a more complicated problem. In addition to holding weights, a structure had to withstand a billiard ball rolling down an eight-foot ramp and crashing into the structure once a minute. I was sure this would greatly reduce the weight held. After all, these were kids....

Result: The 18-gram structure by the world champion team from Pine Bluffs, Arkansas, held an astounding 978 pounds while absorbing 10 impacts.

Achievements like this have abounded during OM's remarkable growth since 1978, when 28 New Jersey high schools and middle schools met at Glassboro State College for the first problem-solving competition. In 1991 membership exceeds 9,000 schools and other institutions.

PRIMARY SCHOOLS, TOO

Schools join the OM Association, a private non-profit corporation, and receive five competition problems for the year (they need not tackle all the problems). As in a sport, teams (of five to seven members) are formed. They compete at local,

regional, and state/province levels for the honor of representing their countries at the OM World Finals. This year teams will represent Canada, China, Hungary, Japan, Mexico, Poland, the Soviet Union, and the United States. Teams are also working in the North Atlantic D.O.D.D.S. (Department of Defense Dependent Schools for the children of U.S. military personnel), the Philippines, and Africa.

There are four divisions: I, kindergarten through grade 5; II, grades 6-8; III, grades 9-12; and IV, colleges and universities.

In addition to the competition problems, one problem is designated for teams at the primary-school level that do not compete in solving it but demonstrate their solutions. At an annual meet in Wisconsin a little boy sat with his arms folded and a sad look on his face after his team demonstrated its solution to a rather complicated problem about

LONG-TERM PROBLEMS FOR 1990-91

The following were solved by participants at regional competitions worldwide—with the winning teams going on to compete in the World Finals, May 23-25, at the University of Tennessee, Knoxville. (The materials used must not exceed $75 in value.)

• OMer's Buggy Lite (Divisions II, III, and IV)
Create a theme that incorporates a lightweight, battery-powered vehicle that the team designs, constructs, and drives. The vehicle must attempt to attach itself to a trailer, tow the trailer, detach the trailer, travel between specific locations, move in reverse, and come to rest in a specific parking place.

• Give and Go (Divisions I, II, and III)
Make four separate devices that relay tennis balls from different locations into containers.

• Classics...Pompeii (Divisions I, II, III, and IV)
Create and present an original performance that includes a scene in the ancient city of Pompeii before or during its devastation. The performance must be supported with team-made works of art/artifacts presented in various media.

• Super Collider (Divisions I, II, and III)
Make and test a balsa wood structure. The structure will be tested to hold weight. The weight stack will be impacted with a collider to cause twisting and vibrations affecting the structure.

• Transformation (Divisions I and II)
Create and present a performance that shows a series of real or imaginary changes or evolutions of something. Photographs and/or drawings illustrating each phase of the transformation must also be presented.

• Bedtime Story (Primary Level, Grades K-2)
Create an original bedtime story and perform a skit in which a team member must tell the story to help someone sleep.

choosing or creating a guest of honor and celebrating his, her, or its birthday. Someone said:

"You did very well. The audience gave you a big round of applause—why do you look so sad?"

"Yeah!" the boy replied. "But now we have to wait a whole year to think!"

For all divisions it's a hands-on project for kids and a hands-off project for adults. After the Kennedy Middle School from Winston-Salem, North Carolina, competed, a judge asked who welded the team's vehicle together. "Michelle Golobic is our welder," said a team member. Michelle says she likes to build things.

'THE LEONARDO DA VINCI SPRING CAR'

There are three scoring categories: long-term (200 points); spontaneous (100 points); and style (50 points). The long-term problems—to be solved before the competition—vary. A few examples:

• "Classics...Poetic License." Create a parody or satire based on a poet and poem selected from a given list, such as "Captain! My Captain," by Walt Whitman; "Trees," by Joyce Kilmer; "The Village Blacksmith," by Henry Wadsworth Longfellow. Read or recite the original work and the parody.

• "Leonardo da Vinci Spring Car." A problem for Divisions II and III. Design, build, and drive a vehicle powered by springs. Make it navigate a course 150 feet long, stop, travel in reverse, and, during its journey, change appearance from a 16th-century vehicle to a modern one. IBM gave Odyssey of the Mind commercial time to feature this problem on a TV special, "I, Leonardo—A Journey of the Mind."

• "Transformation." Create and present a performance that shows a series of changes or the evolution of something. Include the start, the first, second, and third changes, and the final appearance of what's been transformed.

The quality of the students' work is amazing. They can do more things better than most adults think they can, and they often exceed their own expectations.

THE JUDGE WHO LEARNED SPANISH

As for the adults involved, I have been overwhelmed by the skill and dedication of the people OM attracts. The World Finals has 225 volunteers who judge or help out with the competition. They pay their own expenses, work for three to five grueling days, and laugh, cry and stand in awe of our youth.

A retired friend from New Jersey, Bobbi Mansfield, knew that she was going to judge a problem called "Classics...Showtime," and that a Mexican team was competing in its native language. Bobbi enrolled for two semesters of Spanish to help her judge the team.

On the day of competition each team is given a spontaneous problem, something to challenge children to think on their feet. The team enters a room with several judges. No other adults or spectators

How to Win Without Actually Succeeding

After the first few Odyssey of the Mind competitions, it became clear that some teams would try something very, very different. They would be exceptionally creative. To them, winning a trophy was of minor importance. But to encourage students to continue to think creatively, take risks—maybe even place last—OM established the Ranatra Fusca Creativity Award.

Ranatra Fusca?

It all began in one of my design classes, when the students were challenged to devise a flotation contraption to carry them one-half mile around a lake. Students sailed trash cans, paper boats, and milk bottle crafts. One made a giant hamster exercise wheel; he would run inside and it would spin on the water. Another student's device imitated a water bug (see below). He would sit on top and pull a rope that moved the legs together. When he let go of the rope the contraption would, theoretically, skid across the water. Unfortunately, he fell off each time. He didn't solve the problem, but his idea was great.

Thus the Ranatra Fusca award, named for a classification of water insect, was born.

Success is not a criterion. The self-styled Nerds of Nashua, N.H., won simply for remaining totally and ridiculously in character throughout a World Finals competition. Another winner was the Chinese team that went far beyond mere success when its rubber-band-powered aircraft flew more than 100 times as far as the problem required.—*C.S.M.*

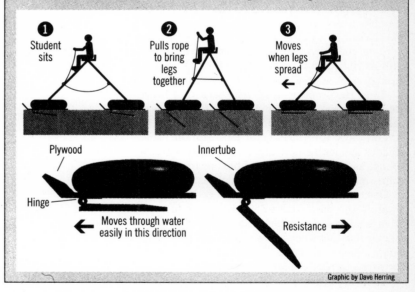

① Student sits

② Pulls rope to bring legs together

③ Moves when legs spread

Plywood

Innertube

Hinge

← Moves through water easily in this direction

Resistance →

Graphic by Dave Herring

are allowed. Here the students must work as a team to be successful.

Sometimes teams are required to respond to a question or statement. For example, they may be given two minutes to name different kinds of light. Common responses (worth 1 point each) include sunlight, moonlight, electric light, flashlight, street light, red light. Creative responses (worth 3 points each) include ultra-lights (airplanes), K-Mart blue light special, aurora borealis (northern lights), delightful, lightning, lightweight (boxer), light-fingered.

Sometimes teams are asked to improvise with something, say, a light bulb. Creative responses

Spectators in an OM competition quickly find that when a team finishes its presentation it receives a round of applause, and most of the people applauding are its opponents.

would be to hold it up to an eye and say, "A tear," or it could be a hot air balloon, an ice cream cone, or a bright idea. One young man from Virginia said, "It looks like a shrine for worshipers of Telly Savalas."

COMPETING WITHOUT HEARING

In the past few years some OM long-term problems have been designated as "nonlinguistic." Teams may not use language in solving them. The purpose is to prevent English-speaking teams from having an unfair advantage.

Although the nonlinguistic problems were implemented for teams that speak such languages as Spanish, French, Polish, and Japanese, they also attracted another group that we hadn't considered—the deaf. Some deaf teams have been state champions and competed successfully at the OM World Finals.

Style, the third scoring category, refers to the elaboration of a long-term problem solution through skits, special effects, music, props, etc.

In all the problems team members must learn not only to work with each other but to depend on each other. Making new friends is encouraged in several ways: Kids meet other kids with the same abilities and interests, sometimes within their own school as well as from neighboring towns and states, and even from faraway countries.

One of the most remarkable aspects of the program is the participants' appreciation of each other's efforts. Spectators in an OM competition quickly find that when a team finishes its presentation it receives a round of applause, and most of the people applauding are its opponents.

Think about young people. They are inquisitive, full of energy, and they love to compete. Why not channel learning in this direction? The teams put a

lot of work into their projects, often in the evenings and on weekends. With so many distractions that have negative, or even disastrous, consequences, it's exciting to see young people having so much fun working on worthwhile activities.

The World Finals are awesome. Last year at Iowa State University a record 634 teams from seven countries competed. At the awards ceremony Yuri Pukas, the Soviet coach, led 14,000 people in singing, "This land is your land, this land is my land, from California to the New York Island...." Afterwards Yuri said, "Of course this land is your land, but it is my land, too."

FOUNDER'S FINDINGS

OM is extending creative problem-solving into the regular classroom through language arts, mathematics, science, social studies, and technology education for primary, elementary, and secondary education. These classroom activities, developed with the support of IBM, are new each year and are free to OM members.

Finally, a few personal observations:

1. Creativity can be taught.

2. Competition makes young people go a step beyond. Just being OK is not good enough. We have to pay attention to details. If all of us do our jobs a little better, or do more than what's required, we will all be better off. This is a life-long skill that should be encouraged.

3. If students can become excited about learning, they will do more, learn more, and feel good about themselves.

4. Be tolerant of kids—give them a pat on the back for trying to achieve something, even if they experience disappointments in the process. After all, Thomas Edison made thousands of mistakes when developing the light bulb.

Different Drummers: The Role of Nonpublic Schools in America Today

Diane Ravitch

Teachers College, Columbia University

When I was growing up in Houston and attending public school, I knew hardly anyone who went to nonpublic school. There were two kinds of students who attended nonpublic schools: the rich and the incorrigible. For the rich, there were two private schools in town; the incorrigible were sent away to military schools, where, according to local lore, they got "straightened out." Perhaps there were religious schools as well, but I was not aware of them. What I did know, because I heard it from my parents and teachers in school assemblies, was that public schools were the best expression of American democracy and that deviations from that norm were only for snobs and misfits. So long as I lived in Houston, this seemed to be incontestable. I did not realize it at the time, but I was enmeshed in a worldview that had a long history and many adherents. I later discovered articles written after World War II with titles like "Our Public Schools Kept Us Free," insinuating that those who did not attend public school were not really committed to a free society. Today one of my prized possessions is a large antique poster displaying a one-room red schoolhouse and proclaiming "Our Public School—the Bulwark of This Country."

Now, on those occasions when the relative virtues of public and private schooling are contrasted, one hears only faint echoes of that perfervid point of view. There are fewer true believers than there were a generation ago. The public school system continues to be an institution of great importance and value in our society, but seldom is it even hinted that nonpublic schools are divisive and that their graduates are unpatriotic. In part, the rise of demands for choice, tuition tax credits, vouchers, or other means to break the public school monopoly indicates a changed political climate. Partisans of nonpublic schooling no longer feel embarrassed to plead their case for tax dollars, and their appeal is clearly reaching an audience that goes far beyond the relatively small number of parents whose children are in nonpublic schools.

The reason for this change in the debate is that the public schools are no longer icons in the nation's civil religion. For many years, their supporters heaped extravagant praise on them, claiming that they and they alone had unified the nation, taught everyone a common language, prepared a work force for a mighty industrial machine, developed a high level of democratic citizenship, and provided equal opportunity to all. They were the guarantors of social stability and the path to social mobility. If the public schools had been able to deliver on all of these promises, then no one would ever have challenged their dominance.

However, the schools were effectively demythologized during the last generation by racial upheavals, by court decisions that held them guilty of intentional racial segregation, by a rising tide of ethnic particularism, by the declining legitimacy of a high school diploma in the workplace, by scholarly and journalistic criticism, and by the burden of their own claims. Free public education was an unquestioned boon for the poor European immigrants, who came from lands where political and religious oppression denied many of them access to schooling. Large numbers of the immigrants stayed in school only long enough to become literate in English, however. The doors of opportunity were wide open, the dropout rate (a modern invention) was high, as was the failure rate.

In the inflamed political atmosphere of the late 1960s and early 1970s, the public schools were accused of every kind of evil: Not only had they failed to do what they promised, but they were *designed* to fail, *designed* to oppress those who were failing. Instead of gaining credit for teaching a common language, they were lambasted for failing to preserve the native language and culture of their millions of pupils. Instead of winning applause for unifying a diverse nation, they were blasted for attempting to destroy ethnic diversity. Pity the poor public school: Once the embodiment of virtue in our civil religion, it became commonplace among Neo-Marxists and other radical pedagogues to characterize it as the instrument of a class conspiracy to repress the children of workers, minorities, and the poor. From archangel to archenemy in one generation!

There were many consequences of this harsh debunking of the public schools, some of which linger in our public policy debates. One was the rehabilitation of the reputation of

From *Teachers College Record*, Vol 92, No. 3, Spring 1991, pp. 409-414. Copyright © 1991 by Teachers College, Columbia University. Reprinted by permission.

nonpublic, private, independent schools. To those who despised the bureaucracy, the uniformity, the sameness of public education, the preferred alternative was schools that were not controlled by the state. In the early 1970s, the radical school movement created hundreds, perhaps thousands, of small alternative private schools. In poor inner-city neighborhoods, community activists opened storefront academies to vie with the public schools. Suddenly, private schools were on the cutting edge of change.

Meanwhile, certain sectors of the middle class abandoned public education. The growth of fundamentalist sects led to a corresponding growth in Christian day schools, mainly in the South. Also in the South, "segregation academies" opened in the wake of desegregation orders. In the northeast, Orthodox Jewish sects created an extensive network of yeshivas, or religious day schools. Where there was a well-to-do black community, in cities like Washington, D.C., and New York, black parents took advantage of declining racial prejudice to place their children in good private schools.

At the same time, Catholic schools, which traditionally had enrolled the great majority of students in nonpublic schools, experienced declining enrollments. As Catholics became more prosperous and left the cities, urban Catholic schools had fewer Catholic children to draw on. Furthermore, the church had fewer religious teachers with which to staff the schools, and lay teachers drove up costs. Although Catholic schools struggled to maintain themselves, hostility toward parochial education abated, in part because tensions between Catholics and Protestants decreased, but also because it was evident that graduates of Catholic schools were just as civic minded and well educated as graduates of public schools.

By 1981, when President Ronald Reagan advocated tuition tax credits and others urged the creation of vouchers to subsidize the cost of private education, the support for these proposals was far broader than the 12 to 14 percent of the population that used private schools. Critics complained that it was wrong to permit tuition tax credits or to allocate funds for vouchers, and they offered a variety of reasons. It was wrong, they said, because such policies would violate the constitutional ban on supporting religion; or because they would encourage racial segregation; or because they would favor the well-to-do over the poor; or because they would be too costly to the public budget. But scarcely anyone said that they should be defeated because public schools were better than private schools or because public schools were the apothesis of American ideals. The most interesting aspect of the entire discussion of public versus private was that the millenarian, patriotic rhetoric once associated with public education had virtually disappeared from the debate.

At present, there is limited interest in funding choice between public and private schools, largely because of the likelihood that the Supreme Court would not permit public funds to go to private schools, but a change in the membership of the Court could cause that issue to rise again. However, continuing advances in learning technology may well change the locus of schooling, and the present definition of a public school may not accord with reality in the not too distant future.

I personally have doubts about the use of public funds for private education, but I confess that I waver in my convictions. I cannot rationally explain why tax dollars support college and graduate students who attend private institutions, but cannot support students in private schools. Yet I worry that federal funding might someday lead to intrusive regulation of a sort that would deprive private education of the very qualities that give it value. Traditionally, there has been little regulation of higher education, no matter how many tax dollars it absorbs; and also traditionally, the schools that receive public dollars are accustomed to close regulation by the state.

As it happens, many states already regulate important aspects of private schools, such as the qualifications of their teachers. At present, however, private schools continue to enjoy a good deal of autonomy. Although there are exceptions, they are relatively free to design their own curricula, hire the teachers of their choice (even if they do not have any education credits), select their own textbooks, create their own tests, and establish their own rules for student conduct. They may require their students to wear uniforms or they may have no dress code at all; if they have more applicants than places, they may admit whomever they wish, and they may suspend or expel students who violate the school's rules. Private schools are the exemplars of school-based management.

Being private precludes access to public funds, but it does have its benefits. When James Coleman compared private and public schools, he pointed out that the Catholic schools were less likely to have vocational programs and to track students, because they could not afford the equipment and the extra staff.[1] So, for economy's sake, most children in Catholic schools are in an academic program, which produces higher achievement in the long run for children of comparable ability. Catholic and independent schools do not have bureaucracies like public schools because they do not need them and cannot afford them. Since they do not get public funds, they do not have administrators to coordinate the many different federal and state programs. In a private school, there are few staff members who do not teach.

Why, however, should there be private schools at all? Why not require all children to attend public schools, so that none can gain special advantages from a private education and none can be excluded from the reach of public policy? If equity were the only value that counted in our society, then private schools might cease to exist, but equity is not the only value that counts in our society. Down that path lies the danger of standardization, homogeneity, and uniformity.

The Supreme Court considered this issue in 1925, in the *Pierce* v. *Society of Sisters* decision. The Court invalidated an Oregon law requiring all children to attend public schools. The impetus for this law came from nativists who wanted faster assimilation of foreign-born children and feared that a private-school education would allow them to remain "un-Americanized." The Court ruled that Oregon had unreasonably interfered "with the liberty of parents and guardians to direct the upbringing and education of children under their control." The Court further held that "the fundamental theory of liberty upon which all governments in this union repose excludes any general power of the State to standardize its children by forcing them to accept instruction from public teachers only. The child is not the mere creature of the State."[2]

In a free society, parents and guardians have the right to send their children to schools that are not controlled by the state. Interestingly, as the democratic movement spread through Eastern Europe in the 1980s, democratic reformers complained about the complete monopoly of education by the omnipotent state. They realized that control of the schools by the state bureaucracy and imposition of the state's official ideology were lynchpins of the Communists' efforts to regulate thought. As Poles and other East Europeans considered how to reconstruct their societies along democratic lines, one of the problems they confronted was the corruption of state schools as vehicles for political propaganda. As they go about the business of creating democratic institutions, it is likely that they will permit religious organizations to open their own schools, if they wish. They will do this not in order to promote religion, but in order to promote divergent thinking, independent centers of thought and activity, removed from state control.

Perhaps the most important lesson to be learned from the Communist debacle in Eastern Europe is that democracy flourishes when government power is broadly decentralized. A free press—free newspapers, free magazines, free television stations, free radio, and free publishing houses—is vital in order to inform public opinion and to encourage unfettered thought. Like a free press, the other institutions of democracy—an independent judiciary, independent religious groups, free trade unions, and so on—act as checks on the power of government.

In education, as in every other aspect of social life,

competition and decentralization are positive goods. In this society, everyone has an obligation to support public education, because it is provided on equal terms to all children. All are not, however, obligated to send their children to public schools. The public schools benefit by the diversity that private education encourages. We look to private education for the off-beat schools, for schools that are out of step with conventional thinking. Some private schools will be experimental and take risks. Some will be rigorously traditional. Others will find their own way of diverging from the mainstream.

It is, in short, their diversity that we value, for private education—whether religious or secular—has the freedom to be different. Whether it is a progressive school like Summerhill [in Leiston, Suffolk, England] (and its American clones) or a traditional Catholic school staffed by old-fashioned nuns, the private school has a special niche in American education. Eliminating these schools, even if it were constitutionally permissible (which it is not), would weaken American education.

Thoreau advised us to be tolerant of the man who "hears a different drummer." In private education, there are many who hear different drummers—religious and secular, progressive and conservative, dogmatic and freethinking, odd and staid. For their own reasons, they do not wish their children to receive what the state offers them at no charge. For their own reasons, they choose to be different. It may be time to acknowledge that the private sector in education, in all its diversity, has helped to keep us free.

NOTES

1. James S. Coleman, Thomas Hoffer, and Sally Kilgore, *High School Achievement: Public, Catholic, and Private Schools Compared* (New York: Basic Books, 1982), p. 78.

2. Pierce v. Society of Sisters of the Holy Name, 268 U.S. 510 (1925).

What Is An Independent School?

Pearl Rock Kane

Teachers College, Columbia University

If asked about "independent schools," most people in the United States would respond with confusion. The term has virtually no recognition value among the general public. So, since independent schools constitute only a small proportion of nongovernmental schools, independent school educators often resort pragmatically to self-definition by exclusion: independent schools are schools that are nonpublic and nonparochial.

Though the term *private schools* embraces both independent and church-controlled schools, the public has a narrower and quite definite conception about "private schools," an image formed by reading popular fiction and viewing films such as the recently acclaimed *Dead Poets Society.* The media have succeeded in giving these schools an aura of exclusivity and elitism more in keeping with the Edwardian world of "Masterpiece Theater" than with current reality. Many still believe that only children of well-to-do, Anglo-Saxon Protestants need apply. The roster of graduates from independent schools also contributes to their reputation. Accomplished professionals, well-known statesmen, and literary figures such as Edward Albee, George Bush, John Irving, John Fitzgerald Kennedy, John Knowles, Franklin Delano Roosevelt, Arthur Schlesinger, Jr., and Gore Vidal are only a few of such distinguished graduates. The popular success of these schools is disproportionate to their numbers: although there are approximately 1,500 independent schools in the United States, that is a small number in comparison to public or parochial schools. Moreover, the reputation is formed from stereotyped images of a few prestigious northeastern schools whose origins date back to the eighteenth and nineteenth centuries. In fact, independent schools are quite diverse in their educational missions, as diverse in character as any comparable number of U.S. citizens—and like those citizens, most independent schools were born in the twentieth century. It is that very diversity that leads independent school educators to resort to definition by exclusion, simply because it is easier than trying to create a definition broad enough to include all these schools and succinct enough to satisfy the casual inquirer.[1]

This article has two purposes: to describe the characteristics that distinguish independent schools from public and other private schools and to point to both self-imposed and environmental challenges that are confronting the schools in the 1990s.

Characteristics of Independent Schools

Although the conditions of the marketplace shape independent schools, they have been relatively free to define themselves. A tremendous range of schools has evolved, varying in philosophy, organization, and style. Some schools are highly traditional, others are progressive in outlook; some are boarding schools, some day schools, some a combination of the two; some are single-sex, some coeducational; some are highly academic and selective, others are "second chance" schools for students who have failed elsewhere; some are free or inexpensive, some have sliding scales of tuition depending on the income of applying families, some have extensive scholarship programs, and some are prohibitively costly, accessible only to the affluent; some have the stability of generations of graduates, others have graduated only a few classes; some have impressive financial endowments and extensive resources in buildings and grounds, others have recourse only to income from tuition and annual fund-raising and operate in modest or even makeshift spaces.

However, varied in their objectives and approaches, all independent schools share six basic characteristics: self-governance, self-support, self-defined curriculum, self-selected students, self-selected faculty, and small size.[2]

Self-Governance

A self-selecting and thus self-perpetuating board of trustees bears ultimate responsibility for an independent school's

From *Teachers College Record*, Vol. 92, No. 3, Spring 1991, pp. 396-408. Copyright © 1991 by Teachers College, Columbia University. Reprinted by permission.

philosophy, resources, and program. Though an independent school may have a religious affiliation, it is the independence of the board of trustees that distinguishes it from a parochial school that is ultimately subordinate to a church hierarchy. The trustees choose the chief administrator, to whom are delegated all aspects of the day-to-day operation of the school.

Self-governance results in responsiveness to the particular needs of the individual school and freedom from the accountability to bureaucratic intrusion from local, state, and federal governments that often comes with financial aid. A metaphor comparing the structure of public and private institutions is found in Gerald Grant's essay "The Character of Education and the Education of Character." Grant compares the contemporary public school to a watermelon: The thick rind represents the accretion of bureaucracy, court orders, union contracts, and measures of accountability that constrain the rightful use of power; the dispersion of such power is like the dispersion of the watermelon's seeds—there is no clearly definable center. He compares the private school to an avocado, where adult power and initiative are akin to the large seed at the center, and there is only a thin skin of externally imposed policy.[3]

In independent schools, which are free of even the centralized bureaucracy present in denominational schools, there is significant autonomy in shaping the institution. The absence of bureaucracy has allowed a more fluid organization where roles of administrators and teachers are less rigidly prescribed. Many administrators have regular teaching responsibility, and many teachers do administrative work as department heads, admissions officers, or college counselors. The blurring of lines between administrators and teachers may explain why most independent school teachers have not chosen an affiliation with a national labor organization. As a result, most independent schools have been unencumbered by the union-sponsored restrictions of tenure and collective bargaining.

Self-Support

Incorporated as not-for-profit, tax-exempt corporations, independent schools rely primarily on tuition for support, supplemented by gifts from parents, alumni/alumnae foundations, and corporations and, for some, income from an endowment. Most independent schools are not eligible for significant financial assistance from local, state, or federal agencies. Although aid is sometimes available for books and equipment and, in many states, for transportation and mandated state services such as attendance monitoring, independent schools are cautious about accepting government subsidies because they pose a threat to self-governance.

That primary dependence on tuition is responsible for the high cost of independent schools, nationally averaging $7,700 for day schools and $14,700 for boarding schools.[4] Those figures reflect the expense of maintaining elaborate facilities, a commitment to low student-teacher ratios, and a recent impetus to increase faculty salaries.

Such high tuitions limit the ability of independent schools to shape the social composition of the student body, tending to favor the economically advantaged. This tendency leads to charges that independent schools are elitist. It is often overlooked that many public schools are less racially and economically diverse than independent schools. Since public school districts are organized within geographic areas, attendance at a particular school is determined by residence. In many affluent communities such as Greenwich, Connecticut, or Newport Beach, California, where the average cost of houses is over half a million dollars, only families that can afford to purchase these expensive houses can send their children to the local public school. The result is that the schools are white, upper-class institutions with little diversity. In affluent communities, private schools are often more diverse than the local public schools because the private schools recruit from a wider geographic area.

Even with public and private schools that are alike in student composition, dependence on tuition in lieu of funding from the government—that is, relying on paying customers—adds an important difference in the way the schools operate and respond to constituents. Independent schools must satisfy their clients, and they are obliged to demonstrate successful outcomes. Driven both by such economic imperatives and a philosophical belief in the primacy of the individual's development as an educational goal, independent schools make a commitment to nurture the students they admit. These schools give personal attention to each student and are determined to help each student achieve personal success. Faculty struggle with reluctant students and, despite popular misconceptions, relatively few students are asked to leave. However, since progress with students is hard to assess individually, the educational achievement of these schools is often measured indirectly, and perhaps unfairly, by the record of admission by graduates to competitive colleges. To the degree that college admission is the dominant client interest, the tuition dependence of independent schools may pressure them away from individualization of instruction that does not directly serve this end.

Self-Defined Curriculum

Each independent school designs its own curriculum, and many independent schools use curricula or books espousing a particular value orientation—for instance, in moral education or in the theory of evolution. Such materials might not be permitted in public schools. The majority of those having a secondary division offer college preparatory programs.

Though free to experiment, most independent schools offer a curriculum that is highly academic and rigorous. Even the so-called second chance schools focus on preparation for college. There is a basic emphasis on English, history, languages, mathematics, and sciences, and because of the small size of most independent schools, a limited range of courses is available to students within these academic areas. The academic, college preparatory orientation allows for cohesiveness in the curriculum, but it usually confines electives to academic offerings and eliminates options for students to take technical and vocational courses, which are regular fare at public schools.[5]

In some states, independent schools are required to include mandated courses, such as the history of the region, or more conventional courses such as American history or algebra. While these are subjects that the schools would choose to teach on their own, most independent schools are not bound by rigid state regulations to teach a specified curriculum. The schools align themselves in state and national organizations to ensure that curricular freedom is maintained, and many schools ignore with impunity the requirements that do pertain.

One of the factors that stimulates faculty intellectually is the continuous assessment and discussion of curriculum that transpires within these schools. The autonomy of the individual teacher to select texts, alone or in consultation within a department, is a key advantage independent schools have over public schools in the attraction of academically oriented teachers. Putting curriculum in the hands of teachers in the school provides a kind of staff development that is not possible if the curriculum is both predetermined and decided outside of the school.

The explicit curriculum has two other facets that are equally emphasized and interconnected: physical development and the overriding goal of character development. Character, or moral development, is nurtured through academics, including courses in religion and ethics that public schools cannot offer. Moral education is also pursued through an extensive program of cultural and athletic activities. In many schools, particularly boarding schools, athletic competition is structured into the school day. Coaching is done by the academic faculty as a way to emphasize that the mind and body work together, and that learning takes place on the field as well as in the classroom.[6]

Self-Selected Students

Although market conditions cause schools to raise or lower their standards of admission, independent schools are at liberty to select the kind of students the school believes will benefit from the type of educational program offered.

Student selection implies mutual selection: The school chooses the student, but the student also chooses the school. There is a psychological advantage to such voluntarism. Although a study of attrition conducted in 1988 showed that only 2 percent of all students in independent schools were asked to leave for academic or disciplinary reasons, the knowledge that their independent school is not obliged to keep them is likely to have an effect on academic and social behavior. Conversely, the school knows the students may decide not to stay, and finds that fact similarly motivating. Beyond the financial contract that exists between the family and the school, there is an unwritten agreement. As Otto Kraushaar has pointed out, "Both the patrons and the school have a stake in seeing that the contract is fulfilled satisfactorily." Mutual freedom of association by students and schools is fundamental to the sense of community that shapes the educational effectiveness of independent schools.[7]

Self-Selected Faculty

Each independent school develops its own criteria for hiring faculty, and in all but a few states, independent schools are not bound by requirements for teacher certification.

Independent schools have latitude in staffing, determining the background and competencies of faculty members they want. In keeping with the academic orientation of independent schools, there is a strong preference, particularly at the secondary level, for teachers with undergraduate and graduate majors in the liberal arts and sciences, and for recruiting teachers who have demonstrated academic achievement by success at colleges with competitive admissions standards. Similarly, these graduates of highly academic colleges may be drawn to independent schools where students are preparing for college.[8]

Most independent school teachers have not taken the education courses necessary for certification to teach in public schools and may regard such courses as of lesser intellectual merit than courses in their academic fields. The schools, too, are not convinced that professional preparation in education is necessary. With the exception of training in early childhood education, many independent school administrators believe that pedagogy is a skill that can be learned on the job. Yet, most schools supply only limited assistance in learning to teach, and young teachers learn the ropes informally, from other teachers or by trial and error.[9]

This distinction between the preparation and academic orientation of public and independent school teachers, together with differences in working conditions and curricular freedom, may in part explain why teachers are willing to work in independent schools for less pay than they would receive in the public sector. It has certainly contributed to the reluctance of independent school teachers to affiliate themselves with public school teachers through unionization. Although a few schools have internal teacher associations that negotiate salary and benefits, the absence of union affiliation has allowed independent schools both to contain salaries and to maintain the freedom to dismiss unsatisfactory teachers without the elaborate procedures of public schools. That freedom of disassociation is seen by independent school administrators as essential to the educational effectiveness of their schools. The freedom to fail is, for independent school teachers, the price of the freedom to teach.

Small Size

Typically small, with a median student enrollment of 321, independent schools resist going beyond a specified size, regardless of the quality of the applicant pool or the number of candidates vying for admission.[10]

When the heads of New York City independent schools were invited to discuss ways to improve public schools with Mayor Edward Koch, they were unanimous in their focus on reducing school size. The average size of a public secondary school, for example, is more than twice the size of the average independent school, and class size is also significantly larger. Independent schools have, on average, six students for every full-time faculty member, fewer than half of the student load of public and Catholic school teachers. Despite having smaller classes and fewer students, independent school teachers report spending more time on the job than their public school colleagues, providing assistance to students, planning lessons, and grading papers.[11]

There is an important consequence of small size for the *average* student. Several researchers have argued that independent schools provide the optimal learning environment for such students, those who are neither top academic achievers nor in need of special support services. Public schools have accommodated those students with abilities on the ends of the achievement spectrum, or those with special needs. Independent schools provide the elements of "personalization" and "push," which are effective in motivating these "unspecial" students in the middle, who would not receive extra attention in a comprehensive public school.[12]

As Leonard Baird has pointed out, it is unlikely that students in independent schools can become like the "socially invisible nonpersons" who pass through large public schools.[13] Smaller schools also allow for increased student participation in extracurricular activities—athletics, clubs, student government, and dramatic productions—which give students opportunities for leadership. Parents who claim to be sending their children to independent schools because of the personal attention afforded their youngsters and the opportunities to participate in the life of the school appear to be getting what they pay for.

Future Challenges

Critics of independent schools have argued that these schools are nothing more than "status seminaries" that furnish upper-class youth with the cultural capital they will need to assume elite group membership.[14] Traditionally, independent schools have served a homogeneous, affluent stratum of the population, but there are indications of change. Independent schools are accepting the challenge to open their doors to a more clinically and socioeconomically diverse student body. This could be a result of several factors: the economic imperative to fill seats at a time when demographic shifts have created a precipitous drop in the number of school-age children available; a desire to set up a more socially equitable school community that reflects American society; or a response to the threat that public school reform is imposing.

Demographic Change

Nationally, demographic trends have a great impact on schools. The number of school-age children in the population began to decline in the early 1970s. Despite two decades of declining population, independent school enrollment has been relatively stable. Although the population trend is beginning to reverse itself as a baby boomlet that started in the 1980s begins to increase elementary school enrollments, schools will face a new challenge. Demographer Harold Hodgkinson predicts that by the year 2000, America will be

a nation in which one of every three people will be nonwhite, and many will be living at the poverty level.[15]

A Commitment to Diversity

The number of students of color in independent schools has increased slowly but steadily over the past two decades, up from 5 percent to an average of 13 percent in 1990. In schools with greater financial resources available, the percentage is even higher. For instance, at Phillips Academy in Andover, Massachusetts, students of color represented 24 percent of the student body in 1991–92. One symbolic and important indication of the independent school commitment to diversity is the increased activity at the National Association of Independent Schools of the Office of Diversity and Multicultural Affairs, whose responsibility it is to promote cultural diversity among the faculty and students of independent schools and to provide resources for the development of multicultural curricula.[16]

As the proportion of minority students has increased, many schools have come to understand that the responsibility for the students they recruit does not end at the admissions office door. Independent schools are becoming sensitive to the needs of students of color in schools that have been unaccustomed to having them and unprepared to meet their needs. Some schools have hired minority coordinators and counselors to assist students of color in adjusting to schools where pressure to achieve is great and social discomfort may be a reality. Attention is also being directed to modifications in the curriculum to allow for a multicultural perspective that includes different voices and a broader conception of education.

This more receptive outlook of the schools has attracted a small number of children of color from middle- and upper-income families. However, since most students of color are recruited from lower socioeconomic groups and must rely on financial aid, further confirmation that the clientele of the so-called elite schools is changing may be gauged by the overall amount of scholarship aid granted. Total financial aid granted by schools that are members of the National Association of Independent Schools increased by 72 percent (50 percent in constant dollars) between 1984 and 1989. In the academic year 1990–91, 33 percent of all need-based scholarships were granted to children of color, averaging $5838 per student. In schools with greater financial resources, financial aid has been even more generous. At Phillips Exeter Academy in New Hampshire, for example, 30 percent of students receive aid, with grants averaging $11,300 per student.[17]

There is evidence that parents who send their children to independent schools are not merely motivated by the perpetuation of old-school ties. According to Leonard Baird, who surveyed the most prestigious independent schools, students at the elite schools do not come primarily from "power elite" families although most are clearly from upper-middle-class and upper-class homes, and there are not significant numbers of alumni children.[18] As the number of dual-career families increases, and there is greater disposable income, independent schools may be attractive to a larger number of middle- and upper-income families willing to pay for the kind of education these schools provide.[19] With a greater commitment to both ethnic and socioeconomic diversity, there will be a need to increase financial aid while keeping the costs of tuition within the range families are able to pay.

Public School Reform

Since the early 1980s, improving our nation's public schools has moved to the top of the political agenda. Several widespread reforms—those specifically aimed at attracting higher caliber teachers and giving parents choice among public schools—have direct implications for independent schools. Modifications in state teacher certification have made it easier for liberal arts graduates to enter public schools. In former years, liberal arts graduates who wanted to enter teaching—even graduates of highly competitive colleges—were forced to teach private schools if they were unwilling to undergo the expensive and lengthy preparation for state certification. It turns out that public schools are now seeking the bright young people whose undergraduate preparation includes a focus on the liberal arts and a major in an academic discipline, the kinds of teachers who traditionally have been attracted to independent schools. Higher salaries and improved working conditions may make the incentives to work in public schools even more appealing. Independent schools have responded modestly to the challenge of increased public school salaries, but as the differentials increase, the schools will have to find greater resources to compete effectively with the public schools.

Choice among public schools—for example, in the magnet-school movement—may provide another challenge to independent school stability. Parents who can choose schools within or outside their district are no longer restricted to deciding between a neighborhood school and a private school. As the magnet-school movement grows, independent schools will be obliged to demonstrate that they are providing something different, or something special, to make the choice of paying tuition worthwhile.

Responses to the Challenge

The collective response in meeting a commitment to diversity in the face of a declining school-age population and a more positive outlook for public schools and public school teaching has been to increase efforts to promote independent schools. Many schools are producing expensive catalogues and videotapes, and some are hiring enrollment and admissions consultants or adding staff to admissions offices to do more intensive recruiting. Day schools estimated spending $400, and boarding schools more than $500, to recruit each new student in 1989 exclusive of the costs of admissions' staff salaries.[20] Although many schools have found a consumerist approach objectionable in the past, the marketing orientation and the escalation of marketing expenditures may become a necessary approach to keep independent schools financially viable. Rick Cowan, director of boarding schools at the National Association of Independent Schools, says, "It is a different, more competitive world and probably will

remain so. . . . The 'market race' is likely to become a permanent feature of the educational landscape." The objective, according to Cowan, is to emerge with stronger enrollments and higher standards.[21]

If the description of independent schools offered here is accurate, then the popular conception of independent schools as exclusive, tradition-bound places that educate the aristocracy to take their place in society appears to be both inaccurate and untenable. The question of definition for independent schools in the 1990s may be reconciling, on the one hand, a profound self-conception as moral communities striving to institute social change through enhanced ethnic and socioeconomic diversity with, on the other hand, the pressures of marketing and the escalation of financial costs. The tension between moral mission and financial necessity has always been present for independent schools, but the moral mission has never been more demanding nor has the market been more unforgiving. Can independent schools be those moral communities and also be successful businesses, driven by a need to stay competitive in the face of multiple challenges?

As open systems, sensitive to environmental conditions, independent schools will no doubt be shaped in unprecedented and unpredictable ways in the next few decades. However, the characteristics that distinguish independent schools—self-governance, self-support, self-defined curriculum, self-selected students, self-selected faculty and small size—provide a strong ethos of personalization and an orientation toward academic success that is not likely to be changed.

Notes

1. The independent schools described here do not include Montessori schools, special education schools, home schools, or street academies.

2. The National Association of Independent Schools lists five features of independent schools: governance, finances, curriculum, student selection, and faculty selection (*A Career in Independent School Teaching*) [Boston: NAIS: 1984], pp. 5–7).

3. Gerald Grant, "The Character of Education and the Education of Character," *Daedalus* 110, no. 3 (Summer 1981): 135–49.

4. Median tuition costs are reported for 895 members of the National Association of Independent Schools (95 percent reporting) in National Association of Independent Schools, *NAIS Statistics 1990–1991* (Boston: NAIS, 1990).

5. James S. Coleman, Thomas Hoffer, and Sally Kilgore, *High School Achievement: Public, Catholic and Private Schools Compared* (New York: Basic Books, 1982), pp. 73–78.

6. Pearl R. Kane, *Teachers in Public and Independent Schools: A Comparative Study* (New York: Esther A. and Joseph Klingenstein Center for Independent School Education, 1986), pp. 41–42.

7. Percentages of attrition based on a study of over 400 NAIS member schools, in NAIS Admission Services, "Survey of Student Attrition in Independent Schools: 1987–1988" (Boston: NAIS, 1989); and Otto F. Kraushaar, *American Nonpublic Schools: Patterns of Diversity* (Baltimore: Johns Hopkins University Press, 1972), p. 93.

8. Telephone survey conducted with administrators in independent schools in New Jersey, February to April 1988; and Kane, *Teachers in Public and Independent Schools*, pp. 21–25.

9. Kane, *Teachers in Public and Independent Schools*, pp. 31–35.

10. Median student enrollment based on a sample of 895 members of the National Association of Independent Schools, *NAIS Statistics, 1990–1991* 2 (Boston: NAIS, 1991), p. 7

11. Meeting with Mayor Edward Koch, January 12, 1988, New York City. For student teacher ratio see Coleman, Hoffer, and Kilgore, *High School Achievement*, pp. 78–81; for a comparison of the work life of

public and private school teachers see Kane, *Teachers in Public and Independent Schools*, pp. 36–48.

12. Arthur G. Powell, Eleanor Farrar, and David K. Cohen, *The Shopping Mall High School: Winners and Losers in the Educational Marketplace* (Boston: Houghton Mifflin, 1985), pp. 207–32.

13. Leonard Baird, "Elite Schools: Recent Research from the Outside and from the Inside" (Paper presented at the annual conference of the American Education Research Association, Washington, D.C., April 1987). p. 3.

14. Peter W. Cookson, Jr. and Caroline Hodges Persell, *Preparing for Power: America's Elite Boarding Schools* (New York: Basic Books, 1985), pp. 22–30.

15. Harold L. Hodgkinson, *All One System: Demographics of Education, Kindergarten through Graduate School* (New York: Institute for Educational Leadership, 1985), pp. 3–10.

16. Statistics on students of color at Phillips Academy based on telephone interview with Robert A. Edwards, assistant director of admissions and director of recruitment of people of color, Phillips Academy, July 18, 1991; and national percentages of students of color reported are for 895 members of the National Association of Independent Schools, *NAIS Statistics* 2, p. 15.

17. Barbara G. Schneider and Diana T. Slaughter, "Educational Choice for Blacks in Urban Private Elementary Schools," in *Comparing Public and Private Schools*, ed. Thomas James and Henry Levin (London: Falmer Press, 1988), v. 1, pp. 294–310; data on scholarship aid in Peter Aiken, National Association of Independent Schools Promoting Independent Education Project, *Briefing*, no. 4, 1991; telephone interview with Paul R. Mahoney, Director of Financial Aid, Phillips Exeter Academy, July 15, 1991.

18. Leonard L. Baird, *The Elite Schools: A Profile of Prestigious Independent Schools* (Lexington, Mass.: D. C. Heath, 1977), p. 10.

19. There has been a rising mean income in real terms and more families in which spouses are working. Adjusted to 1989 dollars, family income has increased for families in the 60 percent to 80 percent quintile: 1970, $42,230; 1980, $43,775; 1989, $49,213. There has also been a steady stream into the work force of wives with children: 1970, 39.3 percent; 1980, 50.2 percent; 1989, 57.7 percent. Data compiled from the following three publications of the U.S. Bureau of Census: "Money, Income and Poverty Status in the U.S., 1989" (Series P-60, no. 168) (Washington, D.C.: 1990), p. 30; "Income in 1970: Families and Persons in the U.S., 1971" (Series P-60, no. 80) (Washington, D.C.: 1972), p. 33; "Money Income of Households, Families, and Persons in the U.S., 1980" (Series P-60, no. 132) (Washington, D.C.: 1982), p. 81.

20. Maguire Associates, Enrollment Management Consultants Division, "National Survey of Independent School Admissions Officers" (Concord, Mass.: Maguire Associates, 1990).

21. Rick Cowan, "The Marketing Race," *Administrative Forum*, Spring 1987: 1–3. Marketing costs based on estimates reported by a national sample of 84 independent schools in Maguire Associates, "National Survey of Independent School Admissions Officers."

The Profession of Teaching Today

The problems facing North American teachers continue to get more complex. Teachers in North America continue to face the demand that they be held accountable for their performance. The many faces of professional accountability are still being discussed. The dialogue about the matter is taken seriously by the public, by public officials, and by school boards and administrative teams. Therefore, we have to consider the many ramifications of professional accountability and the several very different alternative means by which it can be achieved.

As the knowledge base on professional practice continues to expand, we will be able to certify with greater and greater precision what constitute acceptable ranges of teacher performance based on clearly defined standards of practice as in medicine and dentistry. Such standards are achievable. Medicine is a practical art as well as a science, as is teaching. The analogy in terms of professional practice is strong and can be made to logically hold. Yet the emotional pressures on teachers to face the idea that theirs is a performing art and that clear standards of practice can be applied to that performing art is a bitter pill to swallow for many of them. Hence, the intense reaction of many teachers to external competency testing and to being held to any rigorous classroom observation standards. Yet the writing is on the wall. The profession cannot hide behind the tradition that teaching is a special art, unlike others, which cannot be subjected to objective observational standards, aesthetic critique, or to a standard knowledge base. Those years are behind us. The public served demands the same levels of demonstrable professional standards of practice as are demanded of those in the medical arts.

Likewise, certain approaches to working with students in the classroom have been effective. Classroom practices such as cooperative learning strategies have won widespread support for inclusion in the knowledge base on teaching. The knowledge base of the social psychology of life in classrooms has been significantly expanded by collaborative research between classroom teachers, and various specialists in psychology and teacher education using anthropological field research techniques to ground theory of classroom practice in demonstrable phenomenological perspectives. So, there are many things to consider as the teaching professional rapidly moves to the dawn of a new century far better grounded in its knowledge base than at the beginning of this one.

Recent research by teachers and teacher educators on their professional practice in classrooms is greatly enriching our knowledge base on the teaching-learning process in schools. Many issues have been raised by basic ethnographic field observations, interviews, and anecdotal record-keeping techniques to more precisely understand how teachers and students interact in the classroom. There is a rich dialectic developing among teachers regarding the description of classroom teaching environments. The methodological issues raised by this research into the day-to-day realities of life in schools is transforming what we know about teaching as a professional activity. These developments are relevant to the concerns of all teachers regarding how to best advance our knowledge of effective teaching strategies.

Creative, insightful persons who become teachers usually find ways to network their interests and concerns with other teachers. There are many opportunities for creative professional practice in teaching in spite of external assessment procedures. President Bush and other political leaders, as well as leaders in the corporate sector, are urging teachers to consider more creative ways to emphasize basic academic standards in written composition, computer literacy, and applied mathematics. The dispute over alternative approaches to teacher certification has hampered efforts to gain a consensus on minimum academic qualifications for beginning teachers.

As already noted, teaching is both an art and a science. The science of teaching involves the observation and measurement of teaching behaviors. The art of teaching involves the humanistic dimensions of instructional activities. Interesting and original conceptions of teaching as a humanistic activity are still being developed. We continue to rediscover older methods of relating what is taught to the interests of students. The art of teaching involves not only alertness to the details of what is taught, but equal alertness to how students receive it. Teachers often guide class processes and formulate questions according to their perceptions of how students are responding to the material.

We are in the midst of a period in which fundamental revisions in the structure of the professional role and status of teachers are being considered and developed. Teachers want more input into how the profession is to be reformed. It will be interesting to see how many of the new proposals for career ladders for teachers will be implemented, and how the teaching profession responds to the recommendations for licensure by the new national board for certification of teachers. National board certification of teachers will stabilize the system, focusing attention on a national set of standard qualifications for teaching at different levels and in different subject areas. We look forward to the emergence of a national consensus within the teaching profession on the qualifications for teaching. In the past 18 years, we have seen the introduction of increased field experience and clinical experience requirements for preservice candidates for the teaching profession. It is a very interesting time to be part of this profession.

How does a nation achieve a dramatic qualitative advance in the field of education if it is unwilling to pay for it? Blaming most of the problems in education on teacher incompetence is like blaming the victim. Some ways to improve the quality of teaching include the funding of inservice education for teachers, revisions in funding so that teachers can earn wages appropriate to their levels of professional preparation, and the implementation of a method for demonstrating teacher competency.

According to the Rand Corporation and other research groups, serious shortages of teachers already exist in mathematics, the sciences, foreign languages, and in the education of children of linguistic minorities. Shortages are expected to develop in most, if not all, areas of teaching in the next 10 years. Children will always need well-educated and competent teachers. However, the profession may not be able to provide them unless more academically talented people can be attracted to the field.

To build their hope as well as their self-confidence, teachers must be motivated to an even greater effort for professional growth. Teachers need support, appreciation, and respect. Simply criticizing them and refusing to alter those social and economic conditions that affect the quality of their work will not solve their problems, nor will it lead to excellence in education. Not only must teachers work to improve the public's image of and confidence in them, but the public must confront its own misunderstanding of the level of commitment required to achieve excellence. Teachers need to know that the public cares about and respects them enough to fund their professional improvement and to recognize them for the important force they are in the life of their nation.

The articles in this unit consider the quality of education and the status of the teaching profession today.

Looking Ahead: Challenge Questions

List what you think are the five most important issues confronting the teaching profession today (with number one being the most important and number five the least important). What criteria did you use in ranking the issues? What is your position on each of them?

Does teaching have some problems that other professions do not seem to have? If so, what are they? What can be done about them?

What appears to be the major issues affecting teacher morale?

What are the best reasons for a person to choose a career in teaching?

What are the most critical social pressures on teachers? Why are teachers sometimes used as scapegoats?

What are the advantages of peer review and observation processes in helping teachers improve their professional performance?

What do you think of classroom-based research? How would you go about doing it?

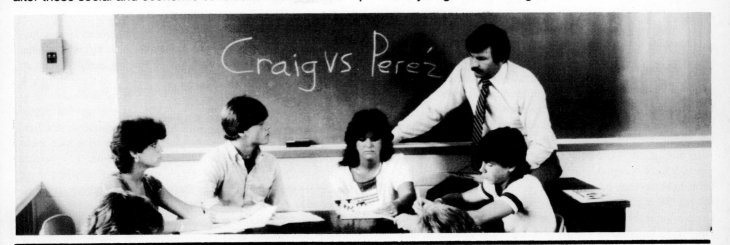

Accountability for Professional Practice

Linda Darling-Hammond

Teachers College, Columbia University

The issue of educational accountability is probably the most pressing and most problematic of any facing the public schools today. Gone are the days when a local town council hired the village schoolmaster and fired him at will for any cause. Gone, too, are the days when schoolteachers were so respected in their office that anything within the schoolroom walls was accepted as the rightful and unquestioned prerogative of school officials. A more highly educated populace has greater expectations of schools, and a more knowledge-oriented economy raises both the costs and benefits of school success or failure. Today, schools are being held to account by politicians, the general public, and parents for results they should be expected to produce and, often, for results over which they have little or no control.

In recent debates about improving American schools and increasing accountability, the professionalization of teaching has surfaced as a prominent strategy, now being pursued in a variety of ways by policymakers and practitioners across the country. Though many changes in the areas of teacher preparation, certification, and compensation have accompanied the reform discussion, many questions remain regarding how schools should operate to sustain and nourish effective teaching based on professional norms and understandings.

At the same time, concerns for school accountability are as pronounced as they have ever been in our nation's history. Policymakers want to find ways to ensure that students learn, and they struggle to find a lever that will penetrate a giant, fragmented system engaged in a difficult and complex undertaking. If the promises of professionalism are to bear fruit, the contributions of professional accountability to improved education must be activated in concrete ways in schools.

In this article, I explore the contributions of professionalism to school accountability in the context of a new phenomenon in American education: the professional development school. Such schools, in their infancy in more than a dozen cities around the country, are intended—like teaching hospitals—to model state-of-the-art practice while simultaneously refining and spreading it. They are to be places where experts train and socialize novices, where research and theory are translated into practice, and where practical knowledge is translated in turn into research and theory. Such schools are, in short, the harbingers of an accountable profession, as they assume the mission of testing, transmitting, and further advancing the ethical norms and knowledge-based standards of professional practice. As models of professional practice, these schools should become models of professional accountability as well.

THE GOALS OF ACCOUNTABILITY

In the current debates about accountability, cacophony rules. There is little agreement, and perhaps even less clear thinking, about what accountability means, to whom it is owed, and how it can be operationalized. Many policymakers seem to equate accountability with something like the monitoring of student test scores, averaged for classrooms, schools, or school districts. Some believe that accountability can be enacted by statutes prescribing management procedures, tests, or curricula. Unfortunately, these approaches to accountability leave the student, the parent, the teacher, and the educational process entirely out of the equation. The production of a test score or a management scheme does not touch the issue of whether a student's educational interests are being well served.

We need to begin to articulate what we mean by accountability, and in particular, what we mean by professional accountability. I suggest here that a meaningful system of accountability for public education should do three things: it should (1) *set educationally meaningful and defensible standards* for what parents and members of the general public can rightfully expect of a school system, school, or teacher; (2) *establish reasonable and feasible means* by which these standards can be implemented and upheld; and (3) *provide avenues for redress or corrections in practice* when these standards are not met, so that ultimately students are well served.

Within this framework, I will explore how current systems of accountability are structured and how they would need to

From *Teachers College Record*, Vol. 91, No. 1, Fall 1989, pp. 59-80. Copyright © 1989 by Teachers College, Columbia University. Reprinted by permission.

be changed to provide honest and useful vehicles for accountability in the context of schools intended to promote professional practice in teaching.

MODELS OF ACCOUNTABILITY

Social transactions in our society are managed in a variety of ways, ultimately subject to democratic control. Through legislative bodies, the populace can decide whether an activity should be a subject of government regulation and where that regulation should begin and end. When legislative government involvement has been eschewed or limited, control of an activity may revert, in whole or in part, to professional bodies, courts, or private individuals in their roles as clients, consumers, or citizens.

In any of these instances, accountability mechanisms are chosen to safeguard the public interest. These include at least the following:

> political accountability—elected officials must stand for re-election at regular intervals so that citizens can judge the representativeness of their views and the responsiveness of their decisions

> legal accountability—courts must entertain complaints about violations of laws enacted by representatives of the public and of citizens' constitutionally granted rights, which may be threatened either by private action or by legislative action

> bureaucratic accountability—agencies of government promulgate rules and regulations intended to assure citizens that public functions will be carried out in pursuit of public goals voiced through democratic or legal processes

> professional accountability—governments may create professional bodies and structures to ensure competence and appropriate practice in occupations that serve the public and may delegate certain decisions about occupational membership, standards, and practices to these bodies

> market accountability—governments may choose to allow clients or consumers to choose what services best meet their needs; to preserve the utility of this form of accountability, monopolies are prevented, freedom of choice is protected, and truthful information is required of service providers

All of these accountability mechanisms have their strengths and weaknesses, and each is more or less appropriate to certain types of activities. Political mechanisms can support the public establishment of general policy directions in areas subject to direct government control. Legal mechanisms are most useful when rights or proscriptions are clearly definable and when establishing the facts is all that is needed to trigger a remedy. Bureaucratic mechanisms are most appropriate when a standard set of practices or procedures can be easily linked to behavioral rules that will produce the desired outcomes. Market mechanisms are helpful when consumer preferences vary widely, when the state does not have a direct interest in controlling choice, and when government control would be counterproductive to innovation. Professional mechanisms are most important when safeguards for consumer choice are necessary to serve the public interest, but the technology of the work is uniquely determined by individual client needs and a complex and changing base of knowledge.

There are, of course, incentives in any of these systems for individuals to shirk their missions or for functional inadequacies to impair performance. (Public servants may use their positions for private gain; courts may become overloaded; bureaucrats may fail to follow regulations; professionals may overlook incompetence; markets may break down due to regulatory or economic failures.) These problems can, presumably, be addressed by efforts to make the systems work more perfectly, often by overlaying another accountability mechanism against the first as a check and balance, for example, enacting an ethics in government law that adds legal accountability vehicles to the electoral process for governing the actions of public officials.

However, even when such mechanisms function perfectly, any given mode of accountability has intrinsic limits that must be weighed in the choice of which to use under varying circumstances. Electoral accountability does not allow citizens to judge each specific action of officials; nor does it necessarily secure the constitutional rights or preferences of citizens whose views and interests are in the minority. Legal accountability cannot be used in all cases: The reach of courts is limited to that which can be legislated; not all citizens have access to courts, and they are buffered from public opinion. Bureaucratic accountability does not guarantee results, it concerns itself with procedures; it is effective only when procedures are known to produce the desired outcomes, and when compliance is easily measured and secured. Professional accountability does not take public preferences into account; it responds to an authority outside the direct reach of citizens and may satisfy its purposes while ignoring competing public goals. Market accountability does not ensure citizens' access to services and relies on the spontaneous emergence of a variety of services to allow choice to operate as a safety valve for poor service provision.

Because of these intrinsic limits, no single form of accountability operates alone in any major area of public life. Hybrid forms are developed to provide checks and balances and to more carefully target vehicles for safeguarding the public interest toward the particular matters they can best address. The choices of accountability tools—and the balance among different forms of accountability—are constantly shifting as problems emerge, as social goals change, and as new circumstances arise.

ACCOUNTABILITY IN EDUCATION

In education, it is easy to see that legal and bureaucratic forms of accountability have expanded their reach over the past twenty years, while electoral accountability has waxed and waned (with local and state school boards operating with reduced authority in some instances, and the purviews of elected and appointed officials shifting in many states). Market accountability is more often discussed as a possibly useful vehicle, but still rarely used, except in a few districts that offer magnet schools or other schools of choice. Professional accountability is gaining in prominence as an idea for strengthening teaching quality, but it is yet poorly defined and partially at odds with other forms of accountability currently in use.

8. THE PROFESSION OF TEACHING TODAY

Bureaucratic Accountability

Bureaucratic organization and management of schools has increased since the early part of this century, when "scientific management" principles were first introduced into urban schools in an effort to standardize and rationalize the process of schooling. The view underlying this approach to managing schools is as follows: Schools are agents of government that can be administered by hierarchical decision making and controls. Policies are made at the top of the system and handed down to administrators, who translate them into rules and procedures. Teachers follow the rules and procedures (class schedules, curricula, textbooks, rules for promotion and assignment of students, etc.), and students are processed according to them.

This approach is intended to foster equal and uniform treatment of clients and standardization of products or services, and to prevent arbitrary or capricious decision making. It works reasonably well when goals are agreed on and clearly definable, when procedures for meeting the goals can be specified, when the procedures are straightforward and feasible to implement, and when following these procedures is known to produce the desired outcomes in all cases. Bureaucratic accountability ensures that rules will be promulgated and compliance with these rules will be monitored. The promise that bureaucratic accountability mechanisms make is that violators of the rules will be apprehended, and consequences will be administered for noncompliance.

When bureaucratic forms are applied to the management of teaching, they rely on a number of assumptions:

that students are sufficiently standardized that they will respond in identical and predictable ways to the "treatments" devised by policymakers and their principal agents

that sufficient knowledge of which treatments should be prescribed is both available and generalizable to all educational circumstances

that this knowledge can be translated into standardized rules for practice, which can be operationalized through regulations and reporting and inspection systems

that administrators and teachers can and will faithfully implement the prescriptions for practice thus devised and transmitted to schools

The circular bottom-line assumption is that this process, if efficiently administered, will produce the outcomes the system desires. If the outcomes are not satisfactory, the final assumption is that the prescriptions are not yet sufficiently detailed or the process of implementation is not sufficiently exact. Thus, the solutions to educational problems always lie in more precise specification of educational or management processes.

In the bureaucratic model, teachers are viewed as functionaries rather than as well-trained and highly skilled professionals. Little investment is made in teacher preparation, induction, or professional development. Little credence is given to licensing or knowledge acquisition. Little time is afforded for joint planning or collegial consultation about problems of practice. Because practices are prescribed outside the school setting, there is no need and little use for professional knowledge and judgment. Thus, novice teachers

assume the same responsibilities as thirty-year veterans. Separated into egg-crate classrooms and isolated by packed teaching schedules, teachers rarely work or talk together about teaching practices. A rationale for these activities is absent from the bureaucratic perspective on teaching work.

In the bureaucratic conception of teaching, teachers do not need to be highly knowledgeable about learning theory and pedagogy, cognitive science and child development, curriculum and assessment; they do not need to be highly skilled, because they do not, presumably, make the major decisions about these matters. Curriculum planning is done by administrators and specialists; teachers are to implement a curriculum planned for them. Inspection of teachers' work is conducted by hierarchical superiors, whose job it is to make sure that the teacher is implementing the curriculum and procedures of the district. Teachers do not plan or evaluate their own work; they merely perform it.

Accountability is achieved by inspections and reporting systems intended to ensure that the rules and procedures are being followed. Teachers are held accountable for implementing curricular and testing policies, grading policies, assignment and promotion rules, and myriad other educational prescriptions, whether or not these treatments are appropriate in particular instances for particular students. As a consequence, teachers cannot be held accountable for meeting the needs of their students; they can only be held accountable for following standard operating procedures. The standard for accountability is compliance rather than effectiveness.

The problem with the bureaucratic solution to the accountability dilemma in education is that effective teaching is not routine, students are not passive, and questions of practice are not simple, predictable, or standardized. By its very nature, bureaucratic management is incapable of providing appropriate education for students who do not fit the mold on which all of the prescriptions for practice are based.

Public Versus Client Accountability

At present, I think it is fair to say that the use of legal and bureaucratic accountability mechanisms in education far outweighs the use of other forms, and that these mechanisms have overextended their reach for actually promoting positive practices and responsiveness to public and client needs. This statement should not be glossed over too lightly, though, for public and client needs are not identical, and positive practices are defined in the eye of the beholder. Indeed, there is a special tension in public education between the goals held by governments for public schools and the goals held by the clients of schools, for which different forms of accountability are needed. Because the needs, interests, and preferences of individual students and parents do not always converge with the needs, interests, and preferences of state or local governments, the question of accountability in education must always be prefaced by the questions "to whom?" and "for what?"

Public schools have been created primarily to meet the state's need for an educated citizenry. Indeed, public education is not so much a right accorded to students as an obligation to which they are compelled by law. State goals include (1) socialization to a common culture (education to meet social needs); (2) inculcation of basic democratic values and preparation of students to responsibly exercise their democratic rights and responsibilities (education to meet political needs); and (3) preparation of students for further education, training, and occupational life (education to meet economic needs). To meet these goals, the state further defines what type of socialization is desired, what manner of democratic preparation is to be given, and what forms of preparation—forms useful to the state's economic goals—are to be offered.[1]

Furthermore, the state has an interest in providing educational services both equitably (sometimes, this state interest has had to be enforced by courts when it is ignored by legislators) and efficiently, so that taxpayers' burdens are not excessive or their tax monies wasted. Since equity and efficiency are difficult concepts to operationalize, they cause special accountability problems for bureaucrats and professionals to resolve. They also frequently stand in conflict with the needs and interests of individual students, as for example when "same" treatment does not produce appropriate treatment, or when "efficient" education does not produce quality education.

Individual consumers (parents and students) often hold social, economic, and political goals different from those of the state government, and they very often disagree about how to pursue even the commonly held goals. Furthermore, child-oriented definitions of student "needs" rarely match state definitions, since the former are unique to the individual child, and the latter are promulgated for all children in a state, or for specified groups of children.

These definitions continually confront a tension that Thomas Green refers to as the dialectic between the "best" principle and the "equal" principle.[2] The best principle is the proposition that each student is entitled to receive the education that is best for him or her; the equal principle is the proposition that each is entitled to receive an education at least as good as (equal to) that provided for others. In translation through legal or bureaucratic vehicles, "equal to" means "the same as," since these vehicles must operate by uniform standards. Efforts to individualize instruction through these vehicles invariably must create groups of children, all of whom are then to be treated alike (hence, the tendency to create identifiable subsets of children, by age, grade level, measured ability, curriculum track, and so on). This may solve the state's problem of specifying inputs and desired outcomes, but it does not solve the student's or teacher's problem that children will still, come what may, fit untidily into the containers designed for them.

Thus, accountability for accomplishing state goals is a very different concept from accountability for accomplishing clients' goals. Indeed, accountability for meeting the needs of individual students is often in conflict—or at least in tension—with accountability for securing the public's preferences for education. Teachers and public school officials are the arbiters of these tensions. They strive to achieve a balance between meeting the state's goals and the needs of

individual students. This requires a great deal of skill, sensitivity, and judgment, since the dilemmas posed by these two sets of goals are complex, idiosyncratic, and ever-changing.

Increasingly, though, attempts to provide public accountability have sought to standardize school and classroom procedures in the hopes of finding "one best system" by which all students may be educated. Codified by law, and specified more completely by regulation, these attempts have both "teacher-proofed" and "student-proofed" schooling, leaving little room for innovation or improvement of education. Indeed, this approach is criticized in recent reports as having created a situation in which "everyone has the brakes but no one has the motors" to make schools run well.[3]

Ironically, prescriptive policies created in the name of accountability have begun to reduce schools' responsiveness to the needs of students and the desires of parents. In the cause of uniform treatment and in the absence of schooling alternatives, large numbers of students "fall through the cracks" when rules, routines, and standardized procedures prevent teachers from meeting individual needs. Those who can afford to do so leave for private schools. Those who cannot are frequently alienated and ill served.

The theory underlying the press for teacher professionalism is that strengthening the structures and vehicles for creating and transmitting professional knowledge will prove a more effective means for meeting students' needs and improving the overall quality of education than trying to prescribe educational practices from afar. This theory is based on a conception of teaching as complex, knowledge-based work requiring judgment in nonroutine situations and on a conception of learning as an interactive and individually determined process. These conceptions limit the applicability of legal and bureaucratic remedies for ensuring learning, by asserting the differential nature of effective interactions between teachers and learners that is beyond the capacity of laws and regulations to predict or prescribe.

Professional Accountability

Professionalism depends on the affirmation of three principles in the conduct and governance of an occupation:

1. Knowledge is the basis for permission to practice and for decisions that are made with respect to the unique needs of clients.
2. The practitioner pledges his first concern to the welfare of the client.
3. The profession assumes collective responsibility for the definition, transmittal, and enforcement of professional standards of practice and ethics.

Professionals are obligated to do whatever is best for the client, not what is easiest, most expedient, or even what the client himself or herself might want. They are also obligated to base a decision about what is best for the client on available knowledge—not just that knowledge acquired from personal experience, but also that clinical and research knowledge acquired by the occupation as a whole and represented in professional journals, certification standards, and specialty training. Finally, professionals are required to take into account the unique needs of individual clients in fashioning their judgments about what strategies or treatments are appropriate.

These are fine goals, but how are they operationalized to result in something that might be called professional accountability? In policy terms, these requirements suggest greater regulation of *teachers*—ensuring their competence through more rigorous preparation, certification, selection, and evaluation—in exchange for the deregulation of *teaching*—fewer rules prescribing what is to be taught, when, and how. This is, in essence, the bargain that all professions make with society: For occupations that require discretion and judgment in meeting the unique needs of clients, the profession guarantees the competence of members in exchange for the privilege of professional control over work structure and standards of practice.

The theory behind this equation is that professional control improves both the quality of individual services and the level of knowledge in the profession as a whole. This occurs because decision making by well-trained professionals allows individual clients' needs to be met more precisely, and it promotes continual refinement and improvement in overall practice as effectiveness, rather than compliance, becomes the standard for judging competence.

It is important to note, too, that professional authority does not mean legitimizing the idiosyncratic or whimsical preferences of individual classroom teachers. Indeed, in other public-service occupations, autonomy is the problem that professionalism is meant to address. It is precisely *because* practitioners operate autonomously that safeguards to protect the public interest are necessary. In occupations that have become professionalized, these safeguards have taken the form of screens to membership in the profession and ongoing peer review of practice. Collective autonomy from external regulation is achieved by the assumption of collective responsibility. Responsible self-governance requires, in turn, structures and vehicles by which the profession can define and transmit its knowledge base, control membership in the occupation, evaluate and refine its practices, and enforce norms of ethical practice.

In theory, then, teacher professionalism promises a more potent form of accountability for meeting students' needs than that which courts and bureaucracies can concoct. It promises competence, an expanding knowledge base, concern for client welfare, and vehicles for enforcing these claims. In many respects, such accountability also serves the needs of the state by promoting better practice; but, because professional accountability is explicitly *client-oriented,* it will not fully represent the preferences of the general public. Hence, in working through a concept of professional accountability, we must keep in mind its limits for achieving public accountability as well as its promise.

THE NATURE OF ACCOUNTABILITY IN PROFESSIONAL PRACTICE SCHOOLS

Professional practice schools have three missions with respect to accountability. First, they should model a professional form of accountability as it might ultimately be seen in all schools. Second, as induction centers, they implement a key accountability function for the profession as a whole. Third, as knowledge-producing institutions, they support and help to build the foundation on which professional accountability ultimately rests. These missions, as suggested by the earlier-stated criteria for accountability mechanisms, require that professional development schools devote considerable attention to defining educationally meaningful *standards* of practice, creating reasonable *means* for upholding these standards, and establishing vehicles for *redress or corrections* of problems that arise.

The goals of professional accountability are to protect the public by ensuring that (1) all individuals permitted to practice in certain capacities are adequately prepared to do so responsibly; (2) where knowledge about practice exists, it will be used, and where certainty does not exist, practitioners will individually and collectively continually seek to discover the most responsible course of action; and (3) practitioners will pledge their first and primary commitment to the welfare of the client.

Preparation for Responsible Practice

The first of the goals listed above—that *all* individuals permitted to practice are adequately prepared—is crucial to attaining the conditions for and benefits of professionalism. So long as anyone who is not fully prepared is admitted to an occupation where autonomous practice can jeopardize the safety of clients, the public's trust is violated. So long as no floor is enforced on the level of knowledge needed to teach, a professional culture in schools cannot long be maintained, for some practitioners will be granted control and autonomy who are not prepared to exercise it responsibly.

Professional practice schools serve a crucial function in the preparation of professional teachers. They are charged with completing the initial education of prospective teachers, by ensuring that they have the tools to apply theory in practice and by socializing them to professional norms and ethics. This mission requires (1) a conception of the understanding and capabilities to be acquired by novice teachers before they are allowed to practice autonomously; (2) means by which these understandings, including ethical and normative commitments, can be acquired with a high probability of success; and (3) safeguards to ensure that those sent forth from such schools are adequately prepared. In addition, as models of responsible professionalism, these schools must offer assurances to parents who send their children to such schools that they will not be harmed by the (literal) practice of novices.

A Conception of Teaching

In highly developed professions, the knowledge expected to be acquired in an apprenticeship or internship is decided by the profession through accrediting bodies that sanction such programs and through certification examinations that are taken after the induction experience is completed. Until such time as these professional structures are available in education, though, professional practice schools will be at the forefront of defining what it is that a teacher needs to know to safely practice without intensive supervision.

In pragmatic terms, this is where the first knotty challenge facing such schools will arise. Although professionalism starts from the proposition that knowledge must inform practice, teacher education is often denounced and frequently avoided on the grounds that either it does not convey the knowledge necessary for real teaching (alternative certification plans argue that this can be acquired on the job), or that there is no knowledge base for teaching anyway. Even trained and licensed teachers will come to their first teaching experiences with variable levels and types of knowledge, given the diversity of preparation experiences and the disparate standards for licensure both within and across states.

In wrestling with a conception of teaching knowledge, then, professional practice schools will form an implicit conception of their "curriculum" that must be based on assumptions—sure to be violated—about what novice teachers might already be expected to know. Even before they have begun, such schools will have to decide whether they will assume the mission of preparing, sometimes from "scratch," the unprepared, or whether they will develop some type of admissions standard that approximates a level of knowledge upon which they feel they can successfully build. A possible middle ground is that the school will diagnose novices' knowledge at entry, requiring supplemental coursework in specific areas where a minimal understanding of rudiments of content or pedagogy has not yet been acquired.

This is more than an academic question, particularly for large city school systems, which have many new entrants admitted on emergency or alternative certificates without prior teacher education, and others who are hired to teach in fields for which they have not had complete subject matter preparation. The choices made in this regard will determine in many respects what methods of preparation and levels of responsibility will be suitable for novice teachers.

There are many statements possible about what kinds of understandings and capabilities professional development schools should seek to exemplify and impart. Shulman, for example, classifies the elements of teaching knowledge as follows:

- content knowledge;
- general pedagogical knowledge, with special reference to those broad principles and strategies of classroom management and organization that appear to transcend subject matter;
- curriculum knowledge, with particular grasp of the materials and programs that serve as "tools of the trade" for teachers;
- pedagogical content knowledge, that special amalgam of content and pedagogy that is uniquely the province of teachers, their own special form of professional understanding;

- knowledge of learners and their characteristics;
- knowledge of educational contexts, ranging from the workings of the group or classroom, the governance and financing of school districts, to the character of communities and cultures; and
- knowledge of educational ends, purposes, and values, and their philosophical and historical grounds.[4]

To this list, I would add a grounding in professional ethics, so that teachers can responsibly resolve dilemmas of teaching practice. The goal, as Shulman puts it, "is not to indoctrinate or train teachers to behave in prescribed ways, but to educate teachers to reason soundly about their teaching as well as to perform skillfully."[5]

Whatever the precise definition of knowledge that is arrived at, the professional development school must have in mind what its expectations are for the understandings that undergird professional practice. It is on this basis that the school selects its staff, develops its program for induction, and assesses whether novices have been adequately prepared to practice autonomously.

STRUCTURING PROFESSIONAL PRACTICE

The basic task here is constructing an organization that will seek, transmit, and use knowledge as a basis for teaching decisions; that will support inquiry and consultation and maintain a primary concern for student welfare. Because knowledge is constantly expanding, problems of practice are complex, and ethical dilemmas result from conflict between legitimate goals, the establishment of professional norms cannot be satisfied by prescriptions for practice or unchanging rules of conduct. Instead, the transmission of these norms must be accomplished by socialization to a professional standard that incorporates continual learning, reflection, and concern with the multiple effects of one's actions on others as fundamental aspects of the professional role.

For a professional development school, the accountability dilemmas associated with structuring practice are at least twofold:

1. How can the school guarantee that novices are given adequate preparation?
2. How can the school encourage the use of appropriate practices for all children it serves?

The induction mission of the school ought to warrant that those working with new teachers are themselves exemplars of good teaching; that the experiences of the new teachers will be structured to explicitly address the understandings they are expected to acquire; and that some means for assessing the progress of new teachers are used.

Faculty who are engaged in the induction of new teachers may or may not be all of the faculty employed in a professional development school. If the school is to be an exemplar of good practice, certainly all of the staff must be committed to the tenets of professionalism and the goals of the school. Those who are specifically charged with the preparation of new teachers must themselves meet the standards of teaching knowledge and disposition toward which new teachers strive. This suggests that these faculty will be carefully selected for their capacities to teach adults as well as children. Selection should be conducted by other teaching professionals according to the standards earlier defined. If the school is to model professional accountability, selection by peers according to professional standards is a fundamental feature of the professionalization process.

What distinguishes the form of professional preparation envisioned here from the usual approaches to teacher induction is that, because a standard of practice is envisioned and articulated, haphazard or idiosyncratic training and experiences will be insufficient to guarantee that the standard has been met. Consequently, pairing of a beginning teacher with a mentor in a single class setting is not adequate to the task. The school must structure the experiences of beginning teachers so that they encounter a range of teaching situations and acquire a set of teaching and decision-making abilities. This suggests that the school has an explicit curriculum for beginning teachers composed of (1) formal instructional experiences, such as seminars, clinical conferences, readings, and observations of other teachers; and (2) clinical experiences in which the beginning teacher, under supervision, systematically encounters and examines the major domains of teaching knowledge.

In order to safeguard the welfare of students and facilitate the learning of novice teachers, beginning teachers should not have sole responsibility for a standard teaching load; they need to be given an appropriate and graduated degree of responsibility for teaching students and the opportunity to review major teaching decisions with expert faculty. Indeed, important decisions about students should not be made in isolation. The requirement for consultation is both a protection for students and a means of transmitting knowledge; it is also a means for socializing new teachers to norms of inquiry and collaboration.

In addition, beginning teachers should acquire experience with a variety of students and types of classes. To develop generalizable teaching skills and the ability to exercise judgment in diverse teaching situations, new teachers should learn to work with students at different cognitive stages and performance levels, from differing family backgrounds, and in different subject areas within the disciplinary or grade-level domain.

Finally, accountability for performing the training mission must be secured by assessing new teachers' progress toward the acquisition of professional knowledge and norms of conduct. Such assessment should be the basis for decisions about according additional responsibility for students to developing teachers and about "certifying" that novices are sufficiently prepared at the close of their experience to practice autonomously. At minimum, this process should include frequent feedback to new teachers, establishment of opportunities to acquire those skills not yet adequately mastered, and consultation at regular intervals.

The conditions for responsible practice in a professional development school obviously must include structures that promote inquiry and consultation among the faculty as a whole, not just those immediately engaged in supervising novices. Teacher isolation promotes idiosyncratic practice and works against the development and transmission of shared knowledge. Changing the egg-crate classroom structure and the groupings of students and teachers that maintain isolation will require major changes in teaching arrangements to promote team efforts and legitimize shared time. Many possibilities for reorganizing instruction, such as those pursued in the Coalition of Essential Schools[6] and other similar initiatives, can be considered. With respect to the accountability question, several features of school structure are particularly important:

the extent to which the organization of instruction fosters responsibility for individual students, that is, client-oriented accountability

the extent to which the school structure fosters the use of professional knowledge beyond that represented in the experiences of individual teachers the extent to which the school structure supports continual self-evaluation and review of practice

Client-oriented accountability requires that teachers primarily teach *students* rather than teaching *courses,* that they attend more to learning than to covering a curriculum. If teachers are to be responsible for students and for learning, they must have sufficient opportunities to come to know students' minds, learning styles, and psychological dispositions, and they must be able to focus on student needs and progress as the benchmark for their activities. This seems obvious, but it is improbable, if not impossible, as schools are now structured. The current structure assures that specific courses and curricula will be offered and students will pass through them, usually encountering different teachers from grade to grade and course to course, succeeding or failing as they may. This system does not offer accountability for student learning, only for the processing of students.

Client accountability entails at least two implications for the organization of schooling: that teachers will stay with students for longer periods of time (hours in the day and even years in the course of a school career) so that they may come to know what students' needs are, and that school problem solving will be organized around the individual and collective needs of students rather than around program definitions, grades, tracks, and labels.

Use of professional knowledge poses other requirements: that decision making be conducted on the basis of available *professionwide* knowledge, not on the basis of individual proclivity or opinion, even collective opinion. When most schools do not even stock professional journals in their libraries, the challenge implied by this requirement is profound. In addition to shared time and expectations of consultation and collective decision making, vehicles must be found for teachers in professional development schools to have access to the knowledge bases relevant to their work and to particular, immediate problems of teaching practice. Linkages to universities and access to professional development opportunities go part way toward solving this problem, but more is needed. Professional practice schools may need to create their own research teams to examine and augment available knowledge if practice is to be thus grounded.

Research in the professional development school setting serves an important function for the development of knowledge, but it poses dangers as well. Experimentation can harm students, if it is conducted without care and appropriate safeguards. Too much innovation for its own sake can result in faddism and lack of a coherent philosophy over time and across classrooms in a school. Thus, research in the professional development school must also be subject to careful faculty deliberation as to its necessity, desirability, and probable effects on children; to monitoring while in progress; and to the informed consent of parents.

Finally, ongoing review of practice is central to the operation of professional organizations. This evaluative function serves the joint purposes of monitoring organizational activities and establishing a continuous dialogue about problems of practice among the practitioners themselves. The very distant analogue in school systems is program evaluation, an activity generally conducted by central office researchers who report findings to government sponsors and school board members. Teachers are neither the major producers nor consumers of such information. Hence, neither they nor their students are the major beneficiaries of such evaluation results.

Teachers must wrestle with and take responsibility for resolving immediate, concrete problems of teaching practice if teaching lore is ever to be transformed into meaningful professional standards. One could envision many methods for achieving this. Standing committees such as those used in hospitals could meet regularly to review practices in various subject areas or grade levels, or to examine other functional areas: academic progress; grading policies; student and teacher assignments to particular courses, programs, or teams; development of student responsibility; organization of instruction; and so on. Or more flexible approaches might be tried. Ad hoc research committees might be formed to examine particular problems, both as they manifest in the school and as they have been addressed by research. Faculty meetings could be used to investigate curricular strategies and other matters within and across departments or grade levels. What is critical is that teachers have both time to pursue these evaluations as part of their role (rather than as "released" or extracurricular time) and authority to make changes based on their collective discoveries.

One other point is worth making here: These evaluative and decision-making functions should be engaged in by all of the teachers within the school, including the novices in training. Some proposals for "teacher leadership" envision a small cadre of lead teachers or master teachers who partake of administrative decision-making authority, while everyone else goes on about their work. The trickle-down theory of expertise does not presume a professional standard for all teachers; professional accountability does. Teachers will learn to weigh and balance considerations, to inquire, consult, and make collaborative decisions, to use and develop teaching knowledge to the extent that they are expected to do so. Socialization into these norms of inquiry and collaboration must be part of the preparation of beginning teachers and part of the daily life of all teachers if they are to begin to permeate the profession.

Safeguards for Professional Practice

Even with all of the professional accountability mechanisms described above, there are dangers that the needs of some students will not be diagnosed or fully met, that the concerns or preferences of parents will be inadequately attended to, that through the continual juggling of multiple and competing goals some will be lost in the effort to secure others. Members of a profession, while setting their own standards, cannot seal themselves off too tightly from public scrutiny or from their clientele. When they do, they endanger their rights to self-governance, as other professions have discovered in recent years.

A number of means for providing safeguards and voice for clients and the public will have to be considered and shaped to fit the requirements for a professional development school:

> hierarchical regulation, which expresses the contract made between a state or district and its populace
>
> personnel evaluation, which establishes avenues for ensuring faculty competence
>
> participation and review procedures for parents, which create clear and meaningful avenues for expression of parent views and concerns
>
> reporting vehicles, which transmit the accomplishments of students in the school to parents and the general public

Standard practices in each of these areas are inadequate to provide genuine accountability. In many cases, standard practice also undermines professional practice. New contracts must be forged with states, districts, teacher associations, parents, and the public. A full exploration of the content of these new contracts is beyond the scope of this article, but the nature of the terrain is sketched briefly in what follows.

The problems associated with hierarchical regulation of teaching have been articulated earlier. In school bureaucracies, authority for decisions and responsibility for practice are widely separated, usually by many layers of hierarchy. Boards and central administrators make decisions while teachers, principals, and students are responsible for carrying them out. It is for this reason that accountability for results is hard to achieve. When the desired outcomes of hierarchically imposed policies are not realized, policymakers blame the school people responsible for implementation; practitioners blame their inability to devise or pursue better solutions on the constraints of policy. No one can be fully accountable for the results of practice when authority and responsibility are dispersed.

Yet policymakers have a responsibility to ensure fairness in the delivery of educational services, and district officials are liable for the actions of schools residing within their jurisdictions. Not all regulations can be dispensed with in the cause of professional practice. A heuristic is needed for sorting those regulations that must be observed from those that must be renegotiated or waived. As a first step, it is useful to divide responsibilities into those that must be centrally administered and those that, by their nature, cannot be effectively administered in a hierarchical fashion.

Wise offers a useful distinction between *equity* and *productivity* concerns. The former generally must be resolved by higher units of governance, since they "arise out of the conflicting interests of majorities and minorities and of the powerful and powerless. Because local institutions are apparently the captives of majoritarian politics, they intentionally and unintentionally discriminate. Consequently, we must rely upon the policymaking system to solve problems of inequity in the operating education system."[7] On the other hand, productivity questions cannot be solved by regulation, since the appropriate use of teaching knowledge is highly individualized, while policies are necessarily uniform and standardized. Thus, policy decisions about methods of teaching and schooling processes cannot ever meet the demands of varying school and student circumstances. These require renegotiation for the accommodation of professional practice.

Personnel evaluation, by this rubric, falls in the domain of professional determination. This could lead to its substantial improvement or to its avoidance and demise. This is a critical function of a profession, as the first promise a profession makes is oversight of competence to practice. The shortcomings of traditional evaluation practices and the outlines of more productive professional practices are described in detail elsewhere.[8] In brief, these entail increased peer involvement in design and implementation of evaluation, and separation of the processes for encouraging professional learning from those for making personnel decisions (by committee and with attention to objectivity and due process safeguards). All of this is more easily said than done, however, and the resolution of issues regarding collective bargaining relationships, appropriate roles for administrators and teachers, and political turf battles will require courage and leadership from teachers.

Parent voice is particularly important and problematic for a professional development school. In the first place, the unique qualities of the school will be uncomfortable for some parents. In addition, professional practice must be guided, to the extent possible, by knowledge, even where that conflicts with client preferences. On the other hand, best practice is never absolute or fully informed by research; it is a matter of judgment and frequently unique to the individual child, about whom the parent has substantial knowledge. The multiple goals of schooling will often stand in tension with one another. Parents must have a voice in determining the balance among goals as they are compelled by the state to entrust their children to schools. Thus, parent voice must be secured in a fashion that few schools have yet managed.

The first requirement, I believe, is that professional development schools must, for their clientele as well as their faculties, be schools of choice. No child should be compelled by neighborhood residence or other criterion to attend the school, although attendance should be open for those in the community who desire it. This both safeguards the rights of parents and students to voice their preferences for a form of education with which they feel comfortable and protects the school from the task of satisfying a clientele that might otherwise have widely differing and even opposing points of view. It also provides the school with information, legitimacy, and a form of external review. If schools of choice are chosen, they are legitimized; if they are not, self-examination is required.

Beyond choice, which is the easy part of the answer, parent voice can be fostered by (1) school structures for shared governance, (2) accessible review and appeals processes, and (3) parent involvement in decision making about individual children. Structures for shared governance, such as school-community councils, can provide a vehicle for the shared interests of the parent community to find legitimized and regular expression in the school context. Perhaps the most proactive form of shared governance among parents, teachers, and administrators is seen in Salt Lake City, where decision-making turf that is the joint domain of parents and faculty (e.g., the school schedule, discipline policies, and curricular emphases) is delegated to councils for determination by consensus and parity vote.[9]

Mechanisms for review and appeal of specific concerns and complaints by a neutral third party supplement the shared governance mechanism, by providing a clear avenue for the resolution of individual problems. These mechanisms also provide information and external review for the school as a whole. Finally, the expectation that parents will be included in discussions of important decisions concerning their children prevents the insulation of the professional decision-making process from exposure to the real-world circumstances and concerns of families and communities.

The issue that most tie knots in discussions of accountability is the question of how individual and school expectations and accomplishments can be transmitted in an educationally productive manner to parents, students, and the public at large. Because school goals are numerous, diffuse, and difficult to quantify, simple statements of objectives and results can never completely capture what schools do or what their students accomplish. The counterproductive outcomes for instruction of mindlessly adopting simple performance measures, such as averages of student achievement test scores, have been well documented.[10] Though less discussed, even student grading mechanisms can work against student success. The assumption behind grading schemes that students are to be ranked against each other and that their accomplishments can be captured in a single letter or number can trivialize the educational strivings of individual students and undermine their motivation and self-esteem, activating the Pygmalion principle rather than supporting learning.

Yet reporting vehicles serve an important accountability function by giving information to parents and policymakers about school practices and student progress. The press for such information is increasing and cannot be avoided. Professional practice schools must be at the forefront of efforts to devise educationally productive means for reporting what they and their students do. Untangling this knotty problem is well beyond the scope of this article, but I can point to a few promising directions.

Recent emphasis in a few school restructuring efforts on "high-fidelity" representations of student accomplishments—demonstrations, exhibitions, and projects, for example—seeks more valid and less artificial tools for educational assessment. Narrative reports of student progress accompanied by cumulative portfolios can better represent what a student has learned than a letter grade. Such forms also better represent what the teacher and school have sought to accomplish by depicting the form of instruction as well. Much can be learned from the assessment systems of other countries, which stress these kinds of representations of learning as a means for both reporting outcomes and supporting meaningful and useful education.[11]

Ultimately, though, to satisfy the press for public accountability, entirely new means of reporting the aggregate accomplishments of students in a school will need to be developed. This puzzle is one that professional development schools will undoubtedly encounter before they, or the profession, have developed a complete answer to it.

POSTSCRIPT

Professional accountability seeks to support practices that are client-oriented and knowledge-based. It starts from the premise that parents, when they are compelled to send their children to a public school, have a right to expect that they will be under the care of competent people who are committed to using the best knowledge available to meet the individual needs of those children. This is a different form of accountability than that promised by legal and bureaucratic mechanisms, which assure that when goals have been established, rules will be promulgated and enforced.

Professional accountability assumes that, since teaching work is too complex to be hierarchically prescribed and controlled, it must be structured so that practitioners can make responsible decisions, both individually and collectively. Accountability is provided by rigorous training and careful selection, serious and sustained internships for beginners, meaningful evaluation, opportunities for professional learning, and ongoing review of practice. By such means, professionals learn from each other, norms are established and transmitted, problems are exposed and tackled, parents' concerns are heard, and students' needs are better met.

In such a system, parents can expect that no teacher will be hired who has not had adequate training in how to teach, no teacher will be permitted to practice without supervision until he or she has mastered the professional knowledge base and its application, no teacher will be granted tenure who has not fully demonstrated his or her competence, and no decision about students will be made without adequate knowledge of good practice in light of students' needs. Establishing professional norms of operation, by the vehicles outlined above, creates as well a basis for parent input and standards and methods for redress of unsuitable practice that do not exist in a bureaucratic system of school administration.

This work is not easy, and will not be accomplished quickly. As Clark and Meloy have noted:

We counsel patience in the development of and experimentation with new organizational forms. We have been patient and forgiving of our extant form. Remember that new forms will also be ideal forms. Do not press them immediately to their point of absurdity. Bureaucracy as an ideal form became tempered by adjectival distinctions—bounded, contingent, situational. New forms need to be granted the same exceptions as they are proposed and tested. No one seriously imagines a utopian alternative to bureaucracy. But realistic alternatives can be formed that consistently trade off control for freedom, the organization for the individual. And they can be built upon the principle of the consent of the governed.[12]

This, in sum, is the challenge that faces professional development schools.

NOTES

1. Arthur E. Wise and Linda Darling-Hammond, "Education by Voucher: Private Choice and the Public Interest," *Educational Theory* 34, no. 1 (Winter 1984): 29-47.

2. Thomas F. Green, *Predicting the Behavior of the Educational System* (Syracuse: Syracuse University Press, 1980).

3. Carnegie Forum on Education and the Economy, *A Nation Prepared: Teachers for the 21st Century* (New York: Carnegie Corporation, 1986), p. 89.

4. Lee Shulman, "Knowledge and Teaching: Foundations of the New Reform," *Harvard Educational Review* 57, no. 1 (February 1987): 8.

5. Ibid., p. 13.

6. See, for example, Ron Brandt, "On Changing Secondary Schools: A Conversation with Ted Sizer," *Educational Leadership* 45 (February 1988): 30-36.

7. Arthur E. Wise, *Legislated Learning* (Berkeley: University of California Press, 1979), p. 206.

8. Linda Darling-Hammond, "A Proposal for Evaluation in the Teaching Profession," *Elementary School Journal* 86, no. 4 (March 1986): 1-21.

9. Arthur E. Wise, Linda Darling-Hammond, Milbrey Wallin McLaughlin, and Harriet T. Bernstein, *Teacher Evaluation: A Study of Effective Practices* (Santa Monica, Calif.: The RAND Corporation, 1984).

10. Walt Haney and George Madaus, "Effects of Standardized Testing and the Future of the National Assessment of Educational Progress" (Working paper for the NAEP Study Group, Center for the Study of Testing, Evaluation and Educational Policy, Boston College, Chestnut Hill, MA, 1986); and Linda Darling-Hammond and Arthur E. Wise, "Beyond Standardization: State Standards and School Improvement," *The Elementary School Journal* 85, no. 3 (1985): 315-36.

11. See, for example, Doug A. Archbald and Fred M. Newmann, *Beyond Standardized Testing: Assessing Achievement in the Secondary School* (Reston, Va.: National Association of Secondary School Principals, 1988); Educational Testing Service, *Assessment in the Service of Learning* (Princeton, N.J.: ETS, 1988); Bobby Fong, *The External Examiner Approach to Assessment* (Washington, D.C.: American Association for Higher Education, 1987); and Clare Burstall, "Innovative Forms of Assessment: A United Kingdom Perspective," *Educational Measurement: Issues and Practice,* Spring 1986, pp. 17-22.

12. D. L. Clark and J. M. Meloy, "Recanting Bureaucracy: A Democratic Structure for Leadership in Schools" (unpublished manuscript, University of Virginia, Charlottesville, Va., October 1987), p. 40.

The What, Why, and How of Cooperative Learning

M. LEE MANNING AND ROBERT LUCKING

M. Lee Manning is an associate professor in the Department of Education, Columbia College, Columbia, South Carolina, and an adjunct professor at the University of South Carolina, Columbia. Robert Lucking is a professor in the Department of Curriculum and Instruction, Darden College of Education, Old Dominion University, Norfolk, Virginia.

The need for people to interact cooperatively and work toward group goals undoubtedly will increase during the 1990s. Yet, American education traditionally has emphasized individual competition and achievement, an approach that results in winners and losers and sometimes produces outright hostility among learners. Although research on competitive versus cooperative learning efforts can be traced to the early 1900s, considerable attention has focused on cooperative learning and its outcomes during the past two decades. In this article, we define cooperative learning, examine reasons for and benefits to students working in cooperative teams, and provide an overview of eight selected cooperative learning methods that hold potential for middle and secondary schools.

What Is Cooperative Learning?

Several scholars and proponents (Slavin 1983, 1985; Johnson and Johnson 1989/1990; Taylor 1989) have either offered definitions or provided the basic essentials of cooperative learning, and Kagen (1989) identified a broad repertoire of cooperative learning strategies. However, it was Slavin (1983) who defined the cooperative learning process as a set of alternatives to traditional instruction systems, or, more specifically, techniques in which students work in heterogeneous groups of four to six members and earn recognition, rewards, and sometimes grades based on the academic performance of their groups. Such a definition does not imply, however, that all methods have the same processes and intended outcomes. Table 1 provides a brief overview of eight cooperative learning methods and shows how instructional efforts can share both similarities and dissimilarities. Commonalities may include cooperative efforts among learners, group goals, and the necessity for social skills (Johnson and Johnson 1989/1990; Slavin 1978; Aronson et al. 1978; Sharan and Sharan 1989/1990). Differences may include the fact that some methods are applicable to most grades and subjects (DeVries and Slavin 1978; Slavin 1978) and still other methods use individualization and are applicable only to mathematics in grades three through six (Slavin, Leavy, and Madden 1986).

The current popularity and interest in cooperative learning, which undoubtedly will extend into the twenty-first century, must be viewed within a historical context. Cooperative learning methods have roots in social and psychological research and theory that focused on cooperation versus competition, some of which date back to the early 1900s (Slavin 1985). Maller (1929) focused his investigation on cooperation in the learning process, although research directed toward practical cooperative methods actually began in the early 1970s. During the 1980s, cooperative learning methods received considerable attention because of their potential to serve as an alternative to the traditional classroom that creates competition among learners rather than fostering a cooperative spirit (Slavin 1985).

Why Is There Current Interest in Cooperative Learning?

The current interest in cooperative learning stems from two broad forces: (1) the recognition that competitive educational environments encourage students to compete with one another rather than learn in a cooperative fashion and (2) evidence that suggests that cooperative learning, when properly implemented, has the potential for contributing positively to academic achievement, social skills, and self-esteem.

Traditionally, students have been taught in schools where competition reigned. Because learners competed with one another for grades and the teacher's attention

From *The Clearing House*, Vol. 64, No. 3, January/February 1991, pp. 152-156. Reprinted with permission of the Helen Dwight Reid Educational Foundation. Published by Heldref Publications, 1319 Eighteenth St., N.W., Washington, DC 20036-1802. Copyright © 1991.

TABLE 1
Overview of Selected Cooperative Learning Methods

Method/Proponent	Brief Description/Comments
Learning Together (Johnson and Johnson 1987, 1989/90)	Emphasizing cooperative effort, Learning Together has five basic elements: positive interdependence (students believe they are responsible for both their learning and the team's); face-to-face interaction (students explain their learning and help others with assignments); individual accountability (students demonstrate mastery of material); social skills (students communicate effectively, build and maintain trust, and resolve conflicts); group processing (groups periodically assess their progress and how to improve effectiveness). Uses four- or five-member heterogeneous teams.
Student Teams–Achievement Divisions (STAD) (Slavin 1978)	Four student learning teams (mixed in performance levels, sex, and ethnicity); teacher presents lesson, students work in teams and help others master material. Students then take quizzes; cooperative efforts are not allowed on quizzes; team rewards are earned. Applicable to most grades/subjects.
Teams-Games-Tournament (TGT) (DeVries and Slavin 1978)	Using the same teacher presentation and teamwork as STAD, TGT replaces the quizzes with weekly tournaments in which students compete with members of other teams to contribute points to team scores. Competition occurs at "tournament tables" against others with similar academic records. The winner of each tournament brings six points to her or his team. Low achievers compete with low achievers (a similar arrangement exists for high achievers), which provides all students with equal opportunity for success. As with STAD, team rewards are earned. Applicable to most grades and subjects.
Jigsaw (Aronson, Blaney, Stephan, Sikes, and Snapp 1978)	Students are assigned to six-member teams to work on academic material that has been divided into sections. Each member reads a section; then, members of different teams meet to become experts. Students return to groups and teach other members about their sections. Students must listen to their teammates to learn other sections.
Jigsaw 2 (Slavin 1987)	Students work in four- or five-member teams as in TGT or STAD. Rather than being assigned specific parts, students read a common narrative (e.g., a chapter). Students also receive a topic on which to become an expert. Learners with the same topics meet together as in Jigsaw, and then they teach the material to their original group. Students take individual quizzes.
Team Assisted Individualization (TAI) (Slavin, Leavey, and Madden 1986)	Uses four-member mixed-ability groups (as with STAD and TGT); differs from STAD and TGT in that it combines cooperative learning and individualized instruction and is applicable only to mathematics in grades three through six. Learners take a placement test, then proceed at their own pace. Team members check one another's work and help with problems. Without help, students take unit tests that are scored by student monitors. Each week, the teacher evaluates and gives team rewards.
Cooperative Integrated Reading and Composition (CIRC) (Madden, Slavin, and Stevens 1986)	Designed to teach reading and writing in upper elementary grades, CIRC assigns students to different reading teams. Teacher works with one team, while other teams engage in cognitive activities: reading, predicting story endings, summarizing stories, writing responses, practicing decoding, and learning vocabulary. Teams follow sequence of teacher instruction, team practice, team pre-assessments, and quizzes. Quizzes may not be taken until the team feels each student is ready. Team rewards are given.
Group Investigation (Sharan and Sharan 1989/1990)	Groups are formed according to common interest in a topic. Students plan research, divide learning assignments among members, synthesize/summarize findings, and present the findings to the entire class.

and approval, students did not promote or encourage one another's academic efforts. Cooperative learning programs encourage students of all performance levels to work together in small groups toward group goals. Rather than competing for grades and other rewards as individuals, students help one another to learn and to achieve (Slavin 1987).

During the 1980s, considerable research (Slavin 1983, 1987; Johnson and Johnson 1987, 1989a) directed attention to the theory and practice of cooperative learning and promoted cooperative efforts over competitiveness. However, a few years earlier, Aronson et al. (1978) proposed a cooperative learning classroom that structured the learning process to make individual competitiveness and success compatible. In fact, success could occur only after the team had engaged in cooperative behavior. Instead of students' equating rewards and success with outperforming their competitors, learners achieved success as a consequence of listening to peers, helping and teaching each other, and helping others in the team to teach.

The second reason for increased interest in cooperative learning has to do with research indicating increases in academic achievement, enhancement of social skills, and the improvement of self-esteem. At the outset, it is imperative to warn against the fallacy of concluding that all cooperative learning methods are equally effective in making these improvements. Slavin (1988, 31) wrote, "I am becoming increasingly concerned about a widespread belief that *all* forms of cooperative learning are instructionally effective. This is emphatically not the case." Nevertheless, research studies have provided convincing evidence that cooperative learning, when properly implemented, can contribute positively to academic achievement, social skills, and self-esteem (see Johnson and Johnson [1989a] for a more comprehensive review).

Academic Achievement

Overall, most studies show that high, average, and low achievers gain equally from cooperative learning experiences; however, some studies have shown greater gains for low achievers and others have shown the greatest gains for high achievers (Slavin 1985). Research studies on cooperative learning and academic achievement have, however, reached agreement on two aspects: (1) cooperative learning methods can and usually do have positive effects on student achievement, and (2) achievement effects do not result from all forms of cooperative learning (Slavin 1988, 1989/1990).

Cooperative learning methods that produce positive academic achievement share two features. First, they have group goals whereby team members work interdependently to earn teacher recognition or other forms of success. Second, they require individual accountability; that is, group success depends on individual contributions and learning of all members. For example, STAD, TGT, TAI, and CIRC (see table 1 for explanations), which require group goals and individual accountability, consistently reveal positive results. The group investigation method (Sharan and Sharan, 1989/1990) revealed positive effects on academic achievement even though it lacked group goals; its use of group rewards (similar to STAD, TGT, TAI, and CIRC) may serve a similar purpose (Slavin 1987).

Social Skills

It seems logical to assume that working and learning together as members of a team would contribute positively to students' social skills and to their overall ability to interact successfully with others. Research on social skills and gains either report positive effects in social areas or suggest the importance of teaching the social skills needed for successful small-group work.

Reporting the basic results of the Jigsaw classroom (see table 1), Aronson et al. (1978) concluded that children grew to like their groupmates even more than others in the classroom. Similarly, Slavin (1987) found that students expressed greater liking for their classmates as a result of participating in cooperative learning methods.

Whether interpersonal and small-group skills are sufficiently important to warrant direct instruction has been an issue of recent debate. Johnson and Johnson (1989/1990) felt that simply placing students in groups and telling them to work together does not produce cooperation and high achievement. Certain social conditions increase students' efforts to achieve and to improve relationships with classmates: positive interdependence, face-to-face interaction, individual accountability, and social skills. For cooperative learning to be effective, students must get to know one another, communicate accurately and unambiguously, accept and support one another, and resolve conflicts constructively. Believing interpersonal and small-group skills to be as important as academic content, Johnson and Johnson (1989/1990) concluded that these skills should be taught just as systematically as a content subject.

Self-Esteem

Several research studies have concluded that cooperative learning teams increase students' self-esteem. This may be true for several reasons. First, feeling liked by peers and experiencing academic accomplishment are important components of students' self-esteem. Research has indicated that cooperative learning addresses both these components. Cooperative learning may lead to increased self-esteem because students have more friends and have more positive feelings about their school experiences and academic achievement (Slavin 1983, 1987, 1989/1990). Second, Aronson et al. (1978) concluded that there was a greater increase in self-esteem among children in the Jigsaw classroom than among the children in competitive classrooms. Third, in typical competitive classrooms, students become either winners or losers, with the latter developing negative attitudes toward themselves and school. With cooperative learning, students see each other as academically and socially competent colleagues rather than competitors. Such improved recognition of peers promotes better interpersonal relationships and leads in turn to increased self-esteem (Towson 1985).

How Can Educators Implement Cooperative Learning?

Implementing cooperative learning requires an understanding of the various types of cooperative learning, of the teacher's role in the process, and of the two previously noted essentials, that is, group goals and individual accountability.

Table 1 contains descriptions of eight cooperative learning methods and gives references for each. These eight methods are the most researched and, it is widely agreed, the most workable and effective methods. Student Teams-Achievement Divisions (STAD), Teams-Games-Tournament (TGT), Team Assisted Individualization (TAI), Cooperative Integrated Reading and Composition (CIRC), and Jigsaw 2 result from Slavin's (1987) work at the Johns Hopkins Center for Research on Elementary and Middle Schools.

> **Working cooperatively seems to have particularly strong effects for Hispanic and black students, regardless of achievement levels.**

Each of the various types of cooperative learning calls for a new role for the teacher. In the Jigsaw classroom (Aronson et al. 1978), the teacher, instead of being the major conveyer of knowledge, becomes the person who creates the process and environment that allow students to see each other as learning resources. Realistically, teachers have to abdicate some of their traditional power, such as being the sole dispenser of knowledge, grades, and discipline. Another change in roles includes viewing students as positive forces capable of learning on their own and from one another (Nickolai-Mays and Goetsch 1986).

As previously discussed, two essentials that significantly determine the degree of academic achievement are group goals and individual accountability (Slavin 1987). Other essentials include the five basic elements (see table 1) proposed by Johnson and Johnson (1989b).

Effect of Cooperative Learning on Intergroup and Multiethnic Relations

People who help one another by joining forces to achieve a common goal generally feel more positively about each other and are willing to interact more positively when performing collective tasks. Rather than treating academic learning and social or intergroup relations as two distinct entities, cooperative learning contributes positively to overall intergroup relations and, particularly, to improving relations with multicultural/multiethnic students (Sharan 1985). Other research shows that students who learn cooperatively have greater liking for their cooperative learning classmates. Cooperative learning increases contact between students, provides a feeling of group membership, engages

learners in pleasant activities, and requires that team members work toward a common goal (Slavin 1983).

Several research studies have indicated that cooperative learning programs can contribute positively to specific multiethnic populations. Aronson et al. (1978) concluded that both black and Anglo students in cooperative learning situations liked school better than did the same ethnic groups in competitive classrooms. Furthermore, for students of diverse populations, learning of this nature requires verbalization of ideas in a context of social interaction (Osterman 1990), and learning takes place through dialogue and conversation. Other research has suggested that working cooperatively seems to have particularly strong effects for Hispanic and black students, regardless of achievement levels (Slavin 1987). One study indicated that Anglo- and Asian-Americans in a learning situation similar to the Jigsaw method had more positive attitudes toward Mexican-Americans than did learners in competitive classes. A study of Jigsaw 2-related classes containing recent European and West Indian immigrants and Anglo-Canadians documented substantially more cross-ethnic friendships than in the control groups (Slavin 1983). Concerning specific cooperative learning methods, positive effects have been documented with STAD, TGT, TAI, and Jigsaw 2 (Slavin 1987). Studies of Group Investigation found that improved student attitudes and behaviors toward classmates of different ethnic backgrounds extended to classmates of different groups (Sharan, Amir, and Ben-Ari 1984). Cooperative learning arrangements also appear to facilitate relationships between handicapped and regular students (Yager, Johnson, and Snider 1985). In conclusion, Slavin (1987) summarized that cooperative learning strategies apparently contribute to students' seeing each other in a positive light and forming friendships based on human qualities.

Summary

The advantages of learning cooperatively continue to become clear. First, social benefits accrue to students of heterogeneous ethnic and achievement backgrounds working together as functioning members of a team that focuses on common goals. Second, increases in academic achievement and self-esteem are also found among these students. Rather than pitting students against one another in competition for attention and grades, educators can select an appropriate cooperative learning method that effectively complements more traditional teaching styles and addresses their students' needs. Emphasizing cooperation over competition requires teachers to change their teaching roles from a power figure or conveyer of knowledge to a guide of learning events or to a resource person. The prospect of changing one's perception of what constitutes an effective teacher will undoubtedly prove unsettling to some educators. Nevertheless, the increasing need for all people to work together during the 1990s and beyond indicates that cooperative learning is an educational practice that contemporary educators must consider for their schools.

REFERENCES

Aronson, E., N. Blaney, C. Stephan, J. Sikes, and M. Snapp. 1978. *The Jigsaw classroom*. Beverly Hills: Sage.

DeVries, D. L., and R. E. Slavin. 1978. Teams-Games-Tournament (TGT): Review of ten classroom experiments. *Journal of Research and Development in Education* 12: 28–38.

Johnson, D. W., and R. Johnson. 1987. *Learning together and alone: Cooperative, competitive, and individualistic learning*. Englewood Cliffs, N.J.: Prentice-Hall.

Johnson, D. W., and R. Johnson. 1989a. *Cooperation and competition: Theory and research*. Edina, Minn.: Interaction Book Company.

Johnson, D. W., and R. Johnson. 1989b. Toward a *cooperative* effort: A response to Slavin. *Educational Leadership* 46(7): 80–81.

Johnson, D. W., and R. Johnson. 1989/1990. Social skills for successful group work. *Educational Leaderhip* 47(4): 29–33.

Kagen, S. 1989. *Cooperative learning resources for teachers*. San Juan Capistrano, Calif.: Resources for Teachers.

Madden, N. A., R. E. Slavin, and R. J. Stevens. 1986. *Cooperative integrated reading and composition: Teacher's manual*. Baltimore: Johns Hopkins University, Center for Research on Elementary and Middle Schools.

Maller, J. B. 1929. *Cooperation and competition*. New York: Columbia Teachers College.

Nickolai-Mays, S., and K. Goetsch. 1986. Cooperative learning in the middle school. *Middle School Journal* 18:28–29.

Osterman, K. 1990. Reflections practice: A new agenda for education. *Education and Urban Society* 22(2): 133–52.

Sharan, S. 1985. Cooperative learning and the multiethnic classroom. In *Learning to cooperate, cooperating to learn*, edited by R. Slavin, S. Sharan, S. Kagan, R. Lazarowitz, C. Webb, and R. Schmuck, 255–76. New York: Plenum.

Sharan, S., Y. Amir, and R. Ben-Ari. 1984. School desegregation: Some challenges ahead. In *School desegregation: Cross-cultural perspectives*, edited by Y. Amir and S. Sharan. Hillsdale, N.J.: Erlbaum.

Sharan, Y., and S. Sharan. 1989/1990. Group investigation expands cooperative learning. *Educational Leadership* 47(4): 17–21.

Slavin, R. E. 1978. Student teams and achievement divisions. *Journal of Research in Education* 12:39–49.

———. 1983. *An introduction to cooperative learning*. New York: Longman.

———. 1985. An introduction to cooperative learning research. In *Learning to cooperate, cooperating to learn*, edited by R. Slavin, S. Sharan, S. Kagan, R. Lazarowitz, C. Webb, and R. Schmuck, 5–15. New York: Plenum.

———. 1987. *Cooperative learning*. 2d ed. Washington, D.C.: National Education Association.

———. 1988. Cooperative learning and student achievement. *Educational Leadership* 47(4): 31–33.

———. 1989/1990. Research on cooperative learning: Consensus and controversy. *Educational Leadership* 47(4): 52–54.

Slavin, R. E., M. B. Leavy, and N. A. Madden. 1986. *Team accelerated instruction—Mathematics*. Watertown, Mass.: Mastery Education Corporation.

Taylor, R. 1989. The potential of small-group mathematics insruction in grades four through six. *Elementary School Journal* 89:633–42.

Towson, S. 1985. Melting pot or mosaic: Cooperative education and interethnic relations. In *Learning to cooperate, cooperating to learn*, edited by R. Slavin, S. Sharan, S. Kagan, R. Lazarowitz, C. Webb, and R. Schmuck, 263–76. New York: Plenum.

Yager, S., R. T.. Johnson, D. W. Johnson, and B. Snider. 1985. The effect of cooperative and individualistic learning experience on positive and negative cross-handicap relationships. *Contemporary Educational Psychology* 10:127–38.

Schools and the Beginning Teacher

Schools can learn to dignify their beginning teachers, according to Ms. Moran. When they do, they will create stewards who care deeply about every aspect of their professional homes.

SHEILA W. MORAN

SHEILA W. MORAN (New Hampshire Profile Chapter) is principal of Thetford Elementary School in Thetford, Vt. She was the director of the Upper Valley Teacher Training Program in Lebanon, N.H., from 1979 to 1988.

NEW TEACHERS yearn for a sense of professional rootedness and community. Too often, however, they know only a sense of dislocation and loneliness, of compromise and inadequacy — feelings that cause them to question their commitment to school life.

"Feeling at home" means feeling safe to explore, to strike out in unexpected directions, to establish a personal identity. Feeling at home as a school professional means both that one is welcomed as an individual within the professional community and that one takes responsibility for seeking and establishing a personal identity. Being creative and powerful as a teacher requires leaving a safe haven to travel unfamiliar paths toward a professional personality.

Many beginning teachers find themselves in school systems that are ill-prepared to welcome them appropriately. These beginners are isolated professionally and socially. They join aging and habit-bound faculties whose members already know the ropes. They become the have-nots among the haves, the ones with neither the tricks of the trade nor the wisdom of experience. The welcoming kindness they feel from some faculty members hardly offsets the hours of isolation in their classrooms. Frequently, beginning teachers are young people who have relocated to unfamiliar communities and have not yet found social support systems to help them endure the emotional hardships of their first tentative years of teaching.

The lot of beginning teachers is made harder still because they are unprepared for the degree of expertise expected of them when they sign their first contracts. Although many states and districts are beginning to develop formal support systems, the oldest myth about teacher preparation still prevails — that newly certified teachers are fully prepared for the rigor and complexity of classroom instruction. Preservice education, even at its most intense and pragmatic, can only begin the process of scientific discovery and artistic creativity that is teaching. Newly certified teachers, however bright and capable, are just ready to begin the meaningful learning that occurs during the first few years of true professional engagement. The most effective preservice preparation stimulates more questions than it answers and erodes the simplistic educational philosophies with which most student teachers gird themselves.

Nonetheless, the public and the employers of beginning teachers usually expect a newly certified teacher to be "competent," to have a full bag of transferable (and often measurable) instruc-

From *Phi Delta Kappan*, November 1990, pp. 210-213. Reprinted by permission of Sheila W. Moran and *Phi Delta Kappan*.

215

tional tricks. They behave as though beginning teachers emerge from their preservice training fully and forevermore responsive, responsible, rational, adaptable, intellectually curious, vigorous, compassionate, imaginative, and open-minded. Because of an inappropriate emphasis on technique, schools have been shy about taking into account such fundamental but nonobjective factors as humanity and the development of attitudes about self and profession when they supervise and evaluate beginning teachers. We expect our beginners to go it alone, especially in the areas of attitude and personality development. But these matters so affect a beginner's sense of competence and worth that they are crucial to professional growth and survival.

Schools often compound the problem. Beginning teachers frequently experience supervision that feels like surveillance and evaluation that feels like a reading of the charges. They are expected to follow lessons prescribed by a commercial textbook series. Instead of requiring that they hone their creativity, schools often require new teachers to replicate the lessons of others. Advice from friendly teachers and supervisors too often comes unsolicited and takes the form of correction of an "error" that was, in fact, a brave but flawed experiment. Rarely are beginners encouraged to take risks and experiment. More rarely are new teachers asked what or how they would like to teach, what they had hoped to accomplish with a "failed" experiment, what others can do to help them achieve their goals. Ironically, all these formal and informal checks — which are in place to protect schools against incompetence — have the effect of encouraging minimal competence at the expense of meaningful and memorable teaching.

We are now in an era of education reform that is flirting with more human aspects of schools and schooling. Acknowledging that beginning teachers need far more than methods and stiff upper lips means seeking a "human reality rather than merely its bureaucratic image. . . . In real schools, excellence is pursued by students and teachers who live complex lives, sometimes in trying circumstances. A wholehearted commitment to excellence will want to go beyond mere labels to nurture intellect broadly and compassionately."[1]

Dispelling the myth that beginning teachers are fully equipped to handle the demands of their profession begins with heartfelt public acknowledgment of what we have always known: that the first months and years of teaching are full of pain, confusion, loneliness, and often humiliation. These conditions all too frequently lay the groundwork for the compromising of ideals and the narrowing and hardening of technique. Dispelling the myth will also involve admitting — even welcoming — into our schools some weak and false starts. "Nurturing intellect broadly and compassionately" is untidy and inconsistent, and bureaucracies are not cheerful in the face of untidiness and inconsistency.

WHAT CAN SCHOOLS DO TO HELP?

New teachers need not be overwhelmed by their burdens. I would like to suggest two methods that could go a long way toward alleviating some of the problems beginners typically confront. The first is an adaptation of the concept of mentoring. The second focuses on an unusual format for the evaluation of beginning teachers.

Beginner peer groups. Public and independent schools have been experimenting with mentoring programs that pair new teachers and seasoned practitioners. Mentoring is understandably receiving attention because of its potential for creating the kind of human environment required for professional development. Certainly a new teacher benefits greatly from spending time with a seasoned practitioner, listening to stories, gaining perspective, watching how experience informs practice. The hope is that the new teacher will also come away feeling liked and welcomed into the fold. It is true, too, that coaching does help many teachers. Bruce Joyce and Beverly Showers found that, while some teachers could learn and apply new skills and models without specific coaching for their application, many others could not do so.[2]

However, mentoring still emphasizes "a thorough knowledge of vocabulary, strategies, skills, and principles related to both general and specific teaching activities."[3] The object in such relationships is usually to pass along the experienced teacher's expertise to the novice. It is rare to find a mentor who has the time or the inclination to engage in the messy work of nurturing intelligent, fulfilling, creative, idiosyncratic teaching[4] or of constructing new and personalized knowledge.[5] It may even be true that the greater professional development accrues to the experienced teacher, who benefits from giving voice to philosophy and practice.

The beginner views the mentor in much the same way that a student views a teacher: as a model, an inspiration, a guide, and, sometimes, as the direct source of a skill or an understanding. The mentor also functions in much the same way as a parent: at first as a mooring and then as a signal light. However, parents cannot replicate themselves in their maturing children. Nor is it appropriate to expect that knowledge and expertise can be transferred in their entirety into our best beginning teachers. The relationship between mentor and beginner is important but essentially unequal.

Equality would be much more likely between teachers who share similarly limited amounts of experience — who have more or less equivalent levels of understanding, skill, accomplishment, and status. Let us consider augmenting existing support systems for beginning teachers by establishing pairs or clusters of relatively new teachers who can meet to define and solve problems, struggle with failures, and celebrate successes. These relationships would be founded, as are peer-coaching relationships among more experienced teachers, on trust and effective communication. They would promote discussions among teachers, promise a nonjudgmental atmosphere for dialogue, and maintain a focus on the development of professional expertise. They would provide opportunities for reflection on those hesitant successes and frightening disasters from which knowledge derives — knowledge that does, in time, translate into teaching skill. Together, beginners would solve problems, search for a philosophy, and exert increasing control over their teaching.

Successful clusters of beginning teachers would need the gift of time to meet, to write, and to reflect. They would not need, and should not have present, administrators or more experienced teachers. In the absence of these "parent figures," beginning teachers would have to take responsibility for their failures and could unequivocally own their successes. They could certainly use the experience of others as a resource, but the beginners themselves should first give voice to their own solutions.

The other side of the teacher report card. Another challenge to schools is to devise a means of evaluation that can inform the way all of us — beginners, mentors, and administrators — look at beginning teaching competence. If we are to "nurture intellect broadly and compassionately," if we are to encourage teachers to make complex judgments, then we must talk about nurturing certain attitudes and personality attributes. We talk about recruiting the right sorts of people into teacher education programs, and we talk about employing the right sorts of people in the classroom, but we fail to nurture the very "rightness" that makes them desirable in the first place.

Consider the metaphor of a report card for teachers. There would be the usual evaluation, which takes into account the development of traditional pedagogical skills and understandings: classroom management and discipline, planning for instruction, implementing instruction, and assessment of student progress. Certainly schools should look for improvement in basic techniques, but the emphasis should be on the improvement of personalized, not generic, techniques.

Now imagine the other side of the report card, which deals with those attitudes and attributes that enhance the "conditions in which [student] learning occurs" — conditions that, taken together, improve the "quality of the teacher-student relationships" and increase the "degree of awareness the teacher has of [his or] her objectives."[6] The beginning teacher will most likely exhibit:

• a reflective posture toward teaching practice and toward interactions with students;

• eagerness to make contact with other teachers;

• a hunger to know more about students, about teaching, about content, about schools;

• a desire to refine and articulate a personal philosophy;

• a desire to develop a personal style;

• a desire to develop personalized curriculum units;

• a sense of perspective and a sense of humor;

• empathy; and

• the courage of his or her convictions.

These are attitudes and attributes that can be developed during the complex early years of employment. In theory, an emphasis on such evaluative considerations draws attention to what is truly of value in the formation of an intelligent, creative teacher. In practice, it is a celebration of promise.

For example, one such evaluation might

celebrate the fact that a beginning teacher, in an effort to refine her discipline technique, labored with two other beginners to clarify, in writing and in discussion, her personal expectations for student behavior. After clarifying those expectations, the beginner accepted the support of the other two in redefining her sense of her relationship with her students. By the end of her first year of teaching, she felt less like an ogre for stopping behavior that looked innocent enough but that she had come to see as a precursor to behavior that could not be tolerated.

A second example would be the celebration of a scholarly new teacher's determination to broaden his repertoire of instructional techniques. This new teacher observed and then experimented with the techniques of several teachers whose varied methods were considered effective by students and colleagues.

Without encouragement, these attitudes and attributes will atrophy. Once affirmed, however, they will grow stronger, and with their strengthening comes the likelihood that new teachers will learn from and be encouraged by their first years in the classroom. These qualities help new teachers become masters, if not owners, of their own instructional ships. They bear directly on the acquisition of teaching skills and understanding.

A CAUTIONARY NOTE

School employment offers few opportunities for advancement. It is difficult (some say impossible) to build in real rewards, such as sabbatical leaves or fully paid positions with diminished teaching responsibility complemented by time for study, curriculum development, peer supervision, or teacher mentoring. Teachers, sanely enough, seek to reduce the amount of time spent in their most punishing tasks if they are not given professionally meaningful incentives. Very often it is the neophytes who, not knowing better, find themselves doing the jobs others have discarded. Beginning teachers too often find themselves teaching the class sections nobody else wants or being hired for two-fifths time in an English department only to have to pick up a three-fifths job as a library assistant to make ends meet, a situation that leaves them no preparation time during the school day. It is almost always the beginning teachers who, in the flush of excitement,

fail to read their contracts carefully and later discover that their jobs don't quite fit the interview description. It is too often beginning teachers who are rotated into certain duties that others know enough to avoid and who are given the least attractive, most awkwardly appointed classrooms.

A spirit of human kindness could help here. Schools could, in this regard only, think of their beginners as children. We protect our young from hazards and then gradually acclimate them to difficult life experiences. There are enough problems in everyday teaching with everyday students that are exceedingly difficult for new teachers to handle. Let them learn to cope with these problems before unleashing the flood.

In every other way, schools can learn to dignify their beginners. Instead of legislating methods and materials that promote dependency, schools can encourage experimentation. Instead of maintaining bureaucracies that subtly require subservience, they can create opportunities for teachers to give voice to their professional ideas. Instead of fearing the power that comes to professionals who have stronger, more meaningful voices, schools can celebrate the changes that occur thereby. Instead of sapping the intellectual and emotional lifeblood of their new teachers, schools can dignify them by expecting intelligent, independent engagement with students and curriculum. Caring schools will find that they have created stewards who care deeply about every aspect of their professional homes.

1. Ronald Gross and Beatrice Gross, eds., *The Great School Debate: Which Way for American Education?* (New York: Simon & Schuster, 1985), p. 19.
2. Bruce Joyce and Beverly Showers, "Improving Inservice Training: The Messages of Research," *Educational Leadership*, February 1980, pp. 379-85.
3. Deborah Burnett Strother, "Peer Coaching for Teachers: Opening Classroom Doors," *Phi Delta Kappan*, June 1989, p. 826.
4. Each year interns in the Upper Valley Teacher Training Program in Lebanon, New Hampshire, are asked to reflect on the most powerful teachers that they can remember. There has been notable consistency in the results. The two most frequent features that impress themselves on a student's memory are, first, strength of personality (seen as the courage to be different) and, second, the ability to teach about life and living while conducting the instructional business of the classroom.
5. Mary Field Belenky et al., *Women's Ways of Knowing: The Development of Self, Voice, and Mind* (New York: Basic Books, 1986).
6. Milton Schwebel, "The Other School System," in Gross and Gross, p. 242.

Put to the Test:

The Effects of External Testing on Teachers

MARY LEE SMITH

MARY LEE SMITH *is Professor in the College of Education, Arizona State University, Tempe, AZ 85287-2411. Her specializations include policy studies and qualitative research methodology.*

Evidence from an extensive qualitative study of the role of external testing in elementary schools led to propositions about the effects of such tests on teachers. Data from interviews revealed that teachers experience negative emotions as a result of the publication of test scores and determine to do what is necessary to avoid low scores. Teachers believe that scores are used against them, despite the perceived invalidity of the tests themselves. From classroom observations it was concluded that testing programs substantially reduce the time available for instruction, narrow curricular offerings and modes of instruction, and potentially reduce the capacities of teachers to teach content and to use methods and materials that are incompatible with standardized testing formats.

Educational Researcher, Vol. 20, No. 5, pp. 8–11

The test raises the anxiety level of everyone. The superintendent likes to use the scores to point out the teachers' weaknesses and create competition among the teachers. He thinks that good scores equal good teaching.

So reported a junior high teacher surveyed by Haas, Haladyna, and Nolen (1989, p. 62). According to their study, substantial percentages of teachers believe that scores from the state-mandated Iowa Test of Basic Skills (ITBS), which at the time of the study was administered to every child from first to eighth grade every year, are "routinely inappropriately used" (p. 8) to evaluate administrators, teachers, and schools and that such inappropriate uses have harmful effects. For the most part, the teachers of Hamilton and Jackson elementary schools, who participated in our qualitative study, concur. An interview with a primary grade teacher produced the following exchange.

Interviewer: Do the ITBS scores ever get used against you?

Teacher: Well, the first year I used Math Their Way [a program designed for conceptual understanding of math concepts through the manipulation of concrete materials], I was teaching a second grade class and they scored at grade level. But other second grades in that school scored higher than grade level, and I had to do an awful lot of talking before they allowed me to use that program again.

Interviewer: So they were willing to throw out the program on the basis of the scores. How did you feel?

Teacher: I was angry. I was really angry because so many of the things I had taught those children about math were not on the test—were not tested by the test. And, indeed, the following year they did extremely well in the third grade. I had no children who were in any of the low math classes and a great many of my children were in the advanced classes doing better than some of the children who had

scored higher than they had on the ITBS. . . . But it's very hard to start a new program knowing that the Iowa may be used against you.

To understand the perceived effects of external testing on teachers, one needs only to ask. Their statements on questionnaires, in interviews, and during conversations in meetings and lounges reveal the anxiety, shame, loss of esteem, and alienation they experience from publication and use of test scores.

To understand fully the consequences of high-stakes external testing on teachers, one must look beyond their verbal statements to underlying meanings within the institution. One must sit with them in the initial faculty meetings when school expectations are laid out, follow them as they collect formidable piles of textbooks, teaching manuals, and the other materials they are required to cover, observe their everyday classroom life throughout the school year, watch their sometimes frenzied preparation for the tests themselves, examine what topics and subject matter gets slighted or left by the wayside for the sake of the tests, and finally learn what reactions to these experiences are incorporated into the teachers' identities and subsequent definitions of teaching.

This is the line of investigation we pursued in a qualitative study of the role of external (mandated) testing on elementary schools (Smith, Edelsky, Draper, Rottenberg, & Cherland, 1989). In that study, we employed direct observation of classrooms, meetings, and school life generally; interviews with teachers, pupils, administrators, and others; and analysis of documents. Data collection spanned more than 15 months in direct contact with the two schools in a Phoenix metropolitan district. Constant-comparative (Strauss, 1987) and analytic induction methods (Erickson, 1986) helped us to generate and test assertions from the data and to establish the evidentiary warrant for those assertions. Among the products of the analysis were a grounded theory of beliefs about testing, a sociological calendar of activities relating to test preparation, and an analysis of the consequences of external testing on what is taught, the methods by which it is taught, and the organization of schools. For the present article, I have drawn from the assertions and data of the larger study and from the work of Haladyna, Haas, and Nolen. Their survey of Arizona educators (Nolen, Haladyna, & Haas, 1989) covered the same topics as ours. Although independent of our study in conception, method, and execution, the findings of their study confirm our own.

Effects of Testing on Teachers

Effects of testing on teachers fall into the following categories.

From *Educational Researcher,* Vol. 20, No. 5, June/July 1991, pp. 8-11. Copyright © 1991 by the American Educational Research Association. Reprinted by permission of the publisher.

1. The publication of test scores produces feelings of shame, embarrassment, guilt, and anger in teachers and the determination to do what is necessary to avoid such feelings in the future.

In the professional literature, a high-stakes testing program is one whose results are used to trigger actions or decisions such as passing or failing a grade, graduating or not, determining teacher or principal merit, or assuming responsibility for a failing district by a state agency (Popham, 1987). But to the teachers involved in our study, high stakes meant the school-by-school and grade-by-grade publication of ITBS scores by the Arizona Department of Education and the unvaryingly brutal treatment of schools with these test results by the newspapers. Test scores are the sole means of describing and judging schools, and there is only minor public or professional debate about the merits of the tests as psychometric instruments. Drawing from media accounts alone, none could deny that the dominant public perception is that Arizona schools are failures, the teachers are not particularly hard-working (test scores "prove" this), and the educational bureaucracy is inept.

Like the teacher quoted in the opening paragraph, teachers feel anxiety and stress about the publication of these test scores, whether grade equivalent scores are low in comparison with grade placement or whether their grade failed to meet the achievement growth standard the state established.[1] Like the second teacher quoted, teachers believe that the districts' drive to keep high scores high and eliminate low scores will prevent them from experimenting with promising programs that are not closely matched to test contents.

Even teachers whose pupils score above grade level are not immune from anxiety and pressure. Administrators in high-scoring districts use these scores to ward off outside interference from parents and patrons and as symbols of status. Thus some apply pressure to teachers to keep scores higher, raise them, or exceed the previous year's achievement growth. Teachers in such schools and districts suffer anxiety because they feel they cannot directly control what their pupils will do on the tests or what the characteristics of the pupils assigned to them will be. Many feel that the test scores are not necessarily related to good or bad teaching, but reflect the socioeconomic standing of the pupils or their native intellectual abilities. Although many teachers approve of the state's achievement growth standard, many are becoming aware that ceiling effects and other technical features of tests make it impossible to exceed the growth standard at every grade every year. Thus, many express frustration, feel off balance, out of control, and held to standards that, if the truth were known, are technically impossible for them to meet.

Teachers also believe that principals are evaluated at least in part on the test scores their pupils attain. Everyone seems to have a story about principals who have been fired or transferred because of low scores. They believe that the pressures on principals get "passed down the line" onto themselves. These beliefs are justified in fact and reinforced every time an administrator singles out for special notice or treatment those teachers whose pupils failed to attain expected standards.

Teachers react to these feelings of anxiety and pressure, as well as fear they will lose autonomy and control over local curriculum and their work lives, by "teaching to the test."

As one teacher stated, "I wanted to keep my literature program, and I knew if my scores were low, they would make us go back to the basal, so I drilled them with *Scoring High* worksheets [that match the objectives and formats of the ITBS]." The double-edged danger for techers, however, is that too much teaching to the test can result in scores that are high enough to draw suspicions of cheating.[2]

2. Beliefs about the invalidity of the test and the necessity to raise scores set up feelings of dissonance and alienation. In conducting our grounded analysis of teachers' beliefs about testing, we discovered that the core category, the category that best explains teachers beliefs, was a conception about educational attainment that was not adequately captured by the achievement tests mandated by the state. That concept of attainment was distorted by the test scores because of the psychometric inadequacies of the test, the mismatch between what was taught and what was tested, and the vagaries of pupil effort and emotional status at the time of the test. In short, the numeric test scores mean little to the teachers we studied, particularly without the interpretive context that teachers alone possess. Against such views about the test and the inability of the test to capture more meaningful conceptions of attainment, the teachers must juxtapose the vigorous demands they receive from district administrators and the public that they raise the scores. This sets up feelings of alienation and dissonance: "Why should we worry about these scores when we all know they are worthless?"

3. Beliefs about the emotional impact of testing on young children generate feelings of anxiety and guilt among teachers. Among elementary teachers particularly, the belief is widely held that the Iowa is "cruel and unusual punishment" for young children. During the testing session, many teachers themselves feel anxious, worrying about whether they have adequately prepared their pupils for the test, whether the pupils will perform their best, and whether there will be incidents of emotional distress (fighting, vomiting, crying, giving up, random marking of answer sheets, and the like). Having experienced or heard about such incidents in the past, they engage in a variety of activities to prevent them: trying to appear calm or nonchalant themselves so as not to communicate their anxieties to their pupils, enlisting the assistance of parents to ensure that the pupils receive a good night's rest and proper breakfast before the tests, repeatedly reading (and sometimes interpreting) written test instructions, promising rewards and breaks to keep the pupils going, offering frequent messages of encouragement. Decreased work loads during and after the test week are also believed to be a means of alleviating the stress of testing. Unlike the teachers of elementary grades, teachers of older pupils are more likely to dismiss negative effects of tests on pupils. Instead, they frequently complain of pupils "blowing off" the test and having no incentive to put in the effort the tests require.

Not every teacher shares these beliefs, and district administrators deny any emotional effects on pupils ("To that I say pfft!") or blame pupils' emotional responses on the "overreaction" of teachers. Still, these beliefs are salient and widespread and may account for the substantial investment of energy teachers spend in test preparation and time spent in recuperation following the tests.

4. Testing programs reduce the time available for instruc-

tion. Time required for the ITBS and the state-mandated criterion-referenced tests, the time teachers elect (or principals require) to prepare pupils to take the tests, and the time spent in recovering from the tests amounted to about a 100-hour bite out of instructional time in the schools we studied. Data from the Arizona survey are consistent with ours. Considering the limited amount of time available for instruction in elementary schools, exclusive of "specials" such as music and various pull-out programs, the reduction caused by external testing means a loss of three to four weeks of the school year. Coupled with the notion of the "packed curriculum," the sheer volume of texts and materials the teachers are required to cover, the time taken up by testing significantly reduces the capacity of teachers to adapt to local circumstances and needs of pupils or to exercise any discretion over what to teach and how to teach it.

5. The focus on material that the test covers results in a narrowing of possible curriculum and a reduction of teachers' ability to adapt, create, or diverge. The received curriculum is increasingly viewed as not amenable to criticism or revision. "Social studies is hashed!" So despaired a sixth-grade teacher in our study. What we saw in one school's sixth grade was a transition, as the school year progressed toward ITBS testing in April, from laboratory, hands-on instruction in science several days a week, to less frequent science out of textbooks (choral reading from the text and answering comprehension and vocabulary questions on worksheets), to no science instruction at all in the weeks before the test, to either no science at all or science for entertainment value during the ITBS recovery phase, to science instruction precisely tailored to the questions in the district criterion-referenced tests, to no science at all. The same group devoted about 40 minutes each day to writing projects in the fall, but the class wrote no more after January, after which they spent the time on worksheets covering grammar, capitalization, punctuation, and usage. Writing instruction returned in late May, when the pupils again began producing poetry, stories, reports on projects for the short time remaining in the school year. Social studies and health instruction disappeared altogether. From January on, teachers spent part of their day on the district's Study Skills Manual, which covers test-taking techniques, as well as the reference, mapping, and graphing skills the ITBS covers. Not only were social studies, science, writing, project work, critical thinking projects, and the like slighted because of the mandated testing, but also teachers tended to slight topics within math and reading that the test does not cover. For example, the sixth grade just mentioned drilled repeatedly on operations with mixed fractions and decimals but skipped over metrics and pre-algebra to stress geometry skills on the basis of teachers' memory of what the math test covers. They never quite got back to the neglected topics or treated them with much less intensity than was true of the tested material prior to the test.

The narrowing of curriculum and neglect of untested subjects were more than just seasonal, however. Primary grade teachers in one school pushed to replace the hands-on science program they used in the past in favor of a text. They felt that setting up the demonstrations and experiments required too much time and energy, and anyway, since no one was stressing science achievement, they had more pressing demands on their time. Some dropped science entirely, using the tadpoles, leaves, and fish tanks only for diversions

and entertainment, rather than serious exploration and study. Another group of teachers rejected the district's writing process curriculum because it did not coordinate with the content of ITBS or district tests.

Narrowing of curriculum happened before our eyes. But what was the impact on teachers? We saw two contrary trends. The first was accommodation by the teachers who incorporated district and principal expectations about the need to focus instruction so as to raise test scores and keep them high. Faced with the "packed curriculum" (a set of requirements—tests, program manuals, scope and sequence, extra programs such as drug resistance education—that exceeds the ability and time of any teacher to cover all of them competently) and the restricted number of instructional hours available, some teachers aligned their actions with expectations. They began discarding what was not to be tested and what was not part of the formal agenda and high priorities of the principal and district administrators. One can imagine a kind of evolutionary process at work, with those teachers who correctly narrow curriculum and maximize scores being those that prosper or escape punishment. Over time, however, teachers who fail to practice instruction in science, social studies, writing, and the like will forget their subject matter knowledge and teaching methods and will gradually lose their capacity to define themselves as, say, science teachers.

The contrary trend we saw was one of resistance (Giroux, 1983) or contesting ideologies of self and role (Ball, 1987), which took various forms at the two schools we studied. "I know what's on the test, but I feel that these children should keep up with current events and trace the history behind what's happening now, so we're going to spend March doing that. I guess I'm saying that the test scores are going to be up for grabs," said one sixth-grade teacher. "My contract doesn't say that I'm here to raise test scores, and if it ever does, I'm out of teaching. So we're going to keep doing what we're doing. They're going to keep writing in their journals and doing math manipulatives and we're going to keep reading stories every day," a primary grade teacher declared.

These teachers, along with any principal whose curricular programs are not well matched with the contents of mandated testing, pay a price for their resistance. They are likely to be subject to frequent demands to defend their programs on other grounds, and to fears that they will suffer sanctions and loss of autonomy because of low scores.

Resistance also took the form of political action. Teachers went outside the school organization to lobby the state legislature in its deliberation over the form of state testing. They were successful in encouraging legislation that removed the mandated testing of first graders.

6. Because multiple-choice testing leads to multiple-choice teaching, the methods that teachers have in their arsenal become reduced, and teaching work is deskilled. Take away the publishers' trappings, and one would be hard pressed to distinguish an ITBS item from a question on a typical work sheet. Both call for the pupil to select among alternative options the one that an outside expert has decided in advance is correct. Over time and with increased testing stakes, teaching becomes more testlike. Some teachers gave up on Math Their Way because they could not make the transition to paper-and-pencil computation quickly enough to prepare

their second-graders for the ITBS. Teaching problem-solving became synonymous with teaching a five-step algorithm for converting math story problems to computational exercises. Teaching spelling became synonymous with providing practice with worksheets on the recognition of which one of three words contained spelling errors. The most telling example we observed of the drift toward testlike teaching occurred between the first and second year of our observation. Hamilton Elementary School met the district's growth standard in most grades and on most ITBS subtests. Third grade, however, achieved about a month less than the standard on the language subtest. Although the difference was small and certainly not statistically reliable, it was large enough to attract negative attention from the district administrators and board members. The message came through that something must be done. The third-grade teachers were assigned the task of designing and implementing a "systematic review" of language, similar to the systematic review they already do in math. What this would consist of, the principal asserted, would be time set aside daily for the pupils to work on exercises that would improve their skills of grammar, punctuation, capitalization, spelling, and usage (the subtests of the ITBS language test). It was clear that these exercises would have formats similar to ITBS items. Besides making certain that subsequent third-grade instruction would be more testlike, this incident had other significance for the teachers. Because the new requirement for systematic review supplemented rather than supplanted other required curriculum, teachers would have even less time at their discretion to pursue alternative topics or methods of teaching language. Because other possibilities for improving pupils' language were not even considered, the idea was reinforced for teachers that there is a single, correct way to teach (reduce a task to simpler components and drill it repeatedly until pupils have mastered it)[3] or revise curriculum (implement changes suggested by authorities). These teachers neither questioned the edict nor offered alternatives from their own expertise and experience.

District administrators use test scores as tools to standardize and control what teachers do. This holds true as much for the results of criterion-referenced instruments as it does for norm-referenced measures such as the ITBS. That is, it is not the form of the test that generates these effects on teachers but the political and social uses made of the scores.

The Teacher After Testing Reform

Whatever the merits are for substituting geometry for metrics, map and graph skills for history and civics, study skills for science, or recognition of grammatical errors in worksheets for editing one's own work, the effects of such substitution on teachers seem obvious. If science, civics, or critical thinking is sifted out of the curriculum because it is not tested and if exploration, discovery, integration methods fall out of use because they do not conform to the format of the mandated test, teachers will lose their capacities to teach these topics and subjects, use these methods, or even imagine them as possibilities. A teacher who is able to teach only that which is determined from above and can teach only by worksheets is an unskilled worker. Far from the reflective practitioner or the empowered teacher, those optimistic images of the 1980s, the image we project of teachers in the

world after testing reform is that of interchangeable technicians receiving the standard curriculum from above, transmitting it as given (the presentation manual never leaving the crook of their arms), and correcting multiple-choice responses of their pupils.

Notes

The study on which this article is based was funded under a subcontract with the Center for Research on Educational Standards and Student Tests, University of California at Los Angeles, with monies from the Office of Educational Research and Improvement, U.S. Department of Education. No official endorsement by the funding agents should be inferred.

[1]Achievement growth or gain is defined locally as the difference between one grade's grade equivalent score in Year 1 and the subsequent grade's grade equivalent score in Year 2. No attention is paid to population differences or attrition in the years compared. In the district we studied, the growth standard was incorporated in the district's strategic plans as the primary goal for pupils. Negative attention was directed to those grade levels within a school that failed to attain this standard or to surpass it in the next yearly growth cycle. Principals were evaluated in part of whether this standard was met for all subtests on the ITBS, and some principals instituted curricular revisions if a grade level "grew" by eight rather than nine months, without respect to the statistical and measurement artifacts embedded in such a standard (Berk, 1988).

[2]The case of Gloria Guzman, which I discussed in Smith (1990), illustrates this conundrum. Charged with "statistically unlikely" high scores in a low socioeconomic school, this teacher attributed them to exceptionally good teaching of objectives that the test covers rather than to cheating. Her case is being considered by a state committee on professional practices.

[3]The following alternatives for improving pupils' language attainment, which were not considered, include inservice training in writing and mechanics for teachers, evaluation of existing texts and materials, providing pupils with more time and opportunities to write and edit their own work, and hiring aides to grade essays and provide individual instruction to pupils.

References

Ball, S. J. (1987). *The micropolitics of the school*. London: Methuen.

Berk, R. A. (1988). Fifty reasons why student achievement gain does not mean teacher effectiveness. *Journal of Personnel Evaluation in Education, 1*, 345–363.

Erickson, F. E. (1986). Qualitative methods in research on teaching. In M. Wittrock (Ed.), *Handbook of research on teaching* (3rd ed., pp. 119–161). New York: Macmillan.

Giroux, H. (1983). Theories of reproduction and resistance in the new sociology of education: A critical analysis. *Harvard Educational Review, 53*, 257–293.

Haas, N. S., Haladyna, T. M., & Nolen, S. B. (1989). *Standardized testing in Arizona: Interview and written comments from teachers and administrators* (Tech. Rep. No. 89-3). Phoenix, AZ: Arizona State University West Campus.

Nolen, S. B., Haladyna, T. M., & Haas, N. S. (1989). *A survey of Arizona teachers and school administrators on the uses and effects of standardized achievement testing* (Tech. Rep. No. 89-2). Phoenix, AZ: Arizona State University West Campus.

Popham, W. J. (1987). The merits of measurement-driven instruction. *Phi Delta Kappan, 68*, 679–682.

Smith, M. L. (1990, April). *The meanings of test preparation*. Paper presented at the annual meeting of American Educational Research Association, Boston.

Smith, M. L., Edelsky, C., Draper, K., Rottenberg, C., & Cherland, M. (1989). *The role of testing in elementary schools*. Los Angeles, CA: Center for Research on Educational Standards and Student Tests, Graduate School of Education, UCLA.

Strauss, A. L. (1987). *Qualitative analysis for social sciences*. Cambridge, MA: Cambridge University Press.

"Our Children Are Dying in Our Schools"

New York City's Teacher of the Year offers an inspiring alternative to confining classrooms, boring lessons, and an educational system that has become "increasingly irrelevant."

John Gatto

John Gatto teaches seventh grade at Junior High 54 on Manhattan's Upper West Side.

WE LIVE IN A TIME OF GREAT SOCIAL CRISIS. OUR CHIL-dren rank at the bottom of nineteen industrial nations in reading, writing, and arithmetic. The world's nar-cotic economy is based upon our own consumption of this commodity. If we didn't buy so many powdered dreams the business would collapse—and schools are an important sales outlet. Our teen-age suicide rate is the highest in the world—and suicidal kids are rich kids for the most part, not the poor. In Manhattan, 70 percent of all new marriages last less than five years.

Our individual social crises are a reflection of this greater social crisis. We seem to have lost our identity. Children and old people are penned up and locked away from the business of the world to a degree without precedent; nobody talks to them anymore. Without children and old people mixing in daily life, a community has no future and no past, only a contin-uous present. In fact, the word *community* hardly applies to the way we interact with each other. We live in networks, not communities, and everyone I know is lonely because of that. In some strange way school is a major actor in this tragedy, just as it is a major actor in the widening gulf among social classes. Using school as a sorting mechanism, we appear to be on the way toward creating a caste system, complete with un-touchables who wander begging through subway trains and sleep on the streets.

I've noticed a fascinating phenomenon in my twenty-five years of teaching—that schools and schooling are increasingly irrelevant to the great enterprises of the planet. No one believes anymore that scientists are trained in science classes, or politicians in civics classes, or poets in English classes. The truth is that schools don't really teach anything except how to obey orders. This is a great mystery to me because thou-sands of humane, caring people work in schools as teachers and aides and administrators, but the abstract logic of the institution overwhelms their individual contributions. Although teachers do care and do work very, very hard, the institution is psychopathic; it has no conscience. It rings a bell, and the young man in the middle of writing a poem must close his notebook and move to a different cell, where he learns that man and monkeys derive from a common ancestor.

OUR FORM OF COMPULSORY SCHOOLING IS AN INVENTION of the state of Massachusetts around 1850. It was resisted—sometimes with guns—by an estimated 80 percent of the Massachusetts population. The last out-post in Barnstable on Cape Cod did not surrender its children until the 1880s, when the area was seized by militia and children marched to school under guard.

Now here is a curious idea to ponder. Senator Ted Kennedy's office released a paper not too long ago claiming that, prior to compulsory education, the state literacy rate was 98 percent, and after education be-came mandatory the figure never again surpassed 91 percent, where it stands in 1990.

Here is another curiosity to think about. The home-schooling movement has quietly grown at such a rate that 1.5 million young people are being educated en-tirely by their own parents. Recently the education press reported the amazing news that children schooled at home seem to be five or even ten years ahead of their formally trained peers in their ability to think.

I DON'T THINK WE'LL GET RID OF SCHOOLS ANYTIME soon, certainly not in my lifetime, but if we're going to change what's rapidly becoming a disaster of igno-rance we need to realize that although the school institution "schools" very well, it does not "educate." That's inherent in the design of the thing. It's not the fault of bad teachers or too little money spent. It's just impossible for education and schooling ever to be the same thing.

Schools were designed by Horace Mann and Barnas Sears and W. R. Harper of the University of Chicago

Reprinted from *New Age Journal*, September/October 1990, pp. 62-64, 99.

Between schooling and television, all the time children have is eaten up. That's what has destroyed the American family: The family no longer is a factor in the education of its own children.

---

and Thorndyke of Columbia Teachers College and others to be instruments of the scientific management of a mass population. Schools are intended to produce, through the application of formulae, formulaic human beings whose behavior can be predicted and controlled.

To a very great extent schools succeed in doing this. But our society is disintegrating, and in such a society the only successful people are self-reliant, confident, and individualistic—because the community life that protects the dependent and the weak is dead. The products of schooling are, as I've said, irrelevant. Well-schooled people are irrelevant. They can sell film and razor blades, push paper and talk on telephones, or sit mindlessly before a flickering computer terminal, but as human beings they are useless—useless to others and useless to themselves.

The daily misery around us is, I think, in large measure caused by the fact that—as Paul Goodman put it thirty years ago—we force children to grow up absurd. Any reform in schooling has to deal with its absurdities.

It is absurd and anti-life to be part of a system that compels you to sit in confinement with people of exactly the same age and social class. The system effectively cuts you off from the immense diversity of life and the synergy of variety. It cuts you off from your own past and future, sealing you in continuous present much the same way that television does.

It is absurd and anti-life to be part of a system that compels you to listen to a stranger reading poetry when you want to learn to construct buildings, or to sit with a stranger discussing the construction of buildings when you want to read poetry.

It is absurd and anti-life to move from cell to cell at the sound of a gong for every day of your youth, in an institution that allows you no privacy and even follows you into the sanctuary of your home, demanding that you do its "homework."

"How will they learn to read?" you say, and my answer is, "Remember the lessons of Massachusetts." When children are given whole lives instead of age-graded ones in cellblocks, they learn to read, write, and do arithmetic with ease if those things make sense in the life that unfolds around them.

But keep in mind that in the United States almost nobody who reads, writes, or does arithmetic gets much respect. We are a land of talkers; we pay talkers the most and admire talkers the most and so our children talk constantly, following the public models of television and schoolteachers. It is very difficult to

teach the "basics" anymore because they really aren't basic to the society we've made.

Two institutions at present control our children's lives—television and schooling, in that order. Both of these reduce the real world of wisdom, fortitude, temperance, and justice to a never-ending, non-stop abstraction. In centuries past the time of a child and adolescent would be occupied in real work, real charity, real adventures, and the real search for mentors who might teach what one really wanted to learn. A great deal of time was spent in community pursuits, practicing affection, meeting and studying every level of the community, learning how to make a home, and dozens of other tasks necessary to becoming a whole man or woman.

But here is the calculus of time the children I teach must deal with:

• Out of the 168 hours in each week, my children sleep 56. That leaves them 112 hours a week to fashion a self.

• My children watch 55 hours of television a week, according to recent reports. That leaves them 57 hours a week in which to grow up.

• My children attend school 30 hours a week, use about 8 hours getting ready, going and coming home, and spend an average of 7 hours a week in homework—a total of 45 hours. During that time they are under constant surveillance, have no private time or private space, and are disciplined if they try to assert individuality in the use of time or space. That leaves 12 hours a week out of which to create a unique consciousness. Of course my kids eat, too, and that takes some time—not much, because we've lost the tradition of family dining. If we allot 3 hours a week to evening meals, we arrive at a net amount of private time for each child of 9 hours.

It's not enough. It's not enough, is it? The richer the kid, of course, the less television he watches, but the rich kid's time is just as narrowly proscribed by a broader catalogue of commercial entertainments and his inevitable assignment to a series of private lessons in areas seldom of his choice.

And these things are, oddly enough, just a more-cosmetic way to create dependent human beings, unable to fill their own hours, unable to initiate lines of meaning to give substance and pleasure to their existence. It's a national disease, this dependency and aimlessness, and I think schooling and television and lessons—the entire Chautauqua idea—have a lot to do with it.

Think of the things that are killing us as a nation: drugs, brainless competition, recreational sex, the pornography of violence, gambling, alcohol, and the worst pornography of all—lives devoted to buying things, accumulation as philosophy. All are addictions of dependent personalities, and that is what our brand of schooling must inevitably produce.

8. THE PROFESSION OF TEACHING TODAY

I want to tell you what the effect is on children of taking all their time—time they need to grow up—and of forcing them to spend it on abstractions. Any reform that doesn't attack these specific pathologies can be nothing more than a facade:

• The children I teach are indifferent to the adult world. This defies the experience of children over thousands of years. A close study of what big people were up to was always the most exciting occupation of youth, but nobody wants to grow up these days, and who can blame them? Toys are us.

• The children I teach have almost no curiosity, and what little they do have is transitory; they cannot concentrate for very long, even on things they choose to do. Can you see a connection between bells ringing again and again between classes and this phenomenon of evanescent attention?

• The children I teach have a poor sense of the future, of how tomorrow is inextricably linked to today. They live in a continuous present; the exact moment they are in is the boundary of their consciousness.

• The children I teach are ahistorical; they have no sense of how the past has predestined their own present, limiting their choices, shaping their values and lives.

• The children I teach are cruel to each other; they lack compassion for misfortune, they laugh at weakness, they have contempt for people whose need for help shows too plainly.

• The children I teach are uneasy with intimacy or candor. They cannot deal with genuine intimacy because of a lifelong habit of preserving a secret self inside an outer personality made up of artificial bits and pieces of behavior borrowed from television, or acquired to manipulate teachers. Because they are not who they represent themselves to be, the disguise wears thin in the presence of intimacy, so intimate relationships have to be avoided.

• The children I teach are materialistic, following the lead of schoolteachers who materialistically "grade" everything—and television mentors who offer everything in the world for sale.

• The children I teach are dependent, passive, and timid in the presence of new challenges. This timidity is frequently masked by surface bravado, or by anger or aggressiveness, but underneath is a vacuum without fortitude.

I could name a few other conditions that school reform will have to tackle if our national decline is to be arrested, but by now you will have grasped my

---

When children are given whole lives instead of age-graded ones in cellblocks, they learn to read, write, and do arithmetic with ease if those things make sense in the life that unfolds around them.

thesis, whether you agree with it or not. Either schools, television, or both have caused these pathologies. It's a simple matter of arithmetic. Between schooling and television, all the time children have is eaten up. That's what has destroyed the American family: The family no longer is a factor in the education of its own children.

WHAT CAN BE DONE? FIRST, WE NEED A FEROCIOUS national debate that doesn't quit, day after day, year after year, the kind of continuous emphasis that journalism finds boring. We need to scream and argue about this school thing until it is fixed or broken beyond repair, one or the other. If we can fix it, fine; if we cannot, then the success of home schooling shows a different road that has great promise. Pouring the money back into family education might kill two birds with one stone, repairing families as it repairs children.

Genuine reform is possible, but it shouldn't cost anything. We need to rethink the fundamental premises of schooling and decide what it is we want all children to learn, and why. For 140 years this nation has tried to impose objectives from a lofty command center made up of "experts," a central elite of social engineers. It hasn't worked. It won't work. It is a gross betrayal of the democratic promise that once made this nation a nobel experiment. The Soviet attempt to control Eastern Europe has exploded before our eyes. Our own attempt to impose the same sort of central orthodoxy, using the schools as an instrument, is also coming apart at the seams, albeit more slowly and painfully. It doesn't work because its fundamental premises are mechanical, anti-human, and hostile to family life. Lives can be controlled by machine education, but they will always fight back with weapons of social pathology—drugs, violence, self-destruction, indifference, and the symptoms I see in the children I teach.

It's high time we looked backward to regain an educational philosophy that works. One I particularly like has been a favorite of the ruling classes of Europe for thousands of years. I think it works just as well for poor children as for rich ones. I use as much of it as I can manage in my own teaching; as much, that is, as I can get away with, given the present institution of compulsory schooling.

At the core of this elite system of education is the belief that self-knowledge is the only basis of true knowledge. Everywhere in this system, at every age, you will find arrangements that place the child alone in an unguided setting with a problem to solve. Sometimes the problem is fraught with great risks, such as the problem of galloping a horse or making it jump, but that, of course, is a problem successfully solved by thousands of elite children before the age of ten. Can you imagine anyone who had mastered such a challenge lacking confidence in his ability to do anything else? Sometimes the problem is that of mastering solitude, as Thoreau did at Walden Pond, or Einstein in the Swiss customs house.

One of my former students, Roland Legiardi-Laura, though both his parents were dead and he had no inheritance, took a bicycle and traveled alone across the United States when he was hardly out of boyhood. Is it any wonder that in manhood he made a film about Nicaragua, although he had no money and no prior experience with film making, and that it was an international award winner—even though his regular work was a carpenter?

Right now we are taking from our children the time they need to develop self-knowledge. That has to stop. We have to invent school experiences that give a lot of that time back. We need to invent a curriculum in which each kid has a chance to develop uniqueness and self-reliance.

A short time ago, two of my twelve-year-old kids traveled alone from Harlem to West 31st Street, where they began an apprenticeship with a newspaper editor. Soon, three of my kids will find themselves in the middle of the Jersey swamps at six in the morning studying the mind of a trucking company president as he dispatches eighteen-wheelers to Dallas, Chicago, and Los Angeles.

Are these "special" children in a "special" program? They're just nice kids from Central Harlem, bright and alert, but so badly schooled when they came to me that most of them couldn't add or subtract with any fluency. And not a single one knew the population of New York City or how far it is from New York to California.

Does that worry me? Of course. But I am confident that as they gain self-knowledge they'll also become self-teachers—and only self-teaching has any lasting value.

We've got to give kids independent time right away because that is the key to self-knowledge, and we must reinvolve them with the real world as fast as possible so that the independent time can be spent on something other than more abstractions. This is an emergency. It requires drastic action to correct. Our children are dying like flies in our schools. Good schooling or bad schooling, it's all the same—irrelevant.

WHAT ELSE DOES A RESTRUCTURED SCHOOL SYSTEM need? It needs to stop acting as a parasite on the working community. I think we need to make community service a required part of schooling. It is the quickest way to give young children real responsibility.

For five years I ran a guerrilla school program in which I had every kid, rich and poor, smart and dipsy, give 320 hours a year to hard community service. Dozens of those kids came back to me years later and told me that this one experience changed their lives, taught them to see in new ways, to rethink goals and values. It happened when they were thirteen, in my Lab School program—only made possible because my rich school district was in chaos. When "stability" returned, the Lab closed. It was too successful, at too small a cost, to be allowed to continue. We made the expensive, elite programs look bad.

There is no shortage of real problems in this country. Kids can be asked to solve them in exchange for the respect and attention of the adult world. Good for kids, good for the rest of us.

Independent study, community service, adventures in experience, large doses of privacy and solitude, a thousand different apprenticeships—these are all powerful, cheap, and effective ways to start a real reform of schooling. But no large-scale reform is ever going to repair our damaged children and our damaged society until we force the idea of "school" open—and include family as the main engine of education. The Swedes realized this in 1976 when they effectively abandoned the system of adopting unwanted children and instead spent national time and treasure on reinforcing the original family so that children born to Swedes were wanted. They reduced the number of unwanted Swedish children from six thousand to fifteen in 1986. So it can be done. The Swedes just got tired of paying for the social wreckage caused by children not raised by their natural parents, so they did something about it. We can, too.

Family is the main engine of education. If we use schooling to break children away from parents—and make no mistake, that has been the central function of schools since John Cotton announced it as the purpose of the Bay Colony schools in 1650 and Horace Mann announced it as the purpose of Massachusetts schools in 1850—we're going to continue to have the horror show we have right now.

The curriculum of family is at the heart of any good life. We've gotten away from that curriculum—it's time to return to it. The way to sanity in education is for our schools to take the lead in releasing the stranglehold of institutions on family life, to promote during school time confluences of parent and child that will strengthen family bonds.

Our greatest problem in getting the kind of grassroots thinking going that could reform schooling is that we have large vested interests profiting from schooling exactly as it is, despite rhetoric to the contrary. We have to demand that new voices and new ideas get a hearing. We've all had a bellyful of authorized voices on television and in the press. A decade-long, free-for all debate is called for now, not any more "expert" opinions. Experts in education have never been right; their "solutions" are expensive, self-serving, and always involved further centralization. Enough. Time for a return to democracy, individuality, and family.

From a speech made by the author upon being named Teacher of the Year, originally published in The Sun *(Chapel Hill, NC).*

A Look to the Future

What is the best preparation of an educator for the encounter with anticipated futures? We know that North American educators will have to adjust to major cultural, economic, and technological changes in the dawning decades of the twenty-first century. Open minds and open hearts, coupled with the willingness to inquire and to learn, are the orders of the day that must guide our anticipation of the effects upon educational institutions to be wrought by the social changes aborning.

Some of the demographic changes occurring to young people in the United States are staggering. Harold G. Shane quotes American Medical Association and National Association of State Boards of Education data to demonstrate this fact. These sources report that 18 percent of girls and 10 percent of boys attempt suicide during their growing-up years. Ten percent of American teenage girls will become pregnant, the highest rate in the developed world. At least 100,000 American elementary school children get drunk once a week. Incidence of venereal disease has tripled among adolescents in the United States since 1965. The actual school dropout rate in the United States stands at 30 percent. A social crisis exists in the United States of America, and we will, in the near-term future, have to face it.

As we enter the 1990s, the forces for change and reform in American education are as real, if not more so, as they were in the latter years of the 1980s. It would appear that we are at a pivotal point in North American educational history if many of the reforms recommended for teacher education in the past decade are actually carried through to implementation. Some of the proposed changes in teacher education and licensure, such as the National Teacher Certification Board, are in advanced planning and development stages. Other proposed reforms would include the elimination of undergraduate teacher education programs.

On other fronts, the student populations of North America reflect vital social and cultural forces at work. In the United States, a massive secondary school dropout problem has been developing steadily through the past decade. The 1990s will reveal how public school systems will address this and other unresolved problems brought about by dramatic upheavals in demographics. There is the issue, as well, of how great a shortfall in the supply of new teachers will be experienced in the 1990s. In the immediate future we will be able to see if a massive teacher shortage is beginning; if it is, how will emergency or alternative certification measures adopted by states affect achievement of the objectives of the reform agenda of the 1980s?

At any given moment in a people's history, several alternative future directions are open to them. Since 1970, North American educational systems have been subjected to one wave after another of recommendations for programmatic change. Is it any wonder that change is a sort of watchword for persons in teacher education on this continent? What specific directions it will take in the immediate future depend on which recommendations of the reform agenda are implemented. The direction of educational change depends on several other factors as well, not the least of which is the resolution of the issue of which agencies of government (local, state or provincial, and federal) will pay for the very high costs of reform.

The major demographic changes that have been occurring on this continent, particularly in the United States, will be critical in determining the needs of our educational systems in the coming years. Increased numbers of students in the schools from the faster-growing cultural groups will bring about shifts in perceived national educational priorities, and perhaps fundamental realignments of our educational goals. We shall see how state and provincial education agencies respond to these trends.

Basic changes in society's career patterns should also be considered. It is estimated that in the United States the average nonagricultural worker now makes a major job change about five times in his or her career. The schools will surely be affected, indirectly or directly, by such major social phenomena. Changes in the social structure due to divorce, unemployment, or job retraining efforts will also have an impact. Educational systems are integral parts of the broader social systems that created them. If the larger social system experiences fundamental change, this is reflected in the educational system.

In the area of information science and computer technologies applicable for use in educational systems, the development of new products is so rapid that we cannot predict what technological capacities may be available to schools 20 years from now. In addition, basic computer literacy is becoming more and more widespread in the population. We are entering—indeed we are in—a period of human history when knowledgeable people can control far greater amounts of information (and have immediate access to it) than at any previous time. As new information command systems evolve, this phenomenon will become more and more meaningful to all of us.

The future of education will be determined by the current debate concerning what constitutes a just, national response to human needs in a period of technological change. The history of technological change in all human societies since the beginning of industrial development clearly demonstrates that major advances in technology and major breakthroughs in the basic sciences lead to more rapid rates of social change. Society is on the verge of discoveries that will lead to the creation of entirely new technologies in the dawning years of the twenty-first century. All of the social, economic, and educational institutions on Earth will be affected by these scientific breakthroughs. The basic issue is not whether the schools can remain aloof from the needs of industry or the economic demands of society, but how they can emphasize the noblest ideals of free persons in the face of inevitable technological and economic change. Another concern is how to let go of predetermined visions of the future that limit our possibilities as a free people. The schools, of course, will be called upon to face these issues. We need the most enlightened, insightful, and compassionate teachers ever educated by North American universities to prepare the youth of the future in a manner that will humanize the high-tech world in which they live.

All of the articles included in this unit touch on some of the issues previously mentioned. They can be related to discussions on the goals of education, the future of education, or curriculum development. They also reflect highly divergent perspectives in the philosophy of education.

Looking Ahead: Challenge Questions

What might be the shape of school curricula by the year 2000?

What changes in society are most likely to affect educational change?

Based on all of the commission reports of recent years, is it possible to identify any clear directions in which teacher education in North America is headed? How can we build a better future for teachers?

How can information about population demographics, potential discoveries in the basic sciences, and the rate and direction of technological change in Canada and the United States assist in planning for our educational future?

How can schools prepare students to live and work in an uncertain future? What knowledge bases are most important? What skills are most important?

Improving Education for The Twenty-first Century

How can today's educators prepare for schooling in the next century? What will tomorrow's students be like and what will they need to know? What kinds of information can help us to prepare for that future? In this article, noted educator and futurist Harold G. Shane provides an overview of the challenges facing us today and their implications for the twenty-first century.

Harold G. Shane

HAROLD G. SHANE is University Professor Emeritus of Education at Indiana University, Bloomington, Indiana.

HEN ONE contemplates improving education for the next century, a potent question arises: Do we actually have the foresight needed to give us reasonably accurate images of tomorrow's world? Roy Amara, a dedicated futurist and the president of the Institute for the Future, cautioned that "anything you forecast is by definition uncertain."[1] Therefore, our planning to shape better ways of life must be based on a blend of interpretations of projections as well as our aspirations.

It is encouraging to note that thoughtful scholars very often have given us a reliable picture of things to come. The work of journalist John Elfreth Watkins provides historical evidence of the reliability of many learned opinions.[2] In 1899 he interviewed a number of scholars and recorded their views regarding probable changes. Among the many accurate predictions: electric kitchen appliances, taller Americans, high-speed trains, airplanes, color photography, global telephone systems, subsidized university education, subsidized medical aid, free lunches for needy children, and dozens of other ameliorative conditions. Thus, it appears that we can study new developments and project with reasonable accuracy outcomes related to education for the twenty-first century.

The Present Challenges the Future

Current books, articles, and statements from a wide spectrum of scholars suggest many contemporary trends that imply social, economic, educational, and diverse other futures.[3] Let us examine a small sampling of these elements with implications that will possibly challenge and complicate educational planning in the next decade or two.

The new minority. Sometime in the new millennium—perhaps even before its debut—our schools will enroll a minority composed of the present white majority. As of 1989, fifty-three of America's one hundred largest cities had schools in which Hispanics,

American Indians, Asians, and African Americans had begun to outnumber children and adolescents of white Anglo-Saxon or European ancestry.[4] Fifteen percent or more of the pupils in our schools speak English as a second language.[5] High birthrates among poor Hispanics and African Americans will further divide the U.S. along ethnic lines.

The accumulation of new ethnic educational admixtures challenges our quest for new ways to teach children with multicultural backgrounds. A recent Carnegie Council on Adolescent Development notes a related difficulty:

By age 15, millions of American youth are at risk of reaching adulthood unable to meet adequately...the responsibilities of participation in a multicultural society and of citizenship in a democracy.[6]

Trends in population and in aging. A rapid increase in the growth of America's older residents is under way and brings with it a myriad of potential problems. By the year 2000, about 13 percent of the population will be sixty-five years old or older, and in the next thirty years, senior citizens will constitute well over 20 percent of an appreciably larger U.S. population.[7] The average life span may well approach over eighty years by the year 2020.[8]

Costs related to medical and custodial care and social security are likely to create an increasing burden for younger employed Americans. Interestingly, present trends indicate that in the next decade the greatest population growth will take place in California, Texas, and Florida.[9]

Environmental problems. So much has been written about threats to the environment that little elaboration is needed. Hazards include land erosion, deforestation in the tropics, acid rain, misuse of energy resources, oceanic pollution, the ozone depletion, and the "green house" effect.

Education that addresses these problems and issues in the 1990s may help young learners understand that our security as a nation does not necessarily depend on numerous, elaborate weapons and large military forces. It also resides in policies regarding our environment and our natural resources and our ability to participate actively and intelligently in these issues.

Changes in the traditional American family. Forty or more years ago most families in the U.S. presented a rather simple profile: fathers worked and mothers reared families, despite the lack of modern conveniences such as garbage disposals, air conditioning, two bathrooms, or second cars.

Today's family is different. Part of the change may be due to a steady decline in home ownership in the past ten years and a dearth of low-cost rental property and subsidized housing for the poor, which is available to only about 25 percent of those who seek it.[10] Other sources of change in family dynamics are single-parent families, endemic homelessness, and working mothers. Approximately 70 percent of U.S. women were employed in 1990 (one-third with children five or younger) as compared with 31 percent in 1950.[11]

Melissa Ludtke succinctly summarized some of the difficulties of our clanking industrial era:

Some call them the sandwich generation, that bulging demographic cohort of thirtysomethings and fortysomethings who face an onerous triple duty: caring for young children and elderly parents while holding down

By the year 2000, about 13 percent of the population will be sixty-five years old or older, and in the next thirty years, senior citizens will constitute well over 20 percent of an appreciably larger U.S. population.

full-time jobs. More than one-third of the U.S. work force confronts this problem, a number that is sure to rise as the population continues to age and as more women, the family's traditional care givers, enter the job market.[12]

Thus, schools may be left with responsibilities formerly assumed by the family, such as providing day care and teaching important values and behaviors.

Debt and inflation. As of 1990, the debt load was staggering—approximately seven trillion dollars owed by our government, U.S. corporations, and individuals! The annual federal deficit was listed by the government at $147 billion last year, but it actually amounted to $244 billion if social security and other trust fund surpluses were included.[13] In view of these figures plus current inflationary trends and an international currency rate reflecting a decline in the value of the U.S. dollar, our national debt may compound the problem of finding funds for schooling.

Meeting Future Challenges to Education

Rebuilding our school environments mandates teacher, parent, and community cooperation to reverse the conditions reported by a thirty-six-member commission of community leaders, doctors, and teachers sponsored by the American Medical Association and the National Association of State Boards of Education. Among the data cited were the following eight points:

1. Suicide is attempted by 18 percent of girls and 10 percent of boys during their growing-up years.

2. Teen pregnancy in the U.S. continues at the highest rate of all developed countries; one in ten teenage girls will become pregnant.

3. Alcohol consumption involves one hundred thousand elementary schoolchildren who get drunk at least once a week.

4. Gonorrhea and syphilis among teenagers has tripled since 1965, with 2.5 million adolescents each year contracting a sexually transmitted disease.

5. Drugs affect more than 3.5 million twelve- to seventeen-year-olds who have tried marijuana and one-third who are regular users; a half-million young people have tried cocaine—half of these are regular users.

6. Arrests—in 1950 youths between fourteen and seventeen years of age had a rate of four per thousand. In 1985, the arrest rate was 118 per 1,000.

7. The dropout rate in the U.S. currently stands at 30 percent.

8. The poverty rate for young people six to seventeen years old living in families with incomes below the poverty line was 13 percent in 1969 and increased to 20 percent in 1985.[14]

Additionally, technological developments are creating other challenges for education and our society. They include the possibility for information overload with the prospect of knowledge increasing fourfold in the next decade and changes in the nature of knowledge and in what we believe. We also must learn to deal with rapidly accumulating innovations such as laptop computers and sophisticated input devices. Interactive video technology will affect our ability to access information. For example, *Compton's Multi Media Encyclopedia* on compact disk adds about ten thousand animated pictures and drawings.[15]

Other technological developments with implications for the future include robots with forms of artificial intelligence, the invasion of privacy by computerized listings (the average U.S. citizen is listed on seventy private and government computer files)[16], and the effects of televised sex, violence, and advertising on children and adolescents.

Insights into challenges of the present and the probable turbulence of tomorrow are of little use unless we consider the redesign of education. Redesigning schooling for students who will live all or most of their lives in the twenty-first century is almost certainly more essential than the swarm of current reform proposals. Since 1983, when *A Nation at Risk* was released by the National Committee on Excellence in Education, we have been overwhelmed by proposals related to improving out-of-date practices rather than preparing young learners for a new millennium.

A few ventures, such as John I. Goodlad's excellent study of schooling,[17] have focused successfully on redesign, but most proposals have failed to consider basic questions such as those raised in a report commissioned by the U.S. House of Representatives. *Information Technology and Its Impact on American Education* presents four key questions that offer guidelines for planning educational policies that need to be developed to prepare learners to cope with a rapidly changing world:

1. What needs to be learned?
2. Who needs to learn it?
3. Who will provide it?
4. How will it be provided and paid for?[18]

A major question should be added to the four listed above: Where will it be provided?

To sum up, educators in the 1990s need to avoid getting stuck with a tar baby like Brer Rabbit did.[19] We must remain diligent in dealing with changes for tomorrow and not be immobilized by trying to polish the aged mosaics of past practices.

Implications for Our Schools

We undoubtedly need to bear in mind possible educational futures to be sought because of their value to learners everywhere. First, the age range of persons served by our schools should be extended to include mature and senior learners as well as children of prekindergarten age. A downward extension of the age range is vital because of the need for benign and instructive learning environments (rather than mere custodial

Insights into challenges of the present and the probable turbulence of tomorrow are of little use unless we consider the redesign of education.

centers) for the care of children of working parents. At upper age ranges, programs for mature learners are essential when innovations may require workers to prepare for ten different jobs during a lifetime that is influenced by technological changes requiring new and diverse skills.

Second, schooling should be developed with an awareness of the flow of technological and social trends that will require substantial changes in curriculum and instruction. With the prospect of living longer, more older Americans will require new "post retirement" jobs. Also to be considered are the challenges facing younger workers who must cope with an increasing information glut.

Third, future-oriented conceptualizations of a school staff should include persons familiar with microelectronic equipment, such as computers and interactive video, combined with an awareness of the diversity and needs among students of varied ages. This also includes people trained with insights into the differences in the cultures of various ethnic groups and their languages and history.

Fourth, we also need to contemplate longer school days and ten- or eleven-month school years during which parents negotiate times when their children will be away from school. This arrangement would imply a future in which there was no traditional "school year." Rather there would be an unbroken flow of learning devoid of the summer break instituted years ago when young people were needed to help on farms where a large majority of Americans lived.

Associated with a rearrangement of the school year, a departure from the traditional K-8-4, 6-6, 6-3-3 or similar elementary-secondary structures may be required. In such a structure, children could advance at their own rate on the basis of maturity and ability rather than on the basis of time spent in a given grade or group.

Since the redesign of schooling will be unique for each district, it should be noted that there are no uniform instructional practices that should be followed in all school districts. Rather we must develop in our schools poli-

We must remain diligent in dealing with changes for tomorrow and not be immobilized by trying to polish the aged mosaics of past practices.

cies which are in keeping with the many different futures that coming decades will demand. We must not look for uniformity but for emerging programs that will help our oncoming generations defuse the socioeducational time bombs with which we are presently challenged.

The Role of Distance Education

Schooling in the home may find a place in the U.S. similar to its role overseas. *Distance education* originated in Britain, where Prime Minister Harold Wilson suggested it as a means "to pull Britain into the twenty-first century."[20] Distance education first began in 1971 with a curriculum transmitted by the BBC at the university level. Today, these television and radio broadcasts serve over 200,000 students with support from a full-time staff of 2,800 and 700 regional personnel.

With the varied needs of American learners that will need to be met in the future, a wide variety of learning materials designed for distance education could be planned by educators in cooperation with our public broadcasting systems. The range of possibilities is virtually infinite.

Depending on the nature of the populations that might be served by distance education, the range of those participating in home learning situations could extend from preschoolers to senior citizens. Depending on learner maturity, virtually all forms of content extending far beyond the traditional classroom could be produced.

As Lord Walter Perry, first vice chancellor of the original Open University pointed out, for mature learners an important goal also would be "...to offer to many people the chance of updating their educations with refresher courses that could be taken without having to drop out of the work force."[21]

As we rapidly approach the new millennium, it is imperative that we develop our foresight with regard to new designs and creative innovations for education. Only in this way can we move from isolation to membership in the global community.

To this task we must bring sincerity and action rather than mere talk. Through education we can strive to abate growing violence, teen pregnancy, poverty, homelessness, disease, and substance abuse. As these goals are attained we will have an infinitely better chance to defend successfully our planet from problems such as pollution, resource depletion, population growth, and other global threats.

As we rapidly approach the new millennium, it is imperative that we endeavor to develop our foresight with regard to new designs and creative innovations for education. Only thus can we move from isolation to membership in the global community.

1. Roy Amara, *The Second Decade* (Menlo Park, CA: Institute for the Future, 1990), 2.
2. John Elfreth Watkins, "What May Happen in the Next Hundred Years," *The Futurist* (October 1982): 8-13. Reprinted from *The Ladies Home Journal*, December 1900.
3. For excellent abstracts of publications dealing with potential futures, see *Future Survey* published monthly by the World Future Society, 4916 St. Elmo Avenue, Bethesda, MD 20814.
4. Joe Cappo, "Future Scope: Success Strategies for the 1990's," *Future* (November 1989): 15.
5. Ibid.
6. Carnegie Council on Adolescent Development, *Turning Points: Preparing American Youth for the 21st Century: A Report of the Task Force on Education of Young Adolescents* (Washington, DC: The Carnegie Council on Adolescent Development, 1989), 21.
7. William Van Dusen Wishard, "What in the World is Going On?" *Vital Speeches of the Day* 56 (March 1990): 314.
8. Ibid.
9. Edward Cornish, ed., *The 1990s and Beyond* (Bethesda, MD: World Future Society, 1990), 156.
10. W.C. Agar, Jr. and H.J. Brown, *The State of the Nation's Housing* (Boston: Harvard University Center for Housing Studies, 1988).
11. Harold G. Shane, "Educated Foresight for the 1990's," *Educational Leadership* 47 (September 1989): 4.
12. Melissa Ludtke, "Getting Young and Old Together," *Time Magazine*, 16 April 1990, 84.
13. H.E. Figgie, Jr., "Surviving Hyperinflation: Lessons from South America," *Vital Speeches*, 1 November 1988, 47-51.
14. "AMA and NASB Report," *Bloomington Herald-Times*, 8 June 1990, p.A3.
15. *Compton's Multi Media Encyclopedia*, (Chicago: Compton's, 1990).
16. Joseph L. Galloway, "How Your Privacy is Being Stripped Away," *U.S. News and World Report*, 30 April 1984, 46-48.
17. John I. Goodlad, *A Place Called School: Prospects for the Future* (New York: McGraw-Hill, 1984).
18. Office of Technology Assessment, *Information Technology and Its Impact on American Education* (Washington, DC: U.S. Government Printing Office, 1983).
19. Joel Chandler Harris, *Uncle Remus, His Songs and His Sayings* (New York: Groffet & Dunlap,1880).
20. "Britain's University of the Air," *The Futurist*, (July-August 1989), 25.
21. Ibid., 26. **EH**

Beyond The Melting Pot

In the 21st century—and that's not far off—racial and ethnic groups in the U.S. will outnumber whites for the first time. The "browning of America" will alter everything in society, from politics and education to industry, values and culture

WILLIAM A. HENRY III

Someday soon, surely much sooner than most people who filled out their Census forms last week realize, white Americans will become a minority group. Long before that day arrives, the presumption that the "typical" U.S. citizen is someone who traces his or her descent in a direct line to Europe will be part of the past. By the time these elementary students at Brentwood Science Magnet School in Brentwood, Calif., reach midlife, their diverse ethnic experience in the classroom will be echoed in neighborhoods and workplaces throughout the U.S.

Already 1 American in 4 defines himself or herself as Hispanic or nonwhite. If current trends in immigration and birth rates persist, the Hispanic population will have further increased an estimated 21%, the Asian presence about 22%, blacks almost 12% and whites a little more than 2% when the 20th century ends. By 2020, a date no further into the future than John F. Kennedy's election is in the past, the number of U.S. residents who are Hispanic or nonwhite will have more than doubled, to nearly 115 million, while the white population will not be increasing at all. By 2056, when someone born today will be 66 years old, the "average" U.S. resident, as defined by Census statistics, will trace his or her descent to Africa, Asia, the Hispanic world, the Pacific Islands, Arabia—almost anywhere but white Europe.

While there may remain towns or outposts where even a black family will be something of an oddity, where English and Irish and German surnames will predominate, where a traditional (some will wistfully say "real") America will still be seen on almost every street corner, they will be only the vestiges of an earlier nation. The former majority will learn, as a normal part of everyday life, the meaning of the Latin slogan engraved on U.S. coins—E PLURIBUS UNUM, one formed from many.

Among the younger populations that go to school and provide new entrants to the work force, the change will happen sooner. In some places an America beyond the melting pot has already arrived. In New York State some 40% of elementary- and secondary-school children belong to an ethnic minority. Within a decade, the proportion is expected to approach 50%. In California white pupils are already a minority. Hispanics (who, regardless of their complexion, generally distinguish themselves from both blacks and whites) account for 31.4% of public school enrollment, blacks add 8.9%, and Asians and others amount to 11%—for a nonwhite total of 51.3%. This finding is not only a reflection of white flight from desegregated public schools. Whites of all ages account for just 58% of California's population. In San Jose bearers of the Vietnamese surname Nguyen outnumber the Joneses in the telephone directory 14 columns to eight.

Nor is the change confined to the coasts. Some 12,000 Hmong refugees from Laos have settled in St. Paul. At some Atlanta low-rent apartment complexes that used to be virtually all black, social workers today need to speak Spanish. At the Sesame Hut restaurant in Houston, a Korean immigrant owner trains Hispanic immigrant workers to prepare Chinese-style food for a largely black clientele. The Detroit area has 200,000 people of Middle Eastern descent; some 1,500 small grocery and convenience stores in the vicinity are owned by a whole subculture of Chaldean Christians with roots in Iraq. "Once America was a microcosm of European nationalities," says Molefi Asante, chairman of the department of African-American studies at Temple University in Philadelphia. "Today America is a microcosm of the world."

History suggests that sustaining a truly multiracial society is difficult, or at least unusual. Only a handful of great powers of the distant past—Pharaonic Egypt and Imperial Rome, most notably—managed to maintain a distinct national identity while embracing, and being ruled by, an ethnic mélange. The most ethnically diverse contemporary power, the Soviet Union, is beset with secessionist demands and near tribal conflicts. But such comparisons are flawed, because those empires were launched by conquest and maintained through an aggressive military presence. The U.S. was created, and continues to be redefined, primarily by voluntary immigration. This process has been one of the country's great strengths, infusing it with talent and energy. The "browning of America" offers tremendous opportunity for capitalizing anew on the merits of many peoples from many lands. Yet this fundamental change in the ethnic makeup of the U.S. also poses risks. The American character is resilient and thrives on change. But past periods of rapid evolution have also, alas, brought out deeper, more fearful aspects of the national soul.

Politics: New and Shifting Alliances

A truly multiracial society will undoubtedly prove much harder to govern. Even seemingly race-free conflicts will be increasingly complicated by an overlay of ethnic tension. For example, the expected showdown in the early 21st century between the rising number of retirees and the dwindling number of workers who must be taxed to pay for the elders' Social Security benefits will probably be compounded by the fact that a large majority of recipients will be white, whereas a majority of workers paying for them will be nonwhite.

While prior generations of immigrants believed they had to learn English quickly to survive, many Hispanics now maintain that the Spanish language is inseparable from their ethnic and cultural identity, and seek to remain bilingual, if not primarily Spanish-speaking, for life. They see legislative drives to make English the sole official language, which have prevailed in some fashion in at least 16 states, as a political backlash. Says Arturo Vargas of the Mexican American Legal Defense and Educational Fund: "That's what English-only has been all about—a reaction to the growing population and influence of Hispanics. It's human nature to be uncomfortable with change. That's what the Census is all about, documenting changes and making sure the country keeps up."

Racial and ethnic conflict remains an ugly fact of American life everywhere, from working-class ghettos to college campuses, and those who do not raise their fists often raise their voices over affirmative action and other power sharing. When Florida Atlantic University, a state-funded institution under pressure to increase its low black enrollment, offered last month to give free tuition to every qualified black freshman who enrolled, the school was flooded with calls of complaint, some protesting that nothing was being done for "real" Americans. As the numbers of minorities increase, their demands for a share of the national bounty are bound to intensify, while whites are certain to feel ever more embattled. Businesses often feel whipsawed between immigration laws that punish them for hiring illegal aliens and anti-discrimination laws that penalize them for demanding excessive documentation from foreign-seeming job applicants. Even companies that consistently seek to do the right thing may be overwhelmed by the problems of diversifying a primarily white managerial corps fast enough to direct a work force that will be increasingly nonwhite and, potentially, resentful.

Nor will tensions be limited to the polar simplicity of white vs. nonwhite. For all Jesse Jackson's rallying cries about shared goals, minority groups often feel keenly competitive. Chicago's Hispanic leaders have leapfrogged between white and black factions, offering support wherever there seemed to be the most to gain for their own community. Says Dan Solis of the Hispanic-oriented United Neighborhood Organization: "If you're thinking power, you don't put your eggs in one basket."

Blacks, who feel they waited longest and endured most in the fight for equal opportunity, are uneasy about being supplanted by Hispanics or, in some areas, by Asians as the numerically largest and most influential minority—and even more, about being outstripped in wealth and status by these newer groups. Because Hispanics are so numerous and Asians such a fast-growing group, they have become the "hot" minorities, and blacks feel their needs are getting lower priority. As affirmative action has broadened to include other groups—and to benefit white women perhaps most of all—blacks perceive it as having waned in value for them.

The Classroom: Whose History Counts?

Political pressure has already brought about sweeping change in public school textbooks over the past couple of decades and has begun to affect the core humanities curriculum at such élite universities as Stanford. At stake at the college level is whether the traditional "canon" of Greek, Latin and West European humanities study should be expanded to reflect the cultures of Africa, Asia and other parts of the world. Many books treasured as classics by prior generations are now seen as tools of cultural imperialism. In the extreme form, this thinking rises to a value-deprived neutralism that views all cultures, regardless of the grandeur or paucity of their attainments, as essentially equal.

Even more troubling is a revisionist approach to history in which groups that have gained power in the present turn to remaking the past in the image of their desires. If 18th, 19th and earlier 20th century society should not have been so dominated by white Christian men of West European ancestry, they reason, then that past society should be reinvented as pluralist and democratic. Alternatively, the racism and sexism of the past are treated as inextricable from—and therefore irremediably tainting—traditional learning and values.

While debates over college curriculum get the most attention, professors generally can resist or subvert the most wrongheaded changes and students generally have mature enough judgment to sort out the arguments. Elementary- and secondary-school curriculums reach a far broader segment at a far more impressionable age, and political expediency more often wins over intellectual honesty. Exchanges have been vituperative in New York, where a state task force concluded that "African-Americans, Asian-Americans, Puerto Ricans and Native Americans have all been victims of an intellectual and educational oppression. . . . Negative characterizations, or the absence of positive references, have had a terribly damaging effect on the psyche of young people." In urging a revised syllabus, the task force argued, "Children from European culture will have a less arrogant perspective of being part of a group that has 'done it all.'" Many intellectuals are outraged. Political scientist Andrew Hacker of Queens College lambastes a task-force suggestion that children be taught how "Native Americans were here to welcome new settlers from Holland, Senegal, England, Indonesia, France, the Congo, Italy, China, Iberia." Asks Hacker: "Did the Indians really welcome all those groups? Were they at Ellis Island when the Italians started to arrive? This is not history but a myth intended to bolster the self-esteem of certain children and, just possibly, a platform for advocates of various ethnic interests."

Values:
Something in Common

Economic and political issues, however much emotion they arouse, are fundamentally open to practical solution. The deeper significance of America's becoming a majority nonwhite society is what it means to the national psyche, to individuals' sense of themselves and their nation—their idea of what it is to be American. People of color have often felt that whites treated equality as a benevolence granted to minorities rather than as an inherent natural right. Surely that condescension will wither.

Rather than accepting U.S. history and its meaning as settled, citizens will feel ever more free to debate where the nation's successes sprang from and what its unalterable beliefs are. They will clash over which myths and icons to invoke in education, in popular culture, in ceremonial speechmaking from political campaigns to the State of the Union address. Which is the more admirable heroism: the courageous holdout by a few conquest-minded whites over Hispanics at the Alamo, or the anonymous expression of hope by millions who filed through Ellis Island? Was the subduing of the West a daring feat of bravery and ingenuity, or a wretched example of white

imperialism? Symbols deeply meaningful to one group can be a matter of indifference to another. Says University of Wisconsin chancellor Donna Shalala: "My grandparents came from Lebanon. I don't identify with the Pilgrims on a personal level." Christopher Jencks, professor of sociology at Northwestern, asks, "Is anything more basic about turkeys and Pilgrims than about Martin Luther King and Selma? To me, it's six of one and half a dozen of the other, if children understand what it's like to be a dissident minority. Because the civil rights struggle is closer chronologically, it's likelier to be taught by someone who really cares."

Traditionalists increasingly distinguish between a "multiracial" society, which they say would be fine, and a "multicultural" society, which they deplore. They argue that every society needs a universally accepted set of values and that new arrivals should therefore be pressured to conform to the mentality on which U.S. prosperity and freedom were built. Says Allan Bloom, author of the best-selling *The Closing of the American Mind*: "Obviously, the future of America can't be sustained if people keep only to their own ways and remain perpetual outsiders. The society has got to turn them into Americans. There are natural fears that today's immigrants may be too much of a cultural stretch for a nation based on Western values."

The counterargument, made by such scholars as historian Thomas Bender of New York University, is that if the center cannot hold, then one must redefine the center. It should be, he says, "the ever changing outcome of a continuing contest among social groups and ideas for the power to define public culture." Besides, he adds, many immigrants arrive committed to U.S. values; that is part of what attracted them. Says Julian Simon, professor of business administration at the University of Maryland: "The life and institutions here shape immigrants and not vice versa. This business about immigrants changing our institutions and our basic ways of life is hogwash. It's nativist scare talk."

Citizenship:
Forging a New Identity

Historians note that Americans have felt before that their historical culture was being overwhelmed by immigrants, but conflicts between earlier-arriving English, Germans and Irish and later-arriving Italians and Jews did not have the obvious and enduring ele-

ment of racial skin color. And there was never a time when the nonmainstream elements could claim, through sheer numbers, the potential to unite and exert political dominance. Says Bender: "The real question is whether or not our notion of diversity can successfully negotiate the color line."

For whites, especially those who trace their ancestry back to the early years of the Republic, the American heritage is a source of pride. For people of color, it is more likely to evoke anger and sometimes shame. The place where hope is shared is in the future. Demographer Ben Wattenberg, formerly perceived as a resister to social change, says, "There's a nice chance that the American myth in the 1990s and beyond is going to ratchet another step toward this idea that we are the universal nation. That rings the bell of manifest destiny. We're a people with a mission and a sense of purpose, and we believe we have something to offer the world."

Not every erstwhile alarmist can bring himself to such optimism. Says Norman Podhoretz, editor of *Commentary:* "A lot of people are trying to undermine the foundations of the American experience and are pushing toward a more Balkanized society. I think that would be a disaster, not only because it would destroy a precious social inheritance but also because it would lead to enormous unrest, even violence."

While know-nothingism is generally confined to the more dismal corners of the American psyche, it seems all too predictable that during the next decades many more mainstream white Americans will begin to speak openly about the nation they feel they are losing. There are not, after all, many nonwhite faces depicted in Norman Rockwell's paintings. White Americans are accustomed to thinking of themselves as the very picture of their nation. Inspiring as it may be to the rest of the world, significant as it may be to the U.S. role in global politics, world trade and the pursuit of peace, becoming a conspicuously multiracial society is bound to be a somewhat bumpy experience for many ordinary citizens. For older Americans, raised in a world where the numbers of whites were greater and the visibility of nonwhites was carefully restrained, the new world will seem ever stranger. But as the children at Brentwood Science Magnet School, and their counterparts in classrooms across the nation, are coming to realize, the new world is here. It is now. And it is irreversibly the America to come.

— Reported by Naushad S. Mehta/New York, Sylvester Monroe/Los Angeles and Don Winbush/Atlanta

EDUCATIONAL RENAISSANCE:
43 Trends for U.S. Schools

More business-and-school partnerships and increased parental participation are among the likely developments ahead, according to two education consultants.

Marvin J. Cetron and Margaret Evans Gayle

Marvin J. Cetron is president of Forecasting International, Ltd., 1001 North Highland Street, Arlington, Virginia 22210. He is author (with Owen Davies) of *American Renaissance: Our Life at the Turn of the 21st Century*, revised edition (St. Martin's Press, 1990, paperback), which is available from the Futurist Bookstore for $14.45 ($13.35 for Society members), including postage and handling.

Margaret Evans Gayle is president of the Triangle Management Group and vice president of the 21st Century Futures Corporation. She is also president of the Triangle Futures Group—Research Triangle Park chapter of the World Future Society. Her address is 3700 Pembrook Place, Raleigh, North Carolina 27612.

In the near future, American schools will have changed dramatically, and so will people's relationship to them. On the outside, most will still be the same brick-and-glass structures—literally the same, half of them nearing 75 years old. But on the inside, the changes will be obvious: Classrooms will be full of personal computers and other high-tech teaching aids. Teaching methods will have changed to reflect a growing understanding of the learning process. Teachers will be backed up by volunteers from the community and from local businesses. Most of all, educational standards will be more demanding, and they will be enforced. We will be asking far more of schools a few short years from now, and giving them more as well. And we will be getting more in return.

The first experiments in reconstruction have already begun. From them, we have learned more than enough to heal most of the ills that now afflict the U.S. school system. There is nothing to prevent school districts across the country from adopting these and many other reforms — nothing but the inertia of 16,000 school districts. But that inertia is rapidly disappearing in the face of political pressure from enraged parents.

The key, of course, is in the hands of parents themselves. If school systems are to recover their lost quality, if the United States is to survive as an economic leader, parents — and all stakeholders — must accept responsibility for the performance of their local school system. They must offer themselves as part-time teachers and teaching assistants. They must work with local political leaders to raise school budgets to pay teachers for performance (merit pay) and with school administrators to see that funds are used to promote effective classes in the core subjects. Above all, they must make certain that their own children understand the importance of a good education and have the support required for the difficult job of learning. In the years to come, more and more people will accept

this challenge. The trend has clearly begun.

In the following pages, we list dozens of examples of key trends and likely developments in education and lifelong learning.

Trends in Education

1. Education will be the major public-agenda item as we enter the twenty-first century.

2. Education will continue to be viewed as the key to economic growth.

3. Technology, coupled with flexible home, work, and learning schedules, will provide more productive time for schooling, training, and working.

4. There is a growing mismatch between the literacy (vocabulary, reading, and writing skills) of the labor force and the competency required by the jobs available. Both ill-prepared new work-force entrants and already-employed workers, who cannot adapt to changing requirements and new technologies, contribute to this mismatch.

● The mismatch between the skills workers possess and the requirements of tomorrow's jobs will be greatest among the "best" jobs, where educational demands are greatest. Three-fourths of new work-force entrants will be qualified for only 40% of new jobs created between 1985 and 2000.

Students

5. The number of public-school enrollments in the United States will increase to 43.8 million by 2000, after having dipped below 40 million in the mid-1980s.

6. One million young people will drop out of school annually, at an estimated cost of $240 billion in lost earnings and forgone taxes over their lifetimes.

7. The number of students at risk of dropping out of school will increase as academic standards rise and social problems (such as drug abuse and teenage pregnancy) intensify.

Teachers

8. The United States will need 2 million new teachers in the public-school system between now and 1995, but historical projections indicate that only a little over a million will materialize.

9. The expected attrition of the aging teaching force, class-size policies, and school-enrollment projections will be major factors determining the numbers of new teachers required to staff U.S. schools.

10. The supply of newly graduated teaching candidates is expected to satisfy only about 60% of the "new hire" demand over the next 10 years.

11. The growing proportions of minorities in the general population and in the student population are not reflected among teachers. This discrepancy will be particularly acute in the southern states, where minority enrollment ranges from 25% to 56% and the proportion of minority teachers ranges from 4% to 35%.

12. Most states will implement alternative routes to certification by 1995 as a solution to teacher shortages, especially in the sciences.

13. We will see a return to teaching laboratories or development schools in the 1990s, as university programs and teaching professionals develop a new vision for schooling from the ground up.

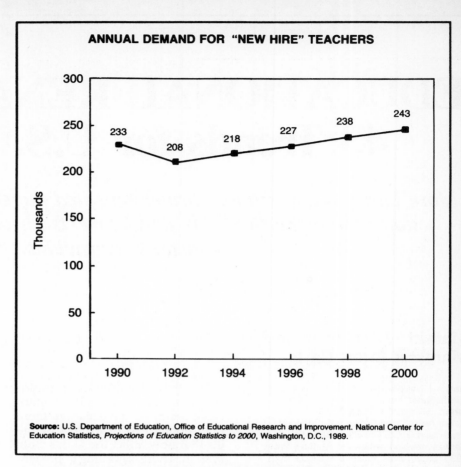

ANNUAL DEMAND FOR "NEW HIRE" TEACHERS

Source: U.S. Department of Education, Office of Educational Research and Improvement. National Center for Education Statistics, *Projections of Education Statistics to 2000*, Washington, D.C., 1989.

The supply of new teachers will fall short of demand by about 40% in the year 2000.

14. Teachers' salaries will continue to be debated in the 1990s while research regarding the relationship of financial incentives to retention of qualified teachers continues.

Curriculum and Instruction

15. Lifelong learning will generate birth-to-death curriculum and delivery systems.

16. A core curriculum for all students will emerge as parents, teachers, business leaders, and other stakeholders debate what is important for the learning enterprise: Basic skills versus arts or vocational education versus critical-thinking skills, for example, will be a major part of the debate.

17. The focus on thinking globally will make foreign language a requirement for all students entering college.

18. Foreign language and bilingual instruction will become a necessity for all students in the twenty-first century. All states will initiate or expand their programs to prepare students for a worldwide marketplace.

19. Vocational education, with emphasis on higher technical literacy, will be required for increasing numbers of students. Access to vocational education will be demanded by more parents and clients.

20. Secondary students will come to value vocational education more highly as reform efforts bring about a restructuring of schools, especially an integration of academic and technical skills.

Higher Education

21. Only 15% of the jobs of the future will require a college diploma, but more than half of all jobs will require postsecondary education and training.

22. There will continue to be an oversupply of college graduates,

The Connection to Jobs and Work

Businesses are increasingly recognizing that their futures depend on an adequately educated work force. Instead of pouring money into training employees once they're hired, more businesses will invest earlier in human resources by forming partnerships with schools.

The trends outlined below show how the world of work is changing and will force schools and businesses to strengthen their relationship.

1. Lifetime employment in the same job or company is a thing of the past. Workers will change jobs or careers five or more times; this will require lifelong training and learning.

2. The decline of employment in agricultural and manufacturing industries will continue. Exception: By 2001, manufacturing productivity will have increased 500% in those industries that have become more automated, added robotics, and remained flexible in their management and production.

3. Information processing (collecting, analyzing, synthesizing, structuring, storing, or retrieving data, text, or graphics), as a basis of knowledge, is becoming important in more and more jobs. By 2000, knowledge workers will fill 43% of available jobs.

4. Work at home will increase as office automation becomes more portable and powerful. Twenty-two percent of the labor force will work at home by the year 2000.

5. A shortage of entry-level workers, especially in the service sector, will create competition among business, the military, and institutions of higher learning for the youth labor force.

6. Eight million jobs in highly skilled occupations — executive, professional, and technical — will become available over the next decade.

7. Small businesses (fewer than 100 employees) will employ most of the labor force by the year 2000. Many of these will be small manufacturing firms.

8. Continued high levels of unemployment in some states will force over-qualified workers to take available jobs, displacing less-qualified workers who will experience longer periods of unemployment.

9. The growth in numbers of part-time workers and workers who moonlight will continue into the twenty-first century as two incomes become increasingly needed to maintain quality-of-life expectations.

— Marvin J. Cetron and Margaret Evans Gayle

Adapted from *Educational Renaissance* (St. Martin's Press, December 1990).

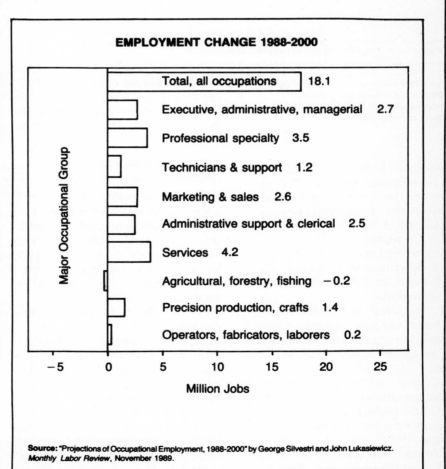

EMPLOYMENT CHANGE 1988-2000

Major Occupational Group

	Million Jobs
Total, all occupations	18.1
Executive, administrative, managerial	2.7
Professional specialty	3.5
Technicians & support	1.2
Marketing & sales	2.6
Administrative support & clerical	2.5
Services	4.2
Agricultural, forestry, fishing	−0.2
Precision production, crafts	1.4
Operators, fabricators, laborers	0.2

Source: "Projections of Occupational Employment, 1988-2000" by George Silvestri and John Lukasiewicz. *Monthly Labor Review*, November 1989.

As changes occur in the world of work, businesses will have to take more responsibility for preparing their future labor force by forming partnerships with schools.

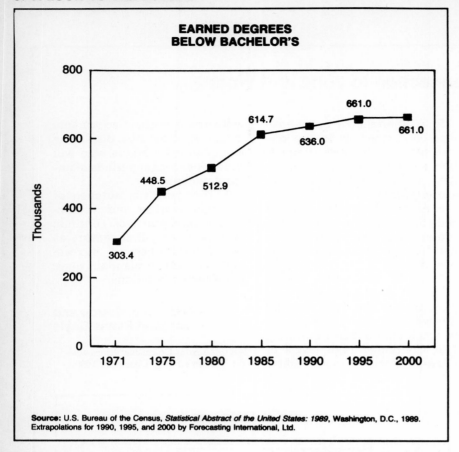

EARNED DEGREES BELOW BACHELOR'S

Thousands

800

661.0

614.7

661.0

636.0

448.5

512.9

600

400

303.4

200

0

1971   1975   1980   1985   1990   1995   2000

Source: U.S. Bureau of the Census, *Statistical Abstract of the United States: 1989*, Washington, D.C., 1989. Extrapolations for 1990, 1995, and 2000 by Forecasting International, Ltd.

Two-year and technical colleges offering degrees below a bachelor's will be significant factors in the technological growth of communities.

especially in liberal arts. A liberal-arts background is valued in principle, but not in pay or in competition for jobs that require specialized skills.

23. Community colleges and technical institutes will become major determinants of technological growth in communities and within regions.

24. The drop in enrollments in teacher-education programs, particularly among minority students, will reach the crisis point in the 1990s.

• Current minority enrollment in teacher education is insufficient even to replace the minority teachers who are leaving the profession.

• Fewer than half of minority teacher candidates, prepared by colleges and universities, pass the required certification tests in some 45 states.

• High failure rates on standardized tests and teacher-certification examinations are also reducing the pool of available minority teachers.

School Reform and Restructuring

25. School-reform efforts will continue to improve elements of the educational system, but without a national philosophy that stresses reform (e.g., merit pay, longer school days and years, etc.) and the commitment to fund it, American schools will remain inferior to those of other industrialized nations.

26. The emphasis on school reform and restructuring will continue throughout the 1990s, but with little improvement of national averages on standardized tests.

27. The "back-to-basics" movement will be superseded by a "forward-to-future-basics" movement, which will include the use of telecommunications technologies, together with other advanced science knowledge and technical skills, for problem solving.

28. Flexible school scheduling will result in more learning time for students.

29. Accountability at all levels will be the buzzword for the 1990s. But will the impetus be top-down or bottom-up? The trend toward school-based management suggests that local schools can carry out national standards. Accountability issues will create major conflict among federal, state, and local agencies.

30. Increased accountability and higher-paid educators will produce more-professional approaches and solutions to educating a democratic and pluralistic society.

Governance and Leadership

31. All community stakeholders (parents, students, teachers, business leaders, and others) will continue to demand more involvement in the decisions governing education, but they will have little knowledge about what should be done to restructure; much is done with little research basis.

32. Centralized control of curriculum, teacher training, and achievement standards will continue, but decentralization of school and classroom management will increase.

33. The current shortage of qualified candidates for school administration positions will continue well into the twenty-first century. Three-fourths of American school superintendents, and as many as half of all principals, will retire by 1994.

34. The principal will become the major change agent for schools. He or she will bear tremendous leadership responsibility in sharing governance with the staff of the school. This school-based-management trend will create a need to place high-quality professionals in school administration — a difficult task in light of projected shortages and the present low test scores of candidates.

35. Educational bureaucracies, local school boards, and other regulatory agencies will lose their power as the second wave of reforms takes hold during the 1990s.

36. The educational system will become more fragmented in the next decade. Implementation of

The Family Connection

Families of the twenty-first century will encounter many stresses and will increasingly turn to the community and the educational system for support. In the Ideal Community School scenario proposed by William L. Lepley, director of the Iowa Department of Education, schools will be the hub of society by the year 2010. Ideal schools will offer a range of family-aiding programs, such as health-care services, job information, child-birth and parenting classes, and pre-retirement planning.

Parents — and even members of the community without children — will form stronger ties with schools as they become increasingly recognized as crucial to the future well-being of communities. Below are just a few of the trends affecting families that will ultimately have an impact on schools and education.

1. By 2000, fewer than 4% of families will consist of breadwinner husband, homemaker wife, and two children.

2. There will be more multifamilies: children living with adults who are not related.

3. Legal redefinitions of "family" will have an impact on schools.

4. By 2000, three-fourths of 3-year-olds will attend nurseries (day-care centers or nursery schools).

5. Both partners in most family units (married and unmarried) will work; this figure could rise to 75% by 2000.

6. The number of single-parent families is steadily growing in size and importance. The major reason why white children are living with only one parent is divorce; for black and

SINGLE-PARENT FAMILIES WITH CHILDREN UNDER AGE 18

Source: U.S. Bureau of the Census, *Statistical Abstract of the United States: 1989*, Washington, D.C., 1989. Extrapolations for 1990, 1995, and 2000 by Forecasting International, Ltd.

Hispanic children it is because the parent was never married. If current trends continue, by 2000:

● Eleven percent of white children will be living with a divorced mother (10% in 1988).

● Forty-two percent of black children will be living with a never-married mother (29% in 1988).

● Seventeen percent of Hispanic children will be living with a never-married mother (10% in 1988).

7. The number of people below the poverty level is not

Growing numbers of single-parent families will look to schools for more services, from pre-kindergarten day care to parenting classes and health care.

improving: Among female-headed families (no husband present) the rates are rising, especially for children.

— **Marvin J. Cetron and Margaret Evans Gayle**

Adapted from *Educational Renaissance* (St. Martin's Press, December 1990).

9. A LOOK TO THE FUTURE

numerous schooling alternatives will erode the traditional schooling pattern.

37. New systems of school governance will be explored that go beyond centralization and decentralization to, for instance, distribution of authority among government, teaching professionals, and families.

School Finance

38. A wide spectrum of school-finance initiatives and experiments will be undertaken. These will range from extreme centralization and financial control at the state level on one end to privatization on the other, where the states will finance education through vouchers to parents (based on their choices of schools) rather than by directly financing schools. Between these extremes, there will be many traditional programs, but with an increasing number of private-sector partnerships.

39. Employers spend $210 billion annually on training. The number and effectiveness of business–education partnerships, to reduce remediation costs and to develop technical skills, will increase.

40. Regional disparities in educational resources will increase.

School Law

41. Making public education work for everyone, especially for minorities and those with low incomes, will be the challenge for the 1990s. Parents and special-interest groups will raise legal challenges to curriculum, methodology, expenditures, access, and a host of other issues.

42. Equity issues will become the major problems faced by policy makers. Legal challenges will increase as standards are raised.

43. Educational equity will be redefined not in terms of access, but in terms of expenditures.

Index

Credits/ Acknowledgments

Cover design by Charles Vitelli

1. Perceptions of Education in North America
Facing overview—The Dushkin Publishing Group, Inc., photo by Richard Pawlikowski.

2. Reconceptualization of the Educative Effort
Facing overview—EPA Documerica.

3. Striving for Excellence
Facing overview—Wharton Econometric Associates, Inc., Philadelphia, PA, photo by Don Walker.

4. Morality and Values in Education
Facing overview—United Nations photo.

5. Managing Life in Classrooms
Facing overview—United Nations photo by Marta Pinter.

6. Equal Opportunity and American Education
Facing overview—United Nations photo by Milton Grant. 149—Illustration by Elaine Cohen.

7. Serving Special Needs and Humanizing Instruction
Facing overview—United Nations photo by L. Solmssen.

8. The Profession of Teaching Today
Facing overview—The Dushkin Publishing Group, Inc., photo.

9. A Look to the Future
Facing overview—Apple Computer.

ANNUAL EDITIONS ARTICLE REVIEW FORM

■ NAME: _____ DATE: _____

■ TITLE AND NUMBER OF ARTICLE: _____

■ BRIEFLY STATE THE MAIN IDEA OF THIS ARTICLE: _____

_____

_____

_____

_____

■ LIST THREE IMPORTANT FACTS THAT THE AUTHOR USES TO SUPPORT THE MAIN IDEA:

_____

_____

_____

_____

_____

_____

■ WHAT INFORMATION OR IDEAS DISCUSSED IN THIS ARTICLE ARE ALSO DISCUSSED IN YOUR
TEXTBOOK OR OTHER READING YOU HAVE DONE? LIST THE TEXTBOOK CHAPTERS AND PAGE
NUMBERS:

_____

_____

_____

_____

_____

_____

■ LIST ANY EXAMPLES OF BIAS OR FAULTY REASONING THAT YOU FOUND IN THE ARTICLE:

_____

_____

_____

_____

■ LIST ANY NEW TERMS/CONCEPTS THAT WERE DISCUSSED IN THE ARTICLE AND WRITE A
SHORT DEFINITION:

_____

_____

_____

_____

_____

*Your instructor may require you to use this Annual Editions Article Review Form in any number of ways:
for articles that are assigned, for extra credit, as a tool to assist in developing assigned papers, or simply
for your own reference. Even if it is not required, we encourage you to photocopy and use this page;
you'll find that reflecting on the articles will greatly enhance the information from your text.

ANNUAL EDITIONS: EDUCATION 92/93

Article Rating Form

Here is an opportunity for you to have direct input into the next revision of this volume. We would like you to rate each of the 41 articles listed below, using the following scale:

1. **Excellent: should definitely be retained**
2. **Above average: should probably be retained**
3. **Below average: should probably be deleted**
4. **Poor: should definitely be deleted**

Your ratings will play a vital part in the next revision. So please mail this prepaid form to us just as soon as you complete it.
Thanks for your help!

Annual Editions revisions depend on two major opinion sources: one is our Advisory Board, listed in the front of this volume, which works with us in scanning the thousands of articles published in the public press each year; the other is you—the person actually using the book. Please help us and the users of the next edition by completing the prepaid article rating form on this page and returning it to us. Thank you.

Rating	Article	Rating	Article
	1. Suffer the Little Children		23. Chapter 1: A Vision for the Next Quarter Century
	2. Emerging Leadership Needs in Education		24. The Search for Equity in School Funding
	3. Education: The Path to Urban Greatness		25. Losing Battle: Schools Fail Hispanics, Whose Dropout Rates Exceed Other Groups'
	4. The 23rd Annual Gallup Poll of the Public's Attitudes Toward the Public Schools		26. *Perestroika* in Chicago's Schools
	5. The Down Side of Restructuring		27. The ABC's of Caring
	6. America's Public Schools: Choice *Is* a Panacea		28. Becoming the Child's Ally—Observations in a Classroom for Children Who Have Been Abused
	7. Inside the Classroom: Social Vision and Critical Pedagogy		29. Children of Divorce
	8. "Restructuring" in Historical Perspective: Tinkering Toward Utopia		30. Teen-Age Pregnancy: The Case for National Action
	9. What Really Counts in Schools		31. The World Finals of Creativity
	10. On Standardized Testing		32. Different Drummers: The Role of Nonpublic Schools in America Today
	11. The Case for More School Days		33. **What Is an Independent School?**
	12. The Standards Debate Across the Atlantic		34. Accountability for Professional Practice
	13. Ethical Education in Our Public Schools: Crisis and Opportunity		35. The What, Why, and How of Cooperative Learning
	14. Caring Kids: The Role of the Schools		36. Schools and the Beginning Teacher
	15. The Good, the Bad, and the Difference		37. Put to the Test: The Effects of External Testing on Teachers
	16. Moral Education: An Idea Whose Time Has Gone		38. "Our Children Are Dying in Our Schools"
	17. Design a Classroom That Works		39. Improving Education for the Twenty-First Century
	18. The Quality School		40. Beyond the Melting Pot
	19. Charm School for Bullies		41. Educational Renaissance: 43 Trends for U.S. Schools
	20. America the Multicultural		
	21. Multicultural Literacy and Curriculum Reform		
	22. Schools That Work		

(Continued on next page)

ABOUT YOU

Name_____ Date_____

Are you a teacher? ☐   Or student? ☐

Your School Name _____

Department _____

Address _____

City _____ State _____ Zip _____

School Telephone # _____

YOUR COMMENTS ARE IMPORTANT TO US!

Please fill in the following information:

For which course did you use this book? _____

Did you use a text with this Annual Edition? ☐ yes ☐ no

The title of the text? _____

What are your general reactions to the Annual Editions concept?

Have you read any particular articles recently that you think should be included in the next edition?

Are there any articles you feel should be replaced in the next edition? Why?

Are there other areas that you feel would utilize an Annual Edition?

May we contact you for editorial input?

May we quote you from above?